The
WILEY
advantage

Dear Valued Customer,

We realize you're a busy professional with deadlines to hit. Whether your goal is to learn a new technology or solve a critical problem, we want to be there to lend you a hand. Our primary objective is to provide you with the insight and knowledge you need to stay atop the highly competitive and ever-changing technology industry.

Wiley Publishing, Inc., offers books on a wide variety of technical categories, including security, data warehousing, software development tools, and networking — everything you need to reach your peak. Regardless of your level of expertise, the Wiley family of books has you covered.

- For Dummies® – The *fun* and *easy* way™ to learn
- The Weekend Crash Course® –The *fastest* way to learn a new tool or technology
- Visual – For those who prefer to learn a new topic *visually*
- The Bible – The *100% comprehensive* tutorial and reference
- The Wiley Professional list – *Practical* and *reliable* resources for IT professionals

The book you now hold, *Lotus Notes and Domino 6 Programming Bible*, contains the most practical and up-to-date comprehensive coverage available for programmers working with this vaunted groupware platform. Written for those new to Notes and Domino programming as well as experienced programmers, the extensive examples, tips, and techniques this book provides are field tested and proven so you can confidently integrate them into your applications. The broad coverage stretches from essential Notes and Domino programming topics to integration with Java and XML and building Web Services, further assuring you'll benefit from *Lotus Notes and Domino 6 Programming Bible* regardless of the simplicity or complexity of your Notes and Domino programming needs.

Our commitment to you does not end at the last page of this book. We'd want to open a dialog with you to see what other solutions we can provide. Please be sure to visit us at www.wiley.com/compbooks to review our complete title list and explore the other resources we offer. If you have a comment, suggestion, or any other inquiry, please locate the "contact us" link at www.wiley.com.

Thank you for your support and we look forward to hearing from you and serving your needs again in the future.

Sincerely,

Richard K. Swadley

Richard K. Swadley
Vice President & Executive Group Publisher
Wiley Technology Publishing

15 HOUR WEEKEND CRASH COURSE

Visual

Bible

DUMMIES

WILEY
Wiley Publishing, Inc.

Lotus Notes® and Domino 6 Programming Bible

Lotus Notes® and Domino 6 Programming Bible

Brian Benz and Rocky Oliver

Wiley Publishing, Inc.

Lotus Notes® and Domino 6 Programming Bible

Published by
Wiley Publishing, Inc.
10475 Crosspoint Boulevard
Indianapolis, IN 46256
www.wiley.com

Library of Congress Cataloging-in-Publication Data: 2003101855

Published simultaneously in Canada

ISBN: 0-7645-2611-1

Manufactured in the United States of America

10 9 8 7 6 5 4 3 2

1O/RX/QU/QT/IN

For general information on our other products and services or to obtain technical support, please contact our Customer Care Department within the U.S. at (800) 762-2974, outside the U.S. at (317) 572-3993 or fax (317) 572-4002.

Wiley also publishes its books in a variety of electronic formats. Some content that appears in print may not be available in electronic books.

About the Authors

Brian Benz, CLI, PCLP, has more than 15 years experience in designing and deploying systems infrastructures, designing and developing applications, migrating messaging systems and applications, and managing projects. He has established his expertise and reputation in the Domino, Web, and e-business application development marketplace since 1992 through hands-on experience working on various projects and by making frequent contributions as a writer, including the IBM Redbook *XML: Powered by Domino*, the upcoming *XML Programming Bible* (Wiley Publishing, Inc., 2003), and trade publications such as *Lotus Advisor*, *e-Business Advisor*, *WebSphere Advisor*, and *e-Pro* magazine. Brian also provides custom technical training to large and small organizations all around the world, and is also a popular technical event speaker for IBM, Advisor Media, and the View at venues worldwide. Brian is CEO of Benz Technologies (www.benztech.com) and can be reached at bbenz@benztech.com.

Rocky Oliver began his "Lotus geek" existence with Lotus Development's Word Processing Division in 1992. A wizened veteran of Lotus technologies, he has since led the development team of a large national consultancy, opened a new branch for a startup, started his own company, and along the way found time to conceive five great kids (with a little help from his wife . . .). Rocky writes quite often, most notably co-authoring *Teach Yourself LotusScript for Notes/Domino 4.6* (MIS Press, 1997). He is also a Technical Editor and writer for *Lotus Advisor* magazine and a writer for *WebSphere Advisor* magazine. Rocky loves to share his knowledge and experience by speaking often at Lotus technology conventions, including Lotusphere, IBM DeveloperWorks Live, and Advisor Devcon. You can reach Rocky at rock@sapphireoak.com.

Contributor **Richard Schwartz** is founder of RHS Consulting Incorporated, a Lotus Business Partner and a founding member of the Penumbra Group. He has spent more than nine years as a consultant, architect, and evangelist for Lotus Notes and Domino technology. He was given the Lotus Beacon Award in 1995 for the Most Significant Contribution to the Lotus Notes Industry. He has served as a consultant to Lotus and Iris Associates' QA teams for Notes R4 and R4.5, as well as NotesView R4, to the product development team for Domino R4.6, and to many Fortune 500 companies. He is a Certified Lotus Professional, past editor of *Lotus Solutions Now*, and a contributing editor for *Lotus Notes Advisor*. He has also been a frequent contributor to other Notes-related publications and has spoken at several major Domino conferences.

Credits

To Yvette, my heart, for her patience. And Gatita, for knowing when I need a break.

To my wife, Debbie, for keeping my world sane during the chaos of writing a book; to my kids — Kris, Kelsey, Rocky, Robin, and Tommy — for making daddysmile when it was needed most. You are my world.

Preface

This book introduces and explains the programming features of Lotus Notes and Domino 6. Because Notes and Domino make use of so many different technologies, several of which are the subjects of numerous other books, and because IBM provides extensive online reference documentation with the Domino Designer software, we have not organized this book in the format typical of so many restate-the-reference-manual books, and we do not attempt to fully describe every detail of every programming feature available to Notes and Domino developers.

Instead, we focus on tips and techniques that make good Domino developers into excellent Domino developers. Novices and experts alike should find the extensive application examples useful for integration with their own applications. The text in the book centers around leveraging the authors' experience to employ the absolutely critical features of Domino 6 to their best advantage. The Domino 6 Help feature is a great place to start learning about many of these tools and technologies. We acknowledge this fact by referring to the Help extensively throughout the book, but without repeating Help text, as many other books do. We add value by providing original examples that help Domino developers get the best out of their applications with the least amount of time and effort.

The material in the book is useful for all developer skill levels, from beginner to advanced. The content does not assume any previous exposure to Notes and Domino, but the presentation of the examples and techniques is not "dumbed down" either. We have an extensive history with this technology—more than 22 years of combined experience as of this writing—which has given us a deep and comprehensive understanding of the fundamental concepts of Notes and Domino, and we also have extensive experience writing about and teaching these topics. This experience enables us to make the material understandable for beginners at the same time that we shed new light on it for experienced professionals.

The book makes extensive use of examples, which are, as much as possible, constructed incrementally—that is, the examples build on one another within a chapter and across chapters. By following these examples, readers actually see several applications developed from scratch, with illustrative features added in contexts that are themselves instructive. Some of the examples are done in the context of "toolbox" applications, and many of the tools are of interest to Domino Administrators as well as to developers.

The Purpose of This Book

Why do we call this book a *bible*? A bible is not an encyclopedia. A bible is not a step-by-step guide. A bible is a book that teaches rules to live by—and, in our case, rules to work by. A bible teaches by weaving together clear explanations of basic principles, rules, and techniques, as well as illustrative examples of their application to real problems. This is what we have set out to do in this book.

We concentrate on covering the advanced principles of Notes and Domino development, each of the various programming and markup languages that are supported, and, especially, the new programming features of Notes and Domino 6. Although we do not ignore the features of the seven earlier releases of Notes and Domino, the newer features get a bit more emphasis. This is, after all, the bible for Notes/Domino 6. We believe that those readers of our bible who are beginners at Notes and Domino development can benefit more from our approach than they can from reading one of the more typical reference-style books, because our bible teaches principles that help beginning and advanced developers learn more about Notes and Domino more efficiently—and more effectively.

Note   You may be asking yourself, "Did they just say that seven major releases of Notes and Domino came before Notes and Domino 6? How could that be?" The answer is that we are counting Notes and Domino 4.5 and 4.6 as major releases.

We should also add that, although Notes and Domino enable developers to use many features of HTML, JavaScript, Java, and XML in their applications, we do not attempt to explain and illustrate the principles and techniques of all these languages in full detail. That, of course, is the subject matter of the bibles devoted to each of those languages. Rest assured, however, that each of these languages is covered in more than adequate detail in the context of Domino applications.

What Hardware and Software Do You Need?

This book was written with the Domino 6.0 version of Notes, Domino Designer, and the Domino Server (the September 26, 2002, release date). The book also uses a number of tools and products in various examples. The following products and tools are used in the examples of this book:

+ Domino 6.0 version of Notes, Domino Designer, and the Domino Server

+ Microsoft Internet Explorer 6.0

+ Netscape Navigator 7.0

+ Sun JDK 1.3.1_01

+ A Java IDE: IBM WebSphere Studio Workbench 2.0.1, SunONE Studio 4.0, or IBM WebSphere Studio Application Developer (for WebSphere shops)

+ IBM Editor/IDE

+ WebSphere 4.0.3 Server (Single server, Advanced, or Enterprise edition)

+ IBM DB2 version 7.02 (if using WebSphere Advanced or Enterprise editions)

+ Apache AXIS version 1.0

+ Lotus Enterprise Integrator 6.0 (for examples in Chapter 45)

+ Microsoft Word 97 or 2000 (for examples in Chapter 31)

We assume that you are running a Notes 6 client and a Domino 6 server and that you are running these applications on a computer that is capable of doing so efficiently. Additionally, we assume that the computer that you use to review the examples is capable of running the software listed in the preceding list, as needed.

The Organization of This Book

This book is organized into the following 11 major sections:

✦ Part I: Introduction to Lotus Notes and Domino

✦ Part II: Domino Designer

✦ Part III: Application Architecture

✦ Part IV: Automating Applications

✦ Part V: Formula Language Techniques

✦ Part VI: LotusScript Techniques

✦ Part VII: Java Techniques

✦ Part VIII: JavaScript Techniques

✦ Part IX: Relational Database Integration

✦ Part X: XML

✦ Part XI: Web Services

In Part I, we provide a general introduction to Lotus Notes and Domino. We briefly cover the history and evolution of the products and their uses. Next, we describe a very simple Notes and Domino application. We introduce the NSF file that is the foundation of all Notes and Domino applications, and finally, we briefly describe the building blocks that Notes and Domino developers put into NSF files to create applications.

In Part II, we take readers on a tour of the features of the WYSIWYG tools and Integrated Development Environment that developers use to build Notes and Domino applications. We go on to describe the Notes and Domino tools and techniques for managing the code in application projects. Finally, we briefly describe the standard application templates that ship with Notes and Domino, which many developers use as starting points for new applications.

In Parts III and IV, we take a close look at all the structural elements that developers use to build Notes and Domino applications and at all the places within those structural elements where developers write code to implement their applications. We also discuss the Notes and Domino features used to implement electronic mail and Web access, as well as techniques used to implement security and workflow in your applications.

In Parts V through VIII, we go into the details of each of the four programming languages that are used to create Notes and Domino applications. Part V covers Formula Language, which was the original programming language for Notes versions 1, 2, and 3. Part VI covers LotusScript, a scripting language similar to Visual Basic for Applications, which was added in Release 4. Part VI also includes information about working with other desktop applications via COM and OLE, as well as working with the C API from LotusScript. Part VII covers Java, which was added in Release 4.6, and Part VIII covers JavaScript, added in Release 5. Each of these sections starts with a chapter that introduces the fundamentals of the programming language and then continues with additional chapters that describe more advanced features.

In Part IX, we describe techniques for integrating Notes and Domino with relational databases, such as DB2, Oracle, Sybase, or SQL Server. We describe both Lotus' Domino

Enterprise Connection Services (DECS) technology, which provides real-time retrieval and update of relational data in Notes and Domino applications, and Lotus Enterprise Integrator (LEI) technology, which provides scheduled and triggered synchronization of data, as well as the capability to "virtualize" documents from a relational database.

In Parts X and XI, we cover features that enable Notes and Domino developers to work with the latest generation of networked application technologies, eXtensible Markup Language (XML) and Web Services. Chapters in Part X explain a wide variety of techniques for generating and processing XML in Domino, and chapters in Part XI discuss and demonstrate how to use Simple Object Access Protocol (SOAP), Web Services Description Language (WSDL), and Universal Description, Discovery, and Integration (UDDI) in Domino so that Domino applications can serve Web Services and Notes applications can consume Web Services.

New and Enhanced Domino 6 Features Highlighted in this Book

Notes and Domino 6 represent a very stable, full-featured application platform that can be used to build a wide variety of applications available to both Notes and Web browser clients. Notes and Domino 6 include a wealth of new and enhanced features from Release 5. These new features can be found in the Notes client, in the programming client known as Domino Designer, and in the architecture and programming languages themselves. This book highlights many of these new features and provides instructions that enable you to get the most out of them. The following list describes some of these features:

✦ **Chapter 3** introduces you to the concepts involved in building an application by walking you through a simple application. This chapter also introduces a few new features, such as shared resources, new @functions, and a few new LotusScript classes. Many of the new features introduced in Chapter 3 are covered in more detail in later chapters.

✦ **Chapter 4** covers the basic building blocks used to create applications. New features highlighted in this chapter include new field types, such as color, time zone, and rich text lite, as well as the capability to have client-specific code in the same event area, such as the `onLoad JavaScript` event in a form. Additionally, new shared code areas such as Java and JavaScript libraries are introduced, although they are covered in more detail in later chapters. New shared resources are introduced as well, such as Cascaded Style Sheets (CSS), shared Java applets, and shared file resources.

✦ **Chapter 5** contains a great deal of new information about the Domino Designer 6 Integrated Design Environment (IDE) features, such as sharing and locking design elements, autocomplete for @Formulas, LotusScript and JavaScript, remote debugging, and the three new DXL utility functions for saving, viewing, and transforming Design elements into DXL. It also covers the use of WebDAV (Web-based Distributed Authoring and Versioning) and offers a tour of the new shared code and Shared Resources sections in the Design bookmarks.

✦ **Chapter 9** dives into the details of creating views. This chapter discusses a plethora of new features available in view design, such as the capability to drag and drop multiple columns, the capability to programmatically set row color, and the capability to enable users to edit an inline document in a view.

✦ **Chapter 12** explores advanced form design concepts and introduces some new features, such as the new captioned table type, layers, and actions in embedded views.

✦ **Chapter 14** explores how to share code by using various code libraries such as LotusScript libraries, as well as the new Java and JavaScript libraries.

✦ **Chapter 15** covers the use of formulas in forms and views, including the new capability to store code for both Notes and Web browser clients in the same event, such as the onLoad event. This chapter also covers the use of hide-when formulas in view columns.

✦ **Chapter 16** covers actions and hotspots and reviews many new features available for actions, such as the use of actions in embedded views, the use of image resources as action button graphics, and the use of a formula for an action button label. The chapter also describes new ways to display menu actions such as check boxes. (Buttons now have new display options available, such as those that enable you to use colors for buttons and to round the corners on them.)

✦ **Chapter 17** reviews the events available in forms, views, and databases. A few events are new in Notes/Domino 6, such as the QueryRecalc, QuerySend, and PostSend events of forms; the QueryEntryResize, PostEntryResize, and InviewEdit events of views; and the QueryDropToArchive and PostDropToArchive database events.

✦ **Chapter 18** discusses the use of agents for automating applications. One of the new features available for agents in Notes/Domino 6 is the capability to change an agent from shared to private or back after it has been saved. Agents can now be activated without being signed by the person activating them; agents can now be run on behalf of someone else; and agents executed in the Notes client can now be run in a background thread. You can now troubleshoot server-based agents remotely by using the new remote debugging feature.

✦ **Chapter 22** covers various ways to workflow-enable your applications, including using a new feature available in Notes/Domino 6 — the capability to lock a document while it is being edited.

✦ **Chapter 24** introduces you to the use of @functions, including new ones such as @AttachmentModifiedTimes, @BusinessDays, and @Count.

✦ **Chapter 25** introduces you to programming with @commands and describes many new features in @commands. These include aliased @commands, which perform the same function as existing @commands except that the new ones execute where they occur in the code. Many new @commands are also available, such as ComposeWithReference and RefreshFrame.

✦ **Chapter 26** discusses the use of @DbColumn and @DbLookup to retrieve data and covers new features such as the ReCache parameter now available for these two functions.

✦ **Chapter 27** covers various ways to interact with the user through the Formula language and introduces many new features, such as the ChooseDatabase keyword for @Prompt and the OKCancelBottom keyword for @DialogBox.

✦ **Chapter 28** reviews quite a few advanced Formula language techniques and describes three new exciting @functions that are available in Notes/Domino 6 — @For, @DoWhile, and @While. These three functions provide looping capabilities to the Formula language. @FileDir, another new @function, is also covered.

✦ **Chapter 29** introduces you to the LotusScript language and reviews such new features as new data types (Boolean, Single), the automatic inclusion of Option Declare in the Options area of your script, and notification of the user when LotusScript Debugger is enabled or disabled — plus many more.

✦ **Chapter 30** reviews the ways that you work with the Domino Object Model through LotusScript and introduces you to many new front-end and backend classes.

✦ **Chapter 31** introduces you to some advanced LotusScript techniques and, along the way, describes some new LotusScript functions such as `ArrayUnique`, new features such as LotusScript to Java (LS2J), and more.

✦ **Chapter 32** shows you how to use the new Java Code Library to centralize the distribution and maintenance of Java code in Domino applications by adding code to a Java Code Library and calling it from Domino design elements.

✦ **Chapter 34** contains our Java application, featuring many J2EE classes and SWING class support that can now be used as a result of the Domino 6 upgrade to JDK1.3.x from JDK 1.18. The application uses advanced Java classes for the Java application's user interface, including the SWING and AWT classes, to create an application that reads and writes to backend Domino classes.

✦ **Chapter 36** highlights two free distribution versions of the most popular third-party J2EE development environments that can now be used with Domino 6, given J2EE support via the JDK 1.3. IBM has added several plug-ins to the base Eclipse Workbench platform and rebranded it as WebSphere Studio Workbench 2.0.1. SunONE Studio 4.0 Community Edition, Sun's open-source, free distribution offering, is based on the former Forte Tools for Java.

✦ **Chapter 37** focuses on accessing and displaying Domino 6 views, documents, and forms via servlets using Domino's custom JSP tags. The chapter illustrates servlet development using Domino JSP tags, the deployment of JSP and Domino access capability on a remote server, and the formatting of JSP content by creating JSP pages and examining the associated servlets that are generated by the JSPs.

✦ **Chapter 38** illustrates techniques for configuring Domino 6 and WebSphere to coexist, the issues involved in deploying a servlet on WebSphere that accesses Domino 6 data, and the issues and procedures arising from deploying and configuring J2EE Web Applications and JSPs using Domino 6 Custom JSP tags on a WebSphere server. It also covers the licensing issues involved in using the version of WebSphere that is bundled Domino 6.

✦ **Chapter 39** covers the issues involved in developing JavaScript solutions for Domino clients and the new features that enable Domino applications to select one JavaScript function for the Web and another for the Notes 6 client. It also shows how to use the new JavaScript Script libraries, which are centralized, shared Domino 6 design elements that support all the Syntax and UI features of a JSHeader object.

✦ **Chapter 40** builds on the basic JavaScript examples in the preceding chapter to develop advanced client functionality for the latest Internet Explorer and Navigator Browsers and for the Notes 6 client.

✦ **Chapter 41** highlights DHTML functionality for Domino, including the new CSS storage object, and shows examples that use Cascading Style Sheet styles and classes and the new HTML Layers to write to DIV tags by using JavaScript.

✦ **Chapter 42** shows some of the ways to expose and manipulate undocumented Java applet parameters and methods by using JavaScript in Web applications.

- ✦ **Chapter 43** introduces developers to the new Data Connection Resource, which is based on DECS (Domino Enterprise Connectivity Services) data integration functionality but does not use the DECS Administration Database (DECSADM.NSF). Instead, the connections and activities are defined in the Domino application database itself, and to function, a DCR-enabled database just needs to be put on a Domino server running the DECS tasks.

- ✦ **Chapter 44** shows the creation of a Domino Web application that uses the DCRs introduced in Chapter 43 to retrieve data from a MS Access Database.

- ✦ **Chapter 45** introduces you to the new Lotus Enterprise Integrator 6, including the exciting new Virtual activities that are available, such as Virtual Documents.

- ✦ **Chapter 46** introduces developers to XML structure, the parsing and transforming of XML, XML data islands, and the uses of XML in Domino applications, including new DXL Exporter, Viewer, and Transformer utilities.

- ✦ **Chapter 47** expands on the introduction provided in Chapter 46 by illustrating DXL utility examples and explains the new Domino 6 StartKey/UntilKey and KeyType ?ReadViewEntries URL command parameters and their uses. Developers are also introduced to the DXL Schema by way of a comparison between the DXL Schema and the Domino DTD.

- ✦ **Chapter 48** provides examples of the NotesXMLProcessor, NotesDXLExporter, NotesStream, and NotesNoteCollection classes and techniques for "pipelining" the results of one NotesStream call to another to generate DXL from Domino Data in LotusScript agents.

- ✦ **Chapter 50** shows techniques for building J2EE applications that can access Domino objects and generate DXL and custom XML formats using support for the J2EE compliant JDK 1.3 in Domino 6. The example is a fully functional Java application that uses SWING classes and AWT events to generate a UI, Domino 6 objects to access Domino 6 data, and Domino and Lotus XML Toolkit classes and methods to generate DXL and other types of XML.

- ✦ **Chapter 51** shows techniques for building Servlets and J2EE applications that can access Domino objects and generate DXL and custom XML formats using support for the J2EE-compliant JDK 1.3 in Domino 6. The example is an adaptation of the application presented in Chapter 50, this time adapting the Java application to call Domino 6 servlets, which access Domino 6 data, and pass data back to the application or a Web browser in a three-tier application model.

- ✦ **Chapter 52** provides examples using the new DOM and SAX LotusScript parsing classes as well as up-to-date J2EE parsing techniques that are supported by JDK 1.3. Examples include LotusScript and Java agents parsing an XML document using DOM, and parsing a DXL document using SAX.

- ✦ **Chapter 53** covers tips and techniques for transforming XML documents into other XML formats and HTML, including options for using the new DXL Transformer utility in Domino Designer and the new Domino 6 LotusScript NotesStream and NotesXMLTransformer classes for DXL documents. It also provides up-to-data J2EE code for transformations and illustrates techniques for building stylesheets to transform custom XML and DXL document output.

✦ **Chapter 54** provides a working example of combining XML, XSL, JavaScript, and DHTML. The example uses the latest version of the Microsoft XML parser, Internet Explorer 6, and Domino 6 design elements to create an XML data island. The data island uses JavaScript-based XML parsing and XSL transformation to create a user-sortable version of a Domino view in a Web browser.

✦ **Chapter 55** introduces developers to the fundamentals of Web Services, which use features in Domino 6 (most critically, J2EE support via the JDK 1.3) to provide service-oriented, component-based, self-describing applications based on an architecture of emerging Web Service standards.

✦ **Chapter 56** focuses on the most practical solution for hosting Web Services in industrial-strength server environments — by serving the Web Service through a third-party application server such as WebSphere or TomCat and calling Domino 6 objects via classes from that server. It includes examples that provide a Web Service for test purposes using the new AXIS SOAP Simple Server, compiled Java 1.3.x classes that call Domino objects, and a sample database on a Domino 6 server.

✦ **Chapter 58** illustrates the great potential for the Notes 6 client to become a full-service Web Services client by introducing developers to SOAPConnect, which enables Web Service access via SOAP from LotusScript. It also shows examples of a Notes client accessing Web Services from a Java agent using AXIS.

Conventions Used in This Book

The following sections explain the conventions used in this book.

Menu commands

Whenever you are instructed to choose a command from a menu, you see the menu and the command separated by an arrow symbol. If you're asked to choose the Open command from the File menu, for example, the directive appears as File ➪ Open.

Typographical conventions

We use *italic* type to indicate new terms or to provide emphasis. We use quote marks ("") to indicate button options on forms, pages, and so on. We use **boldface** type to indicate text that you need to type directly from the keyboard.

Code

We use a special typeface to indicate code, as demonstrated in the following example of Java code:

```
PrintWriter pw = new PrintWriter();
```

This special code font is also used within paragraphs to make elements such as method names — for example, `invoke()` — stand out from the regular text.

Icons

Several types of icons appear in the margins of the book to indicate important or especially helpful items. Following is a list of these items and their functions:

 Tips provide you with extra knowledge that separates the novice from the pro.

 Notes provide additional or critical information and technical data on the current topic.

 Cross-Reference icons indicate other chapters in the book where you can find more information about a particular topic.

 New Feature icons point out features new in Domino 6.

 These icons direct you to relevant material on the book's companion Web site.

Navigating This Book

This book is designed to be read from beginning to end, although if you have already been introduced to the basics of Domino, you can easily skip over the first set of chapters and return to them at some other time.

Companion Web Site

This book provides a companion Web site where you can download the code from various chapters. All the code listings reside in chapter-specific .zip files that you can download by going to www.wiley.com/compbooks/benz, selecting the Downloads link, and then choosing the link for the chapter files that you want to download. Although the Wiley site is the official site for this book, we are also maintaining a separate site, NDBible.com, which is where we provide up-to-date information about this book, as well as general information about Notes/Domino 6 and Lotus technologies in general. The NDBible site provides quite a few goodies not found on the Wiley site. In particular, many of the code examples from the book are actually running on this site. Advisor Media and its *Lotus Advisor* magazine are instrumental in supporting the NDBible.com site.

After you download a file, you can open the file and extract the contents by double-clicking the downloaded file or selecting the Open option for the download dialog box. If you don't currently have WinZip or another archive tool on your workstation, you can download an evaluation version from www.winzip.com.

The files should be extracted to a drive on your system that has at least 50 MB of available space. Included with each chapter's download is a text file named README.TXT that contains instructions for file placement, application installation, and workstation setup requirements for the downloaded files.

Additional Information

You can obtain updated information on Lotus and Domino 6 at our Web site, NDBible.com.

Feel free to contact us with any questions or comments. We greatly appreciate any feedback that you have about the book (good or bad). It will enable us to update any future editions to ensure that you have the most current information you need to write the best applications you can.

Enjoy!!

Brian Benz
bbenz@benztech.com

Rocky Oliver
rock@sapphireoak.com

Acknowledgments

As with all books, this was a team effort, and all members of the team deserve credit. I'd like to thank the whole editorial team at Wiley for their patience in putting up with our schedules during the writing of this book, especially Jim Minatel and Sara Shlaer. I apologize for any pain and suffering endured during status meetings. And a special thanks to the technical editors for their help in making sure the code said what we said it said. And to the editors for making me rewrite sentences like that.

Special thanks go to the members of Penumbra for their help and support in the development of the book and its content.

Brian Benz

As Brian stated, this is a team effort and would not have been possible without the perseverance and undaunting efforts of Project Editor Sara Shlaer, Technical Editor Carolyn Kraut, and the other Wiley editors who made this book possible.

On a personal note, I feel a need to thank a few others for their support, encouragement, patience, and occasional kick in the pants to get this book done. These include, in no particular order: Henry Newberry, Rob Novak, the staff at *ADVISOR* (including Liz Olsen, Ellie MacIsaac, John and Jeanne Hawkins, and Christa Coleman), the folks at Lotus Software and IBM, the participants in the Lotus BP Forum, and the members of the Penumbra Group. You are all exceptional people.

In an unusual note, I want to thank the new owner of the Atlanta Falcons, Arthur Blank. Mr. Blank bought my favorite hometown team, the NFL Atlanta Falcons, and turned a perennially moribund team into a contender by infecting the organization and the fans with his enthusiasm. During the writing of this book, I always looked forward to my breaks from writing to watch our Atlanta Falcons play, and it was a very enjoyable experience thanks to the magic that Mr. Blank worked with our team. Mr. Blank, you have revived our franchise and my hopes along with it. Thanks.

No acknowledgement would be complete without mentioning my amazing wife, Debbie Oliver. She continues to support me through thick and thin, good times and bad, and I would not be half the man I am without her by my side. She has given me five amazing children, and most of all, she gives me love. She is, quite simply, the best thing that has ever happened to me.

Rocky Oliver

Contents at a Glance

Contents

Part VI: LotusScript Language Techniques   401

Chapter 29: Introduction to LotusScript 403

Chapter 30: Working with the Domino Object Model in LotusScript 423

Chapter 31: Advanced LotusScript Techniques 469

Part VII: Java Techniques   511

Part IX: Relational Database Integration — 667

Chapter 43: Integrating Enterprise Data with Domino Applications 669

Chapter 44: Developing Domino Applications for Data Integration 685

Part X: XML   715

Part XI: Web Services   867

Introduction to Lotus Notes and Domino

The History of Notes and Domino

By Richard Schwartz

Eighteen years after Ray Ozzie struck a deal with Mitch Kapor, the founder of Lotus Development corporation, and formed Iris Associates to start developing a product based on his vision of collaborative software for networked PCs, Lotus Notes and Domino 6 has been released by IBM. Ray's vision, which has survived corporate changes and even his own departure to form a new company, Groove Networks, has grown into one of the most successful software products in history, with an installed base of some 80 million users. Notes and Domino owe much of their current success to the fact that Lotus and IBM (which acquired Lotus in 1995, shortly after Lotus acquired Iris) have kept up with emerging trends in information technology at every step along the way. The credit for this goes back to the original vision for the product.

The Notes Vision

The vision for Lotus Notes was never really about any specific technology. The proof of this is that software development done at Iris was cross-platform right from the very beginning. The code that Ray and the other engineers at Iris wrote was designed to be portable to many different operating systems and network protocols, and versions of Notes and Domino have been released for a half dozen different processors, five network protocols, and more than a dozen operating systems. The vision for Lotus Notes was a vision of the way people work and the tools they need to work together.

Ray Ozzie first began to piece together his vision when he was a student at the University of Illinois. While there, he had access to a system called PLATO, which was a mainframe-based timesharing platform for educational computing. In 1973, a programmer named David Woolley wrote a program that allowed users of the PLATO system to send problem reports to the system managers. The program also allowed the system managers to respond to the reports, and the users to respond to the responses. As far as anyone knows, this was the first software implementation of a multi-user, online, threaded discussion system. The system, which was called Notes, was soon adapted for other purposes besides reporting problems.

A module called Personal Notes was added to PLATO in 1974. This was essentially an e-mail system for PLATO users. Nobody really knows who invented e-mail, and Personal Notes was far from the first e-mail system, but even in the late 1970s e-mail was a foreign concept to most people. Ray Ozzie may have been the first person to see both a threaded discussion and e-mail and realize that a system that combined the features of both could be an incredibly powerful tool for businesses.

Note   Nobody really knows who invented e-mail, but it is known that it dates back to the early 1960s. We have heard credible claims for unknown students at both MIT and Dartmouth College. Since most people credit MIT, we're willing to accept that, but the Dartmouth story is actually more interesting because it claims that a student developed the system to communicate with his girlfriend, who could log in to the Dartmouth computers from a terminal at her college more than 90 miles away. Even if this is true, however, the first e-mail system that worked by sending messages between two computers across a network, however, is credited to Ray Tomlinson, an engineer at BBN, the company that did much of the early development work on ARPANET.

Ray also saw a PLATO module known as Group Notes, which extended the original Notes program to allow users to create their own private threaded discussions. One of the key concepts of Group Notes was the Access List, which defined whether individual users could create new threads, read threads, and respond to threads. Ray's vision included similar security mechanisms, and more, because he realized that a system for sharing information among workers could be successful only if it could be trusted to enforce limits on sharing.

Another PLATO feature that influenced Ray Ozzie was networking. By the late 1970s, both Personal Notes and Group Notes had been adapted so that users on different PLATO mainframes in different locations could exchange messages and participate in the same threaded discussions. In the early 1980s, the IBM PC exploded onto the business scene, and Ray correctly predicted that PCs would eventually be networked, allowing software that worked like PLATO Notes to revolutionize the way office workers collaborate with each other.

Ray Ozzie was not the only person to see and be inspired by PLATO Notes. The list of software that traces its lineage back to PLATO Notes includes DEC Notes, which was written for Digital Equipment Corporation by another former U of I student, Len Kawell, who was one of the four co-founders of Iris with Ray. Another descendant of PLATO Notes is the Usenet News system, which provides tens of thousands of newsgroups to millions of users of Internet servers around the world.

Realizing the Vision

Lotus Notes, which was initially released in 1989, began the realization of Ray Ozzie's vision. Ray combined the e-mail, threaded discussion, security, and networking concepts that he had seen in PLATO with five more key concepts to complete the vision. These concepts include:

✦ The idea of the container object model, the "note" database

✦ The ability to create and manage loosely defined data schemas

✦ The concept of rich text, and creating a rich text object as a container for text with effects (for example, bold, italic, color) as well as objects

✦ The ability to create fairly robust database programs with user-friendly programming interfaces

✦ The concept of portability and remote access — what is commonly referred to as replication

The first of these new concepts was the "note" database.

Ray and the other engineers at Iris devised the Notes Storage Facility, or NSF file. It's a bit of an oversimplification, but the best way to think of an NSF file is as a container full of different types of notes. Some notes are *data notes*, also known as *documents*, which contain the data that users work with. Some notes are *design notes*, also known as *design elements*, which contain meta-data that controls the formats in which users see and edit the data documents. We describe these types of notes, and others, more thoroughly in Chapter 4.

The second of the new concepts was loosely structured data. Most database architectures require that all data conform to a rigidly defined schema. The database management software validates all data to make sure that it follows all the rules laid out in the schema so that required data is always present, all data elements have the correct type, and all relationships between records are maintained correctly. Notes does not do this. Over the years, many critics picked on the fact that Notes is not relational, but the real root of criticism is that Notes doesn't enforce a schema, and in Ray's vision this was a strength of Notes, not a weakness. There are many good points for both sides of this argument, but the philosophy behind Notes is that enforcing a schema makes it harder for real-life Notes applications to include all the data that users really need. Managing a database schema, and managing the data to make sure that it conforms to any changes in the schema, takes time and requires a fairly high level of skill and discipline. Ray and his associates at Iris wanted the management of Notes databases to be simple so that applications could be created quickly and modified easily.

The third new concept that Ray added to the vision was rich text editing. By giving users word processing style features for control over colors, fonts, and text layout, as well as the ability to insert non-text elements, such as graphics or file attachments, Ray elevated Lotus Notes' functionality far above the simple text processing offered in PLATO and the other collaboration systems that preceded Notes.

The fourth new concept was programmability. By creating what you see is what you get (WYSIWYG) design tools for generating forms for displaying and editing documents, views for displaying lists of documents, and a simple programming language for doing computations, Ray made Lotus Notes much more than a set of single-purpose applications. It became a platform for developing custom, client-server applications.

The fifth new concept was remote access. Ray extended the networking concept in PLATO to include mechanisms for dialing in to connect to a Notes server, and for replicating databases between servers and clients. This allowed users to take Notes with them when they traveled with their laptop computers, and to connect with a modem in order to resynchronize the data. Local area networks (LANs) were just beginning to become commonplace during Notes' early years, and dial-in network access (Microsoft's RAS) was not in widespread use. Inexpensive high-speed network connections didn't exist either. Notes users, however, could take their work with them wherever they went, and this was an extremely important advantage for Lotus.

The Evolution of Notes into Domino

Groupware is a term that evolved in the mid 1980s to refer to software that helps users in workgroups collaborate more effectively. When Lotus Notes hit the market for the first time, adoption was a little slow. But by the time Release 3 came out in 1993, Notes was clearly the dominant groupware platform. The early releases of Lotus Notes were clearly targeted at workgroups, but with Release 4 in January 1996, it became obvious that Lotus was positioning Notes as an enterprise solution and that this positioning was going to be successful. Groupware became something of a passé term, and the Notes became the leader in the new, less limiting buzzword: collaboration.

At about the same time that Notes was experiencing rapid growth as an enterprise collaboration platform, the World Wide Web was taking the world by storm. There was a great deal of hype about how the Web was going to be a Notes killer. Lotus recognized that Web technology had certain advantages over any system that relied on a proprietary fat client, but that it also had many weaknesses. The standardized technologies used on the Web addressed only a small part of what Notes did. Still, it was clear that tremendous momentum was building up behind Web technologies, and it was only a matter of time before someone overcame the limitations and developed solutions that delivered a rich set of collaboration features via the Web. Lotus decided to be that someone.

In December 1996, less than a year after releasing Notes R4, Lotus changed the name of the Notes server, and released versions 4.5 of the Lotus Notes client and the Lotus Domino server. This release included an HTTP server that could make Notes applications accessible to users of Web browsers. The HTTP portion had actually been released earlier in the year as an add-on to the R4 Notes server, and was an immediate hit with developers. Domino made six of the seven key features (all except replication, and Lotus later released Domino Off-Line Services to take care of that), which had made Notes into a success available to browser users.

The next releases of Notes and Domino continued to embrace evolving standard technologies. By the time Notes and Domino Release 5 shipped in 1999, Domino was a mature and robust platform supporting proprietary technologies such as @formulas and LotusScript and standard technologies such as HTML, JavaScript, Java, and XML, delivering solutions to both the proprietary Notes client and to standard Web browsers. Few, if any, software products have as long a history as Notes and Domino. And few, if any, software product visions have been so successful or so successfully adapted to new technologies.

Notes and Domino 6

Notes and Domino 6 follows in the tradition of preceding releases, adding more power and flexibility for end-users, system administrators, and developers, and adding support for even more standard technologies such as SOAP, UDDI, and WSDL. The IBM development team continues to build on the foundations that were established by the earlier releases, maintaining a level of backward compatibility that is probably unparalleled in any other application development environment. Almost all applications written for previous releases, all the way back to Release 1 from 1989, run on Notes and Domino 6 exactly as they did before. This is all the more remarkable for Notes and Domino 6 because IBM engineers completely rewrote a key component of almost all applications, the engine for executing @Formulas. The new engine is considerably faster than the old version, and it adds many new features to make programming easier, and yet fully compatible with previous versions.

Some of the key new features in Notes and Domino 6 are

✦ Looping in the function language

✦ Accessing list elements with array syntax in the Formula language

✦ Functions @GetField, @ThisName, and @ThisValue for referring to a field and field value without any hard-coding

✦ Improved list processing functions in the Formula language

✦ Improved error processing in the Formula language

✦ Remote debugging of agents

✦ Trusted agents accessing data on remote servers

✦ Boolean and Byte data types in LotusScript

✦ NotesXML, NotesXSL, NotesDOM, NotesSAX, and NotesStream classes in LotusScript for processing XML data

✦ NotesUIScheduler class in LotusScript for embedded schedulers

✦ NotesNoteCollection class in LotusScript for working with design elements or other types of non-data notes in a database

✦ New NotesRichText classes in LotusScript for navigating and editing rich text items

✦ Separate event handling for Notes clients and browsers

✦ The InViewEdit event allowing users to edit documents in views without opening or previewing them in the Notes client editor

All of these features, and many others, will be covered in-depth in later chapters. The preface contains a listing of these features, so if your primary interest in this book is catching up on what's new, you may want to make that your focal point. However, even developers with extensive Notes and Domino R5 development experience will find valuable insights into many of the older Notes and Domino programming features throughout this book.

✦   ✦   ✦

A Simple Application

By Richard Schwartz

✦ ✦ ✦ ✦

In This Chapter

Creating the application

Creating a form

Creating a view

Creating a page

Setting the application's home page

Testing the application

✦ ✦ ✦ ✦

It's been a tradition for the past twenty years or thereabouts for computer programming books to start with an example called Hello, World. The example code simply displays the text "Hello, World" on the user's screen. In this chapter we pay a bit of homage to that tradition, but we don't really stick to its spirit. Our first example application does a little bit more than just say "Hello".

The Purpose of This Example

In this book, most of the examples are either part of a sample Web site or part of a toolkit for Notes and Domino system administrators. This example is part of the Web site. It's a simple user feedback mechanism for the site, and it has the following features:

   ✦ It says "Hello" to the user.

   ✦ It displays the user's name.

   ✦ It enables the user to enter a comment.

   ✦ It allows users to see comments posted by all users.

Note that a real Web site feedback application would probably not allow users to see each other's comments. You return to this application in Chapters 11 and 22 to add security features that prevent this while still allowing site administrators to see all comments.

The application consists of one form, one view, and one page. Users open the application to the page, which contains links to the form and view. Users use the form to enter their own comments. They use the view to see an index of all the comments that have been entered thus far. Because the links on the page can't be created until after the form and view are created, you're going to build the form and view first.

On The Web

This example can be downloaded from www.wiley.com/compbooks/benz.

Creating the Application

To create an application from scratch, the first thing you must do is start Domino Designer. After that, you create a database file and add some design elements. All applications use one or more database files. You learn more about these files in Chapter 3. Design elements are the basic building blocks of the application, the containers for what-you-see-is-what-you-get (WYSIWYG) designs and code. You learn more about design elements in Chapter 4, and throughout the book.

To create the application's database file, choose File ➪ Database ➪ New to open the New Database dialog box (as shown in Figure 2-1), and fill in the fields as follows:

> Server: **Local**

> Title: **Ch. 2 Ex. A: User Feedback**

> Filename: **Ch2-A-Fe edback.nsf**

Figure 2-1: The New Database dialog box

Domino Designer creates a new file on your PC's hard drive, and displays the Forms index. As you will learn in Chapter 5, Domino Designer presents indexes of the different types of design elements (forms, views, pages, and so on) that make up an application. If you were working with a pre-existing Domino application, you would see a list of all the forms in the index. Because this is a new application, there are no forms to see yet. You learn a lot more about forms in Chapters 8 and 12, but for now the only thing you need to know is that a form is what Domino developers create when they want to allow users to enter data.

Creating a form

Follow these steps to create a form in Domino Designer and add text and fields to it:

1. Click the New Form button. This opens the Form editor. You see Untitled in the window title bar, and on the Designer's workspace tab, because the new form has not yet been named and saved. The cursor appears at the top of the form.

2. Type **User Feedback** at the top of the form and press the Enter key twice.

3. Using your mouse, go to the top of the form and select the text that you just entered (User Feedback), being careful not to select the two empty lines that you created below it. Click the B icon on the toolbar to change the text to boldface.

4. Position the cursor at the second of the two empty lines below the title (User Feedback). Type **Enter your comments here** and press Enter twice.

5. Choose Create ➪ Field from the menu. Designer inserts a field element in the form where your cursor is positioned with a placeholder title of Untitled, along with the Field Properties box. Change the following items in the dialog box:

Name: **CommentBody**

Type: **Rich Text**

Note   Whenever you are instructed to modify parameters of a properties box in this chapter it is presented in the preceding fashion, which is *property name: value*. So in this instance the Name property should be set to CommentBody, and the Type property should be set to Rich Text.

6. Close the Field Properties box, click to the right of the placeholder for the CommentBody field, and press the Enter key twice.

7. Choose Create ➪ Hotspot ➪ Button from the menu. Designer inserts a standard button in the form and then displays the Button Properties box. Change the following item in the dialog box:

Label: **Save**

8. Click the Hide-When tab in the Button Properties box. (This is the third tab from the right, with an icon that looks like a horizontal line with a small loop under it.) Put checks in the boxes labeled Previewed for Reading and Opened for Reading. Another check automatically appears in the box labeled Printed.

9. Close the Button Properties box.

10. The pane in the lower-right of the Designer workspace is known as the Programmer's pane. Click in that pane to place your cursor there, and type **@Command([FileSave]);@Command([FileCloseWindow])** as shown in Figure 2-2. Then click the green check that appears at the top of the Programmer's pane. This Notes formula code instructs Notes to save your data and then close the form's window.

11. Choose File ➪ Save from the menu. The Save Form As dialog box opens. Type **Feedback** into the dialog box and click OK. You now see Feedback listed in the Forms index.

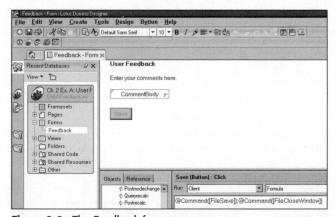

Figure 2-2: The Feedback form

Creating a view

On the left side of the Designer workspace, you should see the Bookmark pane, with a rectangular bookmark block representing your application, and an Explorer-style navigation tree inside the block. You should see the Feedback form that you just created in the tree. You should also see a branch in the tree labeled Views. *Views* are design elements used to present groups of documents to a user. Views are also used to allow a user access to a document so that he can work with it; for example a user might want to open it, edit it, or delete it. All databases are required to have at least one view, which is why there is always one view — Untitled — in every database you create. Of course this view is either modified to be usable or deleted (because you create your own views) during the development of your application. Follow these steps to create a view for this application:

1. Click the Views entry in the tree. The Views index appears.

2. Domino always provides a default view for every application, which appears in the index as "(untitled)". Double-click it to open it in the View editor and bring up the View Properties box.

3. Fill in the name property in the dialog box as follows:

   Name: **Main**

Now that you have created a view and given it a more meaningful name, it is time to add some columns to the view to make it usable for your users.

Modifying a column

Columns in a view present individual item values from the documents displayed in a view, or you can also enter @functions to compute data to display. Without columns your users wouldn't know what they are looking at. Follow these steps to modify a column in the view:

1. Close the View Properties box and click the pound symbol (#) that appears inside the rectangular section of the gray bar at the top of the View design pane. The gray bar represents the column header that appears at the top of a view displayed in Notes client. The rectangular area of the bar represents a column in the view. Domino Designer created a default column for this view, and configured it to display an unsorted list of documents identified only by simple index numbers that start at one and go up to the number of documents contained in the view.

2. Notice that a list of Simple Functions appears in the Column Value pane on the lower right of your Designer window. Change the selection in this window from # in view to Author(s) (Simple Name). This selection causes Domino to display the name of the person who created each feedback document.

3. Double-click the # symbol to open the Column Properties box. Change fields in the dialog box as follows:

   Title: **User**

   Width: **20**

4. Click the Sorting tab in the dialog box (it looks like a pair of arrows with one pointing up, and the other pointing down). Change fields in the dialog box as follows:

   Sort: **Ascending**

Note that the # sign has now been replaced by the word User, and that the rectangular area representing the column has grown and is highlighted to indicate that it is currently selected.

Adding a new column

You have modified the existing column in your view—now you are beginning to build a view that is useful to your users. The next step is to add additional columns to your view to make it even more useful. Follow these steps to add a new column to the view:

1. Double-click in the gray area to the right of the first column to create a second column. Note that the Column Properties box and the Column Value pane now display information for a new column.

2. Enter the following in the dialog box:

   Title: **Date**

   Width: **20**

3. Close the Column Properties box, and then change the Simple Function selection in the Column Values pane to Creation Date. This selection causes Domino to display the date that each feedback document was created.

4. Choose File ➪ Save from the menu. Be sure to click Yes when you are asked whether you want to save your changes.

The view, which is now complete, is shown in Figure 2-3. Notice that the entry for (Untitled) in the View index has been updated and now says Main.

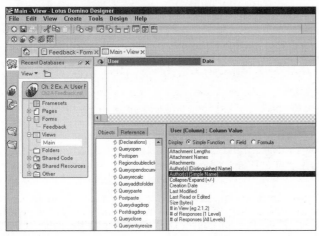

Figure 2-3: The Main view

Creating a page

You should now see three tabs running along the top of your Designer workspace. One is labeled Ch. 2 Ex. A: User Feedback. Domino Designer keeps one tab open for an index of design elements in each database that you are working on. If you click this tab, you return to the View index because the most recent type of element you created was a view. The other tabs are labeled Feedback - Form and Main - View. These represent the design elements that you have created so far.

You can tie these design elements together into a complete application in many ways. You could, for example, use a frameset and an outline (see Chapter 11) to provide links to the form and view. Or, you could set the application to launch directly into the view and add a View action (see Chapter 16) that opens the form. Instead, however, you're going to have the application launch into a page, and put links to the form and view on that page. You're also going to display the user's name on the page by using Domino's computed text feature. Follow these steps to create the page:

1. Click the Pages branch of the navigation tree in the Bookmark pane. This opens the Pages index. As was the case with the Forms index, this will be empty because it's a new application.

2. Click the New Page button. This creates an empty page in the Designer workspace. Pages are similar to forms. You learn all about them in Chapter 8. For now, the most important thing to know is that the Domino Page editor lets you use WYSIWYG techniques to lay out text, graphics, and links for a page that can be viewed in the Notes client or a browser.

3. Type **User Feedback** at the top of the page and press the Enter key twice.

4. Using your mouse, go to the top of the page and select the text that you just entered (User Feedback), being careful not to select the two empty lines that you created below it. Click the B icon on the toolbar to change the text to boldface.

5. Position the cursor at second of the two empty lines below the title (User Feedback). Type **Hello** and press Enter twice.

6. Choose Create ⇨ Computed Text from the menu. This inserts the words `<computed value>` as a placeholder in the page, and opens the Computed Text Properties box. Close this dialog box and place your cursor in the Programmer's pane at the lower right of the Designer workspace.

7. Type **@UserName** in the Programmer's pane and click the green check box at the top of the Programmer's pane. Figure 2-4 shows the computed text formula you just entered.

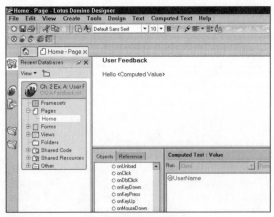

Figure 2-4: Computed text on a page

8. Click to the right of the `<computed value>` placeholder and press Enter twice; then type **Click Here to Submit Feedback**.

9. Select the text you just created with your mouse, and then choose Create ➪ Hotspot ➪ Link Hotspot from the menu. The Hotspot Resource Link Properties box opens. You will create a link from this page to the Feedback form you created earlier.

10. In the dialog box, locate the Type field and select Named Element from the selection list. Another selection control appears immediately to the right. Select Form from this second list. Also, type **Feedback** in the Value field of the dialog box. Close the dialog box. If you move your cursor to another place, you'll notice that your text has turned blue.

11. Position your cursor at the end of the text and press Enter twice; then type **Click Here to View Feedback.**

12. Select the text you just created with your mouse, and then choose Create ➪ Hotspot ➪ Link Hotspot from the menu to display the Hotspot Resource Link Properties box again. You are about to create a link to the Main view you created earlier, just like you did with the Feedback form.

13. Select Named Element again in the Type field in the dialog box, but this time select View from the second list and type **Main** in the Value field of the dialog box. Close the dialog box. Notice that the new text has also turned blue.

14. Choose File ➪ Save from the menu. The Save Page As dialog box opens. Type **Home** into the dialog box and click OK.

The finished page, with the Hotspot Properties box still open, is shown in Figure 2-5.

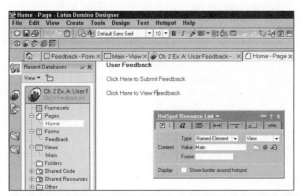

Figure 2-5: The Home page

Setting the application's home page

The last thing you need to do is tell Domino to use the page you just created as the application's home page. To do so, follow these steps:

1. Choose File ➪ Database ➪ Properties from the menu. The Database Properties box opens.

2. Click the Launch tab. (This is the third tab from the right, with an icon that resembles a rocket ship tilted on a 45 degree angle.)

3. Select Open Designated Page in the When Run in a Browser drop-down list. Another drop-down list labeled Page appears. Select Home in the Page drop-down list. These settings are shown in Figure 2-6.

4. Close the Database Properties box.

Figure 2-6: Setting the Launch properties

Testing the application

After all the design elements are done, you must test and deploy an application to a Web server. Because this is just a simple sample the actual deployment isn't described in this chapter. You learn about that in Chapter 6. Instead, this chapter describes how to use Domino Designer's built-in Web preview server to test your application.

Only one step is left to prepare for testing. Domino Designer's Web preview server does not know how to prompt users for a login name and password, but it does enforce Domino's rules that control who can use an application. Without a login prompt, however, the Web preview server considers all users to be anonymous. The default for Domino applications, however, is to disallow anonymous access, so this setting must be changed before you use the Web preview server. To do so, follow these steps:

1. Choose File ➪ Database ➪ Access Control. The Access Control List dialog box opens.

2. Select Default in the large listing window in the dialog box.

3. Select Author in the Access field on the right of the dialog box.

4. Close the dialog box.

You're now ready to test the application. If you followed all the directions exactly, the page that you created should still be visible on your Domino Designer workspace. (If it isn't, click the Home - Page tab at the top of the workspace, or click Home in the Bookmark pane to bring it up.) Choose Design ➪ Preview in Browser from the menu. You see a submenu listing the browsers available on your system. The list also includes the Notes browser, which is installed automatically with your Notes 6 client software.

Select the browser that you want to use for your testing. The application's home page appears in the browser's window. To complete your test, follow these steps:

1. Click link Click Here to Submit Feedback link. Your Feedback form appears in the browser, as shown in Figure 2-7.

2. Type a few words in the field that appears on the form, and then click the Save button. The words Form processed appear.

3. Click your browser's Back button twice to return to the application's home page.

4. Click link Click Here to View Feedback link. The application's main view appears. It's not pretty, but it is functional. You should see one entry in the view, with an Anonymous link.

5. Click the link in the view. A read-only version of the Feedback form appears, and you see the words you typed earlier.

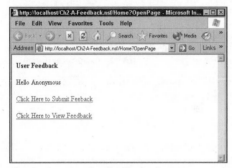

Figure 2-7: Previewing in the browser

You can also test your application in the Notes client by selecting Design ⇨ Preview In Notes from the menu. The application is shown in the Notes client in Figure 2-8. The only noncosmetic differences that you should notice while testing in the Notes client are as follows:

✦ Form processed does not appear after you click the Save button. Instead, you automatically return to the application's home page.

✦ Instead of Anonymous, you see your own name listed in the main view because the Notes client knows your identity.

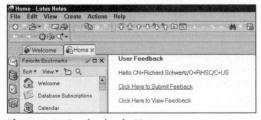

Figure 2-8: Previewing in Notes

Improving This Sample

This sample application is functional, but basic. Here are some ways to improve it:

✦ When run directly from the Notes client (rather than being previewed), the Home Page does not appear. To launch a page in the Notes client, you must create a frameset and put the page into it. You learn how to do this in Chapter 11.

✦ When run in the Notes client, your name appears on the Home Page in an ugly format known as the canonical form fully distinguished name. You can clean this up by using the @Name function, which you learn about in Chapter 15.

✦ When run in the browser, the Form Processed feedback provided when the user submits the form is not very helpful. Also, users have to use the browser's Back button to return to the Home Page. You learn how to provide customized responses and navigation links in Chapter 19.

✦ When run in the browser, the Main view looks ugly. You learn how to customize views in Chapter 10, and you learn to use view templates to improve their appearance in Chapter 19.

✦ Whether you run it in the Notes client or a browser, the application lacks the visual appeal that users expect. You learn how to use colors and graphics to enhance the appearance of pages and forms in Chapter 12.

Summary

In this chapter, you saw that it's possible to create a simple application consisting of three design elements:

✦ A Feedback form with some static text, a modifiable field, and a button.

✦ A Feedback view that lists the author and creation date of documents created with the Feedback form.

✦ A Feedback page that contains computed text to display the user's name, along with links to the form and view.

While this seems overly simplistic, you do need to crawl before you walk. This was a "crawling" chapter. Later in this book you get your legs under you and begin walking, and by the end you will be a world-class Domino Developer sprinter. So hang in there, and you'll be building robust applications in no time at all. Now that you've crawled by building your first application, the next chapter helps you understand the ground you're covering by explaining the Notes Storage Model.

✦   ✦   ✦

The Notes Storage Model

By Richard Schwartz

If you followed along with the example in the preceding chapter, you may be wondering what `Ch2-A-Feedback.nsf` was for. Every Notes application and every Domino-based Web site consists of one or more NSF files. The file extension .nsf, which stands for Notes Storage Facility, indicates that the file is a Notes database file. The NSF file, and the related NTF file, which you'll learn about in Chapter 6, is the fundamental container for everything in Notes and Domino.

The NSF file is a container of a container of containers. It contains notes that contain items that contain values, lists, or compound data. The notes represent data stored in documents, and application GUI and logic stored in design elements within the file. The items represent data fields within the documents, as well as code and user interface components in the design elements. Lists and compound data are ways of storing more than one simple value in an item. Understanding this architecture in detail is the key to understanding why Notes and Domino programming is so different from other programming models.

In addition to describing the NSF file, this chapter also describes some of the programming mechanisms that are closely related to elements of the file's architecture. These features are described in more detail later in the book. For the purposes of this chapter, however, it is important that you understand a little bit of basic terminology:

- ✦ Formula language is a programming language similar in appearance and function to spreadsheet programming languages. The names of functions in Formula language begin with the @ symbol. Some examples are @Sum, which adds a list of numbers, and @DbLookup, which retrieves data from documents. Formula language is used for selecting documents, and for setting, validating, and transforming data values for storage and display. Formula language is covered in Part V, Chapters 23 through 28.

- ✦ LotusScript is a programming language that is similar in syntax and semantics to Visual Basic. It runs in the Notes client and on the Domino server. It has object-oriented features, and it uses a powerful set of predefined classes that represent elements of Domino data. The same classes that are available to LotusScript programmers are also available to Java programmers. These classes have methods and properties, which provide access to data and predefined operations on the data. The names of the classes all begin with the word Notes. Some examples are `NotesDatabase` and `NotesDocument`.

Note   The same classes that are used in LotusScript and Java are also available in Visual Basic or any other programming language that supports Microsoft's COM standard. We cover COM/OLE in Chapter 31, but we omit mention of it elsewhere in the book, unless there is an important point to make about how a specific feature works with COM.

Servers and workstations

The Notes Storage Facility (NSF) is the container for all elements that comprise the design and data of a Domino database. But before discussing the NSF file itself, let's first consider where you might find an NSF file. In Chapter 2, you created `Ch2-A-Feedback.nsf` on the hard drive of the computer where you were running Domino Designer. In Chapter 6, you learn how to deploy an NSF file to a Domino server. One of the strengths of the Notes and Domino architecture is that the same file architecture is used both on the Domino server and the Notes client.

When accessing a database, the user interface of the Notes client often gives a choice between selecting a local or a specific server name. Local refers to the hard drive of the user's own computer. We refer to NSF files stored on the user's hard drive as local databases. By default, Local databases are located in the directory specified in the User Preferences as the Local database folder; however, they can be stored anywhere on the user's hard drive. When writing Notes and Domino code to open a database file, the word local is not used. It is actually possible for a Domino administrator to create a server called Local. Although this would be a very bad idea, that's what any code that actually used the word local would assume you are trying to work with a server named Local. Instead of the word local, code uses an empty string to refer to the user's computer. Here are some examples of code that opens a database:

- ✦ `@Command([FileOpenDatabase];"MyServer/MyOrg";"MyDatabase.nsf")`

- ✦ `session.GetDatabase("MyServer/MyOrg","MyDatabase.nsf")`

- ✦ `@Command([FileOpenDatabase];"";"MyDatabase.nsf")`

- ✦ `session.GetDatabase("","MyDatabase.nsf")`

The first and second examples open a database on a server called `MyServer/MyOrg`. The third and fourth examples, which use `""` instead of a server name, open a database on the user's computer. You learn more about programming with `@Command`, as shown in the first and third examples, in Chapter 24. You find out more about programming with LotusScript, as shown in the second and fourth examples, in Part VI—Chapters 29, 30, and 31.

Whether an NSF file is local or on a server, it has the same structure, essentially the same capabilities, and looks and acts essentially the same to a user.

Notes Storage Facility

The NSF file is the fundamental container for everything in Notes and Domino. Deployment of a Notes or Domino application is normally a matter of placing one or more NSF files in the appropriate directory on a server or workstation's hard drive. It is a rare occasion when there are additional files to copy.

The NSF is the container for Notes and Domino code. In most cases, there are no DLL or EXE files to install on a server or a user's workstation. Installing separate code files is only necessary if an application makes use of COM, the Notes C or C++ API, an LSX (LotusScript Extension), or an LSS (external LotusScript library). Although these are all powerful tools, most applications don't need them.

The NSF file is also the container for many of the resources that a Notes or Domino application uses. The NSF file can contain files, graphics, OLE objects, and Java applets.

New Feature Notes and Domino 6 support some new resource types, such as stylesheets and files, which you learn about in Chapter 4. It has always been possible to include any type of file within an NSF file by attaching it to something else that Domino knows about, and writing special code to get at it. Notes and Domino 5 supported images as a resource type, making it possible to organize all GIF and JPEG files in one place. The new resource types in Notes/Domino 6 make life easier for developers by organizing all resources in one place and providing an easy way for developers to reference the resources.

If you followed along with the example in Chapter 2, you may have noticed that you never created any other files or tables for the data in the application. You also never created a schema to define records for the data. That's because the NSF file is also the container for the data created and used by the Notes or Domino application, and data is stored in the NSF file in documents, which are flexible or loosely structured, not in records that have to conform to a predefined schema.

Storing all code, resources, and data in one file that can exist on a server or on a user's workstation is one of the keys to a feature that differentiated Notes from all of its early competitors, and it is still a major factor in the ease of development and use of Notes and Domino applications. The NSF file was designed specifically to support replication, which allows many servers and workstations to have copies, known as replicas, of the same NSF file and to keep everything in them — data, code, and resources — synchronized. Replication made it possible to build large networks with many Notes servers sharing the workload for an application. It also made it possible for users to take Notes with them on the road on a laptop, work with up-to-date code and data, and send changes to the data back to a server later. Maintaining the synchronization would be a lot harder if Notes used separate containers for code, data, and resources.

The Replica ID

Replication allows many servers and workstations to keep replica copies of the same NSF file. Notes and Domino need some way of knowing that two NSF files are replicas of one another. Lotus realized that using the filename, or even the full path plus the filename, was not a good way to identify replicas. That approach has two problems: Developers of different applications might coincidentally choose the same name for their file, and users could easily break replication by renaming or moving a file. Instead, Lotus decided to set a unique value within a new NSF file, and copy that value to any new replicas that are made from that file. All replicas therefore share that value, which is known as the Replica ID.

The Replica ID is string of eight bytes. Its contents are actually interpreted by internal code in Notes and Domino as a date and time encoded in a condensed format, but there is almost never a reason for a Domino programmer to care about that. In this book, the Replica ID is simply a unique value that is created by Notes software and used to identify all the NSF files that are replicas of each other.

The eight bytes of a Replica ID are normally represented in hexadecimal notation, in one of two formats. It takes 16 hexadecimal characters to represent eight bytes. One format for Replica IDs separates the 16 characters into two groups of four, with a colon character in between, like this:

```
85256C39:001AF5EA
```

This is the format displayed by the Notes client when you open the Database Properties dialog box, and by the Domino Designer when you use the Database Synopsis feature (see Chapter 5). It is also the format used in the Notes and Domino Formula language, in functions like @Command([FileOpenDbRepID]) (see Chapter 24), @DbLookup, and @DbColumn (see Chapter 26).

The other format for the Replica ID omits the colon character, like this:

```
85256C39001AF5EA
```

This is the format used in the LotusScript and Java object models for Notes and Domino, in the NotesDatabase.OpenByReplicaID method and the NotesDatabase.ReplicaID property (see Chapter 30), and by the Domino COM classes in the NotesDbDirectory.OpenDatabaseByReplicaID method. You can also use the @ReplicaID function to get the Replica ID of the current database.

New Feature

The @ReplicaID function and the NotesDatabase.ReplicaID property are both new to Notes/Domino 6.

It can also be used when constructing a URL to access a document from a browser. The following URL, for example, retrieves a document with a key field set to Index in a view called Main in an NSF file with the preceding Replica ID:

```
www.mysite.com/85256C39001AF5EA/main/index?OpenDocument
```

Finding an NSF file

Notes users normally find an NSF file by choosing File ➪ Database ➪ Open from the menu, or by clicking a bookmark or link that someone else has created for them. Browser users normally find an NSF file by clicking a bookmark or link, by typing a URL that specifies the path to the NSF on the server, or an alias that was set up by the server's Web master. (A Domino server feature also enables browser users to view a list of links to all database files on the server, but this is usually considered a security weakness and therefore should be disabled.)

Notes and Domino programmers have four programmatic ways to find an NSF file. The Replica ID, discussed earlier, is one of the ways. Sometimes the Replica ID is used alone, and sometimes it is used in combination with a server name. A programmer can pass only the Replica ID to the @DbLookup and @DbColumn functions in the Notes Formula language, which tells Notes to first look for the NSF file on any server that the user has accessed it on previously; then on the server that contains the database that contains the code that is calling @DbLookup or @DbColumn, and then on the user's local workstation. A server hint can optionally be supplied to @Command([FileOpenDbRepID]). Notes uses the same strategy as described earlier for @DbLookup and then checks the server named in the hint if the NSF file hasn't already been located. In LotusScript and Java, the server name can be specified as an argument to the NotesDatabase.OpenByReplicaID method.

Cross-Reference   @DbColumn and @DbLookup are covered in more detail in Chapter 26: Using the Formula Language to Retrieve Data.

The second way to find an NSF file is by the path name. This is always done in combination with a server name, with a blank server name indicating that Notes should look for the NSF on the local hard drive. In LotusScript, the server and path name are supplied as separate arguments to `NotesSession.GetDatabase` and `NotesDatabase.Open` methods. In Formula language, the server and path names are supplied as a single argument formatted as a list (see Chapter 23) for `@DbLookup`, `@DbColumn`, or `@Command([FileOpenDatabase])`. The path name can also be used in URLs for Web applications. The following URL, for example, opens a document with a key field set to Index in a view called Main in the file `myDir/myAppliction.nsf` stored on a Domino server.

```
www.mysite.com/myDir/myApplication.nsf/main/index?OpenDocument
```

Using the path name to find an NSF file in code is subject to the same disadvantages discussed earlier about using the path name to uniquely identify an NSF for replication, but you can guard against this to some extent. In an application that consists of several NSF files, for example, you can store the path names of various databases in a known location that is configurable for each server or workstation where replicas exist, and have your code look up the path names. Another way, which is less foolproof but easier, is to require that the paths to the various NSF files be related to one another in such a way that code can ask Notes for the name of the NSF file that it is contained in (using the `@DbName` function in Formula language, see Chapter 23, or `NotesSession.CurrentDatabase.FilePath` in LotusScript or Java, see Chapter 30) and calculate the name of the other NSF files by varying the filename or path in a predetermined way.

The third way to find an NSF file is simply to presume that the NSF file that you are looking for is the same one that the code is running in. This may seem at first like a trivial point, but it's not. Developers often want to write code that can be reused in many applications. Reusable code needs to be able to access something that could be in any NSF file, but happens to be in the same NSF file as the code. In LotusScript and Java, the `NotesSession.CurrentDatabase` method can always be used to access the database that contains the running code. In Formula language, this is done by specifying a single empty string to functions `@DbLookup` and `@DbColumn`.

The fourth way is through the `GetFirstDatabase` and `GetNextDatabase` methods of the `NotesDbDirectory` object in LotusScript, Java, or COM. This way implicitly specifies a server name because the server name (or an empty string, indicating the local hard drive) was required to create the `NotesDbDirectory` object itself.

Inside the NSF

You've already learned that an NSF file is a container for code, data, and resources. All of these different things are actually stored using a generic storage format, which is called a *note*. An NSF file contains a header, some information used to track replication, some information that is used to track which users have read which notes, object storage for attachments and embedded objects, and some other internal data structures. For all intents and purposes in this book, however, the file can be thought of simply as a container for notes.

Understanding notes

As the basic unit of storage within an NSF file, a note has to be able to represent many different things. It needs to be able to represent WYSIWYG user interface components for applications, code, various types of resources, and data created by users. Lotus designed the note to be an extremely flexible container for data.

As you see later in this chapter, a note contains data units known as *items*. For now, the only thing you need to know is that items have a name, and they have a data type. You examine items in more detail later.

Every note also contains two other structures:

✦ A header that contains important information about the note itself. This header includes identifiers for the note, the type of note, the parent (if any) of the note, a count of the number of items in the note, the dates and times the note was last accessed and modified, various flags, and a count of the children of the note.

✦ A list of notes that are children of this note, also known as response notes.

The concept of a hierarchy of parent and response notes is extremely important in Notes. As noted in the introduction, it's one of the features of the PLATO system that inspired Lotus Notes. The inherent tracking of response hierarchies that Notes does automatically is often a key architectural consideration in applications. You learn more about responses later in this chapter and elsewhere in the book.

Types of notes

One field in the header of a note contains the Note class, which identifies the type of the note. There are about a dozen different classes of notes, but this section considers four types of classes: Admin notes, Design notes, Design Collection notes, and Data notes. One way of thinking about the distinction between these types is that system administrators create Admin notes to control security and replication, and programmers add Design notes to a Design Collection note to allow users to find and manipulate Data notes within an NSF file.

Admin notes

Admin notes are special notes that contain information that is neither part of the programming of an application, nor part of the data stored by the application. Two classes fall into this category:

New Feature

Generally, the only programmers who need to be aware of the presence and structure of these system notes are those who are working with the Notes C API. But Notes and Domino 6 provide a new class, `NotesNoteCollection`, which allows adventurous LotusScript programmers to manipulate the details of these notes. See later in this chapter, for more information.

The classes of Admin notes are

✦ **Access Control List (ACL).** This note establishes security for the application by assigning permissions to users and groups of users. Domino Designer provides a special interface for editing this note, and the `NotesACL` class for LotusScript and Java allows programmers to manipulate the security information stored in the note. The

`NotesNoteCollection.SelectACL` property can also be used to get lower-level access to this note, but the authors' past experience indicates that a damaged ACL can have crippling consequences and can be extremely difficult to repair, so it is probably not a good idea to use this property to make changes to the ACL note.

✦ **Replication Formula**. This note contains server or user names, some flags, and a formula that Notes and Domino use during replication to determine whether two replicas should be kept fully or partially synchronized. The `NotesNoteCollection` `.SelectReplicationFormulas` property can be used in LotusScript or Java to access these notes.

An NSF file may contain only one ACL note, but it can contain many different Replication Formula notes. The `NotesNoteCollection.SelectAllAdminNotes` method can be used in Java or LotusScript to access all Admin notes.

Design notes

Design notes are notes that contain WYSIWYG user interface elements, code, or both. They define the appearance of the application for Notes client and browser users, the logic that controls all interaction with users and workflow for the application, and resources that are used in the user interface or code. Programmers create Design notes using Domino Designer.

There are only eight classes of Design note. Many of these classes are used to store more than one type of design element. A flag stored in the note tells Notes and Domino which type of design element is actually in the note.

Programmers normally work with these notes in Domino Designer. It is also possible to write code that manipulates some properties of these notes.

The note classes in this category are as follows:

✦ **Form:** These notes represent forms, subforms, pages, image resources, framesets, Java resources, stylesheet resources and shared actions. The `NotesForm` class is available to LotusScript and Java programmers who want to write code to manipulate Form notes that represent actual forms. The `NotesNoteCollection.SelectAllFormat-Elements` method can also be used to access all Form notes, and there are additional select properties in that class that provide access to specific types of Form notes.

✦ **Field:** These notes represent shared fields, which can be inserted into forms and subforms. The `NotesNoteCollection.SelectSharedField` property allows LotusScript and Java programmers to work with these notes.

✦ **View:** These notes represent views, folders, and navigators. Views and folders are tabular representations of collections of documents. Navigators are graphical objects that contain code that can be used to open documents or other Design notes to provide a user-friendly way through an application. Why these two very different types of things share the same type of Design note is a mystery to everyone except the programmers and architects at Lotus who set it up that way. The `NotesView` class is available to LotusScript and Java programmers who want to write manipulate views and folders. The `NotesNoteCollection.SelectAllIndexElements` method can also be used to access all View notes, and there are additional select properties in that class that can be used to provide access to specific types of View notes.

✦ **Filter:** The name of this note class is a reference to the filter feature of Notes Release 2, which was expanded into the agent feature in Release 3 (incidentally, agents were referred to as macros back then, but agents and macros are the same thing). These notes represent agents, outlines, script libraries, and database scripts. The `NotesAgent` and `NotesOutline` classes are available to LotusScript and Java programmers who want to manipulate Agent and Outline notes. The `NotesNoteCollection.SelectAllCodeElements` method can also be used to access all Filter notes, and there are additional properties in that class that can be used to select specific types of Filter notes.

✦ **Help Index:.** This note class is not described in detail in any official Lotus documentation. It is only used in the help databases that Lotus provides with the Notes, Domino Designer, and Domino Administrator products. It can be accessed in LotusScript and Java via the `NotesNoteCollection.SelectHelpIndex` property, but there's little point in doing that since its sole function is to provide a way for the various client applications (i.e., Notes, Designer, Administrator) to link features in the client code to individual help documents in the help database. These documents are displayed when a user presses the F1 key for context-sensitive help because of this link.

✦ **Info:.** This note, also known as the Help ➪ About note, is normally used as a place to record general information about what the application is used for, how it is deployed, and what the security requirements are. Domino Designer provides a special interface for editing this note. Formula language provides a function for displaying this note, `@Command([HelpAboutDatabase])`, and in LotusScript or Java the `NotesNoteCollection.SelectHelpAbout` property can be used to find this note.

✦ **Help:** This note, also known as the Help ➪ Using note, is normally used as a place to record instructions for users of the application. Domino Designer provides a special interface for editing this note. Formula language provides a function for displaying this note, `@Command([HelpUsingDatabase])`, and in LotusScript or Java the `NotesNoteCollection.SelectHelpUsing` property can be used to find this note.

✦ **Icon:** This note contains the graphic that is displayed by the Notes client to represent the application, along with the database title and a few other items. The `NotesNoteCollection.SelectIcon` property can be used to find this note in LotusScript or Java code.

An NSF file may contain only one Info note, Help note, Icon note, and Help Index note. It may contain many Form, Field, View, and Filter notes. `NotesNoteColleciton.SelectAllDesignNotes` can be used in LotusScript and Java to access all these notes.

Design Collection notes

The Design Collection note in an NSF is essentially a hidden View note containing an index of all the Design notes in an NSF file. There is no direct programmatic access to Design Collection notes, but LotusScript and Java developers can use the `NotesNoteCollection.SelectAllDesignElements` property to get the same index that is contained in the Design Collection note.

Data notes

Data notes represent documents in the NSF file. There is only one notes class in this category, which is (not surprisingly) known as the data class. There are actually two types of data, known as documents, and profile documents. You learn more about the difference between these two types of Data notes later in this chapter.

Forms and documents

Notes and Domino programmers also create their own distinctions between different types of documents and profile documents. These distinctions are not really part of the architecture of the NSF file itself, but the most common way of making these distinctions is closely related to a fundamental concept that all Notes and Domino programmers must understand: the relationship between a form and a Data note.

Whenever the Notes client displays a document or profile document to a user, it uses a form to format the display, and it uses the Data note to supply the values that are displayed. Notes and Domino programmers often draw distinctions between different documents or profile documents by using different forms.

Some people like to think of the form as if it were a stencil or mask that is placed on top of the Data note in such a way that only certain items inside the note show through. In reality it is more complicated than that, because the Form note also controls manipulation of the data in the note when the note is displayed, when it is saved, and at various other times. In any case, it is very important to realize that every Data note representing a document or profile document is always presented through a form.

There are two ways that Notes and Domino can select a form for presentation of a Data note. The most common way that Data notes are related to forms is through a pointer value contained within the Data note. The less common way is for the Data note to actually contain a copy of the Form note, a feature known as Store Form In Document, or SFID for short. Notes and Domino help developers maintain the relationship between Data notes and forms by automatically storing either an item called Form, or an item called $Title inside every Data note that is created with a form.

Notes and Domino examine the note to see if it contains an item called Form. If so, this item contains the pointer value, which is simply the name given to a form's Design note. Notes and Domino locates a Form note in the same NSF file as the Data note, with a name that matches the contents of the Form item in the Data note. If no such item exists in the Data note, Notes and Domino look for an item called $Title in the Data note. If that does not exist, Notes locates the default form for the NSF file that contains the Data note it used. If no default form is found in the NSF file, Notes and Domino handle the situation as an error.

You can change the appearance of a document at any time by modifying the form used to display the document. This does not change the document or its items at all. If you add new fields to the form, they will be treated as uninitialized data the next time the document is viewed. If there are no formulas or scripts in the new form design that are dependent on the values of the new fields, no errors will occur when you do this. You can also delete fields from the form, but bear in mind that this does not delete the corresponding items from the document. If you want to reclaim the storage space, you can write code to remove the items using the @DeleteField function.

Replication and save conflicts

Notes and Domino applications inherently have multiuser features. In any multiuser system, it is conceivable that two users might try simultaneously to update the same piece of data. Many systems take steps to prevent this, often by implementing some sort of record locking mechanism. Notes and Domino have not, until Release 6, either tried to prevent conflicting updates from happening or provided tools specifically to help developers prevent this from happening. The Notes and Domino architecture was designed to permit replication of the same NSF file between many servers and workstations, and allowing conflicts was a deliberate design decision that was made in order to make replication "safe" by making sure conflicted data isn't lost. By tracking replication conflicts and keeping both "versions" of the document, the NSF file places the onus of reconciliation of the error on the user.

A locking scheme requires that some central authority, presumably one of the servers, keep track of which users hold locks on which notes. But the designers of Notes and Domino built a product that was designed to run in an era before high-speed networking was common in business environments. They did not want to assume that all replicas of an NSF would exist on the same network, and they wanted users to be able to take NSF files on the road on laptop computers, update information in documents, and dial into their servers to replicate the changes later; therefore, they did not assume that one central authority could always be kept informed of all locks.

A save conflict occurs when two users access the same note in the same replica of an NSF file, in the following sequence:

1. Alice opens the note.

2. Bob opens the same note.

3. Alice changes an item in the note and saves the change.

4. Bob changes the same item in the note and also saves the changes.

A replication conflict occurs when Alice uses replica 1 of an NSF, and Bob uses replica 2 of the same NSF, and the following sequence of events occurs:

1. The two NSF file replicas are synchronized.

2. Alice opens a note, changes an item, and saves the change in replica 1.

3. Bob opens a note, changes an item, and saves the change in replica 2.

4. The two NSF file replicas are resynchronized with each other via replication directly with each other, or through one or more intermediary replicas.

When a save or replication conflict occurs in a Data note that is a regular document (not a profile document), Notes and Domino create a new note called a conflict document, and add an item called `$Conflict` to it. In all other cases, Notes and Domino simply discard the older note and keep the new one.

A conflict document becomes a response to the original Data note. Notes and Domino display conflict documents in any views that display their parent documents, flagging the conflict with a gray diamond on the left margin of the view and also displaying `"[Replication or Save Conflict]"` in a column within the view. A user or system administrator normally examines the conflict document and its parent, selects one or the other to save it, edits it to update fields as needed — which, if done to the conflict document, automatically promotes it so that it becomes the parent, and the parent becomes the conflict — and then deletes the conflict document.

Many developers use the security features of Notes and Domino to control who will be allowed to update documents at specific times, essentially creating locks, and helping to minimize the probability of conflicts. This level of control is not foolproof, and it is not appropriate for some applications, so conflicts do sometimes happen. Developers can also write code that locates conflict documents by searching for notes containing the `$Conflict` item, and automatically resolves the conflicts by updating either the conflict note or its parent note, and deleting the other note.

Finding a Note

The NSF file, which is a container for notes, would be pretty useless if you couldn't find notes inside it when you wanted to work with them. The Notes client provides mechanisms for users to find documents, either by scanning through views, which are lists of documents, by clicking links or bookmarks created by other users, or by executing a search. Browser users have similar capabilities, thanks to Domino server's ability to interpret URLs as paths to specific documents and to present views as lists of links. The Notes client and the Notes Admin client provide dialog boxes for access to information in Admin notes, and the Domino Designer client also provides developers with ways to find Design notes.

Developers also need ways for their code to find specific notes, and the programming languages supported by Domino Designer provide several mechanisms. There are two identifiers for every note, the UNID and the Note ID. Code that knows a Universal Note ID (UNID) or Note ID of any note of any type can retrieve the corresponding note. Notes can also be found in collections. Data notes can normally be found in collections that are associated with views or folders stored in the NSF file. Data notes that represent documents can also be found through their parent-child relationship with each other in a response hierarchy. Other collections, containing any type of note, can be built as needed. There is also a special mechanism for retrieving profile documents.

The UNID

Every note has an identifier: the UNID. A note's UNID is the same for that note in all replicas of the NSF file in which that note exists, and different from the UNIDs of all other notes in the same replica. The UNID is actually a subset of a larger identifier known as the Originator ID, or OID, which uniquely identifies each revision of each note. The OID, which is fully described in the Note C API User Guide and is downloadable from the www.lotus.com/ldd Web site, is generally of interest only to the Notes and Domino replication code, which needs to know when two replicas of the same NSF file contain different data within the same note. The UNID, however, can be useful in ordinary Notes and Domino application development.

The UNID is a string of 16 bytes. The first eight bytes are set randomly when the note is created, and the next eight bytes are set to a condensed representation of the date and time when the note was created. Like the Replica ID, however, it is almost never necessary for a Notes or Domino developer to know how to interpret the contents of a UNID. It can simply be thought of as a unique 16-byte key for every document.

The following programming features in Notes and Domino work with UNIDs:

✦ In Formula language, @DocumentUniqueID returns the UNID of the current document, @InheritedDocumentUniqueID returns the UNID of the current documents, and @GetDocField and @SetDocField use a UNID to locate a document in order to read or modify an item value.

✦ In LotusScript and Java, the NotesDocument.UniversalID returns the UNID of a note, and the NotesDatabase.GetDocumentByUNID method retrieves a note with a given UNID. Doclinks in a document contain UNIDs for the linked document and the "parent" view it was linked from. You can access these two UNIDs by using the NotesRichTextDocLink.ViewUNID and NotesRichTextDocLink.DocUNID properties.

Note   Doclinks are hyperlinks within Notes, similar to URL links between Web pages, which are created by users using facilities in the Notes client, or by code in Notes applications. See Chapters 28 and 30 for more information about creating doclinks.

✦ In Domino applications for browsers, URLs can be constructed using the UNIDs of documents and views. URLs constructed this way are extremely ugly, but the Domino server usually generates them automatically for you. The following URL, for example, opens a document with UNID 699a94011f907ce585256bac00765b12 in a view with UNID 38d46bf5e8f08834852564b500129b2c in an NSF file called `sample.nsf` on a Domino server:

```
www.mysite.com/sample.nsf/38d46bf5e8f08834852564b500129b2c/699a94011f
907ce585256bac00765b12?OpenDocument
```

Cross-Reference   You may be wondering why, because a UNID uniquely identifies any note, it's necessary to include both a document UNID and a view UNID in a URL. The same question actually applies to doclinks, which were discussed earlier. The truth is that you don't have to include a view UNID in either case, but it does serve a purpose if you do. You can replace the view UNID in a URL with a zero, retaining the slash characters that surround it. If you do this, Domino will not be able to execute a form formula, which you may have included in the code of one or more views in your application. See Chapter 15 for more information about form formulas.

The Note ID

In addition to the UNID, which is always the same for any given note in all replicas of an NSF file, every note also has a Note ID, which uniquely identifies the note only within one replica. You may wonder why, if there is already one unique ID, should there be another ID, particularly one that is only useful within one replica? The keys to the answer are that the Note ID, is only four bytes long — much shorter than the UNID — and many of the internal functions and data structures in Notes and Domino use Note IDs for efficiency.

The following programming features of Notes and Domino work with Note IDs:

✦ In Formula language, the @NoteID function returns a string containing a representation of the Note ID, in the format NTxxxxxxxx where each x represents a hexadecimal digit.

✦ In LotusScript and Java, the NotesDatabase.GetDocumentByID method retrieves a note with a given Note ID. It expects its input in the format returned by the NotesDocument.NoteID property or the NotesViewEntry.NoteID property, both of which return the Note ID as a string of hexadecimal characters without the leading letters NT and without any leading zeros.

Using the Note ID is usually the fastest way to access a note, but programmers need to be careful about its use. Even in situations where a database is not replicated to other servers or to user workstations, using the Note ID can be risky because system administrators sometimes need to make a new replica of a database to solve a problem or to swap hard drives on a server. The Note ID should, therefore, never be used as a durable identifier. In other words, a Note ID should not be stored by code running at one time for use by code running at some indeterminate future time.

Collections

When an application needs to examine or manipulate many notes, it is usually not possible to run through a list of known UNIDs or Note IDs. Fortunately, the NSF file contains stored indexes of notes in views, folders, and several built-in indexes, and there are ways that Notes and Domino developers can use these stored indexes or create temporary indexes and write code that walks through them to find documents. In Notes and Domino programming, access to indexes of notes is done through collections.

Some collections have sort keys. Programmers can write code to locate all notes in a collection that match a key value. Although Notes and Domino do not guarantee that a key value is unique to only one note in a collection, an application programmer can write code that does assure this.

Notes and Domino programmers can work with collections that are implicit in the `NotesView` object, or they can create an explicit collection using a variety of techniques to create a `NotesDocumentCollection` object.

Views and folders are the two types of indexes that programmers can add to NSF files. Both are stored in View notes. They are similar to each other, but there is one important difference. Programmers set up selection formulas that establish the criteria that determine which documents are included in View indexes, whereas users have the ability to put any arbitrary documents into Folder indexes.

Both views and folders can have sort keys. Every view and folder has one or more columns defined, and if at least one column has a sort order specified in its properties, the view or folder is keyed. The key is always the first (left-most) sorted column in the view or folder.

Notes and Domino developers can use View and Folder indexes to find documents in an NSF file, using the following features:

✦ In Formula language, `@DbLookup`, `@DbColumn`, and `@Command([OpenView])` all locate documents in views or folders by matching a key that is specified in their argument list.

✦ In LotusScript and Java, the `NotesView` class provides methods `GetFirstDocument`, `GetLastDocument`, `GetNextDocument`, and `GetPrevDocument` for iterating through notes in a view or folder. It also provides `GetParentDocument`, `GetChild`, `GetNextSibling`, and `GetPrevSibling` for navigating through a view or folder's response hierarchy, and `GetNthDocument` and `GetAllDocumentsByKey` methods for finding specific documents in a view. There is also a `NotesViewNavigator` class that provides similar methods, and also provides methods that navigate through view or folder categories (see Chapter 9 for more information about categories).

Collections resulting from a search

The Notes and Domino products have had several different built-in search capabilities for many years. Using *full-text searching*, end-users can type simple queries and get a list of all documents that contain certain words or combinations of words. And by creating personal views or private agents, end-users can run queries called *selection formulas* that use features in the Note Formula language to examine the values of items in documents and return a collection of documents that matches whatever criteria the user is interested in. See Chapters 9, 15, and 18 for more information about selection formulas in views and agents.

LotusScript and Java programmers can use full-text queries and selection formulas to build collections of documents. The `Search` and `UnprocessedSearch` methods of the `NotesDatabase` object can be used to implement a selection formula search. The `Search` method searches all documents in the NSF file, and the `UnprocessedSearch` method is used in an agent (see Chapter 18) to run a selection formula against only documents that are new or modified since the last time the agent was run.

Full-text searches can be performed for several different scopes. An entire NSF file is searched using the `FTSearch` and `FTSearchRange` method of the `NotesDatabase` class. There is a special case using a deprecated feature from Notes R4 called multidatabase search, in which these methods actually return a result set comprised of documents from multiple databases. A feature that was introduced in Domino R5, however, the `FTDomainSearch` method of the `NotesDatabase` class, is preferred over this. An agent, which is a LotusScript or Java program that runs either on a schedule or when a document is created orchanged, can use the `UnprocessedFTSearch` and `UnprocessedFTSearchRange` methods in the `NotesDatabase` class to do a full-text search limited to documents that are new or modified since the last time the agent ran. The `FTSearch` method (but not `FTSearchRange`) for the `NotesView` class can be used to limit the results of a full-text search to only those documents that appear in a specific view or folder.

All the previous selection formula and full-text search methods return a `NotesDocument Collection` object containing the results of the search. Developers can also do full-text searches on arbitrary collections of documents using the `NotesDocumentCollection .FTSearch` method, which creates the possibility of doing a full-text search on the results of a selection formula search.

Other collections

Notes and Domino programmers often want to work on a collection of all documents in an NSF file. You can create a view that includes all documents, but if you don't care about the order in which your code works on the documents, it's not necessary to do so. The `NotesDatabase.AllDocuments` and `NotesUIDatabase.Documents` methods both return a collection containing all the data notes in the NSF file.

When writing agents (see Chapter 18), Notes and Domino programmers are often interested in only the documents that are new or have been changed since the last time a particular agent was run. The `NotesDatabase.UnprocessedDocuments` property makes those documents available as a `NotesDocumentCollection` object.

Response hierarchy

Programmers often use the relationships between documents within a response hierarchy as an important part of their application's architecture. In such cases, finding a note by its UNID, by its Note ID, or through a collection, may be only the first step in a process that a programmer is implementing. As mentioned earlier in this chapter, every note contains a list of its children. Notes also always creates a special item, called `$Ref`, in every child document. The `$Ref` item contains the UNID of the parent document. The programming languages for Notes and Domino use these features to support mechanisms that allow programmers to write code that navigates up and down within a response hierarchy.

The Notes Formula language provides only limited support for working with the response hierarchy. The functions `@AllChildren` and `@AllDescendants` are useful only for selecting documents for inclusion in a view or in a replication formula. The functions `@DocChildren`, `@DocDescendants`, `@DocSiblings`, and `@DocParentNumber` are only useful for displaying information in view column or window title bar. The `$Ref` item or the `@InheritedDocument-UniqueID` function mentioned earlier in this chapter, however, can be used in combination with @GetDocField and @SetDocField to implement logic for updating a document's parent. You can also use Formula language techniques for updating a response document from its parent.

LotusScript and Java programmers can navigate up through a response hierarchy using the NotesDocument.ParentDocumentUNID property in conjunction with NotesDatabase .GetDocumentByUNID, and down through the hierarchy using the NotesDocument .Responses property, which returns a NotesDocumentCollection object containing all of the document's children.

Profile documents

Profile documents are special data notes that are cached in memory by Notes and Domino. Because the caching makes access to profile documents fast, caches are often used for storing configuration information for an application or user defaults or preferences.

Profile documents don't appear in any view. They also do not appear in the NotesDatabase/AllDocuments collection available to LotusScript and Java programmers. Finding profile documents requires the use of special functions in Formula language, LotusScript, or Java. In Formula language, the @GetProfileField and @SetProfileField functions are used to work with profile documents. In LotusScript and Java, the NotesDatabase.GetProfileDocument and NotesDatabase.GetProfileDocColleciton methods are used.

Inside a Note

The beginning of this chapter described the NSF file as a container of containers of containers. The note is a container of containers. Every note contains items, which are data elements with a name, a type, and a set of values. The number of items in a note is variable. Even notes representing the same type of document may have different number of items.

There isn't a limit on the number of items in a note per se, but some other limits do come into play. There are two limits that apply to the names of items. The names are stored in a part of the NSF file known as the UNK Table. A setting in the Database Properties dialog box for an NSF file determines which limit applies. Normally, the total length of all item names must be less than 64,000 characters. If, however, the Allow More Fields in Database property in this dialog box is checked, as it is in Figure 3-1, up to 65,535 item names can be stored, regardless of their total length.

Figure 3-1: Database property for the UNK Table

The other limit that comes into play applies to items that store summary data. The portion of a notes' storage that is devoted to summary data is only 64K, so the total size of all summary items in a note must fit within that limit. Also, no individual summary item can be larger than 32K.

Items

Items themselves are containers. As you'll soon see, there are several different types of items. Most items contain a list of values of a particular type. Rich-text items are complex containers that are organized into paragraphs, sections, tables, and MIME entities, which in turn can hold styled text, file attachments, images, embedded OLE objects, and embedded Design notes representing views and other Notes application features. We'll take a closer look at each item type shortly, but first it's important to understand the relationship between items stored in a document and fields on a form that access the items.

Items versus fields

We described the relationship between a document and form earlier in this chapter using the analogy relating the form to a stencil or mask that is placed over a document. The holes in the mask correspond to fields, which you'll learn about in Chapters 8 and 15, and the things you see through the holes are items.

The analogy isn't quite right, however, because holes are empty space that lets information pass through unchanged, and fields on a form can have formulas. These formulas can transform data from items, changing its appearance either on the way in or the way out. Field formulas can also build new values by aggregating data from more than one item, and even by looking up item values in other documents in other databases. A better analogy, therefore, might be that the fields are lenses instead of holes, and the lenses can come in all sorts of funny shapes that transform whatever information passes through them.

In any case, the difference between fields and items is an extremely important concept to understand. In the next few sections, we talk about item types, and it's very important to understand that field types and item types are only loosely connected with one another. As mentioned earlier in this book, Notes and Domino do not enforce a schema that matches item types and field types. Mismatches can and do occur, and programmers sometimes need to take special steps to deal with these situations.

Data types

Notes and Domino items come in many different types. In most Notes and Domino programming, only the following seven field types are used: Text, Names, Author Names, Reader Names, Number, Date/Time, and rich text. These field data types map to internal item types that are actually stored in the document. Table 3-1 shows the actual item types that are stored in a document, and how they map to field data types that you use when constructing fields in a form. We'll cover the first six within this section, along with a few miscellaneous types that aren't normally used in application programming, but that you may run into occasionally. Rich text is covered in a section of its own at the end of this chapter.

Table 3-1: Domino Item Types

Item Types	Field Types
Text List	Text, Password, Timezone, Color, Authors, Readers, Names
NoteRef_List	Response Reference List ($Ref) - data type only, not used in a form as a field type
NoteLink List	DocLink reference list ($Links) - data type only, not used in a form as a field type
Number Range	Number
Time Range	Date/Time
Composite	Rich text, Rich text lite, Embedded Objects (Embedded objects can be embedded in a form at design time, or into a rich text item. If embedded in a rich text item, internally a pointer to the embedded object is stored there and the actual embedded object is stored in its own item in the document.)

Other types are only accessible to Notes C or C++ API programs. These types are used for storing security information, for storing information related to the GUI definitions in Design notes, and a variety of other purposes that are beyond the scope of this book.

It is important to understand that item types and field types are actually different concepts in Notes and Domino. There are many more field types available on forms than are listed earlier in this section, but all of the field types map to one of the item types, as shown in Table 3-2.

Table 3-2: Item and Field Types

Item Types	Field Types
Text	Text, Dialog List, Checkbox, Radio Button, Listbox, Combo Box, Password, Timezone, Color
Names	Names
Author Names	Authors
Reader Names	Readers
Number	Number
Date/Time	Date/Time
Formula	Formula
Rich text	Rich text, Rich text lite

Rich text is a complex topic that warrants its own section of this chapter. The rest of the data types are briefly described in the remainder of this section.

All of these data types can store either a single value, or a list of values. The internals of the NSF file treat a single text value and a list of text values as different item types, and the same is true of all the types. In LotusScript and Java, however, all items are treated as if they contain a list even if they really contain only a single value, and Formula language can always treat a single value item as though it were a list. So, for our purposes here, we'll ignore the fact that the types are really different.

Fields on forms can be set via the Field Properties dialog box (see Figure 3-2) to restrict the item that represents the field to a single value, or to allow multiple values.

Determines whether the
item that stores the field
is a single value or a list

Figure 3-2: The Multiple Values
property for fields

A mismatch between the setting of this property for a field and the actual values stored in the item represented by the field is one of the more common programming errors that Notes and Domino programmers run into. It can be quite difficult to debug when it happens.

Text items

Text items store, as the name implies, character string data. The characters are stored in a proprietary multibyte character set known as Lotus Multi-Byte Character Set, or LMBCS. All conversions between LMBCS and the native character sets supported by PCs that Notes runs on or the character sets supported by browsers are handled automatically in Formula language and LotusScript, so programmers normally don't have to worry about the details of LMBCS. Programmers who work with the C or C++ API, however, are usually responsible for setting up the conversions properly.

Dialog lists, check boxes, radio buttons, list boxes, and combo boxes are simply special types of text fields that present a list of choices for users to select using the familiar types of user interface controls implied by their names. Radio buttons and combo boxes only enable the user to select one item, so the multivalue property for fields of this type is always turned off and the item always has a single value instead of a list. Check box fields, on the other hand, always allow multiple values, but the item may be either a single value—if the user only checks one box—or a list. Programmers can decide whether the other text types allow multiple values.

Password fields are special text fields that won't actually display their contents to users. The Notes client or browser will display a row of asterisks when a user is entering data or displaying the field. The multiple value property is always turned off for password fields, so the text item is always a single value. Note that password fields only provide minimal protection from people reading over a user's shoulder, and do not actually store the password in any sort of encrypted fashion.

Time zone and color fields provide special user interfaces for making a selection, but they store the selection as a single valued text item. If a user is working with a Notes or Domino application from a location that is thousands of miles away from the Domino server, it may be necessary for the server to know what time zone the user is in. Time zone fields provide a convenient way for users to specify time zone information, and it is automatically stored as a string in a special format. Formula language functions @TimeZoneToText, @TimeToTextInZone, and @TimeMerge work with this special format.

Color fields can be used to select colors for customizing user interfaces built with Notes and Domino. They store their value as a text item in a form that is similar to the format used in HTML, which is a variation on the hexadecimal values for the RGB (i.e. Red, Green, Blue) color.

Names, Author Names, and Reader Names items

Names items are actually text list items with a special flag assigned to them—SUMMARY NAMES. Names items are used to store user, server, or group names in a special text format known as canonical names format. The Notes and Domino security and authentication system uses distinguished names, which consist of a common name (a normal name, like John Smith), an organization name, up to four optional organization unit names, and an optional country name. Here are two examples of canonical names:

✦ CN=John Smith/OU=Sales/O=My Company/C=US

✦ CN=Jane Smith/O=My Company

Names fields provide automatic conversion of data in Names items so that the names can be entered and displayed in a format known as the abbreviated names format. The abbreviated versions of the previously listed names are as follows:

✦ John Smith/Sales/My Company/US

✦ Jane Smith/My Company

Names items are useful for creating lists of people or groups to receive mail messages and for tracking people or groups involved in a workflow process.

Reader Names and Author Names store names in the same canonical format as Names items, and Readers and Authors fields provide automatic conversions to an abbreviated format. Also like Names items, these items are simply text list items with a special flag assigned to them—SUMMARY READ-ACCESS NAMES and SUMMARY READ/WRITE-ACCESS NAMES, respectively. These items have special meaning for Notes and Domino's security system. If there is one or more Reader Names item in a note, only people whose names are listed in one of the items, or who are part of a group that is listed, will be able to read the note. Notes and Domino will not even display the note as part of an index to people who are not listed in a Reader Names item. Author Names items similarly provide control over which users can make changes to a note.

Cross-Reference Document security is covered in more detail in Chapter 10 and Chapter 21.

Number items

Number items provide storage for numbers in a format known as 64 IEEE floating point. They can store numbers with values that range from approximately -10^{308} to 10^{308}, and fractions as small as approximately 10^{-308}. Although these numbers can range from very low to very high values, their precision is limited to only 14 places.

If you are programming an application that deals with U.S. dollars and cents, you might think that 14 decimal places will always be enough, because it can accurately deal with quantities as large as $999,999,999,999.99. It is much easier than most people first suspect, however, to run into accuracy problems with numbers like this. This is especially true if you are doing multiplication and division operations.

It is important to understand that when you think you are entering a fractional value like 3.1, what your computer is actually going to do is break it into two parts and convert each part to a string of binary bits. The integer part, 3, is stored accurately, but the fractional part, 0.1, is only approximated. Just as a fraction like ⅓ can't be expressed accurately as a decimal, many decimal fractions can't be expressed accurately in binary.

The only fractions that can be accurately represented in binary are fractions that can be expressed as a sum of fractional powers of two. In other words, 0.5 and 0.25 can be expressed accurately because they are equivalent to the fractions ½ and ¼, and the denominator of each fraction is a power of two. But 0.1 is ¹⁄₁₀, and the denominator of 10 is not a power of two, therefore it can only be approximated as a series of smaller and smaller fractions: ¹⁄₁₆ + ¹⁄₃₂ + ¹⁄₂₅₆ + ¹⁄₅₁₂ + ¹⁄₄₀₉₆ + ¹⁄₈₁₉₂. This series would be represented in binary as 0.0011001100110011, with the pattern of repeating 0011 going on forever. A Number item in Notes and Domino has enough storage space to repeat the pattern 13 times, but then it runs out of room. The actual value stored will be a very tiny amount less than 0.1.

The inaccuracy in Number items is less than a factor of .00000000000001, but multiplication and division operations on numbers that are slightly inaccurate give answers that are slightly more inaccurate. And when you do a sequence of these operations, the errors can accumulate quickly.

New Feature In previous releases of Notes and Domino, programmers frequently needed to use the @Round function to compensate for the inherent inaccuracy of floating point computer arithmetic. In Notes and Domino 6, you may still want to use @Round when you are displaying number items that are the results of a series of calculations, but when you are comparing two numbers, a new function, @FloatEq, is somewhat easier to work with than @Round.

Date/Time items

Date/Time items in an NSF file store a combination of a calendar date and a time of day. The dates can range all the way back to January 1, 4713 BC, and to approximately the year 39,218 in the future. Times are stored in units of ¹⁄₁₀₀ of a second, with a time zone indicator and a daylight savings time indicator.

Date/Time fields in Notes and Domino represent a simplified view of Date/Time items. They only work with dates as early as January 1, 0001, and as late as December 31, 9999. They also ignore the hundredths of a second stored in the time portion of the item.

Many functions deal with dates/times in Formula language. The most powerful of these functions is @Adjust, which is used to perform date and time arithmetic operations, such as adding two weeks to a document creation date to set an expiration date for a workflow process. LotusScript and Java programmers can use the NotesDateTime class to manipulate date retrieved from Date/Time items. This class provides methods and properties for setting, adjusting, and comparing dates and times, converting to different time zones, and for extracting only the date or only the time.

Other item types

Formula items are used to store compiled Formula language code. Notes and Domino programmers can work with these fields when setting up a database to work with the subscriptions feature of the Notes client. There are no functions for working with formula items in Formula language, and no classes for working with them in LotusScript and Java.

Response Reference List is a special item type used to store UNIDs that point to the parent of a note. The $Ref item in response documents, and the $Orig item in mailed response documents have this type.

The data stream for an attachment or embedded object is not actually stored in the same part of the NSF file as the note that contains the attachment. Documents with attachments or objects always contain items called $FILE, which have the Attached Object type. These items are pointers to the storage area for the data stream. API programmers have to be aware of these items, but Formula language, LotusScript, and Java all deal with attachments through higher-level constructs, so that most developers don't have to deal with them directly.

RFC822 Text is a special item type used to store certain data in received Internet mail messages. LotusScript, Java, and Formula language treat these items as if they were normal Text items, so programmers generally do not need to be aware that they are a separate type.

MIME Part items are also used to store data in Internet mail messages. MIME, which stands for Multipurpose Internet Mail Extensions, is the standard method for representing electronic mail on the Internet. Like rich text in Notes and Domino, MIME allows e-mail to contain more than simple ASCII text. In Notes and Domino 6, MIME Part items can be manipulated in LotusScript and Java via the NotesMIMEEntity and NotesMIMEHeader classes.

Rich text

The NSF file was specifically designed to be a loosely structured database for loosely structured data. Its lack of a rigid schema dictating the names and types for each item in each document make it a loosely structured database. Rich text items make it the ideal container for loosely structured data. They allow users to put just about anything that can be stored on a computer into the NSF file, including images, files, Java applets, and OLE objects. Rich text items also, of course, can store text in multiple fonts, colors, and styles. To avoid having to repeat ourselves constantly when describing what can be put in rich text items, we refer to all the various things that can be stored there as *elements*.

Individual rich text items are not unlimited in size, but a key feature of the NSF file that we have not mentioned yet allows them to store an almost unlimited amount of data. A rich-text field on a form can split its data into many rich text items. All of these items have the same name, because the NSF file architecture allows a note to contain many items of the same type with the same name.

We haven't mentioned this feature until now because, except in the case of rich text items, there is almost never a good reason to take advantage of this capability, and barely even a need to be aware of it. LotusScript and Java programmers are reminded of it by the name of the `NotesDocument.GetFirstItem` method, but the fact that there is no `GetNextItem` method available to find additional items with the same name should be taken as a clue that writing code explicitly to take advantage of this feature is rarely, if ever, necessary.

Notes API programmers who work with rich text, who are a rare and very brave breed of programmers, do have to deal with the fact that rich-text storage is split across multiple items. Other Notes and Domino programmers do not. The tools for working with rich text in Formula language, LotusScript, and Java programs automatically handle all the details of dealing with storage in multiple items.

Formula language provides relatively few features for manipulating rich text. The `@Abstract` function, which is described in Chapter 28, is the only function in Formula language that can work with rich text. LotusScript and Java programmers, however, can use the `NotesRichTextItem` class to access rich text items.

New Feature

In Release 5, LotusScript and Java programmers had the ability to append styled text and doclinks to rich-text fields, but little else. Notes and Domino 6 have introduced a new `NotesRichTextNavigator` class and many other new methods and classes for locating specific elements within rich text, modifying elements in-place, and inserting new elements.

Paragraphs

The basic unit of organization in rich text is the paragraph, which is a stream of rich-text elements that ends with a new line, at the start of a table or section, or at the end of a table cell or section. Every paragraph can have a style attribute that identifies a predefined font, text color, size, and various other format attributes for the paragraph.

Paragraphs can also have formulas associated with them. These formulas are known as *hide-when formulas*. They are executed whenever Notes or Domino is displaying the rich-text field. The result of the formula is either a `true` or `false` value, which determines whether or not the paragraph should appear. We look at hide-when formulas in detail in Chapter 12.

Sections

Sections are groups of paragraphs. They were originally used to organize portions of rich text into a separate unit for security purposes. Sections can have an access list that determines which users are allowed to modify their data, and they can be digitally signed.

In Release 4 of Notes, the concept of collapsible sections was introduced. Users can click the header of a collapsible section to show or hide the paragraphs that it contains. See Figure 3-3 for an example showing two collapsible sections in the rich-text field of a Notes mail message.

New Feature

Notes and Domino 6 have a new `NotesRichTextSection` class that enables LotusScript and Domino programmers to access and manipulate the properties of a section.

Tables

Tables are rectangular areas divided into rows and columns of cells. Each cell can contain one or more paragraphs. Notes and Domino recognize five types of table. In addition to ordinary rectangular tables that display all rows simultaneously, there are four special types of tables that display only one row at a time. The types are as follows:

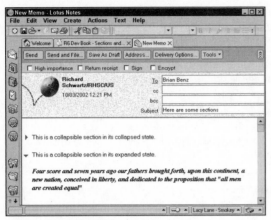

Figure 3-3: Collapsible sections

✦ **Tabbed tables:** Each row is given a name. All row names appear in a row or column of index tabs that are drawn above, below, or to the side of the table display. Users click a tab to select which row appears. See Figure 3-4 for an example. The headings Chapter 1, Chapter 2, and so on are the names of the tabs.

New Feature The tabs in tabbed tables can be set to a uniform size and positioned in different places, like on the side or below a table, in Notes/Domino 6.

✦ **Caption tables:** Like tabbed tables, rows are given names and the names are displayed in a set of caption bars that are stacked one on top of the other. Users click a caption bar to select which row is displayed. Figure 3-4 shows a two-row caption table inside a tabbed table. The captions are Text and Figures.

New Feature Caption tables are new in Notes/Domino 6.

✦ **Animated tables:** The display is cycled through the rows one at a time, with each row displayed for a configurable number of milliseconds.

✦ **Programmable tables:** Like tabbed tables and caption tables, a name is assigned to each row. A name is also assigned to the table. Notes and Domino check for an item with the same name as the table. The row with the name that matches the value of that item appears.

For more information about timed and programmable tables, see Chapter 12.

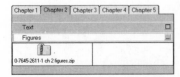

Figure 3-4: Tables can be embedded in each other, which is very useful. Here a tabbed table contains a caption table.

In theory, any rich-text element can be put into a paragraph within a table cell, but there are many practical restrictions on this — both for users and for code. Users, for example, can easily set tab stops with table cells, but because the Notes client always moves the cursor into the next table cell if a user presses the Tab key, there's no way to type tabbed text in a cell. You can, however, cut and paste tabbed text into a cell, and it aligns with the tab stops. Code can sometimes do things in rich-text fields that the Notes client won't actually let users do, but pushing the envelope of rich-text fields further than the Notes client does is living pretty dangerously. Crashes and damaged documents are potential consequences for Notes API programmers who do this.

New Feature   LotusScript and Java programmers can use the new `NotesRichTextTable` class to manipulate the rows and columns of tables.

OLE objects and Java applets

OLE is the acronym for Microsoft's Object Linking and Embedding technology. It is a close cousin of Microsoft's newer COM and ActiveX technologies. OLE is used to allow two applications to work together so that a container application can store embedded data from an OLE server application. The OLE server program is used to manage any changes to the embedded data. This can be done by in-place editing, in which the server application takes over a portion of the container application's window, or out-of-place editing, which launches the server application into a separate window. In addition, scriptable containers can use an OLE server's automation classes to manipulate the embedded data.

Notes is both an OLE container and OLE server. LotusScript programmers can use the `NotesEmbeddedObject` class, the `GetObject` function, and OLE automation classes from any OLE server to manipulate the data in embedded OLE objects. See Chapter 31 for more information about OLE.

Attachments

File attachments have been available in e-mail systems since the very earliest implementations in the 1960s. We mentioned Attached Object items earlier in this chapter. Notes and Domino store the actual data stream associated with a file in those items, but they also store pointers to those items in elements within rich text items. These pointers establish a context for the attachment within a document, allowing users to place icons for file attachments in the middle of the text and other elements of rich text. The `EmbedObject`, and `GetEmbedded-Object` methods, as well as the `EmbeddedObjects property` of the `NotesRichtTextItem` class and the `NotesEmbeddedObject` class allow LotusScript and Java programmers to work with file attachments.

Images and image resources

Rich text items may contain imported or pasted images and image resources. In both cases, the rich text item itself contains only a pointer to the storage for the image. Imported or pasted images are actually stored in an Attached Object item in the same document as the rich text item. Image resources in rich text are pointers to Design notes containing the images.

New Feature   In Notes and Domino 5, image resources used in Notes-based applications had to be located in the same database as the note containing the rich text item that referred to them. In Notes and Domino 6, image resources can be referenced in any database.

Embedded elements

You have already seen references to file attachments, OLE objects, and images that are actually stored elsewhere — in other items or in Design notes. Rich-text elements can also contain embedded elements, which are pointers to other types of Design notes. Rich text items, for example, can contain embedded views and folders that allow a rich-text field to actually contain a reference to a live display of the contents of the view or folder. The display of the embedded design element, which may also be an outline, navigator, date picker, or folder pane (the built-in navigational UI for selecting folders within a database), occurs in the midst of other rich-text elements, therefore a view can be displayed in a section or in a table cell.

Computed text

Computed-text elements in rich text allow personalization of the information so that it looks different to different users, or on different days. A user named Bob, for example, might open a document containing a computed-text element and see, "Hello, Bob. Today is Monday and there are 51 days left before Lotusphere." A user named Carol might open the same document 24 hours later and see, "Hello, Carol. Today is Tuesday and there are 50 days left before Lotusphere."

DocLinks

As mentioned earlier in this chapter, DocLinks are hyperlinks within Notes. They are elements within rich text items that represent icons that users can click to navigate from a document to another database, to a view, or to a document.

Links to databases consist of a Replica ID and a server hint. The Notes client attempts to open the database with the given Replica ID on the server specified in the hint. If that fails, it attempts to find that database on other servers. Links to views consist of a Replica ID, a server hint, and the UNID of a View note. As with a database link, the Notes client first attempts to open the appropriate database on the server named in the hint, and then searches other servers, and opens the view in the first replica of the database that it finds. Links to documents consist of a Replica ID, a server hint, the UNID of a View note, and the UNID of a Data note. The View note UNID identifies the view that the user accessed the document in when the link was first created. Even though the document UNID is sufficient to identify uniquely the desired document, the View note UNID is stored in the doclink so that a form formula stored in the View note can be run prior to display of the document.

HotSpots

HotSpots are clickable regions within rich text that trigger an action. HotSpots can contain most other types of rich-text elements, making them clickable. Several different types of actions are supported by HotSpot elements:

✦ DocLink HotSpot elements act like DocLink elements. The difference is that DocLinks are represented by a small icon, and DocLink HotSpots can contain any text or graphics, which becomes clickable, and can link to any document, view, or database. The `NotesRichTextItem.AppendDocLink` method and the `NotesRichTextDocLink` class for LotusScript and Java work with DocLink HotSpots.

✦ URL Link HotSpot elements act like hypertext links in browsers.

✦ Named Element HotSpot elements are similar to DocLink elements. Like a DocLink, they can link to a view. They can also link to any page, frameset, navigator or form (see Chapter 4 for more information about these design elements). They can't link to documents or databases.

✦ Text HotSpots and Formula HotSpots cause text to pop up when the HotSpot is activated either by clicking it or by passing the mouse over it. Text HotSpots contain the actual text that will appear. Like computed-text elements, these HotSpots allow personalization of rich text. Formula HotSpots contain code written in the Notes Formula language, and that code computes the text that will pop up.

✦ Button and Action HotSpots both cause code written in Notes Formula language to be executed. Unlike Formula HotSpots, the code does not return text that appears. Instead, the formula manipulates data in documents and executes commands, such as `@Command([FileSave]` to save new or modified data into the NSF file. Button HotSpots simply display a generic gray button graphic with an optional title. Action HotSpots can enclose almost any type of rich-text elements to make them clickable.

Rich text lite

Rich text lite fields are a new feature in Notes and Domino 6. They are stored in the same rich text item type as ordinary rich-text fields, but developers can set the properties on the field to restrict which type of rich-text elements can be put in the field. Note, however, that only the rich-text editor in the Notes client enforces the rich-text content restrictions. Browser users are not restricted by the properties of rich text lite fields, and Formula language, LotusScript, or Java is also not restricted.

Forms and rich text

Earlier in this chapter, you learned that forms are used as if they were stencils or masks that allow data items in a document to show through. The items in documents themselves do not have any inherent order or placement instructions. That is all controlled by the layout of the form that is used to display the document's items.

All the options available while working with rich text in Notes are available to programmers when designing a form. Forms can contain paragraphs with hide-when formulas, sections, tables, OLE objects, file attachments, computed text, HotSpots, and doclinks, just like rich text in documents can. That is because a form itself contains a rich text item that defines its layout. The Forms editor in the Domino Designer IDE allows programmers to create and modify the elements in the form's rich text. In addition to the elements mentioned earlier, the Forms editor allows programmers to create fields and the code associated with them, to program event scripts and to insert subforms into forms.

This is an extremely important concept, and there are important consequences to understand, so let's follow it through from the beginning. A document is a Data note containing items, some of which may be rich text items. A form is a Design note that contains items. One of the form's items is a rich text item that describes the visual appearance of documents displayed using the form. When a document appears, what the user is really seeing is the contents of the rich text item from the form, merged with data from the document's items. In other words, the document's items are loaded into the fields in the form's rich text.

As you learned earlier in the chapter, the basic unit of organization in rich text is the paragraph. Because a document's rich text item is viewed within a form's rich text, you may wonder what the relationship is between the paragraphs of the form and the paragraphs of the document's rich text. The answer is that paragraphs do not ever nest. In other words, you can't have a paragraph inside a paragraph. When a new paragraph starts, the preceding paragraph ends. This means that the fonts, sizes, and other attributes of the paragraphs within a document's rich text item are always observed. They can't simply be overridden by changing attributes on the paragraph in the form that contains the field that displays the rich text item.

Summary

This chapter has gone into great detail about the NSF file and its contents. You have learned that

- ✦ The NSF file is a container of containers of containers.
- ✦ The primary unit of data in the NSF file is the Note.
- ✦ Data notes are documents or profile documents.
- ✦ Documents are always viewed through a form.
- ✦ Design notes are used to build the user interface and the logic of applications.
- ✦ Admin notes store security and replication information.
- ✦ Notes contain items of various types.
- ✦ Notes can be found through their UNID, their Note ID, through collections, and by following a response hierarchy.
- ✦ Rich text items are containers for various types of elements.
- ✦ The layout of a form is stored in a rich text item in the form's Data note.
- ✦ Forms can be thought of as a mask or stencil that allow some items in a document to be seen and manipulated.

The next chapter dives into the building blocks used to create applications.

✦　　✦　　✦

Application Building Blocks

By Rocky Oliver

In This Chapter

Introducing design elements

Understanding data entry and display elements

Working with navigation elements

Working with code elements

Working with resource elements

Domino databases are comprised of data, and many design elements enable you to build applications that work with that data. Over the years, more of these design elements, such as Web-enabled databases, data integration, and so on, have been added to the database structure to support the ever-changing demands of the market. This chapter introduces you to these application building blocks, providing a brief introduction to each element.

Introducing Design Elements

Design elements are what you use to construct applications. You can use design elements to present data to a user in the Notes client, on the Web, or both. You can use design elements to manipulate data; you can also use them to navigate through your application so users can find the functionality or data they need. This chapter breaks down these fundamental building blocks into four major areas:

- ✦ User interface elements
- ✦ Navigation elements
- ✦ Code elements
- ✦ Resource elements

This chapter should give you an idea of what these elements are, how they are used, and how they can help you build great applications. Other chapters later in the book describe how you get the most out of these elements.

User Interface Elements

User Interface elements are data entry and display elements that you use to provide your users with the ability to manipulate the data in your application. You can use these elements for other reasons, but their primary use is to enable your users to view or manipulate your data. The following design elements are considered User Interface elements:

✦ Forms

✦ Subforms

✦ Pages

✦ Views and Folders

Forms

A *form* is a design element that acts as a lens for viewing or modifying information in a document. A form is a collection of other elements used for showing or modifying data. These other elements can be a variety of things, such as fields, buttons, embedded views, subforms, embedded objects, hotspots, and so on. A form in the Notes/Domino world is similar to a form used in the paper world — a structured interface, comprised of many smaller elements organized in a consistent fashion, used to prompt users to input data in a structured format. The next two sections review some of the most common elements used in a form.

Fields

A *field* is a design element used to present or modify a particular piece of data from a document. Fields can collect a wide array of data types, including the following:

✦ **Authors/Readers:** This field determines who can edit or read a document. It can also be a keyword field that enables the user to choose a name from their Personal Address book or the Domino Directory.

✦ **CheckBox/Radio Button:** This keyword field enables the user to choose one item (radio button), or one or more items from a list (check box).

✦ **Color:** A Color field displays a color picker dialog box when the user selects the field (see Figure 4-1), and returns the hexadecimal value of the chosen color.

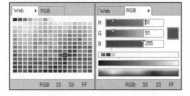

Figure 4-1: The Color field enables you to provide a color picker for your users. The color picker shows the Web palette to the user, or enables the user to choose the RGB color values.

New Feature

The Color field type is new in Notes/Domino 6.

✦ **ComboBox:** This keyword list field shows a single value at a time, or shows the whole list if you click the Helper button.

✦ **Date/Time:** This field displays a perpetual calendar picker and returns the date chosen by the user.

✦ **Dialog List:** This keyword list field displays the choices in a dialog box.

✦ **Formula:** This field enables the user to enter and validate a formula.

✦ **ListBox:** This keyword list field shows the list of values directly on the form.

✦ **Names:** This field displays a concatenated name as an abbreviated name. It can also be a keyword field that enables the user to choose a name from their Personal Address book or the Domino Directory.

✦ **Number:** This field enables the user to enter a number, formatted as desired (fixed, currency, and so on).

✦ **Password:** This field enables a user to enter text into a password field, and the text is obscured by asterisks (*).

✦ **Rich text, rich text lite:** A rich text field is a container within the form element. A rich-text item can contain almost anything, including text, pictures, attachments, embedded objects, and so on. Rich text lite fields are similar to rich text fields, but the developer can limit what the field can contain.

New Feature   Rich text lite fields are new in Notes/Domino 6.

✦ **Text:** This field enables the user to enter text.

✦ **Time Zone:** This field enables the user to choose a time zone from a list of the world's time zones.

New Feature   Time Zone fields are new in Notes/Domino 6.

Buttons, action buttons, action hotspots

A button, action button, or action hotspot enables a user to execute a predefined action. A *button* is a little gray box that can have a text label, an *action button* is part of the form design and appears at the top of the form, and an *action hotspot* enables the user to specify that text or a graphic acts as a button when the user clicks it.

You can add many other items to a form, some of which are covered later in this chapter. Refer to Chapter 5 for more detail.

Forms and documents

In the previous sections, you may have noticed a distinction between the use of the word *document* and the use of the word *form* — this distinction is intended. Although a user may view a form and a document as the same thing, under the hood they are quite different.

A *document* is where the information of the database is stored. If you are familiar with relational databases, a document is analogous to a record. A document is a collection of *items*, which are collections of one or more individual bits of information. Items can be of various data types, such as text, rich text, number, or date/time. Documents can be main documents, response documents (documents that are children of a main document or another response document), or design documents (yes, even design elements are documents).

Note   When reading about Notes/Domino, especially the API, you may hear of documents referred to as *notes*. A note and a document are basically the same, except that most of the time someone using the word *note* is referring to a design element structure.

A *form* is a lens, or template, for viewing, creating, or modifying information on a document. Forms do not store data. Forms, and the fields contained on them, are simply used to view documents and items contained in them. A form is for viewing a document, and a field is for viewing an item.

A form must always have a related document associated with it when it is opened in the UI. But a document does not have to have any form associated with it — you can create documents programmatically all day long without having any form associated with them. Or a document can have more than one form associated with it — maybe a supervisor views a document with a different form, which gives her more options or displays more information to her, than a normal user sees using his related form viewing the same document.

The separation of application and data is an important concept to grasp, not only for Notes/Domino development, but also for development in general. One of the most powerful features of Notes/Domino is that while there is a logical separation of application functionality and data, there is a physical connection in that it is all stored in one physical file. This makes Notes/Domino objects easily maintainable and portable.

A profile document is a special breed of document that doesn't behave like a normal document. A *profile document* is a special document that is normally used to cache semistatic data in a database. Profile documents have some peculiar properties that set them apart from a regular document:

✦ Profile documents can't be listed in a view or folder.

✦ Profile documents aren't normally part of a `NotesDocumentCollection`.

✦ Profile documents don't show up in the database document count.

✦ Profile documents don't respect replication/save conflicts; they act like a design element in that the last one saved *wins*.

Profile documents are extremely useful for storing information that needs to be readily available but doesn't change often. Some uses of profile documents include specific user profile information, keywords that don't change much (for example, state abbreviations), or application functionality — information that needs to be globally available.

Two types of profile documents exist: general profile documents and unique-keyed profile documents. A general profile document has a name that identifies it — this name is the name of the form you use to present it to a user for modification. Only one profile document in a database can use a name. You can, however, add an optional unique key to a profile, and then you can have multiple profiles based on the same (form) name. But even then only one profile can exist for each name/key combination. The ability to store a profile with a unique key can be useful to store profiles for particular application functions, or by user name.

Profile documents are useful for storing cached information, because they can be accessed quickly, especially if the information you're retrieving is normally stored in another database. Suppose, for example, that you centralized all your keywords and configuration documents in a central control database. Normally, you must perform a lookup to the other database to get the needed information. Performing the lookup can be expensive, time-wise, because you are going from one database to another. Instead, you could push this information into one or more profile documents in the database at the time that the keyword or configuration information is saved, and then you would have that information available to you locally. Many LotusScript, Java, and Formula methods are available for getting to profile information to make your code even more streamlined. For more information on profile documents, refer to the Domino 6 Designer help.

Forms in Notes versus forms in browsers

A form is like two design elements in one — a form design element that is useful in a Notes client, and a form design element that is useful in a Web browser. Some of the functionality overlaps, but some of it is designed for one specific client. Figure 4-2 shows the various events and areas available in an example form.

```
♦ Window Title
◇ HTML Head Content
◇ HTML Body Attributes
◇ WebQueryOpen
◇ WebQuerySave
◇ Target Frame
◯ JS Header
◯ onHelp
◯ onLoad
◯ onUnload
◯ onClick
◯ onDblClick
◯ onKeyDown
◯ onKeyPress
◯ onKeyUp
◯ onMouseDown
◯ onMouseMove
◯ onMouseOut
◯ onMouseOver
◯ onMouseUp
◯ onReset
◯ onSubmit
⌖ (Options)
⌖ (Declarations)
⌖ Queryopen
⌖ Postopen
⌖ Querymodechange
⌖ Postmodechange
⌖ Queryrecalc
⌖ Postrecalc
⌖ Querysave
⌖ Postsave
⌖ Querysend
⌖ Postsend
⌖ Queryclose
⌖ Initialize
⌖ Terminate
```

Figure 4-2: Many events and areas are available for both Web functionality and Notes functionality in a form design element.

The items with little diamonds by them are Formula-based areas. You can use most of these in the Notes or browser client, except for the WebQueryOpen and WebQuerySave events. You can use these two areas to list formula code, usually in the form of @Command([ToolsRunAgent]), which is executed right before a document is loaded into the browser or right before a document is saved to the server from a browser. These areas with names that start with HTML — HTML Head Content and HTML Body Attributes — are used to compute HTML, using the Formula language, which you can use for the HTML head and body areas of a Web document.

The little circles indicate JavaScript events that are a part of the form object. You can use four of these JavaScript events — onHelp, onLoad, onUnload, and onSubmit — in both the Notes client and the Web browser. The little curled document icons indicate events that fire in the Notes client. These events can contain LotusScript, Formula, or JavaScript. These events do not fire in a Web browser.

Many design elements used on a form are useful in both client types. If you design your forms right, you can use the same form for both the Web browser and the Notes client. A new feature in Notes/Domino 6 makes this even easier — the ability to have Web-specific and Notes-specific code in the same area. Figures 4-3 and 4-4 show how this is achieved, and what it looks like.

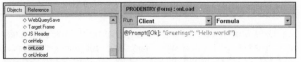

Figure 4-3: The onLoad event of this form has an @function that fires when the client loads.

The little circle indicator to the left of onLoad is two-colored. This means that there is code for both the browser and Notes clients in this event. Figure 4-3 shows the @function code that fires when the form loads into the Notes client.

Figure 4-4: The onLoad event of this form also has a JavaScript alert function that fires when the form loads into a Web browser.

Figure 4-4 shows that, in the same event, there is also a JavaScript alert that fires when the same form is loaded into a Web browser. Now you can have the same form used for both Web browser and Notes clients much more easily than in past releases.

Subforms

Subforms are parts of a form that you can insert into a form. A subform enables you to have the same part of a form available to multiple forms, thereby allowing you to create it once and use it in multiple places. You can even dynamically load subforms into a form based on an @function.

Tip   Don't overuse subforms. Using shared resources, especially subforms, has a speed cost. Subforms are heavy and take a bit of effort to load. They are useful, but the speed hit becomes worse with each additional subform you use in the same form.

Pages

Pages are similar to forms, with a couple of exceptions. The main difference is that pages are not related to documents. Because pages are not related to documents, pages are not allowed to have fields on them. Pages are mainly used to create navigation elements for your databases, as well as for embedded view display. Pages are especially useful as Pass-Thru HTML documents for Web applications. You can only edit pages through the Domino Designer, so pages are design elements, not end-user elements. If your users need to modify them, you should use a document.

Tip   Navigators became a deprecated element with Release 5, which means that you shouldn't use them any more because they're no longer being updated. For future applications use pages: They provide the same functionality as navigators, and much more.

Special pages

The term *special pages* refers to using a page as a library of code. In Release 5, pages were useful for storing JavaScript libraries, which are normally text files with a `.js` extension used to store JavaScript code. But Notes/Domino 6 now has JavaScript libraries available as a separate design element. Pages are, however, still useful for storing one type of code library — XSL stylesheets, which are text files ending in `.xsl` that contain XSL stylesheet code.

Cross-Reference You can learn more about XSL stylesheets and using pages as XSL stylesheets in Chapter 53.

Views and folders

Views and folders are design elements used to organize documents. Think of them as a table of contents (view) or bookmarks you use in a book (folder). In a table of contents, you expect to see the pages of the book listed in order. A view is like a table of contents on steroids — the developer can specify any order for displaying the documents, the view can be filtered to show a subset of documents, documents can be opened from a view, and in Notes/Domino 6 you can edit a document as it's listed in a view.

Views also extend the table of contents metaphor by introducing the concept of categorization. You can cause documents to be grouped by like values, creating categories for each value. A categorized view is like an index to a book — you want to know all the documents that pertain to Triumph Motorcycles, so you go to the index and look up the word *Triumph*, where it lists four documents. The same concept applies to a categorized view, except that you look for the category *Triumph Motorcycles*, and you can expand the category to see all the documents that had that value in the specified field in the view.

Folders are similar to views in that they are designed the same, work the same, can do the same things, and so on. The major difference is that folders, unlike views, do not automatically display documents based on selected criteria (known as a *selection formula*). Instead, folders contain a tag that tells them what folder(s) to show up in. Users normally add documents to folders, but occasionally developers place documents into folders by programmatic means.

Navigation Elements

A Domino developer uses three main elements to provide application navigation to her users: framesets, outlines, and navigators.

Framesets

Framesets were introduced in Release 5 and are similar to the framesets used in browser-based applications. *Framesets* enable the developer to quickly create a framed user interface without knowing complex code. The frameset appears in the Designer as an element instead of code, which makes it much easier to adjust as needed. Framesets work as well in a Web browser as they do in a Notes client. The contents of frames in a frameset can be pages, views/folders, forms, Notes links (such as document links, view links), or an external Web page URL. The contents can also be dynamically determined by formula at runtime. You can also control the appearance of the borders of a frameset during design time.

Outlines

Outlines enable you to automatically generate a tree-based navigation system for your Domino database. The display of an outline object can use text, graphics, colors, or a combination. You can set an outline used in a browser to appear as a Java applet or as HTML. Domino automatically generates the needed HTML for an outline based on the design of the outline.

You can also set outlines to automatically generate changes if the design of the application changes. This is especially useful on sites in which the view or document structure changes regularly, or the design is complex and changing the navigation is otherwise a pain.

But as nice as outlines are, they also have some annoying limitations — most of which center around how the application appears. Things such as margins, some font settings, and graphics/icon displays are somewhat limited with an outline. The recommended rule-of-thumb is that if your site is fairly simplistic, your graphical navigation needs are minimal, and you need to get a site up *fast*, use an outline. In fact, you may want to try an outline regardless of your needs. If you can, do so — it will save you maintenance pains later. If, however, you find outlines limiting, it's probably best to invest the time to develop an alternative navigation feature.

Navigators

Navigators are a decremented element as of Release 5 and the introduction of pages. Navigators were introduced in Release 4 to provide the developer a navigation creation tool for developing Notes/Domino applications. Navigators, however, have many drawbacks, so Lotus introduced pages in Release 5 to overcome these limitations. Lotus told the development community that navigators would continue to work, but that development effort was no longer being applied to them and pages should be used instead.

Shared Code Elements

Shared code elements are elements where code is stored. Most of the elements described in the following sections are considered shared code elements because they enable you to write code in one place and use it in many places. These shared code elements include agents, script libraries, and more.

Agents

Agents are one of the most powerful design elements in Notes/Domino. *Agents* (known as macros in Release 3) are stand-alone chunks of code that can perform actions in one or more databases. Agents are extremely powerful and flexible — a user can trigger an agent in the Notes client and in Web-based applications, a developer can schedule an agent to run periodically, and an agent can be triggered when a particular event happens, such as mail arrival. Agents can also be invoked programmatically — agents can even call other agents. Agents also can work against subsets of documents determined in a variety of ways. Agents respect the powerful security model of Notes/Domino, and can be run as the user executing the agent or as the signer of the agent (the person who last saved the agent).

 Cross-Reference   For more on agents, refer to Chapter 18.

Script libraries

Script libraries enable you to store code in one place and use it in many places. Three main types of script libraries exist: LotusScript libraries, Java libraries, and JavaScript libraries.

 New Feature Java libraries and JavaScript libraries are new to Notes/Domino 6.

Script libraries store subroutines and functions and make them available to other design elements throughout your database. These script libraries are referenced in other design elements by using a `Use` statement in the (Options) area of the code. If, for example, you have a script library called `UtilityLibrary`, you could make it available to a form by using the following statement:

```
Use "UtilityLibrary"
```

All the code in the library is immediately available to the elements of the form for use.

The great thing about script libraries is that they make your code much easier to maintain. Suppose that you have a function that you use in 14 different places in your application. You place that function in each area by copying and pasting it. A week after deploying the application, you find a bug in the function. Now you have to go to all 14 areas and correct the code—opening yourself up to making a typographical error in one or more places, causing even more headaches. Contrast this with placing the function in a Script Library. You reference the script library in the 14 places where you need it. When that bug is found, you simply correct it in the script library, and it's automatically corrected everywhere it is used.

Shared fields

Shared fields enable you to design a field in one place and use it in many places. While this may sound like a good thing, shared fields can be troublesome. Any time you use a shared resource, such as a shared field, shared action, script library, and so on, you trade a bit of code reusability and maintenance for a speed hit. It's a "pay me now or pay me later" proposition. In some shared elements, the tradeoff is worth it: Script libraries, for example, are extremely useful. The tradeoff of the speed hit for the reuse provided by shared fields is debatable. Exceptions to this rule exist, but it's generally recommended that you not use shared fields.

Shared actions

Shared actions are similar to other shared elements in that they enable you to create a single action that can be used in multiple forms, views, or folders. Shared actions have the same drawbacks as shared fields, but not to the extent of shared fields. Shared actions can be useful in designing applications, especially in those applications that have complex actions. It's much more efficient, however, to place the code you would have had in the shared action into an agent, and then call the agent with a simple `@Command([ToolsRunMacro])`. You get the benefit of centralized, shared code (the agent) without the extra weight and speed degradation of a shared action.

Shared Resource Elements

Like shared code elements, shared resource elements are designed to be stored in one place and be available for use in multiple places. The major difference between a shared code element and a shared resource element, however, is that shared code elements are programmatic Notes/Domino elements, and shared resource elements are externally created objects that are made available to other elements. These elements are typically files of some type, such as graphics, Java classes, and so on. While these elements also have the usefulness versus speed dilemma of shared code elements, the price you pay in speed is worth the advantages you get by using shared resource elements. Some of these benefits include the following:

✦ **Portability:** These elements must be on the file system if they aren't shared resources. By placing them in the database, they replicate just like other design elements.

✦ **Ease of access:** These elements are referenced simply by name because they are available as a part of the same object store.

You should use these shared resources whenever you need this type of item in your database design.

You can reference and use any of these resources in the same way. Simply choose Create ➪ Resource ➪ Insert Resource, and then choose the type of resource you want to insert. The Insert Resource dialog box appears, as shown in Figure 4-5.

Figure 4-5: The Insert Resource dialog box is a handy way to access all available shared resource elements in the current database or other databases.

New Feature

One of the most exciting new features in Notes/Domino 6 is the ability to use resources from other databases in your current database. If you look at the Insert Resource dialog box shown in Figure 4-5, you see the combo box at the top that enables you to choose the current database or other databases for selecting the desired shared resource.

Stylesheets

Stylesheets control the presentation of your documents. Usually associated with Web-based applications, stylesheets are now used to control the appearance of documents displayed in the Notes client as well.

To add stylesheets to your application design, you simply choose Shared Resources ⇨ Style Sheets, click the New Style Sheet Resource button, and find your CSS file on your file system. The file is then imported into your database design. Use the Properties box of the stylesheet to name it. You can add a stylesheet to your design element, such as a page or form, by using the method described at the beginning of this section: Create ⇨ Resource ⇨ Insert Resource.

 New Feature   Stylesheets are a new resource element in Notes/Domino 6.

Shared Applets

Although this resource is called an applet, it really means any Java class — whether it's stored in a class, .jar, archive, or resource type file. You can add applets to your application by choosing Shared Resources ⇨ Applets, clicking the New Applet Resource button, and selecting the Java resource files that you need. Figure 4-6 shows the Locate Java Applet Files dialog box.

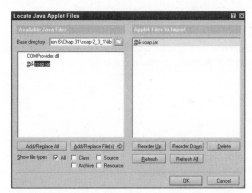

Figure 4-6: The Locate Java Applet Files dialog box enables you to choose Java resource files to add to your application.

 New Feature   Shared applets are a new resource element in Notes/Domino 6.

Images

Image resources have been around since Release 5. Image resources enable you to store BMP, GIF, or JPG files as a part of your database design. These images are available for use in both the Notes client and Web browser applications, in any design element that enables you to place graphics in it.

You can add an image resource to your application by choosing Shared Resources ⇨ Images, and then clicking the New Image Resource button. A Windows common File dialog box appears, and you can choose the graphics file(s) you want to import into your application. You can then use the Properties box to provide an alias for the image.

Besides using the method described at the beginning of this section (Create ⇨ Resource ⇨ Insert Resource) to add a resource to your design element, you can also add an image resource by choosing Create ⇨ Image Resource and selecting the desired graphic.

Files

File resources are basically a catch-all area for files you want to have as a part of your application that don't fit into any other category. But if you place an HTML file here (a file with the extension .html), it's available for insertion by using the method described at the beginning of this section (Create ⇨ Resource ⇨ Insert Resource).

You can add a file resource to your application by choosing Shared Resources ⇨ Files, and then clicking the New File Resource button. A Windows common File dialog box appears, and can choose the file(s) you want to import into your application.

New Feature   The files resource is a new resource available in Notes/Domino 6.

Data Connection Resources

Data Connection Resources (DCRs) enable you to define a connection to an external data resource, and then use that DCR object in your forms to populate one or more fields with data from the external resource.

New Feature   Data Connection Resources are new in Notes/Domino 6.

DCRs are based on the same technology as Domino Enterprise Connection Services (DECS), except that they provide the developer a way to manage the DECS connection in the target database, without the need to use the Domino Administrator.

Cross-Reference   For more information on using DCRs, please refer to Chapters 43 and 44.

Summary

This chapter provided you with a quick review of the various application building blocks available in Lotus Notes/Domino. These design elements were broken down into functional areas:

- ✦ **User interface elements:** These elements include forms, subforms, pages, views, and folders. These elements are used to interact with the user, and allow her to work with the data stored in the database.

- ✦ **Navigation elements:** These elements include framesets and outlines, which can be used to easily provide the ability to locate information in your application, either through a Web browser or the Notes client.

✦ **Shared code elements:** Shared resource elements include script libraries, shared fields, and shared actions. Shared code elements allow you to write your code once and use it in multiple places in your application.

✦ **Shared resource elements:** There are quite a few shared resource elements, including image resources, Cascaded Style Sheets, file resources, and so on. These elements allow you to maintain all of the items needed for your application in one object store, which preserves the portability of your application and makes it easier to maintain.

You build applications that solve you customer's needs by using the powerful design elements covered in this chapter. From here we move on to Part II, Domino Designer. The chapters there will introduce you to the Domino Designer, and how you can use it to develop world-class Domino applications exploiting the design elements covered here.

✦   ✦   ✦

Domino Designer

The Designer IDE

By Brian Benz

Earlier versions of Lotus Notes had user and designer components built into the same client software. With the release of Lotus Domino R5, and extended with Domino 6, Domino Designer has been a separately installable, separately executable product. With Domino Designer, developers now have separate end-user and developer environments, each organized for efficiency of the task at hand. This chapter presents the major elements of the Designer IDE to alert you to all its features and their functions.

Getting Started

To open Domino Designer on a Windows workstation, select the Lotus Domino Designer submenu option under the Lotus Applications menu, double-click the installed Lotus Domino Designer icon on the Windows desktop, select the Domino Designer icon from the Notes client bookmarks, or right-click a database in the Notes Workspace and select Open in Designer from the pop-up menu.

Note Database users must have Designer or Manager access to a database to be able to open and/or change the design of that database in Domino Designer. See your system administrator if you should, but do not, have Designer or Manager access to a database.

Whether you choose to open the design of an existing database, create a new database design with an existing template, or create a new database design from scratch, the first thing you see when you open the Designer is the Domino Designer workspace. The Designer workspace is visually designed around the concept of folders containing bookmarks. The following sections take you on a quick tour of the features of the Designer workspace, shown in Figure 5-1.

Design bookmarks   Menu bar

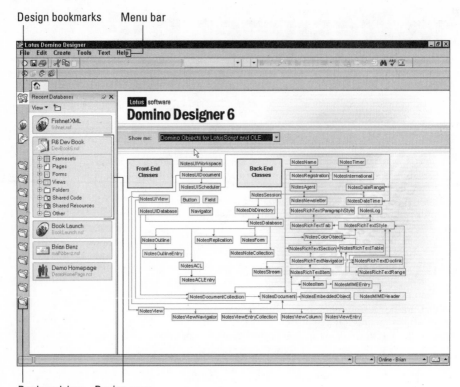

Bookmark bar   Design pane

Figure 5-1: Designer workspace — Main screen

UI Overview

As shown in Figure 5-1, at the top of the Domino Designer is a menu bar, a tool bar, a bar displaying formatting, properties, and preview buttons, and a fourth bar that contains tabs of any currently open database design elements. To the left of the screen icons represent design bookmarks. Each design bookmark opens a list of database design elements, such as views and folders, in the Design pane to the right of the bookmarks. The large open space to the right of the Design pane is called the Work pane, because this is where the developer will do most of his or her developing when an object is open in Domino Designer.

Figure 5-2 offers a look at the interactive elements of the UI.

Design bookmarks

Clicking a folder icon within the bookmarks opens a list of related database design objects. Database objects can be dragged and dropped into and sorted within folders. Design objects can also be placed in multiple bookmark folders that are shared by several different projects. The first folder in this section, for example, is called Recent Databases. The Designer UI automatically maintains a list of recent database objects. You can also place the same database object in one or more separate project folders for future reference.

Properties   Preview
box button   buttons   Window tabs

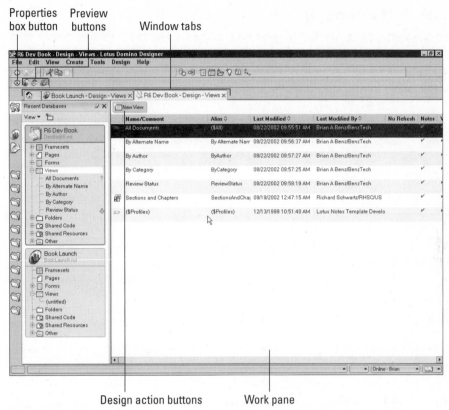

Design action buttons   Work pane

Figure 5-2: Designer workspace — with view objects open in the Work pane and the Design pane

The Design pane

Each database object contains a representation of design elements related to that database in the Design pane, directly to the right of the design bookmarks. You can open design elements in the Work pane by either clicking the design element type and selecting from a list of elements in the Work pane, or by clicking the expand icon (+) to the left of the design element type in the Design pane and selecting one of the design elements. Each time a new element is opened, a tab appears along the top of the Work pane, just under the menu. This allows fast access to multiple open elements by clicking object tabs. Clicking the X displayed for each tab closes the element in the Work pane.

When the pushpin toggle in the Design pane is clicked to the out position, the Design pane and design bookmarks hide whenever you click a new design element, giving you more space for reviewing and editing. When the pin is clicked to the in position, the Design pane and bookmark areas are kept open, even when working with design element in the Work pane.

The Work pane and Programmer's pane

After a design element is opened in the Work pane, several other UI features come into play. The space at the top of the Work pane contains a WYSIWYG (What You See Is What You Get) display of all objects contained in the design element. Figure 5-3 shows the default form in the BookLaunch database, which is currently empty, but does contain JavaScript in the JSHeader, which is displayed in the Programmer's pane, below the Work pane.

Figure 5-3: Designer workspace — The Work pane shows JavaScript references

To the lower left is the Objects tab, which lists all associated objects nested in the design element in a hierarchical format. Clicking the Reference tab to the right of the Objects tab opens a language-sensitive reference list of classes, methods, or functions, reflecting the Domino-supported language the developer is working with at the time.

The right side of the Work pane is the Programmer's pane. The drop-down list in the title bar of the Programmer's pane lists all script and language types available for the selected object.

Design elements

In addition to supporting several languages in objects and design elements, the Domino Designer UI also supports a multitude of design elements in a Domino database to create truly world-class Notes and Web applications. The next few chapters cover these Domino design elements in detail. This section introduces Domino design elements in the order that they are listed in the Design pane (refer to Figure 5-2).

✦ **Framesets:** Framesets divide screens into independent application elements. Framesets and frames are supported in major Web browsers including Netscape and MS IE, as well as the Notes client. Designer R5 contains a built-in frameset designer, eliminating the need for a hand-coded solution. Other Domino design elements, such as outline entries, forms, and pages can specify a target frame when opened in a frameset context.

✦ **Pages:** Pages permit static content to be included and served up quickly in Notes and Domino applications. Pages are very much like Domino forms, with the limitation that they can't include certain interactive design objects, including fields.

✦ **Forms:** Forms are used to display data contained in Domino documents. They are the face of the data and facilitate the separation of data storage and display in Domino applications. Forms are the versatile centerpiece of Domino applications and can contain and/or call any Domino design element.

✦ **Views:** Views are used to collect and display groups of Domino documents. Views are made up of rows and columns of data using a grid model, somewhat like a spreadsheet, but with much more data behind each cell. Views can display data from documents and from computed values.

✦ **Folders:** Folders have all the properties and features of views, but are designed to store groups of documents rather than collect and display them, the same way that files can be stored in subdirectories on a file system.

✦ **Shared Code:** The shared code section of the Design pane includes objects that are shared by many design elements. This section includes agents, outlines, subforms, shared fields, shared actions, and script libraries.

- **Agents:** Agents are shared pieces of code that are callable from other design elements and events, such as buttons and form events. Agents can also be scheduled to run as a result of predetermined events or at timed intervals, either on a local client or on a server. Agents can be developed using simple actions (chosen from menu options), formulas, LotusScript, imported Java (from the file system as class files), and Java.

- **Outlines:** Outlines are design elements that provide a reusable tree-structured navigation facility for Notes and Web applications. Each entry of an outline represents a navigational choice in an application, with hide-when formulas that give the outline context-sensitive dynamic capabilities. Entries are also modifiable by computed formulas that select different display attributes.

- **Subforms:** Subforms are designed to be embedded into forms and represent shared objects and code that become part of the form. Subforms can be referenced directly by subform name or by calculated references based on form data. Subforms are great time-savers for application maintenance. An object change on a single subform automatically changes that object on all the forms in which that subform has been embedded.

- **Shared fields:** Shared fields are objects that can contain code and properties that can be reused across multiple instances of the shared field. Like subforms, a change to a shared field changes the properties and related code in all the forms on which that shared field has been embedded. Some field properties, such as font and color are set in an individual field's property box in the form that they are embedded in. These properties are not affected by changes to a shared field, but are set on an individual basis.

- **Shared actions:** Shared actions are similar to agents, but are designed to be directly related to action-oriented design elements. Shared actions can be referenced from forms and subforms, but not scheduled.

  Shared actions can contain simple actions (chosen from menu options), formulas, LotusScript, JavaScript (coded directly into the Programmer's pane for the shared action), or common JavaScript (calling a reference to a function stored in a Script Library).

- **Script Libraries:** Script Libraries are shared pieces of LotusScript, JavaScript, and Java code that are stored in the Domino database container and referenced by design elements such as fields or form events. Creating code libraries facilitates centralized storage, transport, and maintenance of core code related to the application in which it is contained.

✦ **Shared Resources:** Shared resources, like shared code, are a selection of design elements that are contained in the Domino database and referenced by design elements. You can add shared resources into a design element by choosing Insert ⇨ Shared Resource from the Create menu, choosing the type of shared resource, and then the name of the specific resource. Shared resources include GIF, BMP, or JPG images, applets, and any files that an application would benefit from having embedded and transported with the database, stylesheets, and data connections via ODBC or IBM RDBMS connectors.

✦ **Other:** The Other section of Domino Designer has always been a grab bag of things that don't fit elsewhere. Some design elements in the Other section graduate to other sections; some are demoted into this section, depending on the Domino Designer version. For Domino Designer 6, the database icon that displays a Domino workspace, the About and Using Database documents that are accessible from the Help menu of a Notes client, and Database Script—LotusScript that can be developed to handle default database events such as drag-and-drop or document delete, are all contained under the Database Resources subsection. Navigators—objects that contain clickable regions over a graphical background—are now stored here as well. Synopsis, also included in the Other section, is a valuable and underrated way of producing.

Additional Features of Domino Designer 6

Domino Designer 6 has many new features, including autocomplete, remote debugging for LotusScript, design object locking in native mode or with WebDAV tools, and DXL tools. This section introduces developers to Designer and then highlights the new Domino 6 features.

Flexible coding in a single container model

One of the greatest features in Domino Designer is the ability to store and use several different types of code in a common database container. Domino database design elements can contain and use Formula language, LotusScript, JavaScript, and Java. This has always been a very practical and useful feature for group-based development models and updates to legacy applications. For example, a Domino form that uses formulas and LotusScript to enforce data entry rules can also use a JavaScript button to call a Java agent that calls a Web service. Within a group-based development team, an experienced Notes developer can code the LotusScript form, a Web developer can create the JavaScript for the button, and a Java developer can supply the agent that calls the Web service.

Syntax Checking and Code Formatting

When a developer selects a type of code or script, Domino automatically adapts the syntax checking, color-coding of code elements such as keywords and variables, and code formatting such as auto-indenting to meet the needs of the language chosen. Each language has specific features, but the default across all languages is that code keywords are in blue, user-defined variables are in black, everything between two quotes is in pink, comments are in green, and lines or functions containing syntax errors are in red. Editing the Programmer's pane properties can control colors, fonts, and other display properties as well as auto-indent and pre-population of LotusScript events.

When a developer is entering LotusScript code, for example, all LotusScript syntax is checked, formatted, and color-coded based on the selection of LotusScript as the chosen language in the title bar of the Programmer's pane. When a developer enters LotusScript code that generates a syntax error in Domino Designer, the code is highlighted in red and the syntax error message is displayed just below the Programmer's pane in the Errors box. Clicking the arrow button to the right of the error bar displays a history of errors and the full messages on the screen.

Context-based help for developers

Domino is very good at helping developers when they need it most, with context-sensitive language reference, both in the Work pane reference tab and via autocomplete. Domino Designer keeps track of each language associated with each design element. The Reference tab in the Work pane adapts to display language-specific objects and methods based on the language a developer has selected for the design element. Autocomplete can also be used for Formula language, JavaScript, and LotusScript. It provides a context-sensitive pop-up box that supplies assistance with methods and properties as well as parameters associated with the current code function. Autocomplete can be turned off and on and the display in milliseconds can be set via the Programmer's pane properties box. Even if autocomplete is turned off, the pop-up box can be temporarily called by pressing CTRL+ALT+T. Figure 5-4 shows the Programmer's pane properties box open to the Developer's tab, which displays the autocomplete properties.

Runtime debugging features in Domino Designer

Aside from syntax checking, color coding, autoformatting, and autocomplete as features of the programming UI, Domino Designer integrates advanced run-time and remote debugging features for LotusScript.

Local debugging can be enabled via the Debug LotusScript option in the File ⇨ Tools menu. Breakpoints can be set, variable values tracked, and code can either be stepped through or allowed to run until a runtime error is detected.

Selecting the Remote Debugger option in the File ⇨ Tools menu enables remote LotusScript agent debugging. A new Lotus Client window opens, and a dialog box prompts the developer to select a database on a server that has the remote debugger (rdbug) task running on it. Most local debugger tasks are also available on the remote debugger, and variables and output can be viewed via the remote debugger console. Figure 5-5 shows the LotusScript remote debugger in action.

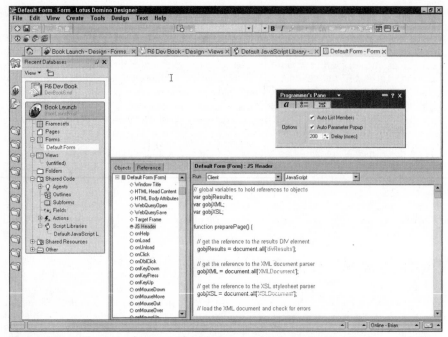

Figure 5-4: Designer workspace — The Work pane shows JavaScript references and the dialog box shows Programmer's pane properties for autocomplete.

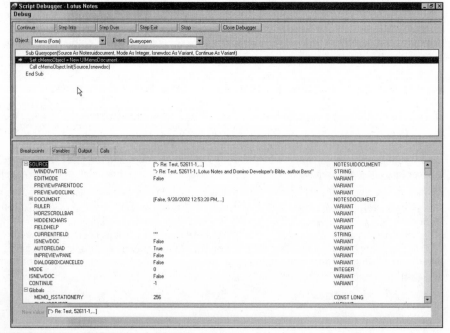

Figure 5-5: LotusScript local debugger in action

Java runtime output can be viewed by selecting the Show Java Debug Window option in the File ⇨ Tools menu. This option enables a basic Java window to which all Java errors and output are printed from the Designer client at Java runtime.

Sharing and locking design elements

One of the most important issues in developing applications in a team environment is preventing multiple developers from working on the same code or object. This becomes even more important in Domino application development models, as developers could be working on different replicas of the application database at the same time. The ability to lock design elements is a very important part of preventing this from happening. Design elements are automatically locked in a single database if a developer is editing them in Designer. To manually lock or unlock a design element, right-click the element and choose the lock or unlock option from the pop-up menu. For design element locking to work across replicas, the database must have an accessible administration server listed in the Advanced tab of the ACL settings, and design locking must be enabled by choosing File ⇨ Database ⇨ Properties from the Domino Designer menu, selecting the Design tab, and enabling the Allow design locking property.

Designing Domino applications with WebDAV

WebDAV stands for Web-based Distributed Authoring and Versioning, a set of HTTP extensions designed to permit remote editing and management of files. Domino Designer supports WebDAV standards for editing design elements such as images, cascading stylesheets, database file resources, and pages using applications such as Microsoft Word, Excel, and Macromedia DreamWeaver. The WebDAV implementation on Domino supports record locking for design elements, as long as Design element locking has been enabled for the Designer client (see the preceding section). Design elements must be available to users via URL, and users have to authenticate in order for WebDAV to function. More information on WebDAV initiatives can be found at www.webdav.org.

XML: DXL Utilities

DXL stands for Domino XML, and as the name suggests, is a standard way of representing Domino data as XML. Designer has three functions built into the Tools menu that allow you to save, view, or transform a DXL representation of the currently selected design element. XML, DXL, and DXL export and transformations are covered in greater detail in part ten of the book. For now, it's good to know where in the UI you can generate and review DXL representations of design elements. Figure 5-6 shows output from a Domino form in DXL format, as displayed in an MS Internet Explorer browser.

Exporter and Viewer

Exporter simply generates DXL for the currently selected design element and saves it to a file on the file system with a .XML file extension. Viewer generates the same DXL to a temporary .XML file and opens a Web browser to display the file to the screen. MS IE 5.01 or higher is recommended to parse and view the output properly.

Transformer

Transformer opens a DXL transformer window. One or more source design elements can be selected for DXL generation, a stylesheet can be selected from a list of defaults or by browsing the file system, and transformation output can be displayed to the screen or written to the file system by selecting the output method from a drop-down dialog box. The DXL transformer dialog box is shown in Figure 5-7.

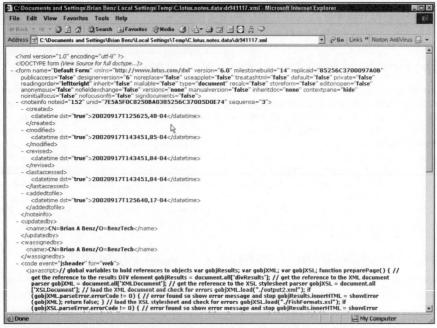

Figure 5-6: DXL for a basic Domino form – displays the form name and properties, followed by Domino system fields represented as XML.

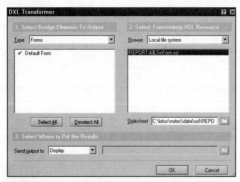

Figure 5-7: DXL Transformer – developers can select one or more design element sources, stylesheets, and output methods.

Previewing your Notes and Domino applications

As part of the Designer IDE, developers can easily preview their Notes or Web applications. Domino Designer checks the registry on your system and displays only the icons representing the browsers that are currently installed. Options for preview are the Notes client and any browser you have enabled on your Domino client machine, including the Notes browser, embedded IE in the Notes browser, Internet Explorer, and Netscape Navigator. This feature enables developers to quickly test application functionality in a multiclient environment.

Summary

In this chapter, developers learned how to navigate the Domino Designer IDE, all about the design elements developers work with in Domino applications, including:

✦ Features for coding and debugging Domino applications

✦ Sharing and locking design resources

✦ Developing applications with WebDAV-compliant development tools

✦ Using DXL utilities to export design elements as XML

✦ How to preview your design in preparation for use in a multiclient application environment

In the next chapter, you learn how to use Domino database templates and database design element updates to manage code and projects in the Domino Designer environment.

✦　　✦　　✦

Managing and Deploying Application Projects

By Richard Schwartz

✦ ✦ ✦ ✦

In This Chapter

Understanding projects, applications and databases

Using templates

Working on multidatabase projects

Working on a development team

Deploying applications

✦ ✦ ✦ ✦

Most programmers are used to working with a development environment that organizes projects containing source files, object files, and executable files. Programmers who work with the Notes C and C++ APIs do work this way, but most Notes and Domino development doesn't use those tools. So, for the most part, source files, executables, and separate data files or database systems are foreign concepts to Notes and Domino programmers. This chapter explains the concepts that Notes and Domino work with to organize projects and deploy applications.

Projects, Applications, and Databases

No consistent terminology exists for describing a unit of work in a Notes and Domino environment. The words *application* and *database* are sometimes interchangeable, and sometimes not, and the word *project* has a variety of meanings. This is somewhat unfortunate, but it really is unavoidable. It's also not unique to Notes and Domino. The following sections try to eliminate some of the confusion surrounding these terms.

Understanding applications

Chapter 3 described the NSF file as a container for both the data and the code of a Notes and Domino application. Notes and Domino programmers often use the words *database* and *application* interchangeably, and in most cases, a Notes or Domino application consists of just a single NSF file. But this is not always the case. An application is a solution to some process or problem that is comprised of one or more databases. A database is a single NSF file that contains data and code that performs work. So in this and other chapters, the word *application* is used to refer to some solution that is one or more databases, and a *database* is a single NSF file.

The fact that Notes and Domino applications store code in NSF files implies that multiple NSF files might be involved in one application. Just as complex applications built in traditional programming languages, such as C or BASIC, sometimes spread their code across multiple EXE and DLL files, Notes and Domino applications sometimes spread their code across multiple NSF files, with each file containing code that provides a portion of the application's functionality — and usually that NSF file also stores the data used by that portion of the applications' code.

The fact that Notes and Domino applications store data in NSF files implies that one NSF file might also be used in multiple applications. Application designers usually don't want to store duplicate copies of the same data, because it can be very hard to ensure that all copies are kept in synch. Many applications built with the traditional tools share use of a data file or SQL table. Notes and Domino developers share information by using a common NSF file to store data that is shared by more than one application.

Understanding projects

Because this chapter is supposed to be about projects, it would probably be helpful to define what the word *project* means. In most traditional application development environments, a project is a collection of source files that are grouped together so that automated tools can be used to build one or more software components — and a component can be a complete application, an executable program, or a library of code used by executable programs. Domino Designer, however, does not provide tools for organizing files into projects this way, so there is no single definition of *project* that all Notes and Domino programmers agree upon.

For the purposes in this book, a *project* is a group of one or more related application features, either for a single application or for a group of related applications, programmed in one or more design elements in one or more NSF files. Although this is a general definition, it can still be useful. A Domino project might be a new application, a set of new applications, a set of new features for an existing application, or a set of new features shared by many applications. Domino projects can be developed directly in the database(s) that are used by the users, but it is a better development technique to perform your development in templates, and use these templates as a basis for the databases that comprise your final application.

Templates

It is often the case that an organization wants to deploy several applications that all use the same code, but have each application maintain its own data. Several different workgroups, for example, may each want their own private application for maintaining employees' weekly status reports. Every NSF file, however, contains code and data, so meeting this common requirement by deploying an NSF file for each group implies that there will be many copies of the actual code. It is impractical, of course, to ask a programmer to duplicate code manually whenever a new version of an application needs to be deployed. It is even more impractical to have a programmer manually update many copies of the same code in order to implement new features or fix bugs. Notes and Domino programmers use templates to automate these processes.

 On The Web

A new feature scheduled for inclusion in Notes and Domino 6 was withdrawn shortly before the product shipped allows NSF files to share a single copy of their code physically. This feature, known as Single Copy Template, is expected to be added to Notes and Domino 6 in the first maintenance release, which should be known as 6.0.1. When this feature is released, a brief description of it will be added to the ndbible.com Web site.

Template files

Templates are files that have the same internal structure as NSF files, but have names that usually end in NTF (but that isn't necessary). Because they have the same internal structure, they are also containers for notes. They are primarily used as containers for Design notes, but they may also contain Data notes. For instance, you may have an application that has a centralized keyword database. You have developed the application using templates, and then you create the application databases from the templates. If you have created the keyword documents in the template version of the keyword database, they are automatically placed in the corresponding keyword application database.

You can choose a template when you create a new database file by choosing File ⇨ Database ⇨ New from the menu of the Notes client or Domino Designer program. See Figure 6-1, and note that the bottom half of the New Database dialog box contains a list of templates that are available on the machine where Domino Designer is running. The combo box labeled Template Server can be used to choose from a list of templates that are available on any Domino server in the network.

Figure 6-1: The template list in the New Database dialog box is used to choose the desired template.

When you select a template in the New Database dialog box, fill in all the fields required for a new NSF file, and click OK, a new NSF file is created. The new database contains copies of all the Design notes and Data notes in the template file. (The Access Control List (ACL) note is not, however, a copy of the template's ACL. See Chapter 10 for more information about how ACLs for databases are created.)

Developers who need to deploy multiple applications that use the same code should always create a template file and use the template to create the database files for the applications.

Template names

Every NSF and NTF file has two names, and an optional third name, used for three different purposes. The first name is, of course, the filename used as a unique identifier on the hard drive of a Notes client or Domino server. The second name is Title, which you set in the New Database dialog box (as shown earlier) and can be seen or modified on the Database Basics (the leftmost) tab of the Database Properties dialog box (see Figure 6-2).

The Database Title

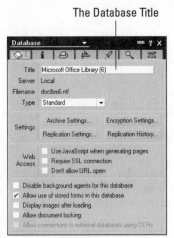

Figure 6-2: The database title

The title of an NSF file is shown to users in the Open Database dialog box, accessed by choosing File ⇨ Database ⇨ Open in the Notes client or Domino Designer. The names shown in the scrolling list of templates in the New Database dialog box, as previously shown in Figure 6-1, are the titles of the NTF files.

The third name that any NSF or NTF file might have is a Master Template name. You view and modify this name on the Design tab (the one with a small picture of a t-square and triangle) of the Database Properties dialog box (see Figure 6-3).

Master Template Name

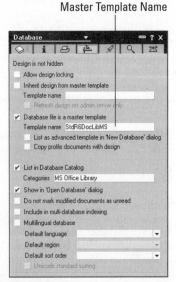

Figure 6-3: The Master Template properties

As you can see in the figure, there is a Database is a Master Template check box and a Template Name field.

Note   The term *Master Template* is new in Notes and Domino 6. In previous releases, the term that was generally used was *Design Template*.

The Master Template name is used to manage design inheritance, which is described in the next section of this chapter. Any NTF or NSF can be designated as a Master Template.

Design inheritance

You can create NSF files from a template, but what happens when the code in the template changes? Because the code in the NSF file is a new copy of the code in the template, you need a way to resynchronize the copy with the original. Design inheritance is Notes and Domino's solution to this problem.

Every NSF file can be set to inherit its design from a Master Template. Figure 6-4 shows the Design tab of the Database Properties dialog box for a database that was created from the Master Template shown in Figure 6-3.

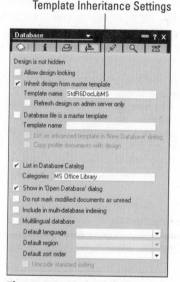

Figure 6-4: Design inheritance properties

Notice that there is a check box labeled Inherit Design from Master Template followed by a field labeled Template Name. The content of this field is StdR6DocLibMS, which matches the value shown in the Database is a Master Template field shown in Figure 6-3. The match between these two settings controls inheritance.

You can manage inheritance automatically or manually. Automatic inheritance occurs only for database files that are stored on Domino servers. But replicas of a database that users keep on the hard drive of their workstations or laptops receive design changes from replicas on servers via the normal client-server replication process, so this restriction does not create problems. Automatic inheritance on servers is managed by the design task, which is normally scheduled to run on servers in the early morning hours.

You can manually initiate design inheritance for any NSF file that inherits from a Master Template by opening the database in the Notes client or in Domino Designer, and choosing File ⇨ Database ⇨ Refresh Design from the menu. A design refresh request does the same thing that the server-based design task does, but for the one requested database only, — which can be on any server, or on the user's local hard drive.

When you initiate a design refresh, the system prompts you for the name of a server to search for a matching template. You can specify Local if the Master Template that you want to use is on your own PC's hard drive, or the name of any Domino server in your network. The system then searches the selected server, looking for any NTF or NSF file that has the Database is a Master Template box checked in its properties, with a template name that matches the Inherit Design from Master Template name in the database that you are refreshing. The system then examines every design element in the database, and determines whether it needs to be refreshed.

Normally, every design element in an NSF is eligible to be refreshed from the database's Master Template, and if there are any differences between the version in the NSF and the one in the template, the design note from the template overwrites the design note in the NSF. In two cases, however, design elements in an NSF will not be refreshed from the Master Template; these two cases are listed here:

✦ **Case one:** Any design element can be set with a property that prevents it from ever being overwritten by either an automatic or manual design refresh. Figure 6-5 shows the Design Properties dialog box, which you open by selecting a design element in Domino Designer and choosing Design ⇨ Properties from the menu. Notice the Prohibit Design Refresh or Replace to Modify check box. This box should be checked for any design element in an NSF that you want to disconnect from its Master Template. You can use this feature to prevent a customization made directly in a design element of an NSF from being automatically replaced with the generic version of the design element from the template.

✦ **Case two:** Design elements can also be set to inherit from an alternate template instead of from the database's Master Template. You accomplish this in the Design Properties dialog box. Enter the name of the alternative template into Inherit from Design Template field, which you can see in Figure 6-5 just above the Prohibit Design Refresh or Replace to Modify check box.

You might use this feature to add one or more common design elements to many applications that were created from several different Master Templates. Design replace, and automatic and manual design refreshes honor this setting, and search for a database that has the Database is a Master Template box checked and a matching template name.

Figure 6-5: Design element inheritance properties

Multidatabase Projects

Choosing whether to build a project in one NSF file, or divide it into multiple NSF files is one of the first things a Notes or Domino developer has to do when beginning a project. Many factors might enter into this decision, but the following guidelines can help you make this decision.

Consider using a single NSF file in the following situations:

✦ It is useful to make all documents part of a single response hierarchy.

✦ All the data stored with the application are unlikely to be useful to any other application.

✦ All users of the application are likely to need access to all the data.

Consider using multiple NSF files in the following situations:

✦ The application stores hundreds of thousands of some types of documents, and smaller numbers of other types of documents.

✦ Some of the data in the application is of a generic nature and may be useful to other applications.

✦ Some of the data in the application needs to be accessible only via the Notes client, or only via a browser, and other data needs to be accessible via the Notes client and a browser.

✦ There are differing security requirements for subsets of the data within the application. Some documents are required to be read-only, while an individual or groups of users edit other documents.

Multiple design inheritance

Multidatabase projects are sometimes managed via multiple design inheritance, in which databases inherit design elements from templates that inherit some of their design elements from other templates. An NTF file that is a Master Template file can also inherit some its own design elements from other Master Templates. You can use a chain of multiple design inheritance to create a common set of features that are shared by all the applications in a project. For example, a project might consist of two NSF files: one for employee status reports, and the other for project plans. Both of these applications may need to support Manager's Comments documents.

1. Create two template files named `Ch6-B-Status.NTF` and `Ch6-B-Plans.NTF` by choosing File ⇨ Database ⇨ New from the Domino Designer menu. Fill in the filenames and appropriate titles for each NTF.

2. Open the Database Properties dialog box, check the Database is a Master Template box on the Design tab, and type **Ch6EmpStatusTemplate** and **Ch6ProjectPlansTemplate**, respectively, in the Template Name field.

3. Next create another template called `Ch6-B-Comments.NTF`, in this case without changing the template selection in the New Database dialog box from its default of None. Open the Database Properties dialog box, check Database is a Master Template on the Design tab, and type **Ch6MgrCommentsTemplate** in the Template Name field.

4. To set up an inheritance chain for this project, create a form in `Ch6-B-Comments.NTF`, add a text field called **Subject** and a rich-text field called **Body** to the form, and save it as **Manager Comments | Response**.

Cross-Reference The basic steps for creating a form and adding fields to it are covered in Chapter 2.

Close the form and copy it from the Forms index, and then paste it into both `Ch6-B-Status.NTF` and `Ch6-B-Plans.NTF`. After pasting the form, the dialog box shown in Figure 6-6 appears.

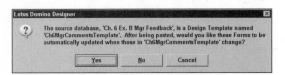

Figure 6-6: The Inheritance dialog box

Clicking Yes in this dialog box tells Domino Designer to set the properties for the Manager Comments form so that it is inherited from `Ch6MgrCommentsTemplate`, as shown in the Design Properties dialog box (see Figure 6-7).

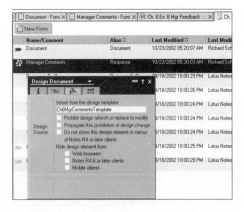

Figure 6-7: Inheritance of the Manager Comments form

If you make changes to the Manager Comments form in `Ch6-B-Feeback.NTF`, and then refresh the designs of `Ch6-B-Status.NTF` and `Ch6-B-Projeects.NTF`, the copies of the Manager Comments forms in those templates are updated with your changes.

On The Web A set of three files demonstrating this technique can be found on the companion Web site at `www.wiley.com/compbooks/benz`. These files were created using the instructions from the preceding section.

Working on a Development Team

A great irony of the Notes and Domino world for the past dozen or so years has been the fact that although Notes and Domino are great tools for developing applications that help people collaborate, Domino Designer did not provide much help for programming teams that needed to collaborate. In past releases of Notes and Domino, the only way teams of programmers could be sure that two or more people weren't trying to modify code in the same design element at the same time was to divide applications into multiple template files and assign individual programmers to each of the templates. There are other third party tools that helped manage a multi-developer environment, but there was no clean way to do it in Notes/Domino itself. Notes and Domino 6 finally addresses this problem.

New Feature Notes and Domino 6 supports locking for documents and design elements. Design element locking enables a programmer to claim exclusive rights to edit any design element in an NSF or NTF file. A master lock server must be designated for the file, and a check box in the Database Properties dialog box must be enabled to activate this feature.

To set up a project for team development, you need to do the following:

✦ Make replicas of each NTF or NSF file in the project on a server so that all team members can access them.

✦ Open each NTF or NSF and open the Access Control dialog box by choosing File ⇨ Database ⇨ Access Control. Click the Advanced tab on the left side of the dialog box, change the Administration Server setting from None to Server, and then fill in the name of a server in the dialog box, as shown in Figure 6-8.

✦ Open the Database Properties dialog box for each NTF or NSF, click the Design tab, and then click the check box labeled Allow Design Locking, as shown in Figure 6-9.

After completing this setup, you can select any design element in the NTF or NSF files, right-click, and select Lock or Unlock. When a design element is locked, other programmers will not be allowed to work with it until either you or someone else with manager access (see Chapter 10) to the database file unlocks it.

You can even set locks on design elements when working with a local replica of the NSF or NTF file on a laptop that is not connected to any server. In such cases, the lock is created provisionally. It is made permanent the next time the programmer replicates his laptop with a server. If someone else locked the design element in the interim, the lock can't be made permanent. The server then sends an e-mail to the programmer, who needs to wait until the lock is released, and then manually merges his changes into the design element.

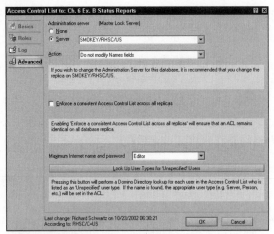

Figure 6-8: Setting the Administration Server for design locking

Enabling Design Locking

Figure 6-9: Setting the design locking property

To minimize the possibility of losing a provisional lock, replicate the NSF or NTF file directly with the Administration server immediately before and immediately after setting the lock.

Application Deployment

Many organizations have strict procedures for deploying applications to Domino servers. For example, some organizations require that programmers submit their applications for testing by a quality assurance team, and then turn them over to system administrators for deployment on servers. There are good reasons for this, mostly having to do with security and operations policy. Programmers are given enormous power over an organization's data and systems. Policies and procedures that control deployment of new applications and changes to existing applications establish checks and balances over the power given to programmers. The larger the organization, the greater is the need for these checks and balances in order to keep programmers from (deliberately or accidentally) compromising the security or reliability of critical systems.

Policies and procedures for Notes and Domino application deployment may be quite elaborate, but the underlying technical requirements are actually simple. Deployment involves the following steps:

✦ Create the NSF files for the application from the template files by choosing File ➪ Database ➪ New from the menu of the Notes client or Domino Designer. (If you did your development work directly in the NSF files, this would be a good time to create a set of templates by choosing File ➪ Database ➪ New Copy from the menu and selecting the Database Design only Option in the Copy Database dialog box.

✦ Set up the Access Control Lists for the NSF files. (See Chapter 10 for more information about database security.)

✦ Replicate the NSF files to a Domino server, or e-mail them to somebody who has the permissions required to do so.

✦ Set up any data in documents that your application's code requires in order to function properly.

Summary

This chapter discussed Notes and Domino applications, projects, databases, and templates. You learned that

✦ Domino applications can consist of a single NSF file or multiple NSF files.

✦ Domino Designer does not define a project the way most traditional development tools do.

✦ Because NSF files are containers for both code and data, it is often the case that an organization needs to deploy many NSF files containing the same code but different data.

✦ Domino programmers can maintain their code in template files.

✦ Database files can inherit all or part of their design elements from other database files designated as templates.

✦ NTF files can inherit parts of their design elements from other NTF files.

✦ Design elements can be locked and unlocked to coordinate the work of programmers on the same team.

✦ Application deployment technically requires just a few simple steps, but in many organizations a formal process must be followed in order to satisfy important policies and procedures.

The next chapter covers the standard templates that ship with Notes and Domino.

✦   ✦   ✦

Standard Templates

By Richard Schwartz

Notes and Domino provide powerful tools for the development of custom applications. Many Notes and Domino users, however, are totally unaware of this fact. They know only that their company uses Notes and Domino for e-mail, calendaring, and address books. Others know only that it provides e-mail and online discussion facilities. What they don't know is that IBM engineers have built all the most popular features of Notes and Domino using the same programming tools that are available to every Notes and Domino programmer for custom applications.

The features of Notes and Domino that end-users know best and that are responsible for much of the popularity of the products are built from ordinary Notes and Domino templates. Every Notes and Domino programmer can examine those templates to learn how those features work.

Notes and Domino ship with more than 30 different template files. Many are employed in system administration tasks and are unfamiliar to most users; others are extremely useful for learning how to develop your own applications.

This chapter briefly describes the templates that are most familiar to end users: the Mail template, the Personal Address Book template, the Discussion template, and the Document Library template.

The Mail Template

As the name implies, the Mail template provides all the e-mail functionality of the mail system for the Notes client. It also provides the calendaring functionality. These two seemingly different areas of functionality are combined into one NTF file, `MAIL6.NTF`, to allow tight integration of sending and receiving invitations, responses to invitations, and the rescheduling of notices for calendar appointments. The standard Mail template also provides a Web user interface for the mail and calendar features. Although it's quite powerful, it is not the nicest Web mail interface for Domino. If you need a powerful Web mail client, check out iNotes Web Access, as it is one of the most impressive Web clients available.

The Mail template is, of course, *the* place to go to find out how to work with e-mail messages in your applications. Of course, the Mail template has evolved over many years and many releases of Notes and Domino, and some of the things that you will find in it are not necessarily always done with the easiest techniques available in Notes and Domino 6. In the Memo form, for example, some action buttons are used in the Notes client, and duplicate action buttons perform the same functionality and are used in a Web browser. The Notes client versions are hidden from Web browsers, and vice versa. This works, but there's a better way of doing this in Notes and Domino 6, which you find out about in Chapter 16.

The Memo form has many other interesting characteristics. The Send action programmed for the Notes client uses Notes Formula language to execute @Command([FileCloseWindow]) in combination with the Present Mail Send Dialog property on that form to cause the message to be sent. The Send action for the browser is written in JavaScript, and it simply submits the message to the server, where a WebQuerySave agent called wMemo is invoked. The agent sets the value of the reserved item MailOptions to 1 to accomplish the same thing. The Memo form uses the reserved fields SendTo, CopyTo, and BlindCopyTo for addressing. Any form using these same field names can be addressed and mailed by Notes and Domino.

One of the most interesting parts of the mail template is the Calendaring and Scheduling (C&S) area. Creating calendars can be tricky if you have never done it before. The Help file is a pretty good start, but there are more advanced features that you will want to use in your applications—and most of these are showcased in the C&S area of the mail template. However, you should avoid the temptation to copy design elements from the mail template and attempt to shoehorn them into your own application. The C&S area of the Notes 6 mail template is one of the most complicated features in *any* Notes application and is comprised of literally dozens of design elements, most of which would make no sense in an application outside of a mail template. A better approach to utilizing the mail template in general, and the C&S features specifically, is to examine how certain features are accomplished. For instance, there are great examples of using the NotesUIView.RegionDoubleClick (for doing things like composing new documents from the date that is double-clicked), NotesUIView .PostEntryResize (for resizing appointment times in the view and recording it to the underlying document), and much more. There are even two really good examples of building LotusScript classes to make it easy to handle an otherwise exceedingly complex task—the CSEventClass and CSUIViewClass, which are housed in LotusScript Libraries of the same name. Therefore it is recommended that you get inspiration from the C&S feature in the Notes mail template, but don't try copying it outright from the template itself.

The Personal Address Book Template

The Personal Address Book database enables users to manage personal and business contacts, to maintain Group documents for mailing lists, and also to maintain some configuration information for the Notes client. There are several features that are of interest, and fortunately the way the pernames.ntf template works is easy to understand. These features include the Preferences dialog box, the Edit Contact Labels button, and the AddressPicker form.

Users can control the display format for contact information using the Personal Address Book Preferences dialog box, which creates a profile document to store the preference information. Users can also customize the labels used to identify various fields within each document. The Contact form, shown in Figure 7-1, makes extensive use of hide-when settings, computed text and computed for display fields, and a programmable table, which is used to implement a highly configurable display for users. This form is also a good example of using nested tables to create a very clean look.

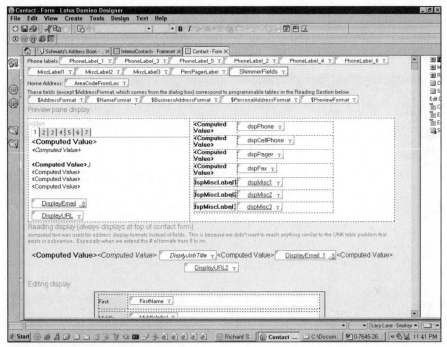

Figure 7-1: The Contact form

The Edit Contact Labels button on the Contact form is an example of the use of the @DialogBox function in Notes Formula language. If you open the form in Domino Designer and select Preview in Browser from the Actions menu, you find that this button does not work. The @DialogBox function is one of several Notes features that doesn't work in browsers. IBM has not Web-enabled the Personal Address Book application. If they were to do so, they would have to change the code in this button to use JavaScript instead of using Notes Formula language.

The Personal Address Book template contains the AddressPicker form, which gives users access to 30 buttons, 26 of which are used (in the U.S. English version of the template) for selecting the letters A through Z for indexing the Contacts list. Although a very straightforward technique could have been used, it would have been harder to adapt for foreign languages, so IBM engineers assigned a number to each of the buttons and used it to look up a letter value in a list stored in a field named AlphList. Modifying this code to work with other alphabets requires only three steps: changing the contents of the AlphList field, entering the number of letters in the alphabet into the AlphNumber field, and changing the caption and alternate text properties on each of the button graphics.

The Discussion Template

Discussion is the archetypal Notes and Domino application. Apart from e-mail, it is probably the application users associate most with Notes and Domino. The Discussion template, `discsw6.ntf`, is a good demonstration of several of the most frequently used Notes and Domino features.

The Discussion template enables Notes clients and browser users to open new topics for discussion using the Main Topic form, and to participate in *threads* by adding new documents using the Response or Response to Response forms. The All Documents view uses Show Response Documents in a Hierarchy to create an indented display that graphically shows the flow of each discussion thread (see Figure 7-2).

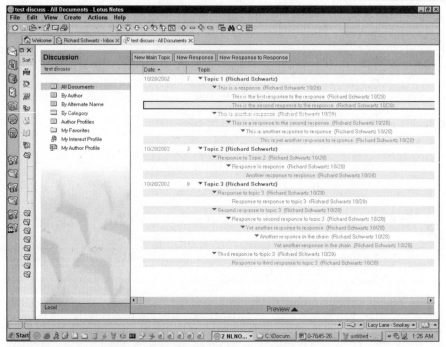

Figure 7-2: Response hierarchy in the Discussion template

The By Author and By Category views demonstrate categorization, a different organizational technique. Chapter 9 covers both response hierarchy and categorization. The By Author view also shows that the Discussion template tracks authorship of documents. An Author Names field is used for tracking purposes and for security. These fields make it possible to design applications that allow users to modify only those documents that they have created. Chapter 21 covers Author Names fields.

Users of Discussion applications can also fill in Personal Profile and Interest Profile forms. An agent called Send Newsletters, which sends out e-mail messages to users to inform them when new documents that match the profile are added to the discussion, uses the Interest Profile forms. This agent is a good example of the use of the `NotesNewsletter` class in LotusScript.

The Document Library Templates

Notes and Domino also ship with a family of three templates known as the Document Library templates. The family includes a generic version, along with versions customized for storing Microsoft Office documents and Lotus SmartSuite documents. The generic version is intended for use with the Notes client and a Web browser. The Office and SmartSuite versions are intended only for use with the Notes client. The Office and SmartSuite versions demonstrate the use of Microsoft's OLE (Object Linking and Embedding) technology, which allows Word, Excel, WordPro, and 1-2-3 documents to appear inside the Notes client window, as shown in Figure 7-3.

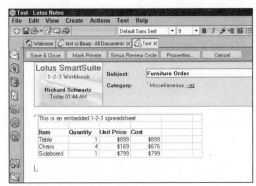

Figure 7-3: An OLE 1-2-3 spreadsheet in the SmartSuite Document Library

The most interesting portion of the Document Library templates is the workflow code, which supports serial and parallel review processes for documents, with facilities for notification of reviewers and setting time limits for each reviewer. The code that manages the workflow is in the DocumentWorkflow subform, which uses the OLERoutines script library. The code is fairly well documented, so you should be able to follow it.

The Document Library templates also support response and response-to-response forms, similar to the ones in the Discussion template. Although there are no new concepts demonstrated by this, it shows how easy it is to add a response hierarchy to any Notes and Domino application, adding value by allowing users to engage in discussions about the data the application manages.

Summary

This chapter examined some of the features of the Mail, Personal Address Book, Discussion, and Document Library templates. You learned that

✦ The Mail template demonstrates reserved fields used for addressing mail, form properties used to send mail from the Notes client, and the MailOptions field used to send mail from a WebQuerySave agent.

✦ The Personal Address Book template demonstrates techniques for designing user-customizable display formats, and is a good example of using tables to control the visual appearance of data on a form. It also shows techniques for writing generic code that is easy to extend.

✦ The Discussion template demonstrates response hierarchy and categorized views. It also demonstrates the use of Author Names fields to control document security, and use of the `NotesNewsletter` class in LotusScript.

✦ The Document Library templates demonstrate techniques for using OLE to embed Microsoft Office and Lotus SmartSuite documents within a document in an NSF file. It also demonstrates techniques for programming serial and parallel workflow processes.

The next part of the book, Part III, dives into the architecture of an application and covers such topics as pages, forms, views, folders, and so on.

✦   ✦   ✦

Application Architecture

Page and Form Basics

By Richard Schwartz

✦   ✦   ✦   ✦

In This Chapter

Creating pages

Creating forms

Formatting text on
pages and forms

Data access through
fields on forms

✦   ✦   ✦   ✦

Pages and forms are design elements used to create formatted data displays in Notes and Domino. If you are familiar with HTML, it is important to understand that it was invented after Notes, so some Notes and Domino terminology does not match up precisely with what most Web programmers would expect. In HTML, a form is a portion of a page that can contain input elements. In Notes and Domino, a *form* is a design element used for displaying data from documents and entering new data into documents, and a *page* is a design element used only for displaying data. Pages are typically used for displaying online help, for menus used to navigate through the features of an application, or for lists of links. This chapter introduces you to the basics of creating pages and forms, and explains how to use them to build your Domino applications.

Creating Pages

To create a new page, choose Create ➪ Design ➪ Page from the Domino Designer menu, or click the Page's entry in the Bookmark panel for the database that you want to create it in, and then click the New Page button at the top of the Pages index. Domino Designer displays an empty window, a blank slate so to speak, into which you can enter text, graphics, and other elements to make up your page.

If you right-click in the Page window and select Page Properties from the menu, Domino Designer displays the Page Properties dialog box, which is shown in Figure 8-1.

You can set a variety of properties for a page on the four tabs in this dialog box. Table 8-1 describes the properties shown on the Info tab (refer to Figure 8-1). The Background tab is shown in Figure 8-2, and the properties are described in Table 8-2. The remaining properties are covered in Chapters 10 and 12.

Figure 8-1: Page Properties
dialog box

Table 8-1: Page Properties — Info Tab

Property	Purpose
Name	Every page must have a unique name, which appears in the Page index, and is used for accessing the page via URLs or for links to the page from other design elements. If you do not enter a name for the page, Domino Designer prompts for it when you save the page. You can also add an alias to a page (or any other design element) by appending the alias to the name with a pipe (	) symbol (for example, My kewl page | KEWL_PAGE).
Comment	This is an optional description of the page, which appears in the Page index for informational purposes only.
No Initial Focus	If selected, this option prevents the page from capturing the cursor focus when first displayed in the Notes client.
No Focus on F6	If selected, this option prevents the page from capturing the focus if the user presses the F6 key.
Render Pass-Thru HTML in Notes	If selected, this option directs the Notes client to interpret any HTML tags on the page that have been marked as Pass-Thru HTML. If you do not select this property, Pass-Thru HTML is displayed as ugly ASCII text in the Notes client.
Content Type	Select Notes if you want to design the page layout using Domino Designer's WYSIWYG features. Select HTML if you want to design the page by coding your own HTML tags to control the layout, or by pasting in HTML that you created with another WYSIWYG page design tool. Select Other if you want to specify the exact value, such as "text/xml", that will be sent to the browser in the content-type header for the page.
Character Set	Select a character set from the drop-down list if you want Domino to send header information to browsers.
Link Colors	Using the color picker, select the colors to be used in a browser for the active link (the one most recently clicked), unvisited links, and previously visited links.

Figure 8-2: The Background tab

Table 8-2: Page Properties — Background Tab

Property	Purpose
Color	Click the drop-down list to bring up the color picker, which is shown in Figure 8-3, to select a solid background color for the page. You can select one of the predefined colors, or click one of the two icons at the upper-right of the color picker. The System Color Selector is used to specify that the client-operating system's default background color should be used for the page. The Custom Color Selector opens a color dialog box that enables you to enter numeric values for the red, green, and blue components of a color and add it to your palette.
Graphic	Click the Paste button to paste a background graphic onto the page. Click the Import button to import a background graphic from a disk file. (Domino Designer supports bitmap, GIF, JPEG, and several other image formats.) It is important that you copy the graphic to the Clipboard before clicking the Paste button. If you want to remove the background graphic, click the Remove button.
Resource	Click the Folder icon to select an Image Resource, either from a list of Image Resources in the current database, or from another database. Click the @ icon to use a formula to select an Image Resource. For example, if you have seven image resources named "1.gif", "2.gif", and so on, you could use the formula @Text(@Weekday) and ".gif" to select a different background for each day of the week.
Hide Graphic In Design Mode	Select this to suppress display of the background image while you are working on your page design.
Hide Graphic On 16 Color Displays	Select this to suppress display of the background image on old computers that might not render the colors reasonably.
Repeat	Select an option for tiling, centering, or repeating the background image. In browser-based applications this setting isn't necessary, as browsers automatically tile background graphics.

Custom Color Selector

System Color Selection

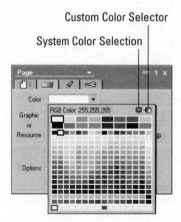

Figure 8-3: The color picker

To save a page, choose File ➪ Save from the menu. You can also press the Escape key or click the X in the tab for your page near the top of the Domino Designer window, and then click Yes when Designer prompts you to save the page.

Creating Forms

To create a new form, choose Create ➪ Design ➪ Form from the menu, or click the Forms entry in the Bookmark panel for the database that you want to create it in and click the New Form button at the top of the Forms index. Domino Designer displays an empty window, in which you can design your form.

If you right-click within the Form window and select Form Properties, Domino Designer displays the Form Properties dialog box, which is shown in Figure 8-4.

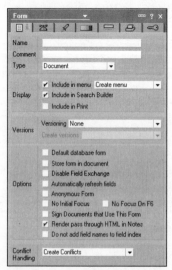

Figure 8-4: The Form Properties dialog box

This dialog box has seven different tabs that enable you to set properties for your form. Table 8-3 describes the properties shown on the Info tab (see Figure 8-4). Figure 8-5 shows the Defaults tab; its properties are described in Table 8-4. The Background tab for form properties is identical to the Background tab for a page, which was described earlier. The remaining properties are covered in Chapters 10 and 12.

Table 8-3: Form Properties — Info Tab

Property	Purpose
Name	Every form must have a unique name, which appears in the Form index and is used for accessing the page via URLs or for links to the page from other design elements. If you do not enter a name for the form, Domino Designer prompts for it when you save the form. It is often useful to create a shorter alias for a form name, which you can do by entering a vertical bar character (|) after name, followed by the alias.
Description	An optional description of the form, which appears in the Form index for informational purposes only.
Type	A Domino database supports three different types of documents, which are used for a structure known as a response hierarchy. A response hierarchy is a thread of documents, similar to a discussion thread at a forum Web site. Select Document for forms that are used to create new documents at the top level of the hierarchy. Select Response for forms that are used to create documents that always appear as responses to the top-level documents. Select Response To Response for forms that are used to create documents that can be a response to a document at any level of the hierarchy.
Include in Menu	If selected, this option tells the Notes client to display the form name in the Create menu or in the dialog box that appears when you choose Create ➪ Other Dialog.
Include in Search Builder	If selected, this option tells the Notes client to enable users to use this form to construct full-text search queries.
Include in Print	If selected, this option tells the Notes client to let users use this form when printing documents that were created with other forms.
Versioning	The Notes client has the ability to make versioned copies of a document each time it is changed. Select New Versions Become Responses to have the Notes client save any document edited with this form as a response to the original document. Select Prior Versions Become Responses to have the Notes client save the original copy of any document edited with this form as a response document. Select New Versions Become Siblings to have the Notes client save any document edited with this form at the same level in a response hierarchy as the original version. Also, select Manual to have the Notes client create a new version if the user selects File ➪ Save As New Version, or select Automatic to have the Notes client create a new version whenever the user chooses File ➪ Save.
Default Database Form	The default form for a database is used to display any document that does not contain an item named *form*.

Continued

Table 8-3 *(continued)*

Property	Purpose
Store Form in Document	Notes and Domino can store the layout and logic of a form in each document created by the form. Selecting this option requires more storage space for each document and can make maintenance of an application difficult if the form design is likely to change in the future.
Disable Field Exchange	If selected, this disables Notes/FX, which is an extension of Microsoft's OLE technology that allows bi-directional data transfer between items in Notes documents and embedded OLE objects. Notes/FX is a deprecated technology, but leaving it enabled is almost always harmless.
Automatically Refresh Fields	If selected, this causes the Notes client to rerun formulas for all fields whenever a field value changes. Warning: This can be extremely inefficient and can lead to poor application performance.
Anonymous Form	If selected, this option prevents Notes and Domino from recording (in an item called "$UpdatedBy") the identity of every user who creates or updates a document.
No Initial Focus	If selected, this option prevents the form from capturing the cursor focus when first displayed in the Notes client.
No Focus on F6	If selected, this option prevents the form from capturing the focus if the user presses the F6 key.
Sign Documents That Use This Form	If selected, this option causes documents created with this form to be automatically signed by the creator of the document. Note: This feature is new to Notes/Domino 6.
Render Pass-Thru HTML in Notes	If selected, this option directs the Notes client to interpret any HTML tags on the form that have been marked as Pass-Thru HTML. Note: This feature is new to Notes/Domino 6.
Do Not Add Field Names To Field Index	If selected, this option prevents Notes and Domino from adding the fields on this form to the UNK table, which is an internal structure in the NSF file that tracks the names of all items. See Chapter 13 for further discussion of the UNK table. Note: This feature is new to Notes/Domino 6.
Conflict Handling	This feature tells Domino what to do when a replication or save conflict occurs. The choices include: **Merge Conflicts:** If the items modified in the two documents are different, merge the two documents into one document, including the changes made to items from both documents. If the same item is modified by two different people, a conflict document is created. **Create Conflicts:** Create a "conflict" response document that shows up in views, and contains a field called $ConflictAction. It is up to the user to resolve the conflict by picking a "winner."

Property	Purpose
	Merge/No Conflicts: Attempt to merge the two documents as in Create Conflicts but if they cannot be merged because the same item was modified in both documents, do not create a conflict document; instead the last one saved wins, and the other one is lost. Note: This choice is new in Notes/Domino 6. **No Conflicts:** Don't create a conflict document ever—the last one saved always wins.

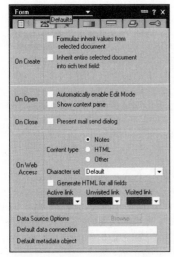

Figure 8-5: The Defaults tab

Table 8-4: Form Properties — Defaults Tab

Property	Purpose
Formulas Inherit Values From Selected Document	When you create a new document using a form, formulas for fields on the form have a one-time opportunity to use the values of items in the currently selected document to set initial values for items in the new document. Selecting this property enables this feature.
Inherit Entire Selected Document Into Rich Text Field	It is frequently desirable, especially when creating documents that will be e-mailed as responses to other documents, to make a WYSIWYG copy of the original document and include that copy in a rich text field in the new document. Selecting this setting enables you to do so. You also have the option of placing a doclink to the original document in the rich text field, or of including the entire document in a collapsible section (see Chapter 12) in the rich text field.

Continued

Table 8-4 *(continued)*

Property	Purpose
Automatically Enable Edit Mode	Normally, users have the choice of opening documents to read or edit. Selecting this property causes Notes and Domino to open the document in edit mode automatically, even if the user requested to open it in read mode.
Show Context Pane	Selecting this setting causes the Notes client to split the screen whenever a document that uses this form is opened. The upper pane shows the document. The lower pane is the context pane. You can specify that the context pane show the document's parent in the response hierarchy, or you can specify that the context pane show a document that is doclinked from the document that you opened. This setting is ignored when accessing documents from a Web browser.
Present Mail Send Dialog	Selecting this setting causes the Notes client to issue a prompt asking the user whether he wants to send the document as a mail message when the user closes the document. This setting is ignored when accessing documents from a Web browser.
Content Type	Select Notes if you want to design the page layout using Domino Designer's WYSIWYG features. Select HTML if you want to design the page by coding your own HTML tags to control the layout, or by pasting in HTML that you created with another WYSIWYG page design tool. Select Other if you want to specify the exact value, such as `"text/xml"`, that will be sent to the browser in the content-type header for the page.
Character Set	This setting enables you to choose the character set (Unicode, Arabic, Japanese, and so on) that is used when this form is loaded in a browser. This choice tells the browser that a different character set is needed, which may cause the browser to prompt the user to obtain this character set if it is not available in the user's browser.
Generate HTML For All Fields	Selecting this setting causes Domino to generate HTML `<input>` tags for all fields on the form, even if those fields are not set up to be editable. The HTML for these fields specifies `type='hidden'` so that they do not appear in the browser. This setting is useful to allow JavaScript running in the browser to access the value of noneditable fields, or to ensure that certain calculations are done only once at the time the form is opened.
Link Colors	Using the color picker, select the colors to be used in a browser for the active link (the one most recently clicked), unvisited links, and previously visited links.
Data Source Options	See Part IX: "Relational Database Integration" for information about these settings.

To save a form, choose File ➪ Save from the menu. You can also press the Escape key or click the X in the tab of your form near the top of the Domino Designer window, and then click Yes when Designer prompts you to save the form.

Formatting Text on Pages and Forms

The layout of pages and forms is stored as a rich text item in the design element. It follows that all the WYSIWYG text-formatting capabilities that Notes gives to end-users for creating documents are available to programmers when laying out their forms. Programmers can select fonts, sizes, colors, and effects on text characters, create bulleted lists, adjust tabs, margins, and line spacing for paragraphs, and set page breaks for printing. Not all Web browsers, however, support these features.

Setting text properties

The Text Properties dialog box, which is available by choosing Text ⇨ Properties from the menu, by right-clicking in a block of text and selecting Properties from the menu, or by using the ALT+Enter keys, contains controls for almost all text features. Like most other properties dialog boxes in Domino Designer, it is a tabbed dialog box.

Font properties

The first tab of the Text Properties dialog box, shown in Figure 8-6, is known as the Font tab. It has controls that apply to sequences of characters. Any changes you make to the settings on this tab affect any characters that you have selected with the cursor. If nothing is selected, the changes take effect for any new characters that you type at the current cursor location.

You select the font in the scroll list on the left side of the dialog box. You can select installed font sizes from the scroll box at the top, or specify a dynamically created size in the box at the bottom. The fonts and sizes listed in the scroll boxes are the ones that exist on the computer where Domino Designer is running. If you select one that does not exist on a user's computer, the Notes client picks a similar font. If your form or page is going to be used from a Web browser on a wide variety of computers, it's best to stick with the more popular fonts, such as Courier, Times, and Verdana.

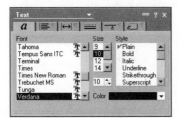

Figure 8-6: The Text Properties dialog box — Font tab

You can select bold, underscore, italic, superscript, subscript, and other effects in the Style scroll box on the right side of the dialog box. These effects work as expected in both the Notes client and Web browsers. Other effects available only in the Notes client include strikethrough, shadow, emboss, and extrude.

The color selector enables you to pick the color for your text. You can select it from a color palette, or you can enter the RGB value in the color selector box.

Paragraph alignment properties

The second tab of the Text Properties dialog box, shown in Figure 8-7, is known as the Paragraph Alignment tab. It has a variety of controls that apply to entire paragraphs. Changes that you make on this tab affect all paragraphs that you select with the cursor. If you have not made a selection, the changes affect only the paragraph in which the cursor is currently positioned.

Figure 8-7: The Text Properties dialog box — Paragraph Alignment tab

The first set of controls on this tab enables you to set paragraphs to align on the left margin, the right margin, the center, both margins, or simply to extend out past the right edge of the window. Browsers recognize only left, right, and center alignment.

The next set of controls enables you to set the first line of a paragraph to indent or outdent. Web browsers do not honor this setting.

The List control lets you set up a group of paragraphs as a bulleted list. Several different styles of bullets are supported, including alphabetic and numeric bullets, which automatically assign consecutive letters or numbers to each paragraph. Both the Notes client and Web browsers support most of these settings. The check box bullet style, however, is supported in only the Notes client.

The Spacing area enables you to set the spacing above and below your paragraph, as well as the spacing between each line of your paragraph. The spacing can be single, 1½, or double.

You can collapse the Text Properties dialog box into a toolbar, as shown in Figure 8-8.

Permanent Pen Icon

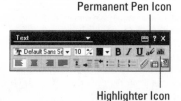

Figure 8-8: The Text Properties toolbar

Highlighter Icon

Most of the properties discussed in this section are available with a single click in this toolbar. The Permanent Pen icon on this toolbar enables you to use a single combination of font, size, and color settings at any location on the page or form where you type new text, regardless of the current settings at that location. You can set the font, size, and color by positioning your cursor in a block of text with the attributes that you want to use, and then choosing Text ➪ Permanent Pen ➪ Set Permanent Pen Style from the menu.

The Highlighter icon is a toggle. When you click it, your cursor changes shape to resemble a pen. If you select text with the cursor while in this mode, the text background changes to yellow. This effect is intended to simulate the use of a highlighting marker pen, to add emphasis to text on a page or form. Only the Notes client, however, supports this feature. To exit from highlighting mode, click the icon on the toolbar again.

The three icons on the right of the second row in the toolbar are discussed in Chapter 12.

Using the ruler and tabs

You can display a ruler at the top of your form or page by choosing View ➪ Ruler from the menu. You can control margin and tab settings from this ruler, as shown in Figure 8-9.

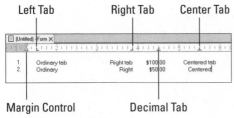

Figure 8-9: The ruler

 Note   Web browsers do not honor ruler and tab settings!

The controls on the ruler are similar to the type used in popular word-processing programs such as Microsoft Word and Lotus WordPro. The margin control consists of three parts. The top triangle controls indentation of the first line of a paragraph. The bottom triangle controls the left margin of subsequent lines in the paragraph, and the rectangular slider at the bottom moves both triangles simultaneously.

You can space text within a line of text according to the tabs on the ruler by using the Tab key to break the line into pieces. By default, Notes assumes that there are tabs located at half-inch intervals on the ruler. You can place tabs in the ruler by right-clicking the desired location in the ruler and selecting the type of tab from the menu. Left tabs are ordinarily used to create left-aligned columns of text. Right tabs are used to create columns that are aligned on the right; center tabs are used to create columns that contain centered text, and decimal tabs are used to create columns of numbers that align on the decimal point.

You can also see margins and tabs in the third tab of the Text Properties dialog box, as shown in Figure 8-10. They can be set from this tab, too, but it's almost always more convenient to work directly with the controls on the ruler instead.

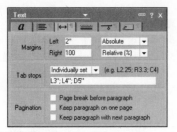

Figure 8-10: Text Properties—
Paragraph Margins tab

Using styles

The right-most tab of the Text Properties dialog box is the Paragraph Styles tab, shown in Figure 8-11. You can use the buttons on this tab to get Domino Designer to "remember" combinations of character and paragraph settings and give them a name.

You can access commonly used styles by pressing the F11 key while editing text. Each press of F11 switches the style to the next one in the list, so you can rapidly cycle through them. You can also easily set the style for a selection of text or at the current cursor position by opening a list of styles from the lower-left corner of the Domino Designer window (see Figure 8-12).

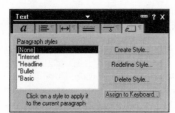

Figure 8-11: Text Properties—
Paragraph Styles tab

Using this dialog box, you can

✦ Click the Create Style button to assign a name to the combination of settings that are applied at the current cursor position The Style pop-up list is shown in Figure 8-12.

✦ Select a name in the scroll box on the left of the dialog box, and then click the Redefine Style button to change the settings for a style that was previously defined.

✦ Click the Delete Style button to remove a named style from the list.

✦ Click the Assign to Keyboard button to add the named style to a list that Domino Designer rotates through when you press F11.

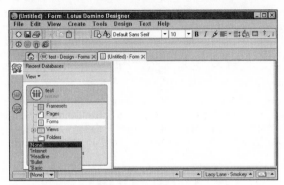

Figure 8-12: The Style pop-up list

Cross-Reference

Styles applied to text in Domino Designer are *not* related to Cascading Style Sheets (CSS). Domino does, however, support CSS. See Chapter 41 for information about using CSS.

Including HTML in page and form text

Although Domino Designer has WYSIWYG features for laying out pages and forms, at times you might want to take control of the HTML layout details for a Web application. There are four ways that you can include HTML in your pages or forms. The first way is through the Content Type property of the page or form. This setting applies to all the text on your page or form, so if you use it you have to generate HTML tags for the entire layout. The other three ways enable you to embed small amounts of HTML in the middle of text to modify or supplement the layout that you have specified with Designer's WYSIWYG features. This is known as using *Pass-Thru HTML*.

The first of the three ways to insert bits of HTML in a page or form is to create a style named HTML and apply it to a paragraph containing the HTML tags. The Domino server ignores the font and all other attributes applied to the text in this paragraph and sends it to the browser without generating any of its own tags; those tags might interfere with what you are trying to do with your own formatting. The Notes client, however, does not interpret HTML tags that are marked this way.

Tip

It doesn't matter what text attributes you apply to this style; they are ignored. However it is a good idea to change the font and color to something distinctive that visually alerts you to the fact that the text is tagged with your HTML style.

The second way to insert bits of HTML is by surrounding the tags with the square bracket characters, [and], as shown here:

```
[<center>This text should be centered</center>]
```

The Domino server strips out the brackets and sends the tags to the browser without generating any tags of its own. Because styles apply to entire paragraphs, this technique is useful when you want to include a few tags within a paragraph. But as is the case with the HTML style, the Notes client does not interpret HTML tags that are marked this way.

The last, and best, method for marking text so that it is treated as HTML is to select the text and then choose Text ➪ Pass-Thru HTML on the menu. The selected text is highlighted in Domino Designer, which makes it easier to locate. The other major advantage of this technique is that, as of Release 6, the Notes client interprets the HTML tags that you mark this way and adjusts the layout of your page or form accordingly — although only if the Render Pass-Thru HTML in Notes property is selected for the page or form.

Text marked as Pass-Thru HTML can also be automatically converted to Notes rich text formatting by choosing Edit ➪ Convert To Notes Format from the menu. This is useful when you want to take some HTML that was generated by hand or by another Web programming tool and use it in a Notes application, but you don't want to have to maintain it in HTML format.

Accessing Data through Fields on Forms

Domino programmers put fields on forms to display items from documents or profile documents, to display values computed from the items, or to get input from users. The input can be saved back to the document or a profile document, it can be e-mailed to another user or to a mail-in database (a special application that is set up to receive documents via e-mail), or it can simply be used temporarily and then discarded.

Cross-Reference   Fields are not supported on pages; they can only be used on forms. Pages do support one feature that allows simple calculations: computed text. See Chapter 12 for more details.

Creating fields

Chapter 3 describes forms in terms of a stencil or mask that allows data from items within a document to show through the holes. The "holes" in a form are fields. You can add a field to a form by choosing Create ➪ Field from the menu, which puts a placeholder at the current cursor position on the form and opens the Field Properties dialog box, as shown in Figure 8-13. You use this dialog box to fill in the name and type information for the field, as well as other properties.

In addition to the name, programmers must specify two different Type properties for a field. The first is the data type, which we'll come back to a little later. The second is, for lack of a better name, the formula type. Notes and Domino support four formula types for fields: editable fields, computed fields, computed for display fields, and computed when composed fields. The formula type describes how the field is populated with data.

Editable fields

Editable fields are used on forms to enable users to enter data when a document is opened for editing. Every field on a form is given a unique name. If the user saves the data on the form in a document, data entered in each editable field is saved in an item with the same name as the field.

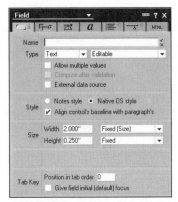

Figure 8-13: The Field Properties dialog box

Three formulas are associated with an editable field: the initial value formula, the validation formula, and the translation formula. These are covered in Chapter 15. At this point, however, it's worth pointing out that the inheritance property for forms mentioned earlier is linked to the initial value formula for editable fields. In other words, if you have an editable field named Subject in a form for a response document, you may want it to take the value of the Subject item from its parent document. This does not happen automatically, even with the inheritance property turned on. You have to enter a formula that references the Subject field. For example, if you want the subject of the response to add the prefix *Re:* to the subject of the parent, the initial value formula for the Subject field in the response document's form would be

```
"Re: " + Subject
```

In this formula, the term Subject refers to the inherited Subject item from the parent document.

Note Inheritance works for all types of fields, not just editable fields. But in all cases, the inherited values are available only when the document is first created with the form.

Computed fields

There are three types of computed fields, with slightly different purposes. Each type has only one formula associated with it, known as the value formula.

Ordinary computed fields

Computed fields are used on forms to allow a formula to compute a value that is stored as an item in a document, but not allow users to modify that value. Computed fields are saved in items whose name matches the field name. For instance, you may have the user entering pricing information, and need to compute a total. You can use a computed field to automatically add up the other field values for a total.

Computed for display fields

Computed for display fields also allow a formula to compute a value that users are not allowed to edit, and that value is not stored in the document. It is a temporary value. Computed for display fields are often used for displaying information that is looked up from other documents and needs to be up to date at the time that the document is opened.

Computed when composed fields

Regular computed fields will recompute any time the document is saved or refreshed, and this is not appropriate for certain things, like time stamps or unique identifiers. Computed when composed fields are used on forms to allow a formula to compute a value only once and save it permanently in an item in the document. Normally this occurs when the document is first created (or *composed* as it was known in Notes R3 and earlier releases, hence the name for this field type), but there are cases where this can occur later on. For example, a programmer can write code to remove an item from a document (for example, using the @DeleteField function in a Formula language agent). In this case, the next time the document is opened, the computed when composed field's value formula will execute. If the document is edited or saved, the new value is saved in the appropriate item.

Setting field properties

Programmers specify many additional properties for fields besides name and type. The Field Properties dialog box has seven tabs. This section covers the Field Info, Advanced, and Extra HTML tabs. The Font and Paragraph tabs were covered previously while discussing text, and their function is the same for fields. The Control tab settings are specific to the data type of the field, and these are covered later in this chapter. The Hide-When tab is covered in Chapter 12.

Field Info properties

The properties on the Field Info tab of the Field Properties dialog box (refer to Figure 8-13) are described in Table 8-5.

Table 8-5: Field Properties — Field Info

Property	Purpose
Name	Assigns a unique name to the field. For fields other than computed for display, this name matches the name of the item in a document that stores the value used in this field.
	Note: You cannot have two fields with the same name.
Type	As described in the main text, fields can be editable, computed, computed for display, or computed when composed. They can be one of 17 data types.
Allow Multiple Values	When selected, this indicates that the field will display and store a list of values rather than just a single value. Separator characters for use in display and input parsing are specified on the Advanced tab.
Compute After Validation	When selected, a computed value formula is executed only after validation formulas have run on editable fields in order to avoid having data entry errors cause a cascade of computation errors.
External Data Source	This property is used to specify a Data Connection Resource, or DCR. DCRs are new to Notes/Domino 6, and are covered in Chapters 43 and 44.

Property	Purpose
Style	The Notes client can display fields Notes style or OS style. For editable fields, most users are more comfortable with OS style, which displays rectangular input boxes. Notes style displays two half brackets. You can see the difference in Figure 8-14. For noneditable fields, however, OS style may not be the best choice, because the rectangular box around the data may be distracting to the user. Notes style fields do not display the half brackets if the field can't be edited. Web browsers understand only one way to display fields, so only the Notes client uses this setting.
Align Control's Baseline With Paragraph	Notes can align the bottom of the rectangle around an OS style field with other text on the same line, or it can align the text within the rectangle with the other text on the same line. Selecting this property chooses the latter option, which usually has a nicer appearance. Web browsers ignore this property.
Size	This property sets the size of the rectangle around an OS style field. For the width, you can either specify a fixed size (in inches), a fixed size in characters, or Fit to Window, which extends the field rectangle out to the right margin. For the height, you can also specify a fixed size (again, in inches), or Dynamic, which expands the field rectangle to fit up to three lines of data and adds scroll bars if needed, or Proportional, which sets the size of the of the field based on the point size of the font selected for the field—but I have never seen it do anything! Web browsers ignore the width and height properties.
Position in Tab Order	The Notes client enables users to navigate between editable fields using the Tab key, normally moving from left to right and top to bottom on the form. Setting a nonzero value for this property in every editable field overrides the default order of navigation. Web browsers ignore this property.
Give Field Initial Focus	The top- and left-most editable field on a form normally takes the cursor focus when the form is used to create or edit a document. Setting this property for one field on a form overrides this behavior, but only in the Notes client. Web browsers ignore this setting.

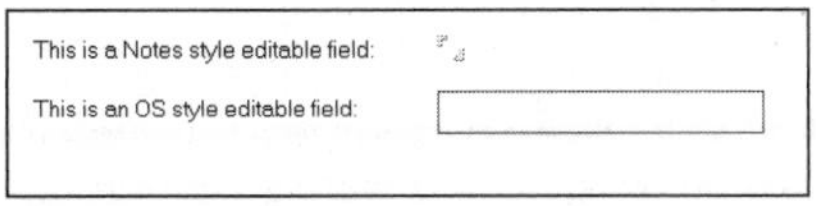

This is a Notes style editable field:

This is an OS style editable field:

Figure 8-14: Notes and OS style fields

Advanced field properties

The Advanced tab of the Field Properties box is shown in Figure 8-15, and each property is described in Table 8-6.

Figure 8-15: The Field Properties dialog box — Advanced tab

Table 8-6: Field Properties — Advanced

Property	Purpose
Help Description	Text entered for this property appears to Notes client users in a one-line area at the bottom of the Notes window, but only if the user has activated this feature by choosing View ⇨ Show@ Field Help. Web browsers do not support this.
Field Hint	Text entered here appears in the actual field on a new document created with the form in the Note client, and it disappears as soon as the user moves the cursor into the field. Web browsers do not support this property.
	Note: This property is new in Notes/Domino 6, and is only available in editable fields.
Separate Values When User Enters	This property, which is available only if the Allow Multiple Values property is checked for the field, specifies values that users can enter as separate individual values within a list. Comma and semicolon are the default separators, but space, newline, and blank line can also be specified.
Display Separate Values With	This property is also only available for fields that have the Allow Multiple Values property checked. It specifies the character that Notes and Domino will use to separate values in a list when displaying data in the field. The default is the semicolon character. Comma, space, newline, and blank line are the other available choices.
Security Options	See Chapter 21 for a description of the available properties.
Run Exiting/OnChange events after value change	If you are using one of the keyword-type fields (combobox, listbox, and so on), you can select this property to cause any code contained in the Exiting and onChange events to be executed when a user changes the value of the keyword field.
	Note: This property is new in Notes/Domino 6.

Extra HTML properties

The Extra HTML tab of the Field Properties dialog box is shown in Figure 8-16. These properties are used to modify the HTML tags that Domino generates when sending a form to a browser.

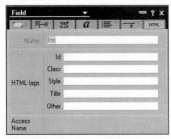

Figure 8-16: The Field Properties dialog box - Extra HTML tab

The first three properties on this tab, ID, Class, and Style, are needed if you want to use DHTML or CSS features. See Chapter 41 for more information about this. The Title property is used to activate ToolTips in Internet Explorer. The Other property enables you to enter any HTML attributes that you want. There are two common cases where this is done.

As mentioned earlier, the size properties for fields are not supported in Web browsers. You can, however, specify the number of characters for the width of a text field by the Other property for the field to

```
size=N
```

where N is the number of characters.

For rich text fields, you can enter the number of rows and columns that the browser should display for the data-entry area by setting the Other property for the rich text field to

```
rows=M cols=N
```

where M is the number of rows that you want, and N is the number of columns.

The second case in which the Other property is used is for hidden fields. As mentioned earlier, the Form property Generate HTML for All Fields causes the Domino server to send <input> elements to the browser for all fields on a form, including all noneditable fields. In some cases, however, you may only want to send the values of one or two noneditable fields to the browser. You can do this by entering the following into the Other property for the selected fields:

```
type='hidden'
```

The value of this field will be accessible to JavaScript running in the browser even though it is not displayed to the user.

Using data types for fields

Table 3-1 in Chapter 3 lists the 17 data types that Notes and Domino support for fields, and shows what item types their values are stored in. The Control tab of the Field Properties dialog box has different options for different field types. The following sections describe field types, and the available properties.

Text fields

Text fields are simple data entry fields into which users can enter unformatted text. The properties available on the Control tab of the Field Properties dialog box for text fields are described in Table 8-7.

Table 8-7: Text Field Control Properties

Property	Purpose
Border Style	This property is only available if OS style has been selected for the field. It enables the programmer to select a single pixel line, or a 3D-appearance for the rectangular border around the field, or to specify that there should be no border at all.
Allow Multiple Lines	This property is also only available if OS style has been selected for the field. If selected, it allows data in the field to contain newline characters.
Show Field Delimiters	This property is available only if Notes style has been selected for this field. If selected, the half brackets (as shown in Figure 8-14) are displayed to mark the input area for the field.

All the control properties for text fields are for the Notes client only. Web browsers ignore the control properties.

Password fields

Password fields are special text fields. The Notes client and Web browser hide the actual value of data typed into these fields. The control properties for password fields are the same as for ordinary text fields, with one exception: The Allow Multiple Lines property is not supported for password fields.

Number fields

Number fields enable users to enter numeric data. The properties available on the Control tab of the Field Properties dialog box for number fields are described in Table 8-8.

Date/Time fields

Date/Time fields enable users to enter dates and/or times. The properties available on the Control tab of the Field Properties dialog box for Date/Time fields are described in Table 8-9.

Table 8-8: Number Field Control Properties

Property	Purpose
Number Format	Select Decimal, Percent, Scientific, or Currency. Decimal displays a number in its normal written format. Percent displays numbers expressed as a percentage, such as 0.33 as 33%. Scientific displays numbers in scientific notation, such as 1,200 as 1.2E3. Currency displays numbers as monetary amounts.
Decimal Places	Specifies the number of decimal places that are displayed for the number, and whether or not the number of places is fixed or variable. For example, fixed with two decimal places would display 1.20 instead of truncating the trailing zero.
Border Style	Same as for text fields. See Table 8-7.
Show Field Delimiters	Same as for text fields. See Table 8-7.
User Preferences From	Select User Setting if you want number formats to be controlled by the settings on the user's computer, or Custom if you want to control the formats within your application. The Custom option may be useful if you want to display numbers representing several different types of national currency in one application.
Decimal Symbol	This setting is available only if Custom is selected. It specifies the character used to separate the whole number and decimal portion of a number, which may vary according to national or user preferences.
Thousands Separator	This setting is available only if Custom is selected. It specifies the character used to separate the groups of three digits in the whole number portion of a number, which may vary according to national or user preferences.
Parenthesis When Negative	This setting causes negative numbers to appear within parenthesis, which is the custom in many accounting applications.
Punctuated At Thousands	This setting determines whether the thousands separator character is used to break the whole number portion of a number into groups of three digits.
Currency Symbol	This setting is available only if Custom and Currency are selected. It determines what character or group of characters is used to represent a national currency amount. A drop-down list of common currency symbols is provided, but programmers can also enter a custom symbol.
Symbol Follows Number	This setting is available only if Custom and Currency are selected. If selected, this setting causes the currency symbol to be displayed after the number instead of before it.
Space Next To Number	This setting is available only if Custom and Currency have been selected. If selected, this setting causes the number and currency symbol to be separated by a single-space character.

Table 8-9: Date/Time Field Control Properties

Property	Purpose
Use Preferences From	Select User Setting to allow the operating system settings on the user's computer to control the format options for dates and times. Select Custom to control the formatting in your application.
Display Date	Select this property to display the date portion of a date/time value.
Display Time	Select this property to display the time value of a date/time value.
Show Date	This property specifies the portions of the date value that should appear. The portions are the year, the month, the day, and the weekday.
Special	This property controls whether the word Today will be substituted in place of today's date, and whether four-digit years appear. Choices for the latter are to always display four-digit years, only display four-digits for years in the 21st century, and to display the year for dates that are not in the current year.
Calendar	This property controls whether dates are interpreted according to the Gregorian calendar or the Hijri calendar. Note: This feature is new in Notes/Domino 6.
Date Format	This property, which is only available if Custom is selected, specifies the order in which the portions of a date are displayed.
Date Separators	This property, which is only available if Custom is selected, specifies the separator characters that appear between portions of a date.
Day	This property, which is only available if Custom is selected, specifies the number of digits displayed for the day, when the date is one of the first nine days of the month (01-09).
Month	This property, which is only available if Custom is selected, specifies the number of digits displayed for the month, when the date is one of the first nine months of the year (01-09).
Year	This property, which is only available if Custom is selected, specifies the number of digits displayed for the year.
Weekday	This property, which is only available if Custom is selected, specifies whether the full weekday name or an abbreviation is displayed. You can also specify whether the name is displayed in parentheses.
Show Time	This property specifies the portions of the time value that should appear. The portions are the hours, minutes, and seconds.
Time Zone	This property specifies whether time zone information appears. Selections are Adjust to Local Time Zone, Always Show Time Zone, and Show Only if Zone not Local.
Time Format	This property, which is only available if Custom is selected, specifies whether the time is displayed in 12-hour or 24-hour format.
Time Separator	This property, which is only available if Custom is selected, specifies the character that appears between the hour, minute, and second portions of the time value.

Property	Purpose
Require User Enter Four Digit Years	If selected, this property, which is available only if the field is editable, specifies that users are required to enter four-digit years. If it is not selected, users may enter two- or four-digit years, two-digit values of 50 and up are interpreted as 20th century, and values below 49 are interpreted as 21st century.
Require User Enter Alphabetic Months	If selected, this property, which is available only if the field is editable, specifies that users enter months by their alphabetical abbreviations instead of by their number.
Border Style	Same as for text fields. See Table 8-7.
Show Field Delimiters	Same as for text fields. See Table 8-7.

Keyword fields

Dialog List, Checkbox, Radio Button, Listbox, Combobox, and Time Zone are all types of keyword fields. These field types enable users to select one or more values from a list. Except in the case of Time Zone fields, the list may be supplied directly by the programmer, or the programmer can write Formula language code to create the list. Dialog List fields have several more options that are explained in the next section. The Choices drop-down on the Control tab of the Field Properties dialog box specifies how the list is supplied.

Checkbox fields display a series of choices with boxes next to them. Users click the boxes to select one or more of the values for the field. Radio Button fields display a series of choices with small circular buttons next to them. Users click one of the boxes to select the value for the field. Listbox fields display a scrolling list of choices. Users may select only one value from the list, unless the Allow Multiple Values property is selected for the field. Combobox fields display a drop-down list of values. Users may select only one value from the list.

The properties available on the Control tab of the Field Properties dialog box for all keyword list fields, except Time Zone fields, are described in Table 8-10.

Table 8-10: Keyword Field Control Properties

Property	Purpose
Border Style	Same as for text fields. See Table 8-7.
Choices	Specifies how the list of choices for the field is supplied. All keyword fields have two choices: Enter Choices (one per line), and Use Formula for Choices. Several other choices are available for Dialog List fields.
Allow Values Not In List	Specifies whether the user can type a value into the field if it does not appear in the list of choices. This property is only available for Dialog List and Combobox fields.
Refresh Fields On Keyword Change	Specifies that the form's formulas should be recalculated when a user selects a new value for this field. This allows fields to be cascaded, so that the choice made in one field can affect the choices available in other fields.

Continued

Table 8-10 *(continued)*

Property	Purpose
Refresh Choices On Document Refresh	Specifies that the formula used to provide the list of choices for the field should be executed whenever the form is refreshed.
Allow Keyword Synonyms	Specifies that the values in the list of choices for the field may have aliases. Aliases are generally abbreviations for the actual choice, and they are specified by using the syntax `value|alias`. For example, if the choices for a radio button field are `Yes|Y` and `No|N`, the user will select Yes or No but the item value for the field will be stored as Y or N.
	Note: Although this is a new property, synonyms have always been allowed. However, there is a speed cost to maintain synonyms, so this property enables you to make your keyword faster if it does not use synonyms.

Dialog List fields

A Dialog List field is always displayed as a Notes style field. It enables users to select from a list of choices by typing the value directly into the field, or by clicking a helper button that opens a dialog box displaying the choices. The helper button appears only if the Display Entry Helper Button property is selected.

Because the Dialog List field is always Notes style, the Show Field Delimiters property is available instead of the Border Style property. This property was described in Table 8-7.

Three additional choices are available for creating the list of values that users can choose for the field:

✦ **Use Address Dialog for Choices:** Specifies that users choose the values for the field from a dialog box that contains the names of all users in the Domino Directory. The Lookup Addresses on Document Refresh property can be set so that partial names that are entered into the field will be checked whenever the form is refreshed.

✦ **Use Access Control List for Choices:** Specifies that users choose the values for the field from a dialog box that contains all the entries in the databases Access Control List. (See Chapter 10 for more information about Access Control Lists.)

✦ **Use View Dialog for Choices:** Specifies that users choose the values for the field from a dialog box that displays a view. The programmer specifies the database, the view name, and the view column that contains the values for the field.

Time Zone fields

A Time Zone field is a special type of keyword field that displays a predefined list of choices. Each choice represents a different time zone. The only property available on the Control tab of the Field Properties dialog box for Time Zone fields is the Border Style property, which was described in Table 8-7.

Names, Reader, and Author fields

Name fields enable users to enter user names or select them from a list, and store them in a format known as *canonical form* (e.g. CN=Richard Schwartz/O=RHS), which is explained in Chapter 3. Reader and Author fields are also used for document-level security, which is explained in Chapter 21. Simply put, readers decide who can see a document and authors decide who can read and edit a document.

Programmers can specify that users must type names into a Name, Reader, or Author field by selecting None for the Choices property on the Control tab of the Field Properties dialog box. The alternatives to None are the three choices listed previously for Dialog List fields, and if one of these is selected, the properties available for Names, Author, or Reader fields are the same as the properties listed above for Dialog List fields.

Rich text fields

Rich text fields allow users to enter formatted text, attach files, embed OLE objects, and import or paste graphics. The properties available on the Control tab of the Field Properties dialog box for rich text fields are described in Table 8-11.

Table 8-11: Rich text Field Control Properties

Property	Purpose
Show Field Delimiters	Same as for text fields. See Table 8-7.
Pressing Tab Key Moves To Next Field	When selected, this property causes the Tab key to act the same way in rich text fields as it does in other types of fields, causing the focus to move to the next field. When not selected, the Tab key advances the cursor within the rich text field, stopping at the next tab stop on the ruler.
Store Contents as HTML and MIME	When selected, this property causes the data entered by users to be stored in one or more Mime Part items instead of in a rich text Item.

Rich text lite fields

Rich text lite fields are a variation on rich text fields. They differ from ordinary rich text fields in two ways. They allow programmers to specify what types of data can be stored in them, and they always display two helper buttons. The right helper button lets the user select one of the data types that the programmer has allowed for the field, and the left button opens a dialog box with choices dependent on the selected type of data. Properties on the Control tab of the Field Properties dialog box for rich text lite fields are described in table 8-12.

Table 8-12: Rich text lite Field Control Properties

Property	Purpose
Show Field Delimiters	Same as for text fields. See Table 8-7.
Pressing Tab Key Moves To Next Field	Same as for rich text fields. See Table 8-11.
Only Allow	Specifies which of the following types of data are allowed in this field: Picture, Shared Image, Attachments, Views, Date Picker, Shared Applet, Text, OLE Object, Calendar, and Inbox. Two additional picks, Help and Clear, are available. Help adds a context-sensitive Help entry to the helper button drop-down, for displaying brief help about the types of data allowed in the field. Clear adds an entry to the drop-down that clears the contents of the field.

Continued

Table 8-12 *(continued)*

Property	Purpose
Display First	Specifies which of the types selected in the Only Allow property will be selected in the helper button when the form is first opened.
Field Help	Provides brief help text that is available in the drop-down helper button menu. To specify different help text for each of the data types selected by the Only Allow property, list the help text in order, and separate the different help stings by vertical bar (	) characters.

Color fields

Color fields display a special drop-down list that allows users to select from a palette of colors or specify numeric red, green, and blue values. The only property on the Control tab of the Field Properties dialog box for color fields is the Border Style property, which was listed in Table 8-7 for text fields.

Formula fields

Formula fields were briefly described in Chapter 3. They are used for storing compiled Formula language code that selects documents from a database for a subscription list that works in conjunction with the Headlines.NSF database and the subscription-monitoring feature on a Domino server.

Formula fields can either be *computed* or *literalized*. If you specify the Literalize property (which is actually on the Field Info tab of the Field Properties dialog box for the special case of Formula fields), then the formula you enter into the field is the formula that will be compiled and saved. If you specify Computed, then the formula you enter must actually compute a string containing the formula that will be compiled and saved.

The only properties available on the Control tab of the Field Properties dialog box for Formula fields are Border Style and Allow Multiple Lines. Border Style was explained in Table 8-7. Allow Multiple Lines simply allows the formula that you are compiling to be more than one line of code.

Summary

This chapter explained numerous properties associated with pages, forms, and fields. You learned that

✦ Pages are used to display information.

✦ Forms are used to display and modify information in documents.

✦ Rich text with fonts, colors, and various effects can be entered onto both pages and forms, and alignment, spacing, and list properties can be assigned to entire paragraphs.

✦ Combinations of fonts, colors, effects, and paragraph properties can be given a name and saved as a style for reuse.

✦ There are four ways to include HTML on pages and forms.

✦ Fields can be added to forms but not pages.

✦ Fields come in four formula types: Editable, Computed, Computed WhenComposed, and Computed for Display, and different properties are associated with each type.

✦ Fields come in 17 data types, and different properties are associated with each one.

Now that you understand forms and fields, take a look at Chapter 9, which covers views and folders. Views and folders allow your users to view data contained in documents in a way that makes sense to them.

✦   ✦   ✦

Views and Folders

By Rocky Oliver

Views and folders provide a robust way to display groups of documents ordered in a meaningful way. But views provide more functionality than just viewing documents. Views are often used as the
starting point for workflow automation, for programmatically accessing documents, for providing calendar-based grouping of documents,
and much more. Views are one of the most powerful design elements
in a Domino database, and this chapter introduces you to some powerful techniques for getting the most out of your views.

One thing this chapter does not do is teach you the basics of building
a view—that's what the Domino 6 Designer help is for. What this
chapter does do is build upon that help file and the basics it teaches,
and it helps you get the most out of your views and folders in both
your Notes and Web-based applications.

Understanding How Views Work

Views are powerful features in Notes/Domino, but that power is a
two-edged sword. Views are a document display metaphor that is
extremely popular with users. Because of this popularity, users (and
developers) have a tendency to make enough views to slice and dice
the data in every conceivable way. Unfortunately, this is an inefficient
practice. Views are the single largest space hog in a database,
because of the way they work under the hood. Everything in a
database is basically a document or, from the design perspective, a
note. Views are no exception. A view is simply a document that stores
information about the view's design and a big table containing the
information that appears in the view—the view index. This index
table contains, at a minimum, a row for every document that is
selected to display in a view. But this table can grow much larger
when categories are added to a table, because each category that
appears in a table adds at least one more row to the index table. The
index table contains a row that corresponds to every row, or line,
that appears in the view. Each category, each response document—
anything that creates a new row in the view—is an additional row in
the index table. A view that has four categories is going to have many
extra rows besides the rows attributed to documents—especially if

the document is listed in more than one category, because then the document will be listed multiple times in the view. All of this contributes to an enormously large index for a single view. This also affects performance. The indexer has to keep that monstrous view updated, because most designers have their views set to automatically update.

Building only the views you need

Because building views is so easy in Domino, most developers build a bunch of views to sort their documents any way they can. This is a mistake. Roughly 80 percent of all views are not used in the typical database, so this is a waste of space, speed, and user patience.

Instead, build only a few views—two or three, at most, that you know you need (the 20 percent that normally gets used). These views should categorize the documents based on the main logical groupings of the documents. For instance, Contact documents may be categorized by Company, State, and Last Name. Product Orders may be categorized by Company, Product, Sales Rep. Additionally, when you are gathering requirements from your users you should ask them how they want to see the data grouped—ask for the top three ways the data should be grouped, and use the consensus top three to build you views. During your beta testing/pilot testing, or even after rollout, wait for your users to complain about what views are needed and don't tell them that this is what you're doing. After you get feedback, you may find that you can simply tweak your existing views to provide the information the users need. You may find that only one or two people need a specialized view. If this is the case, rather than penalize everyone for the needs of a couple of people, teach these individuals how to build private views to store on their desktops. Or create a Shared, Private on First Use view that creates the view for them locally without penalizing everyone else who uses the database.

Remembering the rule of threes

An old design adage, called the rule of threes, states that you should have about three of anything visually on a screen for the user—no more than three fonts, no more than three font effects, no more than three colors, and so on. Of course, there are exceptions, but this is a good rule that produces clean user interfaces. This rule also applies to categories. A *category* is a grouping of documents under a heading. This heading is usually based on one or more items contained in the documents. In most circumstances, your users don't need more than three categories in a view. If they say they do, dig a little deeper to try to find out what they *really* need, and then build the right solution. Exceptions exist, but you shouldn't need more than three categories in any view.

Think Twice About Adding Those Database Views

To illustrate the point, I once had a client that complained that their contact management database was exceedingly large, and it only had about 12,000 documents in it (that's not too many documents). The database was about 1.2GB in size—much larger than a normal database with 12,000 documents should be. I looked at the database and found that they had added many views to the database, some that were categorized six levels deep! I explained that the problem was the views they had added. They were skeptical, so I made a copy of the database—when you make a new copy or replica of a database, the views are not indexed until they're opened. The database size shrunk to a paltry 250MB. Eighty percent of that database's size was view indexes! After I made my point, I gave them pointers to help them reign in their runaway database views, which are the same pointers provided here.

Tip   Developers frequently build multiple large views that show all the documents in a database, sorted a variety of ways. Notes/Domino is much more efficient if you build many smaller views that show subsets of documents, rather than building large views that show a ton of documents.

Three types of views

A good design practice is to know what types of views you are building, and then build them accordingly. Views used in applications (noncalendar views, that is) can be categorized into one of three types:

✦ **User views:** These are views used to gain access to the documents. These views are also used as reports, presenting summary data about document collections. User views are volatile, as is any user interface — it's likely that you will modify these views to suit the needs of your users.

✦ **Programmatic views:** These are views accessed only programmatically. UI doesn't matter too much in these views, as these views are used as objects for access by your code. Programmatic views are usually added to, but the columns are rarely rearranged because of the danger of breaking the application.

✦ **Picklist views:** These views live in the worlds mentioned in the preceding two bullet points. These views are used for picklists, and they have a user interface component because they must present the documents in a way that assists the user in choosing one or more documents. Picklist views have a programmatic component as well, because the code calling the picklist is looking for a particular column as the return value. These views must be polished, but should not be modified after deployment without good reason.

Many developers make the mistake of using the user views programmatically for such things as @DbColumn, @DbLookup, NotesView.GetDocumentByKey, and so on. But these views are the ones most likely to change as users begin using the system, which inevitably means that the code will break because the column order changes. You should segment your views into one of the three groups mentioned earlier. This will minimize the maintenance effort on your application while it is deployed.

You should adhere to a few suggestions when you develop your programmatic views. First, unless there is a specific reason, don't categorize programmatic views. From the programmatic perspective, no difference exists between a sorted view and a categorized view — categorization is a user interface convention that makes information easier to find and digest by humans. The only exception to this rule is if you are using a @DbColumn to get a list of categories from a view, or a list of unique values, as @DbColumn returns the categories only, not the category value for every document listed over and over. Another suggestion is to take a look at your existing hidden views and see if there is one that already uses the key you need for document access and lookup. If a view already exists, simply add a new column to the existing view and access it. Do not rearrange the order of the existing columns, because you will break your code in other places. But a view sorted on the key you need already exists, you don't need to add the overhead of a new view that uses the same key.

When you name your views, you should have an alias that describes what the view is sorted by, and then add an extension to it that indicates if it's a user view, a programmatic view, or a picklist view. Here are a few examples to illustrate the suggestion:

✦ `contacts.by.company.FE`: This is a user view (`FE` for front-end) that lists contact documents by company name. Even though this is a user view, it's still a good idea to have an alias for it. The alias can be more descriptive for the developer than trying to read a long, cascaded view name.

✦ `contacts.by.contactkey.BE`: This is a programmatic view (`BE` for back-end) that lists contacts sorted by the unique key of the contact document.

✦ `contacts.by.company.PL`: This is a picklist view (`PL` for picklist) that also sorts the contacts by the company name. The difference here is that while the users can dictate how the front-end view is sorted, displayed, what columns are used, and so on, this view is not allowed to be dictated by the users because it is used programmatically.

Organizing your views in this way makes the development and maintenance of your application much easier in the long run.

Tuning your views appropriately

One of the neglected areas of developing views is tuning them appropriately to get the best performance out of them. To tune a view, you need to understand how the view is going to be used, how often it is going to be used, and how volatile the documents in the view are (how often the documents change). The next three sections detail ways to tune your views.

Adjusting your auto-update properties for the index

When you create a view, the index updates automatically, which means that whenever a document is added, deleted, or modified, the indexer automatically updates the view index. If you have a large view, this can take some time. You can modify the index update options by opening the View properties box and clicking the Advanced, or propeller head tab, as shown in Figure 9-1.

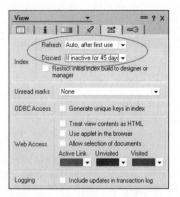

Figure 9-1: You can modify the auto-update frequency and other parameters in the Advanced options tab of the View properties box.

If the documents in your view aren't updated often, or if it isn't critical to show the most up-to-date information, adjust the index update options to update the view index less frequently. Additionally, if you're unsure whether the view is used much, you can discard the view index after 45 days (as shown in Figure 9-1), or even after each use. Experiment with the indexing options to ensure that you're indexing your views only when necessary.

Disabling the response hierarchy feature if it isn't needed

Views, by default, are automatically set up to support response documents. This support comes at a cost of speed, especially when indexing the view. If you're not going to use response documents in your view, disable the feature in the Information tab of the View properties box, as shown in Figure 9-2.

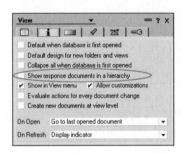

Figure 9-2: The Show Responses in a Hierarchy feature should be disabled in views that don't need to display responses.

If you don't use responses in your database, you can gain even more database performance enhancements by disabling the storage of specialized response document information in the Database properties box, as shown in Figure 9-3.

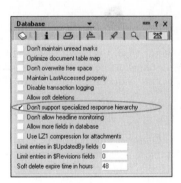

Figure 9-3: Disabling the specialized response hierarchy property in a database greatly enhances performance, but disables some response features.

Only disable this feature if you're not using response documents in your database.

Enabling table bitmap optimization

If you follow the previous suggestion of using smaller, specialized views for databases containing large documents, enabling the Optimize Document Table Map property of the Database properties box, as shown in Figure 9-4, helps make the indexer operate more efficiently.

This feature helps optimize the way the indexer updates the index table for a view, but only on views that use Form= in the view selection formula. It allows the indexer to look only for documents based on that form for the view, which enables it to be much more efficient.

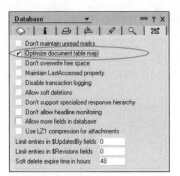

Figure 9-4: The Optimize Document Table Map property, when enabled, makes the indexer much more efficient for smaller views using Form= in the view selection formula.

Using the New Features in Notes/Domino 6

Views are greatly enhanced with the release of Notes/Domino 6. These enhancements, when properly used, provide great functionality to your users. Standard and calendar views include a variety of new features.

Rearranging columns

One of the nicest new view features is the ability to enable users to rearrange the columns of a view and have the rearrangement stick between opening and closing the database. The rearrangement is user-specific as well, so if one user rearranges some columns, it only shows up for that user. If you teach the ability to rearrange columns to your users, it greatly reduces the number of additional views you need to build for your users. By combining this feature with sortable columns, your users can create almost any view arrangement they need. This ability is controlled by the Allow Customizations property on the Information tab of the View properties box, as shown in Figure 9-5.

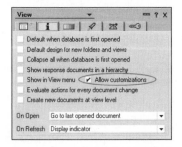

Figure 9-5: The Allow Customizations property enables users to drag columns around in a view so that the view displays the information the user wants.

Setting view colors programmatically

You can now define the text color and background color of rows in your views by specifying the RGB (red green blue) values you want in a hidden column to the left of the columns with the colors you want to change.

In the following example, some documents represent sales records. The view, as shown in Figure 9-6, is coded to show different colors for different sales amounts: red (with a faint red background) for sales under $1000, green (with a faint green background) for sales over $2000, and blue (with a faint blue background) for sales between $1000 and $2000.

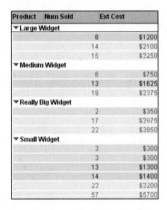

Figure 9-6: Notes/Domino 6 enables you to programmatically code the colors of rows in your views.

You can't see the colors — the graphic is in black and white — but you can check out the example in the ND6 View Examples database (ND6ViewEx.nsf), which you can download from ndbible.com.

To set the view colors, you must add a hidden column as the first column of the view (you can add farther to the right, but it will only colorize the rows from that column to the right). The Column properties box for this column, as shown in Figure 9-7, shows the Use Value as Color property marked.

Figure 9-7: To programmatically color rows in a view, select the Use Value as Color property of the Column properties box.

Choosing this option enables the colors to be changed programmatically. The formula for this column is shown in Listing 9-1.

Listing 9-1: Column Formula for Color Column

```
red := 255:0:0;
redbkgd := 255:221:221;
blue := 0:0:255;
blue2 := 0:0:128;
bluebkgd := 221:221:255;
purple := 128:0:128;
darkgreen := 0:160:0;
greenbkgd := 221:255:221;
brown := 130:66:0;
yellow := 255:255:0;
paleyellow := 255:255:208;
tan := 224:161:117;
DefaultColor := 0:0:0;
pink := 255:193:253;
white := 255:255:255;
black := 1:1:1;
apricot := 255:155:133;
@If(
    ExtCost > 2000; greenbkgd:darkgreen;
    ExtCost < 1000; redbkgd:red;
    bluebkgd:blue2
)
```

For columns marked to use the value as a color, Domino expects to receive three numeric values, each between 0 and 255, concatenated with a colon (which makes them a number list). The first value is red, the second value is green, and the third value is blue (hence RGB). The value for the red variable, for example, is 255:0:0, which means all red. The red position is the maximum value, and the green and blue values are zero (pure red has no blue and green in it). If you want to have a background color along with the text color, specify three more values. Remember that the background color always precedes the text color. To review, your two options are as follows:

✦ For just text colors, use three numeric values (such as 255:0:0 for red text).

✦ For background and text colors, use six numeric values, where the first three numbers specify the background color RGB values, and the second three numbers specify the text RGB values (such as 255:221:221:255:0:0 for light red background and red text).

Alternatively, you could specify one new variable that contains all 6 values. For instance red (255:0:0) and redbkgd (255:221:221) could be concatenated into a new variable, newred (255:221:221:55:0:0).

Tip   Use variables for your RGB values to make your code more readable (for example, light_red := 255:221:221).

In the previous example, if the ExtCost item is more than $2000, the text of the row is colored green with a light green background; if the ExtCost item is less than $1000, the text is colored red with a light red background; otherwise, the text is colored blue with a light blue background.

One bonus of this new feature is that it works in the Notes client and in Web browsers. This can potentially save you many lines of code to accomplish the same results, because the code normally required to change table row color and text color dynamically is quite significant.

Because views are designed to provide a wealth of information visually to a person, colored view rows can enhance the impact and usefulness of this information for your users.

Enabling users to create or edit documents directly in a view

A new feature in Notes/Domino 6 enables your users to create or edit a document directly in a view. This feature is tricky to set up, so you're going to walk through the steps to see how it's done. The example uses the same view and documents used in the previous example. In the 09.01 Products Sold view, you can click the value of the Num Sold column of a document and edit the number sold directly in the view, as shown in Figure 9-8.

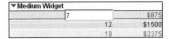

Figure 9-8: You can edit documents directly in a view in Notes/Domino 6, but it takes a bit of effort on the developer's part to enable it.

The first step to enable in-place editing is to select the Editable Column property of the Column properties box, as shown in Figure 9-9.

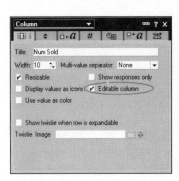

Figure 9-9: The Enable Column property of the Column properties box allows fields to be edited in-place in a view.

Although you can now edit the field in the view, anything you change won't be saved; you have to write a bit more code first.

All in-place editing is controlled through the Inviewedit event of the view. Think of this event as having many *sub* events — events that are similar to the events that exist for a field or a form. The events are as follows:

✦ Query_Request: Similar to the entering event

The QueryRequest event is not available in Release 6.0, but may be available in a future release.

✦ Validate_Request: Similar to the validation formula of a field. This request event only fires against an individual editable column when it is exited.

✦ Save_Request: Similar to the QuerySave event of a form. This request event can fire against accumulated edited columns.

✦ NewEntry_Request:: Used to establish a document with some items (similar to the queryopen and postopen events of a form), and to handle the save of a new document (similar to the querysave event of a form). This request event can fire against accumulated edited columns.

Listing 9-2 presents the code for editing an existing document. For more information on using this feature to create a new document, refer to the Domino 6 Designer help.

Listing 9-2: Inviewedit Event for Products Sold View

```
Sub Inviewedit(Source As Notesuiview,_
Requesttype As Integer, Colprogname As Variant,_
Columnvalue As Variant, Continue As Variant)
%REM
In this view, the programmatic name of each editable column
is the same as the name of the field whose value it holds.
There is only one field, the NumCost field, that is editable in
the view.
%END REM
  REM Define constants for request types
  Const QUERY_REQUEST = 1
  Const VALIDATE_REQUEST = 2
  Const SAVE_REQUEST = 3
  Const NEWENTRY_REQUEST = 4

  REM Define variables
  Dim db As NotesDatabase
  Dim doc As NotesDocument
  Dim caret As String

  REM Get the CaretNoteID - exit if it does not point
  REM at a document
  caret = Source.CaretNoteID
  If caret = "0" Then Exit Sub

  REM Get the current database and document
  Set db = Source.View.Parent
  Set doc = db.GetDocumentByID(caret)

  REM Select the request type
  Select Case Requesttype
  Case QUERY_REQUEST
    REM Reserved - do not use in Release 6.0

  Case VALIDATE_REQUEST
    REM Cause validation error if user tries to exit
    REM column with no value
    If Isnumeric(Columnvalue(0)) Then
```

```
      If Cint(Columnvalue(0)) < 1 Then
        Messagebox "You must enter a quantity greater" &_
        " than 0",, "Negative value"
        Continue = False
      End If
    Else
      Messagebox "Quantity must be numeric",,_
      "Non-numeric value"
      Continue = False
    End If

  Case SAVE_REQUEST
    REM Write the edited column view entries back
    REM to the document
    Call doc.ReplaceItemValue("NumSold",_
    Cint(Columnvalue(0)))
    doc.ExtCost = doc.GetItemValue("NumSold")(0) *_
    doc.GetItemValue("SalePrice")(0)
    REM Save(force, createResponse, markRead)
    Call doc.Save(True, False, True)
  End Select
End Sub
```

In Listing 9-2, four integer constants are established to make the code easier to read.

```
Const QUERY_REQUEST = 1
Const VALIDATE_REQUEST = 2
Const SAVE_REQUEST = 3
Const NEWENTRY_REQUEST = 4
```

These integer constraints are used in the Select Case statement, which is how the request events are handled later in the code. But before covering that, you need to understand CaretNoteID.

The Source parameter of the Inviewedit sub contains the NotesUIView object representing the current view. The NotesUIView.CaretNoteID property contains the NoteID of the document being edited in-line. If the document is new, or if the user is attempting to edit a non-document row (such as a category), this property contains a zero value. In Listing 9-2, this property value is obtained and tested for a zero value; if it's zero, the subroutine is exited.

```
caret = Source.CaretNoteID
If caret = "0" Then Exit Sub
```

After the code determines that a real document is being edited, the actual NotesDocument object is obtained by using the NoteID returned by the CaretNoteID property.

```
Set db = Source.View.Parent
Set doc = db.GetDocumentByID(caret)
```

The Source parameter is the NotesUIView object, the view property is the corresponding NotesView object, and the NotesView.Parent property is the NotesDatabase object representing the current database. The NotesDatabase.GetDocumentByID method is used to get a handle on the document being edited.

The rest of the code is the `Select Case` statement that processes the various request events. The particular request event being processed is carried in the `RequestType` parameter of the `Inviewedit` subroutine. The `Select Case` statement checks the parameter, and the appropriate code is run.

```
Select Case Requesttype
Case QUERY_REQUEST
  REM Reserved - do not use in Release 6.0

Case VALIDATE_REQUEST
  REM Cause validation error if user tries to exit
  REM column with no value
  If Isnumeric(Columnvalue(0)) Then
    If Cint(Columnvalue(0)) < 1 Then
      Messagebox "You must enter a quantity greater" &_
      " than 0",, "Negative value"
      Continue = False
    End If
  Else
    Messagebox "Quantity must be numeric",,_
    "Non-numeric value"
    Continue = False
  End If

Case SAVE_REQUEST
  REM Write the edited column view entries back
  REM to the document
  Call doc.ReplaceItemValue("NumSold",_
  Cint(Columnvalue(0)))
  doc.ExtCost = doc.GetItemValue("NumSold")(0) *_
  doc.GetItemValue("SalePrice")(0)
  REM Save(force, createResponse, markRead)
  Call doc.Save(True, False, True)
End Select
```

The `Query_Request` case is a placeholder and may be useful in future releases.

The `Validate_Request` case ensures that the value entered by the user is numeric and greater than 0. If either case is `False`, the user is informed of the validation error, the `Continue` parameter is set to `False`, and the subroutine is exited.

The `Save_Request` case sets the entered values into the document, processes any other related items that are dependent upon this item (in this case, the `ExtCost` item), and saves the document. When the value is set into the document, it's converted to an integer. The reason for this is that the value, as it exists in the UI, is a text value. It must be typecast to the correct type before it's set into the document. In this case, the `Cint` function converts the text value to an integer.

Using hide-when formulas for view actions

View actions now support hide-when formulas, so action buttons can show up based on item values in the selected document. This enables you to give context-sensitive actions based on the document the user selects in the view.

Enabling this feature requires a few steps. If you take a look at the GetViewInfo/SetViewInfo Example view, you see a view action called Example Action. This action has a hide-when formula that uses a new @function called `@GetViewInfo`. The `@GetViewInfo` function returns the value of the specified column for the selected document in a view. Using this @function, you can cause action buttons to hide when the desired condition is met. The following code is in the hide-when formula for the action in the example view:

```
@GetViewInfo([ColumnValue]; 2) = "No")
```

If this formula evaluates to `True`, the action button is hidden. You can see this happen by selecting various documents in the view.

To enable this function, you must also select the Evaluate Actions for Every Document Change property on the Information tab in the View properties box (see Figure 9-10).

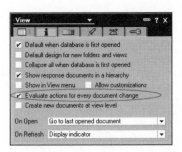

Figure 9-10: The Evaluate Actions for Every Document Change property allows your hide-when formulas to be evaluated whenever a new document is selected.

Using @SetViewInfo to filter views

This is one of the most exciting new functions in Notes/Domino 6. The `@SetViewInfo` function enables you to filter a view dynamically by passing in the category you want to filter it by. Activating this function is useful, especially for views you want to filter by the user's name. The GetViewInfo/SetViewInfo Example view has an action button named SetViewInfo Example, which includes the following code:

```
filterlist := "" : @DbColumn("" : "NoCache"; "";
"SetViewInfo Example View"; 1);

filter := @Prompt([OkCancelList]; "Filter";
"Pick a category for filtering..."; @Subset(filterlist; 1);
filterlist);

@SetViewInfo( [SetViewFilter] ; filter ; "Category" ; 1)
```

The first line gathers the categories from the view using an `@DbColumn` function. The second line prompts the user to choose a value by which to filter the view. The third line sets the filter on the view. The first parameter passes in the category name. The second parameter is the programmatic name of the column to be used for filtering. The third parameter indicates whether the column being used for filtering is a categorized view (1) or not (0). This code causes the view to filter to the chosen category. The user can also choose a blank line to reset the view back to showing all categories.

Tip   In the past if you wanted to have a view that contained a subset of documents based on a user's name, you had to use a "Shared, Private on First Use" view. In Notes/Domino 6 you can use the @SetViewInfo function in the PostOpen event of the view to set the filter, thereby filtering the view to the desired user's name automatically.

Summary

Views are one of the most powerful features in Notes/Domino. Notes/Domino 6 includes many new features that make views even more powerful. This chapter introduced you to the following concepts:

✦ Learning how views work

✦ Optimizing your views for performance

✦ Making views more powerful than ever through the use of new features in Notes/Domino 6

This chapter introduced you to some of these new features for views. Chapter 17 adds on to the concepts learned in this chapter, and also introduces you to calendar view features and folder features. Chapter 10 introduces you to the concepts surrounding database security.

✦   ✦   ✦

Database Security

By Rocky Oliver

In This Chapter

Learning about the Access Control List

Exploring roles

Learning about Authors Names and Readers Names

One of the cornerstones of Lotus Notes and Domino is security. Unlike other applications where security is an obvious after-thought, Notes/Domino is built from the ground up with a rock-solid security infrastructure in place. This chapter helps you understand this security structure and what it means to your applications. You will be introduced to server security, database security, and document security.

Security Starts at the Server

Security for a Notes/Domino environment begins at the server level. The Domino Directory defines who can and can't access the server, and what those who are allowed in are able to do, access, and so on. Most security is defined in the Server document — things such as who can run restricted and unrestricted agents, who can access the Domino Directory, who can use the server as a pass-thru server, and much more. Remember, there is one and only one Server document per server in a Domino Directory database.

After you determine who can access the server and what the individual is allowed to do, the next security level is at the database.

Next Stop: Database ACL

The database Access Control List (ACL) defines who has basic access to the database, and, *at most*, what those who have access are allowed to do.

Note   The Domino database ACL is often pronounced *ackle*, although some pronounce it by the letters — A C L; however, A C L usually refers to the ligament in you leg known as the Anterior Cruciate Ligament (the ligament many football players tear), not the security on your database. You should be familiar with both terms in case you hear them when speaking with other Domino professionals.

The ACL also controls what level of access a user, group, or server has to the database, and what user-defined roles a user may have. *Access level* refers to what an entity can do in a database, such as read or create a document. *User-defined roles* refer to roles in an ACL that usually map to some functional role in an organization. The following sections break down each part of a database ACL to better understand what is available.

User types

The ACL can contain user names, server names, or group names (groups of servers, groups of users, or a mixed group). Two other entries are usually present in an ACL—*default*, which is where you set the access level for users or servers who are not otherwise listed in the ACL, and *anonymous*, which is used for Web applications and is applied to unauthenticated users.

Note   User type was added to database ACLs in Release 4. Before then, you could *spoof* another entity, such as a server, by creating a new user ID with the server's name, and that gave you access to everything to which the server had access. The important thing about user types is that users are allowed to open databases in the Notes client or through a browser, whereas servers are not allowed to use any client to open a database. Explicitly assigning a user type helps the ACL keep track of who, and what, each entity is. Make sure that you explicitly list a user type for each entity in your ACL.

Access levels

After you decide who should have access to your database, you can begin to add entities to the list. When you add an entity to an ACL, you should indicate the user type (person, server, person group, server group) and the overall access level to the database. The access levels available are as follows:

✦ **No Access:** This access level completely blocks the entity from accessing the database.

✦ **Depositor:** The entity can add content to the database (compose a document), but can't open the database and look at the content.

✦ **Reader:** The entity can read content, but can't contribute content.

✦ **Author:** The entity can read and create content, and can modify any document that the entity has author access to, which is usually any content created by that entity.

✦ **Editor:** The entity can edit any document that it has access to.

✦ **Designer:** The entity can change the design of the database, and can edit any document it has access to, but can't change the ACL.

✦ **Manager:** The entity can change the design, edit any document it has access to, and can change the ACL of the database.

The term *entity* is used throughout. An *entity* can be a user, a server, or a group of users and/or servers.

Document-level access is applied through the use of Author Names and Reader Names items. Reader Names items determine who can read, or access, a document. Reader Names items override ACL settings, which determines database access level—even though a user may have the *ability* to delete a document as granted through the ACL, he has to be able to *access* it first—and the ability to view and access a document can be governed by using a Reader Names item.

Tip   The easiest rule of thumb for understanding what you can and can't delete is that you have to be able to see it before you can do anything to it. Reader Names items are extremely important, because even if a user with manager access opens the database, he can only do things to the documents he sees.

You learn more about Author Names and Reader Names items later in this chapter.

After you determine user type and access level, you can assign one of many attributes to the entity.

Attributes

You can assign numerous attributes to an entity in the ACL. Many of these attributes are assigned by default based on the access level; others are optional. The attributes available for assignment are as follows:

✦ **Create Documents:** This attribute enables the entity to create new documents.

✦ **Delete Documents:** This attribute enables the entity to delete documents based on their access level to the document. Authors, for example, can only delete documents they create; whereas editors, designers, and managers can delete any document they see — if this attribute is enabled for them.

✦ **Create Private Agents:** This attribute enables the entity to create private agents that are allowed to perform any operations against the database that are allowed by the entity's access level to the database. This attribute is cross-checked against the server document's security settings before the user is allowed to use an agent on the server.

✦ **Create Personal Folders/Views:** This setting enables users to create *server-based* personal folders and views.

✦ **Create Shared Folders/Views:** This setting enables an entity to create shared views/folders.

Tip   Unless you *really* need to grant this ability to your users, you should not enable the Create Shared Folders/Views attribute. Views are tremendous resource hogs in a database, taking up precious server disk space and causing various maintenance tasks of the server to work much harder. Allowing users to create views can have a serious impact on database and server performance.

✦ **Create LotusScript/Java Agents:** This attribute enables the entity to create agents in your database. The ability to run agents is controlled by the server document's security settings.

Tip   It's strongly recommended that you not enable the Create LotusScript/Java Agents attribute. A user who is allowed to create an agent can seriously mess up any document he has author access to, because an agent is allowed to add, delete, or change any document that the user has access to. Without this ability, a user can only affect a document's structure and content to the extent allowed by the form(s) the user uses to access the document.

✦ **Read Public Documents:** This attribute is for users who normally don't have access to the database. It enables them to be able to access documents that have the $PublicAccess item set to 1.

✦ **Write Public Documents:** This attribute enables users to create documents with forms that have the Available to Public Access Users property enabled.

✦ **Replicate or Copy Documents:** This attribute prevents the user from creating a local replica or copy of the database, and it prevents the user from copying or printing from the database. This attribute affects only Notes clients.

Note   The Replicate or Copy Documents property is *not* a security measure. Users can still use print-screen or other screen capture applications to get copies of documents from a database.

Table 10-1, which was gathered from the Domino 6 Designer help, shows what attributes are defaults and what attributes are optional based on access level. The table makes it easier to understand how access level affects available attributes.

Table 10-1: Privilege Attributes Based on Access Level

Access Level	Default Privileges	Optional Privileges
Manager	Create Documents Create Private Agents Create Personal Folders/Views Create Shared Folders/Views Create LotusScript/Java Agents Read Public Documents Write Public Documents	Delete Documents Replicate or Copy Documents
Designer	Create Documents Create Private Agents Create Personal Folders/Views Create Shared Folders/Views Read Public Documents Write Public Documents	Delete Documents Create LotusScript/Java Agents Replicate or Copy Documents
Editor	Create Documents Read Public Documents Write Public Documents	Delete Documents Create Private Agents Create Personal Folders/Views Create Shared Folders/Views Create LotusScript/Java Agents Replicate or Copy Documents
Author	Read Public Documents	Create Documents Delete Documents Create Private Agents Create Personal Folders/Views Create LotusScript/Java Agents Write Public Documents Replicate or Copy Documents
Reader	Read Public Documents	Create Private Agents Create Personal Folders/Views Create LotusScript/Java Agents Write Public Documents Replicate or Copy Documents
Depositor	Create Documents	Read Public Documents Write Public Documents
No Access	None	Read Public Documents Write Public Documents

Roles

Roles are similar to groups in the Domino Directory, except that they are database-specific. A role enables you to group entities listed in the ACL and provide them access to documents, forms, views, and so on.

Roles are defined in the Roles tab of the Access Control List dialog box for a database, as shown in Figure 10-1.

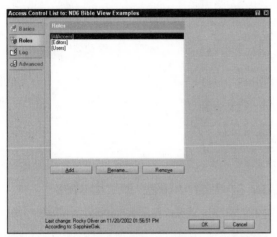

Figure 10-1: The Roles feature of a database's Access Control List is useful because it enables you to specify database-specific groupings of entities listed in the ACL.

Tip Always add at least one role to every database you develop. You should add this role to all AuthorName and ReaderName fields so that you always have a back door to access all the documents in your database. You should restrict this role to the person responsible for the maintenance of the database, and the servers where the database resides. The [AllAccess] role serves this purpose in Figure 10-1.

You assign roles to an ACL entity by highlighting the entity and clicking the role. In Figure 10-2, my name is highlighted, and the [AllAccess] role is enabled for my name.

Note Roles were unavailable locally before Notes/Domino 6, unless an ACL feature called Enforce Consistent Access was enabled for the database. In Notes/Domino 6, roles (and the database ACL) are applied locally, whether or not Enforce Consistent Access is enabled.

The database ACL has more features available, including Enforce Consistent ACL, Administrative Servers, and more. Consult the Domino 6 Designer help database for more information.

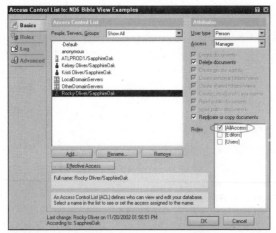

Figure 10-2: Roles are easy to enable for entities listed in the Access Control List. In this figure, the [AllAccess] role is enabled for Rocky Oliver/SapphireOak.

Nuances of access level and privilege attributes

A user may have multiple entries in the ACL of a database. Maybe the user is listed explicitly and is also the member of a group listed in the ACL. Or maybe a wildcard entry includes the user, such as */SapphireOak. If this is the case, what access level and privileges does the user have?

If listed explicitly in the ACL, this entry takes precedence over all other entries. If you are listed explicitly as an author, but are a member of a group with manager access, you still have only author access to the database.

If you are listed in more than one group, you have a *union* of all the privileges and the highest access level. If one group you're in has author access and does not have delete document privileges, but another group you're in has manager access and does have delete document privileges, you have manager access *with* delete document privileges. Additionally, you are a member of all roles from *both* groups.

Document Level Access

The main way to access a document is through the use of Author Names items and Reader Names items. These are items of a special data type — SUMMARY READ ACCESS for Reader Names, and SUMMARY READ/WRITE ACCESS for Author Names. Here's how these items affect access to a document:

✦ If a document has neither type of item, the only entities who can edit the document after it's created are people and servers with editor or above access to the database.

Note   If a user who has author access to the database creates a document, that document *must* have an Author Names item in it listing the author (or a group or role the author is in) for the author to be able to edit the document in the future.

✦ If a document has one or more Reader Names items only, entities who are listed in the Reader Names item(s) (either explicitly or through a group or role) have access to read the document, at a minimum. Their ability to edit the document is based on their access level in the ACL of the database—if they have editor access or above, they can edit the document as well.

✦ If a document has one or more Author Names items only, any entity listed in those items has the ability to read and edit the document, if, and only if, they have at least author access in the ACL. A user who has reader access to a database, but is listed in an Author Names item, still can't edit the item.

✦ If a document has both Author Names and Reader Names items, a combination of the rules for both items applies.

You can use more than one Author Names or Reader Names item on a document; the members of each item are concatenated together to provide the reader and/or author access list for the document. It's not a good practice, however, to use multiple Reader Names and/or Author Names items on a form. Create one of each type on your form, such as AllowedReaders and AllowedAuthors, and add code to them that pulls in the various entity names and roles that you want to have access to documents created with the form. This makes your code much easier to maintain.

You should always use the canonical name for any server or person you list in an Authors/Reader Names item. This is how Notes/Domino stores names internally, and you'll have fewer hassles if you get in this habit now.

Tip   At a minimum, every form you create should contain a computed, multivalue Author Names field that contains the following code: @UserName : "[AllAccess]". [AllAccess] is the name of you role that you use for global access. This field ensures that authors (and database administrators) have the ability to edit the documents created with these forms.

Field-Level Encryption

Field-level encryption is the lowest level of security in a database. You can use a key to encrypt certain items in a document so that only others with a matching key can read those fields. If the user doesn't have the appropriate, matching key, she is unable to see the information. Field-level encryption is extremely secure and is used in a variety of places where data security is important.

The Domino 6 Designer help has a great deal of information on field level encryption.

(Non)Security Through Obscurity

Hiding a design element, such as a view or form, or hiding documents by not providing views containing them, is *not* secure. This is known as "security through obscurity," and it relies on the belief that your users aren't smart enough or inclined enough to find the hidden information. A myriad of ways exists to see hidden views and documents. For example, holding down the Ctrl+Shift keys and choosing View ➪ Go To in a database gives you access to all the hidden views in the database. All that one of your users has to do is read a Notes forum somewhere, or a Notes magazine, such as *Lotus Advisor*, and they may also know this trick.

In some applications, where the data isn't sensitive or mission critical, security through obscurity may be acceptable. But if you're storing sensitive data, such as salary information, medical information, and so on, you should consider severely restricting access to the database and/or using field-level encryption.

Plan Your Security from the Beginning

One of the biggest mistakes developers make is to build an application without giving consideration to security until the application is well under way, or worse yet, completed. Trying to shoehorn security into an existing application is an exercise in futility. Instead, plan your application with security in mind from the beginning. Ask your customers the following questions:

✦ Who is going use the application?

✦ What roles (user roles, not Notes roles, although there is usually a correlation) will these users assume in the application?

✦ What information and functionality do these roles need access to?

✦ What information and functionality do these roles *not* need access to?

✦ Is there any information that is for public consumption?

✦ Is there any information that is highly sensitive?

Obviously, these are just a few of the questions you can ask to understand your customer's needs. But beginning with these questions should lead you toward planning an effective security strategy for your application.

Summary

Notes/Domino 6 offers one of the most secure data models on the market. This chapter explained:

✦ Setting up security on your databases, from the database level down to the document level

✦ Using the Access Control List

✦ Using roles

✦ Using ReadersNames and Author Names fields to safely secure your information

✦ Discovering the security needs of your customer

Chapter 11 explains the usefulness of framesets and outlines for presenting and organizing data for your users.

✦   ✦   ✦

Framesets and Outlines

By Brian Benz

O utlines and framesets augment the Menu and Action bar navigational features built into the Notes client, and add more options
for control and display of an application UI, especially on the Web.
This chapter focuses on using framesets and outlines in Notes client
and Web applications, as well as tips, tricks, drawbacks, and alternatives for each feature.

Tip   Navigators are legacy features that create image maps with
embedded URLs associated with a fixed range on the image map.
Navigators have traditionally been used to create navigational
menus in Notes applications. Although navigators still have their
place in Notes client applications, they are considered inferior to
outlines in Web applications in terms of functionality and compatibility. This can be compared to the way image maps on the Web
have been replaced by URLs. Despite lingering support in Domino
6 for navigators, you should convert any navigators in Notes and
Web applications to outlines.

Outlines were first introduced in R5, and are a great tool for creating
flexible, reusable, and mostly code-free navigational structures for
Notes client and Web applications. Outlines are available under the
Shared Code section of the database design bookmarks in Domino
Designer. Outlines are created as stand-alone application elements,
which are then embedded on a form, subform, or page to be integrated into an application.

Framesets and frames enable several modal windows to function as a
single application. Framesets are available under their own section of
the database design bookmarks in Domino Designer. Framesets
define properties that describe attributes for each frame. Framesets
contain frames only, and frames contain URLs, links, pages, forms,
views, folders, navigators, and other framesets. Framesets containing
up to four frames can be nested within other frames and framesets.

Working with Outlines

Domino Designer provides an easy way to create a default outline under the Shared Code section of the database design bookmarks in Domino Designer. Open the Outlines view of any database and click the New Outline button that appears at the top of the Programmer's pane, and then click the Generate Default Outline button from the menu that appears. An outline for the current database is created, including all views and folders with nested design elements, such as cascading views listed as nested outline entries. You can then click the Use Outline button to simultaneously create a new page and embed the new outline on the page. You can then embed the new page into a frameset. The result is a basic design structure for navigation around a Notes database that will function in a Notes client or on the Web. Of course, the simplest solution is seldom the best, and chances are that you'll have to do some work to customize the outline and the outline entries before the default outline is useful.

Outline elements

Table 11-1 shows the five types of elements that you can use in an outline.

Table 11-1: Outline Element Types and Their Descriptions

Outline Entry	Description
(None)	Nothing linked — used for the top level of a navigational hierarchy.
Action	Used to call and run any @function formula.
Link	Domino doclink, view link, database link, or HTML page anchor.
Named Element	The most popular option for Web navigational menus. Links to named elements in the current database or any other database on the same machine. Choices include pages, forms, framesets, views, folders, and navigators.
URL	HTTP URL — can contain a URL.

Notes outlines offer numerous entry attributes to choose from, and even more options after an outline is embedded in another design element. The Domino Designer 6 help has more than adequate coverage of all the outline entry properties and attributes. Refer to the "Outlines" section of the Designer Help Index for more information on the details of entries and their configuration options.

The Notes Welcome page, and client bookmark navigational elements are excellent practical examples of the implementation of outlines. The Welcome page and a large number of example outlines are the bookmark.nsf database. You can easily open bookmark.nsf in Designer by right-clicking the Bookmarks (6) database icon in a Notes 6 workspace and selecting Open in Designer from the pop-up menu. This option is available if Domino Designer is installed on your workstation and places the database in Domino Designer, with a display of the Forms section of the Designer bookmarks. To view the outlines, move to the Shared Code section and select the Outlines Subsection. Figure 11-1 shows the outlines listed in Domino Designer for bookmark.nsf.

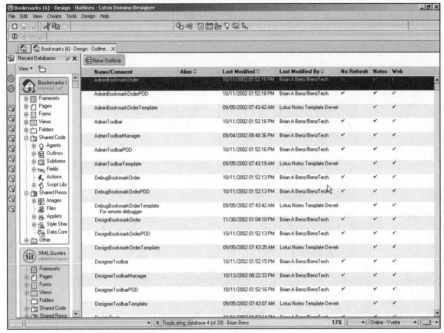

Figure 11-1: The outlines listing in Domino Designer for bookmark.nsf

You can break up the outlines in `bookmark.nsf` into five specific types: Admin, Debugger, Design, Help, and User. Each group corresponds to a Notes client UI element for its corresponding parts. The Domino administrator uses the Admin outlines; Domino Designer uses the Design outlines, and the Help outlines are used by Help databases to provide the forward and back navigation between Help documents. The User grouping of outlines manages the Notes client UI bookmarks and client navigation. The debug bookmarks are part of the remote LotusScript debugger UI.

The Welcome page settings determine which outline is displayed when users open their Notes client workstation. The UserBookmarkOrder outline is a great starting point for understanding outlines and can be copied to other databases and applications as a default outline. Figure 11-2 shows the UserBookmarkOrder outline in Domino Designer.

Testing links in outlines

The first two UserBookmarkOrder outline entries link to a frameset for the user's address book and calendar. Right-clicking one of these outline entries in Designer and choosing Go to Element from the pop-up menu enables you to follow the link to its destination, which is a great way to test the outline and to get to know what each type of entry does.

Figure 11-3 shows the properties for the first outline entry (Address Book) in the UserBookmarkOrder outline.

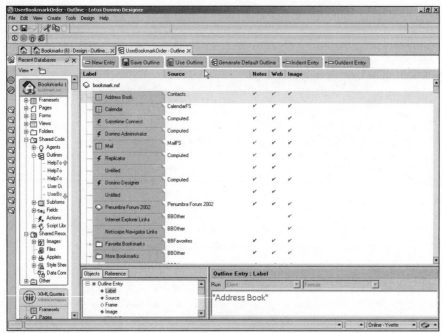

Figure 11-2: The UserBookmarkOrder outline in Domino Designer

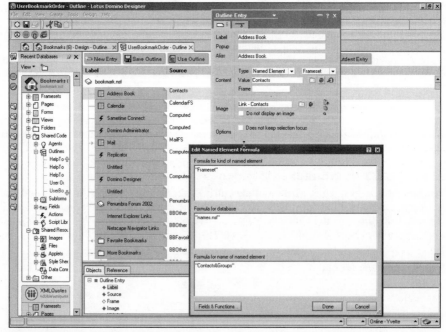

Figure 11-3: The first entry (Address Book) in the UserBookmarkOrder outline in Domino Designer, and the outline entry properties

Linking to named elements

As shown in Figure 11-3, the Address Book link connects to the Contacts&Groups frameset in the `Names.nsf` database. The names.nsf frameset contains another navigational outline that is similar to the UserBookmarkOrder outline in `bookmark.nsf`.

Assigning images to Outline Entries

The graphic for the Address Book outline entry is referenced via the image resource called Link-Contacts. Link-Contacts is located in the `bookmark.nsf` database and is a horizontal image set with three separate sizes. Users can change the bookmark image size by choosing File ⇨ User Preferences from the main Notes menu, and editing the Bookmark Icon Size setting on the Basics page to Small, Medium, or Large.

Using actions

The next two outline entries are computed, and they execute the SameTime client and the Administrator client, if that client is installed on the workstation. The following @Formula, for example, calls the `SameTime` client:

```
@If( @IsAppInstalled(@RegQueryValue("HKEY_LOCAL_MACHINE";
"Software\\Lotus\\Sametime Client"; "BasePath") + "\\Connect"); @Return(
@Command([Execute]; @RegQueryValue("HKEY_LOCAL_MACHINE";
"Software\\Lotus\\Sametime Client"; "BasePath") + "\\Connect")); "");
ip := @DbLookup("":"";
@LocationGetInfo([SametimeServer]):"names.nsf";"$ServersLookup";@LocationGe
tInfo([SametimeServer]);"NetAddr_0");
@URLOpen("http://" + @If(!@IsError( ip) & @Trim(@Text(IP)) != ""; IP +
"/STCenter.nsf"; "www.sametime.com"))
```

The code checks whether the `SameTime` client is installed on the workstation by checking the Windows Registry. If the `SameTime` client has been installed on the workstation, the code gets a URL from the current location document for the `SameTime` server and tries to connect to `STCenter.nsf` at that location; otherwise, it tries to connect to `www.sametime.com`.

The Admin client execution is limited to the local machine and part of the Notes client core code, so it is easier to invoke:

```
@launchApp("ADMIN")
```

Using hide-whens

In addition to @Formulas for execution, display of the `SameTime` connect, and Domino administrator outline entries are governed by hide-when options. Hide-when formulas optionally hide Domino design elements if the hide-when formula returns a positive result.

For the SameTime outline entry, if the Notes client application platform is Macintosh, the SameTime application will not show as installed according to the Windows Registry, because there is no Windows Registry, so the outline entry is hidden. Similarly, if the SameTime server field is blank in the location document, there is no SameTime server specified, so the outline entry is hidden. Here's the SameTime connect outline entry hide-when code:

```
@Begins(@Platform; "Macintosh") |
(!@IsAppInstalled(@RegQueryValue("HKEY_LOCAL_MACHINE";
"Software\\Lotus\\Sametime Client"; "BasePath") + "\\Connect") &
@LocationGetInfo([SametimeServer]) = "")
```

As with the Admin client outline entry invocation code, the hide-when coding is simple:

```
!@IsAppInstalled("ADMIN")
```

Linking to other outlines

The Internet Explorer Links entry links to another outline. The link points to a page with the outline embedded on it instead of the outline directly. Although the page is not used and the outline appears in the bookmark bar, a direct reference to an outline is not permitted. This is good and bad news, because although it's an extra step, linking to an embedded design element doesn't represent any overhead for the application. Additional outline and outline entry properties enable developers to customize the default outline and reuse it in several places, in different ways, with different display properties.

Note   Outlines have to be embedded on another design element before Notes and Domino can reference them.

Accessing outlines with @Formulas, LotusScript, and Java

You can use @Formulas to dynamically generate values for outline entry links, images, and hide-whens. In addition, outlines and outline entries can be created, navigated, deleted, and otherwise manipulated from LotusScript and Java, using the `NotesOutline` and `NotesOutlineEntry` classes in LotusScript, and the `Outline` and `OutlineEntry` classes in Java. The Notes and Domino 6 Designer help has extensive documentation on the properties and methods available, as well as examples.

Outline entry display control

Outline entry display can be unpredictable, especially when displayed on the Web without the outline applet. Another limitation is that you can't implement hide-whens based on associated form values, even if the outline is embedded on that form. Outlines also have a bad habit of automatically indenting the first line of a set of outline entries, and then wrapping any text on the next line without indenting, which makes for a confusing display of navigational elements on a Notes or Web application. To compensate for this, you must use small fonts or keep the outline entry display descriptions short.

Performance considerations for outlines

Unless absolutely necessary, don't embed outlines in forms or documents, as this will cause poor performance when compared to the same outline embedded in a page. Also, although the outline applet provides a rich feature set for Web navigation of Domino sites, the price you pay is dealing with the applet's notoriously poor performance, and the possibility that the browser, or a firewall between the server and the browser, has Java disabled for security reasons, corporate policy, and so on.

Working with Framesets

When combined with outlines, framesets and frames provide a powerful navigational structure for Notes client and Web applications. You can embed outlines in framesets and control and call other frames from a frameset.

The frameset examples in this chapter use many of the same `bookmark.nsf` database Welcome page elements that were used for the outline examples. `Bookmark.nsf` is a great place to start when developing framesets and embedding outlines, because of the large base of framesets and outlines examples that are already set up for the Welcome page.

You can easily open `bookmark.nsf` in Designer by right-clicking the Bookmarks (6) database icon in a Notes 6 workspace and selecting Open in Designer from the pop-up menu. This option is available if Domino Designer is installed on your workstation and places the database in Domino Designer, with a display of the Forms section of the Designer bookmarks. Move to the Framesets section, where all the framesets for the Notes client Welcome page are stored. Figure 11-4 shows the framesets listed in Domino Designer for `bookmark.nsf`.

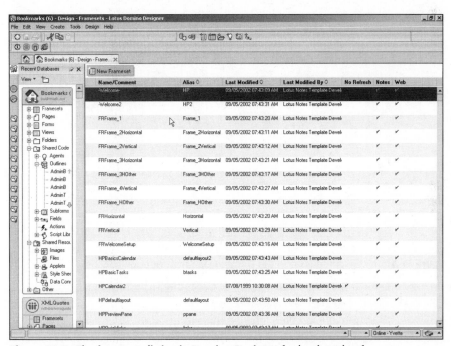

Figure 11-4: The framesets listing in Domino Designer for bookmark.nsf

Framesets can include an unlimited number of nested framesets, but each frameset is limited to four frames. Framesets contain frames only, and frames can contain URLs, links, pages, forms, views, folders, navigators, and other framesets.

The outlines in `bookmark.nsf` are split into client type groups for display purposes, but the framesets are mainly used for the Notes client and Web display. At the top of the frameset listing in Figure 11-4 are two Welcome screen formats, followed by various Notes client layouts, with a few Web client frameset layouts at the end.

The Welcome frameset is the first entry in the frameset listing in `bookmark.nsf`. Figure 11-5 shows the standard layout of the frameset.

Note   Your frameset may look different depending on any client customization that has been done since the Notes 6 client was installed.

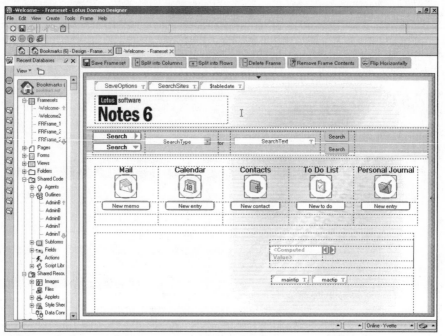

Figure 11-5: The Welcome frameset in Domino Designer for bookmark.nsf

Calculating target framesets

The layout in Figure 11-5 is in a single frame called WelcomeContent in a single frameset, which appears to defeat the purpose of using framesets. But the frameset links to a computed value based on a profile document in `bookmark.nsf`. This formula facilitates customization of the Welcome page. If the page is customized, the layout configuration is stored in a special kind of Notes document called a *profile document*. The @getProfileField function automatically retrieves the value of a field on the named profile document. In this case, a profile document called CurrentLayout is retrieved, and the value of CurrentLayoutKey is assigned to the tKey variable. Next the SetupScreen field value is retrieved from the HPSettings document and assigned to the tSetup variable. If the tSetup variable is not assigned yet, the Welcome screen has not been customized, and the WelcomeSetup frameset is displayed.

The WelcomeSetup frameset links to a form that contains the start of the Welcome screen setup procedure. Otherwise, the Welcome2 frameset (with the alias name of HP2) is selected, which displays the current custom frameset to the users.

```
tKey := @GetProfileField( "CurrentLayout"; "CurrentLayoutKey");
tSetup := @GetProfileField("HPSettings"; "SetupScreen");

@If(tSetup = "" | @IsError(tSetup) | tSetup != "1"; "WelcomeSetup"; "HP2")
```

The Welcome2 frameset contains another @Formula that links to another computed frameset value. The @Formula gets values from four profile documents that describe a custom layout chosen by the user. The first @If statement checks for the tShowOther variable. If the tShowOther variable exists, the @If statement gets the value of the custom frameset to show. The custom frameset display is based on the rest of the calculations in the @If statement, which are recorded as a result of the user customizing the Welcome page. Otherwise, the HPdefaultlayout frameset is chosen, which has an alias name of defaultlayout. The computed value in the defaultlayout frameset links to a named element, which is the WPDefaultBasics form, a single form with the default Welcome screen configuration:

```
tKey := @GetProfileField( "CurrentLayout"; "CurrentLayoutKey");
tShowOther := @GetDocField( tKey; "ShowOtherFrameset");
tLinks := @GetDocField( tKey; "QLinks");
tPreview := @GetDocField( tKey; "PreviewPane");

@If (@IsError( tShowOther); "defaultlayout"; tShowOther = "1";
@GetDocField( tKey; "OtherFrameset");
tPreview = "1" & tLinks = "1"; "QLinks1Prev";
tPreview = "1" & tLinks != "1"; "Qlinks0Prev";
tLinks = "1"; "QLinks1"; "QLinks0")
```

If you drill down further, you see that the last option in the @Formula, Qlinks0, is a three-frame frameset, with a Notes Mail inbox on the left, icons and a search box on the right, and a calendar on the bottom (see Figure 11-6).

But when you open the Qlinks0 frameset, you're greeted with another single frame, calculated by the following formula:

```
tKey := @GetProfileField( "CurrentLayout"; "CurrentLayoutKey");
tShowOther := @GetDocField( tKey; "ShowOtherFrameset");
tLayout := @GetDocField(tKey; "Layout");
tType := @GetDocField( tKey; "Type1");

@If( @IsError( tShowOther); "defaultlayout"; tShowOther = "1";
@GetDocField( tKey; "OtherFrameset");
tLayout = "1a"; "Frame_1";
tLayout = "4b"; "Frame_4Vertical";
tLayout = "d" : "c" : "2b":"3c":"4a":"5c"; "Horizontal";
"Vertical")
```

The code performs a profile document retrieval using the @GetProfileField function as it did in the last two @Formulas, but you also have several frameset references in the @If statement. If the Basics Plus Welcome page is selected from the Welcome page options, the Horizontal frameset is chosen.

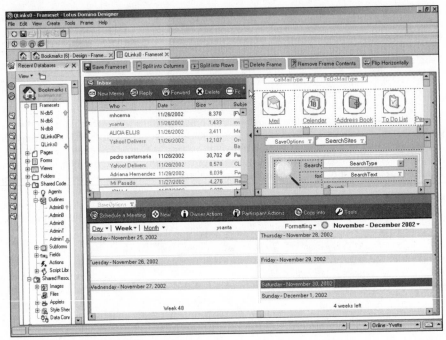

Figure 11-6: The Qlinks0 frameset

The Horizontal frameset is made up of two frames: one for the top half of the screen, and one for the bottom half. The top half of the screen contains another computed frameset reference. The nested frameset references continue one or two more layers for the Frame_2 vertical frameset, which represents the top half of the Horizontal frameset. The bottom half also references another frameset. In the end, all the framesets link to the Split1, Split2, Split3, or Split4 framesets, which in turn refer to named elements for the Notes inbox, search form, Notes calendar, and icon page. Which frame displays which named element is based on the configuration that the user has chosen, which determines the nesting of the framesets.

```
tUNID := @GetProfileField( "CurrentLayout"; "CurrentLayoutKey");
tLayout := @GetDocField( tUNID; "Layout");
@If(@IsError(tLayout); "defaultlayout"; @IsError( tType); "defaultlayout";
tLayout = "d" : "c" : "3c" : "4a"; "Frame_2Vertical";
"split1")
```

So the Welcome page treats the references to framesets independently, allowing each part of the Welcome page to reference it's own framesets, frames, and named elements using a Russian-doll structure of nested framesets and frames.

Working with target frames

Now that you know how and why to nest framesets, frames, and named elements in a frameset structure, you can review the next most critical part of framesets: specifying a target frame for a user action. Target frames are set in the Properties box of Domino pages, forms, outline entries, outlines, hotspot design elements, and frames and framesets.

Specifying target frames in design elements

Because nested frames and design elements could potentially, and usually do, contain more than one nested target frame specification in their Properties box, you must understand the way that Domino chooses the target frame when Design elements are nested.

You can set multiple target frames that appear to conflict with each other. You can set a target frame, for example, on an outline entry, an embedded outline that contains that outline entry, the page that contains that embedded outline, or on a frame that contains the page. The target frame that takes precedence is the most deeply nested design element. In the previous examples of the Qlinks0 frameset, if the named element in the Split1, Split2, Split3, or Split4 framesets contains a target frame specification, actions in that element are carried out in the target frame specified. If no target frame is contained in one of those named elements, a target specified in the Split1, Split2, Split3, or Split4 frameset is chosen. If these framesets don't contain target frame references, the target frames in the Frame_2 vertical frameset are chosen, then the Horizontal frameset, then the Qlinks0 frameset. Any further target frames in parent framesets are chosen in order if their children don't specify a target frame.

Using @SetTargetFrame

There may be times when you want to programmatically set the target frame, instead of relying on frameset, frame, or named element references in design objects. You can use the `@SetTargetFrame` function in conjunction with the `OpenFrameset`, `RefreshFrame`, `Compose`, `OpenView`, `EditDocument`, and `OpenPage` @Commands to override the design element target frame settings. See the Notes 6 help for more details on usage, especially with regard to several exceptions to the target frame specification when using the `@OpenView` function.

Using the SetTargetFrame method in LotusScript

If the application is using LotusScript for navigation instead of @Formulas, target framesets, frames, and named elements can be specified in LotusScript by using the `SetTargetFrame` method in `NotesUIWorkspace`, along with `OpenFrameSet`, `OpenPage`, `ComposeDocument`, and `EditDocument`, as well as the `OpenView` method defined in `NotesUIDatabase`, to override design element target frame settings.

Using naming conventions for frames and framesets

Because nested and target framesets and frames rely on frame names for reference, you must establish effective frameset naming conventions before developing framesets and linking frames together. Name a child frameset with some part of a related parent's frameset name. In a three-frame frameset called MainFrame, for example, you could name the top-left nested frameset MainFrame_TL via the frameset name or an alias name. This groups framesets together in the Designer Outline view, and they are easily distinguished when it comes time to specify target frames in design elements, or via @functions or LotusScript.

Tip
Use unique names for frames, but avoid using underscores at the beginning of frameset names. HTML uses the _ at the beginning of an HTML target frame name, such as `_self` and `_parent`.

Embedding design elements into frames

You can't embed most design elements into a frame alone. In folder panes, outlines, date pickers, graphics with hotspots, and other design elements that don't show up in the Named Element list of a frame Properties box, you must embed the element on a page first, and then embed the page in a frame.

Domino Web Application Navigation Using Outlines and Framesets

Most of the frameset and outline development techniques in this chapter apply to the Notes client application environment and the Web. However, there are a few additional features that need to be highlighted when using framesets and outlines on the Web.

Web outlines

One of the great features of outlines is their reusability across several design elements. The navigation menu for the `ndbible` Web site, for example, is a single outline, which is embedded in all the Domino database forms and pages that make up the Web site. This ensures the same navigation capabilities are available consistently throughout the site, and makes maintenance much easier. When a link is added, edited, or removed in the ndbibleDefault outline in the `ndbiblehomepage.nsf` database, the design change cascades through all the embedded instances of the outline in all the other databases. Figure 11-7 shows the ndbibleDefault outline for the `ndbible.com` Web site.

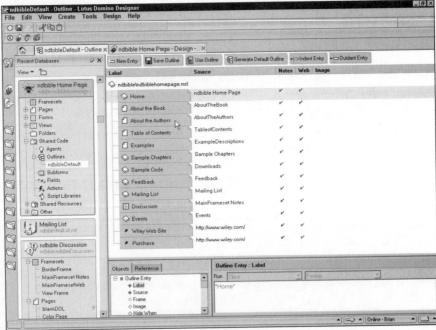

Figure 11-7: The ndbibleDefault outline used for the ndbible.com Web site

In addition to the consistency of using the same outline for the entire `ndbible.com` Web site, each embedded instance of the outline can have different display options selected via the Embedded View properties. The Embedded View properties facilitate control over the look and feel of the embedded outline. The Embedded View properties also control the outline entries that display for the embedded instance of the outline via hide-when formulas, without affecting the source outline.

Web framesets

As with Notes applications, framesets are a quick and easy way to manage Web site user interfaces. On the `ndbible.com` Web site, the discussion forum uses a multipaned frameset template that is part of the standard Domino 6 Discussion Database. The left navigation pane is a Domino outline embedded in a Domino page. The page is formatted for display on the Web and embedded in the frame, which is embedded in the frameset. The frame on the right is an embedded All Documents Domino view. The Action bar above the view is the Action bar associated with the All Documents view, not with the frame. Deselecting the Show Action Bar option in frame properties hides the Action bar. Figure 11-8 shows the MainFrameSetWeb frameset for the `ndbible.com` discussion forum in Domino Designer.

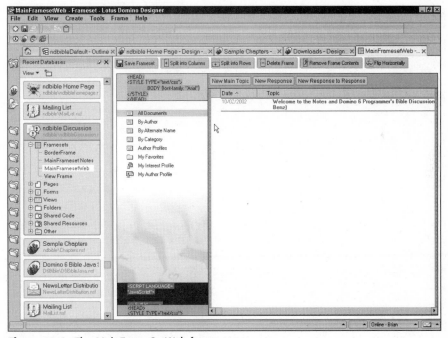

Figure 11-8: The MainFrameSetWeb frameset

Summary

This chapter introduced you to outlines and framesets. It included the following information:

✦ Outline examples: The Notes client Welcome page outlines

✦ Frameset examples: The Notes client Welcome page framesets

✦ Using Web outlines to define the `ndbible.com` navigational structure

✦ Advanced tips and tricks for creating Notes and Web outlines

✦ Advanced tips for specifying Notes and Web target framesets

The next chapter reviews advanced form designs, and provides some valuable tips for using forms, subforms, layout regions, layers, hide-when formulas, sections and tables, embedded elements, actions, and hotspots.

✦　　✦　　✦

Advanced Form Design

By Rocky Oliver

Chapter 8 introduced you to the basics of designing a form. This chapter shows you how to take your form design to the next level, and helps you exploit forms in ways you may not have thought of before. This chapter exposes you to various design elements that you can use with forms. Some practical uses are provided as examples, which are broken down so you can use these techniques in your applications.

Element Integration Overview

This section introduces you to some of the most commonly used design elements that are integrated with forms. The basics of using these elements are not covered here; this section concentrates on the tips and techniques that help you get the most out of these elements.

Tables

Tables are one of the most commonly used elements inside a form. Tables present information in an easily digestible format, and are highly configurable. Five types of tables exist:

- ✦ **Normal:** This is a standard table with columns and rows that you can set to fixed or variable widths.

- ✦ **Tabbed:** Each row is a separate tab in the table.

- ✦ **Animated:** This table shows one row at a time, cycling through each row at a predetermined interval.

- ✦ **Captioned:** This table expands and collapses similar to a section in a form; the caption heading appears with an expand/collapse button similar to the one that appears in the upper-right corner of a window.

New Feature

Captioned tables are new in Notes/Domino 6.

- ✦ **Programmable:** This table shows one row at a time, based on the value of a field on the form.

These tables provide you with a wide variety of options for organizing and presenting information to your users. This flexibility is extended because you can combine tables within tables, which enables you to have granular control over your presentation.

Captioned tables present collapsible rows like a section in a form. This can be a hard concept to grasp, so take a look at Figure 12-1 to see how a captioned table appears.

Figure 12-1: Captioned tables combine the functionality of a collapsed section with the flexibility of a table.

The little gray squares to the right of the captions for each row expand or collapse the row. These little gray boxes are similar to the minimize and maximize buttons in the upper-right corner of an application window.

Caption tables appear as tabbed tables on the Web. The same table from Figure 12-1 is shown in a browser in Figure 12-2.

Figure 12-2: Caption tables appear as tabbed tables in a Web browser.

The other table types are covered in the examples later in this chapter.

Sections

A *section* is a collapsible and expandable section on a form used to group and organize related information for a user. Sections enable a user or developer to provide a great deal of information in logical groupings. Sections can be used in the design of a form, or in a rich text field on a document. Although the most common use of sections is by end-users in rich text fields, they are also useful in form development. Many developers forget two useful features of sections:

✦ The ability to base the section title on an @function formula

✦ The ability to restrict access to a section by defining who can expand or collapse a section

The ability to base the section title on an @function formula is nice, and is not a feature available in the label for a tab in a tabbed table. You can have contextual titles for your sections in a form based on some formula or field value. You can also restrict access to fields or functionality by placing the fields or functionality in a controlled access section.

Hide-whens

Hide-whens are useful for showing information based on predefined criteria, such as whether the document is opened in read or edit mode, or as a result of a formula, such as a formula that checks to determine whether a user is in a certain database role. You can hide most elements based on predetermined criteria, which makes them powerful for disclosing information and functionality when needed. Hide-whens are used extensively in the examples section of this chapter.

Layers

Web developers are familiar with layers. Layers enable you to overlap blocks of information or elements on a form, subform, or page.

New Feature   Layers are a new feature in Notes/Domino 6.

Layers are much more useful in Web applications, but they also have usefulness in the Notes client.

Cross-Reference   Chapter 19 covers the use of layers in Web applications.

You can use layers for exact placement of items on a form, which is useful for doing things such as placing fields over a graphic. For instance, let's say you have a paper form that you want to create as a form in a database. You can scan the form and create a graphic of it, place the graphic as the background of the Domino form, and then use layers to place fields over the appropriate areas of the form graphic, thereby allowing your users to create Domino documents based on a paper form they may be familiar with.

Buttons and action hotspots

Buttons enable you to provide users the ability to take action in a form in context. You may, for example, place a button next to a field to perform some complex operation. The only real drawback to buttons is that they normally appear as little gray boxes, which isn't visually appealing (although in Notes/Domino 6 you can now change the color of a button, as well as give it "rounded" corners). That's where action hotspots come in.

Action hotspots enable you to turn any chunk of text or a graphic into a button. This allows you to provide much more visually appealing buttons in your forms. Buttons and action hotspots give you contextual placement of the functionality — this means that the button or hotspot is placed exactly where it makes sense, such as next to a field that it populates. Form actions, on the other hand, are always at the top of the form.

Form actions

Form actions are the action buttons that appear at the top of a form. Form actions enable you to provide a set of buttons that appear at the top of the form, even when the form scrolls. You can hide form actions based on edit mode of the document or a predetermined @function formula. You can also cascade form actions. You can customize the appearance of form actions, enabling you to blend your form actions with the overall look and feel of your application. You can even create cascaded action buttons, that present your actions in a drop-down menu.

You can also create shared actions, which are shared code resources that can be used in multiple locations within your database. Shared actions enable you to code your action buttons in one place and use them in multiple places.

Image resources

Image resources enable you to store your graphics as a part of your database application, and then reference those graphics throughout your application. Image resources also have the ability to store image wells, which provide mouse-over and selected, or clicked, versions of your images for use in your application without any coding effort. So when the user's mouse goes over the graphic, it shows one version of the image, and when the user clicks the graphic, it shows a different version of the image.

Embedded views

Embedded views enable you to have truly integrated applications. You can display related documents, such as item records for an order or discussion threads for a discussion database, in a form.

New Feature   Embedded views have become more powerful in Notes/Domino 6. Now action buttons from the embedded view can appear with the embedded view, and you can restrict embedded views to show only documents in the same thread the current document is in (which is useful for discussion databases).

You can also use embedded views with the new in-line editing feature for views, allowing you to have really innovative designs for your application. Take a look at some of the examples later in this chapter for more ideas.

Advanced Form Design Examples

This section introduces you to various examples for advanced form development. These examples are available in the example database, which is available from the download site.

On The Web   You can download the database, Bubba's Shrimp Ordering System (BSOS.nsf) used for the examples in this section from the companion Web site, www.wiley.com/compbooks/benz.

Figure 12-3 is an example of an order application for a fictional company known as Bubba's Shrimp (BS) Wholesalers. BS sells many different types of shrimp. This database is used to order products from the list of products in the database.

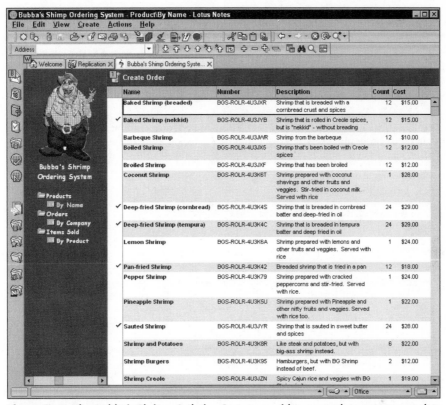

Figure 12-3: The Bubba's Shrimp Ordering System provides a seamless way to complete a shrimp order.

Application architecture

The architecture of the Bubba's Shrimp Ordering System (BSOS) application is as follows. Product documents contain the basic information about each product, such as the product number, description, number of shrimp in that product (count), and cost. Orders are tracked in the same database. Orders are made up of an Order document and 1 to *n* Item documents. The Item documents contain the information from the product that the Item document represents. There is one Item document per product ordered. This is done for a couple of reasons. First, it's easier to manage from a programmatic standpoint, as well as for displaying. Second, it makes it very easy to create multiple views that slice and dice the information. Management, for example, can check the Items Sold view and see how many of each type of product were sold in the last month. These Item documents do not have any user interface (no form used to display them). The items are managed by the Order document.

Application design details

The application uses a main frameset called *BSOS FSet*. This frameset is designated as the design element that is opened whenever the BSOS database is opened. The left frame of the BSOS FSet frameset contains a page called *BSOS Menu*. The graphic in the BSOS Menu page used in the frameset is an image resource. The views listed in the navigation frame are listed by using an embedded outline called *BSOS Outline*.

You can create an order two ways. The first way is to select some products in the Products view, and then click Create Order. This composes an Order document and adds the selected items to the order automatically. All you have to do is update the amounts.

The Order form uses many of the elements mentioned earlier in this chapter. The Order form is shown in Figure 12-4.

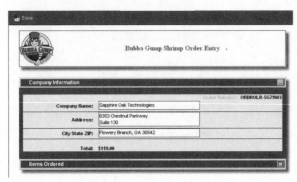

Figure 12-4: The Order form

The graphic and title of the form are contained in a table with a drop shadow, which appears to the right and below the table, and the graphic is an image resource in the database. The special table used for the main part of the form is a captioned table. The first section of the table is the Company Information, shown in Figure 12-4. The first section of this table contains another table, which formats the labels and fields for collecting the company information. The table simply uses a background color that is lighter than the captioned table to give a contrasting color, and various table borders are shown and hidden to make it more aesthetically pleasing.

If you are filling out the Company Information section and tabbing from field to field, you can tab straight to the Items Ordered section. Alternatively, you can click the caption title to collapse the Company Information section and open the Items Ordered section, which is shown in Figure 12-5.

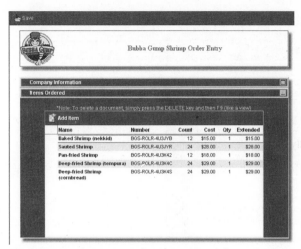

Figure 12-5: The Items Ordered section of the Order form features an embedded view element.

The Items Ordered section of the Order form uses an embedded view that is set to display only the items for this form by using the Show Single Category feature.

The application is designed so that the individual items of an order are stored in separate response documents to the main Order form. These Item documents are not designed to have a UI. In fact, nothing happens if you attempt to open one of these documents. Preventing the user from opening an Item document is accomplished by setting a form item on the Item document that is set to the value of ITEM. A form called ITEM exists, but the form has the Continue parameter of the QueryOpen event set to False; this setting prevents the form from ever loading, thereby preventing any Item document from being opened in a view.

Users can modify the quantities ordered in the Order document by using the in-view edit feature that is new to Notes/Domino 6. By combining the embedded view feature and this feature, you can create a truly unique and useful interface for your applications. Figure 12-6 shows the in-view editing feature adjusting the quantity ordered for an item.

When a quantity is updated, the extended cost and total fields on the Company Information tab are updated as well — but you need to know some tricks to accomplish this.

The name of the embedded view is Items.By.OrderNumber.EV. This tells you that the view is a list of items sorted or categorized by the OrderNumber item, and that it is an embedded view (as indicated by the EV suffix). The view's Inviewedit event contains the code used to update the necessary documents. The code is listed in Listing 12-1.

Figure 12-6: You can combine the in-view editing feature with the embedded view feature to provide useful and innovative functionality to your users.

Listing 12-1: **Inviewedit Event of the Items.By.OrderNumber.EV View**

```
Sub Inviewedit(Source As Notesuiview,_
Requesttype As Integer, Colprogname As Variant,_
Columnvalue As Variant, Continue As Variant)
  REM Define constants for request types
  Const QUERY_REQUEST = 1
  Const VALIDATE_REQUEST = 2
  Const SAVE_REQUEST = 3
  Const NEWENTRY_REQUEST = 4

  REM Define variables
  Dim db As NotesDatabase
  Dim doc As NotesDocument
  Dim caret As String

  REM these variables are used to update the Order
  REM document containing this embedded view
  Dim ws As New NotesUIWorkspace
  Dim parentdoc As NotesDocument
  Dim results As Variant

  REM Get the CaretNoteID - exit if it does not point
  REM at a document
  caret = Source.CaretNoteID
  If caret = "0" Then Exit Sub

  REM Get the current database and document
  Set db = Source.View.Parent
```

```
Set doc = db.GetDocumentByID(caret)
Set parentdoc = ws.CurrentDocument.Document

REM Select the request type
Select Case Requesttype

Case QUERY_REQUEST
  REM Reserved - do not use in Release 6.0

Case VALIDATE_REQUEST
  REM Cause validation error if user tries to
  REM exit column with no value
  If Isnumeric(Columnvalue(0)) Then
    If Cint(Columnvalue(0)) < 1 Then
      Messagebox "You must enter a quantity greater" &_
      " than 0",, "Negative value"
      Continue = False
    End If
  Else
    Messagebox "Quantity must be numeric",,_
    "Non-numeric value"
    Continue = False
  End If

Case SAVE_REQUEST
  REM Write the edited column view entry back to
  REM the document
  Call doc.ReplaceItemValue("Quantity",_
  Cint(Columnvalue(0)))

  REM compute the extended cost and set that into
  REM the Extended item in the Item document that
  REM is being updated
  doc.Extended = doc.GetItemValue("Quantity")(0) *_
  doc.GetItemValue("ProductCost")(0)
  Call doc.Save(True, False)

  REM this performs a lookup for the extended costs
  REM of all items related to this Order document,
  REM and then adds the costs together using the
  REM @Sum function
  results = Evaluate(|@Sum(@IfError(@DbLookup("" | &_
  |: "NoCache"; ""; "Items.By.OrderNumber.EV"; | &_
  |OrderNumber; 7); 0))|, parentdoc)

  REM update the Total field on the parent Order document
  REM of the embedded view; the results variable
  REM is an array, because the Evaluate function
  REM always returns an array
  parentdoc.Total = results(0)
  End Select
End Sub
```

The use of the `Inviewedit` event is covered in Chapter 9, so every line isn't covered here in detail. Focus on the last large chunk of code, beginning at the `SAVE_REQUEST` case. The first part of this case statement is fairly average—the `columnvalues` property sets the new value in the `Quantity` item. The `Quantity` item value and the `ProductCost` item value are then multiplied to compute the `Extended` item value. After these two items are updated, the Item document is saved. An `Evaluate` function call then does a lookup of all the items associated with this order, and the extended values from these items are added together. The result is set into the `Total` item of the parent document, which is the Order document.

Tip   You don't want to get into a habit of using `Evaluate` to compute @functions in LotusScript, but sometimes it's more efficient than attempting to code the same functionality in pure LotusScript. In Listing 12-1, for example, it's much easier (and more efficient) to perform the `@DbLookup` and `@Sum` using an `Evaluate`, because neither of these functions have an equivalent function in LotusScript.

Because the UI document automatically updates whenever an item in the corresponding back-end document changes, the Total field in the UI document automatically updates without any additional effort.

Using an embedded view also enables you to take advantage of standard view functionality, such as deleting a document. You can select the documents you want to delete, and, just like a normal view, press the Delete key and the F9 key (the Refresh key) to delete the documents. Figure 12-7 shows three documents marked for deletion.

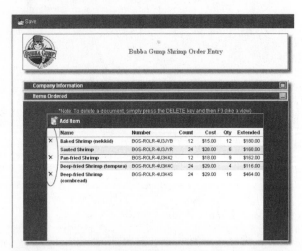

Figure 12-7: Using an embedded view lets you take advantage of basic view functionality, such as deleting documents.

Pressing the F9 key deletes the documents marked for deletion. Another view feature available to you in an embedded view is the ability to use View Actions.

New Feature The ability to use View Action buttons in an embedded view is a new feature in Notes/Domino 6.

In the embedded view in this example is an action button called Add Item. If you click this button, you are presented with the dialog box shown in Figure 12-8.

This dialog box enables the user to add more items to an order. As items are added to the order, they are removed from the available choices in the Product field of the dialog box. This prevents duplicate listings in the order. (A user can modify the values of existing items by using in-view editing). You're going to explore another use of a form, the dialog box, by dissecting the Add New Item dialog box. Figure 12-8 shows the Add New item dialog box form (add.item.dlg) in design mode.

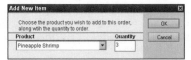

Figure 12-8: Forms are useful for creating dialog boxes.

The table has fields above and below it. These fields are hidden and hold the values of the chosen product. Any item in the dialog box is added to the related document, unless you specify otherwise. The names of the fields below the table correspond to the item names found on the Item document. The fields above the table contain the OrderNumber from the parent document, and the CurrentProductList field contains a list of products that are still available (that have not already been added to the order). The code in the CurrentProductList field is shown in Listing 12-2.

Listing 12-2: **CurrentProductList Field**

```
orderlist := @IfError(@DbLookup("" : "NoCache";
""; "Items.By.OrderNumber.EV"; OrderNumber; 8);"");

productlist := @IfError(@DbColumn(""; "";
"Product.By.Name.BE"; 6); "");

@Trim(@Replace(productlist; orderlist; ""))
```

The orderlist variable looks up the existing items that have already been added to the order, and returns a concatenated list of the values of the item in the following format: ProductName~ProductNumber~ProductCount~ProductCost. If no items are found, the orderlist variable contains an empty string (compliments of the @IfError function). The productlist variable does a cached lookup — after the first time the lookup fires, it is cached for subsequent lookups requesting the same information — and returns an empty string if there is an error. The @Trim @Replace combination then removes any items in the orderlist variable that are found in the productlist variable, resulting in a list of products, with associated information, not yet chosen. This field is used for the choices presented in the ChosenProduct combo box field.

The ChosenProduct combo box field is a keyword field with choices based on the CurrentProductList field. The choice formula for the ChosenProduct field is listed in the following code:

```
@Word(CurrentProductList; "~"; 1) + "|" + CurrentProductList
```

This syntax, using the pipe symbol to concatenate the user friendly version of the list and the actual list, takes advantage of the synonym feature of keyword fields to present the product names as choices to the user. The actual value of the choice is all the product information concatenated together. When a choice is made, the programmatic value is the concatenated information discussed earlier. This chosen value is then parsed in each of the computed fields on the form using the @Word function. The ProductName field, for example, has a formula of @Word(ChosenProduct; "~"; 1), which returns the first value from the concatenated information.

Note   The dialog box works by utilizing the separation of the form from the document. The dialog box gathers and computes the values to be passed back to the document, and then only the values are passed back in the indicated items.

The Add Item action button calls an agent called AddItem. The code for the AddItem agent is shown in Listing 12-3.

Listing 12-3: **AddItem Agent**

```
Sub Initialize
    Dim ws As New NotesUIWorkspace
    Dim s As New NotesSession
    Dim db As NotesDatabase
    Dim orderdoc As NotesDocument, itemdoc As NotesDocument
    Dim retflg As Boolean

    Set db = s.CurrentDatabase
    Set orderdoc = ws.CurrentDocument.Document
    Set itemdoc = db.CreateDocument
    itemdoc.Form = "ITEM"
    itemdoc.OrderNumber = orderdoc.OrderNumber

    REM DialogBox( form$ , [autoHorzFit] , [autoVertFit] ,_
    REM [noCancel] , [noNewFields] , [noFieldUpdate] ,_
    REM [readOnly] , [title$] , [notesDocument] ,_
    REM [sizeToTable] , [noOkCancel] , [okCancelAtBottom] )
    retflg = ws.DialogBox("add.item.dlg", True, True, False,_
    False, False, False, "Add New Item", itemdoc, True, False)
    Call itemdoc.MakeResponse(orderdoc)
    Call itemdoc.Save(True, False)
End Sub
```

Action buttons in embedded views are different, as the code that executes in an action button is aware of the documents in the view as well as the parent document of the embedded view. In this agent, an object handle is obtained to the Order document, a new Item document is created, and the `OrderNumber` from the Order document and the form name of `ITEM` are added to the new Item document. The dialog box is opened, and the Item document is provided as the related document for the dialog box. After the Item document is returned from the dialog box, it is saved as a response to the Order document.

In the Add Item action button, right after the `AddItem` agent is called, an `@Command([View-RefreshFields])` is called. This causes the new document to appear in the embedded view.

Note   When the BSOS database example was created (as of Notes/Domino 6.0), a bug was discovered with action buttons in embedded views. If you attempt to call `NotesUIWorkspace.ViewRefresh` or `NotesUIDocument.Refresh` against the current document containing the embedded view, Notes crashes. Hopefully, this has been addressed. You should be aware of this discrepancy just in case you run into the same problem.

Another handy technique is to remember that `@Commands` return values — usually `True` or `False`. If you have validation formulas in your form, you can use the following code in your Save and Close button:

```
@If(@Command([FileSave]); @Command([FileCloseWindow]); "")
```

If the form saves successfully, close the document; otherwise, do nothing. In a related note, the CompanyName field has the following validation formula:

```
@If(@IsDocBeingSaved & @ThisValue = ""; @Failure("You must provide a
value for " + @ThisName + "..."); @Success)
```

If the document is being saved and the value of the field is an empty string, the field didn't pass validation.

Tip   If you're using validation formulas, you should always add `@IsDocBeingSaved` as a part of the validation test. This prevents the validation formula from returning a `False` failure when the document is being refreshed.

Summary

This chapter introduced you to some advanced techniques for form design, specifically using some of the newer features of Notes/Domino 6, such as:

✦ New table features, such as caption tables

✦ New Form action features

✦ New embedded view features, such as view action buttons and in-line editing

You were introduced to various items that you can use in a form, and you were shown an in-depth example that made use of many of these elements. Chapter 13 goes into detail about the various database properties available to you and explains how you can exploit them to get the most out of your database design.

✦   ✦   ✦

Database Properties

By Richard Schwartz

Developing Notes and Domino applications is not just a matter of designing pages, forms, views, and other design elements. As discussed in Chapter 10, security settings are another important part of the application. In this chapter, you examine many other database-wide settings that help determine aspects of an application's behavior. The database properties dialog box provides a wealth of information about your database, and enables you to customize many behaviors of your database. Let's begin by learning how to access database information.

Accessing Database Information

The settings for a database are all contained in the Database Properties dialog box, which you access by choosing File ➪ Database ➪ Properties from either the Domino Designer or Notes client menu. The Database Properties dialog box contains seven tabs:

- ✦ **Database basics:** The title of the database is set here, and it contains general settings.

- ✦ **Information:** General information about the database size, number of documents, and amount of whitespace is contained here.

- ✦ **Print settings:** This tab is used to define printing options, such as default headers and footers for printed documents.

- ✦ **Design settings:** This tab is where you specify design properties, such as templates that this database inherits from, and the template name used for this database if it is a template.

- ✦ **Launch settings:** This tab defines what is presented when the user opens the database.

- ✦ **Full-text index settings:** This tab is used to create and manage the full text index for the database.

- ✦ **Advanced settings:** Most of the settings on this tab are used to optimize database performance.

Let's take a more in-depth look at each of these tabs.

Database basics tab

The first tab in the Database Properties dialog box is the Database basics tab, which is shown in Figure 13-1. Properties that are set on this tab identify the database and control many different aspects of application behavior, security, and data management. These settings are described in Table 13-1. You can access some of these properties with LotusScript, or Java programmers can use the `NotesDatabase` class. The corresponding property names in this class are in the table's third column.

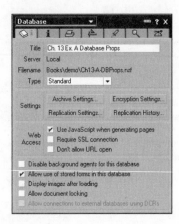

Figure 13-1: The Database Properties dialog box — Basics tab

Table 13-1: Database Information Properties

Property	Purpose	NotesDatabase Property
Title	This is the name of the database that is displayed to users in the Open Database dialog box, on bookmarks, and in various other places in the Notes client.	Title
Server	This read-only property identifies the server where the NSF file for this database is located. Local indicates that the file is on the hard drive of the machine where Domino Designer or the Notes client is running.	Server
Filename	This read-only property identifies the pathname for the NSF file.	FilePath

Property	Purpose	NotesDatabase Property
Type	This property identifies the type of database for certain special-purpose processing on the Domino server. Applications developed outside of Lotus should always be set to Standard. This property is editable because the Lotus template developers need to be able to set this property, and they use the same tools available to "normal" developers—namely the Domino Designer—to develop the templates.	Type (A new property in Notes/Domino 6)
Use JavaScript when Generating Pages	This property determines whether the Domino server generates pure HTML or a combination of HTML and JavaScript when rendering design elements and documents for a browser. Many programming features of Domino applications depend on JavaScript, but some simple applications can run without it.	None
Require SSL Connection	If enabled, this setting issues a redirect to any browser that attempts to access the database via an ordinary HTTP connection instead of an HTTPS connection.	None
Don't Allow URL Open	If enabled, this setting causes the Domino server to issue a Not Authorized response to URLs that attempt to access this database. Web access to databases with this setting can only be done indirectly, such as through a servlet.	None
Disable Background Agents	If enabled, this setting prevents any agents in this database from running on the server. It can be used to temporarily disable agents without losing all the scheduling information.	None
Allow Use of Stored Forms	If disabled, this setting prevents any documents with stored forms (see Chapter 3) from being stored in the database. Stored forms consume more memory and disk space, and they can create security risks in some environments.	None

Continued

Table 13-1 *(continued)*

Property	Purpose	NotesDatabase Property
Display Images After Loading	If enabled, this setting causes the Notes client to delay image display until all data in a document is loaded, which enables users to begin reading text portions of the document while large graphics are still being transmitted over the network.	None
Allow Document Locking	If enabled, this setting allows code to create locks that grant exclusive update rights to specific users. This setting requires that an Administration server be specified in the database's ACL. See Chapter 10 for more information.	IsDocumentLockingEnabled
Allow Connections to External Databases Using DCRs	If enabled, data connection resources can be used to establish a connection to an external data source. See Chapter 43 for more information.	None

In addition to the properties listed in Table 13-1, there are four buttons on the Database basics tab. These buttons are as follows:

✦ **Archive settings:** Archive settings are primarily of interest to application users and data owners, not programmers.

✦ **Encryption settings:** Encryption settings are more often of interest to programmers.

✦ **Replication settings:** Replication settings are more often of interest to programmers.

✦ **Replication history:** Replication history is primarily of interest to system administrators.

The Encryption Settings dialog box, shown in Figure 13-2, controls encryption that is applied to the entire NSF file when it is stored on the hard drive of a server or Notes client. Don't confuse this with encryption of data in items within the NSF file, which is described in Chapter 21. File-level encryption protects against the possibility that someone may steal a laptop or break into a server and steal the file, and then try to read it. If the file is encrypted, it can't be read unless the hacker also steals the Notes ID file of the user whose name appears in the dialog box along with its password. Settings in this dialog box determine whether the NSF file is encrypted, and what the strength of the encryption is. You can choose Simple, Medium, or Strong encryption. There is a performance trade-off for encryption. The stronger the encryption, the more CPU power and time it takes to access data in the NSF file. Simple encryption is not very strong at all, and could probably be broken by any professional code-breaker in a reasonable amount of time. It is strong enough, however, to keep out anyone who merely has casual interest in your data. Strong encryption is very secure, and should resist any effort to break it with any technology known to the private sector at any cost for at least ten years, but it incurs the maximum performance penalty. Medium encryption should be strong enough to resist any practical attempt to break it, but could be broken by someone willing to invest several years and a large amount of money. When deploying applications that contain sensitive data, programmers should advise system administrators about the appropriate level of encryption that should be applied to the NSF files.

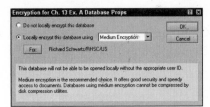

Figure 13-2: The Encryption settings
dialog box

The Replication settings dialog box, shown in Figure 13-3, contains many options, most of which are of interest to only system administrators or end-users. The selective replication settings, shown in Figure 13-3, however, may be of interest to programmers. Programmers may be asked to make some accommodations in their application designs to make selective replication easier for users to manage. For example, programmers may be asked to create views or folders that are set up as Shared Private on First Use to enable users to use the Documents in Specified Views or Folders setting in this dialog box. Programmers may also be asked to create a generic selection formula that users can paste into the dialog box after selecting the Documents by Selection Formula setting in the dialog box.

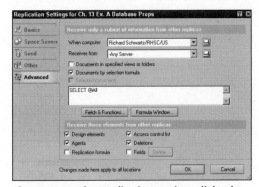

Figure 13-3: The Replication settings dialog box

Information tab

The second tab in the Database Properties dialog box is the Information tab, which is shown in Figure 13-4. There are no settable properties on this tab. Programmers should be aware, however, of two things that are visible on this tab:

✦ The database's replica ID appears on the tab. This value may be required in some code.

✦ The database's *ODS*, or *on disk storage*, level appears on the tab. Some new features in Notes and Domino 6 work only if the level is at least 43, which is the level supported by the Release 6.0 code.

Figure 13-4: The Database Properties dialog box —
Storage tab

Print settings

The third tab in the Database Properties dialog box is the Print settings tab, which is shown in Figure 13-5. The properties on this tab are used to control headers and footers that are printed with all documents from the database. These settings are described in Table 13-2. None of these settings can be accessed via LotusScript or Java code.

Figure 13-5: The Database Properties dialog box —
Print tab

Table 13-2: Print Properties

Property	Purpose
Specify	This radio button determines whether the settings currently shown in the dialog box apply to the header or footer for printed pages. Both sets of settings can exist, but only one can appear at a time.
Header/Footer Text	This property stores the actual text that you want printed in each header or footer. Several buttons appear below the text entry box for this property. These buttons insert codes into the text that represent values that are calculated when the document is printed. The buttons, from left to right, generate codes for the page number, the total number of pages in the document (new in ND6), the date, the time, a tab to the next stop, and the document's window title formula value.

Property	Purpose
Font	This property selects the font used for printing the header or footer.
Size	This property selects the size of the font used for printing the header or footer.
Style	This property selects effects (bold, italic, and so on) that are applied to the font when printing the header or footer.
Print Header and Footer on First Page	If selected, the header and footer print on all pages. If not selected, the header and footer are printed on all pages except the first.

Design settings

The fourth tab in the Database Properties dialog box is the Design Settings tab, which is shown in Figure 13-6. The settings on this tab are a mixed bag. Most of the settings have to do with templates and design elements, but several of them do not. The properties on this tab are described in Table 13-3. You can access some of these properties by LotusScript or Java programmers can use the `NotesDatabase` class. The corresponding property names in this class are in the table's third column.

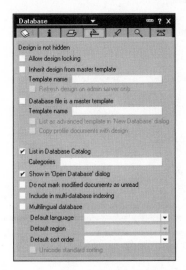

Figure 13-6: The Database Properties dialog box — Design tab

Table 13-3: Design Properties

Property	Purpose	NotesDatabase Property
Allow Design Locking (new in Notes/Domino 6)	If enabled, this setting enables programmers working on a development team to lock design elements. This setting requires that an Administration server be specified in the database's ACL. See Chapter 6 for more information.	IsDesignLockingEnabled
Inherit Design from Master Template	If enabled, this database's design is inherited from at template.	None
Template Name	This setting specifies the template name of the template from which this database's design inherits.	DesignTemplateName
Refresh Design on Admin Server Only (New in Notes/Domino 6)	If enabled, the automated design refresh process modifies the design of the database only on the Administration server selected in the ACL.	None
Database File is a Master Template	If enabled, this database is used as a template to refresh the design of other databases.	None
Template Name	This setting specifies the template name of this database.	TemplateName
List as an Advanced Template in New Database Dialog	If enabled, the template name of this database is available only if users check the Show Advanced Templates option when creating new databases.	None
Copy Profile Documents with Design	If enabled, new databases created using this database as a template will copy all profile documents contained in this database.	None
List in Database Catalog	If enabled, the overnight process on Domino servers that maintains the database catalog obtains information about this database for the catalog.	None
Categories	This setting specifies the categories in the database catalog that list this database.	Categories
Show in Open Database Dialog	If selected, the title of this database appears in the Open Database dialog box in the Notes client.	None

Property	Purpose	NotesDatabase Property
Do Not Mark Modified Documents as Unread	If enabled, documents are marked as unread only when they are first created. The marks are not changed if the document is edited.	None
Include in Multi-database Indexing (New in Notes/Domino 6.)	If enabled, this database is indexed and searchable via the Domain Index feature of the Domino server.	IsInMultiDbIndexing
Multilingual Database	If enabled, this feature enables programmers to create versions of design elements that use different languages.	None
Default Language	This setting specifies the default language for design elements in this database.	None
Default Region	This setting specifies the default region for design elements in this database.	None
Default Sort Order	This setting specifies a national collate sequence used in this database.	None
Unicode Standard Sorting	If enabled, the collate sequence for the database is the Unicode standard sequence.	None

Launch settings

The fifth tab in the Database Properties dialog box is the Launch settings tab, which is shown in Figure 13-7. These settings control the actions that take place when a user opens a database. Making sure that users see meaningful information every time they start an application is an important aspect of user friendliness. The properties on this tab are described in Table 13-4. None of these settings can be accessed via LotusScript or Java code.

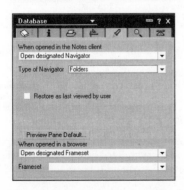

Figure 13-7: The Database Properties dialog box — Launch tab

Table 13-4: Launch Properties

Property	Purpose
When Opened in Notes Client	Specifies the action that takes place when a user opens the database with the Notes client. Choices are Restore as Last Viewed by User, Open About Database Document, Open Designated Frameset, Open Designated Navigator, Open Designated Navigator in its own Window, Launch First Attachment in About Database, and Launch First doclink in About Database.
Frameset Name	If Open Designated Frameset is the Notes client launch option, this property specifies the name of the frameset.
Type of Navigator	If a navigator is specified for the Notes client launch option, this setting determines whether the navigator is a standard navigator, a folder navigator, or a page.
Navigator Name	Specifies the name of a standard navigator or page to launch.
Restore as Last Viewed by User	If selected, the database is always opened to the same location that the user last visited.
When Opened in a Browser	Specifies the action that takes place when a user opens the database from a Web browser using the ?OpenDatabase URL command. Choices are Use Notes Launch Option, Open About Database Document, Open Designated Frameset, Open Designated Page, Open Designated Navigator in its own Window, Launch First doclink in About Database, Launch Designated doclink, and Launch first document in view.
Frameset	If Open Designated Frameset is the browser launch option, this property specifies the name of the frameset.
Page	If Open Designated Page is the browser launch option, this property specifies the name of the page.
Navigator	If Open Designated Navigator in its own Window is the browser launch option, this property specifies the name of the navigator.
View	If Launch First Document in View is the browser launch option, this property specifies the name of the view.

There are three check mark properties in the Launch tab as well:

✦ **Restore as last viewed by user:** This property causes the database to "remember" where the user was when he closed the database, and then opens it back to that place.

✦ **Show "About database" document if modified:** This property causes the database to open the "About database" document if the design of the database is changed.

✦ **Show "About database" document when database is opened for first time:** This property causes the "About database" document to be presented to the user the first time she opens the document, and then it is not presented anymore (unless the previous property is also enabled).

The Launch tab also includes a Preview Pane Default button. The Preview pane is a Notes client feature that enables users to view documents without actually having to double-click them to open them from a view. Programmers can force the Preview pane to open automatically whenever a user opens a database by clicking this button (Figure 13-8).

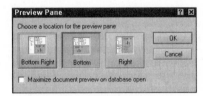

Figure 13-8: The Preview Pane dialog box

Settings in the Preview Pane dialog box enable programmers to specify the position on the screen where the Preview pane appears and to specify whether the pane opens to its maximum size or to the size that the user last set it to.

Full-text index settings

The sixth tab in the Database Properties dialog box is the Full-text settings tab, which is shown in Figure 13-9. Full text indexing is one of the most powerful features of Notes and Domino. It enables users to locate documents by searching for specific words that they think may be contained in them. Many system administrators try to avoid storing full-text indexes for databases because they take up additional disk space on servers. Programmers should be familiar with the full-text indexing options so that they can make good recommendations to administrators.

Figure 13-9: The Database Properties dialog box — Full-text index tab

The Full–text index setting tab contains only one modifiable property, the Update Frequency. If this is set to Immediate, new and modified documents are indexed as soon as they are saved in the database — there may actually be a brief delay if the indexer task on the server is busy. Other options are Daily, Hourly, or Scheduled. The latter indicates that a system administrator must manually set up a program document in the Domino Directory to set the schedule for updating the index. This setting enables administrators to control when the server absorbs the indexing-documents hit. If users expect to be able to find new documents as soon as they are created, however, Immediate is the best setting.

This tab also contains four buttons:

✦ Create Index

✦ Delete Index

✦ Update Index

✦ Count Unindexed Documents

The first three buttons are self-explanatory. Count Unindexed Documents is useful if the update frequency is not set to Immediate.

The Create Index button opens a dialog box that controls several options for the index. This dialog box is shown in Figure 13-10. The settings in the dialog box are described in Table 13-5.

Figure 13-10: The Create Full Text Index dialog box

Table 13-5: Full-Text Index Settings

Setting	Purpose
Index Attached Files	If enabled, this property causes the indexer to open all file attachments in documents and search for text to index. This option should be enabled if the database is primarily used for storing attachments that contain large amounts of text, such as word-processing documents.
Conversion Filters	Select Using Conversion Filters for the most accurate indexing of documents in popular file formats. (If Notes and Domino can import a particular type of document, a filter for that type is available.)
Index Encrypted Fields	If enabled, information stored in encrypted fields will be indexed, but only if the server's Notes ID file contains the appropriate encryption key. Use this setting only in environments where the physical security of the server and its ID file are ensured.
Index Sentence and Paragraph Breaks	If enabled, this setting enables users to create queries using special syntaxes that find matches only if the target words are in the same paragraph or the same sentence.

Setting	Purpose
Enable Case-sensitive Searches	If enabled, this setting enables users to create queries that find a match only if the text in a document exactly matches the case of the text in the query.
Update Frequency	This setting specifies Immediate, Daily, Hourly, or Scheduled updates to the index.

Advanced settings

The final tab in the Database Properties dialog box is the Advanced settings tab, which is shown in Figure 13-11. Most of the settings on this tab are related to performance and storage optimization. The settings are described in Table 13-6.

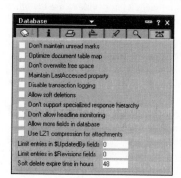

Figure 13-11: The Database Properties dialog box — Advanced tab

Table 13-6: Advance Settings

Property	Purpose
Don't Maintain Unread Marks	If enabled, this property prevents the Domino server from keeping lists of unread documents for each user, saving space and CPU cycles.
Optimize Document Table Map	If enabled, this property creates tables within the NSF file that selects documents by the name of the form from which they were created. This setting helps optimize performance for views that contain a form = clause in their selection formulas, saving CPU cycles.
Don't Overwrite Free Space	If enabled, this property stops the Domino server from writing a random bit pattern over space that becomes free within the NSF file, saving CPU cycles but removing a feature that is important in some high-security installations.
Maintain LastAccessed Property	If disabled, this property stops Domino from tracking the date and time that each document in the database was most recently read, saving storage and CPU cycles.

Continued

Table 13-6 *(continued)*

Property	Purpose
Disable Transaction Logging	If selected, this property prevents Domino from making a record of all changes made to documents in the database in the server's transaction log. The transaction-logging feature improves reliability and performance if configured properly, so this property should only be selected if there is evidence that logging is causing problems.
Allow Soft Deletions	If enabled, this property causes all documents that are deleted by users to remain in the NSF file, accessible only through a view with the Shared, Contains Deleted Documents property, for a specified number of hours. Documents can be undeleted from the view.
Don't Support Specialized Response Hierarchy	If enabled, this setting prevents Notes and Domino from storing a list of child notes within the header of every note. This setting saves storage and CPU cycles, but it makes it impossible to use the functions @AllChildren and @AllDescendants in any formula within the database.
Don't Allow Headline Monitoring	If enabled, this setting prevents the Domino server's headline-monitoring feature from searching for new or modified documents in the database. This setting saves CPU cycles but prevents users from being automatically notified about information that may be of interest to them.
Allow More Fields in Database	If enabled, this property sets aside more space in the NSF file for a structure known as the UNK Table that tracks the names of all items contained in all notes in the file. This property costs extra storage and CPU cycles, but it is necessary for very large applications that use several thousand item names.
Use LZ1 Compression for Attachments (New in Notes/ Domino 6)	If enabled, this property uses a more efficient algorithm for compression than previous releases of Notes and Domino, thereby saving space.
Limit Entries in $UpdatedBy Fields	If enabled by setting a nonzero value, this property puts a cap on the number of names that are stored in $UpdatedBy items that are automatically maintained for all documents. In applications where documents are frequently updated, this setting can save a significant amount of storage.
Limit Entries in $Revisions Fields	If enabled by setting a nonzero value, this property puts a cap on the number of date/time stamps that are stored in $Revisions items that are automatically maintained for all documents. In applications where documents are frequently updated, this setting can save a significant amount of storage.
Soft Delete Expiration Time in Hours	If enabled by setting a nonzero value, this property determines the number of hours that deleted documents remain in an NSF file before being overwritten.

Summary

This chapter covered a variety of properties that apply to an entire NSF file. You learned that

✦ You can access some, but not all, database properties in the `NotesDatabase` class by LotusScript and Java.

✦ File encryption settings protect against loss of data due to theft of a laptop or hacking a server, but strong encryption incurs a performance penalty.

✦ Some new features of Notes and Domino 6 do not work properly if the ODS level in the Database Properties dialog box is less than 43.

✦ Full-text indexing can be a powerful feature for end-users, but requires additional storage and CPU cycles on the server. Setting appropriate options for the indexing is important.

The next chapter covers one of the most useful design features in Domino, the ability to share and reuse code. This reduces maintenance effort, and makes code changes much easier. Learn more about sharing code in Chapter 14.

✦　　✦　　✦

Sharing Code with Libraries

By Rocky Oliver

S cript libraries are one of the most handy design elements in Lotus Notes and Domino. Script libraries enable you to reuse code in multiple design elements throughout your database application. Three types of script libraries exist — LotusScript libraries, JavaScript libraries, and Java libraries.

Cross-Reference   Java libraries and JavaScript libraries are new features in Notes/Domino 6. Using JavaScript libraries is covered in Chapters 39 and 40; Java libraries are covered in Chapters 32, 33, and 34.

This chapter doesn't cover all the basics of using a LotusScript library — that is covered in the Domino 6 Designer help. This chapter concentrates on more useful techniques for creating and using LotusScript libraries, and provides examples along the way.

Tips for Creating a LotusScript Library

While you're encouraged to use LotusScript libraries to make your code easier to maintain and reuse, the tips described in the following sections can help to ensure that you get the best performance out of your script libraries.

Note   Because Java and JavaScript libraries are new to Notes/Domino 6, the common reference for LotusScript libraries is script libraries. Therefore to make it easier to read, this chapter refers to LotusScript libraries as script libraries.

Going deep instead of wide

Any time you use a shared resource, you trade speed for reusability and maintainability. It takes longer to load a resource from somewhere else (even in the same database) than if the code or element is local. When you load a script library, for example, your code is located by name (from the `use` statement) and loaded into memory. Most of the time, this tradeoff is worth it; however, if you create your libraries incorrectly, this performance hit could be exacerbated. Through trial and error, real-world experience, and testing, it's been determined that loading a bunch of little script libraries is much

✦ ✦ ✦ ✦

In This Chapter

Getting the most out of script libraries

Exploring examples that demonstrate these techniques

✦ ✦ ✦ ✦

more expensive (speed-wise) than loading larger, more monolithic libraries. Therefore, you should go deep and create larger libraries rather than trying to create many granular libraries.

Note All the code you place in a script library loads when a library is referenced with a `Use` statement, not just the sub and functions you use in the loading design element.

Tip You need a few functions that you write over and over. Rather than inventing the wheel every time, create a couple of script libraries that you can paste into any database. An example utility library is demonstrated later in this chapter.

Segmenting your libraries

Because script libraries are built for reuse, segment your code to get the maximum use out of it. One of the most useful ways to do this is to divide your script libraries, especially any general utility libraries, into front-end libraries and back-end libraries. Web, server-based, and scheduled agents, as well as agents executed using the `NotesAgent.Run` method, can't use *any* UI-based classes. In previous releases, you couldn't even have a `Dim ws as New NotesUIWorkspace` in the code, as it would throw an error.

New Feature You can now use `Dim` UI classes in a server/Web-based agent without causing an error. An error does occur, however, if you call any of the properties or methods.

By segmenting your script libraries by front-end and back-end subs and functions, you can safely use these libraries without error.

Commenting your libraries

You may have difficulty knowing when and where to use script libraries. A little documentation can go a long way toward making script libraries easier to understand and use. Any comments you can add to a library are good, but being consistent about your comments makes it that much easier to follow. The following are recommendations that you include in the comments of your script libraries:

✦ A definition of all subs and functions in your library, such as what they do, the parameters they take, and so on

✦ A description of where the library is used, and what libraries it uses

✦ A modification history, so others (and you) know what was modified, who modified it, and when

These comments go in the (Options) area of your script library.

Chaining libraries

Libraries can load other libraries. But this can be tricky if you don't plan your libraries well. It's easy to have errors when your code compiles or runs, because the same variables are declared globally (in the Declarations area) in the library being loaded and in the library doing the loading. One of the main ways to make sure this works is to segment your libraries into front-end and back-end subs and functions. Another more thorough way requires you to change the way you build your functions and code.

The main reason that developers declare global variables is to make them available to functions and subs being used. This is not a good practice, as it is sloppy programming that takes unneeded shortcuts. A much better practice is to steal a page from the C API coders and pass in the variables you need to each function and sub. A parameter passed into a function is passed By Ref, or by reference, as a default. This means that a reference to the variable in the parameter passes into the function by the calling code, and changes made to that variable remain after the function completes executing. In other words, you can pass more than one parameter to a function, have that function modify them all, and pass them back. Then you can use the return value of the function to indicate whether the function completed successfully.

If you can minimize or eliminate the global declarations in the (Declarations) area of your script libraries, you should avoid any problems loading multiple libraries. Also, if you load a library into another library, the first library is included when the second library loads.

Example Time!

This section walks through some examples that demonstrate many of the concepts mentioned earlier in this chapter. Not all functions in each library are covered, but you learn about pertinent areas that demonstrate specific techniques.

 A ND6 Script Library Examples database (nd6ScriptLibEx.nsf) on the companion Web site (www.wiley.com/compbooks/benz) contains all the examples in this section.

You're going to work with the LS.utilities.BE script library, located in the example database located on the companion site. This library is a utility library that contains a collection of useful functions. All these functions are safe to use in Web- and server-based agents because none of them contain UI elements (note the BE extension). The LS at the beginning of the name indicates that the library is a LotusScript library.

Listing 14-1 shows an example of the comments in this library, and how you can format your comments to provide meaningful information to your users.

Listing 14-1: **Comments from LS.utilities.BE**

```
REM This is a utility library containing a set of functions that
are useful in many applications

REM This library is used by the following elements:
REM    LS.utilities.FE library
REM    SortArray Example form

REM *********** Functions in this lib ***********
REM
REM getDbPath(sourceDB As NotesDatabase, dbpath As String)
REM As Boolean
REM    returns the file path of the provided database,
REM    without the file name
REM    the path is returned on the dbpath parameter.
REM    the function returns True if successful,
```

Continued

Listing 14-1 *(continued)*

```
REM    False otherwise (and throws error to calling code)
REM
REM DayOfWeek(d As Integer, abbnum As Integer) As String
REM    provide the number of the day of the week
REM    (1 through 7) and the function returns the name of
REM    the day (1 = Sunday, 2 = Monday, etc.)
REM    if you provide an abbnum integer greater than 0
REM    it will return an abbreviation for the day.
REM    for instance if the day is 1 and the abbnum is 3,
REM    then SUN is returned.
REM
REM MonthOfYear(m As Integer, abbnum As Integer) As String
REM    provide the number of the month of the year
REM    (1 through 12) and the function returns the name of
REM    the month (1 = January, 2 = February, etc.)
REM    if you provide an abbnum integer greater than 0
REM    it will return an abbreviation for the month.
REM    for instance if the month is 1 and the abbnum is 3,
REM    then JAN isreturned.
REM
REM SortArray(sArray As Variant, orderflag As String)
REM As Boolean
REM    this function sorts the provided array in either
REM    ascending or descending order, based on the order
REM    flag: A sorts ascending, D sorts descending.
REM    this function uses four private subs to do the
REM    "work" - DoQS_A, DoQS_D, DoInsertSort_A,
REM    and DoInsertSort_D
REM
REM URLEncode(inString As String) As Boolean
REM    encodes a string for a URL
REM
REM URLDecode(inString As String) As Boolean
REM    decodes a string from a URL
REM
REM detachFile(doc As NotesDocument, rtname As String,
REM fname As String, fpath As String) As Boolean
REM    this function detaches the specified attachment to
REM    the indicated location
REM    the parameters are as follows:
REM    doc = the document containing the attachment
REM    rtitem = the rich text item containing the attachment
REM    fname = optional. the name of the attachment
REM    fpath = optional. the filepath where the attachment
REM    is to be saved
REM    If the fname is an empty string, then the first
REM    attachment found in the specified rt item is used
REM    If the fpath is an empty string, then the file is
REM    saved to a subdir of the Windows temp dir
REM
REM initApp(hwd As Variant, appname As String) As Boolean
```

```
REM    retuns an application object handle to the provided
REM    application name.
REM    the parameters are as follows:
REM    hwd = handle to the object. Passed in as an
REM    empty variant, the handle is returned on this param
REM    appname = the programmatic name of the application,
REM    e.g. Word.Application for MS Word

REM *********** Modification History ***********
REM  WHO    WHEN        WHAT
REM  Rock   11/15/02    Initial creation of this library
REM  Rock   11/21/02    Added detachFile function
```

The comments in Listing 14-1 tell you or any other developer what's available in this library, where the library is used, and when it was last modified. This enables you to make use of the function immediately, or reminds you what you added to this library if you come back to it later.

A piece of information that is missing from this comment segment is the *hosting* database for the library. In multidatabase applications, you can use the same script library in more than one database. You should choose one database to be the hosting database for the library, and make sure that all changes are made to that library (and are documented in the comments). This ensures that your functionality stays consistent across applications. You can simply add another line in the comments stating the following:

```
REM This library is hosted in ND6ScriptLibEx.nsf. Any changes
REM made to this library should be made there, and then
REM propagated to the other databases listed below:
REM    anotherdb.nsf
REM    abigdb.nsf
```

Listing 14-2 shows a comment segment from LS.utilities.FE. This is a utility library containing front-end functions, which means that these functions use UI objects or interact with the UI directly.

Listing 14-2: **Comments from LS.utilities.FE**

```
REM This is a utility library containing a set of functions
REM that are useful in many applications. The functions in
REM this library contain UI objects; therefore this library
REM should not be used in Web or server-based agents

REM This library is used by the following elements:REM   Save and Open
Attachment Example form

REM This library uses the following elements:
REM    LS.utilities.BE - the detachFile function

REM ************* Functions in this lib *************
REM
```

Continued

Listing 14-2 *(continued)*

```
REM detachFileOpen(doc As NotesDocument, rtname As String,
REM fname As String) As Boolean
REM    this function detaches an attachment to the specified
REM    location, and then opens it with the associated
REM    program. the parameters are as follows:
REM    doc = the NotesDocument containing the attachment
REM    rtname = the name of the RT Item containing
REM    the attachment
REM    fname = optional. the name of the attachment
REM    If the name of the attachment isn't provided,
REM    then the first attachment in the RT item is used.
REM    This function also uses a C API function that is
REM    defined in the Declarations of this library.

REM ************* Modification History *************
REM   WHO     WHEN         WHAT
REM   Rock    11/21/02     Initial creation of this library
```

The comments in Listing 14-2 warn you not to use this library in Web- or server-based agents. The purpose of these comments is to ensure that you understand what the FE extension means in the library name. These comments also indicate any libraries that are used by this library (including the function used), and what design elements use this library.

You're now going to take a look at an example that uses these script libraries. The example uses the following design elements:

✦ Save and Open Attachment Example form

✦ DetachOpen agent

✦ Save and Open Example view

✦ LS.utilities.FE script library

✦ LS.utilities.BE script library

To explore this example, perform the following steps:

1. Navigate to the document contained in the Save and Open Example view and click the Detach and Open button.

2. A prompt appears with the attachment names of the attachments in the document. Choose one of these attachments that prompt you for a location where you want to detach the attachment.

3. After specifying a location, the attachment detaches where specified and launches in the associated application.

Listing 14-3 provides the code for this example. The Detach and Open button on the Save and Open Attachment Example form calls the DetachOpen agent.

Listing 14-3: **DetachOpen Agent**

```
Options
Option Public
Option Declare

Use "LS.utilities.FE"

Initialize
Sub Initialize
  On Error Goto errHandler
  Dim ws As New NotesUIWorkspace
  Dim doc As NotesDocument
  Dim attachname As Variant, attachnamelist As Variant
  Dim retflg As Boolean

  Set doc = ws.CurrentDocument.Document
  attachnamelist = doc.Attachments
  If Ubound(attachnamelist) = 0 And_
  attachnamelist(0) = "" Then
    Error 900, "No attachments in this document."
  End If
  If Ubound(attachnamelist) > 0 Then
    attachname = ws.Prompt(PROMPT_OKCANCELLIST,_
    "Attachment", "Choose the attachment to open...",_
    attachnamelist(0), attachnamelist)
    If attachname = -1 Then Exit Sub
  Else
    Attachname = attachnamelist(0)
  End If

  REM detachFileOpen(doc As NotesDocument,
  REM rtname As String, fname As String) As Boolean
  retflg = detachFileOpen(doc, "Files", Cstr(attachname))

getOut:
  Exit Sub
errHandler:
  Select Case Err
  Case 900
    Msgbox Error$,,"Error"
  Case Else
    Msgbox Error$ & " (" & Err & ")",,"Unhandled Error"
  End Select
  Resume getOut
End Sub
```

The Attachments field on the form contains the names of all the attachments in the document. If there are no attachments, the user is informed and the code exits. If there is one attachment, the code automatically chooses that attachment; otherwise, the user is prompted to choose one of the attachments. The detachFileOpen function is then called, which resides in the LS.utilities.FE script library, as shown in Listing 14-4.

Listing 14-4: **detachFileOpen Function from LS.utilities.FE**

```
Options
Option Public
Option Declare

Use "LS.utilities.BE"

<<and the comment code listed in Listing 14-2>>

Declarations
REM this C API call is used to find the executable
REM associated with a file
REM this function is used by the detachFileOpen function

Const MAX_FILENAME_LEN = 260
Declare Function FindExecutable Lib "shell32.dll" _
Alias "FindExecutableA" (Byval lpFile As String,_
Byval lpDirectory As String, Byval lpResult As String) _
As Long

DetachFileOpen function
Function detachFileOpen(doc As NotesDocument,_
rtname As String, fname As String) As Boolean
  Dim ws As New NotesUIWorkspace
  Dim rtitem As NotesRichTextItem
  Dim fpath As Variant
  Dim retflg As Boolean, res As Long, res2 As Integer
  Dim exepath As String, shellpath As String

  REM this holds the executable path
  exepath = String(MAX_FILENAME_LEN, 32)

  REM prompt the user for where to save the attachment
  fpath = ws.SaveFileDialog(False,_
  "Save Attachment and Open", "", "", fname)
  If Isempty(fpath) Then
    detachFileOpen = False
    Exit Function
  End If

  REM detach the file (this function is from the
  REM LS.utilities.BE lib)
  retflg = detachFile(doc, rtname, fname, Cstr(fpath(0)))

  REM use the C API call to find the associated executable
```

```
    res = FindExecutable(Cstr(fpath(0)), "", exepath)

    REM shorten the executable, removing the extra spaces
    exepath = Left$(exepath, Instr(exepath, Chr$(0)) - 1)

    REM prep the string to pass to the shell command
    If Fulltrim(exepath) = "" Then Error 900,_
    "Unable to locate associated program"
    REM open the file with the associated executable
    res2 = Shell(shellpath)

getOut:
  Exit Function
errHandler:
  On Error Goto 0
  Error Err, "(" & Err & ") " & Error$ & " [in detachFileOpen]"
  Resume getOut
End Function
```

The Use `LS.utilities.BE` statement in the Options area script library loads the
LS.utilities.BE library, which is an example of chaining script libraries together. When the
`LS.utilities.FE` script library loads into the `DetachOpen` agent, the `LS.utilities.BE`
Script Library loads as well.

The code in Listing 14-4 uses a C API function call to determine which application executable
is associated with the attached file.

The function prompts the user for the location in which to store the file, and sticks the filename in the dialog box as the default. After choosing the location for the file, the file detaches
to that location using the `detachFile` function from the `LS.utilities.BE` script library.
After successfully detaching the file, the associated executable is determined by using the C
API function loaded in the Declarations area. The returned value is trimmed of extra spaces,
and the file location is concatenated to the executable location, which is passed to the `Shell`
function to launch the file.

Along the way, the necessary objects and variables pass in and out of the functions being
called without any global variables being declared. This is the most efficient way to use functions from various script libraries, especially when chaining the libraries, to ensure there are
no errors at compile or runtime.

Listing 14-5 shows the `detachFile` function, which is in the `LS.utilities.BE` script library.

Listing 14-5: **detachFile Function from LS.utilities.BE**

```
Function detachFile(doc As NotesDocument, rtname As String,_
fname As String, fpath As String) As Boolean
  On Error Goto errHandler
  detachFile = True
  Dim rtitem As NotesRichTextItem
  Dim tmpdir As String
  Dim retflg As String
```

Continued

Listing 14-5 *(continued)*

```
Dim obj As NotesEmbeddedObject
On Error Goto errHandler
If doc.HasEmbedded = False Then Error 900,_
"No Attachments found."

Set rtitem = doc.GetFirstItem(rtname)
If rtitem Is Nothing Then Error 900,_
"Unable to find RT item: " & rtname

If fname = "" Then
  Set obj = rtitem.EmbeddedObjects(0)
Else
  Set obj = rtitem.GetEmbeddedObject(fname)
End If
If obj Is Nothing Or obj.Type <> EMBED_ATTACHMENT Then_
Error 900, "Unable to locate file."

If fpath = "" Then
  tmpdir = Environ("TEMP") & "\SapphireOak"
  retflg = Dir(tmpdir, 16)
  If retflg = "" Then Mkdir tmpdir
  tmpdir = tmpdir & "\"
  fname = obj.Source
  fpath = fpath & fname
  retflg = Dir$(fpath, 0)
  If retflg <> "" Then
    fpath = tmpdir & "DUP"  & Minute(Now) &_
    Second(Now) & "-" & fname
  End If
End If

Call obj.ExtractFile(fpath)

getOut:
  Exit Function
errHandler:
  detachFile = False
  On Error Goto 0
  Error Err, Error$ & " [in detachFile]"
  Resume getOut
End Function
```

This function detaches the attachment to the specified location. If the fname parameter doesn't contain a filename, the first attachment in the specified rich text item is used. If the target location for the file isn't specified in the fpath parameter, a subdirectory is used in the Windows temp directory.

Additional utility functions are provided in the example database — take a look at them to learn more about using script libraries in your applications.

Summary

This chapter introduced you to various techniques for getting the most out of your LotusScript libraries, including the following:

✦ You learned that larger libraries are more useful than smaller ones.

✦ You learned techniques for chaining libraries together.

✦ You were shown some recommended commenting techniques.

For examples of using Java libraries and JavaScript libraries, refer to Chapters 32, 33, and 34 for Java, and Chapters 39 and 40 for JavaScript.

The next section, Section 4, shows you techniques for automating your applications. Chapter 15 begins this section with using formulas in forms and views.

✦   ✦   ✦

Automating Applications

Formulas in Forms and Views

By Rocky Oliver

In This Chapter

Understanding how to use formulas in view events

Learning the various ways to use formulas in forms

The Formula language is extremely powerful, as discussed in Part V. This chapter concentrates on the various places you can use the Formula language in forms and views. You also learn helpful tips and techniques to use the Formula language in your forms and views to get the most out of your applications.

Using Formulas in Forms

Formulas are useful in forms because they provide amazing functionality with little effort. Because the Formula language provides ways to perform commonly needed tasks simply, such as retrieving data with an @DbLookup, the Formula language enables you to add the "r" back in rapid application development. This section introduces you to the many areas that you can use formulas in forms, such as the events of a form, fields on a form, and much more. At the end of this section is an example that uses a few of these areas to create a feature called a keyword table.

Formulas in form events

Formulas can be used to provide functionality in numerous events in a form. Events refer to places in which you can place code that is executed when an event, such as the opening, closing, or saving of a form, occurs. This section covers the ways you can use the Formula language in the events of a form, such as the Window title, and the various query and post events. You can even use the Formula language on the Web through the use of the WebQueryOpen and WebQuerySave events, among others.

Window Title

The Window Title area of a form enables you to specify what appears in the title of the window containing the form when it is open. Most developers keep it simple and place only static text in this area; however, you can use @functions and field names to provide more information to the user. For example, in the Bubba's Shrimp Ordering System application used as an example in Chapter 12, the Order form has the following code in the Window Title area:

```
@If(@IsNewDoc; "New"; CompanyName + "'s") + " Bubba's Shrimp Order"
```

If the document is new, the New Bubba's Shrimp Order appears; if the Order has been saved, the title bar shows the name of the company with an apostrophe and *s* along with Bubba's Shrimp Order. If the company name were Newbs Consulting, for example, the title bar would say Newbs Consulting's Bubba's Shrimp Order.

You can also use @functions to display information, such as when the document was created, the number of responses there are to the document, and so on.

Tip You should always put *something* in the Window Title of a form; otherwise, you see (Untitled), which is neither informative nor attractive.

HTML head contents and HTML body attributes

You use the HTML head contents and HTML body attributes areas to create the HTML head and HTML body sections for your Web-based form. You can place static text here, but you can also place dynamic content here using @functions and field names, and then concatenate it together so it's a text string at runtime. Suppose, for example, that you have a form that you don't want cached. The form uses a Cascaded Style Sheet (CSS) from another database in the same directory. You could place this in the HTML head contents area of a form to prevent it from being cached and to specify where the CSS file is stored, as shown in the following code:

```
{<META HTTP-EQUIV="Pragma" CONTENT="no-cache">}+
@NewLine + {<link REL="StyleSheet" TYPE="text/css"
HREF="} +
dspHome + {/main.styles.css">}
```

The `Pragma` and `no-cache` portions of the string prevent this form from being cached in the user's browser. The stylesheet link uses the contents of the dspHome field to create a path to the `main.styles.css` file, which is a shared resource in the Home database of this application.

WebQueryOpen and WebQuerySave

You also use the `WebQueryOpen` and `WebQuerySave` events when creating Web-based forms. These events are used to execute code in a Web-based form (Web) right before (query) a form is loaded (open), or right before it is saved. You can use `@Command([ToolsRunMacro])` or `@Command([RunAgent])` in this area to specify the agents to run; however, many developers don't realize that this area can hold other @functions as well. You could, for example, have different agents that run based on the role of the authenticated user. That type of code would look something like this:

```
agentname := @If(@Contains(@UserRoles; "[Administrator]");
"admin.invoice.WQO"; "user.invoice.WQO");
@Command([RunAgent]; agentname)
```

In the preceding code, the @Contains function is used to check the list of roles in which the user is a member to see if she is an administrator. If the user is an administrator, the agent named `admin.invoice.WQO` is used; otherwise, the user is assumed to be a normal user and the `user.invoice.WQO` agent runs for the `WebQueryOpen` event.

Tip Name your agents to make attributes about them easily identifiable. The names used in the preceding `WebQueryOpen`/`WebQuerySave` event example, for instance, are broken down by role (admin or user), the form name (invoice), and whether it is a `WebQueryOpen` (WQO) or `WebQuerySave` (WQS) agent.

Target frame

The target frame area indicates the frame where the form should load. This can be extremely useful if you have a button or some other action that loads a form into another frame in a frameset, you can list the frame where the form should load in the target frame area and the form will load there without any additional coding. Like the previous areas, this area can contain static text or a formula that evaluates to a string, which should be the name of a frame.

onHelp

If a form is loaded in the Notes client, the code in the onHelp event executes when the user presses the F1 key. This is especially helpful if you take the time to create a help database for your application. You can extend the usefulness of your help database by adding context-sensitive help to your application by using the onHelp event in conjunction with @Command([OpenHelpDocument]). Take a look at the following code:

```
dbserver := @Subset(@DbName; 1);
dbname := @FileDir(@Subset(@DbName; -1)) + "MyHelp.nsf";
@Command([OpenHelpDocument]; server : dbname;
"HelpDocsByKey"; "Order")
```

The preceding code assumes the following:

✦ That your help database is named MyHelp.nsf

✦ That the help database is in the same directory as your application database

✦ That you have created a help document in your help database for the Order form using the name of the form as the help document key

When the user presses the F1 key, the code executes, and finds the help document for the Order form in the HelpDocsByKey view, and opens it in a help window.

New Feature   The onHelp event is new with Notes/Domino 6.

Form events

There are really two groups of form events — the "normal" form events that Domino developers know and love (such as QueryOpen, QuerySave, and so on), and three new events that were previously used for JavaScript only, onLoad, onUnload, and onSubmit. Let's take a quick look at these events and discuss how they can be used with the Formula language.

onLoad, onUnload, onSubmit

These events are traditionally JavaScript events that were previously used for Web browser-based applications only. Notes/Domino 6 now provides a couple of nice new features. The first is the ability to use the Formula language as well as JavaScript in these events. The second is the ability to actually store two sets of code in the same vent — code that is executed in the Notes client, and code that is executed in the Web browser client.

New Feature   The ability to write client-specific code in these events is new in Notes/Domino 6.

Normal form events

Although developers use the normal form events (QueryOpen, PostOpen, QueryRecalc, QuerySave, PostSave, QueryClose, and so on) for LotusScript, many developers are unaware that they can also use the Formula language in these events. You may, for example, want to set other fields right before the document is refreshed. Most people write lines and lines of LotusScript code to do so, and fail to realize that a simple line or two of Formula language in the `QueryRecalc` event accomplishes the same thing. For instance, say you wanted to set a field named LastOpened with the current date/time when a document is opened. The following code, contained in the `PostOpen` event, accomplishes this:

```
LotusScript
Sub Postopen(Source As Notesuidocument)
  Dim doc As NotesDocument
  Set doc = Source.Document
  doc.LastOpened = Now
End Sub
```

```
Formula
@SetField("LastOpened"; @Now)
```

Both versions of the code accomplish the same thing. As you can see, the Formula code is much shorter, and this is a simple example. There are many other examples where the amount of code written would be vastly different, because the Formula language makes so many tasks much, much simpler. Therefore it is a good idea to remember that you can use the Formula language in form events.

Event execution order

Now that you know you can use the Formula language in both the "on" events (such as `onLoad`, and `onSubmit`) and "normal" form events, it may be confusing to figure out which event executes first between the similar events. For instance, `onLoad` is similar to `PostOpen`, `onUnload` is similar to `QueryClose`, and `onSubmit` is similar to `QuerySave`. But how do you know which one to use, and when?

One of the first things to consider when determining which event to use is the execution order. When, exactly, does `onLoad` execute when compared to `PostOpen`? The following lists the execution order for the on and normal events that are related.

When opening:

1. `QueryOpen`

2. `PostOpen`

3. `OnLoad`

When saving:

1. `QuerySave`

2. `OnSubmit`

3. `PostSave`

When closing:

1. `QueryClose`

2. `OnUnload`

It is interesting that the on events fire after the normal events when opening and saving, but the `onSubmit` event fires between the `QuerySave` and `PostSave` events, because there is no

Web equivalent of PostSave, so the onSubmit is actually occurring after the QuerySave, but before the actual save of the document. In reality it is easiest to think of the events to be related thusly:

- ✦ onLoad is functionally equivalent to PostOpen when used in the Notes client.

- ✦ onSubmit is functionally equivalent to QuerySave when used in the Notes client.

- ✦ onUnload is functionally equivalent to QueryClose when used in the Notes client.

How do you know when to use the on event, and when to use the normal event equivalent? The best rule of thumb is that if you are creating a form that is used in the Notes client and a Web browser, use the on event equivalent. And take that a step further; if possible, use the Common JavaScript language entry in the Domino Designer. Why? Because code added using Common JavaScript executes in both client types, which enables you to write and maintain one set of code that is used in both clients. But don't worry if you can't do this; you can still use the same event in both clients, and add code for the Notes client under Client, and code that runs in the Web browser under Web in the event in Domino Designer.

Formulas in fields

The Formula language is used frequently in fields — in fact, it's often the only language used in fields. The Formula language enables you to do many things by using well-placed code in the various areas capable of holding a formula in the field object.

Note   Fields can use only @functions. You can't use @Commands in field formulas.

The areas in which you can place code in a field are largely based on the edit type of the field (editable, computed, computed for display, and computed when composed). You must know when these different edit types are evaluated so that you can choose the right edit type for your fields. Each edit type is covered in the upcoming sections. The formulas placed in fields should result in a value for the field.

Editable field event formulas

A user can modify editable fields. Editable fields have five formula events — default value, translation, and validation. Placing formulas in any or all of these events is optional. These formula events are described as follows:

- ✦ **Default value:** Any formula in this event is evaluated when a form is first composed and provides an initial value for the formula. If code is omitted from this event, the initial value of the field is blank.

- ✦ **Translation:** The formula placed in this event is executed whenever the document is refreshed, and it is executed before the validation formula. The translation formula transforms the value in the field (affect some change to it). The result of the formula is placed as the value of the field.

- ✦ **Validation:** The formula placed in this event validates the values of the field. @Failure returns an error message if the field does not pass validation, and @Success if it does pass validation.

✦ **Input Enabled:** The formula placed in this event enables or disables the field from being edited by the end user. The formula entered here must return a value of True (enabled) or False (disabled). Fields using this feature must use the Native OS display type, and they must not be a rich text or rich text lite field.

✦ **HTML Attributes:** The formula placed in this event is used to set the HTML attributes of the field. HTML attributes are normally added to a field in one of two ways — through the use of this area, or through the HTML tab of the Field properties box. Incidentally, the HTML tab of the Field properties box is the more commonly used area for HTML attributes of the two.

In the ND6 Form & View Formula Examples database (ND6 FV Formula Examples.nsf) is a form called 15.01 Translation Formula Example. It contains a single field called Phone, and this field has a translation formula that takes the contents of the field and formats it as a United States seven or ten digit phone number. The formula automatically detects extensions and formats them appropriately. This field also has a validation formula that makes sure the field isn't empty before the document is saved. The translation formula for the Phone field is shown in Listing 15-1.

Listing 15-1: **Phone Field Translation Formula**

```
REM {This tests the contents of the Phone field to see if it
is already formatted correctly as a 7 or 10 digit US phone
number. If it is, then the number is left alone.};
@If(@Matches(@Left(Phone; 14); "{(}{0-9}{0-9}{0-9}{)}{ }{0-
9}{0-9}{0-9}{-}{0-9}{0-9}{0-9}{0-9}") |
    @Matches(@Left(Phone; 8); "{0-9}{0-9}{0-9}{-}{0-9}{0-
9}{0-9}{0-9}");
    @Return(Phone);
    "");

REM {These characters are removed from the string so that it
can be formatted correctly};
letters := "A" : "B" : "C" : "D" : "E" : "F" : "G" : "H" :
"I" : "J" : "K" : "L" : "M" : "N" : "O" : "P" : "Q" : "R" :
"S" : "T" : "U" : "V" : "W" : "X" : "Y" : "Z";

symbols := "~" : "`" : "!" : "@" : "#" : "$" : "%" : "^" :
"&" : "*" : "(" : ")" : "_" : "-" : "+" : "=" : "{" : "[" :
"}" : "]" : "|" : "\\" : ":" : ";" : "'" : "\"" : "," : "<" :
"." : ">" : "/" : "?";
transform := @Trim(@ReplaceSubstring(@UpperCase(Phone);
letters : symbols; ""));

REM {The transformed string of numbers is now broken down.
The string length is checked and any "stray" characters are
placed used as an extension.};
phlength := @Length(transform);
ext := @If(phlength < 7; transform;
        phlength > 10; @Right(transform; phlength - 10);
```

```
          phlength > 7 & phlength < 10; @Right(transform;
phlength - 7);
          "");

REM {if there is an extension, get the base phone number from
it};
transform := @If(ext = ""; transform; @Left(transform; ext));

REM {Get the area code and the base 7 digits};
base := @Right(transform; 7);
ac := @Left(transform; base);

REM {now string it all together - this is the value
returned};
@Trim(@If(ac = ""; ""; "(" + ac + ") ") +
      @If(base = ""; ""; @Left(base; 3) + "-" + @Right(base;
4)) +
      @If(ext = ""; ""; " EXT " + ext))
```

The first @If statement in this code uses @Matches to check the value to see whether it is already formatted. The code checks for seven or ten digit formatting, without any extensions.

The next few lines remove any non-numeric values from the field. You may think that you can use the @TextToNumber function to do this more cleanly, but you can't — if the string begins with a character instead of a number, it doesn't translate the number. It's more straightforward to use a list of all characters and symbols as a basis for removal from the value using @Trim and @ReplaceSubstring.

The next section of code checks for an extension. The check occurs as follows:

✦ If the value is less than seven characters long, the whole thing is treated as an extension.

✦ If the value is greater than ten, the extra characters on the right are treated as an extension.

✦ If the value is greater than seven but less than ten, the characters to the right of the first seven characters are treated as an extension.

✦ If the value is exactly seven or ten characters long, there is no extension.

If there is an extension, the phone number (seven or ten characters long) is extracted from the whole value.

The base number (right-most seven characters) and the area code (left-most three characters) are broken out.

The whole thing — area code, base number, and extension — is strung together where appropriate, and the resulting value is returned as the value of the Phone field.

Computed formulas

Three types of computed fields exist: computed, computed when composed, and computed for display.

✦ **Computed**: Computed fields reevaluate each time the document is refreshed. The result of the formula is saved to the document when the document is saved. Computed fields are powerful, and you can use them to modify the values of other fields.

✦ **Computed when composed:** Computed when composed fields evaluate when the document is first composed, and then never reevaluate. The resulting value of the formula is saved to the document if the document is saved. Computed when composed fields often show values of fields that are set programmatically, or are used for static fields such as creation date, composed by, and so on.

✦ **Computed for display:** Computed for display fields are similar to Computed when composed fields in that they evaluate only when a document is first opened, but not during subsequent refreshes of the document. The difference is that the values of Computed for display fields are never saved to the document when the document is saved.

Tip Although Computed for display fields are not saved to the document if/when the document is saved, the item *does* have a programmatic value while the document is loaded into the UI. This means that the value(s) of the Computed for display fields are available to other bits of code. You could, for example, place an @DbLookup for keyword values into a Computed for display field and use it as the choices for a keyword. When the document is saved, the values in the Computed for display field are not saved to the document.

Computed text

Computed text isn't a field, but it's a useful place to use @functions. Computed text is what it sounds like — a chunk of text whose value is dependent upon what is returned from a formula. The @functions that are usable in computed text are those that return a value — you can't use any @functions that interact with the user, such as @Prompt. Computed text also is useful when used as Pass-Thru HTML, as you can have dynamic HTML content in computed text that is computed when the form is loaded.

Keyword choice

All the various keyword types — check box, radio button, dialog list, list box, and combo box — can get their values from at least two places: a static list that is entered into the properties box for the keyword field, or the list can be derived from a formula. One simple thing to do is create a Computed for display field that computes using an @DbLookup or @DbColumn formula. The resulting list is displayed in the keyword field by entering the name of this field as the formula for the keyword choices. You might do this because you can also use that same field to set the default value for the keyword field by using the field name with @SubSet.

Hide-when formulas

You can hide most elements and text in a form using hide-when formulas. When you use hide-when formulas, if the formula evaluates to True, it hides the element or text. Some developers get confused by this and think that True means to show the element, and the opposite is true. Make sure you keep this in mind when working with hide-when formulas.

Edit field examples

The following example shows off a few of the edit types of fields, and a unique use of a keyword field. This example is a columnar table of values that is editable by the end user. The end user can add, modify, or delete rows from the table. This example uses @functions only — no LotusScript. Figure 15-1 shows the keyword table with some data in it.

15.02. Keyword Table Example

This example shows off a variety of ways of using the Formula language in a form to achieve a novel and useful result. In this example a columnar table of values is presented to the user. The user can easily add, modify, or delete values from the table. This entire example uses the Formula language only - no LotusScript, JavaScript, etc.

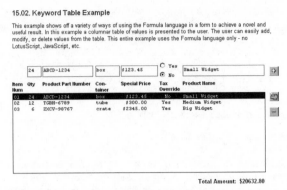

Total Amount: $20632.80

Figure 15-1: The keyword table is an innovative use of fields and functions, providing powerful functionality to your users.

The keyword table is used as follows: The user enters the desired values in the editable fields along the top of the table, and then clicks the plus button to add the new entry to the table below. If the user wants to modify an existing row, she clicks the row, which places the row's values into the editable fields. The user then changes the desired values, and uses the modify button (the button above the minus button) to update the selected row. The minus button removes the selected row from the table. If you remove a row from the table, the item number (the first column of the table) is automatically updated to correctly reflect the row numbers.

General form design

Figure 15-2 shows the form in design mode.

Hidden Text

Form T	CWC - the form name
AllowedAuthors	CWC - the user that composed the document and the [AllAccess] role
OrderEntry_set T	C - sets the entry fields when user selects an order entry, since the Order_Key field is set to refresh the document when the user selects a row
NumList T	CWC - contains the item number list for the table
OrderTable T	CWC - The OrderTable field holds the actual data, delimited as indicated below: <spaces>-quantity-<spaces>-partnum-<spaces>-container-<spaces>-s_price-<spaces>-taxovrd-<spaces>-prodname

15.02. Keyword Table Example

This example shows off a variety of ways of using the Formula language in a form to achieve a novel and useful result. In this example a columnar table of values is presented to the user. The user can easily add, modify, or delete values from the table. This entire example uses the Formula language only - no LotusScript, JavaScript, etc.

Qty$	PartNumEntry T	tainerEn	S_PriceEntry	OvrdEnt	ProdNameEntry T	
Item Num	Qty	Product Part Number	Con- tainer	Special Price	Tax Override	Product Name

Order_Key

Total Amount:
ReqPayAmount #

Figure 15-2: The Keyword Table form uses various field types to provide the keyword table functionality.

Font widths: An explanation

Two types of fonts exist: fixed-width, also known as monospace, and variable-width, also known as proportional. Proportional fonts were invented to make text easier to read, because they adjust the space allotted for each character based on the actual width of the character. Monospace fonts use the same width for every character. Take a look at the following lines:

American Football is a game of inches. (proportional)

```
American Football is a game of inches. (monospace)
```

These two lines contain the same number of characters, but the monospace line (in this case Courier New) is much longer than the proportional line (in this case Arial Narrow). The i in a proportional font is narrower than the w, and in a strange twist, the size of the space character is variable, depending on the characters to either side of the space. This makes it extremely difficult to use proportional fonts for presenting columnar data — the columns appear to snake because the spaces used are not the same size on each line. Monospace fonts, however, are all the same width — an i, a w, and a " " (space character) are all the same width. That's why Courier New was used as the font for the keyword table, which is presented using the Order_Key Listbox field. Spaces are used between the values to space out the data into columns.

The fields at the top of the form, above the title, are hidden. If you look at the form in Designer, you see that the hidden area is green — this is to make it easily identifiable as hidden. The hidden fields are also in a table, so that comments about each field can be entered, making it easier to know what the fields are doing. The comments also include the edit type of each field — CWC = Computed when composed, CFD = Computed for display, and C = Computed.

Order_Key keyword field

The keyword table is possible because of a couple of things: a synonym for keyword values, and a monospace, or fixed-width font — in this case Courier New.

The Order_Key Listbox field is populated from the OrderTable field. The actual table data is stored in the OrderTable field, which is a multivalue text field. The format of the data in the keyword table is as follows:

```
<spaces>~quantity~<spaces>~partnum~<spaces>~container~
<spaces>~s_price~<spaces>~taxovrd~<spaces>
```

A tilde (~) is the delimiter for the values in the rows. Spaces are added before and after the values to provide the columns; however, you can't use actual spaces, because any @Trim used against the values removes the spaces, destroying the columnar presentation. A holder character represents the spaces — in this case, the pound sign (#) represents a space. To present data in a user-friendly fashion, you must use the keyword choices formula, which appears as follows:

```
numlist + @ReplaceSubstring(OrderTable; "#" : "~"; " ") + "|" + OrderTable
```

This formula uses @ReplaceSubstring to replace all pound signs and tildes with spaces, and then the numlist field contents are added to the result — this is what is presented to the user. The actual values of the OrderTable field are concatenated to the user-friendly version of the data using a pipe symbol (|), which keyword fields use to delineate between a synonym and a value. When the user clicks one of the user-friendly rows, the keyword `table` returns the value represented by the selected user-friendly row. This is the value that is used by the form's code when working with the data.

Note   If you add lists of values, the two lists are concatenated together, pair-wise, to create a third list. Adding A : B : C to 1 : 2 : 3 creates a new list of A1 : B2 : C3. This is how the `numlist`, the user-friendly rows, and the data rows are concatenated together for the keyword choices.

There are two properties of the `Order_Key` keyword field that are enabled: `Refresh Fields on Keyword Change` and `Refresh Choices on Document Refresh`. The first property, `Refresh Fields on Keyword Change`, causes other fields on the form to be recomputed whenever the user selects a row in the Order_Key. One of the fields that is refreshed is the OrderEntry_Set field. This field populates all of the fields used for data entry with the data from the selected row. If the `Refresh Fields on Keyword Change` property were not enabled, this data would not be populated.

The Refresh Choices on Document Refresh field causes the keyword table to regather the values from the OrderTable and redisplay them whenever the document is refreshed. If this property were not enabled, the user would not see additions, deletions, or modifications to the values in the OrderTable field, thereby rendering the keyword table useless.

The buttons in this form — Add, Modify, and Delete — are all action hotspots assigned to graphics stored as image resources in the database.

Add button

Now that you understand how data is presented, examining the Add (plus) button code offers insight into how the keyword table works (see Listing 15-2).

Listing 15-2: Add Button for Keyword Table

```
REM {Constants for max values or lengths of fields in error
checking (below)};
maxval_QuantityEntry := 999999;
maxlen_PartNumEntry := 15;
maxlen_ContainerEntry := 3;
maxval_S_PriceEntry := 999999;
maxlen_ProdNameEntry := 25;

REM {Error checking for entry fields.};
@If( QuantityEntry = "" | !@IsNumber( QuantityEntry) |
QuantityEntry > maxval_QuantityEntry; @Return(@Prompt([Ok];
"Entry Error"; "You must enter a valid Ordered Quantity for
the item that is less than " + @Text( maxval_QuantityEntry +
1) + " ."));
        PartNumEntry = "" | @Length( PartNumEntry ) >
maxlen_PartNumEntry; @Return(@Prompt([Ok]; "Entry Error";
"You must enter a Product Part Number for the item that is
less than " + @Text( maxlen_PartNumEntry + 1) + " characters
long."));
```

Continued

Listing 15-2 *(continued)*

```
    S_PriceEntry = "" | !@IsNumber( S_PriceEntry) |
S_PriceEntry > maxval_S_PriceEntry; @Return(@Prompt([Ok];
"Entry Error"; "You must enter a valid Special Price for the
item that is less than " + @Text( maxval_S_PriceEntry + 1) +
" ."));
    ProdNameEntry = "" | @Length( ProdNameEntry ) >
maxlen_ProdNameEntry ; @Return(@Prompt([Ok]; "Entry Error";
"You must enter a Product Name for the item that is less than
" + @Text( maxlen_ProdNameEntry + 1) + " characters long."));
    "" ) ;

REM {Set values for Item Number column.};
lastnumber_1 := @If( NumList = ""; 0; @TextToNumber( @Subset(
NumList; -1 ))) + 1;
lastnumber := @If( lastnumber_1 < 10; "0" +
@Text(lastnumber_1); @Text(lastnumber_1));
itemnum := @Trim( NumList :  lastnumber );

REM {Entry conversion};
quantity := @Trim(@Text( QuantityEntry ));
partnum := @Trim( PartNumEntry );
container := @Trim( ContainerEntry );
s_price := @Text( S_PriceEntry; "C" );
taxovrd := @Trim( TaxOvrdEntry );
prodname := @Trim( ProdNameEntry );

REM {Entry concatenation};
entry := @Repeat("#"; (4 - @Length(quantity)))+ "~" +
quantity + "~" + "#" + "~" + partnum + "~" + @Repeat("#"; (16
@Length(partnum))) + "~" + container + "~" + @Repeat("#";
(15 - @Length(s_price) - @Length(container))) +  "~" +
s_price + "~" + @Repeat("#"; (6 - @Length(taxovrd)))  +
"~" + taxovrd + "~" +@Repeat("#"; 2) + "~" + prodname;

REM {Addition of entry to field};
@SetField("OrderTable"; @Trim(@Unique(OrderTable : entry)));
@SetField( "NumList"; @Subset(itemnum;
@Elements(OrderTable)));

REM {Compute Pay Amount, set field};
qty := @TextToNumber(@Word(OrderTable; "~"; 2));
price := @TextToNumber(@Word(OrderTable; "~"; 8));
subtot := qty * price;
total := @Sum(subtot);
@SetField("ReqPayAmount"; total);

REM {Refresh it all};
@SetField("QuantityEntry";"");
@SetField("PartNumEntry";"");
```

```
@SetField("ContainerEntry";"");
@SetField("S_PriceEntry";"");
@SetField("TaxOvrdEntry";"No");
@SetField("ProdNameEntry";"");
@Command([ViewRefreshFields])
```

The first few variable declarations define the maximum width of the text fields, and the maximum value for the numeric fields. These variables are placed at the beginning of the code so that it's easy for you to make adjustments to the column and value sizes without finding it in the code every time.

```
maxval_QuantityEntry := 999999;
maxlen_PartNumEntry := 15;
maxlen_ContainerEntry := 3;
maxval_S_PriceEntry := 999999;
maxlen_ProdNameEntry := 25;
```

The next chunk of code validates the fields to ensure they are the right length, values, and so on, based on the variables set in the previous chunk.

```
@If( QuantityEntry = "" | !@IsNumber( QuantityEntry) |
QuantityEntry > maxval_QuantityEntry; @Return(@Prompt([Ok];
"Entry Error"; "You must enter a valid Ordered Quantity for
the item that is less than " + @Text( maxval_QuantityEntry +
1) + " ."));
        PartNumEntry = "" | @Length( PartNumEntry ) >
maxlen_PartNumEntry; @Return(@Prompt([Ok]; "Entry Error";
"You must enter a Product Part Number for the item that is
less than " + @Text( maxlen_PartNumEntry + 1) + " characters
long."));
        S_PriceEntry = "" | !@IsNumber( S_PriceEntry) |
S_PriceEntry > maxval_S_PriceEntry; @Return(@Prompt([Ok];
"Entry Error"; "You must enter a valid Special Price for the
item that is less than " + @Text( maxval_S_PriceEntry + 1) +
" ."));
        ProdNameEntry = "" | @Length( ProdNameEntry ) >
maxlen_ProdNameEntry ; @Return(@Prompt([Ok]; "Entry Error";
"You must enter a Product Name for the item that is less than
" + @Text( maxlen_ProdNameEntry + 1) + " characters long."));
        "" ) ;
```

The next chunk sets the NumList field. If a row is being added to the table, the next sequential number is added to the list. If the number is less than ten, a zero is prepended to the number to keep it two-digit, which keeps the column sizes correct. The NumList field values are then concatenated to the OrderTable presentation list in the Order_Key field.

```
lastnumber_1 := @If( NumList = ""; 0; @TextToNumber( @Subset(
NumList; -1 ))) + 1;
lastnumber := @If( lastnumber_1 < 10; "0" +
@Text(lastnumber_1); @Text(lastnumber_1));
itemnum := @Trim( NumList :   lastnumber );
```

Then the values entered by the user are all converted to text, because the OrderTable and Order_Key fields are text fields. The formatting option of the @Text function is used to format the S_PriceEntry value as a currency field.

```
quantity := @Trim(@Text( QuantityEntry ));
partnum := @Trim( PartNumEntry );
container := @Trim( ContainerEntry );
s_price := @Text( S_PriceEntry; "C" );
taxovrd := @Trim( TaxOvrdEntry );
prodname := @Trim( ProdNameEntry );
```

After all the values are converted, they are concatenated with the space padding that provides the columnar formatting. The number of spaces is computed by subtracting the length of the value from the value in the corresponding size variable at the beginning of the code. The pound sign is used as a placeholder for spaces, and is replaced with actual spaces in the Order_Key keyword field.

```
entry := @Repeat("#"; (4 - @Length(quantity)))+ "~" +
quantity + "~" + "#" + "~" + partnum + "~" + @Repeat("#"; (16
@Length(partnum))) + "~" + container + "~" + @Repeat("#";
(15 - @Length(s_price) - @Length(container))) + "~" +
s_price + "~" + @Repeat("#"; (6 - @Length(taxovrd)))  +
"~" + taxovrd + "~" +@Repeat("#"; 2) + "~" + prodname;
```

After formatting the new entry, it is added to the OrderTable field. Additionally, the updated number list is added to the NumList field.

```
@SetField("OrderTable"; @Trim(@Unique(OrderTable : entry)));
@SetField( "NumList"; @Subset(itemnum;
@Elements(OrderTable)));
```

The quantity values and price values are gathered from the OrderTable field, are converted to numeric values, and are multiplied together. If two lists are multiplied together, the multiplication occurs pair-wise, resulting in a new list of numbers of each product of the multiplication. After the values are multiplied, the resulting list is added together using @Sum. The total is placed in the ReqPayAmount field.

```
qty := @TextToNumber(@Word(OrderTable; "~"; 2));
price := @TextToNumber(@Word(OrderTable; "~"; 8));
subtot := qty * price;
total := @Sum(subtot);
@SetField("ReqPayAmount"; total);
```

All the entry fields are set back to empty values, and the entire form is refreshed so the changes are visible.

```
@SetField("QuantityEntry";"");
@SetField("PartNumEntry";"");
@SetField("ContainerEntry";"");
@SetField("S_PriceEntry";"");
@SetField("TaxOvrdEntry";"No");
@SetField("ProdNameEntry";"");
@Command([ViewRefreshFields])
```

Now that you understand the Add button, let's take a look at the Modify and Delete buttons.

Modify button

The Modify button code is identical to the Add button code, with the exception of the following line:

```
@SetField("OrderTable"; @Unique(@Trim(@Replace(OrderTable; Order_Key;
entry))));
```

Instead of adding the values as a new entry, the @Trim and @Replace functions replace the selected row with the new values. This gives the appearance of modifying the values of the selected row.

Delete button

The Delete button is quite small compared to the Add and Modify buttons, as shown in Listing 15-3.

Listing 15-3: **Delete Button**

```
REM {Error checking for deletion fields.};
@If(Order_Key = ""; @Return(@Prompt([Ok]; "Entry Error"; "You
must select an entry for deletion.")); "");

@SetField("OrderTable"; @Trim(@Replace(OrderTable; Order_Key;
"")));

REM {Reset number values for Item Number column.};
@SetField( "NumList"; @If(OrderTable = "";"";@Subset( NumList
; @Elements( OrderTable ))));

REM {Compute Pay Amount, set field};
qty := @TextToNumber(@Word(OrderTable; "~"; 2));
price := @TextToNumber(@Word(OrderTable; "~"; 8));
subtot := qty * price;
total := @If(@IsError(subtot);0;@Sum(subtot));
@SetField("ReqPayAmount"; total);

@Command([ViewRefreshFields])
```

This code does five things:

1. The code makes sure that the user has selected a row (value) in the Order_Key field.

2. The selected row is removed from the OrderTable field using @Trim and @Replace.

3. The code resets the NumList by removing the last number from the list by using @Subset.

4. The total is recomputed and is set into the ReqPayAmount field.

5. The form is refreshed to show the changes.

Miscellaneous uses

The Formula language in forms has some other miscellaneous uses. Most are related to embedded elements in forms. This section discusses these miscellaneous uses, and provides some tips along the way.

Computed section titles

You can compute section titles in a form with a formula. You can have a section in which the title is based on a field value, an @function, or both. For instance, you have a section on a form for Approvals, and have the section set to Auto-collapse section when the form is opened. You use the ApprovalStatus field in the title of the section so the user knows the status of the document's approval process without needing to expand the section.

Computed subforms

You know that you can embed a subform into a form; but not many people know that you can base which subform is used on a formula. The formula should result in the name of the subform to be used.

Note Don't get too crazy using computed subforms. Subforms, especially computed subforms, have a substantial speed penalty for using them. Sometimes it makes sense to use a computed subform, but use them only when the design of the application calls for it.

Computed embedded views

You can determine the view that will be embedded when the form is loaded by using a formula for the embedded view name. Make sure that the formula you use resolves to a view name or view alias. This can be useful if you want to use the same view template for multiple views. You create a computed view formula that, based on conditions you define, loads the appropriate view.

Tip Although this section talks about computed views, you can also use computed folders. In fact, any place in code that references using a view, you can also use a formula, unless otherwise noted.

Computed single category value for an embedded view

If you use an embedded view, you can reduce the documents that appear in the view to a single category by specifying a string, a field name, or a formula that results in a string that matches one of the categories in a view. If you use a single category value, you must categorize the first column of the embedded view. Additionally, that first categorized column won't appear in the embedded view.

Cross-Reference You can see an example of an embedded view with a show single category value in the Bubba's Shrimp Ordering System Example database in Chapter 12.

Other ways exist for you to use the Formula language with your forms; you've been introduced to the most common ways, with a couple of useful examples to illustrate these uses. Views are another area in which the Formula language is useful.

Formulas in Views

Formulas are the predominant language in views. Although there are events in views that can hold other languages, the language of the columns in a view is the Formula language.

Formulas in view events

A number of events and areas in a view exist where formulas provide functionality.

View Selection

The View Selection formula is where you define what documents are going to appear in your views. The formula in this area begins with a SELECT statement, and then is comprised of a combination of field/value pairs that narrow the documents that are going to appear. One field that you should use in most of your View Selection formulas is the Form field. You should refine the documents that appear in your view by the form used to create them (or the form formula in the document), because it makes your views more efficient.

Tip If most of your views display smaller subsets of documents based on the Form item, you should select the Optimize Document Table Map property of the database. This property makes views that use Form= in the View Selection formula more efficient.

You can also specify that response documents appear in your view by adding @AllDescendants to your SELECT statement using a Boolean OR symbol, which is a Pipe symbol (|). The following View Selection formula, for example, shows all documents based on the Main Topic form, and all responses to those documents:

```
SELECT Form = "Main Topic" | @AllDescendants
```

Tip If you've been a Domino developer for a long time, you may have been taught to use @IsResponseDoc to show responses in a view. But @IsResponseDoc is much less efficient than @AllDescendants for View Selection formulas. @IsResponseDoc causes the view to index all response documents in the database, while @AllDescendants causes the view to index only those responses related to the documents in the view.

Form formula

The form formula area enables you to override the form associated with the documents in a view, and use the form specified in the form formula area. You can use a formula to determine the form to use, as long as the formula results in a valid form name. You can use this event in the Notes client and on the Web.

One use for the Form formula is to use a different form for a document based on the role of a user. For instance, you may load one form for administrators that provides additional features and functionality for working with the document, while the standard user is presented the same document without the administrative functionality.

HelpRequest

The code in the HelpRequest event is executed when the user presses the F1 key in the Notes client while the view is loaded. HelpRequest is useful for providing context-sensitive help in your applications. This feature only works in the Notes client.

Note Take a look at the onHelp section in this chapter for an example of using the context-sensitive help feature.

Target Frame events

The Target Frame (single click) and Target Frame (double click) events indicate the frame where a document is loaded whenever the user single- or double-clicks the document. You can use these two events in the Notes client and on the Web.

Normal view events

While developers use the normal view events (QueryOpen, PostOpen, QueryRecalc, QueryPaste, PostPaste, QueryClose, and so on) for LotusScript, many developers are unaware that they can also use the Formula language in these events. You may, for example, want to set other fields right before the document is pasted by placing code in the QueryPaste event. Most people write LotusScript to do so, and fail to realize that a simple line or two of Formula language in the QueryPaste event accomplishes the same thing.

Column formulas

Column formulas are where the power of views exists. Columns contain one of three things: basic document information (authors, created date), field values, or formulas. The formulas entered in a column are evaluated for each document in the view to present a value. You can reference items on the documents in the view by item name, which is why column formulas are often used to present useful data that isn't stored in the document. You should, for example, concatenate multiple values together for return from an @DbLookup. You can do this at the form level in a hidden field, or you can do it in the view using a column formula.

A useful example of concatenating data for presentation in a view is for contact information databases. These databases typically have a form that captures address information such as address, city, state, and zip code. It's useful to present this information in a view. To do so, you could use the following formula:

```
Address : (City + ", " + State + " " + ZIP)
```

Set the multivalue separator in the column properties to New Line, and set the rows height in the View properties to four (or more) lines. Make sure that you also select the Shrink Rows to Content property, as shown in Figure 15-3.

Another use for column formulas is to provide Pass-Thru HTML for presentation of information on a Web page. You can, for example, provide HTML in a column that presents a check box for each document in the view.

Cross-Reference Column formulas are useful when presenting HTML or XML information in a Web application. Refer to Chapters 48 through 51 for numerous examples of using columns for XML presentation. In particular, pay attention to the GetXMLQuotesWithViewInfo view. It has some cool Pass-Thru HTML that calls other views to generate links.

You can use columns to present other types of interesting information as well. You can, for example, present graphics in a view from your image resources by setting the column to Display Values as Icons and the specifying the name of the icon. This can even be a formula, as long as it results in the name of an image resource.

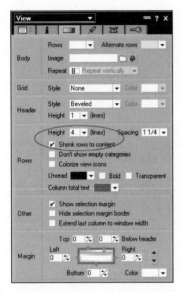

Figure 15-3: The third tab of the View properties box is busy. The highlighted area is where you can set the number of lines to display per row (1 to 9). Below that you can select Shrink Rows to Content to keep your view attractive (and readable).

Hide-when formulas

New Feature

Hide-when formulas for columns are a new feature in Notes/Domino 6.

Hide-when formulas are now applicable to columns. You can specify a hide-when formula, and when the condition evaluates `True`, the column is hidden to the user. The hide-when formula is evaluated as the view loads, but is not reevaluated until the view is loaded again.

Note

Hiding a column from a user is *not* a security measure. It is simply a way to present the relevant information to the user. The only way to truly secure information is through ReaderNames fields on a document, or encryption for a view.

You can use hide-when formulas for a view column to customize information for a user. You may, for example, have a column that displays one set of figures for a sales manager, and a different set of figures for accounting in an order application.

Summary

The Formula language is powerful, especially when combined with forms and views. This chapter introduced you to many ways you can use the Formula language in forms:

- ✦ Form events
- ✦ Various ways you can use formulas in fields
- ✦ How to use formulas with other elements

You were also introduced to the ways that you can use formulas in views:

- ✦ View selection formulas
- ✦ Column formulas

You can now work with formulas with more confidence in your applications. Chapter 16 explores using actions and buttons, which allow your users to execute code when clicked.

✦   ✦   ✦

Actions, Buttons, and Action Hotspots

By Rocky Oliver

◆ ◆ ◆ ◆

In This Chapter

Learning about action
buttons in views

Learning about action
buttons in forms

Learning about buttons
and action hotspots

Learning about
new features

◆ ◆ ◆ ◆

A user can execute a predefined set of code by clicking an action button (otherwise known as an action), a button, or an action hotspot. Actions are available in forms and views, while buttons and action hotspots are available in forms and pages.

Each item is an agent that you call by clicking it instead of choosing it from a menu. What you can do in an agent, you can do in an action or button. You can use each of these items in various ways, many of which are described in this chapter. Actions and buttons can contain simple actions, LotusScript, formulas, and JavaScript. Additionally, in Notes/Domino 6 you can place client-specific code in each — one set of code for the Notes client, and one set of code for Web browsers.

New Feature

Notes/Domino 6 now enables you to place client-specific code in actions and buttons. You can have @functions that fire in the Notes client and JavaScript that fires in a Web browser — all in the same action or button.

Most examples in this chapter use the Formula language, because it is the easiest to use; however, many examples in the book use other languages. Bubba's Shrimp Ordering System example in Chapter 12 makes extensive use of LotusScript.

Action Buttons

Action buttons are a part of the form and view design elements, as well as the subform design element. This section concentrates on forms and views, although the information presented for a form also applies to a subform.

Note

Subform actions load into the form's action bar after the form's actions load.

Agents are shared code

One of the strengths of Notes/Domino is the ability to reuse many objects and bits of code, so that you maintain your code in only one place and use it in multiple places. You know about some elements, such as script libraries and Cascaded Style Sheets. But one element often forgotten as a type of shared code is an agent. You can place LotusScript or formula code in an action button directly, but doing so reduces the reusability of the code. If you need that code in more than one place, you end up pasting it over and over — and this isn't easy to keep straight. You can use shared actions (which are covered later), but they have their drawbacks. Because a shared action must be loaded remotely, it's slower than a native action. Additionally, when you place code into the shared action, you must load all that code with the shared action. This can also reduce the speed with which your shared actions load. Instead, think about using agents for your formula- and LotusScript-based actions. You can perform the functions from either an agent or an action, you maintain code reusability, and you don't have the performance degradation of a shared action — the action is native and the only code that loads when the form loads is the one line used to call the agent (@Command([RunAgent])). You should place your action code in an agent and call the agent from the action.

The following are a few reasons for using an action button over an action hotspot or button:

✦ Action buttons stay at the top of a form, even when scrolling down through the form.

✦ Action buttons can be cascaded with subactions, which provides a way to give a great deal of functionality in a limited amount of space.

✦ Individual action buttons in forms, and now in views as well, can use formula-based hide-whens.

✦ Action buttons can be shown and used in embedded views.

✦ Action buttons can use graphics, text, or both. The graphic used can be from the action icon palette (as in previous releases), or can be chosen from an image resource.

✦ The label for an action button can be generated by a formula.

New Feature Showing and using action buttons in embedded views, using an image resource as an action button graphic, and basing an action button label on a formula are new in Notes/Domino 6.

Using action buttons in forms

Action buttons have become more useful in forms with the release of Notes/Domino 6 because of the new action-based features it brings. The following sections take a look at each of these newer features.

Using formula-based hide-whens

Action buttons in forms can be hidden based on a formula, such as the value of a field. A form in the ND6 Actions and Buttons Examples database called 16.01 Hide-when Example includes an action button with a formula-based hide-when. This formula is hidden if the ShowAction field is set to No, and shown if it is set to Yes. The formula for a hide-when works like all hide-whens — the action is hidden if the formula evaluates to True. In this example, the formula is as follows:

```
ShowAction = "No"
```

If you're in Edit mode, you can change the value of ShowAction, between Yes and No. The action appears and disappears appropriately.

Note If you want an action button to appear and disappear dynamically, you have to refresh the form. In the preceding example, the ShowAction radio button is set to Refresh Fields on Keyword Change, so changes made to the field cause the form to refresh.

Using formulas to control the appearance of actions is useful in applications that have automated workflows. You could, for example, have Approve and Disapprove action buttons that appear only for users who are a part of the approval process.

Using action menus with subactions

Actions can act as menus with subactions. Figure 16-1 shows an example action menu with a subaction.

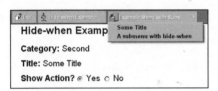

Figure 16-1: The ability to include action menus with subactions in an application has become easier and more intuitive in Notes/Domino 6.

You could create action menus with subactions in Release 5. In Designer 6, however, the subactions are much easier to manage, because a subaction is a separate type of action. Figure 16-2 shows the Action pane of the same form shown in Figure 16-1.

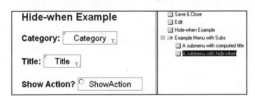

Figure 16-2: Subactions are easier to work with in Domino Designer 6.

If you create subactions, the top-most action can't contain any code, as it is just a menu item at that point. Subactions can't have graphics assigned to them nor can the background color be changed, either. Subactions can, however, use hide-whens like normal actions.

The Java applet used for actions on the Web has been modified, and now supports subaction menus much more cleanly than in Release 5. Figure 16-3 shows how the same document from 16-1 looks in a Web browser.

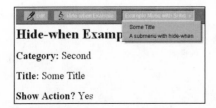

Figure 16-3: The action bar Java applet works much better in Domino 6 than it did in previous versions of Domino.

Using computed action labels

The labels that appear for an action can now be based on the result of a formula. The first subaction in Figure 16-1, for example, is based on the Title field of the underlying form (they are the same).

Using action icon graphics from image resources

In previous releases of Notes/Domino, the only graphics available for actions were from a pre-defined icon palette. As of Notes/Domino 6, you can use image resources as the icon for your actions. If you want to create your own action icon, it must be 21 pixels by 21 pixels. The Hide-when example action in Figure 16-1 uses an image resource for an icon. Additionally, you can write a formula that results to an image resource name.

Note   If you use graphics in an action that contains subactions, the graphic will not show up when that action is loaded in a Web browser as a part of the Action bar Java applet.

Displaying actions with check boxes

Action buttons can now appear with little check boxes included.

New Feature   Displaying action buttons with check boxes is new in Notes/Domino 6.

The check box is checked if the formula in the Value parameter of the display area in the action properties box evaluates to True. In the 16.01 Hide-when example form, a couple of check box-style action buttons set the Show Action field from Yes to No. This causes the hide-when action to either hide or appear, and it causes the check box to become checked or unchecked where appropriate. Figure 16-4 shows the check box action buttons.

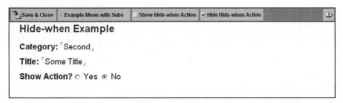

Figure 16-4: The check box action button is new in Notes/Domino 6.

The Show Action field is set to No, which causes Hide Hide-when action to be checked. If the field value were Yes, Show Hide-when action would be checked. This example demonstrates that you can check and uncheck actions based on values on a form. For instance, you may have an application that checks or unchecks actions based on status, making it easy for your users to determine the status and then take action on the form from one interface.

Note   Check box actions show up as normal actions in a Web browser.

Check box actions provide another innovative interface for action buttons.

Note The appearance of actions can be modified in a myriad of ways. You can modify things such as background graphics, borders, position, size, color, and much more. Refer to the Domino 6 Designer help for more information on ways to customize the appearance of action buttons.

Action button use suggestions

This section provides some general tips and techniques for using action buttons.

✦ **Provide some default buttons for your users:** Older Notes veterans know that they can place a document into Edit mode by double-clicking the document, and they can close a document (and be prompted to save if appropriate) by double-right-clicking it (if the user has enabled it in User Preferences), or by hitting the ESC key. Most users don't know these shortcuts, so always include the following two buttons in your applications:

- Save & Close: Hide this button when the document is in Read mode. The button contains the following code:

```
@If(@Command([FileSave]; @Command([FileCloseWindow]); "")
```

- Edit: Hide this button when the document is in Edit mode. The button contains the following code:

```
@Command([EditDocument])
```

Note There is an Edit icon that appears on the toolbar when a document is open in the Notes client. If you have experienced users who know about and use this button, you may not need the Edit action button.

✦ **Don't forget right-aligned buttons:** If you provide global buttons, such as a help button or a design suggestion button, consider right-aligning these buttons. This helps to separate these general-purpose buttons visually from the context-specific ones. Figure 16-5 shows the example form with a help button on the right.

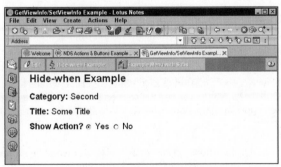

Figure 16-5: Right-aligned action buttons are great for general-purpose or global icons, such as a help icon. The action button at the right is used as a help button for this application.

✦ **Image resources can also be image wells:** Because you can use image resources for action buttons, you can also use image wells. An *image well* is three graphics in one — the first graphic is the default graphic, the second graphic is the mouse-over graphic, and the third graphic is the clicked graphic. These three graphics are in the same physical graphics file, and are separated by one pixel. You indicate that a graphic is an image well in the Image Resource properties box, as shown in Figure 16-6.

Figure 16-6: You indicate image wells in the Image Resource properties box by selecting how many images are either across or down in the graphic.

In the 16.01 Hide-when Examples form, you see that the Example Menu with a Subs action menu uses a *twistie* image well.

Image wells also work in the action bar Java applet.

✦ **Put complex code in agents:** As stated earlier, put complex code in an agent, and then call the agent from the action button. Refer to the sidebar "Actions Are Shared Code" at the beginning of this chapter for more information.

Using action buttons in views

Most of the suggestions for action buttons in forms also apply to action buttons in views. Most of the same features are available, including the ability to use hide-when formulas on view actions. The following sections address some of the new things that are different from action buttons in forms.

Using formula-based hide-whens

Formula-based hide-whens are similar to form actions — the action is hidden when the formula evaluates to True, and is reevaluated when the view is refreshed. But Notes/Domino 6 also enables you to have action buttons show or hide based on conditions per document.

The easiest way to do this is with a combination of formula-based hide-whens and the use of a new @function called @GetViewInfo. @GetViewInfo retrieves the value from a column of the selected document. You place code similar to the following into the hide-when of the action:

```
@GetViewInfo([ColumnValue]; 2) = "No"
```

In this instance, the @GetViewInfo function retrieves the value of the *third* column in the view, and if it is equal to No, the action is hidden. This is important: @GetViewInfo, like LotusScript, uses a zero-based array to count views (first column = 0, second column = 1, and so on), instead of the way @DbColumn and @DbLookup reference columns, which is a one-based array (first column = 1, and so on).

You must do one more thing when you want to use document-specific hiding of view actions. You need to enable the Evaluate Actions on Every Document Change option in the View properties box so that the actions are refreshed every time a new document is selected. The View properties box is shown in Figure 16-7.

Figure 16-7: The Evaluate Actions on Every Document Change option causes the actions to be refreshed every time a new document is selected in the view.

If you don't do this, the hide-when only evaluates when the view is first opened.

 Note   Make sure that you really need to use this feature, as it can cause performance issues with larger views.

Using check box actions

Just like form actions, view actions can be check box-style actions as well. View actions work the same as the form check box actions, but view actions require you to enable the Evaluate Actions on Every Document Change option for the view as outlined in the preceding section.

 Note   Check box actions show up as normal actions in a Web browser.

Check box actions are useful for presenting contextual information to the user without requiring the user to open the document. For instance, let's say you have an application that is an "in/out" application used by your users to indicate if they are in or out of the office. Your users highlight their name and click the Punch action button in the view. The Punch action button expands to show "In" and "Out", and the current status of the selected user is checked. The user then clicks the appropriate action and the user is prompted for a comment. The status and comment fields are then updated appropriately.

Using agents in view actions

If you heed the suggestion made earlier to use agents for your action code, you must remember one thing when using them in view actions: Code in a view action acts like an agent with a `Target` parameter of All Selected Documents. If your action is designed to work with selected documents, and if you use an agent to house your code, you need to make sure the target is set to All Selected Documents.

The rest of the information about view actions is the same as the information discussed about form actions. Rather than duplicate that information here, you can refer to earlier sections of the chapter.

Using shared actions

Shared actions are a type of shared code resource. Shared actions enable you to create one action and use it in any form or view. Shared actions take on the formatting of the action bar where they are placed, just like any other action in that action bar.

Shared actions are useful, but using too many can slow down the loading of your views. Make sure that it makes sense to use a shared action. In the example database for this chapter, the help icon in the view and form is a shared action.

Actions are useful for providing functionality to your users, but you can also use buttons and action hotspots.

Buttons and Action Hotspots

Buttons are similar to form actions in that they enable you to package code that can be executed when the user clicks it. Buttons aren't as configurable as actions, but they perform the same task. Buttons and action hotspots are basically the same thing — buttons are gray boxes that can have labels, while action hotspots are text and/or graphics tagged to act like a button. You can format buttons to a certain extent — you can adjust things like color and border in the Button properties box. Action hotspots are aesthetically more pleasing than buttons (if the graphic used for the action hotspot is aesthetically pleasing), so it's nicer to use action hotspots with graphics rather than buttons. But if your needs are simple, buttons work just fine.

Figure 16-8 shows a button with a label, a button without a label, and an action hotspot. Each performs the same action.

16.02 Buttons and Action Hotspots Example

This page contains a button and an action hotspot that performs the same action.

Here is a button

Here is a button without a label:

Here is an action hotspot:

Figure 16-8: Buttons and action hotspots are able to perform the same tasks, even though their appearance is different.

You can't see it, but the second button — the one without a label — is dark green and has rounded edges. This makes it more interesting than the standard gray button.

Buttons have one other unique feature that is useful. Buttons have a property where you can specify that the button act like an OK or Cancel button in a dialog box without the need to add any code in them.

New Feature The ability to define a button type is new in Notes/Domino 6.

Additionally, you can specify that one of the buttons is the default button. If the user presses Enter without clicking the box, the default button activates. Another button besides OK and Cancel is Help. But the Help button type only works for the Macintosh client.

A dialog box in the example database shows how these buttons work. You can access this example by executing the Button Type Dialog Test agent, the result of which is shown in Figure 16-9.

If you execute this agent and click one of these buttons, a prompt box appears telling you what button you clicked. This proves that the button type feature is working, because there's no code behind these buttons. Take a look at the code in the Button Type Dialog Test agent, as shown in Listing 16-1.

Figure 16-9: The OK and Cancel buttons in this stylish dialog box do not have any code behind them, yet they perform their respective functions.

Listing 16-1: Button Type Dialog Test Agent

```
results := "Cancel" : "OK";

retflg := @DialogBox("Button.Type.Example.dlg";
[AutoHorzFit] : [AutoVertFit] : [NoCancel] : [SizeToTable] :
[NoOKCancel]; "Button Type Example");

@Prompt([ok]; "You Clicked..."; results[retflg + 1])
```

The preceding code uses the new list indexing feature in the Formula language. The beginning of the code contains a list consisting of two elements: Cancel and OK. @DialogBox returns a one if the user clicks OK, and a zero if the user clicks Cancel. The @Prompt at the end of the code uses the return value from the @DialogBox function as the index of the results list to choose the right value to return in the @Prompt. A one is added to the return value from the @DialogBox, because all lists are one-based arrays. You save the use of a couple of @functions—namely @Trim and @Replace.

If you're going to use action hotspots, place your graphics in the database as image resources so they're more easily maintained (especially if you need to switch the graphic later).

Tip   If you're going to use buttons, place the label outside of the button as text and leave the button as a simple button (see Figure 16-2). This makes your form much more attractive.

Creating an action hotspot using a graphic is easy—just follow these steps:

1. Add your graphic to the form as an image resource.

2. Highlight the graphic and choose Create ➪ Hotspot ➪ Action Hotspot.

3. In the Action Hotspot properties box, turn off the Show Border Around Hotspot option.

4. Add your code to the action hotspot.

Action hotspots are great for providing appealing user interfaces to your Notes and browser users.

Summary

This chapter covered the ways you use actions and hotspots in forms and views. This included:

✦ Using hide-when formulas on form and view actions

✦ Using computed labels on actions

✦ Using check box actions in views and forms

✦ Using shared actions

From here you move on to Chapter 17, which explores using events in forms, views, and databases.

✦   ✦   ✦

Form, View, and Database Events

By Rocky Oliver

Chapter 29 introduces object-oriented programming and event-driven programming. In case you haven't read Chapter 29 yet, let's discuss briefly what an event is.

An *event* occurs when an object, such as a form, does something. In object-oriented programming (OOP) languages, such as LotusScript, there are places to put code that is executed when an event occurs, usually before (Query) or after (Post) the event takes place. Therefore you can write code in these Query and Post events, and that code is executed before and/or after the event occurs, respectively. This chapter explains why events are important and what you can do with them.

An entity known as an object model represents the contents of a database. An *object model* is a way to represent the data of a database as things, or objects, that you can access and work with. These objects include ways to access the data in the object (through properties) and ways to take action against the object (through methods).

Objects that exist in the UI also perform actions as well—they are opened, closed, refreshed, saved, and so on. When an object does something, it's an *event*. You sometimes have the opportunity to bind code to these events—either right before or right after the event happens. Creating an application that performs based on when object events happen is known as *event-driven programming*. LotusScript, JavaScript, and Java are object-oriented languages that are used in event-driven programming. Even the Formula language is event-driven (although it really isn't an object-oriented language), as you can use formulas in events as well as the other languages mentioned.

The events for forms, views, and databases are available only in the Notes client. The Web client uses the JavaScript Document Object Model (DOM) to provide access to documents in a Domino database. The events described in this chapter are the ones used by the Notes client only.

Cross-Reference For more information on using the JavaScript events of a form, refer to Chapter 40.

Even though JavaScript and the Formula language are available in events, the language used most of the time is LotusScript. The bulk of the examples in this chapter are LotusScript examples, with the occasional Formula example thrown in for good measure.

This chapter introduces you to the events available in the form, view, and database objects. These events enable you to provide the right functionality at the right time for your users.

Understanding Form Events

The form object includes quite a few events, and more have been added in each release since the introduction of LotusScript. Before diving into the specific events available in a form object, you need some general information about form events.

You shouldn't use two events — Initialize and Terminate. These two events are called when the form object is first created in memory (before a document is loaded into it, and before any properties or events are available), and right before an object is unloaded from memory (after all references are gone, no properties or events available, and so on). These two events are basically used internally for instantiating the object and cleaning up after its closed. The Terminate event also cleans up anything that was created in memory while the object was open. You may find it useful to use these events, but it's best to leave them alone until you're an expert in LotusScript.

The Source parameter is in all form events, while the Continue parameter is in all Query type events. The two events are explained as follows:

✦ **Source:** This is a NotesUIDocument object representing the document as presented in the UI (the marriage of the form and the document). Source is a nice shortcut for getting a handle to the document, rather than needing to get to it through the NotesUIWorkspace.

✦ **Continue:** You can use this Boolean data type parameter to stop the form from actually performing the event. If, for example, you set Continue = False in the QuerySave event, the document won't save.

Each event is explained later in the chapter, with the occasional example to show how the event is used. These events are demonstrated in an example application called ND6 Simple Company Address Book (company address book). The Company Address Book database has two forms: Company, which collects company information, and Contacts, which holds information about contacts at the company. The Company form is shown in Figure 17-1.

The Contact documents are responses to the Company documents. The Contact documents inherit the address information, company name, and company key from the parent Company document.

QueryOpen

The QueryOpen event fires before the NotesUIDocument object is loaded into memory. The QueryOpen event has the following parameters:

✦ **Source as NotesUIDocument:** As stated earlier, this is the NotesUIDocument object representing the document loaded into the UI.

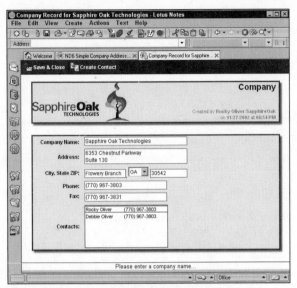

Figure 17-1: The Company Address Book database contains two forms, Company and Contact. The Company form is shown here.

Note   Even though `Source as NotesUIDocument` is listed in the `QueryOpen` event, none of the methods of the `NotesUIDocument` object are available. The methods of `NotesUIDocument` are interacting with the document as it appears in the UI. In this event, the document hasn't loaded to the UI yet, so none of the methods are available.

✦ `Mode as Integer:` The `mode` parameter indicates whether the document is going to be in Edit mode (1) or Read mode (0).

✦ `IsNewDoc as Variant:` This parameter is a Boolean, but since the Boolean data type didn't exist before Notes/Domino 6, the parameter is listed as a `Variant` to maintain backwards compatibility. `True` indicates that the document has never been saved to disk; `False` indicates that the document has been saved to disk.

✦ `Continue as Variant:` This parameter is a Boolean, but it's stored as a `Variant` for the same reasons mentioned in the preceding bullet. If you set this parameter to `False`, the document isn't opened.

One example of using the QueryOpen event is in the Bubba's Shrimp Ordering System application example. The Item documents for an order store information about an individual item in the order, but no UI or form manipulates this data. To keep users from double-clicking the Item documents and getting an error, a dummy form called Item exists that has `Continue=False` in the `QueryOpen` event. This prevents the Item document from being opened in the UI.

In the Simple Company Address example database, the Company form has the code in Listing 17-1 in the `QueryOpen` event.

```
Sub Queryopen(Source As Notesuidocument, Mode As Integer,_
Isnewdoc As Variant, Continue As Variant)
  saveflg = False
  REM capture the current company name so that it can be
  REM checked in QueryClose to see if it has changed
  If Not(Source.IsNewDoc) Then company =_
  source.Document.GetItemValue("CompanyName")(0)
End Sub
```

The Company has three global declarations:

- ✦ saveflg, which is a Boolean data type
- ✦ company, which is a String data type
- ✦ company2, which is a String data type

In the QueryOpen event, saveflg is set to False. If the document is saved, it is set to True in the PostSave event — how it is used there is explained in the "PostSave" section of this chapter. The company string variable is set to the value of the CompanyName item, but only if the document is not a new document. This string is validated in the QueryClose event to see whether the company name has changed, so that the Contact documents can be updated with the new company name — this will be explained in more detail in the "QueryClose" section of this chapter.

PostOpen

The PostOpen event uses only the Source parameter. PostOpen comes in handy for setting up the initial form for use by a user. You may, for example, want a wizard to appear to help a user fill out a complex form. You could then enable the user to choose not to show the help anymore.

In the PostOpen event of the Company and Contact forms, the following code is used:

```
Sub Postopen(Source As Notesuidocument)
  Source.FieldHelp = True    ' show the field help bar
End Sub
```

The code uses the NotesUIDocument.FieldHelp property to enable the field help in the form when it is in edit mode — the result of which appears in Figure 17-2.

QueryModeChange, PostModeChange

These two events occur before and after the document changes between Read and Edit modes. The QueryModeChange event has a Continue parameter that, if set to False, prevents the changing of the document's mode. The PostModeChange event has only the Source parameter.

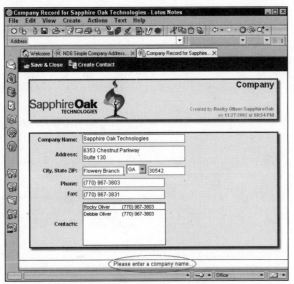

Figure 17-2: Field help, which is highlighted here, is useful in assisting your users with the use of your application.

Tip
You need to know the current Edit mode of the document when using these events. You can determine the Edit mode of the document by using the `NotesUIDocument.EditMode` property, which is read-write and returns a Boolean value indicating the Edit mode of the document (`True` for Edit, `False` for Read). If you need to change the mode, you can set it; if you need to find out the document's current mode, you can get it from this property.

Let's say you have an application that, once a document's status has been set to Completed, can't be edited anymore. You could place code in the `QueryModeChange` event to check the status and prevent the document from being edited if the status is Completed.

Note
The QueryModeChange event is an example of an event where you can use an @Command or LotusScript. For instance, you can use `@IsDocBeingEdited` to determine if the document is being edited, and then use `@Command([EditMode])` to change the Edit mode of the document, if needed.

QueryRecalc, PostRecalc

The `QueryRecalc` and `PostRecalc` events occur before and after the document is recalculated, respectively. As with other `Query` events, the `QueryRecalc` event has a `Continue` parameter that, when set to `False`, prevents the document from being refreshed. The `QueryRecalc` event comes in handy when you need to perform complex retrieval of information not possible with a simple @DbColumn or @DbLookup, and place the resulting data in the document.

New Feature

The QueryRecalc event is new in Notes/Domino 6.

QuerySave, PostSave

The QuerySave and PostSave events happen before and after the document is saved, respectively. The QuerySave event has a Continue parameter that, when set to False, prevents the document from being saved.

The QuerySave event happens *before* any validations have occurred, so you don't know during the QuerySave event whether the document will save successfully. The QuerySave event is handy if you want to do some additional validation, or check some other conditions before you allow the document to be saved. If you need to perform some action after the document is successfully saved, you should use the PostSave event.

The PostSave event is a great place to check conditions after a document is successfully saved. If the user attempts to save a document, and it fails for whatever reason, the PostSave event doesn't fire. You can be sure that the document is successfully saved when the PostSave event fires.

The PostSave event in the Company form accomplishes two things — the saveflg variable and the company2 variable is set — as shown in Listing 17-2.

Listing 17-2: **Company PostSave Event**

```
Sub Postsave(Source As Notesuidocument)
  saveflg = True
  company2 = Source.Document.GetItemValue("CompanyName")(0)
End Sub
```

The saveflg variable is a global variable that is initially set to False in the QueryOpen event. After the document is successfully saved, savedflg is set to True. The company2 variable is also a global variable. Because the document is successfully saved, it's set to the current value of the CompanyName item. The company2 and saveflg variables are used in the form QueryClose event, which is covered in the "QueryClose" section found later in this chapter.

QuerySend, PostSend

These two events happen before and after the document is mailed. The QuerySend event has a Continue parameter that, when set to False, prevents the document from being mailed.

New Feature

The QuerySend and PostSend events in the form are new in Notes/Domino 6.

If the document is being closed and sent at the same time, setting Continue to False in the QuerySend event prevents both the send and the close, in case the user needs to make a modification to correct some error.

QueryClose

The QueryClose event occurs right before a document is closed. Like all other Query events, this event has two parameters: Source and Continue. If the Continue parameter is set to False, it prevents the document from being closed.

Three global variables exist: saveflg, company, and company2. These flags are all used in the QueryClose event of the Company form, as shown in Listing 17-3.

Listing 17-3: Company QueryClose Event

```
Sub Queryclose(Source As Notesuidocument,_
Continue As Variant)
  On Error Goto errHandler
  REM this event does two things:
  REM    1) if contact documents are created,
  REM    but this document is new, then delete the responses
  REM    2) if the doc isn't new, and it has been saved,
  REM    then check and see if the company name
  REM    has changed. if it has, stamp all the contacts
  REM    with the new company name
  Dim thisdoc As NotesDocument
  Dim db As NotesDatabase
  Dim view As NotesView
  Dim col As NotesDocumentCollection

  Set thisdoc = Source.Document
  If Source.IsNewDoc Then
    Set db = thisdoc.ParentDatabase
    Set view = db.GetView("Contacts.by.CompanyKey.EV")
    If view Is Nothing Then
      Error 900, "Unable to get view handle:" &_
      " Contacts.by.CompanyKey.EV"
    Else
      Set col = view.GetAllDocumentsByKey(thisdoc._
      GetItemValue("CompanyKey")(0), True)
    End If
  Else
    Set col = thisdoc.Responses
  End If

  If Not(col Is Nothing) Then
    If col.Count > 0 Then
      If Source.IsNewDoc Then
        Print col.Count & " Contact document(s) removed" &_
        " because the new Company document wasn't saved..."
        Call col.RemoveAll(True)
      Else
        If saveflg = True Then
```

Continued

Listing 17-3 *(continued)*

```
            If company <> company2 Then
              Call col.StampAll("CompanyName", company2)
            End If
          End If
        End If
      End If
    End If
getOut:
  Exit Sub
errHandler:
  Select Case Err
  Case 900
    Print "Error: " & Error$
  Case Else
    Print "Unhandled Error: " & Error$ & " [" & Err & "]"
  End Select
  Resume getOut
End Sub
```

A handle is given to the current document, which is the Company document, by using the `Document` property of the Source object, which is a `NotesUIDocument` object representing the document open in the UI. If the document is a new document any responses created are gathered using `NotesView.GetAllDocumentsByKey`. If the Company document isn't new, the `NotesDocument.Responses` property gathers the responses. The `NotesDocument` `.Responses` property isn't populated for new documents (for example, documents that have never been saved), even if there are responses to the new document.

The `QueryClose` event accomplishes two tasks—the second task is easier, so it's covered first. If the company name of an existing document (not new) is changed, all the Contact document's `CompanyName` items are updated with the new name. The company name is validated by comparing the `company` variable, which is set in the `QueryOpen` event, with the `company2` variable, which is set in the `PostSave` event. If they are different, the items are updated using the `NotesDocumentCollection.StampAll` method.

Note   The update to the Contact documents isn't performed immediately in the `PostSave` event, because it's unnecessary work if the user saves the document multiple times, which causes the Contact documents to be updated each time the documents are saved. Instead, the new name is captured, and the Contact documents are updated one time, when the document is closed.

The code that accomplishes the second task, and the reason why it's needed, is more complicated. The Create Contact action button of the Company form contains the following code:

```
@If(@IsNewDoc; @Command([RunAgent]; "(CreateContact)");
@Command([Compose]; "Contact"))
```

The preceding code is used because users want to be able to compose Contact documents even if they don't remember to save the Company document first. If the action button simply had an `@Command([Compose])`, and the user tried to compose a response without saving the Company document, she would be presented the error message shown in Figure 17-3.

Figure 17-3: If you attempt to compose a response document against a document that hasn't been saved, you get this lovely error message.

The error message isn't user-friendly, as most users believe that the current document they are working on is the selected document. You may think that you can add an @Command ([FileSave]). You can, but it's never a good idea to save a document that the user is working on without the user controlling it or initiating it. By using the preceding code, you call an agent (the CreateContact agent) that creates a Contact document using LotusScript as a response to the unsaved Company document.

You may encounter a situation in which the user begins composing a Company document, composes and saves a Contact document, and then closes the Company document without saving it. Normally, an orphaned document is created, which can create problems in your application. To avoid this, the code in the QueryClose event is used. This code checks the NotesUIDocument.IsNewDoc property to see whether it's a new document. If it is, all the Contact documents are deleted. If these documents aren't deleted, they become orphaned response documents (responses without parent documents in the database). Orphaned documents are bad because they normally do not show up in any views, but they do take up space in the database. That's why it is important to clean up any orphaned responses.

Now you're ready to take a look at the events available in a view.

Understanding View Events

Views have many of the same events that forms have, and others that are quite different. And as with form events, quite a few new events are available in Notes 6. One similarity is that the Query events in a view usually contain two parameters: Source, which in this case contains a NotesUIView object representing the view; and Continue, which can prevent the related event from occurring. A few events are specifically for use with calendar views, and a new, powerful event called Inviewedit is used with in-view editing.

As with form events, you should avoid using Initialize and Terminate. These two events are called when the view object is first created in memory (before a document is loaded into it, and before any properties or events are available), and right before an object is unloaded from memory (after all references are gone, no properties or events available, and so on). These two events are basically used internally for instantiating the object and cleaning up after it's closed. The Terminate event also cleans up anything that was created in memory while the object was open. You may find it useful to use these events, but it's best to leave them alone until you're an expert in LotusScript.

Here is a short listing of the standard events available in View objects:

✦ QueryOpen **and** PostOpen: These events are similar to the events of the same name in a form, in that they are called right before and right after a view is opened. You can prevent a view from opening by setting the Continue parameter to False.

✦ RegionDoubleClick: The RegionDoubleClick event is for calendar views only. It fires when a region, such as a day, is double-clicked. This event is usually used to create a new document. An example of using the RegionDoubleClick event is in the calendar view of your Notes mail file.

✦ **QueryOpenDocument:** The QueryOpenDocument event fires right before a document is opened from the view. You can get a handle to the document being opened by accessing the Source.Documents property, which is a NotesDocumentCollection object containing only one NotesDocument object — the document being opened.

✦ **QueryRecalc:** The QueryRecalc event fires right before the view is refreshed. You can set the Continue parameter to False to prevent the view refresh. If, for example, you have a large view, you may want to ask the user if he's sure that he wants to refresh the view.

✦ **QueryAddToFolder:** The QueryAddToFolder event fires before one or more documents are added to a folder. This event has an additional parameter to the Source and Continue parameters — the Target parameter, which is a string variable containing the name of the target folder for the documents. You can access the documents being added to the target folder by using the Source.Documents property, which is a NotesDocumentCollection object containing the documents being moved. You can use this event to enable only users in certain roles to place documents in folders, or you could only allow users in certain roles to put documents in specific folders by setting the Target parameter of the event.

✦ **QueryPaste and PostPaste:** These two events happen right before and right after a document is pasted into the view. You can prevent users from pasting documents in a view, or from pasting duplicate documents into a view. You can also modify documents before or after pasting.

✦ **QueryDragDrop and PostDragDrop:** These two events occur before and after a calendar entry is dragged from one region to another in a calendar view. Additionally, these events are valid only in calendar views.

✦ **QueryClose:** QueryClose fires right before a view is closed. It has the ever-present Continue parameter that, when set to False, prevents the view from being closed.

✦ **QueryEntryResize and PostEntryResize:** These two events fire right before and after an entry is dragged and resized in a calendar view. You use these events to validate and reset the time and/or date fields in your calendar entry as a result of the resizing. You can find examples of these events, as well as the other calendar entry events, in your Notes 6 mail file calendar view.

New Feature   The QueryEntryResize and PostEntryResize events are new in Notes/Domino 6.

The next event, InViewEdit, is new and rather complicated, so let's explore it a bit more in depth.

InViewEdit

The InViewEdit event fires when a document is edited in-line in a view.

New Feature
The `InViewEdit` event and the ability to edit and create documents in-line in a view are new in Notes/Domino 6.

This event is different from most events, because it has four subevents. The four subevents are as follows:

✦ QUERY_REQUEST (1) occurs before the column becomes editable.

Note
`Query_Request` is not available in Notes/Domino 6, but it is rumored that it will be available in the future.

✦ VAIDATE_REQUEST (2) occurs as you leave an entry being edited, and is used to validate the value.

✦ SAVE_REQUEST (3) occurs when the modified document is saved. This is similar to the `QuerySave` event in a document. This event can be pooled so that you can take action against multiple documents that have been edited at one time.

✦ NEW_REQUEST (4) occurs when the user creates a new document. This event is only available if the developer has enabled the Create New Documents at the View Level option in the view. This subevent enables users to create new documents in the view level. Figure 17-4 shows this new property in the View properties box.

Figure 17-4: The Create New Documents at the View Level option enables users to create a new document in the database from the view by editing the new document in-line in the view.

Note
If you create new documents in-line in a view, no form creates them. All items must be set in this event, including reader and author names items, the form item, all items based on computed fields, and so on.

Cross-Reference
You can see a detailed example of the use of the InViewEdit event in the Bubba's Shrimp Ordering System application in Chapter 12.

Database Events

The database events occur when things happen at the database level, such as opening and closing the database. The database events can, however, be difficult to find. Database events are located in the Database Scripts area of the database design, which is shown in Figure 17-5.

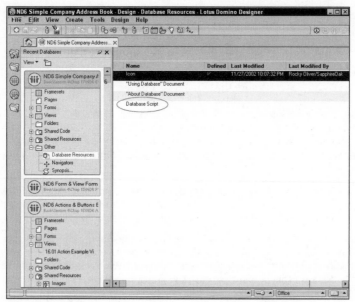

Figure 17-5: The database events are hard to find, but you can find them labeled as Database Scripts in the Data Resources area.

As with the form and view events, database events also have `Initialize` and `Terminate` events. For the reasons mentioned earlier, you should avoid writing code in these events. These two events are called when the database object is first created in memory (before any properties or events are available), and right before an object is unloaded from memory (after all references are gone, no properties or events available, and so on). These two events are basically used internally for instantiating the object and cleaning up after its closed. The `Terminate` event also cleans up anything that was created in memory while the object was open. You may find it useful to use these events, but it's best to leave them alone until you're an expert in LotusScript.

All events have the `Source` parameter, which contains a `NotesUIDatabase` object that represents the database being opened. The `Query` events contain a `Continue` parameter that, when set to `False`, prevents that event from occurring.

PostOpen

The `PostOpen` event fires after a database opens. The firing of the various events can be confusing, so the next paragraph goes over it in detail.

Databases almost always open to a view. When a database opens to a view, the `QueryOpen` and `PostOpen` events of the view fire *before* the database `PostOpen` event fires. The database `PostOpen` event fires after the database is finished opening completely. This means that the view finished opening before the database finished opening. The same thing applies, in reverse, with the view and database `QueryClose` events. The view `QueryClose` event fires before the database `QueryClose` event. Remember these tips if you try to intercept the opening or closing of a database.

QueryDocumentDelete, PostDocumentDelete

These two events fire before and after one or more documents are deleted from a database. Many developers wonder why these are not part of the view events. The main reason is that deleting a document is a database level event, in that it affects the entire database, not just one specific view. You can also write code in one place to handle all deletions in your database. If you set the Continue parameter to False in the QueryDocumentDelete event, the document(s) are not deleted.

Listing 17-4 shows the QueryDocumentDelete event of the Simple Company Address Book database. This event checks whether the document being deleted has any responses, and if so, removes those responses. The code prevents orphans from occurring in the database.

Listing 17-4: Database QueryDocumentDelete Event

```
Sub Querydocumentdelete(Source As Notesuidatabase,_
Continue As Variant)
  REM this code removes all contact documents if the
  REM company document is being deleted.
  Dim delcol As NotesDocumentCollection
  Dim deldoc As NotesDocument

  Set delcol = Source.Documents
  If delcol.Count > 0 Then
    Set deldoc = delcol.GetFirstDocument
    Do While Not(deldoc Is Nothing)
      If deldoc.Responses.Count > 0 Then
        Call deldoc.Responses.RemoveAll(Force)
      End If
      Set deldoc = delcol.GetNextDocument(deldoc)
    Loop
  End If
End Sub
```

The Source.Documents property contains a NotesDocumentCollection containing all documents that are being worked on by the event. In Listing 17-4, it contains all the documents being deleted. The code ensures that there is at least one document being deleted, and then it checks each document being deleted for responses. If responses are found, the collection is removed using NotesDocumentCollection.RemoveAll.

QueryDocumentUndelete

The QueryDocumentUndelete event fires before the deletion mark for one or more documents is removed from it. If, for example, you press the Delete key on a selected document in a view, a little *x* appears next to it. If you press the Delete key again, the little *x* disappears, removing the mark for deletion. This event fires right before that little mark is removed.

QueryDragDrop, PostDragDrop

These two events fire right before and after a document is dragged and dropped into a folder. These events have an extra parameter, EntryName, which contains the name of the target folder where the document(s) are going to drop. These events are available to both calendar and standard view types.

One use of these events would be to create a Completed folder and allow users to actually mark a document as complete by dragging the document to the Completed folder and dropping it. Then the code in the QueryDragDrop could verify that required items contain the needed values, and the PostDragDrop event could set the status field to complete.

QueryDropToArchive, PostDropToArchive

These two events fire right before and after one or more documents are added to an archive. They contain an extra parameter, EntryName, which contains the name of the archive folder where the documents are being dropped.

New Feature   The QueryDropToArchive and PostDropToArchive events are new in Notes/Domino 6.

Summary

This chapter introduced you to the many events available in forms, views, and databases, including:

✦ Various query and post events in a form, such as QueryOpen, PostSave, and QueryClose.

✦ The events found in a view were reviewed, and the new event InViewEdit was explained.

✦ Database events were reviewed.

Examples and techniques were provided to help you better understand how to exploit these events.

Chapter 18 covers the agents, and explores the power of using agents in your applications.

✦   ✦   ✦

Agents

By Rocky Oliver

Agents are small, miniprograms that you can create in Notes and Domino to perform tasks. An agent can be initiated by a user, scheduled, triggered when a certain event occurs, or initiated from a browser. Agents can run on the server or run locally, and can run as the person who called it or the person who last saved it. Agents are an extremely powerful component of Notes and Domino development.

This chapter introduces you to various agent parameters, types, and uses. Tips and tricks are provided along the way, as well as cross-references to other examples in the book. This chapter concentrates on agents in the Notes client and from a server. As always, this chapter is not a rehash of the Domino 6 Designer help; this chapter offers some insight into the use of agents.

If you have developed agents in the past, be aware that the way you control the parameters of an agent has changed considerably. In the past, a pane at the top of the development area controlled such things as triggers, targets, and so on (see Figure 18-1).

In This Chapter

Learning about agent triggers

Learning about agent targets

Discovering the ways and places you can run agents

Finding out about techniques for troubleshooting agents

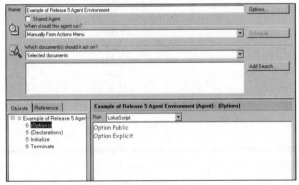

Figure 18-1: In Domino Designer Release 5, you configured an agent's parameters within the development environment.

In Domino 6 Designer, the agent configuration parameters moved to where they belonged all along, the Agent properties box, as shown in Figure 18-2.

Figure 18-2: Agent configuration in Domino 6 Designer is in the Agent properties box.

Many of these configuration parameters are covered later in this chapter, especially the ones that changed in Notes/Domino 6.

Another feature that has changed (for the better) in Notes/Domino 6 revolves around shared and private agents. A *shared* agent is an agent that is available publicly and can be executed by other users. A *private* agent is an agent that is created by someone and is only available to that person.

New Feature

In prior releases of Notes/Domino if you created and saved an agent, its type could never be changed. This was frustrating, as agents, by default, were created as private agents. If you forgot to mark it as a shared agent and saved it, it was private forever. In Notes/Domino 6, this pain is alleviated. Whether an agent is shared or private is now simply a property in the Agent properties box.

Understanding Agents

Agents are packaged chunks of code, or miniprograms that you can call by various methods and execute. Agents are also considered a type of shared code, because they are "write once, use everywhere." You can find agents in your database in the Designer database bookmark under Shared Code.

You can write agents with simple actions or with a variety of languages, such as Formula language, JavaScript, and Java. This chapter concentrates on Formula language and LotusScript agents; you can learn more about Java agents in Part VII.

Chapter 17 told you to avoid using the `Initialize` or `Terminate` events of those objects. That is not the case with agents — the `Initialize` event is where you write the main part of your code, which may use other subroutines and functions. Agents don't have any other events, because they're not UI-based objects.

Front-end versus back-end

As in LotusScript and the Formula language, front-end and back-end agents exist. Front-end agents can use front-end LotusScript classes and formulas; whereas back-end, or server-based, agents use only back-end formulas and classes. This means that any function or class that interacts with the UI doesn't work in a server-based agent, and worse, causes the agent to fail. Front-end formulas include @DialogBox, @Prompt, and all @Commands. Front-end classes are all LotusScript classes that have UI in the name, such as `NotesUIWorkspace`, `NotesUIDocument`, and so on. Be careful to keep your UI front-end agents out of your back-end agents.

Another important difference between front-end and back-end agents concerns permissions. A front-end agent is an agent that executes in the Notes client, and executes with the permissions of the person who triggered the agent. Back-end, or server-based, agents are triggered on the server or through a Web browser and generally run with the permissions of the person who signed the agent. But the signer of a server-based agent is checked against a list in the server document to determine what the agent can or can't do. The next section talks about how these permissions are determined.

Setting agent permissions

Because agents are such powerful design elements, you can enable special security settings that provide granular control of the amount of access given to the signer of server-based agents. This is determined in the server document, in the section shown in Figure 18-3.

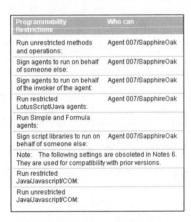

Figure 18-3: This section, in the Security tab of the server document in the Domino Directory, shows which ID(s) have permission to execute various agent actions for scheduled agents.

You can set various levels of access in the Domino Directory. This section doesn't review each one—the Domino 6 Administration help does a good job of explaining them, and you can also click the labels of these fields for help. You should, however, make sure that you set these fields appropriately for your environment.

Many of the permissions and security variations depend on where the agent is executing (server, client), who signed it, what parameters are set, and so on. Additional situation-specific permission variances are mentioned throughout the chapter where appropriate.

Understanding agent targets

A *target* for an agent indicates which document(s) the agent should run against (take action against), if any. The documents that fit within the `target` parameter can be accessed through the `NotesDatabase.UnprocessedDocuments` property. This property includes a `NotesDocument Collection` object containing the documents that match the target criteria. Other methods exist for retrieving these documents, but this is the most commonly used method. The following list describes each of the targets available:

Signing scheduled agents

If you've ever received e-mail from a server or from someone you know didn't send it, it's most likely because a server-based agent sent out the e-mail. Because server-based agents run as the signer of the agent (usually the last person to save it), it appears that e-mails generated by this agent are from the signer. And because many people sign agents with an agent's server ID, it appears the e-mail came from the server.

The best way to avoid this is to create a special user ID only for signing agents. Call this agent by some name that makes it readily available—in Figure 18-3, the only user ID allowed to execute any agents (except for personal agents) is a user called Agent 007. This is a special ID used to sign agents. The only people with access to it are the administrators. Setting up this type of system enables the following: You can control which agents are allowed to run, and, if warranted, institute a testing system ensuring that the agent is safe to run in a production environment. It makes it more readily apparent to your users when they are receiving an e-mail from an agent, if that is appropriate (keep in mind that you can also create an item named Principal in your automated e-mails and populate it with the appropriate e-mail address if needed). An agent-signing ID also gives you the security of an ID that has a password (something most server IDs don't have), and continuity in case the person who signs your agents leaves (your agents continue to be signed by the same ID).

So, create an agent-signing ID, give it only permission to run agents in your server document, and regain control of your production environment—at least where agents are concerned.

✦ **All documents in the database:** Although this is technically possible, only use this target setting if you're absolutely sure you need to do this. Running an agent that modifies every document can have a significant impact on your database in a variety of ways:

- Modifying every document causes excessive replication times for your users, especially those that replicate over a modem.

- Modifying every document causes every index in every view to be updated. Because every document is modified, all view indexes are rebuilt. This also significantly impacts the time it takes your users to open the database the first time after the agent has run, and it causes the server indexer task to take more time running against the database.

- You run the risk of creating replication/save conflicts if the database is in production when your agent executes.

✦ **All new and modified documents:** This agent runs against new and modified documents, as it says—but what constitutes new and modified? It isn't as simple as it appears. An agent considers a document new or modified *every* time the agent executes, if it is not marked as processed by using the `NotesSession.UpdateProcessedDoc` method. You must use this method to mark the document as processed so that the agent does not run against it again the next time the agent executes. When you use the `UpdateProcessedDoc` method, it marks only the document processed for that agent, not for any others. Also, if you edit and save the agent, it resets the processed tag for *all* documents previously marked, and the agent subsequently processes all documents again.

✦ **All unread documents in view:** This trigger causes the agent to execute against all unread documents in the currently open view. You don't have to mark documents gathered with this trigger with the `NotesSession.UpdatedProcessedDoc` method. The unread documents are relative to the person whose rights the agent executes under, which could be the signer of the agent or the person executing the agent, or someone else if the agent is running on behalf of someone else.

✦ **All documents in view:** This trigger causes the agent to run against all documents in the currently open view.

✦ **All selected documents:** This trigger causes the `UnprocessedDocuments` property to return a collection of all the selected documents in the currently open view.

✦ **None:** Use this trigger when you are going to gather your documents through your own means, rather than using the `UnprocessedDocuments` property. You must also use this trigger if you're going to use an agent in areas where a view isn't opened (such as back-end agents), and in formula-based agents that use `@Commands`.

You can further refine the documents on which the agent operates by using the Document Selection area. The Document Selection area enables you to filter the documents the agent executes against at a level deeper than the `Target` property setting. The Document Selection area appears right above the Options area of the agent in Domino Designer. The Document Selection area uses simple conditions to filter the documents that the agent will act upon. Figure 18-4 shows the Document Selection dialog box that is accessed by clicking the Add Condition button at the bottom of the Document Selection area in Domino Designer.

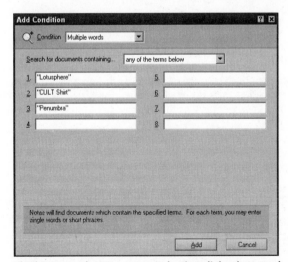

Figure 18-4: The Document Selection dialog box can be used to filter the documents upon which the agent acts.

The Document Selection feature isn't available to agents whose target is set to None. If you need more information about using the Document Selection feature, please consult the Domino 6 Designer help.

Note Using the Document Selection feature causes the agent to conduct a full-text index search of the database to gather the documents meeting the defined criteria. If your database is not full-text indexed, this will adversely affect performance in an extreme way. In fact, in Notes/Domino 6 if you attempt to use the Document Selection feature in an agent on a database that is not full-text indexed, an error message similar to the following appears on the server console and in the Notes log:

```
Warning: Agent is performing full text operations on database
'apps/signin.nsf' which is not full text indexed.
```

This is extremely inefficient.

Now that you know how to gather the appropriate documents for processing by your agent, you need to know how to execute your agent.

Setting agent triggers

The term *trigger* refers to the way your agent is executed. Two main types of triggers exist — on event, which means when something happens; and on schedule, which means on a certain interval. You can schedule agents to run locally in a Notes client, or on the server. You can trigger agents for execution a number of ways.

Scheduled triggers

You can schedule triggers as follows:

✦ **More than once a day:** This trigger setting enables you to specify an interval less than 24 hours in duration — from as short as every minute up to every 11 hours 59 minutes (which is the same as twice/day).

Note Although you can set an agent to run every minute, the quickest I have seen them fire is every three minutes or so. Make sure that you really need to run your agent on a short interval. Really short intervals — anything less than 15 minutes — can adversely affect your server performance. In cases where you think you need a short duration, you can accomplish the same task in other, less costly, ways.

✦ **Daily:** This trigger runs your agent once a day.

✦ **Weekly:** This trigger runs your agent once a week, starting on the specified date and at the specified time, and then executes weekly thereafter.

✦ **Monthly:** This trigger runs your agent monthly, starting on the specified date and at the specified time, and then executes monthly thereafter.

✦ **Never:** This setting is handy when the agent is called programmatically. This disables all triggering.

You can specify the time when your agent will run, and you can also specify things such as start date, end date, no weekends, and so on. You can also specify the server where the agent will execute, to prevent it from executing in multiple replicas of the same database on different servers.

New Feature

When you enabled a scheduled agent in prior versions of Notes/Domino, it automatically signed the agent with the ID of the person enabling the agent. Notes/Domino 6 has a new feature that enables you to activate an agent, which means enabling the agent without signing it. This feature is controlled by the Allow User Activation option of the Agent properties box, as shown in Figure 18-5. Only users who have Editor access or above to the database can activate an agent if this property is set.

Figure 18-5: The Allow User Activation option enables activation of an agent.

Agents scheduled to run locally run with the access permissions of the user. Agents scheduled to run on a server run with the permissions of the signer of the agent.

New Feature

The Run on Behalf of feature is new in Notes/Domino 6.

The Run on Behalf of feature enables you, as the designer, to specify who the agent runs with the permissions of, as if that person had signed the agent herself. When this feature is used, the agent executes as if the name listed in Run on Behalf of signed the agent, not the person who actually saved the agent. This means that things like e-mails are sent with that person's name instead of the signer's. Using this feature, however, does have some caveats. You need to have unrestricted rights to run agents in the Security tab of the Server document in the Domino Directory to be able to set the Run on Behalf of feature of an agent. If you have only restricted rights in the server document, this agent throws an error when it executes. For more information on this feature, refer to the Domino 6 Designer help.

Setting event triggers

Event triggers cause the agent to execute when the chosen event occurs. The events available as triggers are described as follows:

✦ **Agent menu selection:** This causes the agent to be listed in the Actions menu of the Notes client when the database is open. Users are then able to execute the agent. The agent runs with the permissions of the user.

✦ **Agent list selection:** This is used for agents that are executed programmatically. The agent runs with the permissions of the calling code; if the calling code was initiated by a user, the agent runs with the user's permissions. If a scheduled agent calls this agent, this agent runs with whatever permissions the calling agent is using.

✦ **Before new mail arrives:** The agent processes a new mail document before it shows up in the database. This agent is useful for filing, rules, and so on. Only one agent per database can use this trigger.

✦ **After new mail arrives:** The agent processes a new mail document after it is placed in the database.

Note   A delay exists between when a new document arrives and when the After New Mail has Arrived agent processes it. The delay is usually about three to five minutes.

✦ **After documents are created or modified:** The agent fires after documents are created or modified. You usually use this in combination with the target setting of New and Modified Documents. A delay exists when this agent fires from when a new or modified document is created—the delay is usually between 5 and 30 minutes, depending on the load and conditions on the server. This is actually a special type of scheduled agent. You can set start dates, end dates, and so on for this type of agent by clicking the Edit Settings button that appears when this trigger is chosen.

✦ **When documents are pasted:** The agent executes whenever a document is pasted into the database.

There are some other new features that are discussed later in this chapter, such as Run in Background Client Thread (in the Agents Executed from the Notes Client section) and Allow Remote Debugging (in the Agent Troubleshooting section). There are other parameters as well. Refer to the Domino 6 Designer help for more information.

Location, Location, Location

Many of the options and functionalities available in agents are largely dependent upon where they are executed. The following sections break down the various areas from which you can run agents, the ways you can run them, and what features are available when an agent is run from a particular place.

Agents executed from the Notes client

Agents executed from the Notes client include agents that are user-initiated and agents that are scheduled to run from the Notes client. These agents run with the permissions of the user who executed them, which means that the user's permissions decide what the agent can and can't access. When an agent is executed from the Notes client, the code runs on the client; however, you can trigger an agent to run on the server by using the `NotesAgent.RunOnServer` method.

Agents are extremely useful for reusing segments of code, especially for actions and buttons. It's a good technique to place code that would be in a button into agents, and call the agent instead. This is convenient when you have multiple buttons in your application that use the same code, because you can write and maintain the code for the multiple buttons in one place.

Cross-Reference   For more on the technique of using agents for action button code, refer to Chapter 16.

Agents executed in the Notes client run in the current thread, by default. But if you have an agent with the trigger set to Action Menu Selection, you can specify that an agent run in a background thread as well. When you execute an agent in the Notes client, it runs in the foreground, or main thread. This means that you can't do anything else until the agent finishes running, which can irritate your users. By setting the Run in Background Client Thread property, your agent executes in the background, freeing up the Notes client for you to do other things, such as read mail, open other databases, replicate, and so on.

New Feature   The Run in Background Client Thread property of an agent is new in Notes/Domino 6.

Figure 18-6 shows this property enabled in the Agent properties box.

Figure 18-6: The Run in Background Client Thread property allows agents run from the client to run in a background thread, freeing up the client for other tasks.

Using this feature includes the following caveats: The agent must follow the same rules as a server-based or back-end agent — it can't have any references to UI objects. Also, the agent trigger must be Action Menu Selection, which means the agent is listed in the Action menu of the client.

Using Background Client Thread feature with agents not listed in the Action menu

The main way you want your users to be able to execute agents is by clicking a button or action. You want to provide the ability to run your agent in context, which means that you want the ability to execute the agent available only when the user is at a certain place in your application (such as a particular form or view). You normally set the trigger to Agent List Selection, which hides the agent from the Action menu. But if you use this trigger, the Run in Background Client Thread property isn't available. You can have the best of both worlds by surrounding the agent name with parentheses, and adding an alias to the agent. The parentheses hide the agent from the Action menu even though you select Action Menu Selection as the trigger; this enables you to select the Run in Background Client Thread property. The alias enables you to call the agent by name without adding the parentheses to the name. Take a look at Figure 18-5 again, and you'll see that this technique is used for the name of the agent.

You can use agents in the Notes client for a wide variety of tasks. An example of this is in the ND6 Simple Company Address Book example database.

You can download the ND6 Simple Company Address Book example database (ND6 Simple Company Addresses.nsf) from the companion Web site, www.wiley.com/ compbooks/benz.

The Company form in this database has an action button called Create Contact. This button performs one of two functions, based on whether the document is a new document. If the document is new, the CreateContact agent is run; if the document has been saved at least once, a simple @Command([Compose]) is used, as shown in the following code:

```
@If(@IsNewDoc; @Command([RunAgent]; "(CreateContact)");
@Command([Compose]; "Contact"))
```

This code is used because some different work must be done if the Company document is new, and hasn't been saved yet. By encapsulating your button code in agents the code is easier to read, and it allows the mixture of LotusScript (the CreateContact agent is a LotusScript agent) and Formula language, using the best tool for the job in each case.

For more information on what the preceding code does, and why it was written this way, refer to Chapter 17.

What you can do with agents is limited only by your imagination. The agents in the Notes client are mainly used to perform encapsulated tasks and to make it easier to maintain and reuse code.

Agents executed based on an event

The trigger for an agent appears in the Agent properties box when the Trigger property is set to On event. Agents executed based on an event refers to agents run when one of the following events occur, which are chosen in the Agent properties box as well:

- ✦ **Before new mail arrives:** The agent processes a new mail document before it shows up in the database. This agent is useful for filing, rules, and so on. Only one agent per database can use this trigger.

- ✦ **After new mail arrives:** The agent processes a new mail document after it is placed in the database.

- ✦ **After documents are created or modified:** The agent fires after documents are created or modified.

- ✦ **When documents are pasted:** The agent executes whenever a document is pasted into the database.

Agents using one of the first three triggers listed are server-based agents, which means that they operate with one of the following permissions:

- ✦ The signer of the agent, which is usually the last person to save the agent

- ✦ The person listed in the On Behalf of option in the Agent properties box

Because the first three events are server-based, or back-end, agents, they're not allowed to have any UI interaction or objects in the code. Any interaction with the UI causes a runtime error when the agent is executed.

The When Documents are Pasted trigger is a Notes client-based agent, which means that it executes with the permission of the user pasting the document.

These agents are handy for use with workflow applications. You don't have to use Before New Mail Arrives and After New Mail Arrives agent triggers for user mail databases; you can also use them for mail-in databases. A *mail-in* database is a database that has a special Mail-in Database document in the Domino directory that defines a name, or alias, for the database, and the location of the database. When an e-mail message is sent to the mail-in database's alias, the mail router delivers the e-mail to the database listed in the configuration document. You can then write Before New Mail Arrives or After New Mail Arrives agents to automate the processing of the newly received documents.

The After Documents are Created or Modified trigger is useful for workflow as well. You may, for example, have an Order database where documents are created by an automated process, such as Lotus Enterprise Integrator (LEI, which is covered in Chapter 45, incidentally) from a mainframe system. You have sales managers who want to be notified when new Order documents are created or modified. You write an agent with After Documents are Created or Modified as the trigger to accomplish this.

The When Documents are Pasted trigger is useful for handling or modifying documents that are pasted into the database. You may, for example, have a Computed when composed item that contains the name of the person who created the document. Because pasting a document is a way of creating a new one, you need to modify that item and place the new person's name in it. You could use this trigger on an agent to do so.

Agents executed on a schedule

All agents triggered on a scheduled basis are server-based agents. Server-based agents run with one of the following two permissions:

✦ The signer of the agent, which is usually the last person to save the agent

✦ The person listed in the On Behalf of option in the Agent properties box

Scheduled agents are the meat and potatoes of workflow applications. These agents operate periodically to check certain conditions. If those conditions are met, the agents perform some task, such as starting or advancing some workflow process.

Cross-Reference   Chapter 22 covers workflow applications.

Agents executed from a Web browser

Agents executed from a Web browser are server-based agents, even though some type of user interaction often initiates them.

You can trigger an agent from a Web browser in the following ways:

✦ As a `WebQueryOpen` or `WebQuerySave` agent

✦ Using the `?OpenAgent` URL command

✦ Using `@Command([RunAgent])` or `@Command([ToolsRunMacro])` in a button, action, or action hotspot (yes, these two `@Command`s work in a Web browser)

When an agent is executed from a Web browser, it runs with one of the following permissions:

✦ The signer of the agent, which is usually the last person to save the agent

✦ The person listed in the Run on Behalf Of option in the Agent properties box

✦ The authenticated user, if the Run as Web User option is set in the Agent properties box

When you use an agent through a Web browser, you can use the `Print` statement to send information back to a browser. But all `Print` statements in a Web agent are cached until the agent finishes running, and then all the `Print` statements are sent to the browser.

Another aspect to consider when using Web agents is performance. Web agents are powerful, but they also can have scalability issues. They're fine to use in moderation, but Domino developers have a tendency to go overboard with Web agents, which can lead to scalability issues. Agents executed from a Web browser must be loaded into memory each time they are invoked. Although this is greatly improved in Notes/Domino 6, you can still hit some performance issues. Additionally, only so many agents can run concurrently. If you have a lot of users accessing areas of your application that use a ton of Web agents, you're going to have some latency issues.

Step back and think about what you're trying to accomplish, and take an objective look at the tools available to you. You can often accomplish what you're trying to do without using a Web agent. I, for example, was working with a developer who was creating a set of dynamic framesets. Based on some configuration parameters passed in on the query string, the frameset could have two, three, or four frames, and the content for each frame was dynamic (so I couldn't use the frameset design element). The developer built an agent that took all the query string information, gathered all the additional configuration information, and proceeded to spew forth a ton of `Print` statements that built the needed frameset with the appropriate content. The agent worked fine in a test environment — his logic for building the frameset was sound — but there were latency issues when the application was loaded with real user interactions.

To work around these problems, we reconsidered what we had. We had some wrapper HTML. When the application was accessed, parameters were passed that indicated what frameset type was needed. We used one of three chunks of HTML that created the appropriate frames based on the parameters provided, and we had some code that did some data retrieval for the content of the frames. We didn't need an agent — we needed a form! We created a form with the HTML used in the `Print` statements in the agent as Pass-Thru HTML. Some fields at the top of the form parsed the query string, and based on those settings were some formula-based hide-whens on the chunks of HTML to ensure the right one was shown to the browser. We also had some fields that did some `@DbLookup`s to retrieve the dynamic content. The form performed the exact same tasks as the agent, but it was much more scalable, much faster, and didn't suffer from any Web agent limitations. Take the time to look for the right solution before diving into development — the obvious solution isn't always the right solution.

Logging Errors and Troubleshooting

Troubleshooting errors in a server-based agent is difficult because the agent is operating remotely. The next few sections describe some ways to help you keep up with your agent, and how to troubleshoot problems when they occur.

Agent testing

When you first build an agent, test the agent from Designer by selecting the agent in the Designer Agent view and choosing Agent ➪ Test. You can ensure that no syntactical or basic runtime errors are in your agent, and test that the effective user has rights to run the agent.

If your agent runs successfully, you're presented with a dialog box similar to the one shown in Figure 18-7.

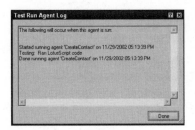

Figure 18-7: Your first step in ensuring that your server-based agent executes successfully

Agent logging

Consider adding some logging features to your agent. Notes/Domino has built-in logging features that are easy to use. You can store log messages in a text file, a Notes database, or a mail memo. Notes/Domino even provides a special class to help you use the log feature — NotesLog for LotusScript and Log for Java. You can record anything you want to in the log, such as variable values, position in code, error messages, and so on. Using the log isn't covered here — it's in the Domino 6 Designer help — but you should know that it exists so you can use it.

Remote debugging

If your log doesn't help you troubleshoot your LotusScript-based server agent, you can also use a new feature in Notes/Domino 6 called the Remote Debugger.

New Feature Remote debugging is a new LotusScript feature in Notes/Domino 6.

The Remote Debugger enables you to use the LotusScript debugger against a scheduled agent that runs on your server remotely. To use the Remote Debugger, you must follow a few steps:

1. First you need to fill out the Remote Debug Manager tab, which is under the Server Tasks tab of the server document. The contents of the Remote Debug Manager tab are shown in Figure 18-8. The tab has the following three fields:

   The *Allow Remote Debugging on this Server* field doesn't enable the Rdebug task; it allows connections to that task.

   The *Turnoff Server Debug After* field keeps the Rdebugtask from hogging resources if you're not using it. Remember to reload the task if you need it. You can, however, prevent it from being automatically unloaded by setting this field to -1.

   The *Agent Wait at StartTime* field causes the agent to delay executing after it is initially loaded into memory. This buys you time to connect to the agent when it starts executing.

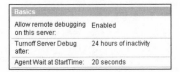

Figure 18-8: The Remote Debugger Manager tab

Note   If you are not actively debugging agents, make sure you set the Turnoff Server Debug After field to a relatively short value, as your agents will be delayed in execution even if you don't have the Rdebug task loaded on the server.

2. You then need to load the remote debugging task in your server by typing **load Rdebug** at the server console, or adding it to the "tasks" entry of your server's NOTES.INI.

3. Next you need to enable remote debugging in the Agent properties box, as shown in Figure 18-9. Make sure you have selected a server on which to run the agent.

Figure 18-9: You must enable remote debugging in the agent to use it.

4. You should also add a STOP statement in your agent code so that the code has a breakpoint for you to see when you connect with the remote debugger.

5. After completing these steps, you need to open your Notes client or Designer client and prepare to debug your agent. Go to your server console and type the following:

```
tell amgr run yourdatabase.nsf agentname
```

The preceding code tells the agent manager to run your agent. If you don't want to do this, or don't have access to the server console, you can increase the schedule frequency to get the agent to run in a few minutes.

6. After you tell the server to run the agent, choose File ⇨ Tools ⇨ Remote Debugger in the Notes or Designer client. The Debugger client loads. Choose your debug target by clicking Select Debug Target on the debugger workspace, which presents you with the dialog box shown in Figure 18-10.

7. If a scheduled agent is running in the chosen server (and your agent should be running because you told it to load), it shows up in this dialog box. Navigate to the agent by selecting the server and database in the dialog box. Select the agent and click OK. The normal debugger appears.

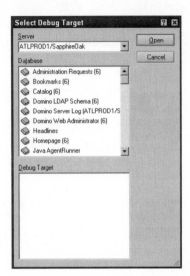

Figure 18-10: The Select Debug Target dialog box is where you choose the agent you want to debug remotely.

Agent troubleshooting references

The information covered in this section is only the tip of the iceberg of troubleshooting agents. Julie Kadashevich is responsible for agents at Lotus. She has written an exhaustive series of articles at the Lotus Developer Domain (formerly known as Notes.Net) about agents, troubleshooting agents, writing agents, and so on. She even has a FAQ called Troubleshooting Agents. Go to www.lotus.com/ldd and enter the Notes/Domino 6 Forum. Once there, go to Resources, and access the Forum FAQs area. Julie's Agent FAQ is there, which not only contains the FAQ itself but links to other agent articles as well. You will find a wealth of information.

Summary

This chapter introduced you to the wonderful world of agents:

✦ You were presented with a description of all the various agent types available.

✦ You learned about agent triggers.

✦ You learned about the targets used for agents.

✦ You learned about the places where you can run agents.

✦ You were given various techniques for troubleshooting your agents.

You also learned about many new features in agents such as remote debugging and running client agents in background threads.

Chapter 19 discusses designing and developing Web applications, and provides you with proven techniques for building solid Domino-based Web applications.

✦   ✦   ✦

Web
Applications

By Brian Benz

By Brian Benz

Because of Domino's advanced container model that naturally
organizes and manages unstructured data, collaborative application capabilities, integrated development environments, and support
for e-mail integration, Domino is a natural choice for a Web application
server. This chapter introduces Domino's advanced Web capabilities
by demonstrating Domino features for collaborative Web applications
and Web sites and illustrates these features by starting to develop the
Web site that will be used throughout the rest of the book.

All of the databases that the Web site is based on can be downloaded from the ndbible.com Web site.

Introducing the Example Web Site

This chapter uses a prototype Web site to illustrate examples. The
Web site is a collection of Web-enabled Domino databases that display Web pages and provide visitors with ways to interact with the
Web site. In this chapter the overall structure of the site is reviewed,
followed by a look under the hood at the elements that make the site
work. The next section of this chapter examines the Mailing List
application database that collects visitor information and signs the
visitor up for a newsletter. In the next chapter, the functionality to the
Mailing List application that manages signup confirmations and mails
the newsletter to everyone that has signed up on the site is added.

Web Design Elements

Figure 19-1 shows most of the elements that you work with in this
chapter. The home page is contained in a Domino form, and Web site
links on the left of the home page are actually a Domino outline formatted for the Web. The IBM banner at the top of the page is
JavaScript stored in a field, and the Amazon Search box is HTML
embedded in a field. The center of the Web page contains a rich text
field embedded in a Domino document, and the What's New listing is
an embedded view.

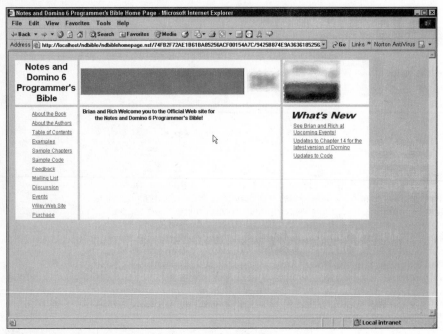

Figure 19-1: The home page for the example Web site

Web Navigation

The Web site is navigable via standard HTML links, most of which are created dynamically by Domino. For example, a Domino outline that generates the links on the left side of the page with links to specific databases, pages, and other Domino design elements. The embedded view that makes up the What's New column on the right side of the home page dynamically links to Domino documents based on the News form in the same Database. This means that if a new document is created using the News form, the embedded view automatically picks up the new document link and displays it on the home page.

Framesets

A frameset is a quick and easy way to manage Web site functionality. Figure 19-2 shows the MainFramesetWeb frameset that is used for the ndbible.com discussion forum, which is part of the standard discussion Database template for Domino 6. In this case, the discussion template uses a multipaned frameset template. The left navigation pane is actually a Domino outline embedded in a Domino page. The page is formatted for display on the Web and, in turn, embedded in the frame, which is embedded in the frameset. The frame on the right is an embedded "all documents" Domino view. The Action bar above the view is actually the Action bar associated with the All Documents view, not with the frame. Deselecting the "Show Action Bar" option in Frame Properties optionally hides the Action bar.

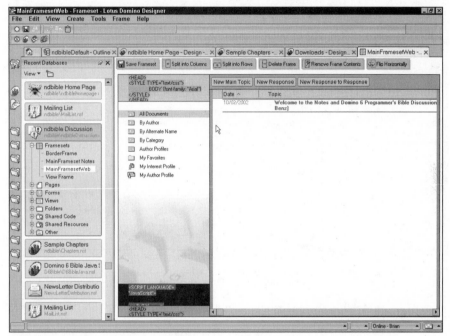

Figure 19-2: The MainFramesetWeb frameset for the example discussion forum open in Domino Designer

Outlines

We created a single outline for the example Web site and embedded the outline in all of the Domino database forms and pages that make up the Web site. This ensures that navigation capabilities are consistent throughout the site and guarantees easy maintenance. Adding, editing, or removing a link in the ndbibleDefault outline in the ndbiblehomepage.nsf database cascades through all of the embedded instances of the outline in all the other databases. Figure 19-3 shows the ndbibleDefault outline, which is used as the default outline for the entire site.

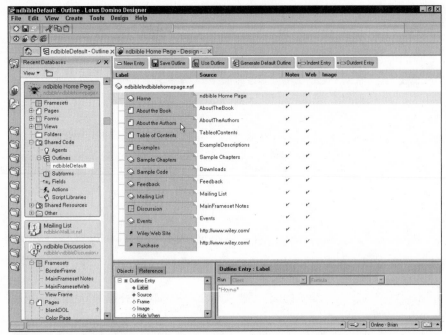

Figure 19-3: The ndbibleDefault outline that is used for the example Web site

Table 19-1 breaks down the navigation structure represented by the ndbibleDefault outline for the example site.

Table 19-1: Outline Navigation for the Example Web Site

Outline Entry	Links To
Home	The ndbiblehomepage.nsf Domino database. When this database is opened by a Web browser, the Web Launch option in the Database Properties opens the first document in the current home page view.
About the Book	The About The Book page in the ndbiblehomepage.nsf Domino database.
About the Authors	The About The Authors page in the ndbiblehomepage.nsf Domino database.
Table of Contents	The Table of Contents page in the ndbiblehomepage.nsf Domino database.
Examples	The Example Descriptions page in the ndbiblehomepage.nsf Domino database.
Sample Chapters	The SampleChapters.nsf Domino database. When this database is opened by a Web browser, the Web Launch option in the Database Properties opens the first document in the current home page view.
Sample Code	The Downloads.nsf Domino database. When this database is opened by a Web browser, the Web Launch option in the Database Properties opens the first document in the current home page view.

Outline Entry	Links To
Feedback	The Feedback.nsf Domino database. When this database is opened by a Web browser, the Web Launch option in the Database Properties opens the Feedback form in edit mode, ready to accept feedback from the Web site visitor. When the visitor clicks the Submit button, the data is validated. After the data passes validation, a new feedback document is saved in the database.
Mailing List	The MailList.nsf Domino database. When this database is opened by a Web browser, the Web Launch option in the Database Properties opens the Newsletter Subscription form in edit mode, ready to accept a subscription request from the Web site visitor. When the visitor clicks the Submit button, the data is validated. Once the data passes validation, a new NewsLetter Subscription document is saved in the database.
Discussion	The ndbibleDiscussion.nsf Domino database. When this database is opened by a Web browser, the Web Launch option in the Database Properties opens the MainFrameSetWeb frameset, which displays a Discussion Navigator outline in the left frame, an embedded discussion view in the right frame, and an Action bar above the view that permits users to create topics and response documents.
Events	The Events.nsf Domino database. When this database is opened by a Web browser, the Web Launch option in the Database Properties opens the first document in the current home page view.
Wiley Web Site	A URL Link to www.wiley.com.
Purchase	A URL link to Amazon.com, where the Notes and Domino 6 Programmer's Bible can be purchased online.

In addition to the consistency of using the same outline for the entire Web site, each embedded instance of the outline can have different display options in the embedded outline properties. This facilitates control over the look and feel of the embedded outline and over which outline entries display for that instance of the outline, without affecting the source outline.

Web Page Display

The example Web site uses Domino documents, based on Domino forms, and Domino pages to display page content. Domino forms and documents are used for home page content and news content because forms, unlike pages, separate the form data display from the document content. This makes it easy for developers to manage the structure and aesthetics of a Web site via forms while delegating the content creation and management tasks to users via documents. Pages require designer access to the database, and some knowledge of HTML and Domino development techniques. For this reason, providing access to the design of a database to inexperienced content editors so they can edit pages is a dangerous option, because they will also have access to other parts of the design of that database. It's usually better to use the forms and document model for Web sites where the design of the site is separated from the content on that site.

Forms design

Figure 19-4 shows the home page form for the ndbiblehomepage.nsf database. This form is the basis of all other forms in the Web site.

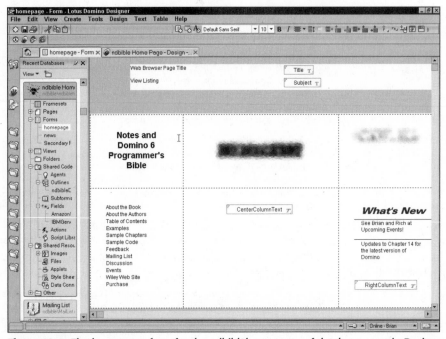

Figure 19-4: The home page form for the ndbiblehomepage.nsf database open in Designer

The next two sections review the most important design elements on the home page form, starting at the top.

Design techniques for Web page display

The home page form is a good example of an advanced Web page design. The background color of the Web page is set to basic gray in the form properties. All visible Web design elements are set in a table in the form. Placing the design elements in table columns and rows rather than directly in the form provides more control over the alignment of design elements when displayed on the Web. Design elements can be contained in a column or row of a table, or in nested tables, and each cell in the table can have its own alignment, color, and graphic options set. In this case, the table is a solid white table on top of the gray background.

Tip

Adding HTML settings directly to the HTML settings in Table properties greatly enhances the control and flexibility in the design of tables on the Web. Note that the designer version of the table appears as a solid table in Figure 19-4, whereas the Web displays spaces between the rows and columns in the table in Figure 19-1. Adding the following line of code to the Other field in the HTML tab of the Table properties places even spacing between the rows and columns when rendered in a Web browser:

```
border="0" cellpadding="3" cellspacing="5"
```

The Title and Subject fields

The Web browser page Title field is where the title that appears in the top bar of a Web browser goes. The Domino server renders this as the HTML TITLE in the HTML heading of the generated Web page. The field named "Subject" is the field that displays the document in views. Both fields are available only when a document is in edit mode, and they are available to Web-page content managers to help in managing their own content on the Web site.

The CenterColumnText field and the RightColumnText field are rich text fields that can contain any type of data that a Domino document can store, including attachments, OLE files, rich text, tables, and embedded views. These fields are where users who have been delegated as content managers can create and edit their own content for the Web site.

The IBMGeneralBannerLink field and the AmazonSearch field are shared fields. The Embedded Navigation outline is used for navigation of the Web site and the embedded What's New view is used to display News documents on the home page.

Domino pages on the Web

Figure 19-5 shows a page on the Web. Because pages require Designer access to a database to edit, and because users with Designer access to the content of a Domino page also have access to the design of a page, pages are best for static Web pages that contain no interactive features and are not often updated. Because there is no access to fields on a Domino form, the IBMGeneralBannerLink field and the AmazonSearch fields that pass HTML to the browser to display the IBM banner and the Amazon Search dialog box could not be used. Pages can, however, handle embedded elements, such as views, outlines, and graphics, so the other design elements of the page remain intact.

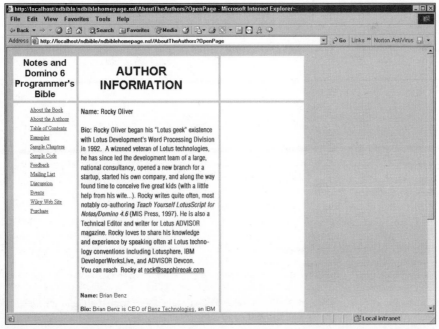

Figure 19-5: The About the Authors Domino page in the ndbiblehomepage.nsf database, as displayed on the Web

Web views

The embedded Web site navigational outline on the left side of the home page is called ndbibleDefault and is formatted for display on the Web by embedding the outline on the page, and then editing the embedded outline properties on the form. In this case, the font was changed to Arial, instead of the default Sans Serif font, which displays as Times Roman in Web browsers. The width and height of the outline were also changed from set values to Fit to Window and Fit to Content. There are literally hundreds of combinations of outline properties, all of which are more than adequately covered in the Domino Designer 6 help database. The basics have been provided here, but refer to Help for a more detailed listing of outline property options features.

The What's New view is an embedded version of the News\1. Current News view, as shown in Designer in Figure 19-6.

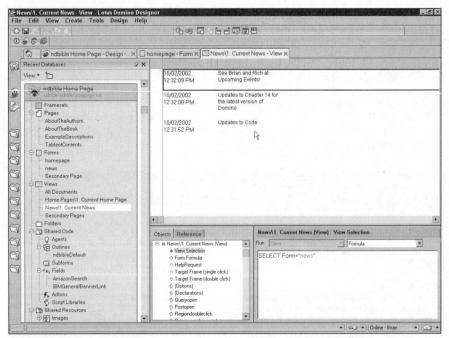

Figure 19-6: The News\1. Current News view, as shown in Designer. It is embedded on the right of the home page as the What's New view.

This is a basic three-column view that contains any documents created using the News form in the home-page database. If a user creates a new news document, it automatically appears in the What's New embedded view in a browser. The only changes to the view were to edit the embedded view properties to change the Font, Height, and Width settings, as with the outline, and also set the view to display as HTML on the Web instead of the default Java applet.

Cross-Reference   Views and Folders were covered in detail in Chapter 9. Refer to that chapter for more information on view display options and choosing between using applets and HTML as the View output on the Web.

The first column of the view is the date and time that the document was last modified, sorted in descending order so that newer documents appear at the top of the screen. The second column is a blank space in the view.

Tip   The blank space column is necessary in the view because Domino views automatically indent the first categorized column in a view that appears on the Web. Adding the space sets all rows in the displayed column to be left aligned, just after the space.

Web Data Entry

Figure 19-7 shows the Mailing List subscription page for the Web site. This is the home page in the MailList.nsf database. A new newsletter subscription document automatically opens in edit mode ready to accept a subscription request from the Web site visitor. When the visitor clicks the Keep Me Updated link, the data is checked for validity using JavaScript functions. After the data passes validation, a new newsletter subscription document is saved in the database, and a confirmation is displayed to the visitor on the screen.

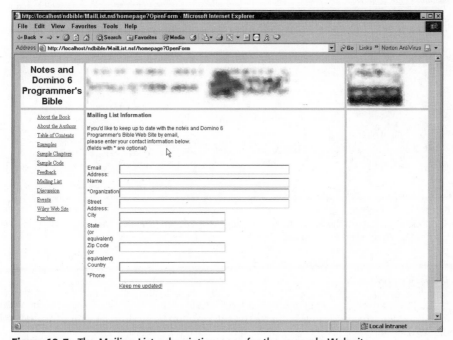

Figure 19-7: The Mailing List subscription page for the example Web site

Forms for data entry

The form is a basic Domino form with fields, JavaScript, and a $$Return field added. Figure 19-8 shows the subscription form open in Domino Designer. There are two paragraphs of text at the top of the data entry section of the screen. When users arrive at the Mailing List subscription page, they are prompted to enter contact information and click the Keep Me Updated link at the bottom of the page to save the data. When the data is saved, the $$Return field reopens the document in read-only mode with a confirmation message; so one form looks like two on the Web.

The first paragraph is visible only when the document is in edit mode, and it appears when the user enters data into the document. The second paragraph is visible only in read-only mode and acts as a confirmation message when the document is reopened after data entry by an @function calculated URL in the $$return field.

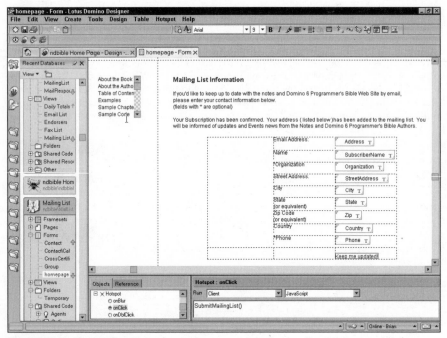

Figure 19-8: The Mailing List subscription page open in Domino Designer, with the Keep Me Updated link highlighted and the JavaScript SubmitMailingList() Hotspot function call displayed at the bottom of the screen

JavaScript

JavaScript is covered in much more detail in Part VIII of this book, but for now it's important to understand what makes each part of the subscription form work, including the function of the JavaScript.

When a Web site visitor submits a page via the Keep Me Updated link at the bottom of the page, the SubmitMailingList JavaScript function is called by the hotspot link to validate the entered data. The SubmitMailingList JavaScript function is contained in the JSHeader container in the form along with other JavaScript functions. If there are any errors, they appear on the screen and the user is prompted to fix the data in the original screen.

$$Return

The $$Return field is a Lotus reserved keyword in Domino forms. When a document is saved on the Web, the Domino server looks for a $$Return field as part of the form. If the $$Return is present, the contents of the form are evaluated and displayed to the user. Aside from text, $$Returns can also contain @functions and HTML links. In this case, a dynamically generated link with the following code is used:

```
"["+@ReplaceSubstring(@Subset(@DbName; -
1);"";"+")+"/MailResponseForm?OpenForm&ParentUNID="+ @Text(@DocumentUniqueID
)+"]
```

The code in the @function instructs the Domino server to open the same document that was just saved in read mode. The database name and the UNID of the document make up the link, and the `OpenForm Domino URL` command tells Domino to open the document without going into edit mode.

Shared Fields

The IBMGeneralBannerLink field and the AmazonSearch field are shared fields and are stored in the homepage database under the Shared Code ➪ Shared Fields section. The IBMGeneral BannerLink field contains HTML code that IBM makes available to affiliates, which accesses a server at `ads.bfast.com` to dynamically pull in graphics for banner ads that IBM places there to display on affiliate Web sites. Here's the actual code that makes up the contents of the IBMGeneralBannerLink field:

```
"<script language=\"JavaScript\" src
=\"http://ads.bfast.com/ad/script?bfmid=<25426813&siteid=38889020&size=468x60&sp
ace=13872148\"> </script>"
```

The AmazonSearch field contains even more HTML code than the IBM field and is used to display an affiliate Search dialog box that sends a search to the Amazon Web site with whatever the user has entered in the Search field.

The reason for storing this code in a field is twofold: portability and design simplicity. Putting the code in a field is good for portability because the code in the field is made into a shared field, which can be embedded anywhere on a form by choosing Create ➪ Resource ➪ Insert Shared Field from the main Domino Designer menu. Putting the code in a field is good for design simplicity because pasting large chunks of HTML code in a column or row of a table makes the design of a form hard to follow, as the resulting display of the HTML code looks vastly different in a browser when compared to the source code. The code still becomes part of the Web page when a new document is created using the form, but the source code itself is hidden in field contents while open in Designer.

Summary

This chapter introduced an example Web site and invited developers to download the Domino databases that the site was based on to follow along with the examples. You also reviewed:

✦ Web design elements that make Domino Web sites dynamic and flexible, and using embedded outlines and views to facilitate Web site navigation.

✦ Tips and techniques for displaying form, document, and page data on the Web.

✦ Examples of Web site functionality for data entry by outlining the functionality of the Mailing List application subscription form.

In the next chapter, you review options for integrating e-mail functionality in your Domino Web site. The chapter illustrates examples by digging deeper into the Mailing List application to see how it manages subscribers and mails newsletters using LotusScript agents.

CHAPTER

♦   ♦   ♦   ♦

In This Chapter

Introducing options
for e-mail integration

Introducing e-mail
options for forms

Using simple actions
for sending e-mail

Using e-mail options
for @functions

Setting e-mail options
using LotusScript

Setting e-mail options
using Java

Viewing an e-mail
newsletter mailing
application

♦   ♦   ♦   ♦

Mail-Enabled Applications

By Brian Benz

Aside from the integrated Domino Designer application development environment outlined in Chapter 5, and the ability to organize unstructured data into Web applications covered in Chapter 19, Domino also has another important feature that makes it a world-class application platform: easy e-mail integration. This chapter covers the advanced e-mail integration options for Domino and Web applications, including creating and managing mail-in applications and generating e-mail newsletters. Developers learn how to add an opt-in e-mail list to a Domino Web site, how to create an application to manage subscriptions, changes, and removals from the e-mail list, and how to develop an application to organize and distribute e-mail newsletters.

Options for E-mail Integration

Over the years, Domino has evolved from a simple way to store data that doesn't belong in columns and rows to a sophisticated platform for building all kinds of applications. E-mail integration capabilities have evolved as well, and as a result, Domino applications can easily integrate with e-mail in a multitude of ways. You can use system fields to automatically control options for e-mailing when a document is saved, @Formula functions, and LotusScript and Java classes and methods can be called from a document or via an agent.

E-mail Options for Forms

Any form in a Domino application can be adapted to become an e-mail form. In the example in Figure 20-1, coding isn't required — all functionality is facilitated via reserved-name fields on the form and through form properties. As an example, the form in Figure 20-1 was created for the sole purpose of using every form-based mailing option available. Please note that not all the fields and their descriptions are visible here; each option is covered in detail in Table 20-1.

A form with an example of all the fields and properties is available in the code samples, under the forms section of NewsLetter-Distribution.nsf. The name of the form is Form Based Email Integration Example.

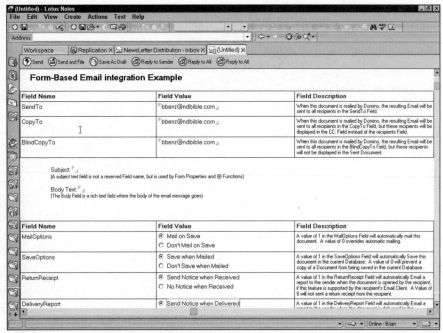

Figure 20-1: A basic Domino e-mail form prototype in the Notes client

Table 20-1: Reserved-Name Fields for E-mail Integration

Field Name	Field Description
SendTo	When Domino mails the document, the resulting e-mail will be sent to all recipients in the SendTo field.
CopyTo	When Domino mails the document, the resulting e-mail will be sent to all recipients in the CopyTo field, but these recipients appear in the CC: field instead of the recipients field.
BlindCopyTo	When Domino mails this document, the resulting e-mail is sent to all recipients in the BlindCopyTo field, but these recipients don't appear in the mailed document.
Subject	Subject is not an officially reserved field name, but is commonly used by Lotus templates to automatically populate the Subject field of an e-mail. It is most commonly a text field.
Body Text	As with the Subject field, Body is not an officially reserved field name, but is commonly used by Lotus templates to automatically populate the Memo Body field of an e-mail. It is usually a rich text field.

Field Name	Field Description
From	Similar to the Subject and Body fields, From is not an officially reserved field name, but is commonly used by Lotus Templates to automatically populate the Sent By field of an e-mail. It is most commonly a Names field that contains the hierarchical Notes user name of the sender. This field converts to an RFC-compliant e-mail address if sent via SMTP.
MailOptions	A value of 1 in the MailOptions field automatically mails this document. A value of 0 overrides automatic mailing.
SaveOptions	A value of 1 in the SaveOptions field automatically saves this document in the current database. A value of 0 prevents a copy of a document from being saved in the current database.
ReturnReceipt	A value of 1 in the ReturnReceipt field automatically e-mails a report to the sender when the recipient opens the document if this feature is supported by the recipient's e-mail client. A value of 0 doesn't send a return receipt from the recipient.
DeliveryReport	A value of 1 in the DeliveryReport Field automatically e-mails a report to the sender when the document is delivered to the recipient's inbox if this feature is supported by the recipient's e-mail client. A value of 0 doesn't send a delivery report from the recipient.
Encrypt	This feature is only available with memos that will be sent to recipients with Notes clients. A value of 1 in the Encrypt field automatically encrypts this message when it is sent. A public key is passed with the message so that the memo can be automatically decrypted using the recipient's private key.
Sign	This feature is only available for memos that will be sent to recipients using Notes clients. A value of 1 in the Sign field automatically sends an electronic signature with the message when it is sent. At least one field in the form has to be sign-enabled so it can store the signature.
	To sign-enable a field, go to the Security tab of a field's properties box and select Sign If Mailed or Saved in Section from the Security Options drop-down box.
DeliveryPriority	When a DeliveryPriority field is added to a document and the document is mailed, a value of L sends the mail with a low priority, a value of N sends the mail with a normal priority, and a value of H send s a high priority e-mail.
MailFormat	This legacy feature is available only for memos that will be sent to CC: mail clients, and is included for backward-compatibility only. A value of E stands for encapsulation, meaning the e-mail is sent with a link to a Notes database on the client's machine where the document resides. A value of T is text of the entire message. B (for both) means that the message will be sent as text and a link will be included for the encapsulated memo in the Notes database. Finally, a value of M instructs Domino to find a body field on the document and sends the contents of the body field as text.
Save This Form button	This button saves the document in the local database. (All e-mail directives are handled by the preceding field values.)

Form Properties for E-mail Integration

Email integration in Domino Designer is automatically available from all Domino documents, when the preceding reserved-name fields are present on a form, or mail-specific @functions, LotusScript or Java are called from the document. Two important form properties affect how a document behaves with relation to e-mail integration. Each one has its own quirks and interactions with other objects in the form.

Advanced Form Properties: Present Mail Send Dialog property

The Advanced tab of the form properties contains the Present Mail Send Dialog property. Figure 20-2 shows the Send Mail dialog box with the message a user sees before a document that has the Present Send Mail Send Dialog property is closed. The options enable the user to send the document and save a copy in the current database, send the document without saving it in the current database, save the document in the current database without sending a copy, discard changes, or cancel the save or send and return to editing the document.

Caution   Several reserved fields in Table 20-1 override the choices in the Mail Send dialog box. If the MailOptions field is set to 1, the document is sent even if the user's choice in the dialog box does not include a Send option. The SaveOption, Encrypt, and Sign options function in the same way and override any choices made by the user for saving, encrypting, or signing the document.

Notes may save a copy of the document in the user's Outbox regardless of the Mail Send Dialog property settings. For instance if a user chooses Send Only from the dialog box and the form contains a SaveOptions field set to 1, the document is saved in the database. If applicable to the application, you can use the @MailSavePreference command to check to see whether the user's preferences are set to Don't keep a copy (0), Always keep a copy (1), or Always prompt (2).

Figure 20-2: The Mail Send dialog box

Security tab property: Disable Printing/ Forwarding/Copying to Clipboard

If this option is checked in the form properties, documents created with that form aren't sent, regardless of the Reserved Field values or Mail Send dialog box options chosen by the user.

Simple Actions for Sending E-mail

When developing a form, default system actions are included as standard parts of every database template and can be added to any form in that database. To add standard actions when creating a new form, open the Action pane to the right of the Programmer's pane by selecting View ➪ Action Pane. Right-click the empty actions section, and select Insert System Actions from the pop-up menu. This installs actions for sending and forwarding the current document, and more. There are several options in Shared Actions for sending, replying, and forwarding documents that can be easily and quickly added to any document as well. To access these, right-click the empty actions section and select Insert Shared Actions from the pop-up menu.

A form with an example of many of the shared and system actions is available in the code samples, under the forms section of NewsLetterDistribution.nsf. The name of the form is Form Based Email Integration Example. Display the actions by enabling the Action pane from the main menu, by selecting View ➪ Action Pane.

To support these actions, a form must have at least SendTo and a Body fields. If the form has a Subject field, it is added to the Subject line of the e-mail.

E-mail Options for @functions

Aside from form properties and reserved field names for e-mail functionality, the formula functions @Command([MailSend]) or @Command([MailForward]) are used for e-mailing forms with an existing SendTo field. @MailSend is used for sending documents that don't contain reserved fields for e-mailing or if the developer wants more programmatic control over recipients, content, subject lines (including document links), and more.

In addition to simple e-mailing and forwarding documents, several additional @functions expose e-mail integration features of Domino to application developers. Adding @Command ([MailAddress]) to a button on a form, enables an e-mail address dialog box to be opened and recipients to be selected from one or more address books depending on Notes client settings. Selected recipients can then be automatically saved to any editable text field. @Command([MailComposeMemo]) can be added to several types of Notes form objects and automatically opens a default mail memo form on a user's machine. @PickList([Name]) opens a special dialog box and enables users to select mail recipients. For more control or to select recipients from a non-address book Domino database, use @PickList([Custom]) and specify the server, database, and view. Figure 20-3 shows the Names dialog box, accessible from @Command([MailAddress]) and @PickList([Name]).

Finally, @Certificate is useful for examining and extracting information about a Domino document certificate, if the document was signed or encrypted.

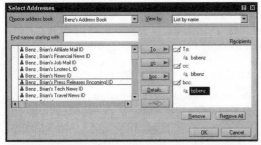

Figure 20-3: The Names dialog box, accessible from @Command([MailAddress]) and @PickList([Name])

E-mail Options Using LotusScript

LotusScript expands the options for Domino e-mail integration even further than @Formulas, form properties, or reserved name fields.

Cross-Reference   This section requires some basic knowledge of LotusScript. For a beginner's guide to using LotusScript, refer to Chapter 29.

LotusScript buttons, events, and agents can take advantage of the NotesDocument or the NotesUIDocument Send and Forward methods, as well as the NotesDocument.Sign and the NotesDocument.CreateReplyMessage methods.

Within a document that is to be sent, you can also use LotusScript to access the SaveMessageOnSend, ncryptOnSend, and signOnSend properties that will be used with the Send method in the NotesDocument.

To access address books for the current session, use the LotusScript NotesSession .AddressBooks property. To create a UI to select recipients from a list and store them in a multivalue string field, use the NotesUIWorkSpace.PickListStrings(PICKLIST_NAMES) method, or for recipients not listed in an address book, use the NotesUIWorkSpace .PickListCollection or the NotesUIWorkSpace.PickListStrings(PICKLIST_CUSTOM) interface and specify the Domino server, database, and view from which to select recipients.

On The Web   A working application for collecting e-mail newsletter recipients and sending e-mail newsletters is available for download at ndbible.com. This application uses several LotusScript and @Formula agents to provide the functionality for the application. Part V (@Formulas) and Part VI (LotusScript) cover the @Formulas and LotusScript that use e-mail integration features.

E-mail Options Using Java

The Java options for working with Notes and Domino objects for e-mail integration closely mirror the LotusScript classes and methods. There are some important limitations and exceptions with Java. First, Java offers no access to the front-end Domino objects, just the back-end objects, so there is no equivalent in Java for the LotusScript NotesUIDocument, just NotesDocument, which is called lotus.notes.Document in Java.

Cross-Reference   This section requires some basic knowledge of Java. For a beginner's guide to using Java in Domino, refer to Chapter 32.

Java can use the Send method of the lotus.notes.Document class, as well as the NotesDocument.createReplyMessage method. E-mail integration document properties are accessed by setting the setEncryptOnSend, setSaveMessageOnSend, setSignOnSend properties to true or false and signing a memo using the Sign method.

Java also has three unique methods for working with e-mail integration. Document.getSigner returns the name of a user who signed a document, and Document.getVerifier gets the name of the certificate that verified the signing. Finally, Document.isSentByAgent returns true if the current document was sent by an agent or some other automatic method.

To access address books for the current session, use the `Session.getAddressBooks` method. Note that there is no way in the Java classes to create a UI to select recipients from, as there is in the @Formula language and LotusScript. Use the AWT and the swing classes, as well as the new JSP features to generate UIs in Java.

 An example database, available as part of the downloads for Chapter 33, illustrates techniques for creating UIs, accessing and creating Domino objects in Java.

Example: An E-mail Newsletter Mailing Application

This section extends the working application for collecting e-mail newsletter recipients and sending e-mail newsletters that was highlighted in Chapter 19. The application consists of two databases. The first database, MailList.nsf, is used in Chapter 19 to enable visitors to access the example Web site to sign up for an e-mail newsletter. MailList.nsf is based on the Domino Personal Address Book template, with a few additional features to facilitate the Web sign-up form. Figure 20-4 shows the Mailing List database and the main Contacts view, with a sample listing of fictitious recipients.

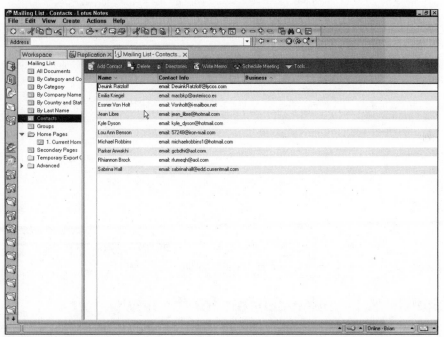

Figure 20-4: The Main Contacts view of the Mailing List database (MailList.NSF), which collects newsletter recipients when they sign up at the example Web site

The second database in the application is the Newsletter Distribution database, which manages all the newsletters that are to go out and to whom they are to be sent. This database is based on the Domino mail template, with a few slight modifications. This database is where most of the action and all of the e-mail integration takes place in the application. Creating and mailing a newsletter is a three-step process.

Step 1: Creating the newsletter text

Creating a slightly modified memo form in the Newsletter Distribution database and adding text for the newsletter accomplish the first step rather easily. All that is needed is the addition of a SentTo field, which is referenced from the LotusScript Agent, and a button for retrieving newsletter recipients from the Mailing List Database, called Get Recipients from the Mailing List:

Figure 20-5 shows the newsletter memo form with an example newsletter.

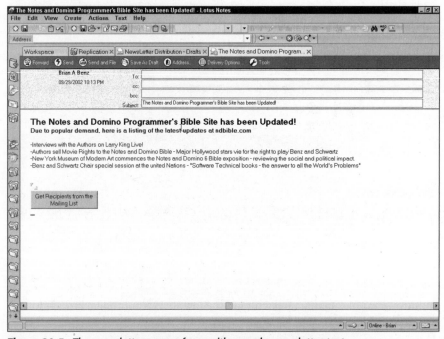

Figure 20-5: The newsletter memo form with sample newsletter text

Step 2: Selecting recipients for the newsletter

Newsletter recipients are selected by using a dialog box, which is called using the @PickList([Custom]) function to access the Contacts By Last Name view in MailList.nsf and display a UI for the user to select recipients:

```
FIELD SentTo:=SentTo;
@SetField("SentTo";@PickList( [Custom] ; "ndbible\\MailList.nsf"
```

```
; "ByLastName" ; "Select NewsLetter Recipients" ; "Please select
the people you want to send this Newsletter to" ; 2 ));
@True
```

The result of this @function is displayed in Figure 20-6. One recipient is selected, the OK button is clicked, and the recipients are added to the multivalue Recipients field at the bottom of the newsletter memo.

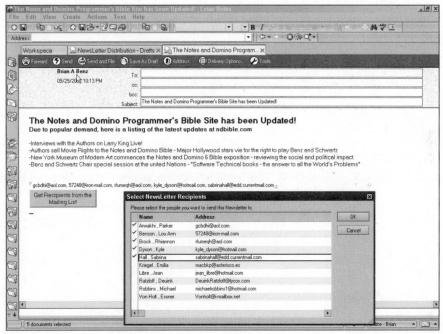

Figure 20-6: The Newsletter Memo form with the recipient Selection window using the @PickList([Custom]) function

Step 3: Mailing the newsletter to the recipients

The newsletter is sent via the Send Group Mail LotusScript agent, which is activated by selecting the Send Group Mail menu option under Actions in the Main Notes menu.

Cross-Reference The inner workings of the code in the Send Group Mail LotusScript agent are covered in detail in Part V, and an example e-mail integration agent is shown in Chapter 22.

After selecting the Send Group Mail menu option, the agent looks for any unsent newsletter memos in the Drafts view of the Newsletter Distribution database. The agent looks for the multivalue recipients field for each unsent newsletter memo, creates a new mail memo for each recipient in the recipients list, saves a copy of the memo to the Newsletter Distribution database, and sends the memo to the recipients, one recipient at a time.

Summary

In this chapter, you were introduced to options for e-mail integration, including options for forms, simple actions, @functions, LotusScript, Java.

✦ You can use system fields to automatically control options for e-mailing when a document is saved, @Formula functions, and LotusScript and Java classes and methods can be called from a document or via an agent.

✦ E-mail integration in Domino Designer is automatically available from all Domino documents, when the preceding reserved-name fields are present on a form, or mail-specific @functions, LotusScript or Java are called from the document.

✦ LotusScript expands the options for Domino e-mail integration even further than @Formulas, form properties, or reserved name fields.

The chapter concluded by introducing a newsletter mailing application. Examples from this application are used later in Part IV, as part of the introduction to @functions, in Part V, which explains the inner workings of a LotusScript agent that mails the newsletters, and in Part VII which discusses converting the LotusScript agent to a Java agent, a multithreaded Java agent, then a Java application, a servlet, and finally a JSP application.

The next chapter highlights options for Domino document security, including new Domino 6 features for document and form locking.

✦   ✦   ✦

Document Security

By Rocky Oliver

Notes/Domino is one of the most secure applications available for storing, sharing, and working with sensitive information. Chapter 10 reviewed database security and mentioned document security. Because you store your information in documents, documents have the most security options available. This chapter helps you better understand the options available for securing your information.

Reviewing Database Security

Security begins at the server and works its way down to the directory, and then the database, and then the document level. Server security is controlled through the Domino Directory and the server document, amongst other documents. Database security is managed through an Access Control List (ACL). The ACL is where you indicate who can gain entrance into your database, what they are able to do, and any roles they may have inside. The ACL is the gatekeeper to your data. Access to the database and replication are controlled by the database ACL. In fact, the ACL is reconciled between replicas before any replication takes place.

The ACL contains a special feature called a role. A role is like a database-specific group; you can group entities listed in the ACL under names you define in the ACL. These roles usually map to some type of business process role that exists in the process you are automating with you application.

Cross-Reference Review Chapter 11 before reading this chapter.

Choosing Document-Level Access

Cross-Reference The information in this section was first introduced in Chapter 10. However, it is important to review what access levels are provided in the Access Control List (ACL) for a database. For more information on Database Security, refer to Chapter 10.

The ACL determines the *most* a user can do to a document or to the design of a database. A database ACL has the following access levels:

✦ **No Access:** Choosing this access level completely blocks the entity from accessing the database.

✦ **Depositor:** Choosing this access level enables the entity to add content to the database (compose a document), but not to open the database and look at the content.

✦ **Reader:** Choosing this access level enables the entity to read content, but not to contribute content.

✦ **Author:** Choosing this access level enables the entity to read and create content, and to modify any document that the entity has author access to, which is usually any content created by that entity.

✦ **Editor:** Choosing this access level enables the entity to edit any document to which it has access.

✦ **Designer:** Choosing this access level enables the entity to change the design of the database, to edit any document it has access to, but not to change the ACL.

✦ **Manager:** Choosing this access level enables the entity to change the design, edit any document it has access to, and change the ACL of the database.

These access levels determine the default access a user or server has to a document. But you can control access to an individual document more granularly through the use of Author and Reader Fields, and through the use of field level encryption.

Understanding Author and Reader Names fields

Author Names and Reader Names fields (Authors and Readers fields) are the front-line security items for a document. They are two special field types — a Reader field translates to a "SUMMARY READ-ACCESS" field type, and an Author field translates to a "SUMMARY READ/WRITE-ACCESS" field type. Reader and Author fields can be single value or multivalue, and can contain user names, server names, group names, and/or roles.

Reader fields determine who can see a document. Further, if a document contains a Reader field, and you are not listed in it, you don't even know it exists. If, for example, you create a local replica of a database that contains documents with Reader fields, and you are not listed in them, your local replica doesn't contain any documents to which you don't have access.

Author fields do the same thing that Reader fields do, and they also enable the people listed in them to edit the document — as long as the user has author access to the database in the ACL. If a user has greater than author access, such as editor or manager, then as long as the user can see the document, she can edit it. If a user has less than author access to the database, such as reader, and is listed in an Author field, she still can't edit the document. Editing a document requires at least author access to the database.

Tip   The easiest rule of thumb for remembering what you can and can't edit and delete is that you have to be able to see it before you can edit it, and you have to be able to edit it to delete it (and you must have the Delete Documents attribute assigned to your entry in the ACL). Reader Names items are extremely important, because even if a user with manager access opens the database, he can only work with the documents he can see.

Add the [AllAccess] role to the ACL of every database you create, and then add that role to all Reader and Author fields you add to your forms. You should always provide a back door to the documents created in your application so that you can correct the occasional, but inevitable, problems that arise. Additionally, any server that is going to host your database should be listed in the ACL and in the Reader and Author fields on your document. You can do so explicitly (bad idea) or through the [AllAccess] role (good idea).

Note If a user has author access to a database, he *must* be listed in an Author field in any document he creates or he will not be able to edit it after he saves and closes it — even though he created it. Add an Author field that contains the formula @UserName : "[AllAccess]" to all forms you create.

You can have more than one Reader Names or Author field on a document — each is aggregated to a universal list of readers and authors, and all entries in all fields are granted the appropriate access to the document. It's best, however, to use only one Reader and one Author field on your forms, set them to be Computed, and have the other Fields aggregate to these fields.

When adding values to these fields, always use the canonicalized name (for example, CN=Kristi Oliver/O=SapphireOak) for any server or person you list in an Authors/Reader Names item. This is how Notes/Domino stores names internally, and you'll have fewer hassles if you get in this habit now.

Creating Reader and Author Names programmatically

You can create and work with Reader and Author Names items programmatically. You can granularly control access to a document by managing these items through the use of code. But when you work with these items programmatically, you need to remember a few concepts.

First, when you create a NotesItem object that you want to be a Reader or Author Names item, you need to set the IsReaders or IsAuthors property to True to convert the item to a Reader Names or Author Names item. The following code, for example, creates a new item named AllowedAuthors, sets it with the canonical name of the current user and the [AllAccess] role, and tags it as an Author Names item:

```
Sub Initialize
  Dim ws As New NotesUIWorkspace
  Dim s as New NotesSession
  Dim doc As NotesDocument
  Dim authoritem As NotesItem
  Dim alist(0 To 1) As String

  alist(0) = s.UserName
  alist(1) = "[AllAccess]"

  Set doc = ws.CurrentDocument.Document
  Set authoritem = doc.ReplaceItemValue _
  ("AllowedAuthors", alist)
  authoritem.IsAuthors = True
  Call doc.Save(True, False)
End Sub
```

If you need to update the value of one of these types of items, you can use any of the normal methods, which preserves the special data type of the items. You can use `NotesDocument-Colleciton.StampAll`, the `FIELD` statement, or extended dot notation, for example, to set the values of these items and preserve the Reader Names or Author Names flags.

Assigning default readers through the form

The Advanced tab of a form enables you to assign default readers to documents created with your form, as shown in Figure 21-1.

Figure 21-1: You can add default readers for documents created with your form through the use of the Form properties box.

You can choose entries from the ACL, or you can add other names from the Domino Directory. Any values chosen with this feature are added to a special item called `$Readers`, which is a Reader Names item. Any values added to this item have at least reader access to documents created with this form, and you can add to this list through the use of your own Reader fields on the form. The default enables anyone who has reader access or above to the database to read documents created with the form.

Working with Author and Reader Names: An example

Bubba's Shrimp Ordering System database (`BGSOS.nsf`) makes use of Author fields to grant access for an approval workflow feature. The Order form has a field on it called AllowedAuthors. The field is an Author field, and the formula in it appears in Listing 21-1.

Listing 21-1: **AllowedAuthors Field Formula**

```
@Unique(
   @Trim(
       CreatedBy : "[AllAccess]" :
       @If(
           FirstApprovalsPending = "";
           SecondApprovalsPending;
           FirstApprovalsPending
       )
   )
)
```

This code always includes the creator of the document and the [AllAccess] role. If first-level approvers have not approved the document yet (as stored in the FirstApprovers-Pending item), they are included as well. This gives them access to the order document long enough to approve it. After they approve it, they're removed from the AllowedAuthors field. After all the first-level approvers approve the document, the second-level approvers are added to the field. @Trim and @Unique keep blank and duplicate values from the field.

Using encrypted fields

The safest way to secure information in an item is to encrypt it. The most common use of encryption is in your Notes mail. You can choose to encrypt an e-mail, and you can encrypt the Body item with the private key of the sender and the public key of the recipient, which is available in the Domino Directory or in the Personal Address Book. This recipient's public key is included in a certificate that you are prompted to accept when you receive a signed document. The only two people who are able to view that encrypted body field are you and the recipient, because only your keys were used to encrypt the item.

An encrypted field doesn't even show up in an opened e-mail. And if you try to access the item programmatically, it isn't interpreted. Encryption is the most secure way to store information in a Domino database.

You can use other users' public encryption keys in your own applications. You can also create your own secret encryption key and share it with others for them to place in their ID file. You can then link that key to fields in the forms in your applications. Only users with this secret key can access the information contained in the encrypted items.

When completing a form that contains fields available for encryption, the boundaries of the fields appear in red. Take a look at a new Memo composed from your Notes mail file, and notice that the body field's brackets are red. This indicates that the body field will be encrypted when the document is marked for encryption.

The Domino 6 Designer help contains a wealth of information on encryption. Refer to it for more information on using encryption in your applications.

Understanding document locking

Document locking works much like an Author field in that it determines who can and can't edit a document. But the document-locking feature ensures that only one person at a time can edit a document, even if multiple people are listed as authors of a document.

New Feature Document locking is a new feature in Notes/Domino 6.

Document locking is also demonstrated in the Bubba Shrimp Ordering System application, which you can download from www.wiley.com/compbooks/benz.

Cross-Reference Chapter 22 covers document locking in greater detail.

Summary

Notes and Domino offer a wealth of security options for your Notes/Domino applications. This chapter introduced you to the various security measures available for documents in a database:

✦ Reader and Author fields

✦ Encryption

✦ Document locking

The Domino 6 Designer help database contains a great deal of information on security, and it is definitely worth a look for more information. Chapter 22 introduces the concept of workflow automation, and how you can add workflow to your applications.

✦   ✦   ✦

Workflow Management

By Rocky Oliver

Notes and Domino make a great container for information. Notes has many tools available out of the box that help you work with, manipulate, and manage your information. But you may want to extend the interaction with the user from just the things that a user initiates to an exchange between the user and the application, even to the point where the application initiates the interaction. A great deal of the power of Notes/Domino resides in its ability to initiate an interaction with a user—routing documents or informing users about things going on with their information in an application. In short, one of the strengths of Notes/Domino is its ability to create and manage automated workflow in an application.

This chapter introduces you to two types of workflow in an application, and then provides an example application that you can play with and examine to gain ideas for your own applications.

Understanding Workflow Concepts

Workflow involves automating the notification of conditions or the routing of documents in your application. Most workflow involves sending an e-mail or routing a document to a user when one or more conditions are met. Workflow often involves security as well, including windows of security where a user has access to a document for a limited amount of time, usually until the user performs some desired action. Another use for workflow is the automated assignment of tasks, the reminders about those tasks, and the escalation of those tasks when they are not performed in a timely manner.

As stated earlier, workflow almost always involves some type of notification being sent to a user. Usually this notification is through e-mail. E-mail notification may be a simple message to update status, a doclink to a document, or even the forwarding of an entire document.

Tip   You can send an entire document with the form as a part of the document, but it can cause long-term issues because those designs can't be updated. Instead, design your applications to use doclinks (or if your application is Web-based, use URL links), and have the user work with the document in the database. This also reduces the traffic on your network, because a doclink/URL is much smaller than a document with a form stored in it.

Understanding Approval Workflows

Most of the e-mail notification and routing that occurs is for approval processing, where a document must be reviewed and approved by one or more individuals. These approval workflows come in two basic flavors: serial routing and parallel routing. *Serial* routing occurs when a document is moved sequentially from one approver to the next approver in order until the approval process is complete. *Parallel* routing occurs when a document is sent to a group of approvers at the same time, and each can approve the document in any order.

Serial routing is good if there are dependencies in the approval process. If you have an expense report application, for example, a serial workflow process is associated with it — the expense report must be approved by the manager before it is sent to accounting for processing, and accounting must process it before payroll can cut the expense check. Each step is dependent upon the previous step.

Parallel routing is handy if it doesn't matter who approves a document first, as long as all of a group of people approve it. You may, for example, have a proposal application, and the technical lead and the project manager must approve the proposal before it is presented to the customer. It doesn't matter which one of them approves it first, as long as they both approve it at some point.

You can also combine serial and parallel routing to create serial-parallel or parallel-serial routing. *Serial-parallel* routing is where you send out a parallel route (multiple people at once), and when that group finishes approving the document, the next group is sent notification, and so on. *Parallel-serial* routing is when the first person in multiple groups of approvers is sent notification, and then as the first person in each group approves the document, the next person in each group gets notification, and so on.

One of the problems that can occur with any approval workflow process is the chance that you create replication/save conflicts. This is a normal risk in a system where multiple people have access to more than one replica of a database. But you can minimize this possibility. Serial workflows are inherently less susceptible to replication/save conflicts. If a serial workflow routing pattern makes sense for your application, this is a good way to go. Notes/Domino 6 introduces a new feature that helps prevent replication/save conflicts called document locking.

Using Document Locking

Document locking refers to the ability to temporarily prevent edits to a document, enabling only specified individuals or groups to edit a document.

To take advantage of document locking, you must complete a couple of steps. First, you must ensure that an administration server is specified in the Advanced tab of the Access Control List dialog box for the database. If you do not have an administration server and you attempt to enable document locking, you're presented with an error message stating, "You must specify a Master Lock (Administration) server for the database. You can set this in the Advanced Panel of the Access Control Dialog."

After specifying the administration server, you can enable document locking by selecting the Allow Document Locking option in the Database properties box, as shown in Figure 22-1.

After you enable document locking for the database, you can build document locking into your code. You can lock a document, unlock a document, and check to see whom has a document locked. The following methods and property are a part of the `NotesDocument` class, and they manage locks on a document.

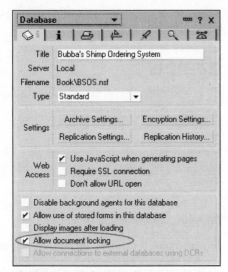

Figure 22-1: Selecting Allow Document Locking enables document locking

The Lock and Unlock methods lock and unlock a document. The Lock method has the following parameters:

✦ **Name:** This is a string or string array containing the name(s) of the entities that can access the locked document. This array can contain user names, server names, or group names.

Note When building an example using document locking, I could not get the lock to work correctly with more than one name passed into the Lock method. This has been reported to Lotus support. Check updated releases to see if it has been addressed.

✦ **Provisional Lock:** The provisional lock parameter is a Boolean value that, when set to True, enables a user to get a provisional lock. A provisional lock is assigned to a document when the database is local or the administration server isn't available. By default, provisional locks are disabled.

The Unlock method doesn't take any parameters. The person with the lock on a document, or a manager of the database, can unlock a document.

Note When you lock a document, an Author Names field called $Writers is created on the document, which contains the names provided in the Lock method. Another field, $WritersDate, is also added and contains the date and time the document was locked.

A benefit of enabling document locking in a database is that documents are automatically locked when a user places the document in Edit mode, and automatically unlocked when the user leaves Edit mode. This means that only one person can edit a document at a time. Obviously, this feature has much more of a benefit if your users are accessing a server replica. But situations may exist where locking documents for disconnected users makes sense, such as a presentation library in which multiple people contribute to the presentation. The document locking feature is especially useful for workflows that use some form of parallel routing.

You now understand some of the basics of workflow. The next section provides an example to illustrate some techniques for integrating workflow into your application.

Integrating Workflow: An Example

You can better understand how workflow is used in your applications if you see it in action. This example is a part of the Bubba's Shrimp Ordering System database (BGSOS.nsf) described in Chapter 12.

 You can download the Bubba's Shrimp Ordering System from the companion Web site, www.wiley.com/compbooks/benz.

This database is an ordering system for the fictitious Bubba's Shrimp Wholesalers, a company that sells all the various shrimp types mentioned in the movie *Forrest Gump*. The ordering system contains the products in a set of Product documents, and then the orders are made from the products. An approval workflow has been added to the system. Two levels of approvers exist: first-level approvers and second-level approvers. The first-level approvers use parallel routing, which means that all the first-level approvers get the document at the same time for approval. After all the first-level approvers approve the order, it is routed serially to the second-level approvers, one at a time. After all the approvers approve the document, or if it gets rejected at any time, the order is routed back to the creator of the order. This database has the document locking feature enabled so only one person at a time can edit the Order documents — this greatly reduces the chances of replication/save conflicts. Now that you have an idea of how the workflow process works for this system, you're going to take a look at each part.

The creator of an order can choose who the first-level and second-level approvers are for the order, as shown in Figure 22-2.

The approval status is listed at the top of the Approvals section. You can start or suspend the approval process by selecting the Begin/Suspend radio button. The creator of the order chooses the first- and second-level approvers in the two list boxes that appear next. As the approval process progresses, the pending and completed approvers are listed so the user knows the status of the approval process. As an approver approves or rejects the document, she can enter comments for either the approval or rejection. The comments and APPROVED or REJECTED are added to the approval history, as shown in Figure 22-2.

The choices available for the first and second approvers come from a profile document. The database administrator chooses the people who are eligible to be first- and second-level approvers, and adds them to the profile document using the dialog box shown in Figure 22-3.

The first- and second-level approvers are retrieved in the Order document using a couple of hidden computed-for-display fields, and those hidden fields are the source for the choices for the first- and second-level approvers list boxes.

After the user finishes creating the order and selects the first- and second-level approvers, she can initiate the approval process by selecting Begin Approvals in the Approvals section, and then saving and closing the document.

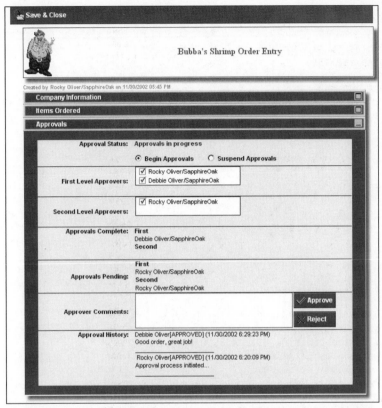

Figure 22-2: The approval feature of the Bubba's Shrimp ordering system is in the Approvals tab of the Order form.

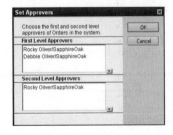

Figure 22-3: The first- and second-level approvers are managed through the Set Approvers dialog box, which maps to a profile document in the database.

Code in the QueryClose event begins the approval process. This code is shown in Listing 22-1.

Listing 22-1: Order Form QueryClose Event

```
Sub Queryclose(Source As Notesuidocument,_
Continue As Variant)
  Dim s As New NotesSession
  Dim db As NotesDatabase
  Dim doc As NotesDocument, maildoc As NotesDocument
  Dim view As NotesView
  Dim col As NotesDocumentCollection
  Dim ordnum As String
  Dim subject As String, bodymsg As String
  Dim linkmsg As String
  Dim recipients As Variant
  Dim histitem As NotesItem, histlist As Variant
  Dim histentry As String

  Set doc = Source.Document

  REM if this is a new doc (i.e. not ever saved)
  REM and it is being closed, then gather the item
  REM docs that were created and delete them
  If Source.IsNewDoc Then
    ordnum = doc.GetItemValue("OrderNumber")(0)
    Set db = doc.ParentDatabase
    Set view = db.GetView("Items.By.OrderNumber.EV")
    Set col = view.GetAllDocumentsByKey(ordnum, True)
    Call col.RemoveAll(True)
  End If

  REM if the document was saved, then check the approval
  REM switch to see if the approval process has
  REM been initiated. if it has, then send an email to
  REM the first level approvers.
  If saveflg Then
    If appswitch2 = "Begin Approvals" And _
    appswitch <> appswitch2 Then
      REM begin the approval process by sending the
      REM first level approver email
      recipients = doc.getItemValue("FirstApprovalsPending")
      If recipients(0) = "" And Ubound(recipients) = 0 _
      Then Exit Sub
      ordernum = doc.GetItemValue("OrderNumber")(0)
      subject = "First Level Approvals Due (" &_
      ordernum & ")"
      bodymsg = "This order is pending your approval. " &_
      "Please follow the doclink to the order and " &_
      "approve or reject it."
      linkmsg = "Link to Order #" & ordernum
      REM SendMail(Subject As String, BodyMsg As String,
      REM recips As Variant, linkdoc As Variant,
```

```
        REM linkmsg As String)
        Call SendMail(subject, bodymsg, recipients,_
        doc, linkmsg)
        doc.ApprovalStatus = "Approvals in progress"

        REM add a comment, user name, and date/time
        REM to the history
        histentry = s.CommonUserName & "[APPROVED] (" &_
        Now & ")" & Chr(10) & "Approval process " &_
        "initiated..." & Chr(10) &_
        "_____" & Chr(10)
        Set histitem = doc.getFirstItem("ApprovalHistory")
        histlist = doc.ApprovalHistory
        Call doc.ReplaceItemValue("ApprovalHistory", histentry)
        Call histitem.AppendToTextList(histlist)
        Call doc.Save(True, False)
    Elseif appswitch2 = "Suspend Approvals" And _
    appswitch <> appswitch2 Then
        REM if the approval process has been suspended,
        REM then set the status appropriately
        doc.ApprovalStatus = "Approval process suspended"
        Call doc.Save(True, False)
    End If
  End If
End Sub
```

Skip the first part that checks whether this is a new document being closed (that part of the code is covered in Chapter 12). Move down to the next section that begins with If saveflg then. The saveflg variable is a global variable that is set to False in the QueryOpen event of the form. If the document is saved, it is set to True in the PostSave event. This flag is used because there's no other way to know whether a document has been saved. The work here isn't performed in the PostSave event because that would cause it to fire over and over each time the document is saved. Instead, a simple flag is set in the PostSave event; then the work is done as the document is closed.

The next line is the following:

```
    If appswitch2 = "Begin Approvals" And _
    appswitch <> appswitch2 Then
```

This line checks two variables that are also global variables. The appswitch variable is set to the value of the ApprovalSwitch item in the QueryOpen event. The ApprovalSwitch item begins or suspends the approval process. The appswitch2 variable is set to the value of the ApprovalSwitch item in the PostSave event. This compares the two values to see if the ApprovalSwitch item value has changed, which prevents the code from executing over and over. The value of the ApprovalSwitch item isn't checked in the QueryClose event, because the user could have enabled the switch, saved the document, disabled the switch, and then closed the document *without* saving, thereby giving the wrong value for the item. Only the value of ApprovalSwitch at the time the document was last saved is useful; any other value doesn't matter.

If the `ApprovalSwitch` item's value is `"Begin Approvals"`, and it was set to this value while the document was open this time, the following code is executed:

```
REM begin the approval process by sending the
REM first level approver email
recipients = doc.getItemValue("FirstApprovalsPending")
If recipients(0) = "" And Ubound(recipients) = 0 _
Then Exit Sub
ordernum = doc.GetItemValue("OrderNumber")(0)
subject = "First Level Approvals Due (" &_
ordernum & ")"
bodymsg = "This order is pending your approval. " &_
"Please follow the doclink to the order and " &_
"approve or reject it."
linkmsg = "Link to Order #" & ordernum
REM SendMail(Subject As String, BodyMsg As String,
REM recips As Variant, linkdoc As Variant,
REM linkmsg As String)
Call SendMail(subject, bodymsg, recipients,_
doc, linkmsg)
doc.ApprovalStatus = "Approvals in progress"

REM add a comment, user name, and date/time
REM to the history
histentry = s.CommonUserName & "[APPROVED] (" &_
Now & ")" & Chr(10) & "Approval process " &_
"initiated..." & Chr(10) &_
"_____" & Chr(10)
Set histitem = doc.getFirstItem("ApprovalHistory")
histlist = doc.ApprovalHistory
Call doc.ReplaceItemValue("ApprovalHistory", histentry)
Call histitem.AppendToTextList(histlist)
Call doc.Save(True, False)
```

The preceding code gathers the values of the `FirstApprovalsPending` item, which contains the approvers that still need to approve the document. If there are values in this item, they are used as the `SendTo` values for your notification e-mail; if there aren't values, the sub is exited. If recipients exist, the subject and body of the e-mail are created, as well as a link comment. The subject, body, and link comment plus the recipients are passed to the `SendMail` sub, which lives in the `order.utils.BE` Script Library. After you send the e-mail, the status changes, the history updates, and the document saves.

Take a look at the `SendMail` sub in Listing 22-2.

Listing 22-2: SendMail sub

```
Sub SendMail(Subject As String, BodyMsg As String,_
recips As Variant, linkdoc As Variant, linkmsg As String)
    Dim s As New NotesSession
    Dim db As NotesDatabase
    Dim bodyitem As NotesRichTextItem
    Dim maildoc As NotesDocument
```

```
        Set db = s.CurrentDatabase
        Set maildoc = db.CreateDocument
        maildoc.Form = "Memo"
        maildoc.Subject = Subject
        Set bodyitem = maildoc.CreateRichTextItem("Body")
        Call bodyitem.AppendText(BodyMsg)
        Call bodyitem.AddNewline(2)
        Call bodyitem.AppendDocLink(linkdoc, linkmsg)
        maildoc.SendTo = recips
        Call maildoc.Send(False)
    End Sub
```

The SendMail sub wraps up the code needed to send an e-mail, making the other code smaller and easier to read. As an example, the e-mail sent by the QueryClose event that initiates the approval workflow appears in Figure 22-4.

Figure 22-4: The SendMail sub enables you to encapsulate the code needed to send an e-mail into a clean subroutine that can be used repeatedly.

The first-level approvers can then follow the provided doclink and approve or reject the order.

The next chunk of code handles what happens when ApprovalSwitch is set to "Suspend Approvals":

```
        Elseif appswitch2 = "Suspend Approvals" And _
    appswitch <> appswitch2 Then
        REM if the approval process has been suspended,
        REM then set the status appropriately
        doc.ApprovalStatus = "Approval process suspended"
        Call doc.Save(True, False)
```

If ApprovalSwitch is set to "Suspend Approvals", the status is set to "Approval process suspended" and the document is saved.

Now that the approval process has begun, your first-level approvers can access the order and approve it. The FirstApproversPending and SecondApproversPending items are both Author Names items, which means that while those individuals are members of those items they have the ability to edit the document. As soon as an approver approves the document, she is automatically removed from the appropriate pending item. This is done by the code in the FirstApproversPending and SecondApproversPending fields, as they are computed fields.

The Approvals section has two graphic buttons: Approve and Reject. These two action buttons contain simple @Command([RunAgent]) calls that execute the (ApprovalButton) and (RejectButton) agents, respectively. Listing 22-3 shows the (ApprovalButton) agent.

Listing 22-3: **ApprovalButton Agent**

```
Options
Option Public
Option Declare

Use "order.utils.BE"

Initialize
Sub Initialize
  On Error Goto errHandler
  Dim ws As New NotesUIWorkspace
  Dim s As New NotesSession
  Dim doc As NotesDocument
  Dim user(0) As String, firstapprovers As Variant,_
  secondapprovers As Variant, comparr As Variant,_
  compfld As String
  Dim ismem1 As Variant, ismem2 As Variant
  Dim apptype As Integer
  Dim histentry As String, histitem As NotesItem,_
  histlist As Variant
  Dim subject As String, bodytext As String,_
  linkmsg As String, ordernum As String, recipient As String

  Set doc = ws.CurrentDocument.Document
  REM get the approver lists, user name
  user(0) = s.UserName
  firstapprovers = doc.GetItemValue("FirstApprovalsPending")
  secondapprovers = doc.GetItemValue _
  ("SecondApprovalsPending")

  REM find out if the user is a first approver
  REM or a second approver
  ismem1 = Arraygetindex(firstapprovers, user(0))
  If Isnull(ismem1) Then
    ismem2 = Arraygetindex(secondapprovers, user(0))
  Else
    apptype = 1
  End If

  If apptype = 0 Then
    If Isnull(ismem2) Then
      Error 900, "You aren't a first or second " &_
      "approver - aborting..."
    Else
      apptype = 2
    End If
  End If

  REM add the user's name to the appropriate complete item
  If apptype = 1 Then
```

```
    compfld = "FirstApprovalsComplete"
  Else
    compfld = "SecondApprovalsComplete"
  End If
  comparr = doc.GetItemValue(compfld)
  Call doc.ReplaceItemValue(compfld,_
  Arrayunique(Fulltrim(Arrayappend(comparr, user))))

  REM add the comments, user name, and
  REM date/time to the history
  histentry = s.CommonUserName & "[APPROVED] (" &_
  Now & ")" & Chr(10) &_
  doc.GetItemValue("ApproverComments")(0) &_
  Chr(10) & "_____" & Chr(10)
  Set histitem = doc.getFirstItem("ApprovalHistory")
  histlist = doc.ApprovalHistory
  Call doc.ReplaceItemValue("ApprovalHistory", histentry)
  Call histitem.AppendToTextList(histlist)
  ordernum = doc.GetItemValue("OrderNumber")(0)

  REM if the first approvers are done then send
  REM to first second approver
  Call doc.ComputeWithForm(False, False)
  firstapprovers = doc.GetItemValue("FirstApprovalsPending")
  If firstapprovers(0) = "" And _
  Ubound(firstapprovers) = 0 Then
    secondapprovers = doc.GetItemValue _
    ("SecondApprovalsPending")
    If secondapprovers(0) = "" And _
    Ubound(secondapprovers) = 0 Then
      REM if there are no more approvers, mark the
      REM document as approved, route to creator of doc
      subject = "Your order has been approved! (" &_
      ordernum & ")"
      bodytext = "Your order has passed through the " &_
      "approval process with flying colors!"
      recipient = doc.GetItemValue("CreatedBy")(0)
      linkmsg = "Link to Order #" & ordernum
      doc.ApprovalStatus = "Approved"
    Else
      REM if it is a second approver, send the msg
      REM to the next approver
      subject = "Second Level Approval Due (" &_
      ordernum & ")"
      bodytext = "This order is pending your approval. " &_
      "Please follow the doclink to the order and " &_
      "approve or reject it."
      linkmsg = "Link to Order #" & ordernum
      recipient = secondapprovers(0)
    End If
    REM SendMail(Subject As String, BodyMsg As String,
```

Continued

Listing 22-3 *(continued)*

```
    REM recips As Variant, linkdoc As Variant,
    REM linkmsg As String)
    Call sendMail(subject, bodytext, recipient, doc, linkmsg)
  End If
  doc.ApproverComments = ""
  Call doc.Save(True, False)
getOut:
  Exit Sub
errHandler:
  Select Case Err
  Case 900
    Msgbox Error$,,"Error"
  Case Else
    Msgbox Error$ & "[" & Err & "]",,"Unhandled Error"
  End Select
  Resume getOut
End Sub
```

After gathering the user's name and the list of first and second approvers, the code checks that the user is a first or second approver. After determining that the user is an approver, the user is added to the appropriate complete field, as shown in the following code:

```
If apptype = 1 Then
  compfld = "FirstApprovalsComplete"
Else
  compfld = "SecondApprovalsComplete"
End If
comparr = doc.GetItemValue(compfld)
Call doc.ReplaceItemValue(compfld,_
Arrayunique(Fulltrim(Arrayappend(comparr, user))))
```

The appropriate item name is determined based on whether the user is a first- or second-level approver. The user is then added to the appropriate complete item.

The history entry is computed and added to the top of the ApprovalHistory item.

```
histentry = s.CommonUserName & "[APPROVED] (" &_
Now & ")" & Chr(10) &_
doc.GetItemValue("ApproverComments")(0) &_
Chr(10) & "_____" & Chr(10)
Set histitem = doc.getFirstItem("ApprovalHistory")
histlist = doc.ApprovalHistory
Call doc.ReplaceItemValue("ApprovalHistory", histentry)
Call histitem.AppendToTextList(histlist)
```

Reading the ApprovalHistory is easier if the most recent entry is listed first. The code takes the value of the ApprovalHistory and assigns it to the histlist variable, replaces the ApprovalHistory item with the new value, and then calls the AppendToTextList method to add the original history back to the item.

The rest of the code checks whether this is the last of the first-level approvers. If it is, a notice is sent to the first of the second-level approvers. If the user is already a second-level approver, the next second-level approver is determined and the e-mail is sent to that approver. If no more approvers exist, an e-mail is sent to the order creator to let them know that the approval process is complete.

The Reject button is a little simpler, as shown in Listing 22-4.

Listing 22-4: RejectButton Agent

```
Options
Option Public
Option Declare

Use "order.utils.BE"

Initialize
Sub Initialize
  On Error Goto errHandler
  Dim ws As New NotesUIWorkspace
  Dim s As New NotesSession
  Dim doc As NotesDocument
  Dim histentry As String, histitem As NotesItem, histlist As
Variant
  Dim appcomments As String
  Dim subject As String, bodytxt As String, linkmsg As
String, recipient As String, ordernum As String

  Set doc = ws.CurrentDocument.Document
  doc.FirstApprovalsComplete = ""
  doc.SecondApprovalsComplete = ""
  doc.ApprovalStatus = "Order REJECTED"
  appcomments = doc.GetItemValue("ApproverComments")(0)

  REM add the comments, user name, and date/time
  REM to the history
  histentry = s.CommonUserName & "[REJECTED] (" & Now &_
  ")" & Chr(10) & appcomments &_
  Chr(10) & "_____" & Chr(10)
  Set histitem = doc.getFirstItem("ApprovalHistory")
  histlist = doc.ApprovalHistory
  Call doc.ReplaceItemValue("ApprovalHistory", histentry)
  Call histitem.AppendToTextList(histlist)

  ordernum = doc.GetItemValue("OrderNumber")(0)

  REM if the first approvers are done then send to first
  second approver
  Call doc.ComputeWithForm(False, False)
  subject = "Order has been REJECTED (" & ordernum & ")"
  bodytxt = "Your order (" & ordernum & ") has been rejected.
```

Continued

Listing 22-4 *(continued)*

```
The approver that rejected your order made the following
comments:" & Chr(10) &_
  Chr(10) & histentry
  recipient = doc.GetItemValue("CreatedBy")(0)
  linkmsg = "Link to Order #" & ordernum

  REM SendMail(Subject As String, BodyMsg As String, recips
As Variant, linkdoc As Variant, linkmsg As String)
  Call sendMail(subject, bodytxt, recipient, doc, linkmsg)
  doc.ApproverComments = ""
  doc.ApprovalSwitch = "Suspend Approvals"
  Call doc.Save(True, False)

getOut:
  Exit Sub
errHandler:
  Select Case Err
  Case 900
    Msgbox Error$,,"Error"
  Case Else
    Msgbox Error$ & "[" & Err & "]",,"Unhandled Error"
  End Select
  Resume getOut
End Sub
```

The RejectButton agent sets all the complete items to empty strings and sets the order status to "Order REJECTED". The ApprovalHistory entry is generated and added to the
ApprovalHistory item, and the same comments are sent to the order creator to inform him
of the rejection and provide the reason. The order creator can then fix the reason for the
rejection and begin the approval process again.

Summary

This chapter introduced concepts concerning workflow, which included the following:

✦ You learned about the basic types of workflow routing.

✦ You were introduced to document locking, a new feature in Notes/Domino 6 that locks
a document while it's being edited to prevent replication/save conflicts.

✦ You walked through an example application that demonstrated a complex workflow,
with techniques on coding it into your own applications.

The next section introduces you to one of the most powerful tools available to Domino developers, the Formula language. Chapter 23 begins with an introduction to the Formula language
that provides a sound foundation for building applications that take advantage of this powerful programming tool.

✦   ✦   ✦

Formula Language Techniques

◆   ◆   ◆   ◆

◆   ◆   ◆   ◆

Introduction to the Formula Language

by Rocky Oliver

In This Chapter

Learning about the Formula language

Exploring the history and future of the Formula language

Exploring the reasons why the Formula language is an important tool

Getting an overview of where and when to use the Formula language

Lotus Notes provides a rich set of programming tools in an integrated environment. The release of Notes/Domino 6 has added to that toolkit by enhancing existing tools, or languages, such as LotusScript and Java, and new tools have also been added, such as integrated XML support. With the variety of choices available, it is easy to overlook the venerable granddaddy of Notes programming languages, the Formula language.

But overlooking the Formula language as an integral part of your toolkit is a mistake. This chapter introduces you to the Formula language, explains the basics of its use, and shows you some advanced techniques for enhancing your Notes/Domino applications. The remaining chapters in Part V expand your knowledge of the Formula language.

Formula Language Defined

Most developers that began developing in Lotus Notes after Release 4 and the introduction of LotusScript have no idea what the Formula language is or what it can do for them. The Formula language is the first language of Lotus Notes, and has been in every release since the introduction of Notes. But the venerability of the language does not mean that it is a legacy language. On the contrary, the Formula language continues to be an integral part of the Notes language feature set. The Formula language, also known as the Notes macro language, is a set of @formulas that provides functionality in a simple, easy-to-use format. Formulas can be used to create Notes client-based applications, Web browser-based applications, or a combination of both. The simplicity of the Formula language enables nonprogrammers to create useful applications without the need to learn a "heavy" language, such as LotusScript or Java. The functionality provided by the Formula language, however, is quite robust. But is the Formula language going to continue to be available?

When asked why they don't use the Formula language in their development efforts, many Notes/Domino developers state that they believe the Formula language is going to go away. "We have LotusScript and Java now! Surely Lotus realizes these languages are much more powerful, and that we don't need the Formula language any more" is often the answer. This couldn't be further from the truth. Lotus continues to update and enhance the Formula language. In Notes Version 1, there were 93 @functions available (@Commands hadn't been invented yet). Today in Notes/Domino 6, there are 256 documented @functions and 381 documented @Commands. In fact, in Notes/Domino 6 the entire Formula Engine was rewritten; there are 48 new documented @functions, and over 20 new or updated @Commands. So, contrary to popular belief, the Formula language continues to be a strategic part of the development toolkit by Lotus — and it should be by developers.

Why Use the Formula Language?

Okay, so Lotus is continuing to enhance the Formula language, and they think it is important. But why should you consider using it? Can't you do everything you need with LotusScript or Java? You probably could do most things with one of the scripting languages, but remember what is important here: writing the best, most efficient application possible in the most expedient way possible. The Formula language helps you do that.

Starting point for novice Notes developers

The Formula language is a simple, easy-to-use language that has a fast ramp-up time for experienced developers and novices alike. There are many "old school" Notes developers out there whose first programming exposure was through the Notes programming language. The Formula language is a gentle introduction into the Notes object model and Notes functionality. Many novice developers use the Formula language as a starting point into the scripting languages offered in Notes.

Architecture of the Formula language

The Formula language is driven by a component of Notes/Domino commonly referred to as the Formula Engine. The Formula Engine is a run-time interpreter of the Formula language. When you write a formula language, the Designer checks your syntax and then saves the instructions — your formula — in a format that makes it easy for the Formula Engine to interpret. Then when your code is executed, the Formula Engine executes your instructions in a very efficient manner when compared to the scripting languages.

Note Given a like set of instructions, the Formula language will *always* be 4 to 5 times faster than the scripting languages executing the same set of instructions.

But why is the Formula language so much faster?

All languages in Notes/Domino access the same core Application Programming Interface, or API. This includes LotusScript, Java, and the Formula language. The scripting languages, however, are compiled and executed differently from the Formula language. When saved, the scripting languages are compiled into a machine language set known as *bytecode*. The scripting languages in Notes/Domino provide the useful capability to enable you to create your own functions, objects, and so forth, enabling you to write code that does exactly what you need. This code is also converted as a part of the bytecode. Incidentally, this bytecode is the same, whether you write your code in Java or LotusScript. When your code is executed, the bytecode representing your instructions is run through a *Bytecode Interpreter*, and the Bytecode

Interpreter carries out your instructions through the API. It's pretty fast. But the flexibility provided by allowing you to create your own functions, subroutines, and classes come at a cost — degraded performance. And this is where the Formula language has an advantage.

The process for executing formulas is a bit different. As mentioned earlier, your formulas are executed by the Formula Engine. The Formula Engine is a highly optimized module that works with the API in a more direct way than the script language bytecode interpreter. Each @Formula and @Command has a direct map to an instruction in the Formula Engine. In old programmers speak, this is known as being "closer to the iron."

Note "Closer to the iron" is a term used in the heyday of mainframes. A common nickname for mainframes was "big iron." Lower-level languages, such as Assembler, were said to be "closer to the iron" because they more closely mapped to the base instruction set of the mainframe. When newer languages were invented, such as Fortran and COBOL, they were said to be "higher level" languages because they were farther away from the base instruction set, which made them not as efficient. The advent of C was a boon to programmers, because it provided high-level language features with the performance of closer-to-the-iron languages.

The only thing missing is the parameters for the formula, which you provide in your code. There are no provisions for creating your own @Formulas, classes, and so forth, so the Formula Engine is not burdened with this additional overhead. These features of the Formula Engine allow it to operate much more efficiently than the Bytecode Interpreter. Figure 23-1 compares the architecture of the scripting languages and the Formula language.

Figure 23-1: The Formula language is faster because it is closer to the iron, or more tightly integrated with the Notes/Domino API.

Formulas are faster to develop

Developers often look for ways to make their applications run as fast as possible, but often neglect to look for ways to help them code as fast as possible. One simple way to do this is to use formulas for common tasks. For instance, a common mistake made by a developer who wishes to provide a Save button to his users is to write the following LotusScript code in a Form Action button:

```
Dim ws as New NotesUIWorkspace
Dim uidoc as NotesUIDocument
Dim doc as NotesDocument

Set uidoc = ws.CurrentDocument
Set doc = uidoc.Document

Call doc.Save(True, False)
```

Unfortunately the developer fails to realize that the same result can be accomplished with one line of formula:

```
@Command([FileSave])
```

Using formulas can help you write code faster, which makes you more productive. Additionally, less code means that understanding and debugging code is much easier for you and others who inherit your code.

Backwards compatibility

Since the Formula language has been around since the dawn of Notes, you can develop an application using the Formula language in Notes 6, and it will run in earlier Notes clients, all the way back to Notes Release 1 — as long as you only use the @Formulas that were available then.

But more importantly, you could run into an application that was developed in an older version of Notes, such as Release 3, and if you know the Formula language you will be able to understand how the application works. This understanding will help you when it comes time to update that application.

Notes/Domino 6 revolutionizes formulas

As mentioned earlier, the Formula Engine was completely rewritten for Notes/Domino 6 — something that hadn't happened since the introduction of Notes itself. When Ray Ozzie (creator of Notes, currently President of Groove Networks) wrote the original Formula Engine for the initial release of Notes, he did it from an assembler programmer's mindset of how to optimize code. It was tightly written and extremely fast. But computer processing power, operating systems, and programming languages have advanced since 1987. Lotus decided it was time to give the Formula Engine, which had been added to but not updated since 1987, a complete rewrite. A young, energetic, and brilliant programmer, named Damien Katz, was assigned the task.

When Damien began working on this task, he made an unprecedented move — he asked the Lotus Business Partner community, "If the sky was the limit, what would you want to see in the Formula language?" The response was equally unprecedented. Over the course of the next couple of months Damien worked with the Lotus Business Partners to refine many of the requests into workable ideas. It was a great example of collaboration, and the results were wonderful.

The result of this collaboration was a new Formula language that not only had many new @functions and @Commands, but quite a few features that were sorely lacking, such as conditional looping (more on that in Chapter 26). One of the biggest enhancements was speed — the new Formula Engine, by unofficial measurements, is approximately two to three times faster than the Release 5 version for most tasks.

So now that you understand why you would use the Formula language, the next questions are *where* and *when* would you use the Formula language?

Where and When to Use the Formula Language

Now you know that the Formula language is efficient, full-featured, and powerful. But where do you use it? And when should you use it? This section introduces you to some ideas for formula usage. It doesn't go into every nook and cranny where the Formula language can be used; instead, it introduces you to some general guidelines for formula usage, and helps lay some groundwork for the subsequent chapters in Part V.

Think "when" first

Often developers get caught up in the details and analysis concerning what tool or language to use before analyzing what their needs are. The easiest way is to not try to force the use of the Formula language (or any language for that matter), but instead analyze your needs first. You should create the workflow and general design of your application first; then while developing it, think about what the characteristics are of the tool you need to write your code.

You know, for example, that you need a keyword in a form you are designing. This keyword is based on the values listed in a column in a particular view. The question you should ask is, "What tool allows me to retrieve a column of values from a view easily and quickly?" Should you write some LotusScript in the QueryOpen event of your form to populate the list? That sounds like a great deal of work. Or should you make your keyword field choices formula based, and then do a @DbColumn to retrieve the list of values? Clearly the latter choice makes more sense. Granted this is an oversimplification, but it helps to illustrate the point — design the application first, as a tool-agnostic design, and then choose the appropriate tool based on what is needed to write efficient code in an efficient manner.

The following list includes some general rules of thumb for deciding when Formula language is a good choice:

✦ Formulas are great for retrieving columnar data from views, or subsets of columnar data from views.

✦ Formulas are great for quick validation and translation of field values in a form.

✦ Formulas are very handy when working with lists of strings (more about this in Chapter 26).

✦ Formulas are great shortcuts for Web development. In fact, there are many @functions that are specifically designed to greatly speed up Web development.

✦ If you need to perform some action that is the same as a Notes client menu action, use an @Command — most of them have a direct correlation to Notes client menu items.

These are just a few guidelines. You will learn quite a few more as you read through the rest of the chapters in Part V.

Looking for code in all the right places

Formulas can be used almost everywhere in a Domino database — but how do you keep it straight? Even after you decide that formulas may be the best tool to use, it is hard to remember all the places where the Formula language is available. The easiest way to determine whether the Formula language is available is to look at the design element in Domino Designer, and then check the second Run keyword at the top of the Programming pane, as shown in Figure 23-2.

Figure 23-2: There are many places where the Formula language can be used — even places you wouldn't normally consider places for formulas, such as the QueryOpen event of a form.

Some practical, common places where the Formula language is used include the following:

✦ The Default Value, Input Translation, and Input Validation events of a field on a form

✦ The Choices area of a Keyword Field property box

✦ The Window title of a form

✦ The Column formula of a view

✦ Actions in forms and views

✦ Buttons on a form

✦ Agents, including user-based, scheduled, and Web-based

✦ The HTML Head Content area of a form

There are quite a few other areas where formulas can be used; these are merely some of the more common areas. Additionally, there are areas where only formulas can be used, such as Input Translation and Validation formulas for fields on a form, and in the HTML Head Content area of a form. Other areas where formulas can and can't be used are covered in subsequent chapters in this section.

Summary

Formulas have always been, and will continue to be, powerful tools for the creation of robust Notes/Domino applications.

✦ The Formula language is simple to use, powerful, and extremely fast.

✦ The learning curve for formulas is relatively easy for novice and experienced programmers alike.

✦ Formulas can be used in a variety of places to enhance your application and shorten your development time.

Take some time to explore the rest of Part V to learn more about what the Formula language has to offer.

✦   ✦   ✦

Working with @Functions

by Rocky Oliver

@Functions are the core components of the Formula language. @Functions were the first component of the Formula language, and originally the only component. Beginning with a simplistic 93 core @functions in Notes Version 1 — all of which are still usable today — the Formula language in Notes/Domino 6 now includes 256 documented @functions. Now, we're not going to attempt to cover all of them here (that's what the Help file is for); instead, you are going to be introduced to programming techniques for getting the most out of @functions, and you will be introduced to some of the more useful @functions. Subsequent chapters in this section dive into the details of using particular @functions for specialized tasks. But you have to crawl before you walk, so let's begin crawling.

Working with @Functions

@Functions are easy to learn and simple to use. This section provides some basic concepts to keep in mind when using @functions, and helps you get the most out of your @function code.

Begin at the beginning

@Functions are used to work with the Domino object model (DOM) API. This simplified language is written as a series of statements that are executed in the order they are written. @Functions usually do one of two things: perform some action, or return a result. The format of @functions is as follows:

```
@Function(Arg1; Arg2;... Argn)
```

You separate arguments with a semicolon, and if an @function takes arguments, you surround the arguments with parentheses; if the @function does not take arguments, you don't use parentheses.

@Functions can work against one or many documents, either in a single instance or iteratively, depending upon where and how the @function statement is written.

Usually the results of @functions are assigned to a variable. This variable can either be an existing item on a document or field on a form, or a temporary variable that is created at runtime. If it is a temporary variable, that variable is only available to the immediate formula code that is executing. For instance, if you want to compute the common name of the user and use it somewhere else, you could assign it to a variable:

```
uname := @Name([cn]; @UserName)
```

Then you could reference the uname variable elsewhere in your code.

Note   If you come from another programming environment, you may be used to predefining the data type of the variable before you use it. Because the Formula language is a simplified language, no typecasting is needed.

To work with an item or a field, you simply have to name your variable the same name as the field or item. An *item* is a discrete piece of information on a document; a *field* is a "lens" that enables a user to view or manipulate an item in the UI. So in the following chapters when an item is mentioned, it is referencing a piece of information on a document, and a *field* is a piece of information presented on a form in the UI. The easiest way to keep it straight is that a field is on a form, and an item is data in a document.

Cross-Reference   You can find more information about the differences and relationships between forms and documents in Chapter 4.

Now that some basic rules for working with @functions have been established, it's time to take a look at some introductory code. Listing 24-1 shows a simple Formula call that prompts the user for a name; then that name is placed in a field called Name on the form, assuming that this code is being executed from a button on the form.

Listing 24-1: Simple @function Formula for Prompting for a Value and Setting a Field on a Form

```
Value := @Prompt([OKCancelEdit]; "Enter a Name"; "Please enter a
name."; @Name([CN]; @UserName));

FIELD Name := Value;
@True;
```

You should notice a few things within this example:

✦ Whenever you assign a value to a variable, you use a colon and an equal sign (`variable := value`).

✦ Formulas are parameter driven. The data types for parameters are fairly simplistic:

   • **Strings:** The most common one.

   • **Action keywords:** Action keywords are like flags, or predefined variables, for a function. They are surrounded by square brackets. In Listing 24-1, `[OKCancelEdit]` and `[CN]` are keywords.

- **Number:** Usually an integer.

- **Date:** Not used often. Dates are passed as a parameter for the few functions that work with dates, such as @Weekday, @Month, and so on.

- **List:** Usually a list, or array of strings.

✦ Parameters can be other @functions. In Listing 24-1, the @Name function is in the default value parameter position for the @Prompt function.

✦ A few leading keywords, or *reserved* keywords, are used with formulas. These include ENVIRONMENT, FIELD, SELECT, DEFAULT, and REM. In Listing 24-1, the FIELD reserved keyword is used to assign the contents of the Value variable to the Name field in the form.

✦ When writing formulas, you must end each line of code with a semicolon (;). A semicolon isn't required at the end of the last line of code.

You can find the examples illustrated in the formula chapters of this book in Domino 6 Bible Formula Examples (d6bibleFormula.nsf), which is available for download from www.wiley. com/compbooks/benz.

Because Formula language has so many @functions available, it is hard to keep up with what's available. The Formula interface in Domino 6 Designer provides a useful context-sensitive list of @functions available to you, as shown in Figure 24-1.

Figure 24-1: As you type your @function, the Domino 6 Designer provides a list of @functions available.

In Figure 24-1, the developer is beginning to type @Prompt, and as he types, the list of @functions jumps to the appropriate @function. This can be useful when you know there is some function that does what you want, but you can't remember the exact way it is spelled.

The @Prompt function has many keywords for it, based on what you need. Keywords, such as [OK], [OKCancelList], and many more define various configurations available for the @Prompt function. So how do you keep up with all of the various choices and parameters for the @functions? Domino 6 Designer has a great new feature that provides you the parameters of the function you are writing. So if you know which @function you need, but you can't remember the parameters for it, you can rely on the context-sensitive help that appears as you type your @function. Figure 24-2 shows what the context-sensitive help looks like for the @Prompt used in Listing 24-2.

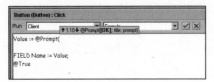

Figure 24-2: The Domino 6 Designer provides context-sensitive help while you are typing your Formula code.

If all else fails, the help file for Domino 6 Designer is excellent, and should be the first place you look whenever you have a question concerning any aspect of Domino development.

The finer points of @function programming

Now that you have learned some basics of @functions, this section discusses some of the finer aspects of them. Like most programming languages, there is both a science and an art to writing good code. The preceding section covered the science, so now it's time to explore some of the finer aspects, or "art" of @functions. This section touches on a couple of them, and as you read through the rest of the chapters in this section, other techniques are introduced where appropriate.

One thing that developers often forget when using @functions is that even if a parameter requires a certain data type, that parameter also optionally takes a variable containing the proper data type. This provides you a great deal of flexibility when writing your code so that you can use less code and gain more functionality. Examples always make complex concepts easier to understand.

The example used here comes from a real problem that I encountered many years ago. My client had a database with many documents, and the form used to modify those documents contained many fields. The client wanted to provide his users the ability to modify a field on multiple documents without requiring them to open each document individually. The client's in-house development staff had written an agent to do this, but the agent was getting increasingly complex to modify and maintain. Additionally, it prompted the user for each document, and users only wanted to be prompted once. The in-house development staff had begun to work around that problem, but had not solved it yet. And because this was like most Notes applications in that it was constantly evolving, the time it took to keep this agent updated was becoming increasingly time consuming to modify, in addition to adding the new requirements for the feature. So the client called me in to help with the situation.

When I first reviewed the code, I could immediately identify some problems. The first problem revolved around the request by the users to be prompted only once for information, and then using that information for all selected documents. This issue stemmed from the fact that formula-based agents run against every document selected in the view if Selected Documents is selected in the Agent property box. This means that if there is an @Prompt in the agent, that @Prompt is executed for every selected document. Therefore, this agent would need to be broken up into two agents: one that prompted the user for information, and one that acted on every document with the information.

Additionally, the code was written in such a way where there was an @If statement for each field that needed to be modified, that included 35 fields or so, and because the code was really long, I don't reproduce it here; however, I do provide an example of what it was like in Listing 24-2.

Listing 24-2: *"Before"* Example of Field Modification Code

```
fieldchoice := @Prompt([OkCancelList]; "Choose a Field";
  "Please choose a field to change."; "Field One";
  "Field One":"Field Two":"Field Three":"Field Four":"Field
Five");

@If(fieldchoice = "Field One";
          @SetField("Field1";
              @Prompt([OkCancelEdit]; "Enter New Value";
"Enter a new value for " + fieldchoice + "..."; Field1)
          );
"");

@If(fieldchoice = "Field Two";
          @SetField("Field2";
              @Prompt([OkCancelEdit]; "Enter New Value";
"Enter a   new value for " + fieldchoice + "..."; Field2));
"");

@If(fieldchoice = "Field Three";
          @SetField("Field3";
              @Prompt([OkCancelList]; "Chooose New Value";
"Choose  a new value for " + fieldchoice + "...";
                  @Subset(
                      @DbLookup("":""; ""; "KEYWORDS";
"States"; 2);
                  1);
                  @DbLookup("":""; ""; "KEYWORDS"; "States";
2)
              )
          );
"");

@If(fieldchoice = "Field Four";
          @SetField("Field4";
              @Prompt([OkCancelEdit]; "Enter New Value";
"Enter a   new value for " + fieldchoice + "..."; Field4));
"");

@If(fieldchoice = "Field Five";
          @SetField("Field5";
              @TextToTime(@Prompt([OkCancelEdit]; "Enter New
Date Value"; "Enter a new value for " + fieldchoice + "...";
Field5))); "")
```

In this example, there are five fields on the form: Field1, Field2, and Field4 are text fields, Field3 is a keyword field, and Field5 is a date field. As you can see, the code is written to first prompt the user to choose the field she wants, and then the code has a series of @If statements that evaluate whether the user chose that particular field. Although this code will work, there are ample opportunities for optimization.

Note One common misconception is that if you write code, and later find or are shown a better way to do it, the old way you wrote the code is wrong or bad. This is not the case. *Any* code that works is good code. But there may be better, more efficient ways to accomplish a given task. If you keep this in mind, you will be more open to learning more efficient ways to write code, and will not be offended if you are shown a better way.

How do you identify opportunities to improve this code? The first things to look for are redundancies in the code. Redundancies or repetitiveness in code usually identify opportunities for optimization. In Listing 24-2, you can see that the @If statements are all remarkably similar, pointing to a prime opportunity for optimization. Now that you have identified that this code could be optimized, how do you go about doing it?

When confronted with this situation, I broke down the problem and tried to identify what the variables were in the problem, and what things were the same. The things that are the same are pretty easy to pick out — the code that assigns the new value to the field. Then what are the variables? The labels of the fields, and subsequently the fields themselves, are variable based on what the user chooses to modify. Listing 24-3 shows a simplified version of code I wrote to solve the problem, based on the "before" example in Listing 24-2. This code has not been broken up into two agents yet — that will be done after the code is optimized.

Listing 24-3: "After" Example of Field Modification Code

```
REM {Define labels and corresponding fields in order};
labels := "Field One":"Field Two":"Field Three":"Field
Four":"Field Five";
fields := "Field1":"Field2":"Field3":"Field4":"Field5";

REM {Define fields requiring a list for choices};
keyfields := "Field3";

REM {Define fields requiring a date};
datefields := "Field5";

REM {Prompt user for label of field to change};
labelchoice := @Prompt([OkCancelList] : [NoSort]; "Choose
Field"; "Choose the field you wish to change...";
@Subset(labels; 1); labels);

REM {Determine corresponding field to change};
fldchoice := @Trim(@Replace(labelchoice; labels; fields));

REM {If it is a keyword field, look up list};
valuelistlook := @If(@IsMember(fldchoice; keyfields);
   @DbLookup("":""; ""; "KEYWORDS"; fldchoice; 2); "");
valuelist := @If(@IsError(valuelistlook); ""; valuelistlook);
```

```
REM {Prompt for new value};
newval := @If(valuelist = ""; @Prompt([OkCancelEdit];
   "Enter New Value"; "Enter a new value for " +
   labelchoice + "..."; "");
   @Prompt([OkCancelList]; "Choose New Value";
   "Choose a new value for " + labelchoice + "...";
   @Subset(valuelist; 1); valuelist));

REM {Set the new value into the field.};
REM {Check to make sure fldchoice isn't blank.};
REM {Check to see if it is a date field; if so, convert};
@If(fldchoice = ""; @Return(@Prompt([Ok];
   "ERROR"; "Missing field name, process aborted."));
   @IsMember(fldchoice; datefields);
   @SetField(fldchoice; @TextToTime(newval));
   @SetField(fldchoice; newval))
```

The example in Listing 24-3 contains many items, from a design and a style perspective that should be pointed out. The overall design flow of the code is explained in the remark, or REM statements in the example. The design is as follows:

✦ Define labels and corresponding field names in order.

✦ Define fields requiring a list of choices (keyword fields).

✦ Define fields requiring a date type of value.

✦ Ask the user what field to change, but use the labels to ask because the user may not know what the underlying field names are, even though she knows the field labels.

✦ After the user chooses a label, determine the corresponding field name.

✦ Determine whether the chosen field is a keyword field; if it is, do a lookup to get a list of possible values.

✦ Ask the user for the new value.

✦ Set the new value into the appropriate field in each document selected.

You define the labels and the field names in order so that the label can be swapped for the corresponding field value easily (more on that in a moment). By defining the labels and field names in a list, the client can easily add fields to the existing code in the future and will not have to modify any other part of the code to support more fields. The client simply adds the new label to the label list, and the new field to the field list. As long as the new label and the new list are in the same relative positions, the code will work correctly.

The solution prompts the user for a new field and then uses a combination of @functions, @Trim and @Replace, to determine the field name that corresponds to the chosen label. @Trim simply trims off extra spaces from within and around text. @Replace is a bit more complex.

@Replace **takes three parameters:** sourcelist, fromlist, **and** tolist. @Replace **checks** fromlist **for the value(s) in** sourcelist; **if the value is found, the** sourcelist **value is** replaced with the value in tolist that is in the same position as the value in fromlist that matches the sourcelist value. Here's a short example to explain it.

Suppose that there are three lists:

```
SourceList := "Apples" : "Oranges" : "Grapefruit"
FromList := "Grapefruit" : "Cherries" : "Apples" : "Bananas"
ToList := "Cantelope" : "Blueberries" : "Grapes" : "Tangerines"
```

The goal is to replace, in SourceList, any instances of what is in the FromList with the corresponding fruit in the ToList. So the @Replace function checks each item in SourceList for a match in FromList, and if it is found, replaces it with the corresponding fruit in ToList. The result is as follows:

```
Result := "Grapes" : "Oranges" : "Cantelope"
```

Now that you have some idea of how @Replace works, explore how it is used in Listing 24-3, in the following code snippet:

```
REM {Determine corresponding field to change};
fldchoice := @Trim(@Replace(labelchoice; labels; fields));
```

In this instance, if the label the user chooses (labelchoice) matches any value in labels, labelchoice is replaced with the corresponding field name, and that value is returned.

Cross-Reference   Chapter 28 covers the @Trim and @Replace combination in more detail.

Now that you know the corresponding field name, you need to know how to prompt the user. Is the field the user wants to change a text field or a keyword field? The following code performs this determination.

```
REM {If it is a keyword field, look up list};
valuelistlook := @If(@IsMember(fldchoice; keyfields);
   @DbLookup("":""; ""; "KEYWORDS"; fldchoice; 2); "");
valuelist := @If(@IsError(valuelistlook); ""; valuelistlook);

REM {Prompt for new value};
newval := @If(valuelist = ""; @Prompt([OkCancelEdit];
   "Enter New Value"; "Enter a new value for " +
   labelchoice + "..."; "");
   @Prompt([OkCancelList]; "Choose New Value";
   "Choose a new value for " + labelchoice + "...";
   @Subset(valuelist; 1); valuelist));
```

To determine this, check the keyfields list and see whether the chosen fieldname is a part of the list using the @IsMember function. If it is, the appropriate list of choices is retrieved from the Keywords view using the @DbLookup function, and the user is presented the list of choices for selection using the [OKCancelList] version of the @Prompt function. If the field name is not in the keyfields list, the user is asked to enter a new value.

Cross-Reference   Chapter 26 explores the @DbLookup function in more detail.

Now you know the field name and the new value to place in the desired field. The following code accomplishes this:

```
REM {Set the new value into the field.};
REM {Check to make sure fldchoice isn't blank.};
REM {Check to see if it is a date field; if so, convert};
@If(fldchoice = ""; @Return(@Prompt([Ok];
   "ERROR"; "Missing field name, process aborted."));
   @IsMember(fldchoice; datefields);
   @SetField(fldchoice; @TextToTime(newval));
   @SetField(fldchoice; newval))
```

Before anything is placed in the listed field, the value is checked to make sure that it isn't blank. Next the field is tested to see whether it is a date field by checking for it in the date-fields list. If it is, the value is converted to a Time value; if not, the value is simply inserted into the field in all selected documents.

One of the keys to all of this working is that flexibility mentioned earlier — that @functions can take variables for parameters. If you check the Domino 6 Designer help files, you will find that the @SetField function takes a string for the first parameter (the field name), and some value as the second parameter (the value to place in the field). Instead of hard coding the field name, use the fldchoice variable for the field name parameter, and the newval variable for the value parameter. This means that the same single @function can be used to set any desired field.

After getting the code optimized, I still had to solve the problem of the user being prompted for each selected document. The client wants the user to be prompted once, and then the change made for all selected documents. To do so, you must use two agents — one to gather the information, and one to set the information in the documents.

The first agent does all of the prompting of the user. The Target property for this agent is set to None so that it only executes once. Listing 24-4 contains the code for the GetFields agent:

Listing 24-4: **GetFields Agent**

```
REM {Define labels and corresponding fields in order};
labels := "Field One":"Field Two":"Field Three":"Field
Four":"Field Five";
fields := "Field1":"Field2":"Field3":"Field4":"Field5";

REM {Prompt user for label of field to change};
labelchoice := @Prompt([OkCancelList] : [NoSort]; "Choose
Field"; "Choose the field you wish to change..."; 
@Subset(labels; 1); labels);

REM {Determine corresponding field to change};
fldchoice := @Trim(@Replace(labelchoice; labels; fields));

REM {Define fields requiring a list for choices};
keyfields := "Field3";

REM {If it is a keyword field, look up list};
valuelistlook := @If(@IsMember(fldchoice; keyfields);
```

Continued

Listing 24-4 *(continued)*

```
    @DbLookup(""::""; ""; "KEYWORDS"; @UpperCase(fldchoice); 2);
"");
valuelist := @If(@IsError(valuelistlook); ""; valuelistlook);

REM {Prompt for new value};
newval := @If(valuelist = ""; @Prompt([OkCancelEdit];
    "Enter New Value"; "Enter a new value for " +
    labelchoice + "..."; "");
    @Prompt([OkCancelList]; "Choose New Value";
    "Choose a new value for " + labelchoice + "...";
    @Subset(valuelist; 1); valuelist));

ENVIRONMENT FieldChoice := fldchoice;
ENVIRONMENT FieldVal := newval
```

Notice that the code is similar to the first part of the "After" code in Listing 24-3. The biggest difference is that right after the new value is gathered from the user and assigned to the newval variable, both the field name and the value are set into NOTES.INI variables so the next agent can get them.

Tip

> The easiest way to pass parameters between two agents is through environment variables in the NOTES.INI. This can be done using the ENVIRONMENT reserved keyword, or by using the @SetEnvironment or @Environment functions. One suggestion: Even though the @Environment function can technically be used to get and set environment variables, it makes your code much easier to read if you use @SetEnvironment to set environment variables and @Environment to read environment variables.

The second agent is used to set the desired field to the new value in all selected documents. This agent's Target property is set to All Selected Documents so that it will process all documents selected by the user. Listing 24-5 provides the code for the ModifyFields agent:

Listing 24-5: **ModifyFields Agent**

```
fldchoice := @Environment("FieldChoice");
newval := @Environment("FieldVal");

REM {Define fields requiring a date};
datefields := "Field5";

REM {Set the new value into the field.};
REM {Check to make sure fldchoice isn't blank.};
@If(fldchoice = ""; @Return(@Prompt([Ok];
    "ERROR"; "Missing field name, process aborted."));
    @IsMember(fldchoice; datefields);
    @SetField(fldchoice; @TextToTime(newval));
    @SetField(fldchoice; newval));
SELECT @All
```

The only part of this agent that may need to be modified if new fields are added in the future is the `datefields` variable, and only if the new field added is a date field. The field name and value are retrieved from the NOTES.INI and are assigned to the `fldchoice` and `newval` variables, respectively. The only other item of note in this code is the last line, the `SELECT @All` statement. Because this runs against selected documents, this line is required to indicate which of the selected documents should be processed. One nice feature of the `SELECT` statement is that you can filter the selected documents even further for processing. Suppose, for example, that you only want to process documents that are based on the `CONTACT` form. You could use a select statement of `SELECT Form="CONTACT"` to filter the agent so that only those documents are processed. Incidentally, it doesn't matter where the `SELECT` statement is in the code, it is processed just the same.

You've explored some of the basics of @function programming. The next two sections dive into some more specific uses of @functions — Notes client programming and Web programming.

Useful @Functions for Notes Applications

Because the Notes client is so feature rich, from both a functionality and design perspective, there is a plethora of ways to effectively use @functions in the Notes client. As stated earlier, there are too many @functions to cover in this book; not to mention that is what the help file is for. Therefore, this section is divided into two parts: @functions you should memorize, and @functions you should know about.

@Functions you should memorize

These are functions that are so useful that you should go ahead and commit them to memory. These functions provide commonly needed useful functionality.

@AllChildren, @AllDescendants

These @functions are used in the selection formula for a view. `@AllChildren` selects all immediate response documents to the main documents defined by the selection formula, and `@AllDescendants` returns all descendants of the main documents defined by the selection formula. You use these as follows:

```
SELECT selection criteria | @AllDescendants
```

@Attachments, @AttachmentNames, @AttachmentLengths, @AttachmentModifiedTimes

These functions are great if you have attachments in your application. You can use these functions to display information in views about attachments, providing more information to your users.

New Feature

@AttachmentModifiedTimes returns the last time the attachment was modified as a Date/Time value. If more than one attachment is in the document, then a list of Date/Time values is returned in the same order as the names returned by @AttachmentNames.

The attachment functions do not take parameters.

✓char(character number)

✓char provides you an ASCII character based on a number you provide. You should memorize the following three:

✦ ✓char(10): Carriage return

✦ ✓char(13): Line feed

✦ ✓char(9): Tab

You use ✓char(10) and ✓char(13) together to simulate a carriage return/line feed. A carriage return is an ASCII character that indicates the end of a line. A line feed is a new line without a carriage return—basically what we think of as line wrapping. Both of these are holdover terms from the ancient days of typewriters. Usually, you use this in places where @NewLine doesn't work, such as an @Prompt. This can be helpful when inserting text into a field programmatically, or with the aforementioned @Prompt.

@DbName

@DbName returns the server and file path of the database where the function is executing, as a list. This function is usually used with @Subset to get one or the other of these values:

✦ @Subset(@DbName; 1): Returns the server name, or "" if the database is local.

✦ @Subset(@DbName; -1): Returns the file path of the database. If the database is on the server, it returns the filepath relative to the Domino data directory; if it is local, it returns the full path, including drive letter.

@DeleteDocument, @DeleteField

These are useful for removing fields from a document (@DeleteField) or documents from a database (@DeleteDocument). To use either function, assign it as the value of a field:

```
FIELD SomeField := @DeleteDocument
```

These functions require no parameters.

@Do(action string 1; action string 2; . . . ;action string n)

@Do executes a list of functions in order. This is useful when used in conjunction with an @If statement:

```
@If(Status = "Complete";
  @Do(
    @SetField("CompletedDate"; @Today);
    @Command([FileSave]);
    @Command([FileCloseWindow])
  );
"")
```

@DocumentUniqueID

This function returns the unique ID of the document where the code is executing.

Tip   If you want to use this function in a field or a view column, you need to use @Text with it, such as @Text(@DocumentUniqueID), as this function returns a special data type, not a text value.

@Environment(environment name), @SetEnvironment (environment name; string)

@Environment can get or set an environment variable in the NOTES.INI. The most commonly used format is shown in the title, although if you use this function to set an environment variable, the second parameter is a string, just like @SetEnvironment.

@SetEnvironment can only set an environment variable in the NOTES.INI.

Tip

> As stated earlier, even though the @Environment function can technically be used to get and set environment variables, it makes your code much easier to read if you use @SetEnvironment to set environment variables and @Environment to read environment variables.

@If(test condition 1; action 1; test condition 2; action 2; . . . ; else action)

@If is one of the most commonly used @functions. @If follows the common If . . . Then . . . Else format, but you can string together your if/then statements sequentially and provide a final else statement. @If requires an odd number of arguments, and the last parameter is always the Else action statement.

If you refer to Listing 24-4, you find an example of using two if/then condition statements in an @If, followed by an else:

```
REM {Set the new value into the field.};
REM {Check to make sure fldchoice isn't blank.};
@If(fldchoice = "";
  @Return(
    @Prompt([Ok]; "ERROR"; "Missing field name, process
aborted.")
  );
  @IsMember(fldchoice; datefields);
  @SetField(fldchoice; @TextToTime(newval));
  @SetField(fldchoice; newval)
);
```

Notice that the first if test is the fldchoice = ""; then, if that is true, the @Return@Prompt sequence fires. The next test is @IsMember; if that is true, the first @SetField fires. If neither statement is true, the final @SetField fires.

@IfError(test condition; error return)

One of the most commonly used combinations of @functions is @If with @IsError. This combination is used to test to make sure @DbLookups and @DbColumns do not return errors before using the results. @IfError replaces this combination with a streamlined function to test a condition, and if that condition is not an error returns the result, but if it is an error returns something else.

Here's what the old way of trapping a @DbLookup for an error would look like:

```
List := @DbLookup("" : ""; ""; "Keywords"; "States"; 2);
List := @If(@IsError(List); ""; List)
```

This can now be replaced with one, simplified line using @IfError:

```
List := @IfError(@DbLookup("" : ""; ""; "Keywords"; "States";
2); "")
```

Chapter 26 covers using @DbLookups, including proper error trapping.

@IsDocBeingSaved

This @function returns @True if the document where the code is executing is being saved, *while* it is being saved; otherwise, it returns @False.

Tip This function should be used in Field Validation formulas. It prevents the Validation formula from firing if the document is only being refreshed and not saved. Here's an example: @IF(@IsDocBeingSaved & SomeField = ""; @Failure("SomeField is blank!"); @Success).

@IsError(condition to test)

This @function tests a value to see if it is an error. If it is an error, it returns @True; otherwise, it returns @False. This function is most often used with @DbLookups and @DbColumns.

Take a look at Chapter 26 for a more detailed explanation of using @IsError.

@Name([format keyword]; RFC 822 string)

@Name is probably one of the most misunderstood @functions. Because @Name has various keywords that allow you to pull out parts of a RFC 822-compliant string, it does not automatically parse Notes names, such as those returned from @UserName. For example, one of the keywords available for @Name is [G] for given name, or first name. Notes does not store this as a part of the Notes ID, so the string returned by @UserName does not contain a G component.

The most commonly used keywords with @Name are the following:

✦ **[CN]:** Stands for Common Name; so @Name([CN]; "CN=Rocky Oliver/O=SapphireOak") returns Rocky Oliver.

✦ **[ABBREVIATE]:** Returns the abbreviated version of a canonical name; so @Name([ABBREVIATED]; "CN=Rocky Oliver/O=SapphireOak" returns Rocky Oliver/SapphireOak.

@NewLine

This @function adds a new line (carriage return/line feed) to text. @NewLine takes no parameters.

@SetField(field name; value)

@SetField sets the specified field name to the given value. This function is similar to the FIELD reserved keyword, except for two things:

✦ @SetField can be used in conjunction with another function, such as an @If or @Do.

✦ @SetField can use a variable for the FieldName parameter.

@Trim(string or string list)

This @function takes the given string or string list and trims the leading and trailing spaces, and extra spaces between words.

Cross-Reference This function is also used in conjunction with @Replace. See Chapter 28 for more information.

@Unique or @Unique(string list)

This function is actually two functions in one. If @Unique is used without any parameters, it returns a unique alphanumeric string. If @Unique is given a list, it removes duplicates from the list.

@UserName

@UserName returns the name of the user in canonical format. If the code is executing on the server, it returns the canonical name of the server.

These are a few functions that are so useful that it is worth knowing them by heart. Another set of functions are also very useful, but don't need to be memorized, either because they are fairly complicated or they are not used as often.

@Functions you should know about

Because there are so many @functions, it is difficult to know which ones you should know and which ones are not as useful. This section introduces you to the functions that are important. Not only do you need to know they exist, but also understand how they are properly used.

@BusinessDays(start date list; end date list; days to exclude; dates to exclude)

New Feature @BusinessDays is a new function in Domino 6.

The code that used to be required to do what @BusinessDays does was very complex and very long. @BusinessDays greatly reduces the complexity of your code when you need to know how many business days are between one or more date ranges. This handy little feature lets you specify one or more pairs of start and end dates, days to exclude (usually Sunday (1) and Saturday (7), and an optional list of dates — say, a list of holidays or vacation days. Given this information, @BusinessDays calculates the number of workdays left.

Suppose, for example, that you want to know the number of working days in November and December 2002. You don't work weekends, and you know you have Thanksgiving and the Friday after off, and you have Christmas Eve and Christmas Day off. The code to calculate your workdays based on these criteria, using @BusinessDays would appear as follows:

```
Weekend := 1 : 7;
Holidays := @TextToTime("11/28/02" : "11/29/02" : "12/24/02" :
"12/25/02");
Workdays := @BusinessDays(@TextToTime("11/01/02");
@TextToTime("12/31/02"); Weekend; Holidays)
```

This would return a number of 39, indicating there are 39 working days based on the parameters provided.

Tip

Notice in the preceding example that the dates had to be converted to date/time values. @BusinessDays needs date/time values, not strings, for the date parameters. The easiest way to convert your date strings into date/time values is with the @TextToTime function.

@Contains(string; string list)

@Contains checks the string list for the string provided. If the string is found, @True is returned.

@Count(list)

New Feature

@Count is a new function in Domino 6

@Count is the same as @Elements, except for one notable difference. If the parameter passed to @Elements is an empty string (""), it returns a 0. If the parameter passed to @Count is an empty string it returns a 1. This can be useful when an empty string is a valid member of the list you are working with in your application.

@Elements(list)

@Elements returns the number of items in a list. If the parameter passed is an empty string (""), then @Elements returns a 0.

@Explode(string; separator)

Other parameters are available for @Explode, but this is the most common format used. @Explode takes a string and breaks the string into a string list at every place the separator is found. So if you had the following string:

```
List := "Apples~Oranges~Bananas"
```

you could explode that string into a string list by using @Explode like this:

```
List := @Explode(List; "~")
```

which would return

```
List := "Apples" : "Oranges" : "Bananas"
```

@Implode(string list; separator)

Other parameters are available for @Implode, but this is the most common format used. Basically, @Implode is the opposite of @Explode. @Implode takes a string list and concatenates the elements of the list together on the provided separator.

@Replace(source string or list; from string or list; to string or list)

@Replace was explained earlier in the area after Listing 24-3 in this chapter. For more information about the intricacies of this example, check out Chapter 28.

@ReplaceSubstring(source string or list; from string or list; to string or list)

@ReplaceSubstring replaces a substring of characters found in text with a different set of characters. @ReplaceSubstring works very similarly to @Replace; in fact, it takes the same parameters:

✦ SourceList: A string or a list of strings that is the target of the function

✦ FromList: A string or a list of strings that is checked for in the SouceList

✦ ToList: A string or a list of strings that is replaced wherever an item in the FromList is found in the SourceList

The following example shows how @ReplaceSubstring works. You have a string that has placeholders for spaces and commas. The string looks like this:

```
MyString :=
"Do#not#meddle#in#the#affairs#of#dragons~#cause~#you're#like#crunchy#an
d#taste#good#with#ketchup."
```

To convert it to something readable, you run it through @ReplaceSubstring like this:

```
MyString := @ReplaceSubstring(Mystring; "~" : "#"; "," : " ")
```

And the result is:

```
MyString := "Do not meddle in the affairs of dragons, cause, you're
like crunchy and taste good with ketchup."
```

 Cross-Reference   @ReplaceSubstring is shown in one of the advanced examples explained in Chapter 28.

@Sort(list; [*order*]; *custom sort expression*)

 New Feature   @Sort is a new function in Domino 6.

@Sort has been requested as a new feature since the release of Notes Release 2. Until now, there was no way to sort a list of values purely in @functions. Given a list of values, @Sort can sort them for you. This function has optional parameters available to it, but the default parameters will suffice for most situations. The default parameters are Ascending, Case Sensitive, Accent Sensitive, Pitch Sensitive. If you need to modify these, please refer to the Domino 6 Designer help for more information.

@StatusBar(string)

 New Feature   @StatusBar is a new function in Domino 6.

The @StatusBar function is a useful function for debugging and informing your user about the status of your code as it is running.

Tip

Users don't like to wait for things. If you have some Formula code that takes a long time to run (a long time being more than a few seconds), then you should provide updates to your user about the progress of the code. For example, if you are processing a view full of documents, then tell them how many documents you have processed, as you process them, with the @StatusBar function. Users are much more tolerant of waiting for something if they are being informed about it during the processing.

@Text(value) or @Text(value; format code)

This @function converts the provided parameter to a string. Optionally, it formats a number or date to the specified format, such as currency or MM/DD/YYYY. For example, if you want to convert a number to text but format it as currency, you could do so as follows:

```
CurString := @Text(123.45; "C")
```

which would return:

```
CurString := "$123.45"
```

@ThisName

@ThisName is a new function in Domino 6.

This function returns the name of the current field. It is useful for many things, including when you are copying and pasting code repeatedly, and that code references the field name of the field containing it. Another use is when you want to validate the name of the current field.

@ThisValue

@ThisValue is a new function in Domino 6.

This function returns the value of the current field. Similar to @ThisName, this feature is extremely useful for areas where you are copying and pasting code over and over, and that code references the field name of the field containing it. The most common place where this is used is in Field Translation and Field Validation formulas.

@Word(string or string list; separator; position)

@Word returns a value from a concatenated string, based on the separator and position provided. For example, suppose that you have the following string:

```
ConcatString := "Red Apples~Orange Oranges~Yellow Pears"
```

and you want the second value in the concatenated string:

```
Value := @Word(ConcatString; "~"; 2)
```

Then Value would be "Orange Oranges". This function is useful in more complex applications when you need to look up multiple values from another document, and then parse the values returned.

@Word is used in examples in both Chapters 26 and 28.

Now that you have explored quite a few @functions that are useful in Notes applications, take a look at @functions that are useful in Web applications.

Useful @Functions for Web Applications

The previous section discussed @functions that are handy for Notes application development. Keep in mind that just because those functions are listed in the previous section, that doesn't necessarily mean that they aren't useful for Web application development. On the contrary, many can be used for Web and Notes application development. If you are unsure whether an @function can be used in Web applications, check the Domino 6 Designer help.

Now review some @functions that are particularly useful for Web application development.

Examples of many of the functions in this section are provided in the "03. Web Function Examples" form in the Domino 6 Bible Formula Examples database (d6bibleFormula.nsf), which is available for download from www.wiley.com/compbooks/benz.

@BrowserInfo(property name)

This feature helps you determine what the capabilities are of the user's Web browser, such as cookies, frames, and so on. The property names that can be tested for include Browser Type, Cookies, DHTML, Java, JavaScript, and many more.

Chapter 39 covers @BrowserInfo in great detail.

@ClientType

If @BrowserInfo is a buffet of information, @ClientType is a snack. @ClientType simply tells you if the client executing the code is a Web browser or a Notes client by returning Web or Notes, respectively. This function is handy if you need to have client-specific code in the same area, such as an action button or agent.

@DbCommand("Domino"; "ViewNextPage"), @DbCommand("Domino"; "ViewPreviousPage"), @DbCommand("Domino"; "FolderList"; prompt string; folders to exclude)

The first two versions of the function enable you to code Previous and Next buttons for your Web-based embedded views, saving you a great deal of manual code. The third version of the function enables you to display a list of folders that are available in the database for Web users.

This function was "semi" documented for Notes Release 5 — it was not a part of the Designer help, but it was documented in examples provided by Lotus. So technically this function is new for Notes/Domino 6, but it isn't really.

@GetHTTPHeader(variable name), @SetHTTPHeader(variable name; value)

New Feature   These functions are new with Domino 6.

@GetHTTPHeader returns the value of a variable in the HTTP header of the document being loaded. For example, if the server is www.sapphireoak.com, @GetHTTPHeader("Host") would return www.sapphireoak.com.

Similarly, @SetHTTPHeader sets the value of a response header variable you specify, such as Set-Cookie.

@LDAPServer

New Feature   @LDAPServer is new with Domino 6.

@LDAPServer returns the URL and port used by the LDAP server in the current domain. It determines the LDAP server by first checking the current server, and then it looks in the server's NOTES.INI for a LDAPServer= entry. If it doesn't have that variable, it checks with the administration server.

The return value of this function is similar to the following:

```
ldap://atlprod1.sapphireoak.com:389
Bottom of Form
```

@URLEncode([format keyword]; string), @URLDecode([format keyword]; string)

New Feature   These functions are new with Domino 6.

Actually @URLEncode was available but undocumented in Release 5. @URLDecode is actually new.

@URLEncode takes any string you provide and encodes it with either a standard character set used by the Domino 6 server (Domino), or with the current server platform's native character set (Platform).

So the string "CN=Rocky Oliver/O=SapphireOak" would appear as follows after being encoded:

```
CN%3DRocky%20Oliver%2FO%3DsapphireOak
```

Conversely, @URLDecode takes an encoded string and converts it back to normal formatting. It takes the same platform parameters as @URLEncode.

```
Bottom of Form
```

@URLOpen(url string)

@URLOpen is a quick way to open a URL for the user. Simply pass a URL into the function, and it will open the page. This function is usually used in a button. This function also has a few optional keywords, but the most common use is for simply opening a Web page. If you are curious about the optional keywords, please refer to the Domino 6 Designer help.

@URLQueryString(optional parameter name)

 @URLQueryString is new with Domino 6.

@URLQueryString is a great new addition to the Formula language. This function can return either the entire query string from the URL of the page where the code is executing, or a single value for a specified name. For example, if the page you were loading had a URL of

```
someURL :=
"http://www.sapphireoak.com/SapphireOak/sapphire.nsf?Open&somena
me=Rocky+Oliver&somecity=Flowery+Branch"
```

@URLQueryString would return a list of

✦ Open

✦ somename=Rocky Oliver

✦ somecity=Flowery Branch

If you wanted a particular value, such as somecity, then @URLQueryString("somecity") would return Flowery Branch.

@WebDbName

 @WebDbName is new with Domino 6.

If you are currently programming Domino Web applications, you will appreciate this function. This function returns the URL-encoded version of the current database's filepath. So if your database's filepath is

```
Domino 6 Bible\d6bibleformula.nsf
```

@WebDbName would return

```
Domino%206%20Bible/d6bibleformula.nsf
```

Now you don't have to write a few lines of code to accomplish this common task. This function makes it much easier to construct URLs to elements of your database, such as views, documents, and so on.

A few functions look like they would be useful for Web development, but they are actually quite a bit more restrictive. These two are @URLGetHeader and @URLHistory. These functions are restrictive in that each one of them can only be used with the native Notes browser (@URLHistory) or with the Personal Web Navigator database (@URLGetHeader). Occasionally, there are times when this is an acceptable limitation, but for general Domino Web development these functions are not very useful.

Summary

This chapter covered a great deal of information about @functions.

✦ You were introduced to some basic techniques for working with @functions, such as syntax and how to use variables.

✦ You were introduced to some useful @functions for Notes application development, such as @Replace, @ThisName, @ThisValue, and so on.

✦ You were introduced to some useful @functions for Web application development, such as @URLEncode and @URLDecode.

✦ You were informed about quite a few new @functions along the way, such as @WebDbName.

Many areas are not covered in this chapter because they are discussed in greater detail in the other chapters in Part V. Take the time to review these other chapters to round out your knowledge of the powerful Formula language in Notes/Domino 6.

✦   ✦   ✦

Introduction to @Commands

by Rocky Oliver

In This Chapter

Working with
@Commands

Exploring @Commands
for Notes application
development

Exploring @Commands
for Web application
development

Chapter 24 took a fairly deep dive into @functions. In this chapter, you explore the companions to @functions in the Formula language, the @Commands. In reality, @Commands are just another type of @function; however they are different from other @functions because virtually all of them are closely tied to things in the user interface (UI). @Commands provide you the ability to take action against things in the UI, and these actions generally map to menus in Notes. This chapter dives into these @Commands and provides you a primer on using them in your applications. The chapter introduces techniques for working with @Commands, and then dives into some of the more useful @Commands that are available to you.

Working with @Commands

@Commands were introduced in Notes Release 2 as an expansion of the Formula language. @Commands basically map to functionality in the UI—menu commands found on the various Notes client menus. So, for File ⇨ Save, there's @Command([FileSave]); for File ⇨ Database ⇨ Open, there's @Command([FileOpenDatabase]). Quite a few specialized commands are also very useful. A good way to think about @Commands is that @Commands represent all the actions you can "do" in a Notes client. Using @Commands can help you write applications,. but before you learn about how to use @Commands, you need to learn a few rules of engagement.

@Commands have a few more restrictions than @functions, and @Commands have a few more quirks. The biggest thing to keep in mind with @Commands is that they are available only in places where UI code is allowed. For example, scheduled agents, agents run on a server, and Web agents are not allowed to have any UI-based functions, including @Commands. If you think about this, it makes sense—there is no UI in these situations, so the @Command has nothing to work against.

Probably the most confusing aspect of working with @Commands is the order of execution, especially when used with @functions. To understand how execution works now, take a look at how things used to be.

Round 1: All @Commands go last

When @Commands were first introduced, all of them fired after all other @functions were evaluated, even if the @Command was in the middle of the code. Take a look at the example in Listing 25-1.

Listing 25-1: Round 1 @Command Execution Example

```
FIELD Status := "Sold";
FIELD Total := Units * Cost;
@Command([FileSave]);
@Command([FileCloseWindow]);
@Prompt([ok]; "New Doc"; "Opening new doc...");
@Command([Compose]; "04.01 EXAMPLE")
```

Note   This code in Listing 25-1 is part of a demonstration that you can find in the Domino 6 Formulas Example database. You can find the demonstration that is set up for the next couple of listings in the form 25-1 @Command Execution Example, the view 25.01 Example View, and the agents Ch25 Round 1 Example (which is the code above) and Ch25 Round 2 Example.

If this code were to execute in the order it is intended, the actions would occur in the following order:

1. The status is set to Sold.

2. The Total is computed based on the values in the Units and Cost fields.

3. The document is saved.

4. The document is closed.

5. A prompt shows up telling you that a new document is being composed.

6. A new document is composed.

If these commands fire in order, the appropriate fields are set, the existing documents are saved and closed, the user gets a prompt, and a new document is created. But the code actually executes in this order:

1. The status is set to Sold.

2. The Total is computed based on the values in the Units and Cost fields.

3. A prompt shows up telling you that a new document is being composed.

4. The document is saved.

5. The document is closed.

6. A new document is composed.

Note   You can see how this code works by opening the 25.01 @Command Execution Example form and clicking the Save: Round 1 Action button.

It's confusing, but after you understand that all @Commands fire at the end, in the order they occur, you can work around that. But it's still a massive pain, and requires that you write code that doesn't flow in a logical order.

The developer masses complained about this, because it required many workarounds to get around this limitation. The next round of @Commands tried to make it easier to understand, but it actually made it more confusing.

Round 2: @PostedCommand

In Notes Release 4 the @Command firing anomaly was addressed, or so the developers were told, by the introduction of the @PostedCommand. Lotus changed the @Commands so that some of them actually fired inline where they occurred. But it turned out that the ones that the developers really needed to fire inline—things like @Command([FileCloseWindow])—still didn't fire in the right place. To keep @Commands firing as they did in Release 3, you had to use @PostedCommand instead of @Command. This forced the @Command to fire at the end of the formula as it did in Release 3, not inline.

In reality, trying to use @Commands inline in Releases 4 and 5 wasn't very predictable. In fact, the same code shown in Listing 25-1 doesn't perform as predictably as it did in Release 3.

Note You can view this anomaly by loading the 25.01 @Command Execution Example form and clicking the Save: Round 2 Action button.

If you run the code in Listing 25-1 but use the Round 2 action button, it fires in the following order:

1. The status is set to Sold.

2. The Total is computed based on the values in the Units and Cost fields.

3. A prompt shows up telling you that a new document is being composed.

4. The document is saved.

5. A new document is composed.

6. The new document is closed.

In Release 5 it is even worse than it was in Release 3! Most developers wound up using @PostedCommands all the time because at least they were predictable.

Round 3: @Commands that actually execute where you want

When the Formula Engine and language was completely overhauled for Notes/Domino 6, one of the areas that was finally addressed correctly was the execution order of @Commands. The developer in charge of the Formula Engine, Damien Katz, realized that he couldn't just change the way all existing @Commands worked, as that would break much of the existing code. Instead, he decided to create new @Commands that had the same functionality as existing @Commands, but these new @Commands were different in that they would execute exactly where they were placed in the formula. Table 25-1 shows the old @Commands that executed after all of @functions, and the new @Commands that execute immediately:

Table 25-1: Old versus New @Commands

Executes after @functions	Executes Immediately
EditClear	Clear
EditProfile	EditProfileDocument
FileCloseWindow	CloseWindow
FileDatabaseDelete	DatabaseDelete
FileExit	ExitNotes
Folder	FolderDocuments
NavigateNext	NavNext
NavigateNextMain	NavNextMain
NavigateNextSelected	NavNextSelected
NavigateNextUnread	NavNextUnread
NavigatePrev	NavPrev
NavigatePrevMain	NavPrevMain
NavigatePrevSelected	NavPrevSelected
NavigatePrevUnread	NavPrevUnread
ReloadWindow	RefreshWindow
ToolsRunBackgroundMacros	RunScheduledAgents
ToolsRunMacro	RunAgent
ViewChange	SwitchView
ViewSwitchForm	SwitchForm

The code in Listing 25-2 is written with the new @Commands, and it executes in the expected order.

Listing 25-2: **Domino 6 @Command Execution Example**

```
REM {This code runs correctly in Noteso 6};
REM {Get the server and filename in case the user composes the
original doc without opening the database};
FIELD Status := "Sold";
FIELD Total := Units * Cost;
@Command([FileSave]);
REM "This is the new version of the FileCloseWindow command that
works inline";
@Command([CloseWindow]);
@Prompt([Ok]; "New Doc"; "Old doc is closed, and a new doc is
being composed...");
@Command([Compose]; "25.01 EXAMPLE")
```

Notice that this code uses the `@Command([CloseWindow])` instead of `@Command ([FileCloseWindow])`. This code fires in the expected order.

The following sections take a look into some of the more useful @Commands for Notes and Web development.

Useful @Commands for Notes Applications

@Commands are primarily used in Notes application development. @Commands interact with the UI—usually the Notes client UI. As with @functions, two sets of @Commands are presented here: @Commands you should memorize, and @Commands you should know about. This section does not cover all 256 @Commands, but does highlight some of the more useful ones.

@Commands that you should memorize

Like @functions, a few @Commands are worth memorizing because they are useful. The @Commands in the following sections also include a small statement about their use, to help you understand how to use them in your development efforts. Unlike @functions, @Commands are almost never used alone; typically, @Commands are a small part of a much larger hunk of Formula code. Additionally, the rest of the chapters in Part V have some more complex examples that utilize @Commands.

Cross-Reference Many of the functions in the following sections also work for Web applications. You can read more about them in the section "Useful @Commands for Web applications" later in this chapter.

@Command([CloseWindow])

New Feature `@Command([CloseWindow])` is a new @Command in Notes/Domino 6.

`@Command([CloseWindow])` closes the window that has focus in the Notes client. `[CloseWindow]` performs the same function as `@Command([FileCloseWindow])`, except that `[CloseWindow]` executes inline where it is called, not at the end of the code like `[FileCloseWindow]`. Listing 25-2 shows the use of `[CloseWindow]`.

@Command([Compose]; form name)

`@Command([Compose])` is one of the most commonly used @Commands. `[Compose]` composes the form listed in the form name parameter. The form name parameter can either be the form name itself, or an alias of the form.

Tip The `@Command([Compose)` function can also take a server and database name as parameters. This is useful when you are composing a form from a different database than the one in which your code is executing, or if your code opens a different database and you want to be able to compose a form from the original one. For example, Listing 25-2 shows capturing the server and database name of the current database, and then using that in the `@Command([Compose])` later in the code in case the user composed the document without having the database open.

@Command([EditDocument]; edit mode; preview pane)

@Command([EditDocument]) is useful in view and form action buttons. Often this function is used in forms because many people are not aware that you can double-click a document to put it into edit mode, or use CTRL+E. The edit mode parameter can be a "1" for edit mode or "0" for read mode. @Command([EditMode]; "1"), for example, would put a document into edit mode. The second parameter is optional, and shows the Preview pane, but it isn't used often.

@Command([FileCloseWindow])

@Command([FileCloseWindow]) closes the window that has focus in the Notes client. [FileCloseWindow] performs the same function as @Command([CloseWindow]), except that [FileCloseWindow] fires at the end of the code no matter where it resides in the code, not inline like [CloseWindow]. Listing 25-1 shows the use of [FileCloseWindow].

@Command([FileOpenDatabase]; server : database)

The @Command([FileOpenDatabase]) command has quite a few variations; the one listed previously is the most used variation. A few more exist, but these three combinations are the ones you will most likely use. The following list discusses each one briefly:

✦ @Command([FileOpenDatabase]; server : database): This is the most commonly used version of the @Command. It simply opens the specified database in the Notes client and gives it focus, or if the specified database is already opened it brings it to the front and gives it focus. Incidentally, there is another parameter, newinstance, which instructs the function to open the database again. You can read more about it in the Domino 6 Designer help.

✦ @Command([FileOpenDatabase]; server : database; view or navigator name): This version opens the specified database, but it also opens the database to the specified view or navigator name.

Tip

If you are still using navigators, it is a good practice to not give the navigator and the related view the same name, as it can cause a great many programming issues, such as with this function. In fact, it is strongly recommended that you never name two design elements with the same name. If you are still using navigators, get out of the habit. They are a *legacy* design element, meaning that Lotus is no longer advancing the development of navigators. Instead, you should be using pages, where you may use buttons, action hotspots, or outlines to provide the same functionality (and more) that you had with navigators.

✦ @Command([FileOpenDatabase]; server : database; view name; view key): Like the previously described version, this one also opens the specified database to the named view, but it also places the focus of the view onto the first document or category represented by the specified key. In order for this to work, the view must be sorted or categorized in the first column. This version can be handy when you want to provide the user the ability to navigate to a document in another database, because you can pass a view and key to the @Command and it will open the view with the desired document highlighted.

@Command([FilePrint])

@Command([FilePrint]) does what you would think it should: it prints the currently open document, the currently opened view, or selected documents within the view. There are also many parameters for this function that enable you to specify such things as the number of copies, from and to pages, and so on. These optional parameters are as follows:

✦ `number of copies:` Used to specify the number of copies to print.

✦ `from page, to page:` These two parameters are used to indicate a starting page, and optionally a page to stop printing at. Use a string to indicate these two parameters ("2" instead of 2).

✦ `draft:` enter the word `draft` to indicate that the print job is to be printed in draft mode.

✦ `printview:` Enter the word `printview` to indicate that you want to print the view that has focus, and not the document that is selected in the view. If you leave this parameter off, or set it to an empty string, the selected document(s) are printed. This parameter has no effect if you are printing an open document.

✦ `form to use:` Specify the name of the form you want to use to print the selected document, rather than using the form that the document is normally associated with. This parameter is available only if you are printing from a view, and has no effect if you are printing an open document.

✦ `break type:` If you specify `pagebreak`, each document is separated by a page break; if you specify `line`, each document is separated by a new line with a horizontal rule across the paper; if you specify an empty string (`""`) each document is printed separated by a blank line. This parameter has no effect when printing an open document.

✦ `resetpages:` If you are printing multiple, selected documents from a view you can set this parameter to `resetpages` to reset the page number to one (1) for each document printed. If you omit this parameter or specify an empty string (`""`) the page number begins with 1 for the first document and increments cumulatively for all pages printed. This parameter has no effect when printing an open document.

✦ `start date, end date:` These two parameters are used in calendar view, and only in conjunction with the print view parameter. These two parameters are used to indicate a date range for printing a calendar view.

@Command([FileSave])

`@Command([FileSave])` saves the currently open document, as long as it is in edit mode. This function is often used in conjunction with `@Command([FileCloseWindow])` or `@Command([CloseWindow])`.

When this function is used in a form action button, it is often paired with `@Command([FileCloseWindow])` or `@Command([CloseWindow])` such as

```
@Command([FileSave]);
@Command([CloseWindow])
```

But this can have an unwanted side effect: if the document fails on any of the field validation formulas, the user is prompted about the validation error, and then is asked to save the document. The user has to cancel out of that to correct the error. This can be confusing to the user, but you can avoid it: Many developers do not know that most @Commands have a return value, usually `@True` or `@False` (and unfortunately it isn't documented in the help for `@Command([FileSave])`). `@Command([FileSave])` returns `@True` if the save is successful and `@False` if the save isn't successful, such as when a field fails validation. Therefore, you can write your Save and Close action buttons like this to avoid the issue:

```
@If(@Command([FileSave]); @Command([CloseWindow]); "")
```

If the `[FileSave]` is successful, the `[CloseWindow]` executes; otherwise, nothing happens, and the user receives only the validation error from the field.

@Command([RefreshHideFormulas])

@Command([RefreshHideFormulas]) refreshes only the hide-when formulas on a document, not all the field values. This can be much more efficient than @Command([ViewRefresh-Fields]) if you have a complex document with many fields and hide-when formulas.

@Command([RunAgent]; *agent name*)

New Feature

@Command([RunAgent]) is a new @Command in Notes/Domino 6.

@Command([RunAgent]) executes the agent named in the agent name parameter. [RunAgent] performs the same function as @Command([ToolsRunMacro]), except that [RunAgent] executes when it occurs inline in code, and [ToolsRunMacro] executes at the end of the code no matter where it occurs inline.

@Command([ToolsRunMacro]; agent name)

@Command([ToolsRunMacro]) executes the agent named in the agent name parameter. [ToolsRunMacro] performs the same function as @Command([RunAgent]), except that [ToolsRunMacro] executes at the end of the code no matter where it occurs inline, and [RunAgent] executes when it occurs inline in code.

@Command([ViewRefreshFields])

@Command([ViewRefreshFields]) actually works in two places. If it is called from a view or folder, it refreshes the view or folder. If it is called from a document that is open in edit mode, it refreshes the fields and hide-when formulas in the document.

Tip

If you need to refresh only the hide-when formulas on a document, don't use @Command-([ViewRefreshFields]). It is not efficient on larger, more complex forms. Instead, use @Command([RefreshHideFormulas]) to refresh the hide-when formulas only.

@Commands that you should know about

The @Commands discussed in the following sections are ones that you should also be familiar with, but not necessarily commit to memory. These are @Commands that you will find yourself using quite often, so it is important to know how they work.

Note

There are 28 @Commands that provide administrative functionality for your environment and server. These functions are not going to be covered in detail here, but it is a good idea to know about their existence, especially if you are one of those "hybrid" developer/administrator types. These administrative @Commands may save you some time if you become familiar with them.

@Command([ComposeWithReference]; server : database; form name)

@Command([ComposeWithReference]) enables you to create a response document to the currently open or selected document. There is an optional flag that follows form name, the reference attribute flag. The optional reference attribute flag enables you to specify how the response document is linked to the main document. If you leave it off, no reference to the main document is provided, except the fact that the new document is a response document.

If you use this parameter, you can combine attributes by adding the numbers. The choices you have for this parameter are discussed in Table 25-2.

Table 25-2: Reference Flag Parameters for @Command ([ComposeWithReference])

Flag	What It Does
1	Includes a doclink to the main document.
2	Includes the body of the main document.
4	Puts the body of the main document into a collapsible section. This parameter requires flag 2 as well (so to use this by itself you would use a flag of 6).
	Note: Even though the help file shows "2+4" for this combination of flags, in fact you can add the flags together and pass the sum in the parameter. This is true of all of these parameter options.
8	Includes an Internet-style copy of the main document, with a title of "author wrote on…" where author is the author of the main document, and each line is prefixed with a greater-than sign (>). This parameter requires flag 2 as well (so to use it by itself you would use a flag of 10). Additionally, you can't use the flag 4 with this one. When you use this option then flag 16 is applied as well, which means that all objects (attachments, graphics, OLE objects, etc.) are removed.
16	Includes a copy of the main document, and removes all large objects (attachments, images, and so on) from it and replaces them with text statements. This parameter requires flag 2 as well (so to use it by itself you would use a flag of 18).
32	This flag is used almost exclusively in the N6 Mail template. You can use it in other applications, but you need to understand what you are doing. Refer to the Domino 6 Designer help for more details.

New Feature @Command([ComposeWithReference]) is new in Notes/Domino 6.

As you can see, this function is used in the Notes 6 Mail template, but it can also be useful for custom applications.

@Command([DebugLotusScript])

@Command([DebugLotusScript]) toggles the LotusScript Debugger on and off. @Command ([DebugLotusScript]) isn't really an @Command you'll use in general code, but it is a good @Command to know nonetheless.

Tip It is a great idea to create a custom toolbar icon (previously known as a smarticon) for turning the LotusScript Debugger on and off. You can do this by choosing File ➪ Preferences ➪ Toolbar Preferences, and then choosing the Customize section. Then select New ➪ Button, as shown in Figure 25-1.

You can then create a new Debug LotusScript icon by giving the icon a name, caption, and entering @Command([DebugLotusScript]) in the Formula box, and clicking OK.

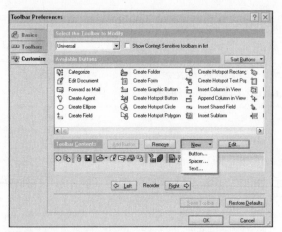

Figure 25-1: The Toolbar Preferences dialog box is where you can create your own useful toolbar icons, such as Debug LotusScript.

@Command([EditProfileDocument]; form name)

`@Command([EditProfileDocument])` enables you to present a profile document to the user for viewing and/or modifying through the associated form named in the form name parameter. Multiple profile documents based on the same form are identified by a unique key, such as a canonical user name, and that unique key is needed to make sure the command is editing the correct document. This optional unique key parameter can be used in this @Command by placing it after the form name parameter, for example. `@Command([EditProfileDocument]; form name; unique key)`.

Note   This is the old version of the @Command. A new version, `@Command([EditProfile])`, executes when it occurs in the code. `[EditProfileDocument]` executes at the end of the code, no matter where it occurs in the code.

@Command([EditProfile])

New Feature   `@Command([EditProfile])` is a new @Command in Notes/Domino 6.

`@Command([EditProfile])` works the same way that `@Command([EditProfileDocument])` does, as listed earlier. It takes the same parameters as well. The only difference is that `[EditProfile]` executes where it occurs in the code and `[EditProfileDocument]` executes at the end of the code no matter where it occurs in the code.

@Command([MailComposeMemo])

`@Command([MailComposeMemo])` composes a mail memo from the user's mail database. Actually, `[MailComposeMemo]` composes the default form that is in the user's mail file. But unless the user has deliberately changed this, it is the Memo form.

@Commands for opening frames, views, and pages

There are three @Commands that are used to open frames, views, and pages. All three @Commands basically take the same parameters, therefore they are listed here together. The basic syntax for these @Commands is @Command([*OpenFlag*]; *element name*) where the available combinations are as follows:

✦ @Command([OpenFrameset]; frameset name)

✦ @Command([OpenPage]; page name)

✦ @Command([OpenView]; view name)

@Command([OpenView]) opens the specified view in the current database. If the specified view is already open, it gives the view focus. Optionally, you can specify a key, and the first category or document that has that key is highlighted. Additionally, the key can be a partial key. If you use the optional key parameter, the first column of the specified view must be sorted or categorized.

A newinstance parameter exists for the [OpenView] command as well. If this parameter is used, a second copy of the specified view is opened.

All of these @Commands are often used with the @SetTargetFrame function, which specifies the frame where the @Command opens the element.

These functions also work for Web applications. You can read more about this in the section "@Commands for Web Applications" later in this chapter.

@Command([RefreshFrame]; target frame name)

@Command([RefreshFrame]) is a new @Command in Notes/Domino 6.

@Command([RefreshFrame]) refreshes the contents of the specified frame. This can be useful if you have some code in one frame that modifies an area of your application that has a direct effect on the contents displayed in another frame. For instance, you have a view in one frame with an action that modifies a document displayed in a different frame. You can use this command to refresh that document after the modification takes place.

This function also works for Web applications. You can read more about this in the "@Commands for Web Applications" section later in this chapter.

@Command([SwitchView]; view name)

@Command([RefreshFrame]) is a new @Command in Notes/Domino 6.

@Command([SwitchView]) opens the specified view in the current database. If you omit the view name parameter, the view selection dialog box is displayed. This can be handy for workflow applications.

[SwitchView] does the same thing as @Command([ViewChange]), except that it executes when it occurs in the code; [ViewChange] executes at the end of the code, regardless of where it occurs inline.

@Commands for refreshing documents in a view

The following two @Commands are used to refresh documents in a view. Refreshing a document causes all computed fields to be recalculated. When you use either of these @Commands you do not need to save the documents. These two @Commands are:

✦ **@Command([ToolsRefreshAllDocs]):** This command refreshes all documents in the current view.

✦ **@Command([ToolsRefreshSelectedDocs]):** This command refreshes all selected documents in the current view.

Note　When you use these @Commands any validation errors that exist are fired.

@Command([ViewChange]; view name)

@Command([ViewChange]) opens the specified view in the current database. This can be handy for workflow applications. [ViewChange] fires at the end of the code, regardless of where it occurs in the code. @Command([SwitchView]) is a new @Command that does the same thing [ViewChange] does, except that it executes where it occurs in the code.

Now that you've reviewed some of the @Commands that are useful for Notes applications, it's time to move on and take a look at @Commands that are useful for Web applications.

@Commands for Web Applications

The @Commands listed in this section also work in Notes applications; in fact, many of them are highlighted elsewhere in this chapter. But these particular @Commands are useful for Domino Web application development, and save you development time.

If you are going to use @Commands to enhance your Web application development, you should enable the Web Access: Use JavaScript when Generating Pages property in the Database properties box, as shown in Figure 25-2.

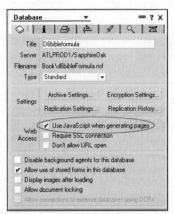

Figure 25-2: The Use JavaScript when Generating Pages property enables many new features for Domino Web application development, including the use of many @Commands on the Web.

This property is enabled by default when you create a new database, but you should probably check it to make sure it is enabled if you are developing a Web application. If this parameter isn't checked, then it causes a few undesirable effects, as shown in Table 25-3.

Table 25-3: Effects of Selecting the Use JavaScript Property

If You Select Use JavaScript	*If You Don't Select Use JavaScript*
Display: Documents and navigators display faster because hotspot formulas are not evaluated until users click each hotspot.	**Display:** Documents and navigators display more slowly because the hotspot formulas are all evaluated at the display time.
Buttons: Domino doesn't generate a Submit button automatically.	**Buttons:** Domino automatically generates a Submit button at the bottom of the form.
To allow users to save and close a form on the Web, you must create a button, hotspot, or action that contains these commands: @Command([FileSave]); @Command([CloseWindow])	If there is already one or more buttons on the form, Domino converts the first button it recognizes to a Submit button automatically and ignores all other buttons on the form.
You can have multiple buttons on a form.	You can have only one button, a Submit button, on a form.
@Commands: The following commands are supported on the Web: @Command([CloseWindow]) @Command([FileSave]) @Command([ViewRefreshFields])	**@Commands:** The following commands are not supported on the Web: @Command([CloseWindow]) @Command([FileSave]) @Command([ViewRefreshFields])
Domino does not check the formulas before displaying pages.	Domino checks the formulas before displaying pages. Actions that contain unsupported @commands or @functions will not be displayed on the Web.

Table 25-3 comes from the Designer 6 Help file, but is reproduced here to make it easier for you.

@Commands to navigate to the previous page

These two @Commands, when used in a Web browser, navigate to the previous page:

✦ @Command([FileCloseWindow])

✦ @Command([CloseWindow])

New Feature @Command([CloseWindow]) is a new @Command in Notes/Domino 6.

`@Command([CloseWindow])` performs the same action as `@Command([FileCloseWindow])`, except that `[CloseWindow]` executes in-line, and `[FileCloseWindow]` executes after all other functions.

@Command([Compose]; form name)

`@Command([Compose])` creates a new document in the current database in a Web browser. If you want to create a response document, the parent document must be open in the Web browser. There is an alternative set of parameters as well, i.e. `@Command([Compose]; "" : database path; form name)`. If you want to compose a document in a different database, specify the path to the database (use the Operating System directory path, not a URL-style path). Notice that where the server parameter is, it is an empty string (`""`). When using this @Command on the Web, you have to specify an empty string for the server parameter, which means that you can't create documents in a database that exists on a different server; the database must reside on the same server where the current database resides.

@Command([EditDocument])

`@Command([EditDocument])` toggles the document currently loaded in the Web browser between edit and read modes. You normally place this @Command in a form action or action hotspot that is hidden when the document is in edit mode. Then the user has an easy way to place the document into edit mode.

@Command([FileOpenDatabase]; "" : database; view)

If you use `@Command([FileOpenDatabase])` in a Web application, you have to use it with `@Command([OpenDocument])`. This @Command also has an optional parameter, full key. This parameter is placed at the end of the other parameters, that is, `@Command ([FileOpenDatabase]; "" : database; view; full key)`. If you leave off the full key parameter, the first document of the specified view is opened. If you use the key parameter, it must be a full key to a document in the view; a partial key will not work.

 Note If you leave off `@Command([OpenDocument])` a 404 error is thrown in the browser.

For more information, check out `@Command([OpenDocument])` later in this section.

@Command([FileSave])

`@Command([FileSave])` saves the document currently being edited in the Web browser. If you use `[FileSave]`, you need to follow it up with some other @Command that opens something else. Domino 6 Designer help states that only `@Command([OpenView])`, `@Command-([CloseWindow])`, and `@Command[FileCloseWindow])` work after `[FileSave]`. This information is incorrect. You can use any @Command that you can use on the Web, or any @Command that opens another design element, such as a form, document, view, or frameset.

If you want to use `[FileCloseWindow]` or `[CloseWindow]`, you should use a $$Return field to specify what should appear after the document is submitted. You can use either HTML or a URL in the $$Return field. Because the $$Return field is simply a Notes field, you can use @formulas to formulate the URL. If you want to display a page in the current database, you use the following code in the $$Return field:

```
{[/} + @WebDbName + {/SubmittedPage?OpenPage]}
```

You can achieve the same effect, however, by placing the following code in your Submit button:

```
@Command([FileSave]);
@Command([OpenPage]; "SubmittedPage")
```

This is a perfect example of the way @Commands can make Web content easier to develop and read.

@Commands for navigation

These @Commands are used for navigating to the previous and next documents in a Web browser. These commands are normally used in action buttons or action hotspots, and provide your users an easy way to move sequentially from document to document in the order listed in a view. The commands are as follows:

✦ `@Command([NavigateNext])`, `@Command([NavNext])`: These commands navigate to the next document in the view, opening the document in the browser.

✦ `@Command([NavigatePrev])`, `@Command([NavPrev])`: These commands navigate to the previous document in the view, opening the document in the browser.

New Feature `@Command([NavNext])` and `@Command([NavPrev])` are new @Commands in Notes/ Domino 6.

The only difference between the commands using `Navigate` and the ones using `Nav` is that the latter ones execute inline in the code, whereas the former execute after all @functions.

These @Commands are only usable in a form, and have no effect in view action buttons. These @Commands are used to navigate from document to document only.

Note If you want to provide Prev and Next functionality for an HTML view embedded in a view template, use `@DbCommand("Domino"; "ViewNextPage")` and `@DbCommand("Domino"; "ViewPreviousPage")` behind the Next and Prev action hotspots or buttons.

@Command([OpenDocument])

`@Command([OpenDocument])` opens a document into the Web browser. But `[OpenDocument]` must be used with `@Command([OpenView])` (for views in the current database) or `@Command([FileOpenDatabase])` for views in a different database on the same server.

When you use `[OpenDocument]` with `[OpenView]` or `[FileOpenDatabase]`, the key you specify must be exact, the view must be sorted in the first column, and the specified key must be listed in the first column. If more than one document has the same key, the first document listed in the view is opened. You use `[OpenDocument]` with `[OpenView]` as follows:

```
@Command([OpenView]; "Main View"; "Newberry");
@Command([OpenDocument])
```

And with `[FileOpenDatabase]`, your command would look something like this:

```
@Command([FileOpenDatabase]; "" : "MyDatabase.nsf"; "Main View";
"Newberry");
@Command([OpenDocument])
```

Tip If you want to open the first document in the view, you can specify `"$first"` as the specific key for either the `[FileOpenDatabase]` or `[OpenView]` commands.

@Commands for opening frames, views, and pages

The following @Commands open the named, frameset, navigator, page, or view, respectively:

✦ @Command([OpenFrameset]; frameset name): Opens the designated frameset.

✦ @Command([OpenNavigator]; navigator name): Opens the designated navigator.

✦ @Command([OpenPage]; page name): Opens the designated page.

✦ @Command([OpenView]; view name): Opens the designated view. This command also takes an optional key parameter, for example @Command([OpenView]; view name; key), which opens the view in the browser with the key as the first row of the view. If you use the key parameter and follow this command with @Command([OpenDocument]), the first document with the specified key is opened.

✦ @Command([SwitchView]; view name), @Command([ViewChange]; view name): Both of these functions switch to the specified view in the current database. The only difference between these two commands is that [SwitchView] executes where it occurs in the code, and [ViewChange] executes after all @functions.

New Feature   @Command([SwitchView]) is new in Notes/Domino 6.

As stated earlier in @Command([FileSave]), you can use these after [FileSave] to load a new item after a document is submitted.

Note   Navigators are a legacy design element and are no longer being supported or enhanced by Lotus. You should use pages containing buttons, hotspots, or outlines instead of navigators in all current and future development work.

@Command([RefreshFrame])

New Feature   @Command([RefreshFrame]) is a new @Command in Notes/Domino 6.

@Command([RefreshFrame]) refreshes the current frame where the code is executing. The Domino 6 Designer help indicates that there is an optional target frame parameter, but in a Web application this parameter is ignored. This command is handy for refreshing documents or views located in a frame in your application.

@Commands that run agents

There are two @Commands that run agents from a Web browser:

✦ @Command([RunAgent]; agent name)

✦ @Command([ToolsRunMacro]; agent name)

Both of these commands run the specified agent from the current database; the only difference between the two is that [RunAgent] runs when it occurs in the code, and [ToolsRunMacro] runs at the end of the @functions in your code.

New Feature   @Command([RunAgent]) is a new @Command in Notes/Domino 6.

@Command([ViewRefreshFields])

@Command([ViewRefreshFields]) refreshes all computed fields on the current document open in the browser in edit mode. This command can be useful if there are computed fields in the form that you need to have recalculated for the user, such as the total of multiple fields, or some type of computed text. This command also causes hide-when formulas to be re-evaluated.

Note Keep in mind that when you use this command in a Web application it causes a server transaction. This may or may not have an effect on the performance of your application.

Summary

This chapter covered @Commands.

✦ You were introduced to some basic techniques for working with @Commands, such as the execution order of @Commands.

✦ You were introduced to some useful @Commands for Notes application development, including many @Commands that you will use often.

✦ You were introduced to some useful @Commands for Web application development, and given some caveats for using them, such as combinations that should be used together.

✦ You were informed about quite a few new @Commands during this introduction, including the many new @Commands that are executed in-line in your formula code.

Many areas were not covered in this chapter because they are discussed in greater detail in the other chapters in Part V. Take the time to review these other chapters to round out your knowledge of how @Commands can help you with your application development efforts in Notes/Domino 6.

✦　　✦　　✦

Using the Formula Language to Retrieve Data

by Rocky Oliver

The earlier chapters of Part V introduced you to the Formula language. You learned some general guidelines for use, and you explored various ways Formula language can help you in your development efforts. This chapter dives into a few ways you can retrieve and work with data using the Formula language, concentrating on various uses of @DbColumn and @DbLookup. The chapter begins by introducing the basic usage of — @DbColumn and @DbLookup for retrieving Notes data, and then explores how to use these two functions to retrieve data from external sources using ODBC.

Introducing @DbColumn and @DbLookup

One of the most powerful features of Formula language is the ability to quickly find and retrieve data from Domino databases and other external data sources. The two functions used to do this are @DbColumn, and @DbLookup.

Retrieving Domino data using @DbColumn and @DbLookup

In this section, you get your first exposure to @DbColumn and @DbLookup. You find out how to use them to retrieve data from Domino databases. The next section shows you a powerful but seldom-used functionality of @DbColumn and @DbLookup — the ability to retrieve external data through the use of an ODBC connection.

@DbColumn

@DbColumn retrieves a column of data from a view in a database. The database can be the current database, another database on the same server, or a database on a different server. @DbColumn uses the following syntax:

```
@DbColumn(data source : cache flag; server : database;
view; column number)
```

Note The separator between data source and cache flag is a colon, as is the separator between server and database; the rest of the separators are semicolons. The Domino 6 Designer help, as of this writing, states that the only colon separator is between data source and cache flag.

New Feature The @DbColumn function isn't new, but it has a new parameter in Notes/Domino 6: the ReCache flag. You learn more about this flag later in the chapter.

The parameters are defined as follows:

Note In this chapter, and in others dealing with @functions, the terms *parameter* and *flag* are used. A *flag* is a variable for a function that is a predetermined value that the function expects, such as a keyword (for example [OK] for @Prompt) or special text (for example, "NoCache" for @DbColumn and @DbLookup). A *parameter* is a user defined variable passed to the function, such as the name of a database, view, or field name.

✦ **data source:** The data source flag indicates what type of data source the function will be accessing. This parameter can be either ODBC or Notes. If the data source is a Domino database, you can also use "" (an empty string) for this parameter.

✦ **cache flag:** The cache flag is an often overlooked but important parameter. The cache flag parameter takes three flags:

- **Cache:** The Cache flag is specified by using an empty string (""). If this flag is used, the results of the @DbColumn are cached so that future calls of @DbColumn with the same parameters happen much faster. Because the data is not retrieved the second time, the cache is used instead.

- **NoCache:** The NoCache flag is specified by using NoCache. If this flag is used, the results of @DbColumn are not cached, so each use of @DbColumn with the same parameters retrieves the data again.

- **ReCache:** The ReCache flag is new with Notes/Domino 6. If this flag is set, the cache from the first call of @DbColumn is refreshed if a subsequent call of @DbColumn is made and all other parameters are the same.

✦ **server and database:** These two parameters are put together because they are related. Here are some rules for these parameters:

- **server:** This parameter can be the canonical or abbreviated name of the Domino server, although it's recommended that you always use the canonical name (for example, "CN=Debbie Oliver/O=SapphireOak") for any Notes name used programmatically, for any server, or for any person. If the database is being accessed locally, specify an empty string ("") for this parameter. Additionally, if the @DbColumn is in a scheduled, Web, or server-based agent, specify an empty string for this parameter.

Caching Tips

Caching can be a performance killer or enhancer, depending upon how it is used. Here are some general rules of thumb for using the cache flag:

If the data you are retrieving is fairly static, cache the data by specifying an empty string.

If the data changes constantly, and it's important that the data retrieved is current, then use the NoCache flag. Caution: Using this flag can cause degradation in performance; make sure you really need to use it. If the data is semi-fluid, you are retrieving the same data a few times in the same area, and it is only occasionally important to get updated data, use ReCache. This is a great new feature, because it gives you granular control over when the cache is updated. Experiment with this new flag and fine-tune your applications.

- database: This parameter is the path to the database relative to the data directory. For example, if the database is D:\Lotus\Domino\Data\Examples\Example1.nsf, you would use "Examples\Example1.nsf" for this parameter. If the database is local, you can either use the full path to the database or the path relative to the data directory.

- If you are performing the @DbColumn against the same database where the code is executing, enter a single empty string (" ") for this parameter, without the colon.

✦ view name: This is the name or an alias of the view that is the target of the @DbColumn.

Tip　Give all your views an alias, especially views that are in a cascaded menu. It makes referencing them programmatically much easier.

✦ column number: This is the column number of the column you want to return. For the purposes of this function, columns begin with number 1, and you count from left to right, including hidden columns.

Note　If a @DbColumn returns a column that is categorized, the @DbColumn returns the categories, not the categories repeated for each related document in the view.

@DbColumn returns a list of values from the column. You should handle the list accordingly, because it is multivalued. Additionally, a @DbColumn that returns a categorized column returns the category names only, not the category value for each document in the column.

Now that you have some understanding of @DbColumn, take a look at a cousin of @DbColumn, @DbLookup.

@DbLookup

If @DbColumn retrieves a column of data, @DbLookup retrieves a subset of data from a column based on the provided key, from a view in a database. The syntax for @DbLookup is similar to @DbColumn, and is as follows:

```
@DbLookup(data source : cache flag; server : database;
view; key; column number or field name; keyword(s))
```

New Feature

The @DbLookup function isn't new, but it has a new parameter in Notes/Domino 6: the ReCache flag. You can learn more about this flag later in this section. Another new feature is the additional keywords parameter. This new parameter is also explained in more detail in this section.

The parameters for @DbLookup are defined as follows:

✦ **data source:** The data source flag indicates what type of data source the function will be accessing. This parameter can be ODBC or Notes. If the datasource is a Domino database, you can also use " " (an empty string) for this parameter.

✦ **cache:** The cache flag is an often overlooked but important parameter. There are three flags that this parameter takes:

- **Cache:** The Cache flag is specified by using an empty string (" "). If this flag is used, the results of the @DbLookup are cached so that future calls of @DbLookup with the same parameters happen more quickly. Because the data is not retrieved the second time, the cache is used instead.

- **NoCache:** The NoCache flag is specified by using NoCache. If this flag is used, the results of @DbLookup are not cached, so each use of @DbLookup with the same parameters retrieves the data again.

- **ReCache:** The ReCache flag is new with Notes/Domino 6. If this flag is set, the cache from the first call of @DbLookup is refreshed if a subsequent call of @DbLookup is made with this parameter set and all other parameters are the same.

✦ **server and database:** These two parameters are put together because they are related. Here are some rules for these parameters:

- **server:** This parameter can be the canonical or abbreviated name of the Domino server, although it's recommended that you always use the canonical name (for example, "CN=Debbie Oliver/O=SapphireOak") for any Notes name used programmatically, for any server, or for any person. If the database is being accessed locally, specify an empty string (" ") for this parameter. Additionally, if the @DbLookup is in a scheduled, Web, or server-based agent, specify an empty string for this parameter.

- **database:** This parameter is the path to the database relative to the data directory. For example, if the database is D:\Lotus\Domino\Data\Examples\Example1.nsf, use "Examples\Example1.nsf" for this parameter. If the database is local, you can use the full path to the database or the path relative to the data directory.

- If you are performing the @DbLookup against the same database the code is executing, enter a single empty string (" ") for this parameter, without the colon.

✦ **view name:** This is the name or an alias of the view that is the target of the @DbLookup.

✦ **key:** This parameter is a string used to retrieve the value(s) from the view. This value is searched for in the first sorted or categorized column of the target view. This is an equality match — you can't use less than (<), greater than (>), and so on. This key is not case-sensitive. You can, however, use the new keyword [PartialMatch] to do a *fuzzy* search. You find out more about that in the keyword parameter, defined later in this list.

✦ `column number` **or** `field name`: This parameter takes one of two values: the name of a field on the documents, or a column number (`@DbColumn`). If you use the `column number`, it is the number of the column you want to return. For the purposes of this function, columns begin with number 1, and you count from left to right, including hidden columns. If you want to retrieve a field name, specify it here in quotes (`"Status"` not Status).

Tip It is much more efficient to retrieve values from columns instead of from a field on a document. If possible, use the column number parameter for the most efficient code.

✦ `keyword`: The `keyword` parameter is new in Notes/Domino 6. It enables you to control the behavior of the `@DbLookup` in useful ways, which are described below. There are three keywords available to you:

• `[FailSilent]`: Normally `@DbLookup` returns an error if there is a problem with `@DbLookup`, such as not being able to find the database or view, or if no documents match the specified key. Using this keyword causes `@DbLookup` to return an empty string (`""`) if there is an error returned.

• `[PartialMatch]`: This keyword causes `@DbLookup` to return partial matches to the specified key. A partial match is defined as matching the beginning characters of the key.

• `[ReturnDocumentUniqueID]`: This keyword causes `@DbLookup` to return a text list of the document-unique IDs of the documents matching the specified key. If this keyword is used, the column value/field name parameter is ignored.

Note You can concatenate the new keywords for `@DbLookup`. For example, if you want to return document-unique IDs and you want the `@DbLookup` to return an empty string if there is an error, you would set the keyword parameter to `[FailSilent]` : `[ReturnDocument-UniqueID]`.

`@DbLookup` returns either a single value or a list of values from the specified column or field. You should handle the list accordingly, since it could be multivalued.

You can specify the database for `@DbColumn` and `@DbLookup` another way — by database replica ID. However, it's not recommended that you use this to identify databases, for a few reasons:

✦ It's a pain to get the replica ID of a database. It is a 32-character alphanumeric string, and the only way to copy it for pasting into your Formula code is to run a design synopsis (File ➪ Database ➪ Design Synopsis) and choose Replication. Then you can copy the replica ID for use in your formulas.

✦ If you make a copy of the target database, it breaks all your `@DbColumns` and `@DbLookups` because the new copy will have a different replica ID.

✦ You have no control over the replica that is used. The replica chosen is based on the first database it finds. It searches for databases in fairly complex order. If you are curious about this order, refer to the help for `@DbColumn` or `@DbLookup`, found in the Domino 6 Designer help.

If you are creating multidatabase applications that retrieve data from each other, it is a good idea to require that the databases reside in the same directory. This makes it easier to write code that is able to dynamically figure out where the other related databases are. By doing this, your database code works no matter where the databases are located on the server, as long as they are in the same directory. The following code can be used to obtain the path to other databases:

```
REM "Indicate the db to navigate to.";
targetdb := "GreatDB.nsf";

REM "Get the server and filepath of this db.";
dbserver := @Subset(@DbName; 1);
dbpath := @Subset(@DbName; -1);

REM "Build the path to go to the target db.";
dbfilename := @If(@Contains(dbpath; "\\"); @RightBack(dbpath;
"\\"); dbpath);
dbname := @ReplaceSubstring(dbpath; dbfilename; targetdb)
```

This code extracts the current database filename from the file path and replaces it with the new filename. Then you can use the `dbserver` and `dbname` variables in your `@DbColumn` or `@DbLookup`.

Using @DbColumn and @DbLookup

A few years ago, I worked with an exceptional developer named Henry Newberry. While we were working for the same company we came up with the idea to build a Quips and Quotes database that would allow us to add a signature to our e-mails with a random quote. We built the Quips and Quotes database, and after a while we decided we also wanted to be able to grab quotes from e-mails and add them automatically to our database. After about five years this database has grown to over 1,100 quotes. The example in this section is the code used to add your name and a quote to a document. As a bonus, I am making this database available to you for download.

The example database described in this section, the ND6 Bible Quips and Quotes database (`ND6 Bible QandQ.nsf`) is available for download from www.wiley.com/compbooks/benz.

Before getting into the code, it's important to review the design of the database to provide some context.

Quips and Quotes general design

The Quips and Quotes database is based on a single form that is used to catalog the quote, where it came from, and when it was added to the database. This simple form is shown in Figure 26-1.

Save & Close	
Date	09/23/98
Source:	Dilbert
Quote:	Do not meddle in the affairs of dragons, 'cuz, like, you are crunchy and taste good with ketchup.

Figure 26-1: A document composed with the Quote form used in the Quips and Quotes database isn't much to look at, but it gets the job done.

Three user views exist, and a hidden view that is sorted by the key of the Quote documents. The key is populated with @Unique, which generates a unique alphanumeric key.

When we were designing this application, we began thinking about when we would want to add a signature and a quote. We quickly realized that there are multiple databases we would want to add a quote—a mail memo, a document in a discussion database, and so on. So the only place that would make this code available everywhere is a smarticon, now known as a toolbar icon. We wrote a basic InsertQuote agent, and Henry and I copied that code into a custom toolbar icon and modified it there to suit our needs—adding things like text formatting, company name, phone number, and even optional ad lines that indicate when and where we were speaking next. For example, I changed my version of the signature code to produce the "formal" signature block shown in Figure 26-2.

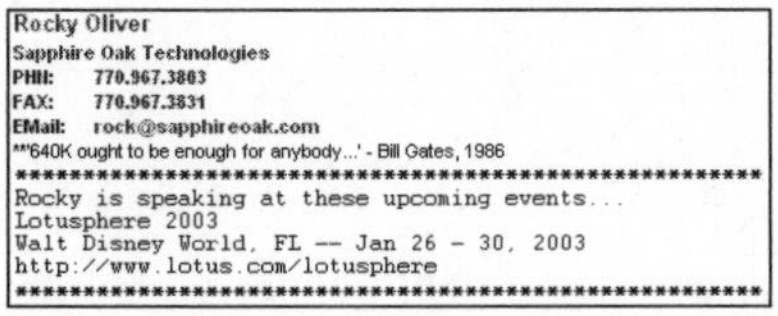

Figure 26-2: This is my "formal" signature quote output. You can customize the code to produce any type of signature block you want.

InsertQuote agent

The InsertQuote agent is designed to be a starting point for creating your own signature block code. You copy the contents of the InsertQuote agent and insert them into the Formula field of the toolbar icon you are creating to be your quote generator. One of the decisions we had to make early on concerned making sure the code in the toolbar icon was able to find the Quips and Quotes database to be able to look up the quote. We made a decision that the database must reside in the root data directory. Take a look at the code shown in Listing 26-1.

Listing 26-1: InsertQuote Agent

```
REM {get a count of how many quotes};
view1 := "QuotesByKey";
dbpath := "ND6 Bible QandQ.nsf";

REM {assume the Quotes db is in the root dir of the local
 machine};
allquotes := @IfError(@DbColumn(""; "" : dbpath; view1; 1);
    @Do(
        @Set("lookerr"; @True);
        "ERROR: " + @Text(allQuotes)
        )
);

REM {generate a random position number to get a single quote,
 then return the corresponding quote key};
rnd := @Integer( ( @Count(allquotes) - 1 )*@Random + 1 );
wquotekey := @If(lookerr = @True;
```

Continued

Listing 26-1 *(continued)*

```
                        allQuotes;
                        @Subset(@Subset(allquotes; rnd); -1)
);

wquote := @If(lookerr = @True;
                allQuotes;
                @DbLookup(""; "" : dbpath; view1; wquotekey; 2)
);

REM {format and set user name};
@Command([TextSetFontSize]; "10");
@Command([TextNormal]);
@Command([TextSetFontColor]; [Blue]);
@Command([TextBold]);
@Command([EditInsertText]; @NewLine + @NewLine +@Name([CN];
 @UserName));

REM {format and set quote};
@Command([TextNormal]);
@Command([TextSetFontSize]; "8");
REM {if there is an error, print the number and the error
message};
@If(@IsError(wquote);
    @Do(
        @Command([EditInsertText];  @NewLine + @NewLine +
"ERROR: " + @Text(wquote));
        @Command([EditInsertText];  @NewLine + " rnd: [" +
@Text(rnd) + "]  elements: [" + @Text(@Elements(allQuotes)) +
"]")
        );
    @Command([EditInsertText];  @NewLine + wquote)
)
```

The first few lines establish the view containing the quotes by key, and the database name and path. Notice that it is just the database name — this means that the code will look for the database in the data directory root.

```
view1 := "QuotesByKey";
dbpath := "ND6 Bible QandQ.nsf";
```

The next part performs an initial @DbColumn to get a list of keys. This list is basically used to get a count of documents in the view:

```
allquotes := @IfError(@DbColumn(""; "" : dbpath; view1; 1);
    @Do(
        @Set("lookerr"; @True);
        "ERROR: " + @Text(allQuotes)
        )
);
```

Notice that the code also uses the new @IfError function. If the @DbColumn succeeds, the result is returned. If it fails, the error thrown by the failed @DbColumn is returned, and another variable, lookerr, is set to @True.

Tip If you are going to return the error code from an @DbColumn or @DbLookup, use @Text to convert the error to a string.

The first parameter of @DbColumn is an empty string (""). This means that the datasource is Notes, and that the results should be cached because the quotes don't change too often. The server parameter is an empty string, indicating that the database is local, and that for the database the variable dbpath is used, which was defined at the top of the code.

The next chunk of code generates a random number. The code then uses that number to retrieve the corresponding quote key from the list generated by the @DbColumn described previously.

```
REM {generate a random position number to get a single quote,
 then return the corresponding quote key};
rnd := @Integer( ( @Count(allquotes) - 1 )*@Random + 1 );
wquotekey := @If(lookerr = @True;
                 allQuotes;
                 @Subset(@Subset(allquotes; rnd); -1)
);
```

The random number generator code generates a number between 1 and the number of items returned by the @DbColumn. If the @DbColumn succeeds, the corresponding quote key is returned based on the random number generated. If the @DbColumn returns an error, that error is returned.

The next chunk of code does a lookup to return the quote that is represented by the quote key the code returned previously:

```
wquote := @If(lookerr = @True;
              allQuotes;
              @DbLookup(""; "" : dbpath; view1; wquotekey; 2)
);
```

If the original @DbColumn errored out, return the error code; otherwise, it does a lookup for the corresponding quote to the key found earlier. The beginning parameters for datasource, cache, server, database, and view are the same as those used with @DbColumn before. The key parameter is set to the variable wquotekey, which contains the quote key that was found earlier, and the column number of 2, which contains the quotes in the view specified in the view1 variable, QuotesByKey.

So why wasn't @IfError used here? Or why wasn't the new [FailSilent] keyword used on the @DbLookup? Because the error that may be generated is needed in the next chunk of code, which formats and enters the quote into the signature, or it detects the error and enters that in the signature:

```
REM {format and set user name};
@Command([TextSetFontSize]; "10");
@Command([TextNormal]);
@Command([TextSetFontColor]; [Blue]);
```

```
@Command([TextBold]);
@Command([EditInsertText]; @NewLine + @NewLine +@Name([CN];
@UserName));

REM {format and set quote};
@Command([TextNormal]);
@Command([TextSetFontSize]; "8");
REM {if there is an error, print the number and the error
message};
@If(@IsError(wquote);
    @Do(
        @Command([EditInsertText]; @NewLine + @NewLine +
"ERROR: " + @Text(wquote));
        @Command([EditInsertText]; @NewLine + " rnd: [" +
@Text(rnd) + "] elements: [" + @Text(@Elements(allQuotes)) +
"]")
        );
    @Command([EditInsertText]; @NewLine + wquote)
)
```

The beginning of this code sets up some formatting and then enters the user's name. This is the area you can modify to format your own signature. The formatted signature is combined with the quote itself, and it is entered into the bottom of the signature. The `@If(@IsError)` code tests the `wquote` parameter to see whether the `@DbLookup` returned an error. If it did, the random number generated, the total number of quotes, and the error message is inserted for the quote. If it did not return an error, the quote itself is returned.

Now that you have seen a fairly simple example of using `@DbColumn` and `@DbLookup` to retrieve data from a Notes database, take a look at how you can use these two functions to retrieve data from an ODBC source.

Retrieving ODBC data using @DbColumn and @DbLookup

You have been introduced to using `@DbColumn` and `@DbLookup` to retrieve Domino data. But an often overlooked ability of these two @functions is the ability to retrieve data from an external data source that is represented by an ODBC connection. This section introduces you to this feature and provides you with a familiar example using this ability. Later in this section you revisit the Quips and Quotes example and demonstrate how you can use these functions together in your applications.

 The databases and files described in this section are available for download from www.wiley.com/compbooks/benz.

This section uses the same example application that was used in the `InsertQuote` agent (Listing 26-1), except that the quotes themselves now reside in a Microsoft Access database.

@DbColumn using ODBC

The syntax for @DbColumn using ODBC is similar to the syntax for using @DbColumn with a Notes datasource, but it is similar enough to be confusing to many people. The syntax for @DbColumn using ODBC is as follows:

```
@DbColumn("ODBC": cache flag; odbc connection name;
user ID; user password; table name; column name;
distinct flag : sort flag)
```

Note

The separator between "ODBC" and cache flag is a colon, as is the separator between the distinct flag and sort flag; the rest of the separators are semicolons.

If the user has NoExternalApps=1 entered in his NOTES.INI, the ODBC versions of @DbColumn and @DbLookup don't work. No error is thrown if this is the case; they simply fail to return any data.

New Feature

The @DbColumn function isn't new, but it has a new parameter in Notes/Domino 6: the ReCache flag. You can learn more about this flag later in this section.

@DbColumn with the ODBC datasource flag retrieves a column of data from the indicated table in the database represented by the named ODBC data connection. This use of @DbColumn requires quite a few parameters, some of them different from the parameters used in the Notes version of @DbColumn.

The parameters are defined as follows. The parameters that are the same as the Notes version of @DbColumn and this one are mentioned, and refer you to that explanation:

✦ **cache:** The cache flag is the same as the Notes version of @DbColumn. This is an important parameter, so make sure you review the explanation for the cache flag.

✦ **odbc connection name:** This is the name of the ODBC connection you have set up to map to your external data source.

✦ **user name:** If your external datasource requires a name and password for access, enter the name here. Some data sources require two names — you can enter two names here, separated by colons (for example, "Allison Janicki" : "Gabriella Davis"). If your datasource does not require a user name, enter an empty string for this parameter ("").

✦ **user password:** If you enter a name in the user name parameter, you need a corresponding password here. If you enter two names, enter two passwords separated by a colon. If no name is needed and you entered an empty string for user name, enter an empty string here as well.

✦ **table name:** This is the name of the table or database view that you are accessing.

✦ **column name:** This is the name of the column from which you want to retrieve data.

Note   You can append an optional parameter to the column name parameter that helps you handle nulls that are returned. The default action is to discard null values and shorten the list, which is usually the preferred option. If you want to learn more about this option, please refer to "@DbColumn(ODBC data source)", the section titled "Specifying null handling" in the Domino 6 Designer help.

✦ distinct: This is an optional parameter. It removes duplicates from the returned list of values, similar to using @Unique on the returned list. The major advantage of this is that the values are removed before the list is returned. But be careful, because not all ODBC drivers support the distinct feature.

✦ sort: This is an optional parameter, and can only be used if you use the distinct flag feature. This feature sorts the returned list in either ascending or descending order. This is the same as using @Sort against the returned list. The advantage is that the sort is performed before the list is returned. But be careful, not all ODBC drivers support the sort feature.

Now that you have some understanding of the ODBC version of @DbColumn, take a look at the ODBC version of @DbLookup.

@DbLookup

Like @DbColumn used with an ODBC datasource, @DbLookup used with ODBC datasource is similar to @DbLookup used with a Notes source; however the parameters are different enough that you should review them carefully. The syntax for @DbLookup using an ODBC data source is as follows:

```
@DbLookup("ODBC": cache flag; odbc connection name;
user ID; user password; table name; column name;
key column name; key; distinct flag : sort flag)
```

New Feature   The @DbLookup function isn't new, but it has a new parameter in Notes/Domino 6: the ReCache flag. You can learn more about this flag later in this section.

@DbLookup with the ODBC datasource flag uses the supplied key value to retrieve one or more values from a table in the indicated ODBC datasource. This use of @DbLookup requires quite a few parameters, some of them different from the parameters used in the Notes version of @DbLookup.

The parameters are defined as follows. The parameters that are the same as the Notes version of @DbLookup and this one are mentioned, and refer you to that explanation:

✦ cache: The cache flag is the same as the Notes version of @DbColumn. This is an important parameter, so make sure you review the explanation for the cache flag.

✦ odbc connection name: This is the name of the ODBC connection you have set up to map to your external data source.

✦ user name: If your external datasource requires a name and password for access, then enter the name here. Some datasources require two names — you can enter two names here, separated by colons (for example, "Kris Oliver" : "Kelsey Oliver"). If your datasource does not require a user name, enter an empty string for this parameter (" ").

✦ user password: If you entered a name in the user name parameter, you need a corresponding password here. If you entered two names, then enter two passwords separated by a colon. If no name is needed and you entered an empty string for user name, then enter an empty string here as well.

✦ table name: This is the name of the table or database view that you are accessing.

✦ column name: This is the name of the column from which you want to retrieve data.

✦ key column name: This is the column containing the key that is used to retrieve the desired data.

✦ key: This is the key you want to use to retrieve data.

✦ distinct: This is an optional parameter. It removes duplicates from the returned list of values, similar to using @Unique on the returned list. The major advantage of this is that the values are removed before the list is returned. But be careful, because not all ODBC drivers support the distinct feature.

✦ sort: This is an optional parameter, and can only be used if you use the distinct flag feature. This feature sorts the returned list in either ascending or descending order. This is the same as using @Sort against the returned list. The advantage is that the sort is performed before the list is returned. But be careful, not all ODBC drivers support the sort feature.

Now that you have some idea of how the ODBC versions of these functions work, take a look at them in the context of a familiar example.

Using the ODBC versions of @DbColumn and @DbLookup together

This section uses the same Quips and Quotes example that was used in the section "Using @DbColumn and @DbLookup," except that now the quotes reside in a Microsoft Access database. If you want to use this example on your own machine, take the Quotes.mdb file that you downloaded from www.wiley.com/compbooks/benz and create an ODBC connection to it. In this example, it's called ND6 Bible Quotes for reference.

Note   You do not need to have MS Access to experiment with this example. The ODBC driver for MS Access is a part of the default ODBC management configuration, so you simply need to configure a System DSN (Data Source) that points to Quotes.mdb.

The Quotes.mdb file contains one table, QuoteTable, and the fields included are Date, Source, Quote, and QuoteKey.

An agent exists in the ND6 Bible Quips and Quotes database used in the earlier example called InsertQuoteODBC. As before, if you want to use this feature you can copy the code from this agent and place it in a toolbar icon. Then you can modify it to format your signature block any way you want. Listing 26-2 shows you the default agent code.

Listing 26-2: **InsertQuoteODBC Agent**

```
REM {get a count of how many quotes};
odbc_connection := "ND6 Bible Quotes";
table1 := "QuoteTable";

REM {get a list of keys from the ODBC resource};
allquotes := @IfError(@DbColumn("ODBC" : ""; odbc_connection;
""; ""; table1; "QuoteKey");
            @Do(
                @Set("lookerr"; @True);
                "ERROR: " + @Text(allQuotes)
                )
);

REM {generate a random position number to get a single quote,
 then return the corresponding quote key};
rnd := @Integer( ( @Count(allquotes) - 1 )*@Random + 1 );
wquotekey := @If(lookerr = @True;
                    allQuotes;
                    @Subset(@Subset(allquotes; rnd); -1)
);

wquote := @If(lookerr = @True;
                    allQuotes;
                    @DbLookup("ODBC" : ""; odbc_connection;
 ""; ""; table1;  "Quote"; "QuoteKey"; wquotekey)
);

REM {format and set user name};
@Command([TextSetFontSize]; "10");
@Command([TextNormal]);
@Command([TextSetFontColor]; [Blue]);
@Command([TextBold]);
@Command([EditInsertText]; @NewLine + @NewLine +@Name([CN];
 @UserName));

REM {format and set quote};
@Command([TextNormal]);
@Command([TextSetFontSize]; "8");
REM {if there is an error, print the number and the error
 message};
@If(@IsError(wquote);
        @Do(
            @Command([EditInsertText];  @NewLine + @NewLine
```

```
          + "ERROR: " + @Text(wquote));
                    @Command([EditInsertText];  @NewLine + " rnd: ["
  + @Text(rnd) + "]  elements: [" +
  @Text(@Elements(allQuotes)) + "]")
             );
             @Command([EditInsertText];  @NewLine + wquote)
  )
```

This code is basically the same as the code in Listing 26-2, except for the @DbColumn and the @DbLookup. Therefore, only the two functions that have changed are covered here.

```
REM {get a count of how many quotes};
odbc_connection := "ND6 Bible Quotes";
table1 := "QuoteTable";

REM {get a list of keys from the ODBC resource};
allquotes := @IfError(@DbColumn("ODBC" : ""; odbc_connection;
  ""; ""; table1; "QuoteKey");
             @Do(
                 @Set("lookerr"; @True);
                 "ERROR: " + @Text(allQuotes)
                 )
  );
```

The variable odbc_connection is used to provide the name of the system DSN that you created earlier, to the @functions. If you name yours differently, here is where you can change it. The user name and password parameters are empty strings (""), because there is no security on the Access database or System DSN. The table1 variable contains the name of the table in the Access file. A column name is used for the data column — remember that the ODBC version of @DbColumn does not take a column number as a parameter, only a column name.

The @DbLookup is similar to the @DbColumn, except a key column name and key value are passed to it so the function knows where to look up the key value, and what key value to look up. Then it returns the desired data from the column specified in the column name parameter:

```
wquote := @If(lookerr = @True;
                    allQuotes;
                    @DbLookup("ODBC" : ""; odbc_connection;
  ""; ""; table1;  "Quote"; "QuoteKey"; wquotekey)
  );
```

The rest of the code is the same as that found in Listing 26-1. Play with this code and you'll see that the response time is not as slow as you would think it would be coming from an ODBC datasource. ODBC datasources are inherently slower when retrieving data than a native datasource, such as a Notes database. With a larger external database, however, the response time could be slower than it would be with a similarly sized data set in a Domino database.

Summary

This chapter covered, in detail, the use of @DbColumn and @DbLookup for retrieving data from both a Notes and ODBC datasource. This chapter introduced the following ways to retrieve data:

✦ Using @DbColumn to retrieve a list of values from the column in a Notes database view

✦ Using @DbLookup to retrieve a subset of data based on a key from the column of a Notes database view or a particular field on one or more documents

✦ Using @DbColumn to retrieve a column of data from the table in an ODBC data source

✦ Using @DbLookup to retrieve a subset of data based on a key value from a table in an ODBC data source

You then saw these functions used in context in a couple of examples.

Chapter 28 covers some more advanced techniques for working with @DbColumn and @DbLookup, and other ways to retrieve data. You also explore some advanced techniques for optimizing the use of @DbColumn and @DbLookup to make your applications as fast as possible.

✦   ✦   ✦

User Interaction through the Formula Language

By Rocky Oliver

✦ ✦ ✦ ✦

In This Chapter

Working with @Prompts

Programming
with @Prompt

Programming
with @PickList

✦ ✦ ✦ ✦

One of the most useful features of the Formula is the ability it gives you to interact with users. You have a great deal of flexibility at your fingertips for informing users, gathering information from users, or for interacting with users. The three main @functions used to interact with users are @Prompt, @PickList, and @DialogBox. These functions have many optional parameters, and using them is an art form in and of itself.

This chapter introduces you to some useful ways to work with @Prompt, @PickList, and @DialogBox, and provides some concrete examples about how to get the most out of them. @Prompt enables you to provide information to a user, or ask the user to enter or choose information. @PickList enables you to use a view as a type of dialog box and allow the user to choose one or more documents. @DialogBox is the most flexible of all — it enables you to use a form as the basis for a dialog box, providing you virtually unlimited customization choices. Before you get to the examples, however, you need to learn the basics of these three complex, powerful functions.

Note

These three functions were so powerful that developers demanded LotusScript equivalents. These were added to the `NotesUIWorkspace` class in Release 5. @Prompt maps to `NotesUIWorkspace.Prompt`, @PickList maps to `NotesUI-Workspace.PickListCollection` and `NotesUIWorkspace.PickList-Strings`, and @DialogBox maps to `NotesUI-Workspace.DialogBox`.

Working with @Prompts

There are many variations of @Prompt available to the developer—from the simple OK box, to complex lists. These variations are determined by using a flag in the @Prompt function call. This section breaks down each one of these flags, and provides some tips along the way. But first you need to review these flags in a general sense, and then explore each type in more detail.

 Note   Throughout this chapter the terms "flag" and "parameter" are used. A *flag* refers to a predetermined keyword or value that the function expects ([OK] for @Prompt). A *parameter* refers to a variable value that the user provides (the title of an @Prompt).

Using @Prompt

The @Prompt function is used to inform the user of something, or to prompt the user for basic information. The general syntax for @Prompt is as follows:

```
@Prompt([type]; title; prompt message; default choice;
list of choices; filetype flag)
```

Not all of these parameters are used for each type of @Prompt. As each type is explained, the parameters needed are discussed as well.

The general parameters for @Prompt are as follows:

✦ [type]: This defines which type of @Prompt you want. You have the following options:

- [ChooseDatabase]: Presents the File ➪ Database ➪ Open dialog box.

- [LocalBrowse]: Presents the common file dialog box appropriate for your operating system.

- [OK]: Presents a text message to the user with an OK button.

- [OKCancelCombo]: Presents a list of choices as a combo box, like the field type combo box.

- [OKCancelEdit]: Presents a message box with a place where the user can enter some text.

- [OKCanceEditCombo]: Presents a list of choices as a combo box and enables users to choose a member of the presented list or enter a new entry.

- [OKCancelList]: Presents the user a list of choices, similar to the listbox field type.

- [OKCancelListMult]: Presents the user a list of choices, but allows the selection of multiple values.

- [Password]: Presents a dialog box where the user can enter a text item, and that text item will be hidden from the screen using asterisks (for example, if you enter **password,** you see ********).

- [YesNo]: Presents the user a text message, similar to the OK prompt, but with Yes and No buttons.

- [YesNoCancel]: Same as the [YesNo] prompt, but with a Cancel button.

- [NoSort]: @Prompts normally automatically sorts the list of choices when a list is presented to the user. If the [NoSort] parameter is used, the @Prompt does not sort the list.

✦ title: The title parameter provides the title displayed in the window title bar for the @Prompt dialog box.

✦ prompt message: The message, or instructions, presented to the user for the @Prompt.

✦ default choice: For @Prompt types that take input from the user, the default choice parameter provides the user a default choice. If you do not want to provide a default choice, use an empty string ("").

✦ list of choices: The list of choices for @Prompts that present a list of choices to the user.

Tip   If your list of choices is dynamic, such as lists generated by @DbColumn or @DbLookup, an easy way to set the default value is to use @Subset, which automatically uses the first value of the list as the default value. More techniques for @Prompt are provided later in this chapter.

✦ filetype flag: This parameter is only used for the [LocalBrowse] type. You can use this flag to specify one of three types to display initially:

- "1" for NSF files

- "2" for NTF files

- "3" for all file types

The following section looks at each type in more detail.

Using @Prompt([ChooseDatabase])

@Prompt([ChooseDatabase]) opens the same dialog box that you get if you choose File ➪ Database ➪ Open. This function returns a list with three variables: server, database path, and database title.

New Feature   Even though @Prompt([ChooseDatabase]) was available in Notes/Domino Release 5, it was undocumented; therefore it is "officially" new now.

The Choose Database dialog box appears, as shown in Figure 27-1.

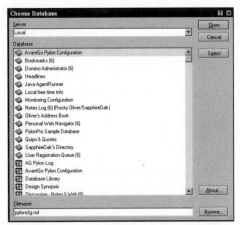

Figure 27-1: @Prompt([ChooseDatabase])
provides the same dialog box you get when
you select File ⇨ Database ⇨ Open.

The Choose Database dialog box is handy when you want to allow the user to choose a
database to take action against. For instance, if you want to allow the users to choose a
database to add to their workspace, you could use the following code to accomplish this:

```
dbinfo := @Prompt([ChooseDatabase]);
@Command([AddDatabase]; dbinfo)
```

Using @Prompt([LocalBrowse])

The syntax for @Prompt([LocalBrowse]) is as follows:

```
@Prompt([LocalBrowse]; title; filetype flag)
```

@Prompt([LocalBrowse]) provides a subset of the functionality that the Windows common
dialog box provides. The dialog box that is presented is like the common dialog box, but the
file choices are not definable beyond the filetypes of NSF, NTF, and all. The filetype flag
takes a "1" to indicate NSF, "2" to indicate "NTF", and "3" to allow the selection of any file
type. If you need greater flexibility, consider using the NotesUIWorkspace.OpenFileDialog
method. This function returns the file path to the chosen file.

Using @Prompt([OK])

@Prompt([OK]) is used to present a simple message to the user. This can be something informative, a notification of an error message, and much more. @Prompt([OK]) uses the following syntax:

```
@Prompt([OK]; title; prompt message)
```

Keep in mind that the prompt message must be text; you cannot provide any other data type
and present it in a prompt. If you want to present non-text information in @Prompt([OK]),
convert it to text using @Text. Additionally, you cannot present a list in @Prompt([OK]). If
you want to present a list of information in this type of prompt, consider using @Implode to
concatenate the list into a string.

This type of prompt is probably the most used, as it can be used to inform the user of anything, such as when an error occurs in your code, or to inform the user of the status of some task. `@Prompt([OK])` is often used for debugging as well.

Tip   If you are writing long Formula code, it is good to build debugging code into your formula. You can do this by creating a role called `Debug` (or whatever you want to call it) in the Access Control List (ACL) of your database, and then add the following statement at any place in your code where you want to have debug prompts:

```
@If(@IsMember("[Debug]"; @UserRoles);
  @Prompt([OK]; "Debug"; @Text(your variable));
  "")
```

Now you simply add yourself to the `Debug` role whenever you need to debug your code, and all of the prompts inform you of what is going on in your code. One thing to keep in mind with this technique is that it only works on server-based databases, since roles are not available locally. However, an alternative method for debugging code is presented later in this chapter, in the section entitled "Using @Prompts for troubleshooting."

Using @Prompt([OKCancelCombo])

`@Prompt([OKCancelCombo])` provides a list of choices, which appears as a combo box to the user. The syntax for `@Prompt([OKCancelCombo])` is as follows:

```
@Prompt([OKCancelCombo]; title; prompt message;
default choice; list of choices)
```

Figure 27-2 shows you how `@Prompt([OKCancelCombo])` appears. The presentation of a list of choices in `@Prompt([OKCancelCombo])` is similar to the formatting of a `combobox` keyword field type. This type of prompt is useful when the list of choices is long, because it is a cleaner presentation of the choices.

Figure 27-2: @Prompt([OKCancelCombo]) presents a list in the same way as the Combo Box type field design item.

This function returns the value chosen by the user. If the user clicks Cancel, the evaluation of the formula stops.

Using @Prompt([OKCancelEdit])

`@Prompt([OKCancelEdit])` enables the users to enter any text they wish to enter. The syntax of `@Prompt([OKCancelEdit])` is as follows:

```
@Prompt([OKCancelEdit]; title; prompt message;
default choice)
```

Remember that this prompt returns a text value; if you need a value of a different data type, such as a date, then you need to convert it using the appropriate @function, such as `@TextToTime`, as shown in the following code:

```
startdate := @Prompt([OKCancelEdit]; "Start Date";
"Please enter the start date."; @Text(@Today));
startdate := @TextToTime(startdate)
```

This code prompts the user for a start date, and then uses @TextToTime to convert the return value from the prompt to a date/time value. If the user clicks Cancel, formula evaluation stops at that point.

Using @Prompt([OKCancelEditCombo])

@Prompt([OKCancelEditCombo]) appears the same as @Prompt([OKCancelCombo]), except that the user can enter a value if the desired value does not appear in the provided list of choices. The syntax for @Prompt([OKCancelEditCombo]) is as follows:

```
@Prompt([OKCancelEditCombo]; title; prompt message;
default choice; list of choices)
```

@Prompt([OKCancelEditCombo]) is useful for working with a user-defined list of values, as it allows the users to choose a value from the existing list or add one of their own, which in turn makes it available for future use as a choice.

This function returns the value chosen or entered by the user. If the user clicks Cancel, the evaluation of the formula stops.

Using @Prompt([OKCancelList]) and @Prompt([OKCancelListMult])

@Prompt([OKCancelList]) and @Prompt([OKCancelListMult]) both provide a list of choices for the user to choose from, which appear as a ListBox field. The difference between the two is that the user can choose more than one value when @Prompt([OK-CancelListMult]) is used. The syntax for @Prompt([OKCancelList]) and @Prompt-([OKCancelListMult]) is as follows:

```
@Prompt([type]; title; prompt message;
default choice; list of choices)
```

In the syntax listed shown, [type] is the flag [OKCancelList] or [OKCancelListMult]. Figure 27-3 shows how @Prompt([OKCancelList]) appears; @Prompt([OKCancelList-Mult]) appears the same way, except that the user can choose more than one value. This prompt type is a nice presentation of choices when the list of choice isn't very large.

Figure 27-3: @Prompt([OKCancelList]) presents a list of choices just as @Prompt([OKCancelCombo]) does, except that this list appears in the same way that a ListBox type of keyword field presents a list of choices.

If @Prompt([OKCancelListMult]) is used, the choices are returned as a text list; otherwise the value chosen by the user is returned. If the user clicks Cancel, the evaluation of the formula stops.

Using @Prompt([Password]; title; prompt message)

`@Prompt([Password])` is similar to `@Prompt([OKCancelEdit])`, except for two things. First, anything entered is shown as asterisks (*), even though the function returns the actual text value entered (it is not obscured or encrypted); and second, the function has a default message that cannot be altered, as shown in Figure 27-4.

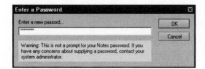

Figure 27-4: @Prompt([Password]) enables you to prompt a user for information that cannot be read by someone else while the user is typing it in.

The default message text of the `@Prompt([Password])` function is there to make it harder for malicious developers to trick an unwary user into believing the prompt was a legitimate prompt for his Notes password.

If the user clicks Cancel, formula evaluation stops.

Using @Prompt([YesNo]) and @Prompt([YesNoCancel])

`@Prompt([YesNo])` and `@Prompt([YesNoCancel])` provide a text message to the user and ask the user to choose Yes or No by clicking the respective button. The syntax of these two functions is as follows:

```
@Prompt([type]; title; prompt message)
```

In the preceding syntax, `[type]` is the flag `[YesNo]` or `[YesNoCancel]`. `@Prompt([YesNo Cancel])` is the same as `@Prompt([YesNo])`, except that the latter enables the user to cancel out by providing a Cancel button. If the user clicks Yes, a 1 is returned. If the user clicks No, a 0 is returned. And if the user clicks Cancel, a –1 is returned.

Note   This is the only version of @Prompt that does *not* stop formula execution when the user clicks Cancel.

You now have a basic understanding of @Prompts and how to use them, so let's explore some suggestions for using @Prompts.

Programming with @Prompt

The following sections describe basic tips for working with and getting the most out of @Prompts.

Using @Return with @Prompt

`@Return` can be used with @Prompt to return some message and stop the rest of the Formula code from executing. For example, consider the following code:

```
REM {Prompt the user for a key. If the user enters an empty
string, prompt them again until he enters a value or clicks
Cancel"};
```

```
@DoWhile(
        key := @Prompt([OkCancelEdit]; "Enter Value";
        "Enter a key value for the lookup..."; "");
        key = ""
);
REM {Once the user enters a value, perform a lookup};
results := @IfError(
            @DbLookup(""; ""; "Main View"; key; 2);
            @Return(
                @Prompt([OK]; "Error"; "There was
                an error performing a lookup on
                this value: " + key)
                )

            )
```

The preceding code does the following:

✦ It prompts the user for some key value.

✦ It makes sure that the user entered a value. If the user doesn't enter a value, it continues to ask for a value until the user enters one or clicks Cancel.

Looping in formulas, such as @DoWhile in the preceding example, is covered in Chapter 28.

✦ It performs a @DbLookup based on that key.

✦ If the @DbLookup fails, it informs the user that there was a problem and then stops the execution of the code.

The @Return function returns whatever is set as its parameter. If the parameter is an @function, it executes the function and then returns the result of the function. This technique is very useful for stopping the execution of your code when an error occurs or when some condition is not met that is required to proceed.

Using variables for parameters

If you are basing the choices in an @Prompt that uses lists on a @DbColumn or @DbLookup, set the lookup to a variable, and then use that variable for the list of choices and the default value. This technique is shown in the following code, where an @Prompt([OKCancelList]) is based on a list of values from a @DbColumn:

```
list := @IfError(
            @DbColumn(""; ""; "Some View"; 1);
            @Return(
                @Prompt([OK]; "Error"; "Unable to
  retrieve values for keyword.")
                )
            );
choice := @Prompt([OKCancelList]; "Choose"; "Please choose
from this list."; @Subset(list; 1); list)
```

The preceding code does the following:

✦ It performs a @DbColumn to get a value.

✦ If the @DbColumn fails, the user is informed of the failure and the formula quits executing.

✦ It prompts the user to choose a value from the list gathered from the @DbColumn. Additionally, the first value of the @DbColumn is used as the default value for the @Prompt.

Using @Prompts for troubleshooting

If you need to troubleshoot your code, @Prompts can be a great help. If you are writing code that is rather long, it may even be worth the effort to establish some periodic checks throughout your code that you can turn off and on with a single variable at the beginning of your code. For example, you could use something like this code:

```
debug := "";
@IfError(debug;
         @Prompt([OK]; "Debug"; "Debug value: " + checkValue)
);
```

To use this example, place the @IfError portion of this code throughout your long formula, and change the checkValue variable to the variable you want to check. Then if you want to debug your code, you change the value of the debug variable from "" to @Error, and all your debug @IfErrors execute, causing your debug @Prompts to display the information to you.

Now that you have a basic understanding of @Prompts, let's move on to @PickLists.

Programming with @PickList

@PickList is a variant of @Prompt that enables you to use a view or folder to present data to the user for selection rather than using one of the list versions of an @Prompt. This provides you the ability to display a great deal more contextual information to the user, because you can show multiple columns in a view. You can also use type-ahead to quickly find the desired value. A couple of specialized @Picklist types enable you to prompt the user to choose a resource, reservation, or folder name.

There are eight different types of @PickLists. The following sections break each one down individually.

Using @PickList([Custom])

@PickList([Custom]) displays the indicated view from the specified database in a dialog box. The title and prompt variables are just like the ones used in @Prompt. Column number returns the indicated column for the selected document(s). Category name is used if you want to display only the documents contained in a single category, similar to using the single category option in an embedded view. If you add the [Single] keyword to the [Custom] one using a colon (:) as a separator, the user can choose only one document; if you omit this optional keyword, the user can choose more than one document, and the results are returned as a text list.

Tip

The column that is used for returning a value from `@PickList([Custom])` can be a hidden column. This can be very useful so that you can return information that isn't necessarily user-friendly.

For example, if you placed the following code into an agent or view action in the ND6 Bible Formulas database, you produce the dialog box shown in Figure 27-5:

```
@PickList([Custom]; ""; "FIELD_REPL_EX"; "Example"; "Choose a
document"; 1)
```

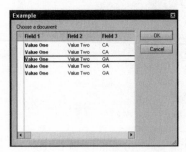

Figure 27-5: The @PickList([Custom]) function can be used to present a view for user choice selection.

Using @PickList([Name] : [Single])

`@PickList([Name])` presents the Domino Directory Name Selection dialog box shown in Figure 27-6.

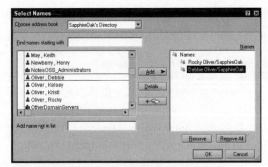

Figure 27-6: The @PickList([Name]) function enables a user to choose names from a Domino Directory or Personal Name and Address Book.

If you use the optional `[Single]` parameter, the user can only choose one name in the dialog box.

Using @PickList([Room]), @PickList([Resource])

`@PickList([Room])` and `@PickList([Resource])` present the Room and Resource Selection dialog boxes from the Domino Directory.

Using @PickList([Folders])

By default, `@PickList([Folders])` displays a dialog box that provides a text list of all the folders in the specified database, and the user can choose one or more of them from the list. You can use a few keywords with `@PickList([Folders])`; however, to narrow the choices. Many of these keywords can be combined to filter the folders list at a granular level:

✦ `[Single]`: The user is allowed to select only one value from the folder list. This keyword can be combined with any of the other keywords.

✦ `[Shared]`: This keyword filters the folder list to only shared folders.

✦ `[Private]`: This keyword filters the folder list to only private folders that are stored in either the desktop or on the server.

✦ `[NoDesktop]`: This keyword, when combined with the `[Private]` keyword, filters out the private folders stored on the desktop and shows only private folders stored on the server.

The syntax for `@PickList([Folders])` is as follows:

```
@PickList([Folders]:[optional keyword];
server : database path)
```

The optional keywords are the four mentioned previously. So if you want to show only shared folders, and allow the user to choose only one folder, you would use the keywords like `@Prompt([Folders] : [Single] : [Shared])`.

`@PickLists` can be a great way to present a list of choices in context to a user. Experiment with them to learn more about how they can help you in your application development.

Cross-Reference Chapter 28 has a good example of using `@PickList`, including the previously mentioned technique of returning concatenated, user-unfriendly values and parsing the values out. This example is in the section entitled "Concatenating values for retrieval" in Chapter 28.

Using @DialogBox

One of the most flexible and useful ways to interact with your users is through the use of a custom dialog box. A dialog box is nothing more than a form that is presented as a window. Because a dialog box is based on a form, the options for customization are quite extensive. In this section, the basics of `@DialogBox`, including parameters, are covered first, and then some tips for designing your dialog box forms are discussed.

Cross-Reference You can invoke a dialog box two ways—through the `@DialogBox` command and through the LotusScript `NotesUIWorkspace.DialogBox` method. The `@DialogBox` command provides quite a bit of functionality, but overall the `DialogBox` method in LotusScript is more powerful. The `DialogBox` method is covered more extensively in Part VI.

This section reviews the parameters of `@DialogBox`. `@DialogBox` has only three parameters: form name, option keywords, and title, but the option keyword parameter can take a variety of keywords. The syntax of `@DialogBox` is fairly simple:

```
@DialogBox(form name; option keywords; title)
```

The form name parameter indicates the form that the dialog box uses. The title parameter indicates what will show up in the title bar of the dialog box window. The option keywords are numerous and can be combined to customize the preferences for your dialog box. Additionally, all of these flags are optional. The option keywords that are available are as follows:

✦ [AutoHorzFit] **and** [AutoVertFit]: These two keywords cause the dialog box to scale to fit the first table or layout region in the form horizontally and vertically, respectively. Usually these two keywords are used together.

✦ [NoCancel]: This keyword removes the Cancel button from the dialog box, but leaves the OK button.

✦ [NoNewFields]: Normally, all fields that are on the dialog box are automatically placed on the associated document. This keyword prevents any new fields from being added to the document and updates only existing fields.

✦ [NoFieldUpdate]: Normally, any changes made to fields in the dialog box are automatically passed to the associated document. This keyword prevents all changes to fields on the dialog box from being passed to the underlying document. This can be very useful when creating a dialog box that is used for workflow but doesn't update the related document. For instance, you may create a dialog box that prompts the user through a variety of choices that determines a series of documents to be created, and what information is contained in those documents.

✦ [ReadOnly]: Normally, dialog boxes are editable. This keyword causes the dialog box to be read-only. You can see an example of this when you use the Domino 6 Designer help — it opens help documents in a read-only dialog box. Incidentally, using this keyword also implies the [NoCancel] keyword, which makes sense because you would only cancel a dialog box that you are editing.

✦ [SizeToTable]: If you are using a table to create your dialog box, this keyword allows the [AutoHorzFit] and the [AutoVertFit] keywords to work with a table instead of a layout region. If you are using a layout region to create your dialog box, you don't need this keyword, because this one is for tables only.

✦ [NoOKCancel]: This keyword removes the gray bar containing OK and Cancel buttons that normally appear on the right of a dialog box. This is very useful if you are making your own custom dialog box, and you want to use your own buttons for it.

✦ [OKCancelAtBottom]: Normally, the OK/Cancel gray bar appears to the side of the dialog box. This keyword causes the OK and Cancel buttons to appear at the bottom of the dialog box.

New Feature   The [OKCancelAtBottom] keyword is new with Notes/Domino 6.

@DialogBox is useful, but knowing a few tips and tricks can make them even more useful. Here are a few basics for using @DialogBox.

Understanding how @DialogBox works

As you learned in Chapter 2, forms are merely a way to view and work with information contained in a document. A document can have one, more than one, or no forms associated with it. But whenever a form is open in the UI, it must have a corresponding document loaded into memory as well. Even when you compose a new document with a form, there is a new, blank document loaded into memory with the new form.

Dialog boxes are forms loaded into a window, usually with OK and Cancel buttons. Because it is a dialog box form, it is held to the same rule that forms are held — all dialog boxes must be associated with a document. Therefore, when you use a dialog box, whether it is the Formula version or the LotusScript version, it must be associated with a document. When using the Formula version of a dialog box, the only way to associate it with a document is to load the dialog box while a document is selected in a view, or while a document is loaded in the UI. All changes made to the dialog box are also made to the associated form, unless you are using one of the optional keywords that alter this behavior. The LotusScript version of a dialog box, NotesUIWorkspace.DialogBox, also requires a document to be associated with it; however there is a way to create a "temporary" document to use with the dialog box that doesn't actually exist in the document.

Therefore, it is a good idea to use an @DialogBox when you need to perform specialized work for a particular, existing document. If, however, you need to use a dialog box for general workflow or other applications where the dialog box isn't being used to modify a specific document, you should use the LotusScript version.

Cross-Reference You can learn more about using the LotusScript version of a dialog box in Part VI.

Even though this section discusses the similarities between dialog boxes and forms, there is one notable difference — you cannot use rich text fields in a dialog box. Rich text fields do not transfer from a dialog box to the associated document. Keep this in mind so you are not tripped up by it in the future.

Knowing when @DialogBox is used or canceled

The Domino 6 Designer help document for @DialogBox incorrectly states that there is no return value from @DialogBox. @DialogBox actually does return a value based on if you click OK or Cancel. If the user clicks OK, then @DialogBox returns a 1. If the user clicks Cancel, then @DialogBox returns a 0. Use the return value of @DialogBox to determine whether the user canceled out of the dialog box — this way you can gracefully exit your code without causing undue errors. For example, the following line of code exits the formula if the user cancels out of the dialog box:

```
@If(@DialogBox("InfoForm"; [SizeToTable]; "Info Prompt") = 0;
@Return(""); "")
```

Using autosize, layout regions, and tables

You do not have to use a table or layout region with a dialog box, but if you don't you can't use the autosizing features of @DialogBox — [AutoHorzFit] and [AutoVertFit]. And if you don't use the autosizing features, the dialog box is presented in a rather ugly fashion, as shown in Figure 27-7.

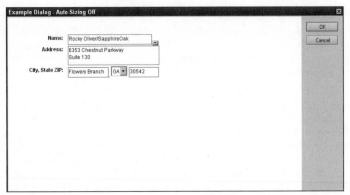

Figure 27-7: If you don't autosize your dialog boxes to a layout region or table, they aren't user-friendly because they are so big.

But if you use the autosizing feature, your dialog boxes are nicely proportioned, as shown in Figure 27-8.

Figure 27-8: If you do use the autosizing keywords [AutoHorzFit] and [AutoVertFit], your dialog boxes are nicely proportioned.

The autosizing features work by shrinking the dialog box to one of two design element sizes — a layout region or a table. Both of these still work; however, if you are developing in Release 5 or later (and hopefully if you're reading this book you're at least beginning to develop in Notes/Domino 6), then you should break any habit you have of using layout regions. Layout regions are a legacy design element and have been superceded by tables since Release 5. Layout regions have a laundry list of issues and problems with development.

Luckily for developers, Lotus has added new features to Domino in general, and @DialogBox specifically, to help break the layout region habit. In @DialogBox, you have the [SizeToTable] feature, which when used with [AutoHorzFit] and [AutoVertFit], provides autosizing to the first table found in your dialog box form.

On The Web   The code mentioned in this chapter is contained in the ND6 Bible Formula Examples database, which is available for download at www.wiley.com/compbooks/benz.

Code in the ND6 Bible Formula Examples database (d6bibleformula.nsf) demonstrates this autosizing feature (and shows off some other techniques). If you open the 27.07 Dialog Example view, and click the Dialog Example action button, you activate the 27.07 Dialog Example agent. This agent provides a set of instructions and then enables you to display a dialog box that either is autosized or not. The agent's code is shown in Listing 27-1.

Listing 27-1: **27.07 Dialog Example Agent**

```
@Prompt([Ok]; "Instructions"; "This agent shows you the
difference between using automatic sizing of your dialog
box," + @char(10) + "or just letting the box show up without
auto-sizing." + @char(10) + "Simply choose YES to view with
auto-sizing on, and NO to turn it off.");

sizechoice := @Prompt([YesNoCancel]; "Auto Size?";
"Do you want to auto-size the dialog box to the table?");

@If(sizechoice = 0; @Return(""); "");

sizeflag := @If(sizechoice = 1; [AutoHorzFit] : [AutoVertFit]
: [SizeToTable]; "");

retflg := @DialogBox("DIALOG_EX"; sizeFlag; "Example Dialog -
Auto-Sizing " + @If(sizechoice = 1; "On"; "Off"));

msgtxt := @If(retflg = 1; "By the way, you clicked OK on the
dialog box."; "By the way, you clicked Cancel on the dialog
box.");

@Prompt([Ok]; "Results"; msgtxt)
```

This agent performs the following actions:

✦ Gives the user an introduction to the agent's functions.

Tip Notice that @char(10) is used to add line breaks to the text of the @Prompt. @NewLine does not work in @Prompt messages, so you can use @char(10) instead to add a line break in @Prompt messages.

✦ Asks the user whether to autosize dialog box.

✦ If the user cancels out, the code is terminated.

✦ Based on the user's choice, sets the sizeflag variable the [AutoHorzFit], [AutoVertFit], and [SizeToTable] flags (if the user has chosen to autosize the dialog box), or it is set to an empty string (if the user has not chosen to autosize the dialog box).

✦ Presents the dialog box. You should notice two things here. First, the @DialogBox function is set to the retflg variable, so that the return value can be captured. Second, the flags are being passed in on a variable — the sizeflag variable to be precise.

✦ Checks the retflg variable and presents a prompt message indicating which button — OK or Cancel — the user clicked.

Incidentally, if you change a value in the dialog box, the associated value changes in the underlying document.

Using the Native OS Style property for dialog box fields

Dialog boxes cannot change in size while they are open. Notes style fields are allowed to dynamically expand to be able to display the entire content of the field. This can cause you problems if your user types in so much text that the field grows in size by a row or more, because some data will be hidden. To avoid this problem, set all your fields to the Native OS Style property. When this property is set, the field does not grow in size; instead, the field automatically displays a scrollbar if the amount of text entered exceeds the display capacity of the field.

Note You learn more about using dialog boxes in your applications in Part VI. Additionally, you should practice building dialog boxes to explore the power and flexibility provided to you with this feature.

Summary

In this chapter, the three main ways of interacting with users — @Prompts, @PickLists, and @DialogBoxes — were explored.

✦ You learned about the various types of @Prompts, and were introduced to a variety of ways to use them.

✦ You learned about @Picklist and how it takes advantage of the power of a view to present choices to a user.

✦ You learned about @DialogBox, and how dialog boxes are extremely flexible and powerful for creating robust applications.

Each @function was broken down, providing you details of how they work, and insight into how you may exploit them in your applications.

Chapter 28 dives into some advanced techniques for working with the Formula language, including dialog boxes.

✦   ✦   ✦

Advanced Formula Techniques

By Rocky Oliver

In This Chapter

Looping in the
Formula language

Working with text lists

Using @DbColumn and
@DbLookup

The chapters in Part V introduced you to the power and flexibility of the Formula language. You've gotten a good taste for what it can do for you, and you have been shown various tips and techniques for using the Formula language effectively. This chapter takes your Formula finesse to a higher level. This chapter takes you from the science of Formula language coding to the art of Formula language coding. The chapter begins by introducing you to the new looping features in Notes/Domino 6, and then it shows you various ways to enhance your applications.

Looping in Formulas

New Feature

Lotus introduced three new @functions in the Formula language in Notes/Domino 6 to deliver the ability to loop iteratively though code. These functions are @For, @While, and @DoWhile.

Before Notes/Domino 6 was released, there was no clean way to perform loops in the Formula language. So if you wanted to execute a block of code until a particular condition was met, you simply couldn't do it. This was severely limiting when working with the Formula language, and forced many Formula newbies to go to LotusScript instead of trying to come up with some convoluted workaround.

The Formula language finally has looping capabilities. Looping is now accomplished through three new @functions: @DoWhile, @While, and @For. Let's take a look at each one. First this section covers the basics of the @function, and then it provides some examples.

Using @DoWhile

@DoWhile executes all the formula statements provided until the test condition is True (1). While the test condition is False (0), @DoWhile continues to execute the statements on each pass. The syntax of @DoWhile is as follows:

```
@DoWhile(formula statement 1; formula statement 2;... ;
test condition)
```

> **Note**   @DoWhile checks the test condition *after* executing the Formula statements.

For example, look at a factorial, a common mathematical function that requires looping. The *factorial* of an integer is the product of the integer multiplied by each smaller integer, down to 1. This means that the factorial of a number is derived by multiplying it by all smaller integers. So the factorial of 4, written as 4!, is computed as 4 * 3 * 2 * 1, or 24. So 4! = 24. Because the number of times you need to loop through a number to determine its factorial is dependent on the number itself, it is extremely difficult to write code in Formula language to compute a factorial based on a user-supplied integer.

The code in Listing 28-1 shows how to prompt a user for a number for computing the factorial, and then how to actually compute it using @functions. This code is in the 28.01 @DoWhile Example—Factorial agent in the ND6 Bible Formula Examples database (d6bibleformula.nsf).

Listing 28-1: **28.01 @DoWhile Example — Factorial Agent**

```
REM "Prompt the user for an integer. If the user enters
a negative number or an empty string,";
REM "prompt them again.";
@DoWhile(
        factnum := @Prompt([OKCancelEdit];
                "Enter an Integer";
                "Please enter an Integer whose factorial
you want to compute."; "5");
        factnum = ""  | @TextToNumber(factnum) <= 0
);

REM "Set up the initial values for the computation.";
REM "factwork is the number that gets decremented";
REM "factorial is the variable that will hold the
final result.";
factwork := @TextToNumber(factnum);
factorial := factwork;

REM "compute th e factorial";
REM "iterate the code, decrementing the factwork
variable until it is = 0";
```

```
@DoWhile(
        factwork := factwork - 1;
        factorial := factorial * factwork;
        factwork != 1
);

REM "return the results to the user.";
@Prompt([OK]; "Results"; "The factorial of " + factnum +
" (" + factnum + "!) is " + @Text(factorial; ","))
```

The first @DoWhile loop makes sure that the user enters a valid entry by testing to make sure that the entered value isn't an empty string, and that it is a number greater than –1. After that, the value entered by the user is converted to a number, and is assigned to two variables — factwork and factnum. factwork is used to decrement the number entered for multiplication to compute the factorial. factorial is the variable that will hold the result and the variable that you are using for the interim computation.

The next @DoWhile actually performs the factorial computation. First, the factwork variable is decremented by 1; then it is multiplied with the factorial variable, and the product is reassigned to the factorial variable. This process continues until the factwork variable is reduced to 1, and then the loop exits.

Note   Before Notes/Domino 6, you could not reassign a variable, so factorial := factorial would not be allowed. With Notes/Domino 6, you can now reassign a variable, which makes factorial code simpler to write and read.

Finally, the result is returned to the user with an @Prompt.

Using @While

@While is virtually identical to @DoWhile, with two notable exceptions: First, @DoWhile evaluates the condition *after* the formula statements have been executed, whereas @While evaluates the condition *before* the formula statements have been executed. The second difference is that the test condition is placed before the formula statements instead of afterward as in @DoWhile. The syntax for @While is as follows:

```
@DoWhile(test condition; formula statement 1;
formula statement 2;...)
```

The significance of this is that at times you want to process the code before a statement is tested, and sometimes you want to test it after the code is executed. For instance, you may want to test to see whether a value is less than a certain value, and if it is, you want to perform some processing. But there may be times when the condition is true before the loop is encountered; and if that is the case, you don't want to do the processing at all. In this instance you would want to use @While to test the condition before the code is executed.

Listing 28-2 shows the agent called 28.02 @While Example—Factorial, which is identical to Listing 28-1 except for the @While statement.

> **Listing 28-2: 28.02 @While Example — Factorial Agent**
>
> ```
> REM {Prompt the user for an integer. If the user enters a
> negative number or an empty string,};
> REM {prompt them again.};
> @DoWhile(
>         factnum := @Prompt([OkCancelEdit]; "Enter an
> Integer"; "Please enter an Integer whose factorial you want
> to compute."; "5");
>         factnum = ""  | @TextToNumber(factnum) <= 0
> );
>
> REM {Set up the initial values for the computation.};
> REM {factwork is the number that gets decremented};
> REM {factorial is the variable that will hold the final
> result.};
> factwork := @TextToNumber(factnum);
> factorial := factwork;
>
> REM {compute the factorial};
> REM {iterate the code, decrementing the factwork variable
> until it is = 0};
> @While(
>         factwork != 1;
>         factwork := factwork - 1;
>         factorial := factorial * factwork
> );
>
> REM {return the results to the user.};
> @Prompt([Ok]; "Results"; "The factorial of " + factnum + " ("
> + factnum + "!) is " + @Text(factorial; ","))
> ```

Notice that the only difference is the @While statement, which lists the test condition at the beginning rather than at the end.

Using @For

@For is similar to a For statement in LotusScript or JavaScript. For statements are typically used to process arrays or lists, because you can use the incrementing variable to reference an array index sequentially.

The syntax for @For is as follows:

```
@For(initial statement;
     test condition
     incremental statement;
     formula statement 1; formula statement 2;... )
```

@For takes the conditions described in the following list:

✦ **Initial statement:** This sets up the initial number for the iterative loop. For example, x := 1.

✦ **Test condition:** This is what the @For function tests to determine whether the condition has been met (it returns True). For example, x <= 10.

✦ **Incremental statement:** This statement is used to increment the initial value until it satisfies the test condition. For example, x := x + 1.

✦ **Formula statement(s):** This is the actual code that is executed while the @For loop is executing.

If you were to write the factorial code used in the original factorial example using an @For loop, it would look like the agent shown in Listing 28-3.

Listing 28-3: **28.03 @For Example — Factorial**

```
REM {Prompt the user for an integer. If the user enters a
negative number or an empty string,};
REM {prompt them again.};
@DoWhile(
            factnum := @Prompt([OkCancelEdit]; "Enter an
Integer"; "Please enter an Integer whose factorial you want
to compute."; "5");
            factnum = ""  | @TextToNumber(factnum) <= 0
);

REM {Set up the initial values for the computation.};
REM {factwork is the number that gets decremented};
REM {factorial is the variable that will hold the final
result.};
factorial := @TextToNumber(factnum);
factwork := factorial - 1;

REM {compute the factorial};
REM {iterate the code, decrementing the factwork variable
until it is = 1};
@For(
        factwork;
        factwork != 1;
        factwork := factwork - 1;
        factorial := factorial * factwork;
);

REM {return the results to the user.};
@Prompt([Ok]; "Results"; "The factorial of " + factnum + " ("

+ factnum + "!) is " + @Text(factorial; ","))
```

There are two main differences in this listing from the previous listings. First, notice that the initial decrement is made against `factwork` before entering the @For loop. This is done because the Formula statements fire before the `factwork` variable is decremented. The other difference is just the formatting of @For itself. Notice that you don't have to place the setting of the initial condition in @For itself. You can set it up before it is placed in @For and simply set a variable into @For instead.

Here's a more practical example for @For. Many Web sites that you encounter have a navigation aide known as a "breadcrumb" across the top of the page. This breadcrumb shows you where you are in the hierarchy of the Web site. For this example open the BreadCrumb .Example view in the D6 Bible Formula Examples database. Notice there are three documents, and each document is at a different categorization level. Click A Third Level Doc, which is shown in Figure 28-1.

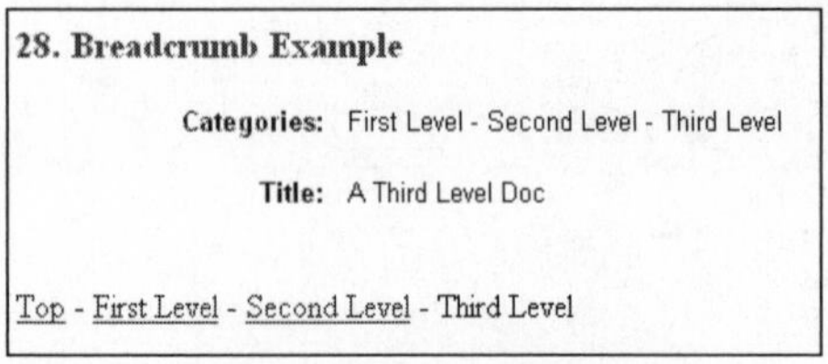

28. Breadcrumb Example

Categories: First Level - Second Level - Third Level

Title: A Third Level Doc

Top - First Level - Second Level - Third Level

Figure 28-1: The BreadCrumb Example document demonstrates a breadcrumb at the bottom of the document.

Notice at the bottom of the document there is a breadcrumb that enables you to walk up the document hierarchy. This breadcrumb is generated automatically using an @For. The code that accomplishes this is shown in Listing 28-4.

Listing 28-4: **BreadCrumb computed text code**

```
catlist := @Explode(@ReplaceSubstring(Categories; " - ";
"~"); "~");
@For(z := 1;
        z <= @Elements(catlist);
        z := z + 1;
        lname := @Trim(lname + @If(z = 1; ""; " - ") +
catlist[z]);
        breadcrumb := breadcrumb + @If(z = 1; ""; " - ") +
                        @If(z < @Elements(catlist);
                            "<a href=\"" +
@URLEncode("Domino"; lname) + "?OpenDocument\">" +
                            catlist[z] + "</a>";
                            catlist[@Elements(catlist)]
                        )
);
"<a href=\"?OpenView\">Top</a> - " + breadcrumb
```

This code takes the value of the categories field and explodes it. Then it uses @For to cycle through each value from the categories field and creates a link to each document up the category tree. Finally a Top link is added that takes the user back to the view level.

Working with Lists

One of the most powerful features in the Formula language is the ability to manipulate lists of data. The Formula language provides many nice @functions that make list manipulation easy. Two of the most useful @functions for list manipulation are @Trim and @Replace.

@Trim and @Replace were briefly discussed in Chapter 24, but it's important to understand how they work, so it is worth taking a few moments to review them.

Using @Trim and @Replace

@Trim simply removes leading, trailing, and extra spaces in a string or a list of strings. @Trim also removes blank entries from a text list. A blank entry is an empty string; for instance @Trim("Apples" : "" : "Oranges") returns "Apples" : "Oranges". @Trim takes the string or string list as the only parameter.

@Replace takes three parameters, sourcelist, fromlist and tolist. The goal is to replace, in the sourcelist, any instances of the values in the fromlist with the corresponding values in the tolist, so the @Replace function checks each item in sourcelist for a match in fromlist. If a match is found, replace it with the corresponding value in tolist. The following short example helps to explain it further.

Let's say there are three lists:

```
sourcelist := "Apples" : "Oranges" : "Grapefruit"

fromlist := "Grapefruit" : "Cherries" : "Apples" : "Bananas"

tolist := "Cantaloupe" : "Blueberries" : "Grapes" :
"Tangerines"
```

The @Replace function compares each item in sourcelist with each item in fromlist, and if it's found, replaces it with the corresponding fruit in tolist. The end result is a list with these values:

```
resultlist := "Grapes" : "Oranges" : "Cantaloupe"
```

Using @Trim and @Replace together

You now understand how @Trim works, and you are beginning to understand how @Replace works. You understand that @Replace can be used to replace values in your list with new values. You can use @Trim and @Replace together to perform the following functions (and so much more):

✦ Remove one or more items from a list

✦ Replace an item with a different item

✦ Return a list of items that appear in two different lists

✦ Return a list of items that do not appear in either of two lists

The following sections take a look at brief examples of each of these functions.

Removing one or more items from a list

Using the fruit example listed earlier, suppose that you have a list of fruits, but you want to remove certain items from the list. The following code demonstrates how this is done.

```
FruitList := "Apples" : "Cantaloupes" : "Oranges" :
"Grapefruit";
YuckList := "Cantaloupes" : "Grapefruit";

GoodFruit := @Trim(@Replace(FruitList; YuckList; ""))
```

The result of this code is as follows:

```
GoodFruit := "Apples" : "Oranges"
```

Let's break this down so you can understand it better. FruitList is a list of fruits. The YuckList variable contains a list of fruits I don't happen to like, so I want to remove them from FruitList. Notice that in place of the fromlist variable is an empty string (""). This causes @Replace to read as, "For each item in the FruitList that matches an item in the YuckList, replace it with an empty string." So if @Trim were left off of @Replace, the result of @Replace would be

```
"Apples" : "" : "Oranges" : ""
```

The yucky fruits have been removed, but there are now unwanted empty strings in the list. @Trim comes to the rescue. @Trim, when applied to the list returned by @Replace (as shown in the line GoodFruit := @Trim(@Replace(FruitList; YuckList; "")))removes all empty strings from the list, and you are left with a list of only the good fruits.

Replacing an item with a different item

In Chapter 24, Listing 24-4 provides code that prompts the user to choose the label of a field she wants to change. The code then figures out the field name that corresponds to the chosen label name, as shown in the following code snippet:

```
REM {Define labels and corresponding fields in order};
labels := "Field One":"Field Two":"Field Three":"Field
Four":"Field Five";
fields := "Field1":"Field2":"Field3":"Field4":"Field5";

REM {Prompt user for label of field to change};
labelchoice := @Prompt([OkCancelList] : [NoSort]; "Choose
Field"; "Choose the field you wish to change..."; 
@Subset(labels; 1); labels);

REM {Determine corresponding field to change};
fldchoice := @Trim(@Replace(labelchoice; labels; fields))
```

In the last line, the `labelchoice` variable contains only a string, not a string list. Developers often forget that the parameters of `@Replace` can be a list or a string. In this case, the label chosen by the user is replaced with the corresponding field name, because the label names in the `labels` variable are in the same order as the field names in the `fields` variable.

Returning a list of items that appear in two different lists

You have two lists. You want to know what the common items between the two lists are. No problem with `@Trim` and `@Replace`. Let's go back to the fruit stand for another example.

You have two lists of fruits. You want to know the common values between the two lists. You can use the following code to accomplish this task:

```
FruitList1 := "Apples" : "Bananas" : "Lemons" : "Oranges" :
"Grapes";
FruitList2 := "Bananas" : "Blackberries" : "Tangerines" :
"Apples";

REM "Remove the items from list1 that are also in list2";
NOTlist := @Trim(@Replace(FruitList1; FruitList2; ""));

REM "Now that we know what isn't common in list1 with list2,
we can easily figure out what is common by removing what
isn't common.";
CommonList := @Trim(@Replace(FruitList1; NOTList; ""))
```

This works because items that are common in both lists are initially removed and assigned to `NOTList`, making the value of `NOTList` equal to `"Lemons":"Oranges":"Grapes"`. Then `NOTList` is compared to the original `sourcelist` — `FruitList1`, once again replacing the common values with `""`. This subtracts those items not found in both lists, leaving those they have in common. As a result, `CommonList = "Apples":"Bananas"`. This would have worked as well with the list positions in `@Replace` reversed; the trick is that whatever list is used in the `sourcelist` parameter (the first parameter) in the first `@Replace` must also be used in the `sourcelist` parameter in the second `@Replace`. If you do this, it will work just fine.

You may be asking yourself, "Why not use `@Keywords` to return the list?" The biggest problem with `@Keywords` is that it returns partial words that match inside the two lists. For example, if you executed the following code:

```
FruitList1 := "Apples" : "Bananas" : "Lemons" : "Oranges" :
"Red Grapes";
FruitList2 := "Bananas" : "Blackberries" : "Tangerines" :
"Apples" : "Red";

Results := @Keywords(FruitList1; FruitList2)
```

The results would be

```
"Apples" : "Bananas" : "Red"
```

And that's not what you want, so it's best to use `@Trim` and `@Replace` to get exactly what you want.

Returning a list of items that don't appear in either list

You now know how to get a list of values that are common between two lists, so it should be easy to take that a step further and get a list of values that is made up of the values *not* common between the two original lists. Here is the code that accomplishes this:

```
FruitList1 := "Apples" : "Bananas" : "Lemons" : "Oranges" :
"Grapes";
FruitList2 := "Bananas" : "Blackberries" : "Tangerines" :
"Apples";

REM "Remove the items from list1 that are also in list2";
NOTlist := @Trim(@Replace(FruitList1; FruitList2; ""));

REM "Now that we know what isn't common in list1 with list2,
we can easily figure out what is common by removing what
isn't common.";
CommonList := @Trim(@Replace(FruitList1; NOTList; ""));

REM "This is a list of items that are not common between the
two original lists";
NOTCommonList := @Trim(@Replace(FruitList1 : FruitList2;

CommonList; ""))
```

Advanced Techniques for Working with @DbColumn and @DbLookup

Chapter 26 covered the basics of @DbColumn and @DbLookup. This section introduces you to some advanced techniques for getting the most out of your @Formulas. This includes better error-trapping, using code that makes it easy to locate other databases, and designing better, more efficient views.

Error-trap @DbColumn and @DbLookup

Fortunately, @DbColumn normally returns an empty string if there is a problem. This may or may not break your application. But @DbLookup normally returns an error if there is a problem, and this almost certainly will break your code. To avoid this, you should always error-trap your @DbColumn and @DbLookup calls. You can error-trap @DbColumn and @DbLookup one of three ways:

✦ Use @If with @IsError. If you do this, make sure you set your @DbColumn or @DbLookup to a variable, and then error-trap the variable. Do not make the rookie mistake of calling the @DbColumn or @DbLookup twice to error-trap it. The following code shows the wrong way to trap errors — see if it looks familiar to you:

```
List := @If(
          @IsError(@DbLookup("" : "NoCache"; ""; "SomeView";
mykey; 2));
          "";
          @DbLookup("" : "NoCache"; ""; "SomeView"; mykey;
2)
          )
```

The correct way follows:

```
List := @DbLookup("" : "NoCache"; "";
"SomeView"; mykey; 2);
List := @IF(
        @IsError(@DbLookup("" : "NoCache"; ""; "SomeView";
 mykey; 2));
        "";
            List
)
```

✦ Use the new @IfError function. Following is a cleaner version of the preceding code:

```
List := @IfError(@DbLookup("" : "NoCache"; ""; "SomeView";
mykey; 2); "")
```

✦ Use the new optional parameter for @DbLookup, [FailSilent]. This parameter causes @DbLookup to work as @DbColumn works, where the function returns an empty string ("") if an error occurs.

Error-trapping your @DbColumns and, more importantly, your @DbLookups can save you and your users many hours of frustration.

Using dynamic paths for related databases

When you began to develop applications using @DbColumn and @DbLookup, especially applications that were comprised of more than one database, then you probably wrote the path to the related databases as a static string. This is not a good practice because if your application gets moved at some later time to a different directory, or if it's replicated locally by your users and they happen to not place the application in the same directory, then all of your lookups break. You can avoid this headache by using *dynamic pathing*.

If you develop applications that require more than one database, then one rule you should establish from the start is to place the related databases in the same directory. If you do so, then you can write your @DbColumn and @DbLookup code to reference the related databases, and always be able to find them no matter what directory the application resides in. I call this technique dynamic pathing. The following code accomplishes this task:

```
REM "Indicate the db to navigate to.";
targetdb := "AnotherDB.nsf";

REM "Get the server and filepath of the current db.";
dbserver := @Subset(@DbName; 1);
dbpath := @Subset(@DbName; -1);

REM "Get the file name of the current database.";
dbfilename := @If(@Contains(dbpath; "\\"); @RightBack(dbpath;
"\\"); dbpath);

REM "Replace the current database file name with the target
db name.";
dbname := @ReplaceSubstring(dbpath; dbfilename; targetdb)
```

Using this code, you can write all your @DbColumns and @DbLookups to use the dbserver and dbname variables for the server : database parameter as follows:

```
list := @DbColumn(""; dbserver : dbname; "KeyView"; 1)
```

This technique provides you much greater flexibility, and reduces potential errors in your applications. Now this code is backwards-compatable — it works all the way back to Release 4. However, you can write a more streamlined version of this technique using some the new @FileDir function in Notes/Domino 6:

```
REM {Indicate the db to navigate to.};
targetdb := "AnotherDB.nsf";

REM {Get the server and filepath of the current db.};
dbserver := @Subset(@DbName; 1);
dbpath := @Subset(@DbName; -1);

dbname := @FileDir(dbpath) + targetdb
```

The new @function here is @FileDir. @FileDir returns the file path of a string, leaving off the filename itself. This comes in very handy for functionality, such as dynamic pathing.

New Feature   @FileDir is a new feature in Notes/Domino 6.

Making smart design decisions for views

If you think about it, there are really two types of views that you build:

✦ Views that are for presentation of information to users

✦ Views that are used programmatically

It is a good design technique to not mix these two types of views. Veiws are some of the most volatile design elements. No matter how you design your views, it is probable that your users are going to want those views changed. This can have disastrous impact on your @DbColumns and @DbLookups, because you build those to use a column based on the column number. If you modify a view used by @DbColumns and @DbLookups, you most likely will rearrange, add, or delete column(s), which will throw off your @DbColumns and @DbLookups. Therefore, it is recommended that you create these two sets of views: one for users, and one for programs. The user views can be changed as much as the users want, because that's what they are there for — to present information to the user in an easily digestible format. Programmatic views are your domain. You have control over these, so that the information contained in them is what you need for your application.

Now that you are building these programmatic, or *back-end* views, how do you design them? Here are a few design concepts:

✦ Do not categorize your back-end views. Categorization is a design concept that makes it easier for users to read information; but to a search or lookup there is no programmatic difference between the two. The reason you don't want to use categories in your back-end views is because categories can cause a view's size in the database to grow exponentially, because a great deal more information must be provided for each document.

Note   There is one exception to the "no categories in back-end views" rule: When you need to do an @DbColumn to retrieve a unique list of values from the categorized column. If this is the need, then categorize the column. A categorized column automatically returns a unique list of values, which greatly reduces the information returned by @DbColumn, and this makes your code more efficient.

✦ If you have different @DbLookups that are using the same key to retrieve information but are returning different sets of information, set up a single back-end view to have columns for each set of information to be retrieved. This makes it easier to trouble-shoot, and reduces the size of your database.

Using back-end views makes your applications more stable and easier to modify and maintain.

Concatenating values for retrieval

Many times, you need to retrieve various columns of information for a form from the same view. Without thinking, you do three, five, ten @DbLookups to the same view using the same key. This is very expensive from a time standpoint. Instead, concatenate the values you need from the view into a single string, and then retrieve that string. Then you can use @Word to parse the returned string back into the respective values.

There is an example set up in the ND6 Bible Formula Examples database (d6bibleformula. nsf) that shows this process in action. This example is comprised of the following design elements:

✦ **28.01 Concatenated Info Example** (form): This form is used for entry of data for the example. It also contains a button that parses concatenated info.

✦ **28.01 Concatenated Example User view** (view): This is a view that is used to display the documents to users. It can be customized any way the client desires.

✦ **28.01 Concatenated Example PickList view** (hidden view): This view is used in a @PickList on the form, and returns a concatenated value from the @PickList.

The example is a simple contact form that captures Company, Name, Address, City, State, and Zip, as shown in Figure 28-2.

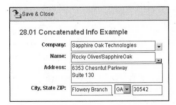

Figure 28-2: This form allows the user to choose an existing contact to prefill in the Company, Address, City, State, and Zip; or the user can simply fill it all in manually.

The button next to the Company field presents a picklist that is based on the hidden view titled 28.01 Concatenated Example PickList view, which has an alias of CONCAT_EX.by.Company.PL.

Tip

Give aliases to your design elements that convey useful information. For example, the name CONCAT_EX.by.Company.PL tells you the form used in the view (CONCAT_EX), how the view is sorted (by.Company), and that it is a view used in a picklist (PL). I typically use FE for user view aliases, BE for programmatic or back-end view aliases, and PL for views used for picklists.

Earlier in this chapter, we recommended that you use two types of views — views for users (front-end) and views used programmatically (back-end). There is also an optional third view type—`PickList` views. Views used for a picklist are somewhere between front-end and back-end views. They have a user-friendly interface, because they are presented to the user, but they are programmatically used because `@PickList` returns a value based on a column number. Because they are used programmatically, they should not be open to customization. They do, however, need to look "nice" for users, so spend a few extra minutes making them presentable.

The code in the button next to the Company name is shown in Listing 28-5.

Listing 28-5: Contact Selection Button from 28.02 Concatenated Info Example Form

```
REM {Right now this is set to pull from the column that
concatenates the values in the formula. You can switch it to
the column that is based on a concatenated field on the
documents by changing the column number from 4 to 5.};

choice := @PickList([Custom] : [Single]; "";
"CONCAT_EX.By.Company.PL"; "Choose Contact"; "Please choose a
contact on which to base this contact."; 4);

REM {Company + "~" + Name + "~" + @Implode(Address; "^") +
"~" + City + "~" + State + "~" + ZIP};
FIELD Company := @Word(choice; "~"; 1);
FIELD Address := @Explode(@Word(choice; "~"; 3); "^");
FIELD City := @Word(choice; "~"; 4);
FIELD State := @Word(choice; "~"; 5);
FIELD ZIP := @Word(choice; "~"; 6)
```

When the user clicks the button, she is presented with a picklist dialog box, similar to the one shown in Figure 28-3.

When the user makes a selection, the information contained in the fourth column is returned to the code in the choice variable. Then `@Word` is used to parse the returned selection into the respective fields. If this code did not use concatenated information, then it would have had to perform four lookups for Address, City, State, and Zip to return the same amount of information. Instead, no lookup was performed. `PickList` returned all of the needed information in a concatenated string, which appeared as follows:

```
Sapphire Oak Technologies~CN=Rocky Oliver/O=SapphireOak~6353
Chestnut Parkway^Suite 130~Flowery Branch~GA~30542
```

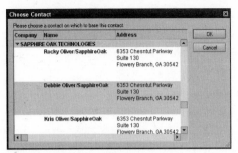

Figure 28-3: The @PickList feature provides a great deal of information to help a user make the best selection for her needs.

@Word parses this string and returns the desired values. Notice that the Address is imploded — this is because the Address field is a multivalue field, so that the user can enter multiple lines for the address. Because a single string needs to be returned, the Address field value is imploded, using @Implode, on a character that is not likely to be used in an address, such as a caret (^). When the address information is later placed into the Address field of the new document, the information is exploded with @Explode.

You have two ways to concatenate information for use, as illustrated earlier — at the form level or at the view level. The CONCAT_EX.by.Company.PL view has two columns that are hidden in it, for demonstration purposes. The fourth column concatenates the information using a column formula, and the fifth column simply lists a field, DocInfo, as its value. Both the fourth column and the DocInfo field contain the same formula, listed as follows:

```
Company + "~" + Name + "~" + @Implode(Address; "^") + "~" +
City + "~" + State + "~" + ZIP
```

If you are building an application from the beginning, add the field to the document, because it allows the view to load much faster. When you use a column formula, the view has to compute the formula for every document listed in the view. Most of the time, the time it takes to do this isn't too noticeable, but it still is less efficient than computing the value on the document. At times, however, using a computed column formula is better.

If you know you are going to need to deliver document information in a concatenated fashion, then it is a good idea to go ahead and create a computed field with the concatenation formula in it, and reference that field in your programmatic and picklist views. If you have an existing application that currently has many lookups to the same view using the same key, then it is a candidate for converting to this concatenation technique. Rather than adding the field to the form and then refreshing every document, it may be a better idea to simply use a column formula to concatenate the values, because if you refresh every document to add the new field, you cause any replica to replicate every document that is updated. Therefore, if you have users who are on dial-up connections and they replicate this database, they won't think nice thoughts about you as their replication time takes forever to replicate all the changes you made.

Summary

A few advanced techniques were presented in this chapter.

✦ You were introduced to looping in formulas.

✦ You began to explore working with lists using the Formula language.

✦ You learned some advanced techniques for working with @DbColumns and @DbLookups.

You can find more examples in the ND6 Bible Formula Examples database that is available at ndbible.com, so review that code to see other ways you can exploit the Formula language to help you build high-quality applications.

The next section introduces you to the power and flexibility of the LotusScript language. Chapter 29 begins by introducing you to object oriented, event-driven programming in general, and LotusScript specifically.

✦   ✦   ✦

LotusScript Language Techniques

◆   ◆   ◆   ◆

Introduction to LotusScript

By Rocky Oliver

Even though Lotus Notes was an innovative, flexible, and powerful collaboration platform prior to Release 4, it took a huge step forward with Release 4 and the introduction of LotusScript. Originally introduced in Lotus Improv for Windows (an innovative but misunderstood spreadsheet product) in 1993, Lotus quickly decided to add a common scripting language to all of its products. LotusScript support was added to Lotus Notes Release 4 in January 1996. But what exactly is LotusScript? This chapter introduces you to the LotusScript language, and a couple of the concepts it is built on — object-oriented programming and event-driven programming. You are then introduced to other basic concepts of LotusScript, such as syntax, classes, and objects, and the Domino Object Model.

Introducing LotusScript

LotusScript is an object-oriented form of BASIC, similar to Microsoft's Visual Basic for Applications (VBA) in that it is specifically designed to be "working compatible" with VBA (syntax is the same, simple code compiles and runs in both). When LotusScript was initially being designed, Lotus went to its lawyers and asked what they would have to change in LotusScript to make sure that Microsoft would not sue them for copying VBA. So LotusScript is really, *really* close to VBA in functionality and syntax. Therefore, if you know Visual Basic or VBA, you already know a great deal about LotusScript.

The following list explains some of the ways LotusScript is similar to VBA:

   ✦ **Syntax:** LotusScript and VBA syntaxes are similar.

   ✦ **Hosted scripting language:** A *hosted* scripting language is a scripting language that is a part of a hosting application, and cannot be used to write stand-alone applications. LotusScript is hosted in Lotus' products, such as SmartSuite and Notes/Domino, and VBA is hosted in Microsoft's products, such as Office and Exchange.

But even though LotusScript and VBA are similar, there are also some notable differences:

✦ **Cross-platform:** Because Lotus Notes/Domino is cross-platform, LotusScript is cross platform. LotusScript is fully functional on all platform versions that Lotus Notes/Domino runs on, such as Windows, OS/2, OS/400, OS/390, AIX, Solaris, and Linux. MS Office only runs on Windows, and recently it is supported in a limited fashion in MS Office for Mac OS X.

✦ **Object oriented:** LotusScript is a near-complete, object-oriented language. You can create your own classes, use class inheritance, and much more. VBA is not truly object oriented.

What can you do with LotusScript? Well, in general you can do pretty much anything you can do with VB or VBA, such as access and work with other programs and work with data. Additionally, you have exceptional granular control of your Domino applications, including application functionality and data management/manipulation. This compelling combination has made LotusScript the most popular programming language for Lotus Notes/Domino.

LotusScript provides scripted access to the Domino Object Model API layer, or the programmatic layer to a Domino database. This API is a subset of the functionality provided by the C API layer, but LotusScript hides a great deal of the ugly part of working with the C API (for example, keeping up with memory allocation, "garbage collection" of old objects, and so on) and exposes most of the good stuff, such as the power of the Domino Object Model. LotusScript also provides some features and functions that assist you with working with various data types and application constructs.

Now that you have a basic understanding of LotusScript, take a look at the structure and syntax of Notes' most popular language.

Introducing LotusScript Syntax Basics

If you know Visual Basic or VBA, LotusScipt syntax will be familiar to you. If you aren't that familiar with VBA, here's a quick primer on the basic syntax of LotusScript.

LotusScript is similar to the Formula language in that you can access data of different types, and you can take actions against that data. You can assign data to a variable, and then reference that data by the variable name. And just like the Formula language, when you use a function to take action against data, you pass that data into the function through a parameter of the function. Let's take a look at your first example, the ritualistic "Hello World" application.

In all programming languages, the first application you create is a dialog box that says, "Hello World!" You're going to do the same thing here. Additionally, you're going to compare the syntax of the Formula language to the syntax of LotusScript, as shown in Listing 29-1.

 On The Web Unless otherwise noted, all examples in this chapter are found in the ND6 LotusScript Examples database (D6LSExamples.nsf), which is available for download from www.wiley.com/compbooks/benz.

You can find this example in the ND6 LotusScript Examples database, in the 29.01 Hello World Example form.

> **Listing 29-1: Comparison of "Hello World" Applications**
>
> ```
> Formula Language:
> result := @Prompt([OK]; "First App"; "Hello World!")
>
> LotusScript:
> Sub Click(Source As Button)
>   result = Messagebox("Hello World!",,"First App")
> End Sub
> ```

A few differences exist between the two versions of "Hello World," but there are also some similarities. The first major difference is the code above and below the actual message code in the LotusScript example — Sub and End Sub. The Sub and End Sub lines are the event constructors for the button object. For now, take a look at the MessageBox function, and compare it to the @Prompt. The first thing you'll notice is that the MessageBox function takes similar parameters, but in a different order. For MessageBox, the first parameter is the message text, the second parameter is the type of message box (OK, Yes/No, and so on), and the third parameter is the title text. So, although the parameters are in a different order from @Prompt, they are quite similar. Another difference you may notice is that the second parameter is empty — not an empty string, but actually empty. The default type of MessageBox is an OK box, so no parameter was provided. Also, assigning a function to a variable does not require a colon with the equal sign (:=); it only requires an equal sign (=). In LotusScript, the equal sign can be used to assign a value to a variable or to test for equality between two values. One other difference between MessageBox and @Prompt is that if you don't want your dialog box to have a title, you can simply leave it off of the MessageBox function; if you want to leave off a title in the dialog box produced by @Prompt, you must enter an empty string ("") for the title parameter.

Understanding Data Types in LotusScript

All data in any programming language is of some *type*. In the Formula language, you were introduced to some basic data types — strings, date/time, and number. You could use @Text, @TextToNumber, and @TextToTime to convert values that were string data types to numbers and date/times, respectively. In LotusScript, there are quite a few more data types, and understanding data types is much more important.

Data type basics

Table 29-1 describes the scalar (numeric and string) data types supported by LotusScript.

Table 29-1: Scalar Data Types in LotusScript

Data Type	Value Range	Size
Boolean	0 (False) or −1 (True)	2 bytes
Byte	0 to 255	1 byte
Integer	−32,768 to 32,767	2 bytes
Long	−2,147,483,648 to 2,147,483,647	4 bytes
Single	−3.402823E+38 to 3.402823E+38	4 bytes
Double	−1.7976931348623158E+308 to 1.7976931348623158E+308	8 bytes
Currency	−922,337,203,685,477.5807 to 922,337,203,685,477.5807	8 bytes
String	Limited by available memory	2 bytes/character

New Feature

There are two new features in the scalar data types for LotusScript. The first new feature is the Boolean data type, which lets you define a variable that will contain either True or False. The second new data type is Byte, which is useful if you are passing values to C API calls that you make from LotusScript.

The following list provides some notes about the different scalar data types:

✦ Boolean is new to Notes/Domino 6. It's useful for capturing values returned by certain properties and functions, and is also handy for using with your own functions.

✦ Byte, another new data type in Notes/Domino 6, is useful when working with the C API of both Domino and Windows, because there are many functions that require a single byte data type.

✦ Long is often used for handles to objects that are passed to C API calls.

✦ Keep in mind that integers are whole numbers, and do not have decimals. If you assign a decimal value to an Integer data type, the decimal portion will be stripped off. If you need to use decimal places, use a floating point precision data type such as Single, Double, Long, or Currency.

✦ If you are coming from Notes 4.x straight to Notes/Domino 6, you need to keep in mind that the String data type now has no theoretical size limit. Before Release 5, String data types were limited to 32K bytes of size. So if you were assigning the size of your string (using the Len function) to an integer variable, you may get an error now because your strings can be larger than the size of an integer.

Besides the scalar data types, LotusScript supports additional complex data types and structures, as described in Table 29-2.

Table 29-2: Complex Data Types in LotusScript

Data Type	Description	Size
Array	A group of elements that have the same data type. A single array can have up to 8 dimensions, and the subscript can range from −32,768 to 32,767.	Limited by available memory
List	A one-dimensional group of elements that have the same data type and is subscripted with a unique string rather than a numeric index.	Limited by available memory
Variant	Variants are the "catch-all" data type, and can contain a value of any other data type.	16 bytes minimum
User-defined data type	One or more elements that are grouped together by user definition, not necessarily of the same data type. User-defined data types are often used for passing complex data structures to C API functions.	64K bytes
User-defined class	Basically the same as a user-defined data type, except that a user-defined class also includes procedures (subs and functions) that operate on the related elements.	
Object reference	A pointer to some object — either a Notes/Domino object, an external OLE/COM object, or an object based on a user-defined class.	4 bytes

Following are some notes about the complex data types:

✦ Arrays and lists are covered some in this chapter, and a great deal more in Chapter 31.

✦ Variants are most often used to work with COM or OLE objects. Variants are also used to capture arrays when you don't know what size array to expect.

✦ Creating user-defined data types and classes is covered in detail in Chapter 31.

Now that data types are defined, you need to know what to do with them.

LotusScript is a bit more structured than the Formula language in that you can (and should) declare the type of data you're going to put in a variable before you use it. Declaring a variable is also known as *dimming* a variable, because the statement you use to declare a variable is known as a `Dim` statement.

Take a look at another example. In this example, you begin to build a simple, functional application. The meat of the application code is shown in Listing 29-2, and it simply converts miles to kilometers. You can find this example in the 29.02 Miles to Kilometers form.

Listing 29-2: Converting Miles to Kilometers

```
Sub Click(Source As Button)
  Dim mi As Single, km As Single

  REM InputBox[$] ( prompt [ , [ title ] [ , [ default ]
  REM[ , xpos , ypos ] ] ] )
  mi = Inputbox("Enter the miles to convert to " &_
  "kilometers...","Miles to Clicks", 5)

  km = mi * 1.610  ' 1 mile = 1.61 kilometers

  Msgbox mi & " miles is the same as " & km &_
  " kilometers.",,"Result"
End Sub
```

This code is in a button on the Miles to Kilometers form.

You should review a few things about this code. Notice the first line of the code below the Sub line:

```
Dim mi As Single, km As Single
```

This is where the variables are declared. The Dim statement, as mentioned earlier, is used to set up the variables as the designated type. This line has two statements, which is acceptable. Simply separate the variable declarations by commas. Do not, however, get too cutesy and try to do this:

```
Dim mi, km as Single
```

This code compiles; however, it is not performing the action you may think. If you declare a variable and you do not assign a data type explicitly, the variable is cast as a Variant data type by default. Using a default data type of Variant is not nearly as efficient, because the Variant data type is much larger (16 bytes minimum) than, say, the Single data type (4 bytes) used in the example. And even though you can still stick a Single into the Variant variable, you are still wasting 12 bytes of space. Although that doesn't seem like much, you should always write your code to be as efficient as possible.

The next couple of lines after the declarations are REM statements. REM stands for remark, or comment.

```
REM InputBox[$] ( prompt [ , [ title ] [ , [ default ]
REM[ , xpos , ypos ] ] ] )
```

REM statements are used to make comments in code — usually remarks about the code itself, the parameters needed for the function you are calling (as it is used here), or explanation about the overall purpose, workflow, and so on. In the preceding example, the REM statement is used to make it easy to know the parameters of the InputBox. The InputBox parameters were copied directly from Domino 6 Designer help.

Tip For LotusScript functions that require many parameters, copy the parameters from the Domino 6 Designer help and paste them into your code with REM statements. That makes it easier for you to code, and easier for you and others to remember later if your code needs to be revised. If the comment you are pasting is large, you can surround it with %REM and %END REM, rather than using many REM statements for each line.

The next statement simply prompts the user for the miles she wants to convert to kilometers.

```
mi = Inputbox("Enter the miles to convert to " &_
"kilometers...","Miles to Clicks", 5)
```

The input box, as shown in Figure 29-1, prompts the user for the miles, and assigns the resulting value to the mi variable.

Figure 29-1: The input box is similar to the @Prompt ([OKCancelEdit]) function. InputBox is prompting the user to enter miles to be converted to kilometers.

The next line computes the conversion of miles to kilometers. There are 1.61 kilometers per mile, so to convert miles to kilometers you multiply miles by 1.61, which appears as follows:

```
km = mi * 1.61    ' 1 mile = 1.61 kilometers
```

The conversion is computed and assigned to the km variable. Notice the comment after the line. Another way to make a comment in code is to use an apostrophe (') to indicate a comment. The difference between using REM and an apostrophe is that you can add a comment to the end of a line of code with an apostrophe, as in the preceding example. The REM statement must be used on its own line.

The final line of code creates the message that appears in Figure 29-2.

Figure 29-2: The MessageBox (which can also be referenced as MsgBox) function is similar to the @Prompt([OK]) function. In this figure, the message box is informing the user of the result of the conversion.

The last line in the example is a prompt informing the user of the result, as previously shown in Listing 29-2:

```
Msgbox mi & " miles is the same as " & km &_
" kilometers.",,"Result"
```

When the MsgBox function, which is the same as MessageBox, is not assigned to a variable, you do not need to use parentheses around the parameters. You do not have to convert the mi and km variables to strings before using them in a message. One difference between LotusScript and the Formula language is also demonstrated in this line of code—you use an ampersand (&) to concatenate strings and variables in LotusScript instead of a plus sign as in Formula language.

You now have a basic understanding of data types, but you may be wondering why this is important when you can just declare everything as a Variant, because it can hold anything. You may have even noticed that you can write code and declare little. Just because it's possible doesn't mean it is the right thing to do.

Explicitly declaring data types

You should get in the habit, right now, of explicitly declaring your data types for the following reasons:

✦ Declaring the right data types is more efficient, and ensures you're only using the memory needed.

✦ Declaring the right data types means that you have planned your application, and know what you should get for each variable.

LotusScript has a feature that can help you remember to explicitly declare all of your variables. The feature is called Option Declare. Basically, it means that you are enabling a feature that forces you to declare all variables.

New Feature

Domino 6 Designer has a new feature that enables you to indicate that you want Option Declare automatically enabled for all LotusScript that you write. This feature is in the Programmer's pane properties, as shown in Figure 29-3. To access the Programmer's pane properties box simply right-click in the code pane of Designer, and choose Programmer's Pane Properties.

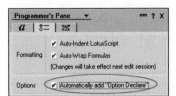

Figure 29-3: Domino 6 Designer provides a new Options property in the Programmer's pane that automatically adds Option Declare to all LotusScript modules.

The Option Declare feature is enabled by adding Option Declare to the (Options) area of your LotusScript code.

Enabling Option Declare also helps you troubleshoot your code. Suppose that you do not enable Option Declare. You are writing a long chunk of LotusScript code, and somewhere along the way you mistype the variable `bookno` as `bokno`. Because you don't have Option Declare enabled, the LotusScript engine enables you to type any variable, at any time, without explicitly declaring it in a `Dim` statement. Therefore, your mistyped variable will compile just fine. When you test your code, it will break—and you will have to find out why, and where.

But if you enable Option Declare and mistype your variable, when you try to save your code, the LotusScript engine generates the error `Variable not Declared - Bokno`. Now you can correct your misspelling and save yourself quite a bit of troubleshooting effort.

Note   As stated earlier, Lotus was told by its lawyers that it must change certain things in the language to avoid being sued by Microsoft for copying VBA. One of the things they changed was Option Declare. In VBA, you use Option Explicit to accomplish the same task. In fact, Option Explicit also works in LotusScript — it's just an alias for Option Declare.

Now that you understand data types and how important it is to declare variables by data type properly, it's time to move on and explore a bit more about LotusScript.

Understanding Subroutines and Functions in LotusScript

LotusScript has a couple of procedures that you can use to group code into reusable chunks. These two procedures are called subroutines, or subs, and functions. A *sub* is a chunk of code that you can call, by name, and it will execute — but it does not return a value. A sub can also take one or more parameters, but that is optional. You can create a sub by writing your code and enclosing it with a Sub and End Sub line. When you create the Sub line, you give the sub a name and define any parameters that you may want to pass into your sub. This first line is called a *signature*. In previous listings, for example, you saw a Sub Click and End Sub statement surrounding the code. The example's signature for the Click subroutine is the following line:

```
Sub Click(Source As Button)
```

Click is the name that identifies the sub. (Source as Button) defines a parameter that is passed into the sub — in this case the sub expects a Button object to be passed into the sub, and the variable that holds the Button object is Source.

Note   Objects, such as the Button object, and classes are covered later in this chapter.

Therefore, when the button is clicked, the code in the Click Sub is executed — which is the code that you write.

A *function* is basically the same thing as a sub, with one notable exception — a function returns a value. Therefore, you can create a chunk of code and have that code return a value. Let's go back to the example, as shown in Listing 29-3.

Listing 29-3: Convert Miles to Kilometers Using a Function

```
Code in the Button:
Sub Click(Source As Button)
  Dim mi As Single, km As Single

  REM InputBox[$] ( prompt [ , [ title ] [ , [ default ]
  REM [ , xpos , ypos ] ] ] )
```

Continued

Listing 29-3 *(continued)*

```
mi = Inputbox("Enter the miles to convert" &_
" to kilometers...","Miles to Clicks", 5)

km = ConvertMIKM(mi)

Msgbox mi & " miles is the same as " & km &_
" kilometers.",,"Result"
End Sub
```

ConvertMIKM Function:
```
Function ConvertMIKM(miles As Single) As Single
  Dim kilometers As Single
  kilometers = mi * 1.61  ' 1 mile = 1.61 kilometers
  ConvertMIKM = kilometers
End Function
```

The example is basically the same as before, except that now a function call is used to determine the conversion instead of doing the conversion computation directly in the main code. Of course, this is a simplified example. But it's important to understand the concepts of constructing a function. The examples later in this chapter and the rest of this section become more complex. Take a look at the ConvertMIKM function in detail.

The signature of the ConvertMIKM function is as follows:

Function ConvertMIKM(miles As Single) As SingleConvertMIKM is the name of the function. Miles is defined as a Single data type, and when the ConvertMIKM function is called the input from the user is passed in on this variable. The function is declared as a Single, which means that the data type of the value passed back from the function will be single.

The next line declares a variable called kilometers and casts it as a Single data type:

```
Dim kilometers As Single
```

This variable exists only inside of the ConvertMIKM function; therefore, the kilometer variable can't be used or referenced in the sub code that called it. When the function returns a value and finishes running, the kilometers variable is removed from memory.

The next line does the actual computation and assigns the result to the kilometers variable:

```
kilometers = miles * 1.61  ' 1 mile = 1.61 kilometers
```

After the computation has been assigned to the kilometers variable, it is assigned to the name of the function:

```
ConvertMIKM = kilometers
```

Values are returned from a function by assigning the value to be returned to the name of the function. The signature of the function declares the function name as a variable of the designated data type, and that is the variable that is returned from the function. So in this example when `kilometers` is assigned to `ConvertMIKM`, it is expecting `kilometers` to be a data type of `Single`—and in this case it is.

Here are a few reasons to use subs and functions:

✦ Subs and functions make your code easier to read, especially if they are used correctly. This means that you use subs and functions to break your code into logical groupings based on functional use.

✦ Subs and functions make your code easier to troubleshoot. When your code is logically broken up into subs and functions where appropriate, you can set breakpoints at your subs and functions in the Debugger and test to see whether they are the problem.

The LotusScript Debugger is covered later in this chapter.

✦ Subs and functions make your code easier to reuse. You may want to use a highly functional piece of code more than once in your application. Compartmentalizing that code into a sub or function makes it much easier to reuse it elsewhere.

If your code is more than a couple of pages in length, your code could probably use a sub or function to make it easier to read and understand. If you see patterns in your code—the same type of code over and over, doing the same work—that code is a prime candidate to become a function.

When you are creating a sub or function, make sure you name it something that explains what it does. This makes your code easier to read and understand.

Using Classes and Objects in LotusScript

Classes and objects are the foundation of object-oriented programming (OOP). LotusScript is, arguably, an OOP language, as it supports many of the things expected in an OOP language, such as event-driven programming, the ability to create developer defined classes, class inheritance, and so on.

But what is a class and what is an object? An *object* is a discreet chunk of code where the data (nouns) and the actions you can use to manipulate the data (verbs) are self-contained. A *class* is the definition of an object that provides a framework for the object, defines what is and isn't a part of the object, and defines the possible things you can do with the object.

When you are declaring a variable to hold an object, you use the class name to tell LotusScript what kind of object you are creating. This defines the structure of the variable required to hold the object. So if you want an orange object, you declare the variable like this:

```
Dim citrus as Orange
```

What Is Object-Oriented Programming?

Object-oriented programming is a concept that has revolutionized computer programming. Before OOP, the focus of a program was to perform some action, usually against data. OOP turned that around, and made the data—how to manipulate it, and how chunks of data relate to each other—the focus of the program. Instead of working procedurally, where you have some code that takes data, does something to it, and returns data, OOP concentrates on the definition of the data itself (the object), how to describe it and work with it, and then models the code around the object of data—hence the term object oriented.

Later, when you have your navel orange in hand, you have a variable ready to hold it:

```
Set citrus = myNavel
```

You wouldn't be able to put an `apple` object in the `citrus` variable, because an apple isn't an orange. Also, a `Set` places the `myNavel` object into the `citrus` variable. Whenever you assign a value to an object variable, you must use `Set` to assign that object. Incidentally, loading an object into memory is known as *initializing* the object.

An object not only contains data, but also contains constructs that describe the object and actions that can be taken against the object. These objects are known as properties and methods. A *property* is a noun that describes some aspect of an object. A *method* is a verb, or action, that you can take against an object.

Suppose, for example, that I have a `car` object. The car is black with four doors. The color and number of doors are properties of the car object. So if I wanted to access one of these properties, it would look something like this:

```
numDoors = Car.Doors
Car.Color = "Black"
```

Some properties are read-only, which means you can access them to get the value stored in the property, but you can't change it. `Car.Doors` is such a property, and the preceding code stores the value contained the `Car.Doors` property in the `numDoors` variable. Some other properties are read-write, which means you can either access the value contained in the property, or you can change the value in the property. The second line in the preceding code changes the `Car.Color` property to `Black`.

When you access a property or method of an object, you reference it by listing the object name, and then the property or method name, separated by a period (`.`). An example is `object.property`.

Working with a method is similar to working with a property. A method of the `car` object would be to start the car, which would look something like this:

```
Call Car.Start()
```

There are many ways to use a method. One way you use a method is to *call* the method by preceding the `object.method` with the `Call` statement, as shown in the preceding line of code. Another way is to assign the result of the method to a variable, or if the method returns an object you can assign the result of the method to an object variable using the `Set` statement. Both of these ways of using a method are shown here:

```
Set Car = New LexusCar
MPH = Car.getSpeed()
```

Another construct that is a part of many objects is an event. An *event* occurs when an object does something, usually before (Query) or after (Post). Events are where you put code you want to execute when that event happens. Suppose, for example, that I wanted to turn my car. Then my car has a QueryTurn event and a PostTurn event, and my code would look something like this:

```
Before the car turns, or the QueryTurn event:
Sub QueryTurn(Source as Car)
  Call Source.Signal("Left")
End Sub

After the car turns, or the PostTurn event:
Sub PostTurn(Source as Car)
  Call Source.Signal("Off")
End Sub
```

The car object is passed into the event subs on the Source variable, which makes all of the properties and methods of the car event available in the event subs. Right before I turn my car, the QueryTurn event fires and executes the code in the QueryEvent sub, the Signal method — in this case, the left turn signal is turned on because "Left" is passed in as a parameter to the Signal method. After the turn is completed, the PostTurn event fires, and the Signal method is called again — this time "Off" is passed as a parameter, which ends the Signal method. Events are usually a part of objects that interact with the UI, because events are almost always tied to actions that users take on objects.

Objects may have events, properties, methods, or any combination thereof. Objects often do not have all three. But all objects have two special events: Initialize and Terminate. These events occur when the object is loaded and unloaded from memory, respectively.

Cross-Reference The Initialize and Terminate events are covered in more detail in Chapter 30.

Let's dive into an example again. This example is a bit more complex. We have now added a field to the form to replace the InputBox dialog box from before. The user enters the miles he wants to convert, clicks the button, and is informed of the result through a MessageBox dialog box, just like before. The code in the Miles to Kilometers button on the form, titled 29.04 Miles to Clicks with a Field, is shown in Listing 29-4.

Listing 29-4: **Miles to Clicks with Field**

```
"What is it in Clicks?" button:
Sub Click(Source As Button)
  REM Always DIM NotesUIWorkspaces as "New"
  Dim ws As New NotesUIWorkspace

  Dim uidoc As NotesUIDocument
```

Continued

Listing 29-4 *(continued)*

```
Dim doc As NotesDocument
Dim mi As Single, km!   ' ! is a data type suffix used to
define a single

REM get a handle to the currently open document in the
workspace
REM using the NotesUIWorkspace.CurrentDocument property
Set uidoc = ws.CurrentDocument


REM get a handle to the back-end representation of the open
document
REM using the NotesUIDocument.Document property
Set doc = uidoc.Document

REM get the value of the NotesItem "Miles" using the
NotesDocument.GetItemValue property
REM remember that ALL Notes items are returned as arrays
mi = doc.GetItemValue("Miles")(0)

REM convert to clicks
km = mi * 1.61

REM return the result
Msgbox mi & " miles is the same as " & km &_
" kilometers.",,"Result"
End Sub
```

There is a great deal of new information here, and much of it isn't going to be covered until Chapter 30. For now, concentrate on a few things. First, the `ws` variable is dimmed as a `New NotesUIWorkspace`. When you are defining a variable that will be used as an object, there are two ways that the object can be assigned to the variable. The first way is to declare the variable and cast it as the appropriate object type, and then assign the object to the variable later using the `Set` statement. The second way, which is demonstrated in the `ws` variable declaration, is to use the `New` keyword when you declare the variable. This creates the object variable, and the new object, and assigns it to the variable all in one line. Therefore, the line

```
Dim ws as New NotesUIWorkspace
```

performs the same function as

```
Dim ws as NotesUIWorkspace
Set ws = New NotesUIDocument
```

The next line that is of interest is the following:

```
Dim mi As Single, km!   ' ! is a data type suffix used to
define a single
```

The km variable has an exclamation point after it (!). The exclamation point is a data type suffix. In the old days of programming, the idea of keeping the code as small as possible was prevalent, so data type suffixes were invented to use fewer characters to perform the same action. In the example, appending an exclamation point casts the km variable as a Single, just as As Single does the same thing.

Table 29-3 shows the data type suffixes available in LotusScript.

Table 29-3: Data Type Suffixes in LotusScript

Suffix	Data Type
%	Integer
&	Long
!	Single
#	Double
@	Currency
$	String

Tip   Even though data type suffixes are available, we recommend not using them. Using them makes your code harder to read and understand. The reason they were introduced is so you can recognize them when you encounter them in someone else's code.

Now skip down to the following line:

```
Set doc = uidoc.Document
```

From this line, you know that an object is being assigned to the doc variable because the Set statement is being used. The Document property of the uidoc object is an object itself — properties of objects can contain any data type, including scalars (strings, numbers, and so on) or complex data types (arrays, objects, user-defined).

Note   Referencing properties, methods, and so on using a period as a separator is known as *dot notation* or *extended dot notation*.

Now you have a brief understanding of classes and objects, and you're beginning to be exposed to more complex code. How do you troubleshoot LotusScript? With Formula language, the only real way to troubleshoot is to place @Prompts everywhere in your code. Lotus gives you a handy tool for troubleshooting LotusScript — the LotusScript Debugger.

Using the LotusScript Debugger

The LotusScript Debugger is a development tool that enables you to execute your code, line by line, and watch the results. You can see what values all the variables are being assigned and when; you can watch functions return values, and you can set breakpoints (places where the code will stop running so you can see what's going on). Throughout the remaining chapters in Part VI, we recommend that you step through the examples with the LotusScript Debugger so you can get a better understanding of what the code is actually doing. Occasionally, the Debugger output is referenced to draw attention to a particular item of interest.

To enable the LotusScript Debugger, choose File ➪ Tools ➪ Debug LotusScript. You are then informed that debugging has been activated.

You can enable the Debugger through the Notes client or through the Domino Designer client. You are notified each time you enable or disable it with a small message box.

New Feature   Notifying the user when the Debugger is enabled or disabled is a new feature in Notes/Domino 6. But some people have complained that it is too invasive; so by the time you read this, the notification may be moved to the status bar of each client.

When you enable Debugger, it is enabled for *all* databases that you open, or code that you execute, including databases that you aren't developing. For example, if Debugger is enabled and you get a new mail notification, when you open your new e-mail, you are immediately thrown into Debugger. This isn't a big deal, but you should be aware of it so that you know it isn't something you did wrong.

Tip   You can toggle the Debugger on and off by using the @Command([DebugLotusScript]) command. We recommend that you create a toolbar icon to make it easier for you to toggle it on and off. Note that if you choose to do this, you need to create a toolbar icon for the Notes client *and* the Domino Designer client separately, as they do not share the custom icons between them.

If you enable the Debugger you get the window shown in Figure 29-4 when you execute any LotusScript code.

You should be aware of a few items. First, take a look at the buttons presented along the top of the window:

✦ **Continue:** Tells the code to execute without stopping unless it encounters a breakpoint, stop, error, or leaves the current code module.

✦ **Step Into:** As you step through your code, you use this button to go into any subs or functions you encounter.

✦ **Step Over:** As you step through your code, Step Over lets you execute the code in a sub or function you encounter without actually walking through the code itself.

✦ **Step Exit:** Exits out of the current sub or function, but continues debugging.

✦ **Stop:** Stops the execution of the code and Debugger at the current position, and closes the Debugger window, but leaves Debugger enabled.

✦ **Close Debugger:** Stops the execution of the code and Debugger at the current position, and disables the Debugger.

New Feature   The Close Debugger button is a new feature in Notes/Domino 6.

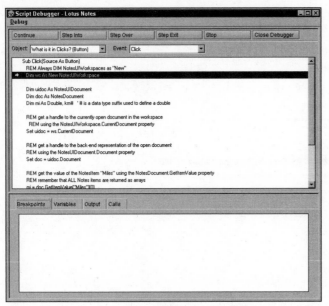

Figure 29-4: The LotusScript Debugger is an extremely useful tool for troubleshooting your LotusScript code.

The next line down contains two combo box selections: Object and Event. The Object button lists all the objects that are in the current scope of the code being executed. The Event button shows all events associated with the currently selected object in the Object combo box. These are useful for finding a particular bit of code, setting a breakpoint, and then using the Continue button to get to that point.

The big window below that is the Script pane. The Script pane shows you the code currently selected in the Object and Event combo boxes, but usually this is the code currently being executed. The black bar and gold arrow indicates the line that is about to be executed.

The next big window below that is the Utilities pane. The Utilities pane has four tabs in it: Breakpoints, Variables, Output, and Calls. These tabs are used to see what is going on, and what is in memory while your code is executing.

There's a term that keeps getting mentioned — *breakpoint*. A breakpoint is a place in Debugger where you have told Debugger to stop execution and wait for you to tell it to continue. Take a look at Figure 29-5.

Figure 29-5 shows the Script pane with a breakpoint assigned and the Breakpoint tab in the Utilities pane, which lists the breakpoint. The gold pointer arrow shows where the code is at in executing, and the black bar highlights the breakpoint line, because it was selected to set the breakpoint. The breakpoint is indicated by the little stop sign icon next to the line where the breakpoint has been set. You can set, clear, or disable a breakpoint by double-clicking the line, selecting Debug ➪ Set/Clear Breakpoint, or by pressing F9. Doing this cycles through setting, disabling, and clearing the breakpoint.

Figure 29-5: Breakpoints are a powerful feature in the LotusScript Debugger and are indicated by a stop-sign icon.

The breakpoints that exist in the code listed in the Script pane are shown in the Breakpoints tab of the Utilities pane. If the code is long and there are multiple breakpoints, you can jump to a breakpoint by double-clicking the desired breakpoint listed in the Utilities pane.

Figure 29-6 shows that the code has been executed to the breakpoint, and the line containing the breakpoint is the currently selected line. The Variables tab is selected in the Utilities pane, and you can see there is a wealth of information there. The two objects initialized thus far, ws (the NotesUIWorkspace object) and uidoc (the NotesUIDocument object), now have information available about them, as indicated by the little plus marks next to their names. The breakpoint line assigns the NotesUIDocument.Document object to the doc variable, but since that's where the code has stopped executing (as indicated by the little gold arrow over the stop sign), that object has not been assigned yet. Also, the data type of the variable appears to the right of each variable. This is handy when you have variable assignment issues and you are trying to figure out why your object or value can't be assigned to your variable.

The bottom of the Variables tab in the Script pane shows the value of any variable that is a scalar data type. You can also change the value for testing if needed.

The use of the LotusScript Debugger is covered in more detail in the other chapters in Part VI. For now, you have a good introduction to Debugger and how it is used.

Figure 29-6: The Variables tab in the LotusScript Debugger contains a great deal of information about the objects and variables that are used in the LotusScript code being executed.

Summary

This chapter provided an introduction to LotusScript. In this chapter

✦ You learned a little about the history of LotusScript and how much it is like VBA.

✦ You were exposed to syntax and data types.

✦ You learned the concept behind object-oriented programming (OOP).

✦ You were exposed to the LotusScript Debugger so that you have some basic understanding of how it can help you troubleshoot your LotusScript code.

The next two chapters take you deeper into LotusScript, exposing you to the details of the Domino object model and providing you a wealth of advanced information to help you get the most out of your LotusScript based applications.

✦　　✦　　✦

Working with the Domino Object Model in LotusScript

By Rocky Oliver

◆ ◆ ◆ ◆

In This Chapter

Understanding the differences between front-end and back-end classes

Learning proven techniques for working with front-end and back-end classes

Discovering how to work with script libraries

Reviewing the most useful front-end and back-end classes

◆ ◆ ◆ ◆

You now have a working knowledge of how LotusScript works, and a basic understanding of classes and objects. This chapter takes that general knowledge and applies it to the LotusScript classes used to define the Domino Object Model.

The Domino Object Model (DOM) is an object model that represents the application programming interface (API). This API provides the interface for working with Domino databases. The API, at its core, is written in C. The other languages available in Domino — LotusScript, Java, C++, the Formula language, and even JavaScript — all provide higher-level access to the API itself, and the object model it represents. Therefore, the features and functions available for working with Domino databases are relatively the same for all programming languages. Of course, some languages offer only a subset of functionality — for example, Java offers access to only the back-end portion of the object model (more on that later) — but the interfaces that do exist between the different languages are all used in relatively the same way, with a few syntactical differences.

Note   Because the DOM interface used between Java and LotusScript is based on the same underlying API, most new features that are added to the API are easily added to Java and LotusScript as well.

The DOM is broken into two major areas: UI, or front-end classes, and data, or back-end classes.

Understanding Front-End versus Back-End Classes

In a general definition, *front-end classes* are used to manipulate the objects that are in the user-interface, such as forms and views; whereas *back-end classes* are used to work with data elements, such as documents. But why is there a separation between the two?

One basic design concept is that data should be separate from the presentation layer and application logic. And even though data and application are combined physically in a Domino database, they are totally separated logically. A perfect (and important) example of this is the difference between forms and documents.

The average Notes user thinks of forms and documents as being the same thing, because the only way an end user sees a form or document is when they are integrated together — when a document is open in the UI. But there is a big difference between forms and documents. A *document* is where your data lives. If you are familiar with relational databases, think of a document as a record. It is a unique entity that contains one or more *items*, or discreet bits of information. Items have a data type, and can have one or more values. Databases have one or more documents, documents have one or more items, and items have one or more values.

Contrast that with forms. A *form* is a lens for viewing the information contained in a document, or for creating/modifying information in a document. Forms are simply for user interaction with a document — nothing more, nothing less. A form is a part of the application layer; whereas a document is a part of the data layer. Forms contain one or more *fields*. Remember analogies on your college prep tests? Well, here's one: A form is to a document as a field is to an item. Fields are simply a way to present the information contained in an item to a user, and a field may allow the user to modify that information. A field is a lens for viewing an item, just as a form is a lens for viewing a document.

When a form is open in the UI (front-end), there must be an associated document loaded into memory (back-end). Even when a new document is composed, there is a corresponding empty document created in memory at the same time. And when the user saves that new document, the back-end document in memory is written to disk.

Note   A document can be used with one or more forms (a form and a dialog box), but a document does not need to have *any* form associated with it. This is a useful concept, and it is explored in detail later in this section.

A document can exist in up to three places at any one time: on disk, in memory (back-end), and loaded into the UI (front-end). Think about this scenario: A user finds a document listed in a view. As the user is looking at the view, the document he sees listed (which is really just a reference to the document) exists in only one place — on disk. The user then double-clicks the document and views it. What actually happened is that the Notes client determined what *form* to use to present the document by first looking for a form formula in the view, and then looking for a form field on the document itself, and then looking for a default form for the database. Once the form to use is determined, the document is loaded from the disk into memory (back-end), and then is presented to the user through the use of the appropriate form (front-end). A form loaded in the UI represents a marriage of a form and a document for presentation to the user.

But aren't the front-end document (the one in the UI) and the back-end document (the one in memory) really the same document? It may seem so, but they aren't, and here's an example. Most of the time when you update a field in a form loaded in the UI (the front-end document), the change is automatically updated to the document in memory (back-end). This happens without any intervention on the developer's part. But as with all rules, there is an exception — and in this case it is an exception that has plagued Domino developers since the dawn of time (okay, since the addition of LotusScript to Notes in Release 4). Rich text fields are the exception. If the user makes a change to a rich text field in the UI, that change is *never* updated to the memory doc. The change stays in the UI version of the document until the user saves the document, and then it is written directly to the disk version of the document, bypassing the memory version of the document altogether. This can be frustrating to a novice LotusScript developer, so it is important to understand the concept now.

The DOM is broken down along the front-end and back-end concept. A set of classes is available for working with the UI, and a set of classes is used for working with data.

Tip   When you are working with documents, even documents open in the UI, you should use the back-end classes to work with the data, not the front-end classes.

The real power of the DOM lies in the back-end classes, because the real value of your application is the data. Lotus has added many new classes over the years to the back-end classes, but few have been added to the front-end classes since Release 4. This is a strong indication that Lotus views the power of the DOM to be in the back-end, working with the data, rather than in the front-end. Another reason why you should get to the back-end version of a document before working with it lies in the way that the front-end classes present data compared with the way the back-end classes present data. All field information accessed from a form in LotusScript is a string, regardless of the data type. "But," you insist, "I set data types on my fields in my forms!" Those field data types that you set when designing your form tell the Notes client what format to save the data as when it is written back to the on-disk document, *not* what data type the field itself is. All fields, from a programmatic perspective, are strings (except for rich text fields). If you access those fields programmatically, you get strings back. Even if the field is a multivalue field, a single concatenated string is returned from it if you access it in LotusScript

Contrast that with a document. The items on a document are the real data, so they have the appropriate data type. In fact, all items on a document are arrays — even single-value items — so multivalued items are returned appropriately. Therefore, working with items from a document is much simpler than working with the corresponding field.

Basic Techniques for Working with the Domino Object Model

The groundwork has been laid for working with the DOM, so now it's time to dive a little deeper into some concrete examples. In fact, this first example (Listing 30-1) is the same example as the one used in Listing 29-4 in the last chapter, but this time you get a bit more explanation of the actual objects being used.

Listing 30-1: **Miles to Clicks with Field, Button Code**

```
Sub Click(Source As Button)
    REM Always DIM NotesUIWorkspaces as "New"
    Dim ws As New NotesUIWorkspace

    Dim uidoc As NotesUIDocument
```

Continued

Listing 30-1 *(continued)*

```
    Dim doc As NotesDocument
    Dim mi As Single, km as Single

    REM get a handle to the currently open document
    REM in the workspace - the front-end version of the doc -
    REM using the NotesUIWorkspace.CurrentDocument property
    Set uidoc = ws.CurrentDocument

    REM get a handle to the back-end representation
    REM of the open document, in memory,
    REM using the NotesUIDocument.Document property
    Set doc = uidoc.Document

    REM get the value of the NotesItem "Miles" using
    REM the NotesDocument.GetItemValue property
    REM remember that ALL Notes items are returned as arrays
    mi = doc.GetItemValue("Miles")(0)

    REM convert to clicks
    km = mi * 1.61

    REM return the result
    Msgbox mi & " miles is the same as " & km &_
    " kilometers.",,"Result"
End Sub
```

The first line sets up an object representing the parent object of all UI objects available in Notes, the NotesUIWorkspace object. There is a corresponding back-end parent class called NotesSession (more about it later in this chapter).

 Note   All front-end classes have UI in the name, such as NotesUIWorkspace and NotesUIDocument.

Whenever you initialize a NotesUIWorkspace object, you need to use the New keyword. You can do this one of two ways:

This code

```
    Dim ws as New NotesUIWorkspace
```

is the same as

```
    Dim ws as NotesUIWorkspace
    Set ws = New NotesUIWorkspace
```

The next few Dim statements set up the variables used in the code. Placing all of your Dim statements at the top of your code makes it easier to read.

```
    Dim uidoc As NotesUIDocument
    Dim doc As NotesDocument
    Dim mi As Single, km as Single
```

The front-end version of the document is assigned to the `uidoc` variable, which is a `NotesUIDocument` object. The `NotesUIDocument` object provides programmatic access to a document that is open in the front-end, which means it is the version that is created by marrying the form to the document for display to the user.

Cross-Reference The Notes UI classes mentioned in this section are covered in more detail later in the chapter.

The back-end version of the document is assigned to the `doc` variable, which is a `NotesDocument` object. This object represents the actual document loaded into memory, which contains the data items that will be used programmatically.

The last `Dim` statement casts the `mi` and `km` variables as Single data types.

The next line (that isn't an `REM` statement) assigns the document that's currently open and has focus to the `uidoc` object variable.

```
Set uidoc = ws.CurrentDocument
```

The `CurrentDocument` property of the `NotesUIWorkspace` class always contains the currently open document that has focus. Because this property contains an object, the `Set` statement assigns it to the `uidoc` variable.

The next line assigns the back-end version of the `uidoc` variable to the `doc` object variable.

```
Set doc = uidoc.Document
```

The `Document` property of the `NotesUIDocument` object contains a `NotesDocument` object that represents the back-end version of the currently open document. Because it is best to work with the back-end version of a document, this code immediately gets a handle to that document.

Note The term *handle* is used for variables that have an object assigned to them, because they can be used to grab the referenced object and work with it.

The next line gets the value contained in the `Miles` item. The `Miles` item is represented in the UI by the `Miles` field on the form, and that's where the user enters the number of miles she wants to convert to kilometers (or *clicks* for short).

```
mi = doc.GetItemValue("Miles")(0)
```

The `GetItemValue` method of the `NotesDocument` class gets the value of the `Miles` item. You may also notice an index number at the end of the `GetItemValue` method. Remember, all items (except rich text items — sound familiar?) are stored as arrays in the document. Therefore, to get the value of the `Miles` item, you have to use an index number of 0. The next two lines simply compute the kilometers value and assign it to the `km` variable, and then present the results to the user using a message box.

```
km = mi * 1.61
Msgbox mi & " miles is the same as " & km &_
" kilometers.",,"Result"
```

A couple of things are of interest here. First, you don't have to convert the `mi` and `km` variables to strings before using them in the `MsgBox` (which is the same as MessageBox). This is because the `MsgBox` function expects a string for the message parameter, and if you place any other scalar (number or string) variable in that parameter, it will convert it for you. The other thing of interest is the last couple of characters on the end of the second line: `&_`. If you are entering a long string in the designer and you want to make it easier to read, you can split the string into multiple lines by ending each string segment with a double-quote ("), and then appending an ampersand and underline to it. This tells the LotusScript compiler that the two string segments concatenated by &_ should be treated as one string programmatically.

Tip

You can split any line in LotusScript with an underline. For instance, these lines:

```
km = mi *_
1.61
```

Are the same as this line:

```
Km = mi * 1.61
```

Listing 30-2 builds upon Listing 30-1, but it uses two fields, Miles and Clicks.

Listing 30-2: **Miles to Clicks with Multiple Fields, Button Code**

```
Sub Click(Source As Button)
  REM Always DIM NotesUIWorkspaces as "New"
  Dim ws As New NotesUIWorkspace
  Dim uidoc As NotesUIDocument
  Dim doc As NotesDocument
  Dim mi As Single, km as Single

  REM get a handle to the currently open document
  REM using the NotesUIWorkspace.CurrentDocument property
  Set uidoc = ws.CurrentDocument

  REM get a handle to the back-end representation
  REM of the open document using the
  REM NotesUIDocument.Document property
  Set doc = uidoc.Document

  REM get the value of the NotesItem "Miles" using
  REM the NotesDocument.GetItemValue property
  REM remember that ALL Notes items are returned as arrays
  mi = doc.GetItemValue("Miles")(0)

  REM convert to clicks
  km = mi * 1.61

  REM return the result to the Clicks field using
  REM extended syntax
  doc.Clicks = km

  REM NOTE: notice there is no reload required;
  REM the front end document is updated automatically
  REM by default; this can be disabled temporarily by
  REM setting NotesUIDocument.AutoReload = False.
End Sub
```

This example is almost identical to Listing 30-1, except that now the result of the computation is assigned to another item, which then appears to the user through a field. The following line assigns the km value to the Clicks item:

```
doc.Clicks = km
```

The item name that holds the result of the computation is Clicks. The form has a computed field of the same name. The new item is added and set to the desired value by simply referencing it like another property or method of the doc object. This shorthand is known as *extended dot notation*, or *dot notation* for short. Dot notation was mentioned in Chapter 29 as the way to access properties and methods of an object. You can reference items in a document as properties of the document, as shown in this example. That dot notation example performs the same action as the following method call:

```
Call doc.ReplaceItemValue("Click", km)
```

Tip You can access the value of an item by using dot notation; however, it is not as efficient as using the NotesDocument.GetItemValue method, because of the different ways the two methods find and retrieve item information. But using dot notation to set an item value is just as efficient as using the NotesDocument.ReplaceItemValue method, so feel free to use it to set item values.

If you load the form titled 30.02 Miles to Clicks with Multiple Fields, enter a value for miles (or use the default value), and click the button, you see that the Clicks field is automatically updated, without any additional code needed in the button. This is because if either the front-end or back-end document is modified, the other one is automatically updated with the change.

Tip If you are updating many items on a large document that is loaded with a form containing many computed fields, it may be more efficient and user-friendly to turn off the automatic refreshing feature so that the user sees the form refresh only once. You can do this by setting the NotesUIDocument.AutoReload property to False. Don't worry, you don't have to remember to turn it back on — the flag is automatically reset when that particular module of code finishes executing.

Using Script Libraries

Subroutines (subs) and functions were introduced in Chapter 29, and one of the reasons for using them is to make your code reusable. This works great if you are using the function in one particular design element. But what if you wanted to share that function amongst multiple design elements in your database? If this is what you want, you need to use a script library.

A *script library* is a type of shared code element that enables you to store functions and subs in one place for access in multiple places in your application. Script libraries help you maintain your code, because you don't have to reinvent the wheel every time you need a particular function. If you need to fix a bug or update your code, you can do it in one place, and the change is implemented everywhere in your database.

You can create a script library one of two ways: by choosing Create ➪ Design ➪ script library ➪ LotusScript library, or by selecting the Shared Code/script library listing in the database bookmark window, and then clicking the New LotusScript library button in the Script Libraries view. Figure 30-1 shows the Script Libraries view.

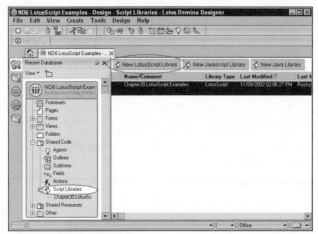

Figure 30-1: The Script Libraries area is under the Shared Code entry of the Designer database bookmark. After you navigate there, you can create a LotusScript library by clicking the New LotusScript library button.

The next example uses a LotusScript library to store a function, and then that script library is referenced in the application's form. Let's break down the example found in form 30.03, Miles to Clicks with Functions and Script Libraries.

The form, when loaded in the Notes client, looks like Figure 30-2.

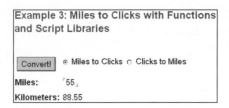

Figure 30-2: The application is now more complex, as it can convert miles to kilometers or kilometers to miles.

The form itself is a bit more complex. It uses a radio button to allow the user to choose to convert miles to kilometers or kilometers to miles, and the labels for the fields switch based on the radio button choice. When the user clicks the button, the conversion is computed and set in the Results field. Take a look at the code in Listing 30-3.

Listing 30-3: **Miles/Clicks Conversion with Function and Script Library**

```
Sub Click(Source As Button)
  REM Always DIM NotesUIWorkspaces as "New"
  Dim ws As New NotesUIWorkspace
  Dim uidoc As NotesUIDocument
  Dim doc As NotesDocument
  Dim inpval as Single, conv as String, result as String
```

```
REM get a handle to the currently open document using
REM the NotesUIWorkspace.CurrentDocument property
Set uidoc = ws.CurrentDocument

REM get a handle to the back-end representation
REM of the open document using the
REM NotesUIDocument.Document property
Set doc = uidoc.Document

REM get the value to be converted
inpval = doc.GetItemValue("Entry")(0)

REM get flag for conversion
conv = doc.GetItemValue("Convert")(0)

REM call the function - it is in the script lib that is
REM referenced in the Globals/Options section of the form
result = ConvertKMMI(inpval, conv)

REM set the result into the Result item
doc.Result = result
End Sub
```

Most of this code is the same as the previous examples in this chapter. A couple of new variables exist — inpval and conv. The inpval variable holds the value of the Entry item, which is the number that is to be converted. The conv variable holds the value of the Convert item, which indicates if the code should convert miles to kilometers or kilometers to miles. These two variables are passed into a function called ConvertKMMI. But where is the ConvertKMMI function?

If you look in the Globals area of the form, four specific areas are listed: (Options), (Declarations), Initialize, and Terminate.

✦ **(Options):** This is an area where you can list various global options for the form, such as Option Declare (or Option Explicit), or you can load LotusScript libraries here as well.

✦ **(Declarations):** This is an area where you can declare variables that will be available globally throughout the form.

Tip

The (Declarations) event can be handy for loading variables that will be used in more than one place in the form. But don't go overboard and place all variables here, because this is highly inefficient and can cause some problems if you have different sets of code reading and writing to the same global variable. Usually this area is useful for loading global flags that can be checked from various events in the form, such as a Saved flag to indicate if the document has been saved while it is open.

✦ **Initialize:** This is the event that is executed when the form object is first being loaded into memory.

✦ **Terminate:** This is the last event that is executed right before the form object is unloaded from memory.

Tip   All objects have an `Initialize` and a `Terminate` event. These events are executed when an object is beginning to be loaded (`Initialize`), and right before it is unloaded (`Terminate`). If the object is a UI object (form, view), you should *not* place code in either of these events because the object cannot be guaranteed to be available. But non-UI objects, such as agents, only have `Initialize` and `Terminate` events; therefore, you should write your code in the Initialize event in this case.

Figure 30-3 shows the (Options) area of the form in Designer. It's at the top of the Objects tab of the Events pane. The (Options) area is loaded in the Script pane, and you can see that the LotusScript library, named Chapter30.LotusScript.Examples, is listed there.

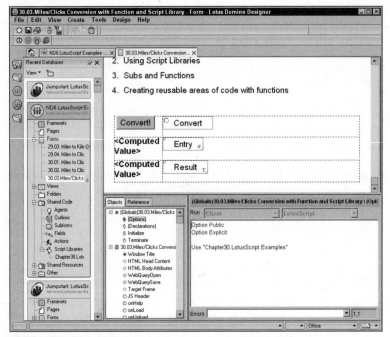

Figure 30-3: The Globals area of a form is where Script Libraries are normally loaded.

Also, the Options Explicit statement is loaded here, which forces all variables to be declared anywhere in the form.

To load a script library, you use a `Use` statement and enclose the script library in quotes. In Figure 30-3, the LotusScript library is loaded with the following line:

```
Use "Chapter30.LotusScript.Examples"
```

The `ConvertKMMI` function is in that LotusScript library, and Listing 30-4 shows that function.

Listing 30-4: **ConvertKMMI Function**

```
Function ConvertKMMI(inputval As Single,_
flag As String) As String
  Dim resultval as Single

  If flag = "K2M" Then    ' clicks to miles
    resultval = inputval/1.61
  Else  ' otherwise, do miles to clicks
    resultval = inputval * 1.61
  End If

  REM return the result as a formatted string
  ConvertKMMI = Format$(resultval, "Fixed")
End Function
```

The function checks the flag variable for a value — K2M means kilometers to miles, otherwise it is miles to kilometers. The result of the computation is assigned to the resultval variable, and this function is formatted and returned as a string value from the function.

How would this look if you use the LotusScript Debugger to walk through it? As you step through this code in the LotusScript Debugger, notice how the value in the conv variable is passed into the ConvertKMMI function at the position of the flag parameter. Then that value is used within the ConvertKMMI function to determine whether the conversion is miles to kilometers ("M2K") or kilometers to miles ("K2M"). If you continue stepping through the code, Figure 30-4 shows the output of the Debugger Variables pane right before the code finishes executing.

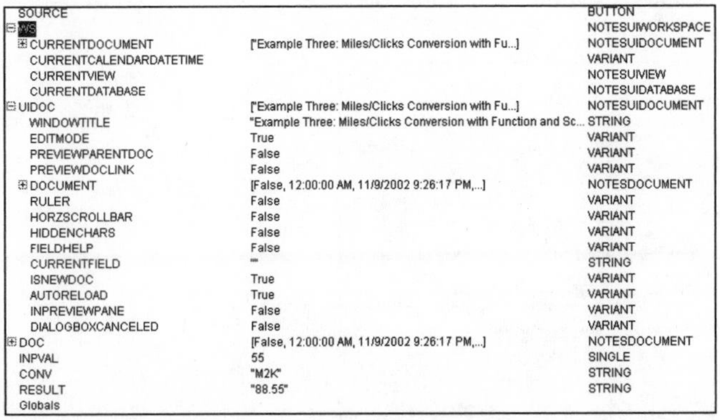

SOURCE		BUTTON
WS		NOTESUIWORKSPACE
⊞ CURRENTDOCUMENT	["Example Three: Miles/Clicks Conversion with Fu...]	NOTESUIDOCUMENT
CURRENTCALENDARDATETIME		VARIANT
CURRENTVIEW		NOTESUIVIEW
CURRENTDATABASE		NOTESUIDATABASE
⊟ UIDOC	["Example Three: Miles/Clicks Conversion with Fu...]	NOTESUIDOCUMENT
WINDOWTITLE	"Example Three: Miles/Clicks Conversion with Function and Sc...	STRING
EDITMODE	True	VARIANT
PREVIEWPARENTDOC	False	VARIANT
PREVIEWDOCLINK	False	VARIANT
⊞ DOCUMENT	[False, 12:00:00 AM, 11/9/2002 9:26:17 PM,...]	NOTESDOCUMENT
RULER	False	VARIANT
HORZSCROLLBAR	False	VARIANT
HIDDENCHARS	False	VARIANT
FIELDHELP	False	VARIANT
CURRENTFIELD	""	STRING
ISNEWDOC	True	VARIANT
AUTORELOAD	True	VARIANT
INPREVIEWPANE	False	VARIANT
DIALOGBOXCANCELED	False	VARIANT
⊞ DOC	[False, 12:00:00 AM, 11/9/2002 9:26:17 PM,...]	NOTESDOCUMENT
INPVAL	55	SINGLE
CONV	"M2K"	STRING
RESULT	"88.55"	STRING
Globals		

Figure 30-4: The LotusScript Debugger is a great resource for understanding what is happening in your code.

The WS.CURRENTDOCUMENT property title is the same as the uidoc variable title. Remember that you assigned the CurrentDocument property of the NotesUIWorkspace object loaded into the wc variable to the uidoc object variable. Also, the UIDOC.DOCUMENT information is the same as the doc variable information, because you assigned the NotesUIDocument.Document property to the doc variable. The uidoc and doc variables are considered handles to the NotesUIDocument and NotesDocument objects, respectively.

You can also see the values of the inpval, conv, and result variables. This is handy to ensure your functions are returning the right values.

You now have a basic understanding of LotusScript techniques and working with script libraries and the Debugger. The rest of this chapter dives into some specific front-end and back-end classes that you should be familiar with so you can write great LotusScript code more efficiently.

Domino Object Model LotusScript Classes

This section introduces you to the Domino Object Model LotusScript classes, often referred to as the Notes classes. Not every class is covered, nor is every property and method of the listed classes covered—that's what the wonderful Domino 6 Designer help is for. Instead, this section concentrates on those events, properties, and methods that are important and useful for getting your job done. Additionally, this section continues to offer tips and techniques to help you get the most out of your LotusScript code.

Most Notes classes are related to other classes, usually in a parent/child relationship. Understanding this relationship can be helpful in working with the classes. But there are so many Notes classes that it's hard to remember them all, much less the relationship between them. Lotus produces a poster called a *class map* to help you figure out what is available. This map became so popular that it is now a part of the Domino 6 Designer. You simply go to the homepage of Designer and choose Domino Objects for LotusScript and OLE in the Show Me field. The class map appears, as shown in Figure 30-5.

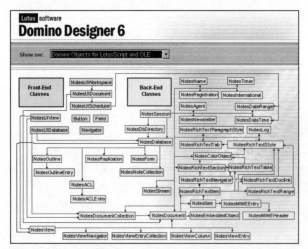

Figure 30-5: Domino 6 Designer has a great class map built into it, which can be helpful for locating the desired class and determining its relationship to other classes.

The Domino objects for LotusScript and OLE map, as well as object maps for DXL (Domino XML Language) and JavaScript, are new features for Domino 6 Designer.

Another nice feature of this map is that you can click any of the class names and the related help document opens for your reference. You may also notice the importance of the back-end classes by the number of back-end classes (about 43) against the number of front-end classes (8). The power of the Notes classes lies in the back-end, but the front-end classes do have some usefulness.

Front-End Classes

As stated earlier, the front-end classes represent the objects used in the UI. These classes are representative of the UI object itself, such as a form, *not* the data object, such as a document. Most times the UI classes are used to either get to the corresponding back-end objects (using the `NotesUIDocument.Document` property to get a handle to the corresponding `NotesDocument` object), or to interact with the user directly (using `NotesUIWorkspace.Prompt` to provide a `combobox` prompt).

Front-end classes can only be used from the Notes client, which means they cannot be used in server-based, Web, or scheduled agents, or in agents called from the API or the `NotesAgent.Run` method. This is because these classes interact with the UI, and because there is no UI in the aforementioned situations, these classes should not be used in these situations.

The classes listed in this section are in a logical order rather than alphabetical. This helps you understand and reinforce the relationship between these classes.

NotesUIWorkspace

The `NotesUIWorkspace` object is the parent object of all of the front-end classes. In most circumstances, you instantiate a new `NotesUIWorkspace` object to get a handle to other front-end objects, such as `NotesUIDocument` or `NotesUIView`. Incidentally, the `NotesSession` class is the parent class of the back-end classes. You can find out more about the back-end classes and the `NotesSession` class later in this chapter.

Properties

The following sections describe some properties that are useful in the `NotesUIWorkspace` class.

✦ `CurrentDatabase`: The `CurrentDatabase` property contains a `NotesUIDatabase` object that represents the currently open database in the UI.

You should not use this property anymore, as it had some problems when the database was open by the user in unconventional ways. Instead, you should use the `NotesUI-Workspace.GetCurrentDatabase` method, which is new in ND6 and works all the time.

✦ `CurrentDocument`: The `CurrentDocument` property contains a `NotesUIDocument` object that represents the currently open document with focus in the UI. This is the most commonly used property of the `NotesUIWorkspace` class, as it is often used to get to the corresponding back-end `NotesDocument` object. The following code shows how this is commonly done.

```
Dim ws as New NotesUIWorkspace
Dim uidoc as NotesUIDocument
Dim doc as NotesDocument
Set uidoc = ws.CurrentDocument
Set doc = uidoc.Document
```

Methods

The following sections describe some useful methods that you should be familiar with in the NotesUIWorkspace class.

ComposeDocument

The ComposeDocument method composes a document with the indicated form in the specified database. The syntax is as follows:

```
ComposeDocument(server, dbpath, form, "", "", return
NotesUIDocument flag)
```

The parameters are:

✦ server: The server where the target database resides. If this is an empty string ("") , the local database is used.

✦ dbpath: The database filepath of the target database. If the server parameter and this parameter are empty strings ("") , the current database is used.

✦ form: The form you want to present to the user to compose your document.

✦ return NotesUIDocument flag: If this flag is True (which is the default value if this parameter is omitted) a NotesUIDocument object is returned; if this flag is set to False, no object is returned. There are times, such as when the calling code is contained in an ancestor frame of the target frame for the document, when this method will throw an error. If you get an error when composing a document in a frame, try setting this flag to False—but be aware that you will not get a NotesUIDocument object back from the method.

Note   The two empty strings in the syntax represent the windowwidth and windowheight parameters. These parameters became obsolete in Release 5, but have been left in the syntax to maintain backward compatibility.

New Feature   The return NotesUIDocument flag is a new flag for the ComposeDocument method in Notes/Domino 6.

The ComposeDocument method is similar to the @Command([Compose]) formula command.

DialogBox

The DialogBox method is useful for interacting with the user. A dialog box is a form that is presented as a dialog window to the user. A dialog box still conforms to the rules of a form in that it must be associated with a corresponding back-end document. This document is either the currently open document or selected document in a view, or it is the NotesDocument provided in the NotesDocument object parameter. The syntax for the DialogBox method is as follows:

```
DialogBox(form, auto-horizontal fit, auto-vertical fit,
no cancel button, no new fields, no field updates, read-only,
title, NotesDocument object, size-to-table, no ok or cancel
buttons, put ok and cancel buttons at bottom)
```

The `DialogBox` method has many parameters, which are listed as follows:

✦ `form`: The form that you are using for your dialog box.

✦ `auto-horizontal fit` **and** `auto-vertical fit`: These two parameters, when set to `True`, cause the dialog box window to size automatically to the first layout region found in the form. If the dialog box is using a table for formatting, set these two parameters to `True` as well as the size-to-table parameter.

✦ `no cancel button`: When this parameter is set to `True`, it causes the dialog box window to not show a Cancel button, only an OK button. This is useful for read-only dialog boxes.

✦ `no new fields`: When this parameter is set to `True`, it prevents any fields that are on the dialog box that aren't in the underlying document from being written to the underlying document. Any changes made to fields that exist in both the form and the document are updated in the document.

✦ `no field updates`: When this parameter is set to `True`, it prevents any changes from being written to the underlying document.

✦ `read only`: When this parameter is set to `True`, it makes the dialog box read only. This is useful for informational dialog boxes, such as a help dialog box.

✦ `title`: This parameter provides the title for the dialog box.

✦ `NotesDocument` **object:** If you provide a `NotesDocument` object for this parameter, the dialog box is associated with this document instead of the selected document in the view or open in the UI.

✦ `size-to-table`: When this parameter is set to `True`, it causes the dialog box to size to the first table found on the form. This parameter must be used with the auto-horizontal fit and auto-vertical fit parameters to work.

✦ `no ok or cancel buttons`: When this parameter is set to `True`, no OK or Cancel buttons appear. Normally, a dialog box has a gray bar along the right side with OK and Cancel buttons, as shown in Figure 30-6. This parameter removes the buttons and the gray bar.

Figure 30-6: By default, a dialog box has a gray bar on the right with OK and Cancel buttons.

✦ `put ok and cancel buttons at bottom`: When this parameter is set to `True`, the OK and Cancel buttons are placed at the bottom of the dialog box instead of the side, as shown in Figure 30-7.

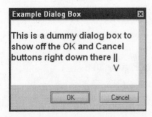

Figure 30-7: You can now put the OK and Cancel buttons at the bottom of your dialog box by setting the put ok and cancel at bottom parameter to True.

New Feature   The put ok and cancel at bottom parameter is new in Notes/Domino 6.

The DialogBox method returns a value of True if the user clicks OK, or False if the user clicks Cancel.

The DialogBox method is extremely useful for building robust Notes applications. In fact, most of the dialog boxes you use in Notes, such as the wizard for customizing the Welcome Page, are just well-done dialog boxes.

Cross-Reference   Dialog boxes are explored in more detail in Chapter 31.

Refer to the Miles/Kilometers conversion example again. The example now uses a dialog box to display the conversion application. The form used is basically the same as the previous example, except that a Cancel button has been added to it with @Command([FileClose-Window]) in it. This new button closes the dialog box. An agent named 30.05 Miles/Kilometer Conversion calls the application, which is listed in Listing 30-5.

Listing 30-5: Miles/Kilometers Conversion Agent

```
Sub Initialize
    Dim ws As New NotesUIWorkspace
    Dim s As New NotesSession
    Dim db As NotesDatabase
    Dim tempdoc As NotesDocument

    Set db = s.CurrentDatabase
    REM all dialog boxes must represent a document, even if
    REM you do not want to save the results of the dialog box,
    REM but are merely gathering information from the user for
    REM further processing; therefore we will create a
    REM temporary "holder" document so the dialog box will have
    REM a document to be associated with. since this document
    REM is never saved, it is removed from memory when this
    REM script has finished running.
    Set tempdoc = db.CreateDocument

    REM DialogBox( form$ , [autoHorzFit] , [autoVertFit] ,
    REM [noCancel] , [noNewFields] , [noFieldUpdate] ,
    REM [readOnly] , [title$] , [notesDocument] ,
    REM [sizeToTable] , [noOkCancel] , [okCancelAtBottom] )
    Call ws.DialogBox("KMMIdlg", True, True, True, False,_
    False, False, "Miles - Kilometers Conversion", tempdoc,_
    True, True)
End Sub
```

The agent in Listing 30-5 loads the dialog box, shown in Figure 30-8.

Figure 30-8: The Convert Miles/Kilometers dialog box is associated with a temporary document that is never saved to disk.

Tip

The parameters for the `NotesUIWorkspace.DialogBox` method are placed in the code using REM statements. This was copied directly from the help document for the `DialogBox` method, and this makes it much easier to fill in the proper parameters for the method call. It also makes it easier for other people to read your code in the future.

This example introduces a new and useful technique — using a temporary document to collect and work with data. When you create a document in memory, it exists only in memory until you call `NotesDocument.Save`, which writes the document to disk. If you never call `NotesDocument.Save`, the document is never saved. Therefore, you can use it to hold information, work with information, and so on. Think of it as a super clipboard. And because dialog boxes must be related to a `NotesDocument` object, the use of a temporary document object can be useful for collecting information from a user without modifying any "real" documents in your database.

In the previous example, a `NotesDocument` object is created and assigned to the `tempdoc` object variable. Then the dialog box is loaded and associated with that `tempdoc`. When the sub finishes running, the `tempdoc` object is automatically removed from memory. In this example, you're using the `tempdoc` object to give the conversion dialog box the `NotesDocument` object it needs to work.

Cross-Reference

The technique of using a temporary document for information is used in a few examples in Chapter 31.

EditDocument

The `EditDocument` method edits the currently selected document or the specified document in either read or edit mode. The syntax for the `EditDocument` method is as follows:

```
EditDocument(edit mode, NotesDocument object, read-only,
document anchor, return NotesDocument object, new instance)
```

The parameters for this method are as follows:

✦ **edit mode:** True opens the document in edit mode, False opens the document in Read mode. You can also change the currently open document's mode using this flag with this method.

✦ **NotesDocument object:** If you provide a `NotesDocument` object, this is the document that is opened; if you don't provide a `NotesDocument` object, the currently selected document is used.

✦ read-only: True means that this document is opened in read-only mode, and cannot be placed into Edit mode. False, or omitting this parameter, means that the document can be placed in Edit mode.

✦ document anchor: If you provide the text of a document anchor, the document opens to the position of the anchor. The document has to be in Read mode (edit mode flag set to False) for this to work.

✦ return NotesUIDocument object: If this flag is True (which is the default value if this parameter is omitted) a NotesUIDocument object is returned; if this flag is set to False, no object is returned. There are times, such as when the calling code is contained in an ancestor frame of the target frame for the document, when this method will throw an error. If you get an error when composing a document in a frame, try setting this flag to False — but be aware that you will not get a NotesUIDocument object back from the method.

✦ new instance: If this flag is set to True, a new instance of the document is opened. If this flag is set to False or is omitted, then if the document is already open it is brought into focus; additionally the document is placed in Edit or Read mode based on the edit mode flag. This flag is ignored if you don't supply a NotesDocument object or if the document is being opened in a targeted frame.

The EditDocument method returns a NotesUIDocument if the return NotesUIDocument object flag is set to True, or is omitted; otherwise the EditDocument has no return value.

 New Feature The new instance parameter is new to the EditDocument method in Notes/Domino 6.

The EditDocument method can be useful if you construct a NotesDocument object, add items to it, and then open it in the UI. This is a cleaner way to set up a document, rather than opening it in the UI and then modifying it, causing it to refresh and flash for the user. By creating the document in the back-end and then loading it into the UI when completed, you provide a cleaner user interaction.

EditProfile

Profile documents are extremely useful for storing and caching information. Profile documents do not show up in any view, and can only be updated programmatically or by loading them with a form so the user can change them. The EditProfile method loads the specified profile so the user can work with it. The syntax for EditProfile is as follows:

```
EditProfile(profile name, unique key)
```

Here are the parameters for this method:

✦ profile name: The profile name is also the name of the form that edits the profile. Profiles do not have to have a form associated with them; however, if the profile is going to be presented to the user for modification, the profile name must be the same as the form name.

✦ unique key: There are two types of profiles — database-wide, or general profiles, and profiles that are specific to the unique key. There is one and only one profile for each profile name and unique key combination. If the unique key is omitted, there is only one profile for the profile name.

Tip Profiles are handy for storing information that is looked up but is fairly static, such as keywords. Rather than look up keywords all the time, you can push them to a profile document in the database and they are accessible much more quickly than looking them up from another database.

GetCurrentDatabase

The `GetCurrentDatabase` method returns the currently open database as a `NotesUIDatabase` object. This method should be used instead of the `CurrentDatabase` property, which has problems when the database is opened by choosing View ➪ Goto.

New Feature The `GetCurrentDatabase` method is new in Notes/Domino 6.

OpenDatabase

The `OpenDatabase` method opens the specified database and, optionally, the view you specify. The syntax for the `OpenDatabase` method is as follows:

```
OpenDatabase(server, database path, view, key, new instance,
Temp flag)
```

Here are the parameters for this method:

- ✦ `server`: The name of the server where the database resides. If this field is an empty string (`""`), the database is accessed locally.

- ✦ `database path`: The file path of the desired database.

- ✦ `view`: The name of a view you want to open in the specified database. If you omit this parameter, the default view of the database is opened.

- ✦ `key`: If you specify a key in this parameter, the first document or category with this key is selected in the specified view. The key is selected in the first sorted or categorized column of the view.

- ✦ `new instance`: If you specify `True`, a new instance of the database is opened if the database is already open. If you specify `False` or omit this parameter, and if the database is already open, that instance is used and is brought into focus.

- ✦ `temp flag`: Normally, when a database is opened with this method, it is added to the user's workspace. If you specify `True` in this parameter, the database is not added to the user's workspace.

OpenFileDialog

The `OpenFileDialog` method presents the user with a file selection dialog box, as shown in Figure 30-9.

The dialog box presented is the native one for the user's operating system. The dialog box shown in Figure 30-9 is the Windows common file dialog box. The dialog box can return one or more file paths. This method returns an array containing the path(s) to the file(s) selected. The syntax for the `OpenFileDialog` is as follows:

```
OpenFileDialog(multiple selection, title, filters, initial
Directory, initial file)
```

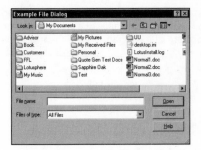

Figure 30-9: The OpenFileDialog method presents a file dialog box to allow the user to choose one or more files. The dialog box presented is native to the OS of the user's machine.

The parameters for the `OpenFileDialog` method are as follows:

✦ `multiple selection`: If this flag is set to `True`, the user can choose more than one file; if set to `False`, the user can select only one file.

✦ `title`: The title of the dialog box. This parameter is optional.

✦ `filters`: This parameter allows the user to specify the filter(s) for the dialog box. The format of the filter parameter is `filter name||file` mask. For example, if the developer wants the user to be able to choose all files or MS Word documents, the filter parameter would be:

```
"MS Word Documents|*.doc|All Files|*.*"
```

This parameter is optional. If you omit this parameter, the mask is all files, so all files are shown in the dialog box.

✦ `initial directory`: This parameter enables you to specify the directory that will initially appear when the dialog box is presented to the user. This parameter is optional; if it is omitted, the user's operating system determines what directory will be used.

✦ `initial file`: This parameter enables you to specify a file to have selected when the dialog box is first presented to the user. This parameter is optional.

SaveFileDialog

The `SaveFileDialog` method presents a dialog box that is used to prompt the user for a directory and filename, just like the `OpenFileDialog` method. The syntax for the `SaveFileDialog` method is as follows:

```
SaveFileDialog(directories only, title, filters, initial
directory, initial file)
```

The `SaveFileDialog` method is basically the same as `OpenFileDialog` method, except for the first parameter. In this method, the directories only parameter gives you the option to show directories only (`True`) or files and directories (`False`). Figure 30-9 shows what this dialog box looks like as well.

ViewRebuild and ViewRefresh

The `ViewRebuild` method rebuilds the currently open view from the associated back-end `NotesView`. The `ViewRefresh` method is similar to the `ViewRebuild` method, except that it simply refreshes the view with any changes made to the back-end NotesView, instead of rebuilding the view from scratch. If you simply need to update the currently open view, use `ViewRefresh` instead, as it is more efficient.

The `ViewRebuild` method is new in Notes/Domino 6.

Other methods

These methods are ones you should know exist, but are either self-explanatory or are not used enough to warrant detailed coverage here. If you want more information about these methods, consult the Domino 6 Designer help.

- ✦ `OpenFrameset`: Opens the specified frameset. You can use the `SetTargetFrame` method to set where the frameset will be opened. This method performs the same action as `@Command([OpenFrameset])`.

- ✦ `OpenPage`: Opens the specified page. You can use the `SetTargetFrame` method to set where the page will be opened. This method performs the same action as `@Command([OpenPage])`.

- ✦ `PickListCollection`: This method is similar to `@PickList` in that it uses a view to display a list of documents to a user in a dialog box, but this method returns a `NotesDocumentCollection` of the selected documents. This is similar to the `@PickList([Custom])` parameter that causes `@PickList` to return a list of document unique IDs.

- ✦ `PickListStrings`: This is basically the same as `@PickList`, with all of the same options.

- ✦ `Prompt`: This method is the same as `@Prompt`, with all of the same options.

- ✦ `SetTargetFrame`: Sets the target frame for such methods as `OpenFrameset`, `OpenPage`, and so on. Performs the same action as `@Command([SetTargetFrame])`.

- ✦ `ReloadWindow`: Reloads the currently open window. This method performs the same action as `@Command([RefreshWindow])` and `@Command([ReloadWindow])`.

- ✦ `URLOpen`: Opens the specified URL using the browser preference indicated in the user's location document. This method performs the same action as `@URLOpen`.

Other properties and methods that aren't covered here are also a part of the `NotesUIWorkspace` class; however, these are the ones that are most useful to you. For more information, refer to the Domino 6 Designer help.

NotesUIDocument

The `NotesUIDocument` class represents the marriage of the form and document in the UI. This class is most often used to get a handle to the corresponding `NotesDocument` object, but a couple of properties and methods are useful in this class.

Properties

You should be familiar with the following useful properties. These properties generally have to do with either updating the front-end document so that any change in data is displayed to the user, or determining the status of various things in the UI, such as the field where the cursor is, or the edit mode of the document.

AutoReload

The `AutoReload` property determines whether the front-end document automatically refreshes when the corresponding back-end document is updated. The default value is `True`, so the updates occur automatically.

Tip   If you are updating many fields on a complex document, set the `AutoReload` property to `False`. This prevents updates from showing up as you make them; instead, the updates won't happen until your code finishes executing, and then all of your updates will show up in the document at once. This is a much more user-friendly approach to updating documents opened in the user interface.

CurrentField

The `CurrentField` property returns the name of the field that currently has focus. This property is populated only when a document is open in Edit mode and the cursor is in a field

DialogBoxCanceled

When you work with dialog boxes loaded using the `DialogBox` method, you can use this property to determine whether the dialog box was canceled. This is useful if you have code in your dialog box that performs some action, instead of letting the values of the dialog box be written back to the underlying document. If the dialog box was canceled, this property returns `True`.

Document

The `Document` property returns a `NotesDocument` object representing the corresponding back-end document. This is probably the most used property in the `NotesUIDocument` class. You should always work with the back-end `NotesDocument` object when modifying the currently open document, instead of attempting to work with the `NotesUIDocument` object. The following code is an example of the way this property is used most often:

```
Dim ws as New NotesUIWorkspace
Dim uidoc as NotesUIDocument
Dim doc as NotesDocument

Set uidoc = ws.CurrentDocument
Set doc = uidoc.Document
```

EditMode

You can use the `EditMode` property to determine whether a document is being edited, or you can use the property to change the edit mode of a document. `True` indicates the document is being edited, and `False` indicates that the document is in Read mode.

IsNewDoc

The `IsNewDoc` property indicates whether the document is new (has never been saved to disk). This property is (obviously) read-only.

Methods

The following `NotesUIDocument` methods are useful in LotusScript programming. Not all methods are listed — only the ones that are most commonly used. Some additional methods that you should know about are listed at the end.

FieldGetText, FieldSetText

These two methods `get` and `set` the value of the specified field. The syntax for each is as follows:

```
FieldGetText(field name)
FieldSetText(field name, field value)
```

Although these two methods exist, I recommend that you *not* use these methods to modify the values of items on a document, because when you retrieve a value from a field, you are getting the text representation of the actual value, not the value itself. That's why the FieldGetText method returns a string—not a string array, and not a value with the appropriate data type. It's not obvious, but it is important to understand that when you create a field on a form and choose a data type, the data type you choose is the data type that the value in the document is stored as, not that of the field as displayed on the screen. All fields are text when they appear on the screen—it is the corresponding item that has the assigned data type.

The form shown in Figure 30-10 has three fields, with the following data types set: multivalue text list, currency, and date/time. You can experiment with this example—it's in the ND6 LotusScript Examples database, which is available at www.wiley.com/compbooks/benz. The name of the form is 30.06 Fields VS Items Data Types Example.

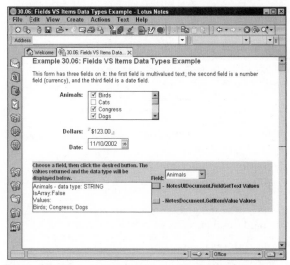

Figure 30-10: In this example, the FieldSetText button is pressed, and what it returns is shown in the field at the bottom.

The buttons on the right of the lower area contain code. The first button uses FieldGetText to get the values from the chosen field (the field chosen in the combobox above the buttons). The second button uses NotesDocument.GetItemValue to get the same item's values. You can use this form to compare the return values of each method. In Figure 30-10, the Animals field returns as a string, not a multivalue text array. The returned value is a concatenated string of the selected values; the values are concatenated on a semicolon.

Now take a look at Figure 30-11. In this example, the second button is pressed and the results are shown. The data type is STRING(), which indicates a string array (the parentheses indicate an array). The values returned are a string array, as shown at the bottom of the results. Therefore, NotesDocument.GetItemValue returns a much more useful result than FieldGetValue—so get in the habit now of working with the NotesDocument object, not the NotesUIDocument object.

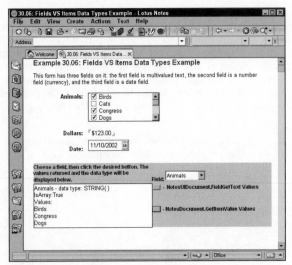

Figure 30-11: In this example, the same field is used and the GetItemValue button is pressed.

Other methods

These are methods that you don't need to know in detail, but may prove useful to you at some point.

- ✦ `Close`: Closes the document.

- ✦ `Copy`, `Cut`, `Paste`: Copies, cuts, or pastes the current selection.

- ✦ `GotoField`: Goes to the specified field and places the cursor in it. Only works when the document is in Edit mode, and only works on editable fields.

- ✦ `Save`: Saves the document. This is the same as `@Command([FileSave])`.

If you are tempted to use this class to work with a document's data, reconsider and make sure that the action you are trying to accomplish isn't available in the `NotesDocument` class.

NotesUIDatabase

The `NotesUIDatabase` class provides UI access to the database that's currently open. The `NotesUIDatabase` class is only used in the Database Scripts area, which is found in the database bookmark in Domino Designer. The Database Scripts area is under Other, Database Resources. The following properties and methods are useful when using the `NotesUIDatabase` class.

Properties

The `NotesUIDatabase` class has only two properties, listed here:

- ✦ `Database`: The `Database` property returns the corresponding `NotesDatabase` object (back-end representation of the database).

- ✦ `Documents`: The `Documents` property returns a `NotesDocumentCollection` that contains the documents that the current database event is working on. If, for example, you want to take some action against documents before they are deleted, you can place code in the QueryDocumentDelete event that uses this property to get a collection of the documents that are about to be deleted. You can then take action on them before they are deleted, including preventing them from being deleted.

Note You can obtain the NotesDatabase object for the currently open database through the NotesSession object, which is covered later in this chapter.

In the Simple Company Address database used as an example for Chapters 29 and 30, there is code in the QueryDocumentDelete event that demonstrates using the NotesUIDatabase.Document property. Listing 30-6 shows the QueryDocumentDelete method.

Listing 30-6: QueryDocumentDelete Event in Simple Company Address

```
Sub Querydocumentdelete(Source As Notesuidatabase,_
Continue As Variant)
  REM this code removes all contact documents if the
  REM company document is being deleted.
  Dim delcol As NotesDocumentCollection
  Dim respcol As NotesDocumentCollection
  Dim deldoc As NotesDocument

  Set delcol = Source.Documents
  If delcol.Count > 0 Then
    Set deldoc = delcol.GetFirstDocument
    Do While Not(deldoc Is Nothing)
      If deldoc.Responses.Count > 0 Then
        Call deldoc.Responses.RemoveAll(Force)
      End If
      Set deldoc = delcol.GetNextDocument(deldoc)
    Loop
  End If
End Sub
```

In the Simple Company Address database there are company documents, which represent companies and contact documents, which are response documents to the company document and represent employees of the company. If a company document is deleted, all related response (contact) documents are deleted as well. In Listing 30-6 the Source parameter in the QueryDocumentDelete sub contains a NotesUIDatabase object that represents the current database in the UI. The Documents property returns a NotesDocumentCollection of all documents being deleted. Each document is checked to see whether it has responses, and if so, all of the deleted document's responses are deleted as well using the NotesDocumentCollection.RemoveAll method.

Methods

The NotesUIDatabase class has just a few methods, which are briefly reviewed in the following sections.

Close

The `Close` method closes the database, including all views, documents, and so on. This method is handy if you need to ensure that your user is completely out of a database, such as when you open one programmatically along with other elements in the database (such as views, documents, and so on), and you don't want to leave all those elements open in the user's Notes client. Now rather than finding each one and closing it, you can simply call this method to close completely out of it.

New Feature   The `Close` method is new in Notes/Domino 6.

OpenNavigator

The `OpenNavigator` method opens a navigator in a database. The `OpenNavigator` method is only in the `NotesUIDatabase` class for legacy purposes, since Navigators are not supported anymore. You should not be using navigators in your new applications.

OpenView

The `OpenView` method opens the desired view, and optionally highlights the first occurrence of the specified key. The syntax for `OpenView` is as follows:

```
OpenView(view name, key, new instance, replace view)
```

The parameters for `OpenView` are as follows:

✦ `view name`: The name or alias of the view you want to open.

✦ `key`: The key is the search criteria used to locate the document or category where the cursor will be placed when the view is opened. The key is compared to the values in the first sorted or categorized column in the view. This parameter is optional.

✦ `replace view`: If this parameter is `False` or you omit this parameter, a new window is opened with the specified view in it. If this parameter is `True`, whatever view is currently open is replaced with the specified view.

Back-End Classes

The back-end classes are where the power lies in LotusScript. The back-end classes are extremely powerful tools for working with Domino data and functionality. Lotus believes that the power lies in the back-end classes as well; this is evidenced by the breadth and depth of the back-end class model, and by the fact that Lotus has exposed only the back-end classes to Java and COM. The following sections take a look at some of the more useful back-end classes.

NotesSession

The `NotesSession` class is the parent class of all other back-end classes, just like the `NotesUIWorkspace` class is the parent class of all front-end classes. Begin by looking at the properties of the `NotesSession` class. When you are instantiating a `NotesSession`, you must use the New keyword. Either one of the following code examples will work:

```
Dim s as New NotesSession
```

or

```
Dim s as NotesSession
Set s = New NotesSession
```

Properties

The NotesSession class has a number of useful properties. These properties are used to gain access to objects and information pertaining to the current "session." Session refers to the overall Notes environment, from a data perspective, that the user is working.

AddressBooks

The AddressBooks property returns an array of NotesDatabase objects that represent all Domino Directories and Personal Address Books that are available to the user in the current session.

> **Note** You can use the NotesDatabase.IsPublicAddressBook and NotesDatabase.IsPrivateAddressBook properties to determine if a member of the AddressBooks property is a Domino Directory or Personal Address Book, respectively.

CommonUserName

The CommonUserName property returns the common portion of a canonical name. The Notes name for a user or server is normally stored canonically. The common name portion of a canonical name is identified by CN. So, in the following canonical name:

```
"CN=Kelsey Oliver/O=SapphireOak"
```

the common name of this canonical name is Kelsey Oliver as identified by the CN= in the canonical name. So, if Kelsey Oliver/SapphireOak were the current user, the CommonUserName property returns Kelsey Oliver.

If the code is running on a server, such as in a scheduled agent, the server's common name is returned.

CurrentDatabase

The CurrentDatabase property is the easiest way to get a NotesDatabase object representing the database where the code is executing.

DocumentContext

The DocumentContext property returns a NotesDocument object that represents one of the following:

✦ The document currently selected in the view.

✦ If the code calling DocumentContext is running from a Web-based agent that was called with the OpenAgent URL command (http://www.someserver.com/mydatabase.nsf/WebAgent?OpenAgent), then it is a new document containing all of the CGI variables supported by Domino.

✦ If the code calling DocumentContext is running from a browser using @Command([ToolsRunMacro]), the NotesDocument object represents the document currently loaded in the browser.

EffectiveUserName

`EffectiveUserName` returns the effective user name. The effective user name is one of the following, depending on the condition:

✦ If the code is executing in a Notes client, it is the canonical name of the current user.

✦ If the code is running on a server, it is the canonical name of the server.

✦ If the code was executed from the Web, then the effective user name is based on the Run as Web User property of the agent. If this property is enabled, it returns the canonical name of the logged-in Web user; if the property is not enabled, it returns the canonical name of the last person to sign the agent.

SavedData

The `SavedData` property returns a `NotesDocument` containing data that you want to persist between invocations of an agent. There is only one `SavedData` document per agent. If you edit and resave the agent, it causes the `SavedData` document to be deleted and a new one is created. The `SavedData` document is only available to agents. If you delete the agent, the related `SavedData` document is deleted as well.

The `SavedData` document is a great tool for storing data between agent invocations.

UserGroupNameList

The `UserGroupNameList` property returns a string array of all groups to which the member belongs.

New Feature   The `UserGroupNameList` property is new in Notes/Domino 6.

UserName

The `UserName` property returns the canonical name of the user. If the script is running on the server, it returns the canonical name of the server.

UserNameList

The `UserNameList` property returns a string array of all names and alternate names that the user has listed in the person document of the Domino Directory.

Methods

The following methods are useful in the `NotesSession` class. Many of these methods are used to get programmatic access to objects representing various data elements of the Notes session, mainly the database and the data elements contained therein.

✦ **GetDatabase:** The `GetDatabase` method returns a `NotesDatabase` object that represents the specified database. If the database can be opened, it is opened as well. The syntax of GetDatabase is as follows:

```
GetDatabase(server, database path, create on fail)
```

The parameters of `GetDatabase` are as follows:

• `server`: The server where the desired database is located, or an empty string (`" "`) if the database is local.

• `database path`: The filepath to the desired database. If both this parameter and the server parameter are empty strings, an empty `NotesDatabase` object is created in memory.

- create on fail: If this flag is set to True or is omitted, a new database object is created in memory even if the specified database isn't found. If this parameter is set to False, the GetDatabase method returns nothing if the specified database can't be opened.

Tip

You can use the NotesDatabase.IsOpen property to determine if the NotesDatabase was successfully opened.

✦ GetEnvironmentString, GetEnvironmentValue: These two methods return the specified environment variable from the NOTES.INI. If the optional system flag is set to True, the specified system environment variable is returned. The only difference between these two variables is that GetEnvironmentString returns a string value, and GetEnvironmentValue returns a numeric value. The syntax of GetEnvironmentString is as follows:

```
GetEnvironmentString(env var name, system flag)
```

The syntax for GetEnvironmentVar is exactly the same as GetEnvironmentString.

What is a system environment variable? When variables are added to the NOTES.INI programmatically, such as using @SetEnvironment or the ENVIRONMENT keyword in the Formula language, the environment variable name is prepended with a dollar sign ($). System environment variables are set by the Notes program itself, and are not prepended with a dollar sign; therefore to retrieve the value of a system environment variable (one that is not prepended with a dollar sign), set the system flag to True.

Note

If you use either GetEnvironmentString or GetEnvironmentVar in server-based code, then the NOTES.INI that is accessed is the server's NOTES.INI, and most of the time that NOTES.INI cannot be accessed programmatically unless you have permission to do so in the server document of the Domino Directory.

✦ SetEnvironmentVar: The SetEnvironmentVar method sets the specified environment variable to the provided value. The syntax for SetEnvironmentVar is as follows:

```
SetEnvironmentVar(env var name, value, system flag)
```

Normally, when you set an environment variable, the variable name is prepended with a dollar sign ($). But if you set the optional system flag to True, the dollar sign is left off.

Other methods

These methods are either discussed in more detail in other chapters, or you should be aware of their existence but you don't have to know the details.

- ✦ CreateDOMParser: Takes XML and puts it into an XML DOM object.
- ✦ CreateDXLExporter: Creates a new NotesDXLExporter object.
- ✦ CreateDXLImporter: Creates a new NotesDXLImporter object.
- ✦ CreateName: Creates a new NotesName object.
- ✦ CreateSAXParser: Creates a new NotesSAXParser object.
- ✦ CreateXSLTransformer: Creates a new NotesXSLTransformer object.
- ✦ GetDBDirectory: Creates a NotesDBDirectory object.

New Feature

The following NotesSession **methods are new in Notes/Domino 6:** CreateDOMParser, CreateDXLExporter, CreateDXLImporter, CreateSAXParser, **and** CreateXSL-Transformer.

Cross-Reference

The following methods are explained more fully, as are their related classes, in the associated chapters: CreateDOMParser **(Chapter 52),** CreateDXLExporter **(Chapter 48),** CreateDXLImporter **(Chapter 52),** CreateSAXParser **(Chapter 52), and** CreateXSL-Transformer **(Chapter 53).**

NotesDatabase

The NotesDatabase class represents the database and the data contained therein. The two most frequently used methods for getting a handle to a Notes database are described in the following text:

To get the current database that is executing the code, use the NotesSession.CurrentDatabase property, as follows:

```
Dim s as New NotesSession
Dim db as NotesDatabase
Set db = s.CurrentDatabase
```

To get another database, use the following code:

```
Dim s as New NotesSession
Dim db as NotesDatabase
Set db = s.GetDatabase("MyServer/MyOrg", "Customers\Kew1DB.nsf")
If db.IsOpen Then
   ... your code here ...
End If
```

Tip

Remember to test the database handle you get with NotesSession.GetDatabase to make sure you actually got it. If it is unable to find the database, it still creates a database object, but the object is closed. Therefore, use NotesDatabase.IsOpen to make sure you actually got the database.

The properties described in the following sections are useful.

AllDocuments
The AllDocuments property contains a NotesDocumentCollection representing all documents in the database. You could use this to get a count of all the documents in the database by checking the NotesDocumentCollection.Count property. But overall it's better to work with smaller, logical subsets of documents based on need.

CurrentAccessLevel
CurrentAccessLevel is a handy property for determining the access level of the user based on the ACL of the database. CurrentAccessLevel returns one of the following integer constants:

✦ ACLLEVEL_NOACCESS: 0

✦ ACLLEVEL_DEPOSITOR: 1

✦ ACLLEVEL_READER: 2

✦ ACLLEVEL_AUTHOR: 3

- ✦ ACLLEVEL_EDITOR: 4

- ✦ ACLLEVEL_DESIGNER: 5

- ✦ ACLLEVEL_MANAGER: 6

FileFormat

`FileFormat` returns an integer value indicating the on-disk structure version (ODS) of the database. This property is useful for making sure the database supports newer features. Soft deletes, for example, were not available until ODS 40. The ODS levels tie to Domino releases as follows:

- ✦ Release 4: 20

- ✦ Release 5.x: 41

- ✦ Notes/Domino 6: 43

New Feature   The `FileFormat` property is a new feature in Notes/Domino 6.

FileName and FilePath

The `FileName` property is the file name of the database without the path. The `FilePath` property is the file name and path of the database.

IsFTIndexed

`IsFTIndexed` returns `True` if the database is full-text indexed, `False` if it's not. This can be useful when determining the best method for searching your database programmatically. You can read more about searching databases in the `FTSearch` method later in this chapter.

IsInService

The `IsInService` property indicates if the database in a cluster is available. You can also set this value to `True` to make the database available to the cluster.

New Feature   The `IsInService` property is new in Notes/Domino 6.

IsLink

The `IsLink` property indicates if the database is referenced by a file link. A *file link* is simply a text file that references a database somewhere else on the disk. The database appears to be at the file link location, not the actual location. You can create a file link by creating a text file containing the actual path of the database, and then setting the extension of the text file to `.NSF`.

New Feature   The `IsLink` property is new in Notes/Domino 6.

IsOpen

The `IsOpen` property indicates whether the database is open. An open database means that you have access to all of its properties. If a database is not open, you only have access to the following properties: `DelayUpdates`, `DesignTemplateName`, `FileName`, `FilePath`, `IsOpen`, `IsPrivateAddressBook`, `IsPublicAddressBook`, `Parent`, `ReplicaID`, `Server`, `Size`, `SizeQuota`, `SizeWarning`, `TemplateName`, and `Title`. You can attempt to open a database by calling `NotesDatabase.Open`.

IsPrivateAddressBook, IsPublicAddressBook

These two properties indicate if the database is a Personal Address Book or a Domino Directory, respectively. These properties are useful when used in combination with the `NotesSession.AddressBooks` property.

Server

The `Server` property is the canonical name of the server where the database resides. If the code is executing locally, the `Server` property returns an empty string (`" "`).

UnprocessedDocuments

The `UnprocessedDocuments` property returns documents that the current agent considers unprocessed, or that are selected in the currently open view. If you are using this property to get a collection of documents that have not been previously processed by an agent, you must also use the `UpdateProcessedDoc` method, found in the `NotesSession` class, to update the documents after being processed.

The more handy use of this property is with documents selected in a view. If you use this property in a view action or an agent set to act on selected documents, this property returns a `NotesDocumentCollection` of all documents selected by the user. You can find out more about this property in the Domino 6 Designer help.

Many other properties of NotesDatabase are not covered here. You should review the Domino 6 Designer help to learn more about the properties of `NotesDatabase`.

Methods

`NotesDatabase` has numerous methods. The following sections cover some of the more important ones.

CreateDocument

The `CreateDocument` method creates a new, empty document in the `NotesDatabase` object. This method does *not* create a new document on disk; if you want to save the document permanently, call the `NotesDocument.Save` method. Also, if you are creating a document manually, remember that you need to set up a few things, such as

- ✦ A form item to associate the document with a form (if needed)

- ✦ Any Readers/Authors items that are needed for security and access

- ✦ If the document is targeted to be a response to another document you will have to manually make the document a response by calling the `NotesDocument.MakeResponse` method

- ✦ Any other items that are needed for the document

CreateView

The `CreateView` method enables you to programmatically create new views. The syntax for the `CreateView` method is as follows:

```
CreateView(view name, selection formula, template NotesView,
prohibit design refresh/replace flag)
```

The following parameters are used for this method:

✦ `view name`: The name you want to give the view. If you want the view to have an alias as well, use a pipe symbol (|) to separate the name from the alias.

✦ `selection formula`: The selection formula to use for this view. If you omit this parameter, the selection formula of the template `NotesView` is used (if the template `NotesView` is specified). Or, `SELECT @All` is used if no template view is provided.

✦ `template NotesView`: The view to copy and base the new view upon. This is a `NotesView` object, not simply the name of the view. If you omit this parameter, the default design view is used. If there is no default design view, a blank view is created.

✦ `prohibit design refresh/replace flag`: Enables you to indicate that you don't want the view design updated or replaced by any process. The default value is `True`.

New Feature   The `CreateView` method is new in Notes/Domino 6.

Fixup

The `Fixup` method runs the `Fixup` task against the database. The syntax for the `Fixup` method is as follows:

```
Fixup(option keyword)
```

You can pass quite a few options into the `Fixup` method, as listed here — the integer value of the flag is listed in parentheses next to the keyword:

✦ `FIXUP_INCREMENTAL (4)`: checks only documents since `Fixup` was last performed on the database. If you don't use this keyword, `Fixup` checks all documents in the database.

✦ `FIXUP_NODELETE (16)`: prevents `Fixup` from deleting corrupted documents, which causes `Fixup` to check the database the next time it runs, or the next time a user opens the database. Use this keyword to try to salvage corrupted documents if the corruption is minor, or if there are no replicas of the database.

✦ `FIXUP_NOVIEWS (64)`: prevents `Fixup` from checking views, which allows `Fixup` to run more quickly. Use this keyword if view corruption isn't a problem.

✦ `FIXUP_QUICK (2)`: Performs a quick, but less thorough, `Fixup` on the database.

✦ `FIXUP_REVERT (32)`: Reverts ID tables to the previous release format.

Note   Do not use the `FIXUP_REVERT` keyword unless Lotus Technical Support tells you to do so.

✦ `FIXUP_TXLOGGED (8)`: Use this keyword if your database is enabled for transaction logging. Normally `Fixup` doesn't run against databases with transaction logging enabled.

✦ `FIXUP_VERIFY (1)`: Verifies the integrity of the database and reports the errors in the Notes Log, but makes no modifications to the database.

New Feature   The `Fixup` method is new in Notes/Domino 6.

You can combine these keywords to perform combinations of options when running Fixup. For instance, if you want to run a quick fix up and exclude views on a database, you could call it in one of the two following ways:

```
Call NotesDatabase.Fixup(FIXUP_QUICK + FIXUP_NOVIEWS)
```

Or

```
Call NotesDatabase.Fixup(66)
```

The second way of calling Fixup with the aforementioned options uses the fact that FIXUP_QUICK equals 2 and FIXUP_NOVIEWS equals 66, which when added equals 66.

FTSearch

The FTSearch method performs a full-text search of the database. The syntax for FTSearch is as follows:

```
FTSearch(query, maxdocs)
```

The parameters shown are the most widely used; there are other parameters that may be useful to you in special circumstances. Review the Domino 6 Designer help for more information. The parameters are as follows:

✦ query: The search query. Remember that the words you search for should be enclosed in quotes. This means that you need to escape your quotes correctly.

Tip   It's much easier to surround your search string with pipes (|) when you are building it, because that enables you to use your quotes normally. If you want to search on a field name, you could enter it as "FIELD = """ & some_variable & """", making it hard to keep up with the quotes, or you could enter it as |FIELD ="| & some_variable & |"|.

✦ maxdocs: An integer value indicating the maximum number of documents to return. If you place a 0 here, it returns all the documents found, up to of 5,000.

The FTSearch method is *extremely* inefficient if the database is not full-text indexed. You can check to see whether database is full-text indexed by using the IsFTIndexed property. If the database is full-text indexed, FTSearch is the fastest way to search a database. If you only need to search the documents in a particular view, use the NotesView.FTSearch method instead.

GetAgent

The GetAgent method returns a NotesAgent object representing the named agent. You can then use the NotesAgent object to schedule the agent, run the agent, or determine the last time the agent ran.

GetDocumentByID, GetDocumentByUNID

These two methods return NotesDocument objects. GetDocumentByID uses the NoteID to identify the desired document, while GetDocumentByUNID uses the document unique ID to return a document. The syntax of these two methods are as follows:

```
GetDocumentByID(note ID)
GetDocumentByUNID(doc unique ID)
```

The NoteID uniquely identifies a document within the same physical database. Different replicas of a database have two different NoteIDs for the same document. The NoteID is a somewhat volatile identifier for a document — it changes whenever the database is compacted, sometimes when a document is saved. The NoteID is simply an internal identifier for the document. Because of the transience of the NoteID, it should only be used if you get the NoteID right before you use the GetDocumentByNoteID method.

The document unique ID uniquely identifies a document across all replicas of a database. This ID does not change while the document exists, so it is safe to use any time. Keep in mind, however, that if you copy and paste a document, the document unique ID of the newly pasted document will be different than the original document.

Using these two methods for retrieval of a document is much faster than other methods of document retrieval, such as getting a document by key from a view.

GetView

GetView returns a NotesView object representing the desired view. The syntax for GetView is as follows:

```
GetView(view name)
```

The view name parameter can be the name of the view or any alias of the view.

Open

The Open method opens a database. The syntax for the Open method is as follows:

```
Open(server, database path)
```

If you already specified a database when you instantiated the NotesDatabase object, you can call this method without any parameters. If you created an empty NotesDatabase object, you can use this method with the parameters listed previously to open the specified database. The following code

```
Dim db as New NotesDatabase("", "Names.nsf")
Call db.Open
```

is the same as

```
Dim db as NotesDatabase
Call db.Open("", "Names.nsf")
```

OpenMail

The OpenMail method is useful for opening the current user's mail file. Simply declare an empty NotesDatabase object and call the OpenMail method against it, like this:

```
Dim maildb as NotesDatabase
Call maildb.OpenMail
```

Note   If the Open method is called in a server agent, the mail file retrieved will be that of the last person who saved the agent, or the signer of the agent.

Search

The Search method performs a search against the database using the provided selection formula, and returns a NotesDocumentCollection of the matching documents. The syntax for the Search method is as follows:

```
Search(selection formula, cutof date/time, maxdocs)
```

The parameters for the Search method are as follows:

✦ **selection formula:** The selection formula parameter is formatted in exactly the same way as a view selection formula. The Search method is actually pretty efficient—not quite as efficient as the FTSearch method when the database is full-text indexed, but still quite usable.

Tip   If you want to see what your Search method should return, create a view and add the selection formula to it. This will show you exactly what documents the Search method should return.

✦ **cutoff date/time:** This is a NotesDateTime object that contains a cutoff date. The Search method only searches documents created or modified after the cutoff date/time provided. Set this parameter to Nothing to indicate you want to search all documents regardless of creation/modification date.

Note   Nothing is an actual value in LotusScript. Nothing is *not* the same as an empty string (" "). Nothing represents an object variable that does not have an object in it.

✦ **maxdocs:** An integer value indicating the maximum number of documents to return. If you place a 0 here, it returns all of the documents found.

Other methods

The following are other methods that you should know about:

✦ **Compact:** Compacts the database

✦ **Create:** Creates a new database on the server and with the name you specify

✦ **GetProfileDocCollection:** Returns a NotesDocumentCollection containing all profile documents that match the provided profile name.

✦ **GetProfileDoc:** Returns the indicated profile document

The NotesDatabase class has many more methods. This section simply introduced you to the most common ones. For more information, review the Domino 6 Designer help.

NotesView

The NotesView class represents a view in a database. Normally, you get a handle to a NotesView object by using the NotesDatabase.GetView method. NotesView objects are handy for retrieving information from one or more documents. The properties and methods described in the upcoming sections are useful in the NotesView class.

Note   The NotesUIView class represents the view as it appears in the UI. The NotesView class represents the view and the documents contained in the view. The NotesView class is a data object, and the NotesUIView is a UI object. I recommend you work with views and documents using the NotesView class.

Properties

The following sections describe some of the useful properties in the NotesView class.

AutoUpdate

When you update a document by modifying and saving it, the corresponding view is updated each time. If you're cycling through many documents in a view, it keeps refreshing after each document, which affects performance considerably. It can also cause your code to run erratically if the changes you make to the documents cause them to be reordered in the view. This property, which is True by default, enables you to temporarily disable this auto-updating feature so that your code will run more efficiently. The following code cycles through each document and sets a new item in the document that is the concatenation of other items:

```
Dim s as New NotesSession
Dim db as NotesDatabase
Dim view as NotesView
Dim doc as NotesDocument

Set db = s.CurrentDatabase
Set view = db.getView("Main")

view.AutoUpdate = False

Set doc = view.getFirstDocument
Do While Not(doc is Nothing)
  doc.ConcatValues = doc.ColumnValues(1) & "~" &_
  doc.ColumnValues(2)
  Call doc.Save(True, False)
  Set doc = view.getNextDocument(doc)
Loop
```

This example takes the value from the second and third columns in the view, concatenates them together using a tilde (~), sets this new string into the ConcatValues item, and saves the document. When the code finishes executing, the view automatically refreshes.

EntryCount

The EntryCount property returns the number of documents in the view as an integer.

 The EntryCount property is new in Notes/Domino 6.

Methods

The methods described in the following sections are useful in the NotesView class. Other methods exist, but these are the ones you will use most often.

FTSearch

The FTSearch method is similar to the NotesDatabase.FTSearch method in that it allows you to perform a full-text search of documents — in this case against the documents in the NotesView object instead of all the documents in the database, as you do when using the NotesDatabase.FTSearch method. The syntax of the FTSearch method is as follows:

```
FTSearch(query, maxdocs)
```

Here are the parameters for this method:

✦ query: The search query. Remember that words you are searching for should be enclosed in quotes. This means that you need to escape your quotes correctly.

✦ maxdocs: An integer value indicating the maximum number of documents to return. If you place a 0 here, it returns all the documents found, up to 5,000.

This method is *much* more efficient when the database is full-text indexed; in fact, I don't recommend using this method if the database is not full-text indexed. You can determine whether the database is full-text indexed by checking the NotesDatabase.IsFTIndexed property. If it is not a part of your deployment plans to ensure the database is full-text indexed, then you should explore other searching options, such as the NotesDatabase.Search method or the NotesView.GetAllDocumentsByKey method, which is described in the next section.

One thing to keep in mind is that this method does *not* return a NotesDocumentCollection like the NotesDatabase.FTSearch method; instead, it simply filters the documents in the NotesView object so that only the documents that match the search criteria are returned. If you want to reset a NotesView that has been filtered by this method, call the NotesView.Clear method.

GetAllDocumentsByKey

The GetAllDocumentsByKey method returns a NotesDocumentCollection that contains all documents that have values that match the key in the first (and subsequent) sorted or categorized column of the view. The syntax for GetAllDocumentsByKey is as follows:

```
GetAllDocumentsByKey(key or array of keys, exact match)
```

If you provide an array of keys, the first key must match a value in the first sorted column, the second key must match a value in the second sorted column, and so on. Keep in mind that the keys are not case-sensitive. If the exact match flag is True, it tells the method that you want to return documents that match the key(s) exactly; if it is False or is omitted, it returns documents that only partially match the key(s).

Keep in mind two important things about the NotesDocumentCollection returned by this method: First, the documents returned by this method are *not* in view order; in fact, these documents are not in any particular order at all (actually they are sorted on the internal NoteID, but that isn't useful). Second, the documents returned from this method do not have ColumnValues, so those are not available to you. If you need either of these features, use the GetAllEntriesByKey, which is described in the next section.

Note The GetDocumentByKey method works the exact same way as the GetAllDocuments-ByKey method, except that it returns a single NotesDocument object representing the first document matching the key(s).

GetAllEntriesByKey (key or array of keys, exact match)

This method is exactly the same as GetAllDocumentsByKey, except for a few useful exceptions:

- ✦ A NotesViewEntryCollection object is returned containing NotesViewEntries of type document instead of NotesDocuments.

- ✦ The NotesViewEntries returned in the NotesViewEntryCollection are in view order.

- ✦ The NotesViewEntries returned have the ColumnValues properties that are available for use.

Therefore, I recommend that you explore using the GetAllEntriesByKey method when you think you need the GetAllDocumentsByKey method—it offers more features for the same amount of effort.

The GetEntryByKey method works the exact same way as the GetAllEntriesByKey method, except that it returns a single NotesViewEntry object representing the first view entry matching the key(s).

GetFirstDocument, GetLastDocument

These two methods get the first document and last document in the view, respectively. These two methods are usually used in conjunction with the GetNextDocument or GetPrevDocument methods to walk all the documents in a view using a DoWhile loop, such as the following loop using GetFirstDocument/GetNextDocument:

```
Dim s as New NotesSession
Dim db as NotesDatabase
Dim view as NotesView
Dim doc as NotesDocument

Set db = s.CurrentDatabase
Set view = db.getView("Main")

view.AutoUpdate = False

Set doc = view.getFirstDocument
Do While Not(doc is Nothing)
   doc.ConcatValues = doc.ColumnValues(1) & "~" &_
   doc.ColumnValues(2)
   Call doc.Save(True, False)
   Set doc = view.getNextDocument(doc)
Loop
```

Notice that I listed the GetFirstDocument and GetNextDocument methods with the first character small-capped. This is actually a good habit to get into, especially if you have any plans to learn Java in the future. LotusScript is not case-sensitive in syntax; Java, on the other hand, is *very* case sensitive. All of the properties and methods in Java do not capitalize the first letter of the property or method. Therefore it is a good habit to get used to writing your properties and methods in this manner, so your transition to Java will be easier.

GetNextDocument, GetPrevDocument

These two methods get the next or previous document in the view, respectively, relative to the provided NotesDocument. The syntax for these two methods is as follows:

```
GetNextDocument(NotesDocument object)
GetPrevDocument(NotesDocument object)
```

As stated in the GetFirstDocument/GetLastDocument section, these two methods are normally used in conjunction with the GetFirstDocument or GetLastDocument methods to walk the documents in a view using the DoWhile loop.

If you are modifying documents in such a way that could change the order of the documents in the view, such as deleting documents, these two methods could return an error. If the order changes, the "next" document may not be there anymore. To prevent this problem from occurring, or if you are modifying many documents in a large view, it's more efficient to set the NotesView.AutoUpdate property to False so the view isn't trying to constantly refresh. Refer to the AutoUpddate property for more details.

GetNthDocument(document position number)

The `GetNthDocument` method returns the document at the indicated position.

Tip It's almost always a bad idea to use the `GetNthDocument` method to walk a view. This has been proven through testing, and was confirmed by the creator of the LotusScript interface for Lotus Notes, Bob Balaban. This method is only as efficient as `GetNextDocument` or `GetPrevDocument` on `NotesViews` that have been filtered by the `FTSearch` method, and only if the database is actually full-text indexed. And even then, it's only as efficient as `GetNextDocument` (or `GetPrevDocument`). To keep it simple, just say no to `GetNthDocument`.

Refresh

The `Refresh` method refreshes the `NotesView` object with any updates that have been made to the view on which the `NotesView` object is based. But, by default, this refresh happens automatically. This method is really only handy if you have disabled the automatic refresh by setting `NotesView.AutoRefresh` to `False`, and then using this method to refresh the `NotesView` object manually.

This method does not cause the actual view index to be refreshed or rebuilt. To do so, take a look at the `NotesUIWorkspace.ViewRefresh` and `NotesUIWorkspace.ViewRebuild` methods.

Other methods

The following methods all create an object called a `NotesViewNavigator`. The `NotesView-Navigator` class provides you with an object that represents data in a view as you see it on-screen — it contains the categories and any category totals, if you have categorized views with totals. The nice thing is, as you can tell by the names of the methods, you can generate `NotesViewNavigators` that contain a subset of the view information. The methods that are used to generate a `NotesViewNavigator` are: `CreateViewNav`, `CreateViewNavFrom`, `CreateViewNavFromCategory`, `CreateViewNavFromChildren`, `CreateViewNavFrom-Descendants`, and `CreateViewNavMaxLevel`.

You can learn more about these methods in the Domino 6 Designer help.

NotesDocumentCollection

A `NotesDocumentCollection` object is a group, or collection, of `NotesDocument` objects. The `NotesDocumentCollection` object is most often generated from the `NotesView.GetAllDocumentsByKey` method or the `NotesDatabase.Search`, `NotesDatabase.FT-Search`, or `NotesDatabase.UnprocessedDocuments` property methods. You can also get a really big `NotesDocumentCollection` object from the `NotesDatabase.AllDocuments` property. There are other ways to get a `NotesDocumentCollection`, but these are the most common.

Properties

Only one property — `Count` — is generally useful. The `Count` property returns the number of documents in the collection. This is useful for testing to see whether your search returned any results. For example, if you were to use the `NotesView.GetAllDocumentsByKey` method to retrieve a set of documents, you could check the `NotesDocumentCollection` property to see whether any documents were found.

Methods

A few methods are useful in the `NotesDocumentCollection` class. Most of the useful methods deal with navigating the documents in the collection.

AddDocument, DeleteDocument

These two methods are used to add and remove documents from the
NotesDocumentCollection object. The syntax for these two methods are as follows:

```
AddDocument(NotesDocument object)
DeleteDocument(NotesDocument object)
```

Note   You cannot create an empty NotesDocumentCollection object and add documents to it.
You have to use one of the methods that returns a NotesDocumentCollection, and then
add/remove documents to it. You can, however, execute a NotesView.GetAllDocuments-
ByKey that returns no documents, and then add documents to it.

GetFirstDocument, GetLastDocument

These two methods get the first document and last document in the NotesDocument-
Collection, respectively. These two methods are usually used in conjunction with the
GetNextDocument or GetPrevDocument methods to walk all of the documents in a
NotesDocumentCollection using a DoWhile loop.

GetNextDocument, GetPrevDocument

These two methods get the next or previous document in the NotesDocumentCollection
relative to the provided NotesDocument. The syntax for these two methods is as follows:

```
GetNextDocument(NotesDocument object)
GetPrevDocument(NotesDocument object)
```

As stated in the "GetFirstDocument/GetLastDocument" section, these two methods are normally used in conjunction with the GetFirstDocument or GetLastDocument methods to
walk the documents in a NotesDocumentCollection using the DoWhile loop.

GetNthDocument

The GetNthDocument method returns the document at the indicated position. The syntax of
GetNthDocument is as follows:

```
GetNthDocument(document position number)
```

As stated in an earlier tip, it is a bad idea to use this method, as it is highly inefficient except
in the most narrow of circumstances.

PutAllInFolder, RemoveAllFromFolder

The PutAllInFolder method places all documents in the collection into the specified folder,
or removes all documents from the specified folder. The syntax for these two methods is as
follows:

```
PutAllInFolder(folder name)
RemoveAllFromFolder(folder name)
```

RemoveAll

The RemoveAll method permanently deletes every document in the
NotesDocumentCollection from the database, permanently. The syntax for RemoveAll is as
follows:

```
RemoveAll(force flag)
```

If the force flag parameter is set to True, all documents are immediately deleted, even if
one of the documents is open. If False, only documents that are not open are deleted, and
those that are open are left in the collection.

Note   Be careful using the `RemoveAll` method, because the documents are gone forever after this method is called.

Listing 30-6, earlier in this chapter, demonstrates the use of the `RemoveAll` method.

StampAll

The `StampAll` method is extremely useful for setting an item with the same value in every document in the collection in one call. When this method is used, the item is either updated or created with the new value and is written to disk immediately, without the need for a save. The syntax for `StampAll` is as follows:

```
StampAll(item name, item value)
```

The `item name` parameter is the name of the item to set or update in the documents in the collection, and the item value parameter is a value or array of values that are to be set into the item on each document. This method bypasses the memory documents, so if the document is opened in memory, and is saved individually after this method is called, the item value may be overwritten.

NotesDocument

Of all the back-end classes, the most frequently used is the `NotesDocument` class. This class represents the actual documents — your precious data — in the database. The upcoming sections cover the most useful properties and methods of the `NotesDatabase` class. For a full review of all properties and methods available, refer to the Domino 6 Designer help.

Properties

The most useful `NotesDocument` class properties are covered here. For a more comprehensive listing of all of the properties, refer to the Domino 6 Designer help.

ColumnValues

The `ColumnValues` property is an array of all of the column values from the parent view of the document. This property is only populated if the document was accessed through a `NotesView` object, or if it was accessed from a `NotesViewEntryCollection` object. The array is a zero-based array, so the first column would be `NotesDocument.ColumnValues(0)`.

Tip   If you are accessing a document from a view to get one or more item values, it is much more efficient to get the item value from the `ColumnValues` property than it is to actually access the item itself through the `NotesDocument`. The reason is that all the values from the columns of the parent view are cached in the "pointer" to the document in the view, so when you access the `ColumnValues` property, the actual `NotesDocument` object doesn't have to be loaded into memory. If you actually get the value from the item, then the whole `NotesDocument` object must be loaded into memory.

EmbeddedObjects, HasEmbedded

The `EmbeddedObjects` property contains an array of all embedded objects in the document, including attachments. The `HasEmbedded` property returns `True` if the document has any embedded objects, and `False` if it does not. Therefore, you can check the `HasEmbedded` property before you actually access the `EmbeddedObjects` property.

Cross-Reference   These two properties are covered in more detail in Chapter 31.

IsNewNote

The IsNewNote property returns True if the document has never been saved to disk, and False if it has been previously saved.

IsProfile

The IsProfile property returns True if the document is a profile document, and False if it is not.

Items

The Items property contains a NotesItem object array of all items in the document. This array includes all system items (usually system items are prepended with a dollar sign).

Responses

The Responses property contains a NotesDocumentCollection object of all the immediate responses to the document. Listing 30-6, earlier in this chapter, provides an example of using the Responses property.

Methods

This section lists a few of the most useful methods available in the NotesDocment class. For a full list of all methods in the NotesDocument class, refer to the Domino 6 Designer help.

ComputeWithForm

This method computes all the items on a document using the associated form. This includes all default value, translation, and validation formulas, and all computed fields. The syntax for ComputeWithForm is as follows:

```
ComputeWithForm(True, raise error)
```

The first parameter is actually ignored, so it doesn't matter if you use True or False. If the raise error parameter is set to True, an error is thrown if validation fails; if False, no error is thrown and the method returns a False if an error occurs instead.

Note   Make sure that your document contains a form item, or your document will be computed with the default form (and that's probably not what you want to happen).

CreateRichTextItem

The CreateRichTextItem method creates a new rich text item in the NotesDocument object. The CreateRichTextItem method uses the following syntax:

```
CreateRichTextItem(item name)
```

The item name parameter specifies the name to use for the new rich text item. This method returns a NotesRichTextItem object that represents the newly created rich text item. Make sure you save the document to commit your new item to the document on disk.

GetAttachment

The GetAttachment method retrieves an attachment from the document. The syntax for GetAttachment is as follows:

```
GetAttachment(attachment name)
```

A NotesEmbeddedObject object is returned that represents the desired attachment named in the attachment name parameter. This method can return attachments that are in a rich text item as well as attachments that aren't, such as attachments that are attached to a document from the Web using a file upload control.

Cross-Reference

The GetAttachment method is used in various examples in Chapter 31.

GetFirstItem

The GetFirstItem method gets the first item with the specified name in the document, and then returns a NotesItem object representing the item. The syntax is as follows:

```
GetFirstItem(item name)
```

GetItemValue

The GetItemValue method returns the value of the specified item. This method returns an array, because all items are stored in a document as arrays. The syntax is as follows:

```
GetItemValue(item name)
```

Tip

You can retrieve an item value two ways: extended dot notation (NotesDocument.Item-Name) or with the GetItemValue. Using the GetItemValue is more efficient than using dot notation, so get in the habit of using this method.

GetItemValueDateTimeArray

This method basically does the same thing as GetItemValue, except that this method returns a NotesDateTimeArray object containing all the values of the item as NotesDateTime or NotesDateRange objects. The syntax is the same as GetItemValue.

New Feature

The GetItemValueDateTime method is new in Notes/Domino 6.

MakeResponse

The MakeResponse method makes the document a response to the supplied document. The syntax is as follows:

```
MakeResponse(NotesDocument object)
```

Remember, you must save the document for the effects of this method to take effect.

RemoveItem

The RemoveItem method deletes the named item from the document. The syntax is as follows:

```
RemoveItem(item name)
```

RemovePermanently

The RemovePermanently method deletes the document from the database, even if soft deletions are enabled. The syntax is as follows:

```
RemovePermanently(force flag)
```

The force flag parameter, when set to True, causes the document to be deleted even if it has been opened after the script obtained a handle to it. If the force flag parameter is set to False, the document isn't deleted if it was opened after the handle was obtained. The method returns True if the document was successfully deleted, and False if it was not deleted.

New Feature

The RemovePermanently method is new in Notes/Domino 6.

ReplaceItemValue

The `ReplaceItemValue` method replaces the named item in the document with the new value. The syntax is as follows:

```
ReplaceItemValue(item name, item value)
```

This method is the same as using dot notation to replace or set an item value, and they are equally efficient. For example, the code

```
doc.ThisItem = "This Value"
```

is the same as

```
Call doc.ReplaceItemValue("ThisItem", "This Value")
```

Save

The `Save` method saves the document to disk. This method returns `True` if the document is saved successfully. The syntax is as follows:

```
Save(force, create response, mark read)
```

The parameters are as follows:

- ✦ `force`: If `True`, this method forces the document to be saved, even if the document is being edited in the UI. If this method is `False`, the create response method determines what will happen.

- ✦ `create response`: The `force` parameter has to be `False` for this parameter to have any effect; if the `force` parameter is `True`, this parameter has no effect. If `True`, the current document becomes a response to the new document, like a version. If `create response` is `False`, the save is canceled.

- ✦ `mark read`: If this parameter is `True`, the document is marked read so it doesn't show up as unread in the view. If `False` or omitted, the document is not marked read.

Other Back-End Classes

The following classes may prove useful to you as you work with the Domino Object Model's back-end classes:

- ✦ `NotesACL`, `NotesACLEntry`: These two classes can modify the database ACL, including adding, modifying, and deleting entries.

- ✦ `NotesAgent`: The `NotesAgent` class can run or schedule an agent, or find out other information about the agent, such as the last time it ran, what the agent runs as, and so on.

Agents are covered in more detail in Chapter 31.

- ✦ `NotesDateRange`, `NotesDateTime`: These two classes work with date/time values in Notes/Domino.

- ✦ `Notes XML`, `SAX`, **and** `DXL Classes`: Notes/Domino 6 now has extensive classes for working with XML natively in LotusScript, including the new Domino XML language.

The classes used for XML, SAX, and DXL are covered in Part X.

✦ **NotesEmbeddedObject:** The NotesEmbeddedObject class works with attachments in Notes. Chapter 31 covers working with attachments.

✦ **NotesItem and NotesRichTextItem:** The NotesItem class represents an item from a document. The NotesItem class is the parent class of NotesRichTextItem, so NotesRichTextItem has all the properties and methods of NotesItem, plus many properties and methods of its own.

✦ **NotesName:** The NotesName class enables you to dissect an RFC-822 compliant string into its component parts. This class is basically the same as the @Name function.

✦ **Notes Rich Text Manipulation Classes:** Notes/Domino 6 has many new rich text manipulation classes. These classes can granularly control the content of a NotesRichTextItem.

✦ **NotesStream:** The NotesStream class enables you to stream text or binary information from one place to another. You can read or write data to the stream.

New Feature   NotesStream is a new class in Notes/Domino 6.

For more detailed information, refer to the Domino 6 Designer help.

Summary

The front-end and back-end classes are extremely powerful for manipulating Domino data and application functionality. Many concepts were covered in this chapter, among them:

✦ The differences between front-end and back-end classes

✦ Proven techniques for working with front-end and back-end classes

✦ The most useful front-end and back-end classes that help you get the most out of LotusScript

The next chapter dives into quite a few advanced examples to help you take your LotusScript abilities to the next level.

✦   ✦   ✦

Advanced LotusScript Techniques

By Rocky Oliver

◆ ◆ ◆ ◆

In This Chapter

Understanding error handling

Working with lists and arrays

Introducing LS2J

Working with COM/OLE

Working with the Notes and Win32 API

Creating your own classes in LotusScript

◆ ◆ ◆ ◆

Chapters 29 and 30 introduced you to LotusScript and to the Domino Object Model. You learned how to work with the language, the syntax, some nice techniques, and some commonly used classes. This chapter takes that knowledge to another level. This chapter exposes you to advanced techniques for getting the most out of LotusScript. Topics such as error trapping, working with COM/OLE, and techniques for working with lists and arrays are presented.

Error Trapping in LotusScript

One of the most overlooked areas of LotusScript is the proper handling of error conditions. Usually, only the expected errors are trapped for, and unexpected errors aren't handled at all. Proper error handling can provide your users with a more user-friendly application, help you in diagnosing problems when they occur (and they *will* occur), and help you make decisions on an alternative course or action.

First, you need to know why error trapping is needed. Suppose, for example, that you try to get a handle to a document, but you are unsuccessful. If you try to use the `NotesDocument` object, the dialog box shown in Figure 31-1 appears to the user.

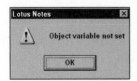

Figure 31-1: The default error messages presented by Notes/ Domino are not informative.

You know that *some* object didn't get set properly; but which one? The first lesson to keep in mind is to trap for the known possible failures.

Trapping for known possible errors

Many situations exist when you may get an error; usually these involve getting a handle to an object. Virtually all methods for obtaining an object return one of two things — the desired object (which is what you wanted in the first place), or the value of Nothing (yes, Nothing really is a value). Returning Nothing is a two-edged sword. The good thing about returning Nothing is that an error isn't immediately thrown, because you didn't get the object. The bad thing about returning Nothing is that if you try to access some property or method of the object, it throws an error. When you get an object, you usually get it so you can perform actions on it (call a method), or get some data from it (access a property). In either case, if you attempt to get the object and that fails, your code throws an error when you try to access the object's properties or methods. Because you know that this is a possibility, this is a known possible error.

The easiest way to trap for a known possible error is to place some code immediately after you attempt to get the object that checks for Nothing, and then handles that condition in a way that is appropriate for the error thrown. Listing 31-1, which is also in the ND6 Advanced LotusScript Examples database (ND6AdvLSEXP.nsf) in the form entitled "31.01 Error Trapping Examples," intentionally throws an error (in the first button) and shows how you can trap for it (in the second button).

The ND6 Advanced LotusScript Examples database (ND6AdvLSEXP.nsf) can be found at the companion Web site, www.wiley.com/compbooks/benz.

Listing 31-1: **Error Trapping Example (Second Button)**

```
Sub Click(Source As Button)
   Dim s As New NotesSession
   Dim db As NotesDatabase
   Dim view As NotesView
   Dim doc As NotesDocument
   Dim fldval As Variant

   Set db = s.CurrentDatabase
   Set view = db.GetView("AllDocs")
   REM this checks to make sure the view "AllDocs" was found
   If view Is Nothing Then
     Msgbox "Unable to access the desired view - sorry",_
     MB_OK + MB_ICONSTOP, "Error"
     Exit Sub
   End If

   Set doc = view.getDocumentByKey("Dummy Key", True)
   REM this checks to make sure a document is found
   If doc Is Nothing Then
     Msgbox "Unable to retrieve the desired document" &_
     " - sorry!", MB_OK + MB_ICONSTOP, "Error"
     Exit Sub
   End If

   fldval = doc.GetItemValue("SomeValue")
End Sub
```

The preceding code traps for the view and the document. If the view or document is not found (that is `Nothing` is returned), a message returns to the user telling him that the object wasn't found. The `sub` then exits by using the `Exit Sub` statement. Figure 31-2 shows the message returned.

Figure 31-2: This type of error message is more user friendly and informative than the default error message shown in Figure 31-1.

Advanced error handling

The method in the preceding section is great for trapping the errors you know may happen; but what about unforeseen errors? Also, the code is a bit lengthy and repetitive. Repetitive code is a good signal that you can optimize. Take a look at this technique for making your error handling more robust.

LotusScript provides some functionality that helps you provide more robust error handling in your code. To begin explaining the use of this functionality, start with the `On Error` statement.

The `On Error` statement determines how errors are handled. Normally when an error occurs, the user is alerted and the code stops executing. The `On Error` statement enables you to gracefully handle the error and continue executing the code. You can use the `On Error` statement for general statements, or you can test for specific errors. The syntax for the `On Error` statement is described in the next few sections.

On Error optional error number Goto label

This is the most commonly used syntax. The error number parameter is optional. If the error number is provided, and if that particular error occurs, the code branches to the label specified. If no error number is provided, the code branches to the given label for any error that occurs.

On Error optional error number Resume Next

This syntax tells the code to keep executing and ignore the error. If an error number is provided, that means that if that particular error occurs, it will be ignored and the code will continue executing.

Tip

In rare circumstances you want to use `On Error optional error number Resume Next`. You should know which errors may occur and handle them accordingly. Additionally, you should have error handling for any condition you didn't plan for. Unfortunately, this syntax is used by developers who don't really understand why they are getting an error, so they use the `Resume Next` statement to keep their code running without returning an error to the user. Doing this can only lead to bad code.

On Error optional error number GoTo 0

This syntax is normally used in functions so that errors that occur in the function are passed back to the calling code.

You're going to take a look at the preceding code again, but this time with some more sophisticated error handling added to it. Listing 31-2 shows the updated code.

Listing 31-2: **Better Error Trapping Example**

```
Sub Click(Source As Button)
  On Error Goto errHandler
  Dim s As New NotesSession
  Dim db As NotesDatabase
  Dim view As NotesView
  Dim doc As NotesDocument
  Dim fldval As Variant

  Set db = s.CurrentDatabase
  Set view = db.GetView("AllDocs")
  If view Is Nothing Then Error 900,_
  "Unable to access the desired view - sorry"

  Set doc = view.getDocumentByKey("Dummy Key", True)
  If doc Is Nothing Then Error 900,_
  "Unable to retrieve the desired document"

  fldval = doc.GetItemValue("SomeValue")
getOut:
  Exit Sub

errHandler:
  Select Case Err
  Case 900
    Msgbox Error$, MB_OK + MB_ICONSTOP, "Error"
  Case Else
    Msgbox Error$ & " (" & Err & ")", MB_OK +_
    MB_ICONSTOP, "Unhandled Error"
  End Select
  Resume getOut
End Sub
```

The first line under the Sub signature is an On Error statement:

```
On Error Goto errHandler
```

This means that on any error (because no error number is provided), the code branches to the label provided after the GoTo parameter, which in this case is the errHandler label.

This example attempts to get three objects (four if you count NotesSession, but if the script is running, it's available). The s.CurrentDatabase line has no error trapping—if the script is running, you can get the database where it is running. The next line attempts to get a view called Main; the line after that attempts to get a document that doesn't exist (the line that you know throws an error). Start by looking at the line that gets the view, and then the subsequent line:

```
Set view = db.GetView("AllDocs")
If view Is Nothing Then Error 900,_
"Unable to access the desired view - sorry"
```

The first line is common—using the `GetView` method to get a view object. Like most methods that return an object, if this method fails, it simply returns `Nothing`—no error. Because the call returns `Nothing` and no error, the earlier `On Error` statement doesn't catch that you do have an error (meaning that the result is not what's desired). You want to have one area that handles all your errors—the expected and unexpected. To do so, you need to create your own error by using the `Error` function, and that's what the next line does. It checks the view object variable, and if it is a value of `Nothing`, the `Error` function fires. The `Error` function takes two parameters: an error number, and an optional error message. How did you know what number to use for your error? Make it up—900 isn't one of the used error numbers, so it's a safe number to use. To confirm that 900 isn't a used number, check the `LSERR.LSS` file.

The `LSERR.LSS` file contains a list of all Notes/Domino error codes. It's a list of constants that map to the error numbers, which are integer values. The error that was thrown in the first example in this chapter (Figure 31-1) is error number 91, which corresponds to the following line in the `LSERR.LSS` file:

```
Public Const ErrObjectVariableNotSet      = 91
```

Tip If you want to simulate an error condition and find out how your error-handling routine handles it, use the `Error` function and the desired condition number. If you want to simulate not getting a handle to a document, you could call `Error 91`.

By checking this file, you know that 900 isn't a known error number, so it's safe to use. You learn more about using the `LSERR.LSS` file later in the chapter.

The other part of the `If` statement provides an error message. You can use this error message to provide a more user-friendly error message, and to provide some additional helpful diagnostic information, such as the module where the error occurs, or the actual document type that was not found.

The next couple of lines are similar to the previous two. The code attempts to retrieve an object from the view, and throws an error if it is not found.

```
Set doc = view.getDocumentByKey("Dummy Key", True)
If doc Is Nothing Then Error 900,_
"Unable to retrieve the desired document"
```

The same error number is needed because the error message is provided by the developer, and you don't need to use a different number. You can, however, design your own specific error numbers and messages and create your own LSS file of them for use in your applications.

Here's the bottom of the code:

```
getOut:
  Exit Sub

errHandler:
  Select Case Err
  Case 900
    Msgbox Error$, MB_OK + MB_ICONSTOP, "Error"
  Case Else
    Msgbox Error$ & " (" & Err & ")", MB_OK +_
    MB_ICONSTOP, "Unhandled Error"
  End Select
  Resume getOut
End Sub
```

If the code completes successfully, it hits the `Exit Sub` statement, which ends the execution of the code. Below this statement is the error-handling routine, which is labeled with `errHandler`. A `Select Case` statement checks the error number and provides the appropriate prompt to the user. The `Error$` function returns the message text of the error condition, if there is one. If the error number is 900, the `Error$` function returns the error message that is then presented to the user through a `MsgBox` prompt. The `Err` function returns the error number of the last error that occurred, or 0 if no error has occurred.

You can use a `Select Case` statement instead of an `If` statement when you want to trap for additional errors, and `Select Case` statements are easier to read for more than three conditions. This code was set up as a `Select Case` statement to make it easier to maintain and modify in the future.

The next line in the error handler is the `Resume getOut` line. This tells the error handler that the code should continue to execute at the label provided. In this case, the label is right above the `Exit Sub` function, so the code jumps there and exits. When you have error handling, you must tell LotusScript what you want to do to resolve the condition. The acceptable ways to resolve the condition are as follows:

✦ `Resume Next`: This tells the code to keep going from where the error occurred. Make sure this is really what you want to do before you use this.

✦ `Resume label`: This tells the code to continue running from the provided label.

✦ `Exit Sub`, `Exit Function`, `Exit Property`: This tells the code to stop executing immediately. Use the statement appropriate to the type of module you are in.

You can't use `End Sub` or `End Function`. If you do not provide an appropriate `Exit` or `Resume` statement, the code throws a `No Resume` error and immediately halts execution.

Note   Error handling is important, but it becomes critical when working with COM/OLE. Review the "Working with COM/OLE from LotusScript" section later in this chapter to learn more about error handling when using COM/OLE.

Using %Include LSERR.LSS

You can include the `LSERR.LSS` file as a part of your code to make it easier to test for particular conditions without knowing the appropriate error number.

Suppose that you have a function that computes a factorial. The factorial function is a *recursive* function; that is, it calls itself until some condition is met. A factorial is a number that is multiplied by all positive integers of a lesser value than the specified number. A factorial of 5, expressed as 5!, is calculated as 5 * 4 * 3 * 2 * 1, which equals 120. The problem with computing a factorial using a recursive function is that you quickly run out of allotted memory, or stack space, because the memory keeps building up until the function quits running. You want to test for this condition. Listing 31-3 shows some code that computes a factorial and has some additional error condition handling.

Listing 31-3: **Error Handling Using LSERR.LSS**

```
Sub Click(Source As Button)
  On Error Goto errHandler
  Dim ws As New NotesUIWorkspace
  Dim doc As NotesDocument
```

```
    Dim factnum As Integer, factres As Integer

    Set doc = ws.CurrentDocument.Document
    factnum = doc.GetItemValue("FactorialNum")(0)
    factres = Factorial(factnum)
    Msgbox "The factorial of " & factnum & " (" & factnum &_
    "!) is " & factres & ".",,"Results"

getOut:
  Exit Sub

errHandler:
  Select Case Err
  Case ErrTypeMismatch, ErrNotAContainer
    Msgbox "You must enter a numeric value into " &_
    "the field." & Chr(10) & "(" & Error$ & "[" & Err &_
    "])", MB_OK + MB_ICONSTOP,_
    "Error"
  Case ErrOverflow
    Msgbox "The factorial of the number you entered " &_
    "is larger than an integer (32K)." &_
    "Please enter a smaller number." & Chr(10) &_
    "(" & Error$ & "[" & Err & "])", MB_OK +_
    MB_ICONSTOP, "Error"
  Case ErrOutOfStackSpace
    Msgbox "The number you have entered is too big. " &_
    "Please enter a smaller number." &_
    Chr(10) & "(" & Error$ & "[" & Err & "])", MB_OK +_
    MB_ICONSTOP, "Error"
  Case 900
    Msgbox Error$, MB_OK + MB_ICONSTOP, "Error"
  Case Else
    Msgbox Error$ & " (" & Err & ")", MB_OK +_
    MB_ICONSTOP, "Unhandled Error"
  End Select
  Resume getOut
End Sub
```

Three types of errors are thrown in this example — type mismatch and variant not a container indicate that the user either entered characters instead of numbers, or didn't enter anything; stack overflow, which occurs when the result of the computation is too big; and out of stack space, which occurs when the result is too big and the number entered is large. Additional conditions have been added that use four constants from LSERR.LSS to check for these error conditions. But how does the code know what the LSERR.LSS constants are?

You can add chunks of code by using a %Include directive. If you use a %Include, the code in the indicated text file is added to your code at compile time. The line

```
%Include "lserr.lss"
```

adds all the constants in the LSERR.LSS file to the code, making them available. This statement is placed in the Global (Declarations) area of the form.

Working with Arrays and Lists

Arrays and lists enable you to work with groups of data efficiently. LotusScript provides good support for arrays and lists.

Arrays

Arrays are a useful data construct in LotusScript. An *array* is a collection of data of the same data type, indexed sequentially by number. The beginning and ending numbers of an array are known as the *upper bound* and *lower bound*, respectively. You can reference a member, or element, of an array by its index number. If you have the following array:

```
Dim geekarray(0 to 4) as String
geekarray(0) = "Rocky"
geekarray(1) = "Henry"
geekarray(2) = "Bob"
geekarray(3) = "Rob"
geekarray(4) = "Andrew"
```

You can retrieve the third member, Bob, by referencing geekarray(2).

An array with the first element numbered 0 is said to be a zero-based array. You can begin an array with any number, but the default in LotusScript is to begin all arrays with a zero. You should stick to the default — it's what most developers expect. One exception to this rule is the function shown in Listing 31-4, which returns the weekday name based on the number of the day. The code for this function is located in the form entitled "31.02 Arrays and Lists Examples," in the button contained on the form.

Listing 31-4: **WeekDayName Function**

```
Function WeekDayName(wdate As Variant,_
abbrevnum As Integer) As String
  Dim dayname(1 To 7) As String
  Dim wd As Integer
  dayname(1) = "Sunday"
  dayname(2) = "Monday"
  dayname(3) = "Tuesday"
  dayname(4) = "Wednesday"
  dayname(5) = "Thursday"
  dayname(6) = "Friday"
  dayname(7) = "Saturday"

  wd = Weekday(wdate)

  If abbrevnum > 0 Then
    WeekDayName = Ucase(Left(dayname(wd), abbrevnum))
  Else
    WeekDayName = dayname(wd)
  End If
End Function
```

This function is one of the few where using a one-based array makes sense. The WeekDay LotusScript function returns an integer representing the day of the week, 1 being Sunday and 7 being Saturday. Because the days of the week are one-based, you should use a one-based array to retrieve the right name. The function can also return an abbreviated version of the day name. You can try out this function in the form, 31: Arrays and Lists Examples, in the ND6 Advanced LotusScript Examples database (ND6AdvLSEXP.nsf).

A few ways exist for you to use arrays in your code. The following sections provide some tips to get the most out of working with arrays and making your array code more efficient.

Items are arrays

All items on a document, except for rich text items, are arrays. You can reference an item value directly using the array index number. This is especially handy if you need a value from an item that has only one value. If that's the case, you can get the value like this:

```
Myval = doc.getItemValue("SomeItem")(0)
```

It's easy to forget that all items are arrays, especially if you get into the bad habit of referencing items using extended dot notation. The previous line returns a single value, as does this line:

```
Myval = doc.SomeItem(0)
```

But this line returns an array with one element:

```
Myval = doc.SomeItem
```

Don't overuse Redim

You can resize an array, or establish a new array, using Redim. If, for example, you have an empty variant and you need to change it to an array, you could use the following line:

```
Redim myvar(0 to 9) as String
```

This line creates an array called myvar that has 10 elements, and is a data type of String. Suppose that you added values to myvar, but you need it to be 12 elements instead of ten, and you don't want to lose the values you already assigned. You can accomplish this by using the following line:

```
Redim Preserve myvar(0 to 11) as String
```

The Preserve keyword tells LotusScript to make the array bigger, but leave the existing values in it. If you do not use Preserve, your values are erased.

While Redim Preserve is a great function, it is expensive, meaning that it's inefficient and slow. Because it's so easy to use, many people make the mistake of using Redim Preserve in loops to build an array of indeterminate length. This is a bad practice. It's better to determine how big of an array you need, establish it with a Redim, and then assign the values to it.

Use arrays to assign values to an item

You can use the NotesItem.AddToTextList method to add values to the end of an existing item. But like Redim Preserve, this is inefficient, especially when used in a loop. Instead of using this method to add an array of values to an existing item, it's much better to establish the array outside of the item, and then reassign the new value list to the item. The following code, for example, takes an item and adds new values to it:

```
Dim NFCSouth(0 to 3) as String
Dim newlist as Variant
NFCSouth(0) = "Falcons"
NFCSouth(1) = "Saints"
NFCSouth(2) = "Panthers"
NFCSouth(3) = "Buccanneers"

teams = doc.NFLTeams
newlist = ArrayAppend(teams, NFCSouth)

doc.NFLTeams = newlist
```

This code takes the existing values from the `NFLTeams` item, appends the new teams, and reassigns the new array back into the item, which replaces the old list with the new, combined list.

Array functions

LotusScript includes quite a few functions for working with arrays. Some of these are reviewed in the following list:

✦ `ArrayAppend(array 1, array 2)`: `ArrayAppend` takes two arrays, combines them, and returns the result as a new array. Look in the previous section for an example.

✦ `ArrayGetIndex(source array, search value)`: This handy little function searches the source array for the specified search value, and returns the index number (variant containing data type long) that matches. If no match is found, `NULL` is returned.

✦ `ArrayReplace(source array, compare array, replace array)`: This function works just like `@Replace`; it searches the source array for matches in the compare array. If any are found, it replaces the match with the element found at the same index number in the replace array as the match in the compare array. Check out Chapter 28 for more examples of using the concept of `ArrayReplace`. Additionally, the Domino 6 Designer help has a good explanation of using this function.

✦ `ArrayUnique(source array)`: This function works just like `@Unique` against a list — it removes duplicate entries from an array and returns the smaller, unique array.

New Feature Even though the Domino 6 Designer help doesn't indicate it, the `ArrayUnique` function is new in Notes/Domino 6.

✦ `FullTrim(source array)`: This feature takes an array and removes any empty elements, returning an array with no blanks. This function, combined with `ArrayReplace`, can perform similar functionality as `@Trim` and `@Replace` combined. See Chapter 28 for ideas of using these types of functions together. The chapter has formula examples, but the usage suggestions apply here.

Lists

Lists are one of the most underutilized features in LotusScript. A list is similar to a one-dimensional array in that it is a collection of indexed elements. But lists have a few differences that make them uniquely useful:

✦ Lists are indexed by a unique string value, not an index number. This means that you can reference things by a name rather than a number, which is useful.

✦ Elements can be added to a list without the use of `Redim`.

✦ You can remove elements from a list by using the `Erase` function. With a list, the `Erase` function can remove individual elements; if you use `Erase` against an array, it blows away the whole array.

Lists are hard to grasp in the abstract, so here's an example. You have a database or some other source that has orders in it. You want a summary of total units sold and total dollar amount of sales. You could build an elaborate bit of code to do it with arrays, but a better way exists — a list!

In the ND6 Advanced LotusScript Examples database is a form called 31.03 List Example, as shown in Figure 31-3.

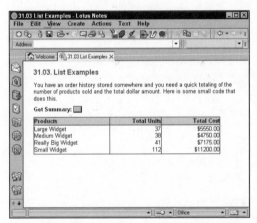

Figure 31-3: The Get Summary button on this form uses a list to summarize the product data.

The form in Figure 31-3 has a table and a button. If you click the Get Summary button, it walks a view (in the same database to keep the example easier to manage, but the source could be somewhere else) and totals the units and cost by product by using a list. Then it takes the list information, transfers it to traditional arrays, and places the data in the table on the form. Listing 31-5 shows the code in the Get Summary button.

Listing 31-5: **Get Summary Button**

```
Sub Click(Source As Button)
   Dim ws As New NotesUIWorkspace
   Dim s As New NotesSession
   Dim db As NotesDatabase
   Dim view As NotesView
   Dim doc As NotesDocument, thisdoc As NotesDocument
```

Continued

Listing 31-5 *(continued)*

```
Dim prodlist List As ProdData    ' units, cost
Dim pname As String, pcount As Integer

Set thisdoc = ws.CurrentDocument.Document
Set db = s.CurrentDatabase
Set view = db.getView("PRODSOLD")

REM walk the view and add up all the units
REM and costs by product
Set doc = view.GetFirstDocument
Do While Not(doc Is Nothing)
  pname = doc.ColumnValues(1)
  If Iselement(prodlist(pname)) = False Then pcount =_
  pcount + 1
  prodlist(pname).units = prodlist(pname).units +_
  doc.ColumnValues(2)
  prodlist(pname).cost = prodlist(pname).cost +_
  doc.ColumnValues(3)
  Set doc = view.GetNextDocument(doc)
Loop

pcount = pcount - 1 ' reduce by 1 since its a 0 based array
REM set up the arrays to place the values in the items
Redim prods(0 To pcount) As String
Redim tunits(0 To pcount) As Integer
Redim tcost(0 To pcount) As Single

pcount = 0  ' reset the counter
REM add the values to the arrays
Forall p In prodlist
  prods(pcount) = Listtag(p)
  tunits(pcount) = p.units
  tcost(pcount) = p.cost
  pcount = pcount + 1
End Forall

REM add the values to the items
thisdoc.Products = prods
thisdoc.TotalUnits = tunits
thisdoc.TotalCost = tcost
End Sub
```

Note   In the real world, Listing 31-5 should have error handling—it was left out to make the listing smaller.

Take a look at the statement that sets up the list:

```
Dim prodlist List As ProdData    ' units, cost
```

The list is declared as a data type of ProdData. ProdData is a user-defined data type. A *user-defined data type* is a complex data type that the developer defines. In this example, the data type is declared in the (Declarations) area of the button as follows:

```
Type ProdData
  units As Integer
  cost As Single
End Type
```

This data type has two parts: an integer variable called units, and a single variable called cost. These two variables hold the totals for units and cost for each product, enabling you to store more than one piece of information per product found.

The next interesting section of the code walks through the view and adds the values to the list:

```
Set doc = view.GetFirstDocument
Do While Not(doc Is Nothing)
  pname = doc.ColumnValues(1)
  If Iselement(prodlist(pname)) = False Then pcount =_
  pcount + 1
  prodlist(pname).units = prodlist(pname).units +_
  doc.ColumnValues(2)
  prodlist(pname).cost = prodlist(pname).cost +_
  doc.ColumnValues(3)
  Set doc = view.GetNextDocument(doc)
Loop
```

The product name is assigned to the pname variable, and that is used as the listtag for the elements of the list. A *listtag* is the unique string that is the index for the list. Because you are gathering the information by product, it makes sense to index the list by product name. The first time a new product name is encountered, the pcount variable is incremented by one. This count eventually holds the total number of products. Then the pname variable references the existing list element or to add the new element to the list. No Redims are needed to add a variable to the list — it is added automatically. The units and cost are added to the existing amount. The next document is gathered and the process starts over until all documents are processed.

After gathering all the information, you want to be able to present it to the user by adding the information to the items on the document. Unfortunately, you can't add lists to an item — you must convert the list to a traditional array. That's why the number of products was counted in the pcount variable — so that arrays could be set up for products (prods), total units (tunits), and total cost (tcost). The following code shows the building of the arrays and their assignment into the respective items:

```
pcount = pcount - 1 ' reduce by 1 since its a 0 based array
REM set up the arrays to place the values in the items
Redim prods(0 To pcount) As String
Redim tunits(0 To pcount) As Integer
Redim tcost(0 To pcount) As Single

pcount = 0  ' reset the counter
REM add the values to the arrays
Forall p In prodlist
```

```
      prods(pcount) = Listtag(p)
      tunits(pcount) = p.units
      tcost(pcount) = p.cost
      pcount = pcount + 1
   End Forall

   REM add the values to the items
   thisdoc.Products = prods
   thisdoc.TotalUnits = tunits
   thisdoc.TotalCost = tcost
```

You must reduce the counter by one because the arrays are zero-based. The arrays are set up; then the list is walked using a `Forall` loop to gather the information from the list for assignment to the arrays. The `Listtag` function returns the listtag of the provided element. You reference the other parts of the custom data type by using dot notation (`p.units`, `p.cost`). After the arrays are built, they are set into the respective items on the form, and the information is presented to the user as shown in Figure 31-3.

Using Java from LotusScript

One of the most intriguing new features of Notes/Domino 6 is LotusScript to Java (LS2J), which is the ability to call Java classes from LotusScript. A wealth of information about this is in the Domino 6 Designer help, but this section briefly shows you what it takes, and the ND6 Advanced LotusScript Examples database has the working example provided here.

Note　The LotusScript to Java (LS2J) example provided here has a few requirements before it will run on your system. First, Notes must be on your Windows path. Next, you must be running on Windows 98 or greater, as Windows 95 doesn't support Java 1.3 (which is required for LS2J and, incidentally, Domino 6 Designer).

First, add the following line to your (Options) area:

```
Uselsx "*javacon"
```

This loads the LS2J handler environment so that you can begin working with LS2J.

LS2J enables you to reference Java classes that are either on your CLASSPATH or are in a Java library (similar to a LotusScript library) in your database. LS2J has an object model similar to a LotusScript or JavaScript object model. This model loads a runtime of the Java class into memory, and translates the calls from LotusScript to Java and the output back to LotusScript.

Figure 31-4 shows an old Java example from many years ago. It is called Bubbles, and shows some little graphic bubbles in a Java application.

Note　It takes a few moments for the Java to initially load, so you may need to try the example a couple of times before it works.

Here's how the Bubbles example works. Listing 31-6 shows the Globals area of the example form.

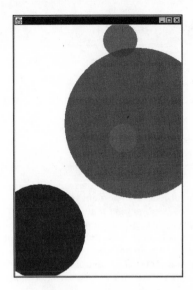

Figure 31-4: The Bubbles example may be silly, but it's a great introduction to controlling Java with LotusScript through LS2J.

Listing 31-6: **Globals Area of Bubbles Example Form**

```
Options
Option Public
Option Explicit

Uselsx "*javacon"   ' this line enables JS2J
REM this line loads the bubbles java code from
REM the Java Library
Use "BubbleClasses"

Declarations
REM this is the LS2J session where the classes are loaded
Dim j As JavaSession
REM this is the wrapper class for the Java class
Dim bubbleClass As JavaClass
REM this is the object that is created from the class
Dim bubbles As JavaObject
```

The Options area loads the LSX to enable LS2J, and it loads the BubbleClasses Java Library. The BubbleClasses Java Library contains the actual Java class code that creates the Bubbles example.

The Declarations area establishes global variables for the JavaSession, the JavaClass, and the JavaObject. These are established globally, because there are buttons on the form loading this code that enable you to control the bubbles application.

Listing 31-7 shows the PostOpen event of the form, which loads the actual Java object.

Listing 31-7: PostOpen Event of Bubbles Example Form

```
Sub Postopen(Source As Notesuidocument)
  Set j = New JavaSession()
  Set bubbleClass =  j.GetClass("BubbleFrame")
  Set bubbles = bubbleClass.createobject(_
  "(Ljava/lang/String;" &_
  "Ljava/lang/String;Ljava/lang/String;IIII)V", "", "", "",_
  16777215, 5, 400, 600)
End Sub
```

The JavaSession is like the NotesSession — it is the object environment that all of the LS2J classes live in. From the JavaSession object a JavaClass object is created using the JavaSession.GetClass method. This method loads the class into the environment. The JavaClass.CreateObject method instantiates the object and takes any necessary parameters. The JavaClass.CreateObject method has one confusing parameter — the Java Native Interface (JNI) signature parameter, which is the first parameter. The rest of the parameters for the CreateObject method are the actual parameters for the newly created Java class.

The JNI signature parameter defines what each of the data types are for the parameters for the Java class. This tells the JavaSession how to convert the LotusScript data types to the equivalent Java data types. Because many data types in Java are objects, many of the data types are actually paths to other Java classes. Take a look at the signature from the code in Listing 31-7. It is broken down as follows:

"(Ljava/lang/String;Ljava/lang/String;Ljava/lang/String;IIII)V"

✦ The first three parameters indicate that the first three parameters of the BubbleFrame class are String objects (Ljava/lang/String;). The L at the beginning of the parameter indicates that these are fully qualified Java classes. The semicolon at the end of the parameter is actually a part of the class name, not a separator for the string.

✦ The last parameter is four parameters — each one of them integers (IIII).

✦ The V at the end of the string indicates that the Java class is a "Void" class, meaning that it has no return value.

If you look at the parameters passed after the signature, you can see that three String objects and four integers are passed to the class.

Now that the object is created and loaded, you can call methods of the object from LotusScript. The form has four buttons: Show, Hide, Start, and Stop. Show makes the application window visible, Hide hides the window, Start causes the bubbles to start, and Stop causes the bubbles to freeze and stop bubbling. Listing 31-8 shows the methods used to do carry out these various actions.

Listing 31-8: Buttons from the Bubbles Example Form

```
Show Button
Call bubbles.show()
```

```
Hide Button
Call bubbles.hide()

Start Button
Call bubbles.start()

Stop Button
Call bubbles.stop()
```

Remember that the methods being called are *Java* methods from LotusScript. You can learn more about this from Domino 6 Designer help, and from the Lotus Notes Net Web site (www.notes.net).

Working with COM/OLE from LotusScript

One of the most useful functions of LotusScript is its ability to work with other desktop applications through COM/OLE. COM stands for Component Object Model, which is the standard used by Win32-based applications to make their functionality available to other applications. COM standards require that an application publish itself to the Registry, and that it self-publish the properties and methods it has available. This makes it is easy for applications to share functionality. OLE, which stands for Object Linking and Embedding, has two flavors: OLE1 is a simple attachment in a document; OLE/2 is an embedded object in a document.

You can't use OLE/2 to work with objects because it is extremely inefficient and slow. OLE has never been stable, and it continues to be unreliable and prone to crashes. Additionally, an embedded object takes up a *minimum* of 500KB (a half a megabyte) of disk space per embedded object — not counting the data. Contrast that with an attached document. A typical 20-page document with some graphics takes up about 200KB on the hard drive. Embedded on a document, it balloons to over 1.1MB of space. As an attachment, it takes up about 170KB of space (attached files are compressed somewhat by Notes). Working with attachments is much more efficient.

Another problem with OLE objects is that only a subset of functionality is available to the full application. This can be confusing and frustrating to users who are already upset that the embedded object took so long to load.

COM and OLE are often used to refer to how you work with other applications. You can boil down the difference between the two as whether the environment is early binding or late binding. *Binding* refers to obtaining a handle to, and working with, an object.

Early binding refers to the ability to declare an object from an application and have its properties and methods available to you while you write your code. One of the most visible examples of early binding is the way the Domino 6 Designer provides type-ahead for Domino objects. Because you are able to explicitly identify and declare the class to be used for the variable, the designer is able to show you the properties and methods available. This also helps the designer test for syntax errors at compile time instead of runtime. Most developers refer to early binding as using the COM interface. VBA in Microsoft Office 95 and above uses a COM interface to work with other applications.

Late binding refers to the way you work with an object without the Designer knowing anything about it. The onus of getting the syntax right is up to you, and errors typically are not found until runtime. Additionally, late binding tends to run a little slower because the code has to find the object registration at runtime, and then figure out if your syntax was right. Most developers refer to late binding as OLE.

Domino 6 Designer uses late binding to work with other application objects. Overall this is fine, but it takes a little bit of effort to work with other applications. How can you find out if you don't have type-ahead in the Designer to tell you the properties and methods available? One place to look is the Designer client.

The Domino 6 Designer client has a pane to the left of the Script pane that contains two tabs. The first tab is an Objects tab that shows you the Domino objects available in the context of your code. The second tab, the Reference tab, has a combo box that has a setting of OLE classes. If you select this choice, it takes a few moments to refresh, but eventually you are presented with a list of all of the COM/OLE registered objects on your system. This is handy for discovering what objects are available, and the properties and methods they have published. Figure 31-5 shows the Reference tab with MS Word expanded.

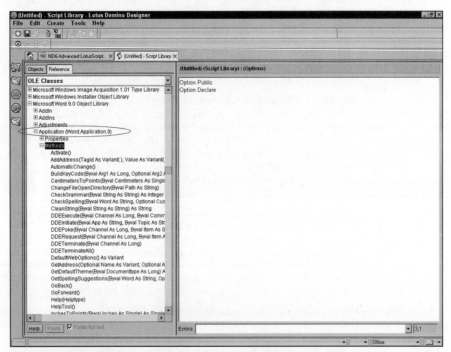

Figure 31-5: The Reference tab in the Domino 6 Designer is useful to learn more about what application objects are available to you.

One of the more desirable functions is performing a mail merge from Notes into Microsoft Word. The agent displayed in the next few listings takes the documents you select from your Personal Address Book and enables you to seamlessly write a letter and perform a merge with those documents.

You can find the NAB Merge Example agent in the ND6 Advanced LotusScript Examples database. To use it, copy the agent and place it in your Personal Address Book; then go into your Personal Address Book, select documents, and execute the agent.

Listing 31-9 shows the main part of the agent that calls the functions used to build the data document and set up the merge document. It also performs all error handling for the agent.

Listing 31-9: **NAB Merge Example Agent (Part 1)**

```
(Options)
Option Public
Option Explicit

(Declarations)
%INCLUDE "lserr.lss"
%INCLUDE "lsconst.lss"

Initialize (main part of the agent)
Sub Initialize
  On Error Goto errHandler
  Dim s As New NotesSession
  Dim contdb As NotesDatabase
  Dim col As NotesDocumentCollection
  Dim cfname As String
  Dim flg As Boolean
  Dim hwd As Variant, hwddoc As Variant

  Set contdb = s.CurrentDatabase
  REM the docs the user selected
  Set col = contdb.UnprocessedDocuments

  REM create the data file if any docs are selected
  If col.Count > 0 Then
    flg = createDataFile(col, cfname, hwd, hwddoc)
  Else
    Error 900, "No documents selected!"
  End If

  REM perform merge if the data file was created successfully
  If flg Then
    flg = openWordMergeDoc(cfname, hwd, hwddoc)
  End If

getOut:
  Exit Sub
errHandler:
  REM all error handling is done here.
  REM when functions have an error,
  REM they are passed up to here for handling and cleanup
  Select Case Err
  Case 900
```

Continued

Listing 31-9 *(continued)*

```
     Msgbox Error$,MB_OK +_
     MB_ICONEXCLAMATION, "Wrong Version"
   Case Else
     Msgbox "Unknown problem (" & Err & ":   " & Error & ")",_
     MB_OK + MB_ICONEXCLAMATION, "Unhandled Error"
   End Select

   If Isobject(hwddoc) Then Call hwddoc.close(0,1)
   If Isobject(hwd) Then Call hwd.Quit
   Resume GetOut
 End Sub
```

The (Options) and (Declarations) areas of the agent are standard (you should always use Option Declare or Option Explicit). The LSCONST.LSS file is included in the (Declarations), because the constants for the MsgBox function are used in the error handler.

The documents that the user selected are gathered using the NotesDatabase.Unprocessed-Documents property. This property, when accessed from an agent set to run against selected documents, returns the documents that the user selected in the view.

The next chunk of code checks to see whether the user selected at least one document. If the user did select one or more documents, the createDataFile function is called. If no documents are selected, the function throws an error and exits. The createDataFile function creates an MS Word document with a table in it that contains information for the selected documents; this document is used as the data source for the merge. MS Word likes using Word documents for data sources. For larger merges this can be slow, but for this application it works fine. You explore the createDataFile function in Listing 31-10.

After creating the data file, the merge document is created by the openWordMergeDoc function. The openWordMergeDoc function creates a new Word document, sets it up for the merge by providing it with a data source file, and then shows the Word document to the user. The user can then create the letter and perform the merge. Figure 31-6 shows a merge document created with the NAB Merge Example agent in progress, with the merge fields available. The merge fields come from the Person document of the Personal Address Book.

The final bit of code is the error handling section. All error handling in this agent is done in the Initialize sub, which is the main segment of code reviewed in Listing 31-9. The Select statement helps decide whether the error is one that is custom (a custom error message is thrown if the user has Word XP or later — this code only works with MS Word 2000 or MS Word 97) or a normal, unhandled error. The end of the error-handling segment cleans up the Word application or document that is open.

 Tip   If you write LotusScript code that works with COM/OLE objects, make sure that you have error trapping and that you clean up all objects in your error-handling code.

The error handling code in the functions helps complete this picture. Take a look at the createDataFile function, as shown in Listing 31-10.

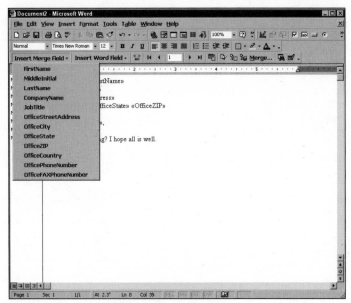

Figure 31-6: The NAB Merge agent seamlessly sets up a merge
document from your Personal Address Book.

Listing 31-10: **NAB Merge Example Agent (Part 2)**

CreateDataFile function

```
Function createDataFile(contcol As NotesDocumentCollection,
cfilename As String, hwd As Variant, hwddoc As Variant) As
Boolean
  createDataFile = True
  Dim myrange As Variant, tst As Variant
  Dim z As Integer, dcount As Integer
  Dim contdoc As NotesDocument
  Dim contfld(0 To 11)As String
  Dim wordver As String
  dcount = contcol.Count
  On Error Goto errHandler

  Print "Creating merge data file for " & dcount & "
documents..."
  REM these are the fields from the Contact form in the
Personal NAB
  contfld(0) = "FirstName"
  contfld(1) = "MiddleInitial"
  contfld(2) = "LastName"
  contfld(3) = "CompanyName"
  contfld(4) = "JobTitle"
```

Continued

Listing 31-10 *(continued)*

```
    contfld(5) = "OfficeStreetAddress"
    contfld(6) = "OfficeCity"
    contfld(7) = "OfficeState"
    contfld(8) = "OfficeZIP"
    contfld(9) = "OfficeCountry"
    contfld(10) = "OfficePhoneNumber"
    contfld(11) = "OfficeFAXPhoneNumber"

    REM create an new Word doc, and set it to not be visible
    REM note that the version number is left off, which means
    REM that this will work with any version of Word
    REM that supports COM
    REM however, avoid Word XP, as the way you do
    REM merges completely changed
    Print "Creating MS Word object..."
    Set hwd  = CreateObject("Word.Application")
    hwd.Visible = False

    REM this merge doesn't work with MS Word XP -
    REM the merge object is completely changed
    REM therefore this tests to make sure the version is 9.0
(2000) or less
    wordver = hwd.Version
    If Cint(wordver) > 9 Then Error 900, "You must use MS Word
2000 or less, not XP."

    REM check to make sure the merge directory exists, and if
it doesn't, create it.
    cfilename = Environ("TEMP") & "\merge"
    tst = Dir(cfilename, 16)
    If tst = "" Then Mkdir(cfilename)
    cfilename = cfilename & "\mrgdata.doc"
    Call hwd.documents.Add   ' create the new doc
    Set hwddoc = hwd.ActiveDocument
    Call hwddoc.SaveAs(cfilename, 0)   ' give it a file name
    Set myrange = hwddoc.Range(0,0)   ' set the range for table
    REM add table to the doc, with number of rows and columns
    Call hwddoc.Tables.Add(myrange, 1, 12)
    REM NOTE: we are automatically in row 1, col 1

    Print "Adding field names..."
    REM set the column titles in the doc
    For z = 0 To 11
      REM ' sets the field value into the current cell
      hwd.Selection.TypeText(contfld(z))
      REM first param is move cell, second param is
      REM how many cells to move over
      Call hwd.Selection.moveright(12,1)
```

```
  Next

  Print "Field names added; now adding Contact data..."
  Set contdoc = contcol.GetFirstDocument
  dcount = contcol.Count
  REM add the field values to the table
  Do While Not(contdoc Is Nothing)
    REM if it isn't a person doc, skip it
    If contdoc.Form(0) = "Person" Then
      For z = 0 To 11
        REM sets the field value into the current cell
        hwd.Selection.TypeText(contdoc._
        GetItemValue(contfld(z))(0))
        REM first param is move cell,
        REM second param is how many cells to move over.
        REM if it is the last cell of the last record,
        REM we don't move again because that causes
        REM a blank row to show up
        If Not(dcount = 1 And z = 11) Then &_
        Call hwd.Selection.moveright(12,1)
      Next
    Else
      Print "Document form is " & contdoc.Form(0) &_
      ", needed to be Contact or Person - skipping..."
    End If
    Set contdoc = contcol.GetNextDocument(contdoc)
    dcount = dcount - 1
    Print dcount & " documents left to process..."
  Loop

  REM save and close this doc once we're done
  Call hwddoc.SaveAs(cfilename, 0)
  Call hwddoc.close(0,1)
  Set hwddoc = Nothing
getOut:
  Exit Function

errHandler:
  On Error Goto 0
  createDataFile = False
  Error Err, Error$ & " [in createDataFile]"
End Function
```

The `createDataFile` function builds the data file used for the merge. The data file is built from the documents selected in the user's Personal Address Book. Take a look at the details of the code, beginning with the signature line of the function:

```
Function createDataFile(contcol As NotesDocumentCollection, cfilename
As String, hwd As Variant, hwddoc As Variant) As Boolean
```

The function takes four parameters:

✦ `contcol`: This is the `NotesDocumentCollection` object containing the contact documents the user selected in the Personal Address Book.

✦ `cfilename`: When this parameter is initially passed in, it is an empty string (" "). The value gets created inside the function, and it is passed back out of the function when the function finishes executing.

✦ `hwd, hwddoc`: These two parameters are the handles to the Word application object (`hwd`) and the data file document (`hwddoc`). You should use separate handles for all objects and sub objects when working with other applications. These two parameters are initially empty when passed into the function, and the objects are created and passed back when the function ends.

One of the neat techniques used in the functions in this agent is the ability to pass modified parameters back out of the function. This allows your functions to do a great deal more, and then you can pass a state back on the actual function — in this example, the functions pass back `True` if they work correctly, and `False` if an error is thrown. The real data is passed back on the parameters. When the `createDataFile` function finishes running, it passes back the filename of the data file, the handle to the Word application, and the handle to the document.

The next few lines establish an array of field names from the Contact form in the Personal Address Book. Because these fields do not change between releases, this agent also works in Release 5, as long as you change the Boolean data types to `Variant`. The establishment of the fields array is as follows:

```
contfld(0) = "FirstName"
contfld(1) = "MiddleInitial"
contfld(2) = "LastName"
contfld(3) = "CompanyName"
contfld(4) = "JobTitle"
contfld(5) = "OfficeStreetAddress"
contfld(6) = "OfficeCity"
contfld(7) = "OfficeState"
contfld(8) = "OfficeZIP"
contfld(9) = "OfficeCountry"
contfld(10) = "OfficePhoneNumber"
contfld(11) = "OfficeFAXPhoneNumber"
```

The next section of the function creates the Word application, and then checks it to see if it is an acceptable version:

```
Set hwd  = CreateObject("Word.Application")
hwd.Visible = False
wordver = hwd.Version
If Cint(wordver) > 9 Then Error 900, "You must use " &_
"MS Word 2000 or less, not XP."
```

The `CreateObject` function creates the specified object. The object name for MS Word was determined by checking the References tab in Designer, as shown in Figure 31-5. In that figure, the name of the application is `word.application.9`. Because this code works with earlier versions of Word other than 2000 (which is version 9), you can leave off the version number from the application name, as shown in this example.

Although this code works with earlier versions of Word, it does not work with Word XP because the merge object model has completely changed. Code has been added to the function to test the version number, and if the version number is greater than 9 (Word 2000), an error is thrown. The error is a custom error message that is passed back to the user to inform her that the version of Word she is using is wrong.

After the Word application is validated as the right version, the directory where the data file is to be stored is determined:

```
cfilename = Environ("TEMP") & "\merge"
tst = Dir(cfilename, 16)
If tst = "" Then Mkdir(cfilename)
cfilename = cfilename & "\mrgdata.doc"
```

The Environ function returns the environmental parameter you specify. In this case, the Windows temp directory is returned from the TEMP variable, and a new subdirectory name is concatenated to it — "\merge". The code determines if the directory already exists. If it does not, the directory is created. Finally, the name of the file is added to the directory path.

The next segment of code creates a table and adds the field names to the table:

```
Call hwd.documents.Add    ' create the new doc
Set hwddoc = hwd.ActiveDocument
Call hwddoc.SaveAs(cfilename, 0)    ' give it a file name
Set myrange = hwddoc.Range(0,0)    ' set the range for table
REM add table to the doc, with number of rows and columns
Call hwddoc.Tables.Add(myrange, 1, 12)
REM NOTE: we are automatically in row 1, col 1

Print "Adding field names..."
REM set the column titles in the doc
For z = 0 To 11
  REM ' sets the field value into the current cell
  hwd.Selection.TypeText(contfld(z))
  REM first param is move cell, second param is
  REM how many cells to move over
  Call hwd.Selection.moveright(12,1)
Next
```

A document is created in the application, and then it is saved using the file name that was created earlier. A range is then established so that the code knows where to place the data table. The data table is created to the size needed with one row — as the code walks the row, it automatically adds a new row at the end of a row, similar to the way Word works when you tab through a table in the UI.

The field names are added to the table using the TypeText method in Word. After the field name is added to the cell, the cursor is moved to the next cell using the MoveRight method. After all the field names are added, the documents in the collection are processed and the data is added to the table using the same technique, as shown in the following code:

```
Print "Field names added; now adding Contact data..."
Set contdoc = contcol.GetFirstDocument
dcount = contcol.Count
REM add the field values to the table
Do While Not(contdoc Is Nothing)
  REM if it isn't a person doc, skip it
  If contdoc.Form(0) = "Person" Then
    For z = 0 To 11
      REM sets the field value into the current cell
      hwd.Selection.TypeText(contdoc._
```

```
       GetItemValue(contfld(z))(0))
       REM first param is move cell,
       REM second param is how many cells to move over.
       REM if it is the last cell of the last record,
       REM we don't move again because that causes
       REM a blank row to show up
       If Not(dcount = 1 And z = 11) Then &_
       Call hwd.Selection.moveright(12,1)
     Next
   Else
     Print "Document form is " & contdoc.Form(0) &_
     ", needed to be Contact or Person - skipping..."
   End If
   Set contdoc = contcol.GetNextDocument(contdoc)
   dcount = dcount - 1
   Print dcount & " documents left to process..."
 Loop
```

The Form item on the document is checked to ensure that the document is a Person document. If it is, the desired fields are added to the data file using the same technique that added the field names.

The document is saved, and the various objects are closed:

```
REM save and close this doc once we're done
Call hwddoc.SaveAs(cfilename, 0)
Call hwddoc.close(0,1)
Set hwddoc = Nothing
```

The Word document object is saved, closed, and the handle is set to Nothing. This is done to clean up memory and prevent crashes.

> **Tip**   Whenever you work with COM/OLE objects, it's a good idea to remove them from memory immediately after you're done. This prevents possible memory leaks, and in the worst case scenario, crashes.

The application object isn't closed, because it's going to be used later on. The Word document is closed, but the handle is still passed out on the function. This is in case an error occurs while the document is open — all error handling and the resolution of those errors is done at the main, calling code level. The handle to all objects should be passed to your error handling code to make sure the object handles get closed.

Take a look at the following code for the error-handling segment of this function:

```
getOut:
  Exit Function

errHandler:
  On Error Goto 0
  createDataFile = False
  Error Err, Error$ & " [in createDataFile]"
End Function
```

At the beginning of this function is the following line:

```
On Error Goto errHandler
```

This line causes the code to jump to the errHandler label whenever an error occurs. In Listing 31-11, the errHandler label is another On Error statement that sets the Goto to 0. LotusScript knows that if an error occurs from here on to pass the error back up to the code that called the function. The next line sets the function to False. The next line is interesting: Because the On Error for this part of the code is reset, you can use this to your advantage by adding your own custom information to the existing error that was originally thrown. In this case, the name of the function is added to the actual error. That error statement and error number are passed back up to the calling code where the main error-handling code resides. This enables your error message to have more useful information, and enables you to concentrate your cleanup code in one place. Listing 31-11 shows the openWordMergeDoc function.

Listing 31-11: NAB Merge Example Agent (Part 3)

```
OpenWordMergeDoc function
Function openWordMergeDoc(cfilename As String, hwd As Variant, hwddoc
As Variant) As Boolean
  openWordMergeDoc = True
  On Error Goto errHandler

  hwd.documents.Add    ' create the new doc
  Set hwddoc = hwd.ActiveDocument
  hwddoc.MailMerge.MainDocumentType = 0    ' tell word this
will be a merge
  REM  open the data source we created in createDataFile
  hwddoc.MailMerge.OpenDataSource cfilename, 5, False
  hwddoc.MailMerge.EditMainDocument  ' put the cursor in the
doc

  hwd.Visible = True   ' show the blank merge letter, ready to
go, to the user
getOut:
  Exit Function
errHandler:
  On Error Goto 0
  openWordMergeDoc = False
  Error Err, Error$ & " [in openWordMergeDoc]"
End Function
```

This function pulls it all together by creating a new Word document, telling that new document that it is a merge document, providing it the file path to the data source file that was created earlier, and then presenting the results to the user. The same type of error handling just described is used here as well, including the addition of the function name to the error message. Various parameters are set for the Word document — but how do you know which parameters to set?

The easiest way to learn how to work with Word is to record a macro performing the action you want to use. In the preceding code, a Word macro was recorded and converted to LotusScript. The hardest part of the conversion is learning what parameters Microsoft uses, because their parameters are all constants that aren't available to you in LotusScript. These constants translate to integer values, so the easiest way to determine the constant value is to write a simple macro in Word that presents an `MsgBox` containing the constant. If you use the constant name for the `MsgBox`, the number is returned to you. If, for example, you need to know the integer equivalent of the constant `wdFieldUserName`, you create a Word macro with the following:

```
MsgBox wdFieldUserName
```

You get a message box with the number 60 in it, which is the integer equivalent of `wdFieldUserName`.

Working with other applications, especially Microsoft Word, can prove useful. Practice these techniques to explore more ways to integrate Notes with other products.

Working with the C API from LotusScript

LotusScript provides tremendous functionality, especially when you include the ability to work with COM/OLE objects. But you may need functionality that isn't available in LotusScript — it may be available in the C API (application programming interface) of Notes/Domino, or even the Win32 C API (the foundation API of Windows operating systems).

Working with the Notes C API

LotusScript is built on a core API, known as the C API. The C API is the foundation of all other languages in Notes/Domino — Formula, Java, JavaScript, and LotusScript. But these other languages don't contain all the functionality available. Sometimes you have to work with the C API from LotusScript, and it can be difficult. Mistakes in working with the C API can cause the dreaded Red Box of Death (RBOD). This section shows you how to safely work with the C API and helps you understand the nuances of working with it.

The biggest difference between the C API and LotusScript is the data types used. Some data types are the same (Integer, Single, Double), some are totally different, and some are named the same but work differently (string). If you can understand the data types, working with the C API is going to be much easier for you.

To begin understanding the C API, refer to the Lotus C API Reference database available for download from the Documentation Library in the Lotus Developer Domain, formerly known as Notes.Net (`www-10.lotus.com/ldd` or `notes.net`). You're going to begin with the function called `NSFDbInfoGet`. This function returns some basic information about a database, such as title, categories, and so on. If you take a look at the help for the `NSFDbInfoGet` call, it defines the syntax as follows:

```
STATUS LNPUBLIC NSFDbInfoGet(
            DBHANDLE   hDB,
            char far *retBuffer
            );
```

The help file shows the data type before the parameter, so `DBHANDLE` is the data type of the `hDB` parameter, and `char` is the data type for `retBuffer`. The `far` word after `char` is for 16-bit legacy applications, so you can ignore it. Now you need to translate the code to LotusScript data types.

`DBHANDLE` is a data type of Long (keep in mind that any object handle you access through the C API is a long). The `retBuffer` variable is where the function places the results of the function — the database info. `retBuffer` is a pointer to a string buffer, which is an allotment of memory of a fixed size used to hold a string. Because LotusScript hides all that messy memory allotment from LotusScript developers, you have to set up strings in a special way for them to be used with the C API. The size of the string must be preset to the maximum size before it is passed to the C API function — this is how you set up the string buffer that the C API expects. You learn how to do that in the next example; first you must learn how to declare a C API function for use in LotusScript.

You declare the NSFDbInfoGet function in the (Declarations) area of your code as follows:

```
Declare Function W32_GetDbInfo Lib "nnotes.dll"_
Alias "NSFDbInfoGet"( Byval hdb As Long,_
Byval dbinfo As String )  As Integer
```

The Declare Function part is self-explanatory. W32_GetDbInfo is the name you want to use to reference the function in your code. Lib "nnotes.dll" tells the declaration where the function you want to use lives. C API functions live in files called Dynamic Link Libraries (DLLs). A DLL is like a Script Library — it's a way to encapsulate code and make it reusable. Alias "NSFDbInfoGet" is the name of the function in the DLL. All published C API functions are accessed through a single DLL; for Windows that file is nnotes.dll. The first letter indicates the operating system — in this case n means Windows. The name of this DLL for other operating systems is as follows:

✦ **nnotes.dll:** all Win32 operating systems

✦ **anotes.dll:** DEC Alpha

✦ **inotes.dll:** OS/2

✦ **libnotes_r.a:** IBM AIX

✦ **libnotes:** IBM S/390

✦ **libnotes.so:** Solaris SPARC, Solaris Intel, Linux

✦ **libnotes.sl:** Hewlett Packard HP-UX

✦ **noteslib:** Macintosh

Tip　　When providing a name to use when calling C API functions, you should prepend the function name with some type of indicator of the operating system. This is because the DLL used is different based on the operating system. In this case, the first n of the DLL name — nnotes.dll — indicates that this is for Win32. W32 is prepended to the function name.

The parameters are as follows:

✦ hdb: This is the handle to the NotesDatabase from which you want to gather information.

✦ dbinfo: This is the String variable that holds the database information.

The function returns an integer value to tell you whether it was successful. A zero (0) indicates success, and any other number indicates an error condition.

You may wonder how you call your newly declared function. Listing 31-12 is the Ch 31.\01. Basic DB Info agent. This agent uses the C API to get the title of the database. A LotusScript way exists for getting this information, but this is an example designed to introduce you more to concepts and syntax than to a useful C API call.

Listing 31-12: Basic DB Info Agent

```
Options
Option Public
Option Explicit

Declarations
REM the first two are used to open and close
REM the Notes database
Declare Function W32_NSFDbOpen Lib "nnotes.dll"_
Alias "NSFDbOpen" ( Byval dbName As String, hdb As Long )_
As Integer
Declare Function W32_NSFDbClose Lib "nnotes.dll"_
Alias "NSFDbClose" ( Byval hdb As Long ) As Integer

REM Here is the one Rocky described.
Declare Function W32_GetDbInfo Lib "nnotes.dll"_
Alias "NSFDbInfoGet" ( Byval hdb As Long,_
Byval dbinfo As String )  As Integer

Const NSF_INFO_SIZE% = 128   ' Max size of the NSFInfo buffer

Initialize
Sub Initialize
  Dim s As New NotesSession
  Dim db As NotesDatabase
  REM this establishes the string for the path,
  REM the variable to catch the returned code,
  REM and the long variable for the database handle
  Dim dbpath as String, rc as Integer, hdb as Long

  Set db = s.CurrentDatabase

  REM Build the path for this database.
  REM if the server is local then we don't want
  REM the double bang (!!) in there
  If db.Server = "" Then dbpath$ = db.FilePath _
  Else dbpath$ = db.Server & "!!" & db.FilePath
  REM notice the double bang (!!) to separate
  REM the server from the database.

  REM Get a C long handle on the db.
  REM When using C API functions that require a database
  REM handle you need to use NSFDbOpen to get the handle,
  REM and NSFDbClose to clean up the memory after you are
  REM done using the db.
  REM If you don't, you leave "garbage" in the memory
  REM that *could* cause problems.

  REM the NSFDbOpen function takes the string containing
  REM the server!!dbfilepath
```

```
    REM from above, and the empty long variable that
    REM will contain the database handle that is returned
    REM by the function
    rc% = W32_NSFDbOpen(dbpath$, hdb& )

    REM error checking to make sure an error isn't returned;
    REM if it is, get out.
    If rc% <> 0 Then
      Messagebox "Couldn't open database.",, "Bummer, Dude."
      Exit Sub
    End If

    REM This is the place where the string buffer is
    REM established for the dbinfo that is returned.
    REM Notice that we first establish the string variable,
    REM  then set an empty string of NSF_INFO_SIZE
    REM (the constant declared in the Declarations area) into
    REM it to establish a 128 character buffer.
    Dim  NSFInfoBuffer$
    NSFInfoBuffer$ = String(NSF_INFO_SIZE%, 0)

    REM now get the db information (title, categories, etc.)
    rc% = W32_GetDbInfo( hdb&, NSFInfoBuffer$ )

    REM make sure that an error isn't returned; if one is,
    REM then tell the user, and close the db then exit
    If rc% <> 0 Then
      Messagebox "Didn't get the title info - sorry.",,_
      "No Soup for You!"
      rc% = W32_NSFDbClose( hdb& )
      Exit Sub
    End If

    REM get just the title, and trim off the extra spaces
    NSFInfoBuffer$ = Left$( NSFInfoBuffer$, _
    Instr( NSFInfoBuffer$, Chr$( 0 ) ) - 1)

    Msgbox "The DB Title is:" & Chr$(10) &_
    NSFInfoBuffer$,, "The Sweet Smell of Success"

    REM clean up after ourselves to keep the memory tidy
    rc% = W32_NSFDbClose( hdb& )
  End Sub
```

Two additional C API functions are declared in the (Declarations) — NSFDbOpen and
NSFDbClose. These functions get a handle to the database, and then close it when you're
through. In many API calls, you must explicitly open and close objects on your own. This
requirement to clean up your own memory is different from normal LotusScript objects,
which automatically get cleaned up out of memory when you're done using them. The automatic cleanup of objects is called garbage collection, and the C API expects you to clean up
your own garbage.

Take a look at this next line, which gets the server and database of the current database:

```
If db.Server = "" Then dbpath$ = db.FilePath _
Else dbpath$ = db.Server & "!!" & db.FilePath
```

The code checks the server. If there is a server name, it's concatenated with the database file path by the use of two exclamation points, otherwise known as double-bang syntax. It's common in the C API to use the double-bang syntax to specify a server and database path.

Review the following lines:

```
rc% = W32_NSFDbOpen(dbpath$, hdb& )
If rc% <> 0 Then
  Messagebox "Couldn't open database.",, "Bummer, Dude."
  Exit Sub
End If
```

The first line opens a C API database handle to the database. The dbpath parameter contains the server!!database syntax, and the hdb variable is passed in empty to the variable. The function then gets a handle to the desired database, and the handle to that database is placed in the hdb variable and passed back to the user. The If statement that follows checks the rc variable to make sure a zero is passed back to the user. A nonzero value indicates that the function failed to get a handle to the database.

Now that you have a handle to the database, you can use the NSFDbGetInfo function, which is aliased as W32_GetDBInfo, to get the database information:

```
Dim  NSFInfoBuffer as String
NSFInfoBuffer$ = String(NSF_INFO_SIZE%, 0)

REM now get the db information (title, categories, etc.)
rc% = W32_GetDbInfo( hdb&, NSFInfoBuffer$ )

REM make sure that an error isn't returned; if one is,
REM then tell the user, and close the db then exit
If rc% <> 0 Then
  Messagebox "Didn't get the title info - sorry.",,_
  "No Soup for You!"
  rc% = W32_NSFDbClose( hdb& )
  Exit Sub
End If
```

The NSFInfoBuffer variable is a String buffer variable that holds what the W32_GetDBInfo function returns. The buffer is set to the size of the integer in the NSF_INFO_SIZE constant, which is 128 characters. The 0 in the String call tells the function to use spaces for the 128 characters. The largest string returned from the W32_GetDBInfo function is 128 characters.

When the W32_GetDBInfo function is called, the handle to the database is passed in as the first parameter, and the 128-character string buffer (full of spaces) is also passed in. The function then returns the results in the NSFInfoStringBuffer, and the function returns a 0 because it was successful. If, for some reason, the function wasn't successful, it returns a value that isn't zero. The If statement below the function call catches that, alerts the user, and closes the database handle.

The final bit of code takes the returned string and removes the title from it, and then provides a prompt to the user informing her of the title of the database:

```
NSFInfoBuffer$ = Left$( NSFInfoBuffer$, _
Instr( NSFInfoBuffer$, Chr$( 0 ) ) - 1)
```

```
Msgbox "The DB Title is:" & Chr$(10) &_
NSFInfoBuffer$,, "The Sweet Smell of Success"

rc% = W32_NSFDbClose( hdb& )
```

Remember that the string that is passed into this function is 128 characters long. The information returned by the function is stored in this 128 character string, which remains 128 characters long — any unused portion of the buffer is still filled with null string characters. Additionally, each bit of information returned by the function is separated by a null character as well. The first line of the code finds the first null character (Char(0)) and returns the part of the string to the left of it, which is the title. It is returned in a message box, and the database handle is closed.

Tip   Make sure you close all handles that you open in your code that calls the C API, or you could experience errors.

This next example is from the Ch 31. DB Info Samples\02. Advanced DB Info agent. It builds on the last example and adds a new function, NSFDbInfoParse. Listing 31-13 shows the agent code.

Listing 31-13: **Advanced DB Info Agent**

```
Declarations
REM the first two are used to open and close the Notes
database
Declare Function W32_NSFDbOpen Lib "nnotes.dll"_
Alias "NSFDbOpen" ( Byval dbName As String,_
hdb As Long ) As Integer

Declare Function W32_NSFDbClose Lib "nnotes.dll"_
Alias "NSFDbClose" ( Byval hdb As Long ) As Integer

Declare Function W32_GetDbInfo Lib "nnotes.dll"_
Alias "NSFDbInfoGet"( Byval hdb As Long,_
Byval dbinfo As String )  As Integer

Declare Sub W32_NSFDBInfoParse Lib "nnotes.dll"_
Alias "NSFDbInfoParse"(Byval info As String,_
Byval what As Long, Byval outMsg As String, _
Byval outLen As Long)

Const NSF_INFO_SIZE% = 128    '*** Maximum size of the NSFInfo
buffer.

Const INFOPARSE_TITLE = 0 ' -  database title.
Const INFOPARSE_CATEGORIES = 1 ' -  database categories.
Const INFOPARSE_CLASS   = 2 '-  template name
Const INFOPARSE_DESIGN_CLASS = 3 '-  inherited template name
```

Continued

Listing 31-13 *(continued)*

```
Initialize sub
Sub Initialize
  Dim s As New NotesSession
  Dim db As NotesDatabase
  REM this establishes the string for the path,
  REM the variable to catch the returned code,
  REM and the long variable for the database handle
  Dim dbpath As String, rc As Integer, hdb As Long
  REM Used to locate and remove the trailing character
  REM that C uses to terminate strings
  Dim wpos As Integer
  REM Set up a memory are that can be used by the
  REM API calls to store the reults
  Dim Buffer2 As String*255
  Dim DBTitle As String
  Dim DBCategories As String
  Dim DBClass As String
  Dim DBTemplate As String

  Set db = s.CurrentDatabase

  REM Build the path for this database.
  REM if the server is local then we don't want
  REM the double bang (!!) in there
  If db.Server = "" Then dbpath$ = db.FilePath _
  Else dbpath$ = db.Server & "!!" & db.FilePath
  REM notice the double bang (!!) to separate
  REM the server from the database.

  REM Get a C long handle on the db.
  REM When using C API functions that require a
  REM database handle you need to use NSFDbOpen to get the
  REM handle,and NSFDbClose to clean up the memory after you
  REM are done using the db.
  REM If you don't, you leave "garbage" in the memory
  REM that *could* cause problems.

  REM the NSFDbOpen function takes the string containing
  REM the server!!dbfilepath from above, and the empty
  REM long variable that will contain the database
  REM handle that is returned by the function
  rc% = W32_NSFDbOpen(dbpath$, hdb& )

  REM error checking to make sure an error isn't returned;
  REM if it is, get out.
  If rc% <> 0 Then
    Messagebox "Couldn't open database.",, "Bummer, Dude."
    Exit Sub
  End If

  REM This is the place where the string buffer is
```

```
REM established for the dbinfo that is returned.
REM Notice that we first establish the string variable,
REM  then set an empty string of NSF_INFO_SIZE
REM (the constant declared in the Declarations area)
REM into it to establish a 128 character buffer.
Dim  NSFInfoBuffer$
NSFInfoBuffer$ = String(NSF_INFO_SIZE%, 0)

REM now get the db information (title, categories, etc.)
rc% = W32_GetDbInfo( hdb&, NSFInfoBuffer$ )

REM make sure that an error isn't returned; if one is,
REM then tell the user, close the db, and get out.
If rc% <> 0 Then
  Messagebox "Didn't get the title info - sorry.",,_
  "No Soup for You!"
  rc% = W32_NSFDbClose( hdb& )
  Exit Sub
End If

REM Parse off the trailing nuill character to make it
REM an LS String again....
Call W32_NSFDBInfoParse(NSFInfoBuffer$, INFOPARSE_TITLE,_
buffer2, NSF_INFO_SIZE )
wpos = Instr(1, buffer2, Chr(0))
DBTitle = Left$(Cstr(Buffer2), (wpos- 1))

REM Parse the Database Categories
Call W32_NSFDBInfoParse(NSFInfoBuffer$,_
INFOPARSE_CATEGORIES, buffer2, NSF_INFO_SIZE )
wpos = Instr(1, buffer2, Chr(0))
DBCategories = Left$(Cstr(Buffer2), (wpos- 1))

REM Parse the Database Class - Template Name
Call W32_NSFDBInfoParse(NSFInfoBuffer$,_
INFOPARSE_CLASS, buffer2, NSF_INFO_SIZE )
wpos = Instr(1, buffer2, Chr(0))
DBClass = Left$(Cstr(Buffer2), (wpos- 1))

REM Parse the Database Design Class
Call W32_NSFDBInfoParse(NSFInfoBuffer$,_
INFOPARSE_DESIGN_CLASS, buffer2, NSF_INFO_SIZE )
wpos = Instr(1, buffer2, Chr(0))
DBTemplate = Left$(Cstr(Buffer2), (wpos- 1))

 REM Display it all
Msgbox "The DB Title is:" & DBTitle & Chr(10) & _
"Categories:    " & DBCategories & Chr(10) & _
"Class:         " & DBClass & Chr(10) & _
"Design Class: " & DBTemplate

REM ' clean up after ourselves to keep the memory tidy
rc% = W32_NSFDbClose( hdb& )
End Sub
```

This code is basically the same as the preceding example, except that now you are using a new C API function that automatically parses the information returned by NSFDBInfoGet. The declaration for the new function is as follows.

```
Declare Sub W32_NSFDBInfoParse Lib "nnotes.dll"_
Alias "NSFDbInfoParse"(Byval info As String,_
Byval what As Long, Byval outMsg As String, _
Byval outLen As Long)
```

The NSFDbInfoParse function takes the info returned by the NSFDbInfoGet function, parses it, and returns the information you want. The constants in the following code defines the types of information you can get from the function, which includes the title, categories (used in the database catalog), the design template name, and the inherited design template name. All this information is available in the Database Properties box.

```
Const INFOPARSE_TITLE = 0 ' - database title.
Const INFOPARSE_CATEGORIES = 1 ' - database categories.
Const INFOPARSE_CLASS   = 2 '- template name
Const INFOPARSE_DESIGN_CLASS = 3 '- inherited template name
```

The NSFDbInfoParse function is then used in the main part of the code (the Initialize event) to parse out the info string, as shown in the following code:

```
REM Parse off the trailing nuill character to make it
  REM an LS String again....
  Call W32_NSFDBInfoParse(NSFInfoBuffer$, INFOPARSE_TITLE,_
  buffer2, NSF_INFO_SIZE )
  wpos = Instr(1, buffer2, Chr(0))
  DBTitle = Left$(Cstr(Buffer2), (wpos- 1))

  REM Parse the Database Categories
  Call W32_NSFDBInfoParse(NSFInfoBuffer$,_
  INFOPARSE_CATEGORIES, buffer2, NSF_INFO_SIZE )
  wpos = Instr(1, buffer2, Chr(0))
  DBCategories = Left$(Cstr(Buffer2), (wpos- 1))

  REM Parse the Database Class - Template Name
  Call W32_NSFDBInfoParse(NSFInfoBuffer$,_
  INFOPARSE_CLASS, buffer2, NSF_INFO_SIZE )
  wpos = Instr(1, buffer2, Chr(0))
  DBClass = Left$(Cstr(Buffer2), (wpos- 1))

  REM Parse the Database Design Class
  Call W32_NSFDBInfoParse(NSFInfoBuffer$,_
  INFOPARSE_DESIGN_CLASS, buffer2, NSF_INFO_SIZE )
  wpos = Instr(1, buffer2, Chr(0))
  DBTemplate = Left$(Cstr(Buffer2), (wpos- 1))

   REM Display it all
  Msgbox "The DB Title is:" & DBTitle & Chr(10) & _
  "Categories:     " & DBCategories & Chr(10) & _
  "Class:          " & DBClass & Chr(10) & _
  "Design Class: " & DBTemplate

  REM ' clean up after ourselves to keep the memory tidy
  rc% = W32_NSFDbClose( hdb& )
```

This code uses the `W32_NSFDBInfoParse` function (which is the alias for the `NSFDBInfoParse` C API function) over and over to get each part of the database info, and then the database information is presented to the user. Finally, the database handle is closed.

Working with the Win32 API

Working with the Win32 API is similar to working with the Notes C API — the biggest difference is trying to find out what is available. Various books can help you, but the easiest way to find out what is available and how to call the Win32 API is from a freeware tool called the API Guide. It's available from `AllAPI.net`, and is also available for download from `ndbible.com`.

You may need the ability to work with the registry from LotusScript. You can't do this cleanly from within LotusScript, so you have to get dirty and work with the Win32 API. The declarations and structure are basically the same as working with the Notes C API, as demonstrated in the following example.

The code shown in Listing 31-14 enables you to get the path to the executable of any program installed on your machine, as long as the program registered itself in the Registry.

Listing 31-14: **Win32 API Example Agent**

```
Declarations
Declare Function RegOpenKeyExA Lib "advapi32"_
Alias "RegOpenKeyExA" (Byval HKEY As Long,_
Byval lpszSubKey As String,Byval dwreserved As Integer,_
Byval samDesired As Long, keyresult As Long) As Long

Declare Function RegQueryValueExA Lib "advapi32"_
Alias "RegQueryValueExA" (Byval HKEY As Long,_
Byval lpszValueName As String,Byval dwreserved As Integer,_
lpdwtype As Long, Byval lpData As String, readbytes As Long)_
As Long

Declare Function RegCloseKey Lib "advapi32"_
Alias "RegCloseKey" (Byval HKEY As Long) As Long

REM the base keys of the registry.
REM we will be drilling into HKEY_LOCAL_MACHINE
REM in this instance
REM these are hex values
Const HKEY_LOCAL_MACHINE = &H80000002
Const HKEY_CURRENT_USER = &H80000001

REM keys used by C function calls.
REM used to navigate registry
Const KEY_QUERY_VALUE = 1
Const KEY_ENUMERATE_SUBKEYS = 8
Const KEY_NOTIFY = 16
Const KEY_READ = KEY_QUERY_VALUE Or _
KEY_ENUMERATE_SUBKEYS Or KEY_NOTIFY
```

Continued

Listing 31-14 *(continued)*

Initialize
```
Sub Initialize
  Dim app As String, AppPath As String

  app$ = Inputbox("Enter the name of an .EXE file you" &_
  " want to locate.", "Name of App", "NOTES.EXE"

  AppPath = LocatePath(app$) ' call the function

  REM test and display the results
  If AppPath = Ustring(Len(AppPath), 32) Then
    Msgbox app & " not found.",,"Not Found"
  Else
    Msgbox "The path to your EXE is:" & Chr(10) &_
    AppPath$,,"Success!"
  End If
End Sub
```

LocatePath Function
```
Function LocatePath(ApplicationName As String)
  Dim happkey As Long
  Dim ValueType As Long
  Dim ReturnedKeyContents As String * 255
  Dim readbytes As Long
  Dim rc As Integer
  Dim basename As String, keyname As String
  Dim valuename As String

  REM C likes to know how long it's strings might be
  REM sets up the returned key variable
  ReturnedKeycontents = String$(255,Chr$(32))

  REM  this is the default part of the key
  BaseName  = "Software\Microsoft\Windows\" &_
  "CurrentVersion\App Paths\"

  REM this adds the user-entered exe to
  REM the basename, creating the key
  KeyName = BaseName$ + ApplicationName

  REM a null or empty string represents the default value
  ValueName  = ""

  REM get a handle on the key
  rc=RegOpenKeyExA(HKEY_LOCAL_MACHINE,_
  KeyName$,0,KEY_READ,happkey)

  REM contains the size of the buffer passed in,
  REM and contains the size of the buffer passed back
  ReadBytes=255
```

```
REM get the value of the desired key
rc=RegQueryValueExA(happkey,ValueName$,0,valueType,_
ReturnedKeyContents$,ReadBytes)

Call regCloseKey(happkey) ' release the handle of the key

REM format and return the result
LocatePath = Left$(ReturnedKeyContents$,ReadBytes-1)
End Function
```

The calls setting up the declarations are basically the same as before. You declare the functions you need, define an alias, and set up the parameters. With this application, you need to have functions to open a key (RegOpenKeyExA), find a value (RegQueryValueExA), and close a key (RegCloseKey). The LocatePath function uses these declarations to find the application path for the executable, and then returns it.

If you want to make some C API functions available to your developers, but you don't want to require them to learn how to work with the C API, you can wrap your functions in a user-defined class. Creating LotusScript classes is covered in the next section.

Creating LotusScript Classes

Creating a LotusScript class enables you to provide an object of your own that represents data and functionality as a single object with which you can work. You have an understanding of how classes and objects work. Now you can leverage that understanding to build your own classes, which will help you understand how classes and objects work.

Classes are defined in the (Declarations) area of your script. You should set up a separate LotusScript library for your classes — it makes them easier to access and modify, and it makes more sense when reading your code.

Creating classes requires a great deal more than what is covered here. This section is just an introduction to creating a class and using an object created from this class. The following class wraps the getting and setting of a Registry value to make it easier for your developers to do this, without the need to understand the many steps needed to work with the C API from LotusScript.

When you create a class, you create the public interface available to objects created from your class. These interfaces include properties and methods. A property in a class is simply a variable that has a value and is available publicly. A method in a class is simply a sub or function that is publicly available. You can also define classes with private variables and functions — these are usually used to do some work internally to present the requested data or complete the requested task.

Note Your class requires two subs — New (used to create the class) and Delete (used to destroy the class and perform cleanup).

RegistryClass is defined in the example database, in a LotusScript library called RegistryClass. All the code of this class is in the (Declarations) area, as shown in Listing 31-15. This listing doesn't contain all the C API declarations or constants — it's a long listing that doesn't show the meat of creating a class. Take a look at it in the example database for details.

Listing 31-15: RegistryClass Code

```
Declarations, below the setup of the C API calls and
constants
REM definition of the RegistryClass
Class RegistryClass
  REM these are private variables available
  REM to the subs and functions
  khdl As Long
  hkey As Variant
  retflg As Integer
  retvalsize As Integer
  rc As Integer

  REM these are the public variables, or properties
  Public keyname As String
  Public  subkeyname As String
  Public wholekeyname As String
  Public subkeyval As String

  Sub new (hk As Variant, kname As String)
    keyname = kname
    hkey = hk
  End Sub

  REM all classes should have a New sub and a Delete sub
  Sub Delete()
    If khdl <> 0 Then
      Call RegCloseKey(khdl)
    End If
  End Sub

  Public Function getKeyValue(skname As String) As String
    Dim skval As String, defval As String
    Dim vtype As Long
    retvalsize = 255
    subkeyname = skname
    wholekeyname = keyname & skname
    defval = ""
    skval = String$(255,Chr$(32))
    rc = RegOpenKeyEx(hkey, wholekeyname, 0,KEY_READ, khdl)
    If rc <> ERROR_SUCCESS Then
      Exit Function
    End If
    rc = RegQueryValue(khdl,defval,0,vtype, skval,retvalsize)
    subkeyval = Trim(Left$(skval,retvalsize-1))
    getKeyValue = subkeyval
  End Function

  Public Function setKeyValue(skname As String,_
  skvalue As String) As String
```

```
      wholekeyname = keyname & skname
      rc = RegOpenKeyEx(hkey, wholekeyname, 0,_
      KEY_ALL_ACCESS, khdl)
      If rc <> ERROR_SUCCESS Then
        rc = RegCreateKey(hkey, wholekeyname, khdl)
      End If
      rc = RegSetValueEx(khdl, skname, 0, REG_SZ,_
      skvalue, retvalsize)
      subkeyname = skname
      subkeyval = skvalue
   End Function
End Class
```

Private and public variables are declared initially. The public variables are the properties of the class. The listing has two subs — New and Delete. The New sub takes a couple of user-defined parameters and assigns them to the needed properties. The Delete sub cleans up the registry handle that is opened when working with the registry. This sub is automatically called when a RegistryClass object is unloaded from memory.

The two functions, getKeyValue and setKeyValue, are declared with the word Public before them. Users can call these functions as methods to a RegistryClass object.

Listing 31-16 shows the Ch 31. Class Test Example agent. It uses the RegistryClass to perform the same work as the example in Listing 31-14, namely returning the file path to the executable named by the user. The agent uses the class to find the path to the executable by searching the Registry.

Listing 31-16: **Class Test Example Agent**

```
Sub Initialize
   Dim kname As String
   Dim subkname As String
   Dim appname As String
   Dim applocation As String
   Dim robj As RegistryClass

   appname = Inputbox("Enter the name of an .EXE file" &_
   " you want to locate.", "Name of App", "NOTES.EXE")

   If appname = "" Then Exit Sub

   Set robj = New RegistryClass(HKEY_LOCAL_MACHINE,_
   "Software\Microsoft\Windows\CurrentVersion\App Paths\")

   applocation = robj.getKeyValue(appname)

   Msgbox "The path to your EXE is:" & Chr(10) &_
   applocation,,"Registry Class Test"
End Sub
```

The class makes it much cleaner and easier to attain some fairly complex functionality. Understanding the building of classes greatly enhances your LotusScript prowess. You should take some time and practice building classes on your own.

Summary

This chapter covered advanced topics for working with LotusScript, including the following:

✦ Error handling in LotusScript: You learned some techniques for writing better error handling in your code.

✦ Lists and arrays: You learned some new tips and techniques for working with these two powerful complex data structures.

✦ You learned about LS2J, a new feature in Notes/Domino 6 that enables you to call Java classes from LotusScript.

✦ You were introduced to the techniques for working with COM/OLE objects from LotusScript.

✦ You learned about working with the Notes and Win32 API from LotusScript.

✦ You were introduced to a powerful feature in LotusScript — the ability to create your own classes.

Section VII introduces you to the wonderful world of Java, beginning with Chapter 32, Java and the Domino Designer. This chapter introduces you to the basics of working with Java through the Domino 6 Designer.

✦   ✦   ✦

Java Techniques

Java and Domino Designer

By Brian Benz

Java certainly has come a long way since a group called the "green team" was locked away in the Menlo Park, California offices of Sun in 1991 to make an interactive TV system. The system was ahead of its time and didn't sell well, but it spawned processor-independent technology to send and display interactive features on a screen. Interestingly for Domino developers, the interactive features and functionality were originally described as agents. The next objects to use Java were *applets*, which were small applications that could be delivered and displayed on a screen via the Internet. This technology took off in 1994, when Netscape announced a Java Virtual Machine (JVM) as a core component of its new Navigator Browser software. In 1997, Lotus added Java to Domino 4.6 and announced that Java would be a core component of the new Domino Designer in R5. At that time Java had come full-circle, from interactive agents on a custom interactive TV system, to interactive agents in Notes clients and on the Web.

Cross-Reference   For those who are unfamiliar with agents, refer to Chapter 18.

Today, Java is still used for applet delivery and functionality, but is more often used for server-side development and is rapidly becoming the back-end server language of choice when developing high-capacity enterprise Web applications. This chapter provides an overview of Java and the details and capabilities of Java in Domino, including building Domino agents and creating Java code libraries.

Understanding Java Functionality in Domino Designer

Domino Designer provides two places to store Java code: Domino agents, under the Agents tab of the shared code section of the Design pane, and Java libraries, under the Script Libraries tab in the same

Shared Code section. Figure 32-1 illustrates the Domino Designer Java UI with the minimum code needed to run Java in a Notes and Domino environment.

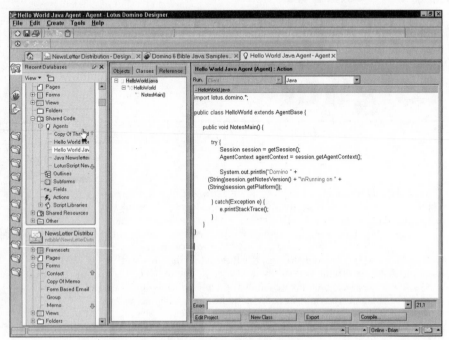

Figure 32-1: Basic Java agent code in the Domino Designer

The Domino Designer window in Figure 32-1 has three tabs. Normally, there are two: Objects lists objects associated with the selected object in the Programmer's pane, and Reference provides references to language syntax, classes, and methods for the language selected in the Programmer's pane. When working with Java in the Designer UI, there is a third tab, Classes. Because Java is an object-oriented language, classes can be defined within classes, and are arranged in the Classes tab in a hierarchical display. The Classes tab enables developers to quickly drill down to specific classes and is useful when coding long agents.

When working with Java in Designer, the Reference tab contains three flavors of Java: *Core Java*, which covers syntax for basic Sun JDK classes and methods; *Notes Java*, which contains references to lotus.domino subclasses; and *Third-Party Java*, which includes references for org.w3c.dom and org.xml.sax, which are used in XML parsing. One important thing to remember is that autocomplete in the Designer UI is only available for LotusScript, @Formulas, and JavaScript, not for Java.

Four buttons run across the bottom of the screen below the Programmer's pane when working with Java in Domino Designer:

✦ The Edit project button opens a dialog box and permits inclusion of references to .java source code, compiled .class files, archived .jar files, and shared Java code libraries contained in a Domino database (shared code libraries are covered later in this section.)

✦ The New Class button appends a new Java class skeleton to the current agent code, ready for developer code to be added to the new class within the agent.

✦ The Export button exports a copy of the source code to a file on the file system.

✦ The Compile button compiles the entire agent or a specific class within an agent. An agent is also automatically compiled when it is saved. A copy of the compiled code is saved behind the scenes. The compiled code is what runs when an agent is called.

Developing an Agent in Domino Designer

Let's go through the basic code in a Java agent by reviewing a simple agent in Listing 32-1:

Listing 32-1: The basic code building blocks for a Domino Java agent

```
import lotus.domino.*;
public class HelloWorld extends AgentBase {
   public void NotesMain() {
        try {
                Session session = getSession();
AgentContext agentContext =
session.getAgentContext();
                System.out.println("Domino " +
(String)session.getNotesVersion() + "\nRunning
on " +(String)session.getPlatform());
        } catch(Exception e) {
                e.printStackTrace();
        }
   }
}
```

Now that you have a big picture of the Java agent, go through the code line-by-line to review what each line does. The first line of the Java agent starts with an import statement, which brings in all the classes under lotus.domino, by using the * wildcard:

```
import lotus.domino.*;
```

The lotus.domino classes are located in the program directory on the file system of the Notes client and server in the Notes.jar file.

Note   A *.jar* file is like a .zip file that contains multiple compiled Java .class files, which are compressed into a single file for portability, in a hierarchical format. You can use any .zip file archival tool to decompress and recompress .jar files.

The next line defines a public Java class object called HelloWorld that extends AgentBase:

```
public class HelloWorld extends AgentBase {
```

AgentBase is a lotus.domino class that contains access to a Domino session. object.Domino sessions access Domino objects on the server or workstation on which the agent is running. AgentBase also redirects any output to a Java Debug console when the agent is run on a Notes client. To view the output of an agent from Designer or a Notes client, enable the Java console by selecting File ➪ Tools ➪ Show Java Debug Console from the Notes client menu.

The next line instantiates the `NotesMain` method:

```
public void NotesMain() {
```

The `NotesMain` method is the starting point for your code, because `AgentBase` uses `NotesMain` as a starting point for instantiating threads for a Domino Java agent. For those already familiar with Java, `NotesMain` is similar to `Main` in a regular Java program.

After extending `AgentBase` and initializing a single thread for this agent by instantiating the `NotesMain` method, you get to the meat of the code, which is contained in the `try` statement of the `NotesMain` method:

```
try {
   Session session = getSession();
AgentContext agentContext = session.getAgentContext();
```

This is a simple, single-threaded agent that queries the current Notes session through an instance of the `AgentContext` object class. The Agent Context enables developers to access Domino system properties. In this simple example, you retrieve and print the current Notes version and the platform of the system that the agent is currently running on, via the `getNotesVersion` and `getPlatform` properties of the `Session` class:

```
System.out.println("Domino " +
(String)session.getNotesVersion() + "\nRunning on "
(String)session.getPlatform());
```

Finally, the error-catching functionality of the agent uses the `catch` command to implement the fun-sounding throwable class, which catches errors that are "thrown" by the Java Virtual Machine (JVM) and include stack trace data. `PrintStackTrace` follows an error through the classes and methods that called it until it reaches the source of the error. It can also contain messages passed from the code that provide more specific information, based on each explicitly named exception. For now, you are just watching for any errors and sending a snapshot of the stack trace if an error occurs:

```
} catch(Exception e) {
        e.printStackTrace();
```

Storing and Referencing Java in a Domino Code Library

Agents and other types of Java code can be stored in a Domino database structure for portability when copying, moving, or replicating a database. To create a code library version of the `HelloWorld` Java agent, cut and paste the Java code into a new Java code library under the Script Libraries tab of the Shared Code section in the Work pane, or export the Java code using the Export button on the Programmer's pane and import it into the code library. The Java code library Java environment is identical to the Agent code environment, so code is imported by clicking the Edit Project button under the Java code library Programmer's pane and bringing in the `.java` source code from the file system. Figure 32-2 shows the Organize Java Agent Files dialog box that is displayed when the Edit Project button is clicked.

To reference a Java code library from an agent, click the Edit Project button below the agent's Programmer's pane, select Java Shared Libraries from the drop-down Browse field in the dialog box, and select the library you want to include. The Java library code can then be referenced like any other Java code from within an agent.

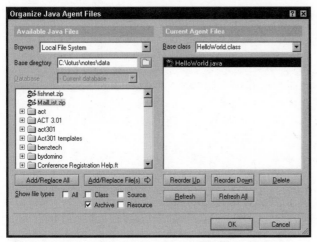

Figure 32-2: The Organize Java Agent Files dialog box

Summary

This chapter supplies developers with a brief introduction to Java. It also reviewed the following:

✦ Some of the Java functionality in Domino Designer

✦ Some of the Java-specific features in the Domino Designer UI

✦ A simple agent to get developers started working with Java in a Domino context

✦ Options for storing code in Domino Java code libraries

In the next chapter, developers will learn additional Domino Java classes to get you more intimately acquainted with using Java with Domino. The rest of the Java part of this book covers methods of accessing Domino objects from Java applications, servlets, JSP tags and tools, and techniques for working with Java that access Domino, such as using third-party developer tools and the IBM WebSphere Application Server.

✦　　✦　　✦

Java Classes and Methods

By Brian Benz

Domino Java classes and methods are an interface to the same Domino back-end classes that LotusScript uses. Developers will find many similarities between the LotusScript classes and syntax in Part VI (LotusScript) and the Java classes and methods in this section.

This chapter converts the LotusScript `NewsLetter` mailing agent example to a single-threaded Java agent by starting with the `Hello World` Java agent from the last chapter and adding Domino Java classes and methods to correspond with the original agent's LotusScript classes and methods. It then discusses the advantages of multithreaded Java and shows an example of what is required to convert the single-threaded Java agent to a multithreaded agent using the `NotesThread` class.

Introducing the Java Domino Classes

Table 33-1 provides a quick review of each of the key Domino Java classes used in the agent examples in this chapter.

Table 33-1: Domino Java Agent Classes Used in This Chapter

Class	*Representation*
Session	Session is used to access all objects on the server or client, including the AgentContext. All Domino objects for the current agent environment are derived from Session.
AgentContext	AgentContext is used to access a Domino agent's context on the server or Notes client that it is running on. AgentContext is derived from the Session class via the session.getAgentContext() method and represents the specific environment properties and methods for the server or the Notes client that the agent is running on.

Continued

In This Chapter

Introducing the Domino Java classes

Developing complex Domino agents in Java

Java agent development for LotusScript developers

Handling multiple classes in a Java agent

Developing multithreaded Java agents

Passing values from one Java agent thread and class to another

Table 33-1 *(continued)*

Class	Representation
Database	Database is used to access a Domino database. Existing databases can be accessed explicitly via the session.getDatabase() method, or the database that the agent is currently running on can be accessed via the agentContext.getCurrentDatabase() property.
View	View is used to access a database view or folder. Views are accessed via the database.getView() method. All views in a database can be accessed by database.getViews().
ViewEntryCollection	ViewEntryCollection is used to access a collection of rows in a View class. This class can contain an entire view via the view.getAllEntries() method or certain rows that match a specified column value via the view.getAllEntriesByKey() method.
ViewEntry	ViewEntry is used to access a row in a View class. ViewEntries are accessed by the ViewEntryCollection.getEntry() method or the view.getEntryByKey() method. ViewEntries can be documents, categorized rows, or total rows.
DocumentCollection	DocumentCollection is used to access a collection of documents. This class can be used to access all documents in a database via the database.getAllDocuments() method, and the view.getAllDocumentsByKey() method to select certain documents that match a specified document value via the View class.
Document	Document is used to access a document in a database. Documents are most commonly accessed by cycling through a DocumentCollection class. Documents can also be accessed via Document Universal ID using database.GetDocumentbyUNID() or Note ID via database.GetDocumentbyID().
Item	Item is used to access an item of data in a document. All non-system fields in Notes and Domino forms and Documents are referred to as items. Items are accessed by cycling through items on a document using Document.getItems().
Name	Name is used to access a user or server name. It's most commonly used to extract the hierarchical name of the current user or server that is running an agent.

Converting LotusScript Agents to Java

To provide a good working example of a complex Java agent in Domino, this section starts with the LotusScript agent created for mailing newsletters in Chapter 20 and recodes it as a Java agent. The newsletter agent is a great example to work with because it interfaces with so many commonly used Domino back-end object classes. To create the newsletter, the agent reads Domino databases, views, and documents, updates document items, changes document properties, creates documents, and sends e-mail. Listing 33-1 shows the new Java agent with the corresponding old LotusScript code just above each line, where applicable.

Listing 33-1: **A LotusScript Newsletter Agent Converted to a Java Agent**

```
import lotus.domino.*;
import java.util.*;

public class JavaAgent extends AgentBase {

    public void NotesMain() {

        try {
            Session session = getSession();
            AgentContext agentContext = session.getAgentContext();

            //Dim MailListFile As NotesDatabase
            //Set MailListFile = Session.CurrentDatabase
            Database MailListFile = agentContext.getCurrentDatabase();

            //Set Drafts = MailListFile.GetView ("($Drafts)")
            View Drafts = MailListFile.getView("($Drafts)");

            //Set NewMessage = Drafts.GetFirstDocument
            Document NewMessage = Drafts.getFirstDocument();

            //While Not (NewMessage Is Nothing)
            while (NewMessage != null) {

                //If (NewMessage.GetItemValue ("Processed")(0) = "") Then
                Item ProcessedItem = NewMessage.getFirstItem("Processed");

                if (ProcessedItem.getValueString() != null); {

                    //Forall x In NewMessage.SentTo
                    // sendList(x) = x
                    //End Forall
                    // Forall y In sendList
                    // End Forall

                    Item SentToItem = NewMessage.getFirstItem("SentTo");
                    Enumeration values = SentToItem.getValues().elements();
                    while (values.hasMoreElements()) {
                        //Dim memo As New NotesDocument(MailListFile)
                        Document memo = MailListFile.createDocument();
                        //Call NewMessage.CopyAllItems( memo, True )
                        NewMessage.copyAllItems( memo, true );
                        //     memo.Recipients=sendList(y)
                        String eMailAddress = (String)values.nextElement();
                        memo.replaceItemValue("Recipients", eMailAddress);
                        //     memo.SendTo=sendList(y)
                        memo.replaceItemValue("SendTo", eMailAddress);
                        //memo.RemoveItem( "SentTo" ) ;
                        memo.removeItem( "SentTo" ) ;
```

Continued

Listing 33-1 *(continued)*

```
                        //memo.SaveMessageOnSend = True
                        memo.setSaveMessageOnSend(true);
                        memo.send( false ) ;
                }

                    // Make sure this document is not processed again
            //Set Processed = New NotesItem (NewMessage, "Processed", "1")
            Item Processed = NewMessage.replaceItemValue("Processed", "1");
                    //Processed.IsSummary = True ;
                    Processed.setSummary(true);
                    //Call NewMessage.Save (True, False) ;
                    NewMessage.save(true, false) ;
                    //Set NewMessage = Drafts.GetNextDocument(NewMessage)
                    NewMessage = Drafts.getNextDocument(NewMessage);
                //End If is not needed in Java, just a close of the bracket
                }
            //Wend is not needed either in Java, just a close of the bracket
            }
        } catch(Exception e) {
            e.printStackTrace();
        }
    }
}
```

As you can see from this listing, many of the familiar LotusScript classes and methods have parallels in the Java classes and methods. As a general rule, most of the objects LotusScript accesses are available through Java, with notable syntax exceptions.

Caution

The most important thing for newbies to remember when working with Java classes is to watch capitalization carefully. If you are getting a compile-time error message, such as `Interface <x> not found in lotus.domino.Database`, and the class can be found in the Domino help, the first thing to check is your capitalization.

Let's drill down into the code line by line to see how a Java agent compares to LotusScript code:

```
import lotus.domino.*;
import java.util.*;
```

For the purposes of this agent, you need to import all Java classes located under `java.util` by using the * wildcard in your import statement. The standard `lotus.domino` classes are also included, as they always are for any Java agent. We'll show you exactly where `java.util` is used later on in the code:

```
import lotus.domino.*;
import java.util.*;

public class JavaAgent extends AgentBase {

    public void NotesMain() {
```

```
try {
    Session session = getSession();
    AgentContext agentContext = session.getAgentContext();

    //Dim MailListFile As NotesDatabase
    //Set MailListFile = Session.CurrentDatabase
    Database MailListFile = agentContext.getCurrentDatabase();
```

As with the simple Java agent example in Chapter 32, the agent gets the `AgentContext` from the Java agent session object. Next, the agent identifies the database that it is currently running on by accessing the `session. CurrentDatabase` property. This returns a fully accessible Domino database object, including all views and documents:

```
//Set Drafts = MailListFile.GetView ("($Drafts)")
View Drafts = MailListFile.getView("($Drafts)");

//Set NewMessage = Drafts.GetFirstDocument
Document NewMessage = Drafts.getFirstDocument();
```

The next step is to get the Drafts view of the Newsletter Mailing database, which contains one or more newsletters waiting to be mailed. This returns a full Domino View object, including all View entries via `ViewEntry` objects, and all documents, via `Document` objects. View entries can be documents, summary categories, or totals. Because the agent is interested in documents, the Document objects are retrieved in the view instead of `ViewEntry` objects. Note the difference in capitalization of the `getView` and `getFirstDocument` methods. Compiling the agent after converting to Java syntax but keeping the old LotusScript capitalization results in errors.

```
//While Not (NewMessage Is Nothing)
        while (NewMessage != null) {
```

Tip   Looping is treated a little differently in Java. In this example, the agent uses a `while` loop that cycles through all the documents in the Drafts database, just as in LotusScript. Note in the following code that while LotusScript requires a `Wend` to finish off the loop, Java requires that the closing bracket be placed in the proper spot. For this reason, indents and other helpful formatting of code is important for following through Java logic.

```
//If (NewMessage.GetItemValue ("Processed")(0) = "") Then
        Item ProcessedItem = NewMessage.getFirstItem("Processed");
        if (ProcessedItem.getValueString() != null); {
```

The Domino `Document` class contains all of the attributes and items in a Domino document or form. In this case, the agent is only interested in documents in the Drafts view. After the agent gets a document, the agent can start working with the items in that document. Items are any objects in a document and can be assigned to the document by Domino itself or by developer code. In this case, the agent is looking for a specific item by using `getFirstItem` with an item name supplied as a parameter. `getFirstItem` with no parameters gets the first item of a document as it appears in the item list.

The preceding code also highlights an interesting difference between LotusScript and Java—in LotusScript nulls can be optionally represented by two double-quotes, while Java requires an explicit null check. By default, Lotus originally designed the value of empty fields as two double-quotes with no space between. LotusScript makes null values the same as an empty string for backward compatibility with @Formula functions. Java syntax, however, looks for a string of length zero, but gets a string of length null, so an error is returned at runtime.

For this reason, any previously undefined strings, such as the processed variable, generate a `can't convert string to Boolean` compile error when you try to save an agent that contains a comparison with empty quotes on an undefined string:

```
//Forall x In NewMessage.SentTo
   //           sendList(x) = x
   //End Forall
   //        Forall y In sendList
  // End Forall
```

The preceding code in LotusScript pulls e-mail address values out of a multivalue text field in LotusScript and loads the values into an array to be processed by the LotusScript agent. Because the new agent is using Java, the agent can take advantage of the `Enumeration` class as shown following, which does the same thing in a much simpler way:

```
Item SentToItem = NewMessage.getFirstItem("SentTo");
                  Enumeration values = SentToItem.getValues().elements();
                  while (values.hasMoreElements()) {
```

The `Enumeration` class is part of the `java.util` classes that were imported earlier (and, incidentally the only class the agent uses from `java.util` in this agent). The `Enumeration` class generates a series of elements from, in this case, a multivalue field in a Domino document represented by the `Item` Java class. The multivalue item elements are cycled through until the end of the multivalue item is reached. If the item contains a single value, the elements property returns a single value and the element cycling stops after the first item, so no test is required to check for single and multivalue items.

```
//Dim memo As New NotesDocument(MailListFile)
Document memo = MailListFile.createDocument();
//Call NewMessage.CopyAllItems( memo, True )
NewMessage.copyAllItems( memo, true );
```

The preceding code starts by cycling to the next value in the multivalue e-mail text field item. For each new value, this code segment creates a new document for each of the values in the e-mail list, and skips out of the `while` loop if it has reached the end. The `copyAllItems` method is used to copy the items from the `NewMessage` document to the memo document. Once again, note the capitalization of `CopyAllItems` in LotusScript and `copyAllItems` in Java.

```
//        memo.Recipients=sendList(y)
String eMailAddress = (String)values.nextElement();
memo.replaceItemValue("Recipients", eMailAddress);
//        memo.SendTo=sendList(y)
memo.replaceItemValue("SendTo", eMailAddress);
//memo.RemoveItem( "SentTo" ) ;
memo.removeItem( "SentTo" ) ;
//memo.SaveMessageOnSend = True
memo.setSaveMessageOnSend(true);
memo.send( false ) ;
```

The rest of the code mirrors the LotusScript in setting values, with a few important exceptions.

Note that the variables cannot be set in the new document by simply using the LotusScript construct of `variable = value;` so `replaceItemValue` is used instead. `appendItemValue` can also be used in Java, but developers run the risk of adding another value to a document with a duplicate field name, because `appendItemValue` doesn't check to see whether there is an existing instance of the item. As the method name suggests, it simply appends the value to the items in the document.

Note that `setSaveMessageOnSend` is used to set a Boolean value of `true` instead of assigning a Boolean using `replaceItemValue` or `appendItemValue`. This is necessary because Boolean values cannot be defined directly via `replaceItemValue` or `appendItemValue` Domino back-end classes in Java. Domino Java classes compensate for this by having methods for setting Domino system fields to Boolean values. Once again, note the lack of capitalization of `true`, compared to `True` for LotusScript.

```
// Make sure this document is not processed again
                //Set Processed = New NotesItem (NewMessage, "Processed",
"1")
                Item Processed = NewMessage.replaceItemValue("Processed",
"1");
                //Processed.IsSummary = True ;
                Processed.setSummary(true) ;
                //Call NewMessage.Save (True, False) ;
                NewMessage.save(true, false) ;
                //Set NewMessage = Drafts.GetNextDocument(NewMessage)
                NewMessage = Drafts.getNextDocument(NewMessage);
```

After breaking out of the `while` loop for the current memo in the Drafts view by cycling through all the e-mail addresses in the `SentTo` multivalue text field using the `Enumerator` class, the agent moves on to the next document or the end of the documents in the Drafts view using the `getNextDocument` method. Before doing that, the agent sets the Domino document item `Processed` with a value of 1. This takes the document out of the Drafts view and places it in the Sent view, using `replaceItemValue`. Note how the agent sets the Boolean summary property to `true` for the item using the `item.SetSummary` method instead of trying to use `replaceItemValue` with a Boolean value:

```
//End If is not needed in Java, just a close of the bracket
                }
//Wend is not needed either in Java, just a close of the bracket
            }
        } catch(Exception e) {
            e.printStackTrace();
        }
```

The rest of the code is simple Java agent cleanup and exception catching. Note that there is no Java equivalent to a LotusScript `Wend`, `End Forall`, or `End If`, just braces to indicate the point of departure for that code segment.

Tip During this exercise some readers may have questioned the point of converting LotusScript agents to Java. In many cases this is a valid point; if LotusScript agents work fine and do everything you need, there's no point to converting them to Java. But there are times when using Java has advantages over LotusScript for agents. The next example covers one of these advantages as developers learn how to take advantage of Java multithreading to potentially speed up Java agents. Additional advantages are also covered in the next few chapters.

Developing Multithreaded Agents

One of the best features of Java is the facility to provide multithreading of Java agents, applications, and servlets. Multithreading of applications allows for multiple tasks to take place in parallel on a single processor, instead of one process having to wait for another to finish before it can begin processing.

One of the ways multiple Java threads could assist in the preceding Java agent example is by creating a separate thread for each of the NewMessage documents that is waiting for mail to be generated. In the preceding single-threaded example, the while loop opens one memo to be sent, processes all of its e-mail addresses from the multivalue SentTo item, and then moves on to the next NewMessage to be sent. Instead, a thread could be opened for each NewDocument, and e-mails could be generated for each document in parallel. Listing 33-2 takes a look at how that happens:

Listing 33-2: **A Multithreaded Java Newsletter Agent**

```
class processEmailsThread extends NotesThread {
    private Database MailListFile;
    private Document NewMessage;

    public processEmailsThread( Database MailListFile, Document NewMessage) {
        this.MailListFile = MailListFile;
        this.NewMessage = NewMessage;
    } // end public processEmailsThread

    public void runNotes() {
        try {
            System.out.println("processEmailsThread Running");
            Item ProcessedItem = NewMessage.getFirstItem("Processed");
            if (ProcessedItem.getValueString() != null); {
                Item SentToItem = NewMessage.getFirstItem("SentTo");
                Enumeration values = SentToItem.getValues().elements();
                while (values.hasMoreElements()) {
                    Document memo = MailListFile.createDocument();
                    NewMessage.copyAllItems( memo, true );
                    String eMailAddress = (String)values.nextElement();
                    memo.replaceItemValue("Recipients", eMailAddress);
                    memo.replaceItemValue("SendTo", eMailAddress);
                    memo.removeItem( "SentTo" ) ;
                    memo.setSaveMessageOnSend(true);
                    memo.send( false ) ;
                } // end if (ProcessedItem.getValueString() != null)
            } // end while (values.hasMoreElements())

        } // end try
        catch(NotesException ne) {
            ne.printStackTrace();
        } // end catch(NotesException ne)
    } // end runNotes()

} // end processEmailsThread
```

This code includes several new and important techniques. In the previous example, the agent was using a single Java thread and a single Java class. In this multithreaded example, the main class (represented by NotesMain) handles the tasks of getting the database from which the agent will be e-mailing newsletters and finding the Drafts view in that database. After the agent has the Drafts view, it calls another class called processEmailsThread that handles the actual creation and sending of the e-mail memo for each document in the Drafts view. To facilitate this, the agent needs to pass values from the main class to the `processEmails-Thread` class. The `multiThreadJavaNewsletter` example is a great introduction to working with multiple Java classes, handling multiple threads in Java, and passing values form one Java class and thread to another Java class and thread. Let's re-examine the code:

```java
import lotus.domino.*;
import java.util.*;

public class multiThreadJavaNewsLetter extends AgentBase {
    public void NotesMain() {
        try {
```

The agent starts with the same code as before, but this time the `NotesMain` call has more significance. `NotesMain` is the main class for Java agents for a good reason: It actually initializes its own Java thread. This means that Domino Java agents always have at least one thread running at all times. Next we start a Domino session:

```java
            Session session = getSession();
            AgentContext agentContext = session.getAgentContext();
            Database MailListFile = agentContext.getCurrentDatabase();
            View Drafts = MailListFile.getView("($Drafts)");
            Document NewMessage = Drafts.getFirstDocument();
            while (NewMessage != null) {
                processEmailsThread processNewsLetter = new
processEmailsThread(MailListFile, NewMessage);
                System.out.println("Starting Thread");
                processNewsLetter.start();
                System.out.println("Joining Thread");
                processNewsLetter.join();
                Item Processed = NewMessage.replaceItemValue("Processed", "1");
                Processed.setSummary(true);
                NewMessage.save(true, false) ;
                NewMessage = Drafts.getNextDocument(NewMessage);
            } //End while (NewMessage != null)


        } // end try
```

The preceding code is identical to the previous example until the instantiation of the `ProcessEmailsThread` class. This is not a Java library class, but actually a class in this code that has been developed to process e-mails when passed a database and a document. The agent passes the database to the new class so that the class knows in which database it needs to create a new e-mail memo and from which database to send the memo. The document is passed because it contains the information about the newsletter, including the text of the newsletter and the list of intended recipients.

After handling the calling of the new class and the passing of objects that the class needs to function, the agent instantiates the class using the `start()` method. The `join()` method tells the code to wait until the thread created by the `processEmailsThread` class is finished. In the following case, the `join()` makes sure that the thread that the agent started to process the e-mails finishes properly before proceeding to the code that marks the newsletter document in the database as processed, so the recipients don't get the same newsletter twice:

```java
            catch(InterruptedException ie) {
                ie.printStackTrace();
            } // end catch(InterruptedException ie)
```

```
        catch(NotesException ne) {
            ne.printStackTrace();
        } // end catch(NotesException ne)
    } // end NotesMain
} // end multiThreadJavaNewsLetter
```

The agent finishes this class with some error catching. Because the join() method is being used in this class, the agent also needs to catch InterruptedException errors along with the regular NotesException for Domino Java classes. InterruptedException errors are thrown when another thread tries to interrupt the current thread before it has a chance to finish running.

Now the agent moves on to the ProcessEmailsThread class in this agent:

```
class ProcessEmailsThread extends NotesThread {
private Database MailListFile;
private Document NewMessage;
```

This is where the agent gets into the actual thread processing. This class extends the Domino NotesThread class. NotesThread is itself an extension of the base object java.lang.Thread class. The agent initializes a couple of private variables based on the previous variables in the calling class that represent the database and the current newsletter Document objects. It's important to note that, at this point, the agent has not actually created a new thread — it's just warned the JVM at runtime that a new thread will be created. The new thread is started in the following code:

```
public processEmailsThread( Database MailListFile, Document NewMessage) {
        this.MailListFile = MailListFile;
        this.NewMessage = NewMessage;
    } // end public processEmailsThread


    public void runNotes() {
        try {
```

The agent pulls in the parameters passed from the NotesMain thread and assigns them to the private objects created for the processEmailsThread class. Now the agent has newly created private objects with which the current thread can work.

After defining the processEmailsThread in the NotesMain class and issuing a start() method extending the NotesThread class, the agent starts a new thread by calling the runNotes class as follows:

```
            System.out.println("processEmailsThread Running");
            Item ProcessedItem = NewMessage.getFirstItem("Processed");
            if (ProcessedItem.getValueString() != null); {
                Item SentToItem = NewMessage.getFirstItem("SentTo");
                Enumeration values = SentToItem.getValues().elements();
                while (values.hasMoreElements()) {
                    Document memo = MailListFile.createDocument();
                    NewMessage.copyAllItems( memo, true );
                    String eMailAddress = (String)values.nextElement();
                    memo.replaceItemValue("Recipients", eMailAddress);
                    memo.replaceItemValue("SendTo", eMailAddress);
                    memo.removeItem( "SentTo" ) ;
```

```
                        memo.setSaveMessageOnSend(true);
                        memo.send( false ) ;
                } // end if (ProcessedItem.getValueString() != null)
            } // end while (values.hasMoreElements())

        } // end try
        catch(NotesException ne) {
            ne.printStackTrace();
        }  // end catch(NotesException ne)
    } // end runNotes()

} // end processEmailsThread
```

The rest of the code is the same as the single-thread, single-class example in Listing 33-1. It simply processes each newsletter document by creating and sending an e-mail memo for each recipient listed in the SentTo item in the document.

Note　The agent didn't have to include the InterruptedException in the error catching at this class level, just the NotesException catch. This is only necessary in the code that includes a join(), which in this case is in the calling NotesMain class, not this one. After the processEmailsThread class is finished, execution returns to the NotesMain code at the point of the join() class, and the rest of the NotesMain class code is executed.

Summary

In this chapter, developers learned all about key Domino Java classes by example that showed how to read from and write to Domino documents and databases, as well as work with Domino views and sending mail.

We also introduced developers to:

✦ Multiple classes in Java code.

✦ Multiple threading in Java by creating a multiclass, multithreaded Domino agent from a single class, single thread agent.

✦ Standard formats for passing values between classes and threads in Java.

Other added bonuses of Java agent code are that Java agents are easily ported to other types of Java, including Java applications and servlets. The next chapter illustrates this by converting some of the code from this chapter from a Java agent to a Java application. Chapter 35 illustrates techniques for adapting the same core functionality for use in a servlet, which can run in the Domino servlet environment and on other application servers, such as WebSphere.

✦　　✦　　✦

Accessing Domino from Java Applications

By Brian Benz

Java applications are stand-alone applications that have been written in Java instead of another programming language, such as C++. This chapter covers the steps necessary to integrate Domino data into a Java application by developing an interactive Java application UI that accesses Domino views, documents, and fields via the same Notes Objects Interface used for agent examples in Chapters 32 and 33.

Prerequisites for Developing Domino Applications in Java

Before developing and running Java applications on a workstation, there are a few things that have to be set up to make sure everything works as it is intended to. The next sections take developers through the process of setting up a workstation to run Java.

Selecting the Java Developer Kit version

Before trying to develop stand-alone applications in Java that access Domino objects, it's important to know which Java Developer Kit (JDK) to use when developing and compiling code. The first step is to determine which Domino version is running on the server. Notes and Domino 5 support Lotus JDK 1.1.8, and Domino 6 supports JDK 1.3. Make sure that you have the corresponding version appropriate for the machine the code will run on loaded on your development machine as well. The help-about Notes screen on a workstation displays the version number of Notes and the Domino Designer client. On a server, typing **version** at the console returns a version number for the server to the screen.

The CLASSPATH, PATH, and JAVA_HOME variables

The CLASSPATH, PATH, and JAVA_HOME variables are usually set when you install a JDK and Domino, but it's best to check these values first if you are experiencing any Java compile or run errors. At a bare minimum, your CLASSPATH system variable should contain accurate references to Notes.jar and NCSO.Jar for developing Java applications. Aside from this, your JDK \bin directory will probably have to be in the PATH environment variable for Java applications to compile and run correctly, and the JAVA_HOME environment variable will have to be set to the main directory of your JDK. For Windows 98 and earlier versions, environmental variables are set in the autoexec.bat file. For Windows NT and later, environmental variables are set by opening the Control Panel, selecting the System icon, selecting the Advanced tab, and clicking the Environment Variables button.

Listing 34-1 offers a look at a sample setup of a typical Java application developer's machine, where the Notes 6 designer client is installed in c:\Lotus\Notes, and the Java JDK 1.3 is installed in c:\JSDK1.3.1_01.

Listing 34-1: Environment Variable Settings for a Typical Domino Developer Client

```
SET CLASSPATH =
.;c:\Lotus\Notes\Data\domino\java\NCSO.jar;c:\lotus\notes\Notes.
jar;
PATH=C:\WINNT;C:\WINNT\COMMAND;C:\jsdk1.3.1_01\bin;c:\lotus\note
s;c:\lotus\domino
set JAVA_HOME=c:\jsdk1.3.1_01
```

The CLASSPATH is a listing of all the java archive (.jar) files on a machine. The PATH refers to .dlls and other windows executable resources that need to be defined on the machine. JAVA_HOME is used to find the root directory of the Java installation.

Converting a Simple Domino Java Agent to a Java Application

Listing 34-2 is a basic single-threaded Hello World Java application based on the multi-threaded Java agent from Chapter 33.

Listing 34-2: The Basic Building Blocks for a Domino Java Application

```
import lotus.domino.*;

public class SingleThreadApp {
    public static void main(String argv[]) {
      try {
        singleThread helloWorld = new singleThread();
        Thread jLThread = new Thread(helloWorld);
```

```
        jLThread.start();
        jLThread.join();
      }
      catch(InterruptedException e) {
      }
    }
}

class singleThread implements Runnable {
   public void run() {
try {
        NotesThread.sinitThread();
        Session s = NotesFactory.createSession();
        System.out.println("Running Domino version " + s.getNotesVersion() + "
on " +

s.getPlatform());
      }
      catch (Exception e) {
         e.printStackTrace();
      }
finally
      {
      NotesThread.stermThread();
      }
   }
}
```

The code starts with the familiar `import` statement for the `lotus.domino` classes, but then things wander quickly into unfamiliar territory when compared to the agent examples in Chapters 32 and 33.

The following snippet shows that main class no longer extends `AgentBase`, telling the compiler right away that this is not a Domino agent. Also note that the main class is no longer called `NotesMain`, but just `main`. For Java applications, the main class provides a starting point for the `SingleThreadApp` class, just as `NotesMain` provides a starting point for any class that extends `AgentBase`.

```
import lotus.domino.*;

public class SingleThreadApp {
   public static void main(String argv[]) {
```

The next thing to notice, in the following snippet, is that the application initiates a thread before it calls the `singleThread` class that is being used in the application. The application instantiates a new `singleClass` object and calls the object `HelloWorld`, and defines the new class as a `java.lang.thread` named `jLThread` by extending the `Thread` class and calling `Notesthread` to create a new thread. The application now has a new object and a thread to run it in, so it can start running the thread by using the start method of `Thread`. The `join` method tells the code to stop executing until the `singleThread` class returns something, so that the main class doesn't finish running before the `singleThread` class is finished.

```
try {
  NotesThread.sinitThread();
  singleThread helloWorld = new singleThread();
  Thread jLThread = new Thread(helloWorld);
  jLThread.start();
  jLThread.join();
}
```

The application finishes this class with some error catching to balance the try, but it's not done yet:

```
catch(InterruptedException e) {
  }
 }
}
```

Take a look at the `singleThread` class that's running when the application starts the thread in the main class:

```
class singleThread implements Runnable {
    public void run() {
try {
    Session s = NotesFactory.createSession();
System.out.println("Running Domino version " + s.getNotesVersion() + " on "
+ s.getPlatform());
    }
    catch (Exception e) {
        e.printStackTrace();
    }
    finally
    {
    NotesThread.stermThread();
    }
  }
}
```

This simple class gets the session object by calling `NotesFactory` and creating a session for the class to access while it's running on the local machine. The application then accesses the Domino platform and version from the session and prints them to the screen.

An Advanced Domino Java Application Example

Listing 34-2 is a good example for learning how Java applications can work, but not a full demonstration of what Java applications can do. The next example uses advanced Java classes for UI handling, including the `Swing` and `AWT` classes, to create an application that reads and writes to back-end Domino classes. Figure 34-1 shows the user interface for the Java application that is used in this example.

The example in Figure 34-1 uses Swing classes to display UI features, such as the text area and the button, and AWT classes to capture the button event and pass values to the multithreaded Java application example. Listing 34-3 shows the code for the application in Figure 34-1.

Figure 34-1: An advanced Domino Java application example, showing the text area for adding a list of e-mail recipients and a button to send mail to the recipients

Listing 34-3: **An Advanced Domino Application Example**

```
import lotus.domino.*;
import java.util.*;
import javax.swing.*;
import java.awt.*;
import java.awt.event.*;

public class DominoBibleJavaAppExample extends JFrame implements ActionListener
{
     JButton sendMailButton;
     JTextArea textArea;
     JLabel actionLabel;
     String Recipients;

     public static void main(String[] args) {
        JFrame frame = new DominoBibleJavaAppExample();

        frame.addWindowListener(new WindowAdapter() {
            public void windowClosing(WindowEvent e) {
                System.exit(0);
            }
        });

        frame.pack();
        frame.setVisible(true);
     }

    public DominoBibleJavaAppExample() {
      super("DominoBibleJavaAppExample");
    actionLabel = new JLabel("Enter a List of Email Recipients and Press the
Send Mail Button.");
      actionLabel.setBorder(BorderFactory.createEmptyBorder(10,0,0,0));
        JPanel textControlsPane = new JPanel();
        GridBagLayout gridbag = new GridBagLayout();
```

Continued

Listing 34-3 *(continued)*

```
        GridBagConstraints c = new GridBagConstraints();
        textControlsPane.setLayout(gridbag);
        c.gridwidth = GridBagConstraints.REMAINDER;
        c.anchor = GridBagConstraints.WEST;
        c.weightx = 1.0;
        gridbag.setConstraints(actionLabel, c);
        textControlsPane.add(actionLabel);
        textControlsPane.setBorder(
        BorderFactory.createCompoundBorder(
BorderFactory.createTitledBorder("Domino Programmer's Bible
JavaApplication Example"),
        BorderFactory.createEmptyBorder(5,5,5,5)));
        textArea = new JTextArea(
"gcbdhi@aol.com, 57248@iron-mail.com, rfumeqh@aol.com,
Kyle_dyson@hotmail.com, sabrinahall@edd.currentmail.com");
        textArea.setFont(new Font("SansSerif",Font.PLAIN, 12));
        textArea.setLineWrap(true);
        textArea.setWrapStyleWord(true);
        JScrollPane areaScrollPane = new JScrollPane(textArea);
areaScrollPane.setVerticalScrollBarPolicy
(JScrollPane.VERTICAL_SCROLLBAR_ALWAYS);
        areaScrollPane.setPreferredSize(new Dimension(250, 250));
        areaScrollPane.setBorder(
        BorderFactory.createCompoundBorder(
        BorderFactory.createCompoundBorder(
        BorderFactory.createTitledBorder("Enter Email Recipients Here"),
        BorderFactory.createEmptyBorder(5,5,5,5)),
        areaScrollPane.getBorder()));
        JPanel leftPane = new JPanel();
        BoxLayout leftBox = new BoxLayout(leftPane, BoxLayout.Y_AXIS);
        leftPane.setLayout(leftBox);
        leftPane.add(textControlsPane);
        leftPane.add(areaScrollPane);
        sendMailButton = new JButton("Send Email");
         sendMailButton.addActionListener(this);
        leftPane.add(sendMailButton);
        JPanel contentPane = new JPanel();
        BoxLayout box = new BoxLayout(contentPane, BoxLayout.X_AXIS);
        contentPane.setLayout(box);
        contentPane.add(leftPane);
        setContentPane(contentPane);
    }

public void actionPerformed(ActionEvent e) {
        System.out.println("Mailing Newsletters");
        String Recipients = textArea.getText();
         multiThreadJavaNewsLetter pnl = new
multiThreadJavaNewsLetter(Recipients);
    }
```

```
class multiThreadJavaNewsLetter  {
private String Recipients;
public multiThreadJavaNewsLetter (String Recipients) {
    try {
            NotesThread.sinitThread();
            Session session = NotesFactory.createSession();
              //AgentContext agentContext = session.getAgentContext();
              //Database MailListFile = agentContext.getCurrentDatabase();
Database MailListFile = session.getDatabase("",
"NewsLetterDistribution.nsf");
              lotus.domino.View Drafts = MailListFile.getView("($Drafts)");
              lotus.domino.Document NewMessage = Drafts.getFirstDocument();
              while (NewMessage != null) {
processEmailsThread processNewsLetter = new
processEmailsThread(MailListFile, NewMessage);
              System.out.println("Starting Thread");
              processNewsLetter.start();
              System.out.println("Joining Thread");
              processNewsLetter.join();
            Item Processed = NewMessage.replaceItemValue("Processed","1");
        Processed.setSummary(true);
              NewMessage.save (true, false) ;
              NewMessage = Drafts.getNextDocument(NewMessage);
              } //End while (NewMessage != null)
    } // end try
catch(InterruptedException ie) {
            ie.printStackTrace();
} // end catch(InterruptedException ie)
    catch(NotesException ne) {
            ne.printStackTrace();
} // end catch(NotesException ne)
    finally
    {
    NotesThread.stermThread();
    }

} //end public
} // end multiThreadJavaNewsLetter

class processEmailsThread extends NotesThread {
private Database MailListFile;
private lotus.domino.Document NewMessage;

public processEmailsThread(Database MailListFile, lotus.domino.Document
NewMessage) {
    this.MailListFile = MailListFile;
    this.NewMessage = NewMessage;
    } // end public processEmailsThread
 public void runNotes() {
    try {
```

Continued

Listing 34-3 *(continued)*

```
System.out.println("processEmailsThread Running");
     Item ProcessedItem = NewMessage.getFirstItem("Processed");
     if (ProcessedItem.getValueString() != null); {
          //Item SentToItem = NewMessage.getFirstItem("SentTo");
Item RecipentText =NewMessage.replaceItemValue("RecipentText",
null);
          RecipentText.setValueString(Recipients);
             Enumeration values = RecipentText.getValues().elements();
              while (values.hasMoreElements()) {
lotus.domino.Document memo =
MailListFile.createDocument();
                     NewMessage.copyAllItems( memo, true );
                     String eMailAddress = (String)values.nextElement();
                     memo.replaceItemValue("Recipients", eMailAddress);
                     memo.replaceItemValue("SendTo", eMailAddress);
                     memo.removeItem( "SentTo" ) ;
                     memo.setSaveMessageOnSend(true);
                     memo.send( false ) ;
                     } // end if (ProcessedItem.getValueString() != null)
                     } // end while (values.hasMoreElements())

} // end try
     catch(NotesException ne) {
            ne.printStackTrace();
}   // end catch(NotesException ne)
} // end runNotes()

} // end processEmailsThread
}
```

 All the source code in this chapter is available at www.wiley.com/compbooks/benz from the downloads section.

The rather long code example in Listing 34-3 takes advantage of several Swing UI classes, some AWT classes to control actions and responses to actions, such as the pressing of the Mail Send button, and uses the multithreaded Domino agent example from Chapter 33, with some slight modifications. The application sends e-mail newsletters to recipients, overriding the values in the newsletters with the values a user enters in the text area of the Java application.

This section breaks down the code and discusses it in segments. You start by reviewing the import statements for the application.

The code begins by importing the regular lotus.domino and java.util classes that you worked with in previous agent examples:

```
import lotus.domino.*;
import java.util.*;
import javax.swing.*;
import java.awt.*;
import java.awt.event.*;
```

You also import the `javax.swing` classes to handle UI features and selected `java.awt` classes to manage the action event when the Send E-mail button is pressed. You create a public class that extends the `JFrame` class, which is the foundation for the Swing UI classes you are using in the application. You also implement the AWT `ActionListener` class here as well, so that any `ActionListener` events attached to a Swing UI object are captured and can be shared among all the subclasses contained in the `DominoBibleJavaAppExample` class:

```
public class DominoBibleJavaAppExample extends JFrame implements ActionListener
{
    JButton sendMailButton;
    JTextArea textArea;
    JLabel actionLabel;
    String Recipients;
```

As with the simple Domino application example in Listing 34-2, instead of initiating a `NotesMain` class, you use the `Main` class in a Java application and implement a new instance of the `DominoBibleJavaAppExample` class, which contains a Swing `JFrame` class and an AWT `WindowAdapter` class, as shown here:

```
public static void main(String[] args) {
        JFrame frame = new DominoBibleJavaAppExample();

        frame.addWindowListener(new WindowAdapter() {
            public void windowClosing(WindowEvent e) {
                System.exit(0);
            }
        });

        frame.pack();
        frame.setVisible(true);
    }
```

When you invoke a new instance of the `DominoBibleJavaAppExample` class, the code starts at the public statement. The super class statement tells the JVM to invoke the superclass version of a class and methods, rather than use any existing classes with the same method names, as this code shows:

```
    public DominoBibleJavaAppExample() {
      super("DominoBibleJavaAppExample");
```

The next code segment initializes a JPanel, on top of which label UI objects will go at the top of the application window. The rest of the code sets up the layout for the label objects and borders in the JFrame by using the AWT GridBagLayout class and the Swing BorderFactory class.actionLabel = new JLabel("Enter a List of Email Recipients and Press the Send Mail Button.");

```
        actionLabel.setBorder(BorderFactory.createEmptyBorder(10,0,0,0));
        JPanel textControlsPane = new JPanel();
        GridBagLayout gridbag = new GridBagLayout();
        GridBagConstraints c = new GridBagConstraints();
        textControlsPane.setLayout(gridbag);
        c.gridwidth = GridBagConstraints.REMAINDER;
        c.anchor = GridBagConstraints.WEST;
```

```
        c.weightx = 1.0;
        gridbag.setConstraints(actionLabel, c);
        textControlsPane.add(actionLabel);
        textControlsPane.setBorder(
        BorderFactory.createCompoundBorder(
BorderFactory.createTitledBorder("Domino Programmer's Bible
JavaApplication Example"),
        BorderFactory.createEmptyBorder(5,5,5,5)));
```

The next segment of code identifies the text area that users will be able to add e-mail recipients into, using the Swing `JtextArea` class. Properties, default size and borders, and border styles are set here as well.

```
        textArea = new JTextArea(
"gcbdhi@aol.com, 57248@iron-mail.com, rfumeqh@aol.com,
Kyle_dyson@hotmail.com, sabrinahall@edd.currentmail.com");
        textArea.setFont(new Font("SansSerif",Font.PLAIN, 12));
        textArea.setLineWrap(true);
        textArea.setWrapStyleWord(true);
        JScrollPane areaScrollPane = new JScrollPane(textArea);
areaScrollPane.setVerticalScrollBarPolicy
(JScrollPane.VERTICAL_SCROLLBAR_ALWAYS);
        areaScrollPane.setPreferredSize(new Dimension(250, 250));
        areaScrollPane.setBorder(
        BorderFactory.createCompoundBorder(
        BorderFactory.createCompoundBorder(
        BorderFactory.createTitledBorder("Enter Email Recipients Here"),
        BorderFactory.createEmptyBorder(5,5,5,5)),
        areaScrollPane.getBorder()));
```

The next segment places the text area pane in a new `JPanel` just below the `JPanel` that displays the message labels. You also add a button for sending the e-mails and implement the `ActionListener` class to watch for the button press action:

```
        JPanel leftPane = new JPanel();
        BoxLayout leftBox = new BoxLayout(leftPane, BoxLayout.Y_AXIS);
        leftPane.setLayout(leftBox);
        leftPane.add(textControlsPane);
        leftPane.add(areaScrollPane);
        sendMailButton = new JButton("Send Email");
         sendMailButton.addActionListener(this);
         leftPane.add(sendMailButton);
        JPanel contentPane = new JPanel();
        BoxLayout box = new BoxLayout(contentPane, BoxLayout.X_AXIS);
        contentPane.setLayout(box);
        contentPane.add(leftPane);
        setContentPane(contentPane);
    }
```

When the `ActionListener` detects that the user has pressed a button, the code contained in `ActionPerformed` executes. In this case, the code gets the string of e-mail recipients that the user has entered from the Swing UI text area using the `JtextArea.gettext` class and stores the string value in a variable called `Recipients`. The code then creates a new instance of `multiThreadJavaNewsLetter` and passes the `Recipients` string value to the new object for processing.

```
public void actionPerformed(ActionEvent e) {
      System.out.println("Mailing Newsletters");
      String Recipients = textArea.getText();
       multiThreadJavaNewsLetter pnl = new
multiThreadJavaNewsLetter(Recipients);
}
```

To readers who have been following the Java examples in sequence, this code segment should look familiar. The code is copied directly out of the multithreaded Java agent example from Chapter 33, and it runs in a Java application with a few minor modifications. Most notably, instead of simply retrieving a Notes session using the getSession method, this code uses the NotesFactory classes to instantiate a Domino session.

In an agent you use the AgentContext to select the current database that the agent is running in. Because this code is now running a stand-alone application that has no reference to a database, it needs to use the getDatabase method of the Session class to explicitly name a database from which to retrieve newsletter memos.

```
class multiThreadJavaNewsLetter  {
private String Recipients;
public multiThreadJavaNewsLetter (String Recipients) {
    try {
            NotesThread.sinitThread();
             Session session = NotesFactory.createSession();
             //AgentContext agentContext = session.getAgentContext();
             //Database MailListFile = agentContext.getCurrentDatabase();
Database MailListFile = session.getDatabase("",
"NewsLetterDistribution.nsf");
             lotus.domino.View Drafts = MailListFile.getView("($Drafts)");
             lotus.domino.Document NewMessage = Drafts.getFirstDocument();
             while (NewMessage != null) {
processEmailsThread processNewsLetter = new
processEmailsThread(MailListFile, NewMessage);
             System.out.println("Starting Thread");
             processNewsLetter.start();
             System.out.println("Joining Thread");
              processNewsLetter.join();
              Item Processed = NewMessage.replaceItemValue("Processed","1");
          Processed.setSummary(true);
              NewMessage.save (true, false) ;
              NewMessage = Drafts.getNextDocument(NewMessage);
              } //End while (NewMessage != null)
      } // end try
catch(InterruptedException ie) {
             ie.printStackTrace();
} // end catch(InterruptedException ie)
      catch(NotesException ne) {
             ne.printStackTrace();
} // end catch(NotesException ne)
finally {
NotesThread.stermThread();
}
} //end public
} // end multiThreadJavaNewsLetter
```

After establishing a session and having a database to work with, the rest of the original Domino Java agent code in this class can run in a Java application with a few notable modifications.

In this code you use the fully extended Java class names for Domino documents and views, because the Swing classes and the Domino classes contain documents and views, so the Java compiler needs the developer to be specific about which view and document type you are referring to when creating new objects. Domino documents must be defined as `lotus.domino.Documents`, and Domino views must be defined as `lotus.domino.views`, as shown here:

```java
class processEmailsThread extends NotesThread {
private Database MailListFile;
private lotus.domino.Document NewMessage;

public processEmailsThread(Database MailListFile, lotus.domino.Document
NewMessage) {
     this.MailListFile = MailListFile;
     this.NewMessage = NewMessage;
     } // end public processEmailsThread
 public void runNotes() {
      try {
System.out.println("processEmailsThread Running");
     Item ProcessedItem = NewMessage.getFirstItem("Processed");
     if (ProcessedItem.getValueString() != null); {
               //Item SentToItem = NewMessage.getFirstItem("SentTo");
Item RecipentText =NewMessage.replaceItemValue("RecipentText",
null);
             RecipentText.setValueString(Recipients);
             Enumeration values = RecipentText.getValues().elements(
             while (values.hasMoreElements()) {
lotus.domino.Document memo =
MailListFile.createDocument();
                     NewMessage.copyAllItems( memo, true );
                     String eMailAddress = (String)values.nextElement();
                     memo.replaceItemValue("Recipients", eMailAddress);
                     memo.replaceItemValue("SendTo", eMailAddress);
                     memo.removeItem( "SentTo" ) ;
                     memo.setSaveMessageOnSend(true);
                     memo.send( false ) ;
                     } // end if (ProcessedItem.getValueString() != null)
                     } // end while (values.hasMoreElements())


} // end try
     catch(NotesException ne) {
             ne.printStackTrace();
}   // end catch(NotesException ne)
} // end runNotes()

} // end processEmailsThread
}
```

In preceding code segment, a bit of trickery was used to lessen the development load and make the code more compatible when running in Java agents and Java applications. Instead of having to create an array and parse the `Recipients` value as a string before looping through the array to send e-mails, it's easier from a coding point of view to create a new item in the in-memory Domino document, add the `Recipients` string value to the new item, and then use the code we already had to send the contents of the item to the `Enumerator` class for parsing and looping.

The rest of the code needs only the specific declarations of `lotus.domino.Document` and `lotus.domino.View` to run in a Java application instead of a Java agent. Note that `Notes-Thread` is used to instantiate multiple threads in a Java application instead of the runnable interface, as shown in Listing 34-2. Either method is acceptable to Java applications, but `NotesThread` can be used only if the application has access to Domino objects; whereas the runnable interface can be used for any thread handling in any Java application.

Summary

This chapter introduced you to Domino Java applications:

✦ Prerequisites for developing and running Domino applications in Java

✦ A simple conversion of a basic Domino Java agent to a Java application

✦ An example of an advanced Domino Java application

✦ Tips and tricks associated with working with Domino objects from Java applications.

The next chapter introduces Java servlets and what is required to run a Domino servlet. After you are introduced to servlets, you move on to extending simple examples that demonstrate how to adapt Domino Java agent and application code for use in Domino servlets.

✦   ✦   ✦

Java Servlets for Domino

By Brian Benz

Java has had adoption issues in the IT marketplace, with the exception of servlets. Java applets have not lived up to the promise of universal, platform-independent application delivery using Web browsers as a front-end, because of performance, reliability, and compatibility issues. Java applications require a Java Development Kit (JDK) or a Java Virtual Machine (JVM) to be loaded on a client's machine to provide any meaningful functionality, and, unfortunately, share the performance, reliability, and compatibility characteristics of Java applets. Java agents in Domino are widely used in Domino applications but can't run outside a Notes or Domino environment. Servlets, however, are a different story. Java servlets are quickly becoming the method of choice for implementing Java solutions in enterprise environments, mainly because of the application servers on the market that support high-volume, high-capacity transactional Web sites using servlets. Servlets are also a natural fit for the middle tiers of multitier application architectures because of their relatively good security model and multithread performance characteristics. Because servlets run exclusively on servers, they are not constrained by the less performance, distribution, and compatibility issues that plague the applet and Java application models.

Servlets are Java code that extends the `HTTPServlet` Java class, which is the core of the Sun Java Servlet Development Kit (JSDK). Servlet class files are loaded on a servlet application server and are called via Web browser requests. Every servlet has a call method, which receives servlet requests, and a response, which returns servlet responses.

Prerequisites for Developing Domino Servlets

Domino has native capabilities for supporting Java servlets, as well as advanced methods of integrating with the IBM WebSphere Application Server. This chapter will take you though the steps needed to code a servlet for use in the Domino environment. Issues surrounding Domino servlet deployment, performance, and security will also be covered. Illustrating the examples are the development and deployment of a simple Domino diagnostic servlet and a servlet that has been converted from the agent examples in Chapter 33.

Before installing and running servlets on a Domino server, the server must be configured for servlet support. Domino servlet support must be enabled in the server document, and the correct JDK and the server's Java-related environment variables must be set up to support servlets. The next few sections will take you through server setup.

Setting up servlet support in Domino

By default, servlet support is not enabled on a Domino server. Domino can manage its own servlet environment as part of the Domino HTTP task, or can delegate servlet management to a third-party servlet manager, such as the IBM WebSphere Server. WebSphere provides a much more robust servlet environment, with more security options, better performance, and more options for running and administrating servlets. Chapter 38 gets into the details of working with WebSphere, but the Domino servlet manager is more than adequate to provide you with an introduction to servlets for this chapter.

Note   Double-check to make sure that the Domino server has the HTTP task running before enabling Java servlet support. If it's not running on the server, load it by typing **LOAD HTTP** into the Domino administrator console.

To enable servlet support, a person with administration rights on the Domino server on which servlets will be running has to edit the server document in the Domino Directory. In the server document, click the Internet Protocols tab, and then select the Domino Web Engine tab. You will find a section called Java Servlets on the right of the document that appears. Change the value in the Java Servlet Support field from None to Domino Servlet Manager.

You should leave the default values for the Servlet URL field (as /servlet) and Class Pass field (as domino/servlet), unless you have a good reason to change them. The Servlet URL field indicates the trigger that causes Domino to look for a servlet as opposed to a Domino object, such as a database. The Class Path field is the location relative to the Domino data directory where the servlet class files are located. If left unchanged, the servlet directory is <Domino default directory>:\lotus\domino\data\domino\servlet.

Java servlet support: JDK and JSDK issues

Before trying to develop servlets that access Domino objects, you must know which Java Development Kit (JDK) to use when developing and compiling servlet code. Domino Server 5 supports the Sun JDK 1.1.8, and Domino Server 6 supports JDK 1.3 and Java Servlet Development Kit (JSDK) 2. Domino Server 6 ships with a JSDK.jar in the default Domino program directory. To download a JSDK.jar for previous versions of Domino from the Sun Web site, go to http://java.sun.com.

Editing the Domino server CLASSPATH, PATH, and JAVA_HOME

You need to add a Java servlet SDK reference if it's not already in the Domino server's CLASSPATH, which is usually in c:\lotus\domino\jsdk.jar. Make sure that the JSDK.jar file is there by searching the c:\Domino directory on your server for JSDK.jar before adding the value to your CLASSPATH environment variable. Aside from the JSDK reference, the CLASSPATH system variable should contain accurate references to Notes.jar and NCSO.Jar for supporting Domino servlets. The JDK \bin directory should be in the PATH environment variable for Java servlets to compile and run correctly, and the JAVA_HOME environment variable should be set to the main directory of the server's JDK.

For Windows NT and earlier server versions, you can set environmental variables via the autoexec.bat file. For Windows 2000 servers and later, you can set environmental variables by opening the Control Panel, selecting the System icon, selecting the Advanced tab, and then clicking the Environment Variables button.

Listing 35-1 shows the minimum required settings to support compiling and running servlets in a Domino 6 server environment. The Domino server is installed in c:\Lotus\Domino, and JDK 1.3 is installed in c:\JSDK1.3.1_01.

Listing 35-1: Minimum Environment Variable Settings for Servlet Support

```
SET CLASSPATH =
.;c:\Lotus\Domino\Data\domino\java\NCSO.jar;c:\lotus\
Domino\Notes.jar; c:\lotus\ Domino\JSDK.jar;
PATH=C:\WINNT;C:\WINNT\COMMAND;C:\jsdk1.3.1_01\bin;c:\lotus\D
omino;
set JAVA_HOME=c:\jsdk1.3.1_01
```

Setting Up JavaUserClasses in NOTES.INI

Servlets are supported as part of the HTTP task on a Domino server and run under the JVM that is installed as part of the JDK. Domino also has its own JVM to run its own classes, such as the lotus.domino classes. To ensure that your servlets are loaded as part of the Domino JVM, add the same JDK and JSDK references to the server's JavaUserClasses variable in the server's NOTES.INI. Listing 35-2 shows a standard Domino server JavaUserClasses variable setting for Domino JVM servlet support.

Listing 35-2: JavaUserClasses Value in a Domino Server's NOTES.INI

```
JavaUserCLasses = .;c:\Lotus\Domino\Data\domino\java\NCSO.jar;c:\lotus\
Domino\Notes.jar; c:\lotus\ Domino\JSDK.jar;
```

Installing the diagnostic servlet

You can download the diagnostic servlet from ndbible.com. The DiagnosticServlet. class file and the DiagnosticServlet.java source code file are also available for download.

To test your Domino servlet configuration, download the `DiagnosticServlet.class` file and copy it to the Domino servlet directory, which is usually `<drive>:\lotus\domino\data\domino\servlet`.

> **Note** After loading and copying new servlets, you must stop and restart the Domino HTTP task. You can do so by entering the `TELL HTTP RESTART` command in the server administrator console.

After restarting the HTTP task, you should see two messages from the Domino server Administration console. The first message is the following:

```
Java Servlet Manager Initialized
```

This message confirms that the servlet manager is running — check the server document setting if this doesn't appear. The second message is the following:

```
HTTP Web Server restarted
```

After the HTTP message appears, it's safe to test the servlet.

Running the diagnostic servlet

After the HTTP task restarts, start up any browser that has access to the server and open the following URL:

```
http://<server IP address>/servlet/DiagnosticServlet
```

> **Caution** The Domino servlet manager is case sensitive. URLs must match the filename exactly. Check the case of URL references if you're having trouble with servlets in the Domino environment.

Because of servlet initialization, the servlet may take 10 to 15 seconds to load the first time. If everything is configured properly, you should get results similar to those in Figure 35-1. The servlet displays system properties and the results of a few basic tests to ensure that the servlet environment can access Domino and system objects.

Troubleshooting the Diagnostic Servlet

If the servlet encounters any problems running, an error message appears in the browser window. The errors are designed to provide clues as to where the problem lies. Start by checking the case of the servlet URL. Next, check the version of JDK and JSDK, and that the `CLASSPATH`, `PATH`, and `JAVA_HOME` environment variables and the `JavaUserClasses` variable in the server's `NOTES.INI` all point to actual files with the same names on the server.

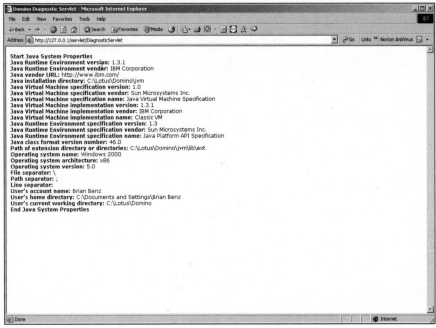

Figure 35-1: The Browser output for the diagnostic servlet

Getting Under the Hood of the Domino Diagnostic Servlet

The diagnostic servlet is a good starting point for discovering how servlets interact with the Domino server. Listing 35-3 shows the full code for the diagnostic servlet.

Listing 35-3: **Code Listing for the Domino Diagnostic Servlet**

```
import java.io.*;
import javax.servlet.*;
import javax.servlet.http.*;

public class DiagnosticServlet extends HttpServlet {

    public void doGet(HttpServletRequest request,
            HttpServletResponse response)
        throws IOException, ServletException
```

Continued

Listing 35-3 *(continued)*

```
{
  response.setContentType("text/html");
  PrintWriter out = response.getWriter();

  out.println("<html>");
  out.println("<head>");
out.println("<title> Domino Diagnostic Servlet</title>");
  out.println("</head>");
  out.println("<body bgcolor=\"white\">");
out.println("<font size=\"2\" face=\"Verdana\">");


  try {

out.println("<b>Start Java System Properties"+"</b><br>");
out.println("<b>Java Runtime Environment version: </b>" +
System.getProperty("java.version")+"<br>");
out.println("<b>Java Runtime Environment vendor: </b>" +
System.getProperty("java.vendor")+"<br>");
out.println("<b>Java vendor URL: </b>" +
System.getProperty("java.vendor.url")+"<br>");
out.println("<b>Java installation directory: </b>" +
System.getProperty("java.home")+"<br>");
out.println("<b>Java Virtual Machine specification version: </b>" +
System.getProperty("java.vm.specification.version")+"<br>");
out.println("<b>Java Virtual Machine specification vendor: </b>" +
System.getProperty("java.vm.specification.vendor")+"<br>");
out.println("<b>Java Virtual Machine specification name: </b>" +
System.getProperty("java.vm.specification.name")+"<br>");
out.println("<b>Java Virtual Machine implementation version: </b>" +
System.getProperty("java.vm.version")+"<br>");
out.println("<b>Java Virtual Machine implementation vendor: </b>" +
System.getProperty("java.vm.vendor")+"<br>");
out.println("<b>Java Virtual Machine implementation name: </b>" +
System.getProperty("java.vm.name")+"<br>");
out.println("<b>Java Runtime Environment specification version: </b>" +
System.getProperty("java.specification.version")+"<br>");
out.println("<b>Java Runtime Environment specification vendor: </b>" +
System.getProperty("java.specification.vendor")+"<br>");
out.println("<b>Java Runtime Environment specification name: </b>" +
System.getProperty("java.specification.name")+"<br>");
out.println("<b>Java class format version number: </b>" +
System.getProperty("java.class.version")+"<br>");
out.println("<b>Path of extension directory or directories: </b>" +
System.getProperty("java.ext.dirs")+"<br>");
out.println("<b>Operating system name: </b>" +
System.getProperty("os.name")+"<br>");
out.println("<b>Operating system architecture: </b>" +
```

```
System.getProperty("os.arch")+"<br>");
out.println("<b>Operating system version: </b>" +
System.getProperty("os.version")+"<br>");
out.println("<b>File separator: </b>" +
System.getProperty("file.separator")+"<br>");
out.println("<b>Path separator: </b>" +
System.getProperty("path.separator")+"<br>");
out.println("<b>Line separator: </b>" +
System.getProperty("line.separator")+"<br>");
out.println("<b>User's account name: </b>" +
System.getProperty("user.name")+"<br>");
out.println("<b>User's home directory: </b>" +
System.getProperty("user.home")+"<br>");
out.println("<b>User's current working directory: </b>" +
System.getProperty("user.dir")+"<br>");
out.println("<b><b>End Java System Properties"+"</b><br>");
    out.println("</font>");
    out.println("</body>");
    out.println("</html>");
} catch (Exception e) {
    out.println( "<h1>exception:
"+e+"Message:"+e.getMessage()+"</h1>" );
    }
  }
}
```

Take a look at the Java classes imported for a servlet.

```
import java.io.*;
import javax.servlet.*;
import javax.servlet.http.*;
```

Importing `javax.servlet` and `javax.servlet.http` enables the `HttpServletRequest` and `HttpServletResponse` classes to handle the communication between the Web browser and the servlet via HTTP. `Java.io` is imported to permit the display for the servlet output to the browser window via the `out.println` class, and to handle any I/O errors.

The servlet uses a `PrintWriter` to handle capturing and sending the servlet output to the current browser window. The servlet sets up a header for an HTML page and prints the header to the browser window.

```
public class DiagnosticServlet extends HttpServlet {

  public void doGet(HttpServletRequest request,
          HttpServletResponse response)
    throws IOException, ServletException
  {
    response.setContentType("text/html");
    PrintWriter out = response.getWriter();

    out.println("<html>");
```

```
    out.println("<head>");
  out.println("<title> Domino Diagnostic Servlet</title>");
    out.println("</head>");
    out.println("<body bgcolor=\"white\">");
  out.println("<font size=\"2\" face=\"Verdana\">");
```

The final step, repeated many times, retrieves all the java.System.Properties via the
system.getProperties method. Because you're displaying the output data in HTML, some
basic HTML formatting is included in the text output to add new lines and bold fonts. The
catch statement at the end of the code catches any system errors while the servlet is running, and then displays the errors to the browser window so the developer can see where the
servlet is having trouble:

```
  try {

out.println("<b>Start Java System Properties"+"</b><br>");
out.println("<b>Java Runtime Environment version: </b>" +
System.getProperty("java.version")+"<br>");
out.println("<b>Java Runtime Environment vendor: </b>" +
System.getProperty("java.vendor")+"<br>");
out.println("<b>Java vendor URL: </b>" +
System.getProperty("java.vendor.url")+"<br>");
out.println("<b>Java installation directory: </b>" +
System.getProperty("java.home")+"<br>");
out.println("<b>Java Virtual Machine specification version: </b>" +
System.getProperty("java.vm.specification.version")+"<br>");
out.println("<b>Java Virtual Machine specification vendor: </b>" +
System.getProperty("java.vm.specification.vendor")+"<br>");
out.println("<b>Java Virtual Machine specification name: </b>" +
System.getProperty("java.vm.specification.name")+"<br>");
out.println("<b>Java Virtual Machine implementation version: </b>" +
System.getProperty("java.vm.version")+"<br>");
out.println("<b>Java Virtual Machine implementation vendor: </b>" +
System.getProperty("java.vm.vendor")+"<br>");
out.println("<b>Java Virtual Machine implementation name: </b>" +
System.getProperty("java.vm.name")+"<br>");
out.println("<b>Java Runtime Environment specification version: </b>" +
System.getProperty("java.specification.version")+"<br>");
out.println("<b>Java Runtime Environment specification vendor: </b>" +
System.getProperty("java.specification.vendor")+"<br>");
out.println("<b>Java Runtime Environment specification name: </b>" +
System.getProperty("java.specification.name")+"<br>");
out.println("<b>Java class format version number: </b>" +
System.getProperty("java.class.version")+"<br>");
out.println("<b>Path of extension directory or directories: </b>" +
System.getProperty("java.ext.dirs")+"<br>");
out.println("<b>Operating system name: </b>" +
System.getProperty("os.name")+"<br>");
out.println("<b>Operating system architecture: </b>" +
```

```
System.getProperty("os.arch")+"<br>");
out.println("<b>Operating system version: </b>" +
System.getProperty("os.version")+"<br>");
out.println("<b>File separator: </b>" +
System.getProperty("file.separator")+"<br>");
out.println("<b>Path separator: </b>" +
System.getProperty("path.separator")+"<br>");
out.println("<b>Line separator: </b>" +
System.getProperty("line.separator")+"<br>");
out.println("<b>User's account name: </b>" +
System.getProperty("user.name")+"<br>");
out.println("<b>User's home directory: </b>" +
System.getProperty("user.home")+"<br>");
out.println("<b>User's current working directory: </b>" +
System.getProperty("user.dir")+"<br>");
out.println("<b><b>End Java System Properties"+"</b><br>");
    out.println("</font>");
    out.println("</body>");
    out.println("</html>");
} catch (Exception e) {
    out.println( "<h1>exception:
"+e+"Message:"+e.getMessage()+"</h1>" );
  }
 }
}
```

Converting Domino Agents to Domino Servlets

Domino agents are usually easy for Domino developers to code when compared to Java applications, applets, and servlets. But Domino agents also suffer from poor performance, due to the fact that they do not stay in memory on a Domino server. This means that they have to be loaded into the JVM each time they are called, which causes application overhead issues. One way to overcome this limitation is to recode the agent as a servlet. Servlets are designed to reside in memory at server startup, or after the first time they load. The servlet can then run in the Domino Servlet environment or on a WebSphere server. The DominoBibleJavaServletExample provides a good example of adapting the multithreaded agent example from Chapter 33 for use in a servlet environment. Listing 35-4 shows the complete servlet code.

You can download the DominoBibleJavaServletExample servlet from ndbible.com. See the notes at the site for full installation instructions. Remember that the Domino-BibleJavaServletExample.java file creates three class files when it is compiled: DominoBibleJavaServletExample.class, multiThreadJavaNewsLetter.class and processEmailsThread.class. Make sure that all of these files are copied to your /servlet directory on the Domino server, and don't forget to restart the HTTP server. (The previous example in this chapter explains how to do this.)

Listing 35-4: Domino Agent Code Converted to a Domino Servlet

```java
import java.io.*;
import java.util.*;
import javax.servlet.*;
import javax.servlet.http.*;
import lotus.domino.*;

public class DominoBibleJavaServletExample extends HttpServlet {

  public void doGet(HttpServletRequest request,
  HttpServletResponse response)
  throws IOException, ServletException {
    response.setContentType("text/html");
    PrintWriter out = response.getWriter();
    try {

      multiThreadJavaNewsLetter pnl = new multiThreadJavaNewsLetter();
      out.println( "<H1>Newsletter Mailing Complete</H1>" );
    }

    catch (Exception e) {
      out.println( "<h1>exception: "+e+"Message:"+e.getMessage()+"</h1>" );
    }
  }
}

class multiThreadJavaNewsLetter  {
  public multiThreadJavaNewsLetter() {
    try {
      NotesThread.sinitThread();
      Session session = NotesFactory.createSession();
      //AgentContext agentContext = session.getAgentContext();
      //Database MailListFile = agentContext.getCurrentDatabase();
      Database MailListFile = session.getDatabase("",
"ndbible\\NewsLetterDistribution.nsf");
      lotus.domino.View Drafts = MailListFile.getView("($Drafts)");
      lotus.domino.Document NewMessage = Drafts.getFirstDocument();
      while (NewMessage != null) {
        processEmailsThread processNewsLetter = new
processEmailsThread(MailListFile, NewMessage);
        System.out.println("Starting Thread");
        processNewsLetter.start();
        System.out.println("Joining Thread");
        processNewsLetter.join();
        Item Processed = NewMessage.replaceItemValue("Processed", "1");
        Processed.setSummary(true);
        NewMessage.save(true, false) ;
        NewMessage = Drafts.getNextDocument(NewMessage);
      } //End while (NewMessage != null)
```

```
    } // end try
    catch(InterruptedException ie) {
      ie.printStackTrace();
    } // end catch(InterruptedException ie)
    catch(NotesException ne) {
      ne.printStackTrace();
    } // end catch(NotesException ne)
    finally {
      NotesThread.stermThread();
    }  //end finally
  } //end public
} // end multiThreadJavaNewsLetter

class processEmailsThread extends NotesThread {
  private Database MailListFile;
  private lotus.domino.Document NewMessage;

  public processEmailsThread(Database MailListFile, lotus.domino.Document
NewMessage) {
    this.MailListFile = MailListFile;
    this.NewMessage = NewMessage;
  } // end public processEmailsThread

  public void runNotes() {
    try {
      System.out.println("processEmailsThread Running");
      Item ProcessedItem = NewMessage.getFirstItem("Processed");
      if (ProcessedItem.getValueString() != null); {
        Item SentToItem = NewMessage.getFirstItem("SentTo");
        Enumeration values = SentToItem.getValues().elements();

        while (values.hasMoreElements()) {
          lotus.domino.Document memo = MailListFile.createDocument();
          NewMessage.copyAllItems( memo, true );
          String eMailAddress = (String)values.nextElement();
          memo.replaceItemValue("Recipients", eMailAddress);
          memo.replaceItemValue("SendTo", eMailAddress);
          memo.removeItem( "SentTo" ) ;
          memo.setSaveMessageOnSend(true);
          memo.send( false ) ;
        } // end if (ProcessedItem.getValueString() != null)
      } // end while (values.hasMoreElements())

    } // end try
    catch(NotesException ne) {
      ne.printStackTrace();
    }  // end catch(NotesException ne)
  } // end runNotes()

} // end processEmailsThread
```

As with Listing 35-3, this servlet imports the `javax.servlet` and `javax.servlet.http` classes to create request and response objects for the servlet and handle requests and responses via HTTP. `Java.io` and `java.util` are used for output to browser windows and error handling. Unlike the previous example, you use the `lotus.domino` classes this time to access the Domino server via the `NotesFactory` session object.

```
import java.io.*;
import java.util.*;
import javax.servlet.*;
import javax.servlet.http.*;
import lotus.domino.*;
```

The next step is to set up the call and response events for this servlet by implementing the `doGet` class with request and response objects as parameters. This is also where errors are caught for the servlet. In this case, this class is watching for any I/O errors, because the servlet creates a response object that writes to the browser window. The class also watches for servlet exceptions thrown by the extended `HttpServlet` class.

```
public class DominoBibleJavaServletExample extends HttpServlet {

    public void doGet(HttpServletRequest request,
            HttpServletResponse response)
      throws IOException, ServletException
    {
    response.setContentType("text/html");
      PrintWriter out = response.getWriter();
```

The code in the `try` section of the main `doGet` class creates a new instance of the `MultiThreadJavaNewsletter` class and names the new class `pnl` (which stands for `ProcessNewsLetters`).

```
    try {

    multiThreadJavaNewsLetter pnl = new multiThreadJavaNewsLetter();
    out.println( "<H1>Newsletter Mailing Complete</H1>" );
}

    catch (Exception e) {
out.println( "<h1>exception: "+e+"Message:"+e.getMessage()+"</h1>" );
      }
    }
}
```

The `multiThreadJavaNewsLetter` class is the same as the class defined in the multi-threaded agent in Listing 33-2 and adapted for use in the Java applications in Chapter 34. You may also recall that Chapter 33 discusses the reasons for converting LotusScript agents to Java. One reason for converting LotusScript to Java is so that the code can later be adapted to a Java servlet or application. In the following example, the code illustrates how easy it is to adapt Java agent code for use in Java servlets. In fact, because of the limited functionality of many Java development UIs when interacting with Domino objects, it's sometimes advisable to write a Domino Java agent that handles the functionality you need for interaction with Domino objects in the Java agent UI of Domino Designer, and then move the proven class code to the Java application or servlet development UI for final integration and testing.

The following code is the same code that was used for the multithreaded agent example, with a couple of exceptions. Instead of having a Domino session object available by extending AgentBase, you have to get a session object by invoking the NotesFactory class for your servlet, just as you did in the application example in Chapter 34. Also, you don't have access to the agent context class, which provides access to the current database via the getCurrentDatabase method. You have to select a Domino database explicitly from the server's default data directory — in this case, the Newsletter Distribution database.

The rest of the functionality is the same as the agent and application examples in Chapters 33 and 34. The multiThreadJavaNewsletter class loops through all the documents in the Drafts view of the Newsletter Distribution database and mails a copy of the newsletter to each of the recipients listed in the multivalue SentTo field. Each draft document is assigned a thread to run on by creating a new processEmailsThread class for each document. When each thread is done, the processEmailsThread class turns code execution back to the join method. The Newsletter document is then marked as processed, which removes the document from the Drafts view in the Newsletter Distribution database so it won't be resent to the same recipients the next time the servlet is run.

```
class multiThreadJavaNewsLetter  {
  public multiThreadJavaNewsLetter() {
    try {
      NotesThread.sinitThread();
      Session session = NotesFactory.createSession();
      //AgentContext agentContext = session.getAgentContext();
      //Database MailListFile = agentContext.getCurrentDatabase();
      Database MailListFile = session.getDatabase("",
"ndbible\\NewsLetterDistribution.nsf");
      lotus.domino.View Drafts = MailListFile.getView("($Drafts)");
      lotus.domino.Document NewMessage = Drafts.getFirstDocument();
      while (NewMessage != null) {
        processEmailsThread processNewsLetter = new
processEmailsThread(MailListFile, NewMessage);
        System.out.println("Starting Thread");
        processNewsLetter.start();
        System.out.println("Joining Thread");
        processNewsLetter.join();
        Item Processed = NewMessage.replaceItemValue("Processed", "1");
        Processed.setSummary(true);
        NewMessage.save(true, false) ;
        NewMessage = Drafts.getNextDocument(NewMessage);
      } //End while (NewMessage != null)

    } // end try
    catch(InterruptedException ie) {
      ie.printStackTrace();
    } // end catch(InterruptedException ie)
    catch(NotesException ne) {
      ne.printStackTrace();
    } // end catch(NotesException ne)
    finally {
      NotesThread.stermThread();
```

```
    }  //end finally
  } //end public
} // end multiThreadJavaNewsLetter
```

The rest of the code is the same as the agent and applications code for the
processEmailsThread class. The specific declarations of lotus.domino.Document and
lotus.domino.View resolve any future compiler issues if another Java Document or View
class is imported into the servlet, both of which are common class names. Swing classes for
applications, for example, use Document and View for object class names, and a Document
class is used to describe XML documents when parsing XML documents using Apache
Xerces, or implementing Apache Xalan classes for XML transformation.

NotesThread can be used to instantiate multiple threads in a Java application instead of the
runnable interface in servlets and Java applications, as long as the lotus.domino classes are
available and you can extend NotesThread (which is an extension of the java.lang.thread
class). Either method is acceptable to Java servlets, but the runnable interface is best used if
the servlet isn't working with Domino objects:

```
class processEmailsThread extends NotesThread {
private Database MailListFile;
private lotus.domino.Document NewMessage;

public processEmailsThread(Database MailListFile, lotus.domino.Document
NewMessage) {
  this.MailListFile = MailListFile;
  this.NewMessage = NewMessage;
  } // end public processEmailsThread


 public void runNotes() {
   try {
System.out.println("processEmailsThread Running");
    Item ProcessedItem = NewMessage.getFirstItem("Processed");
    if (ProcessedItem.getValueString() != null); {
    Item SentToItem = NewMessage.getFirstItem("SentTo");
      Enumeration values = SentToItem.getValues().elements();
    while (values.hasMoreElements()) {
lotus.domino.Document memo =
MailListFile.createDocument();
    NewMessage.copyAllItems( memo, true );
    String eMailAddress = (String)values.nextElement();
    memo.replaceItemValue("Recipients", eMailAddress);
    memo.replaceItemValue("SendTo", eMailAddress);
    memo.removeItem( "SentTo" ) ;
    memo.setSaveMessageOnSend(true);
    memo.send( false ) ;
    } // end if (ProcessedItem.getValueString() != null)
    } // end while (values.hasMoreElements())


} // end try
   catch(NotesException ne) {
   ne.printStackTrace();
} // end catch(NotesException ne)
} // end runNotes()


} // end processEmailsThread
```

Summary

This chapter introduced you to Domino servlets. It included the following topics:

✦ Prerequisites for developing Domino servlets

✦ A review of a simple Example: The diagnostic servlet

✦ Troubleshooting a Domino servlet environment

✦ How to port Domino Java agent and application code to servlets

✦ A review of a more complex example: Recoding the multithreaded Newsletter Java agent example into a multithreaded Java servlet

Now that you have a basic understanding of Java application and servlet code, you need to learn how a developer actually creates code for Domino Java applications and servlets. Java code for anything but Java agents is difficult to develop in the Domino Designer UI. In the next chapter, you review options for developing Domino applications and servlets using third-party development tools.

✦   ✦   ✦

Java Servlets Using Third-Party Developer Tools

By Brian Benz

Chapters 34 and 35 reviewed techniques for making Java applications and servlets work with Domino, but an important detail was glossed over — how are Domino Java servlets and applications developed? The Domino Designer UI is a great place to build Java agents, and it can even store and compile some simple applications and servlets. But most Java applications require classes and methods that the Domino Designer UI was never meant to handle.

Complex application and servlet Java can usually be loaded into the UI, and the interface can even break up and list the classes in the Work pane to the left of the Programmer's pane. Unfortunately, saving and compiling are not so predictable. Figure 36-1 shows an error message generated by Domino Designer when trying to save the `DominoBibleJavaServletExample.java` in the Java agent UI. Note that the classes on the left of the code recognize the classes in the code, but the compiler can't handle some of the imported classes and sends a message that `javax.servlet` cannot be found in the import (and that's just the beginning).

This chapter outlines the steps for enabling Domino object support for the two most popular Java application development environments: WebSphere Studio Workbench, and SunONE Studio. Two options are discussed, partly because most large organizations with J2EE development initiatives have standardized on one of these platforms, and partly because of the different approaches taken in the user interface and features. Both platforms need some customization, which is covered in detail in this chapter, to enable the compiling and running of Domino applications, applets, and servlets. If you already have one of these environments set up, running, and configured for access to Domino objects, you can probably skip this chapter.

Note   You will need to set up one of these environments (WebSphere Studio Workbench, or SunONE Studio) to compile and run the Java application and servlet examples in Chapters 37, 38, 50, 51, and 57.

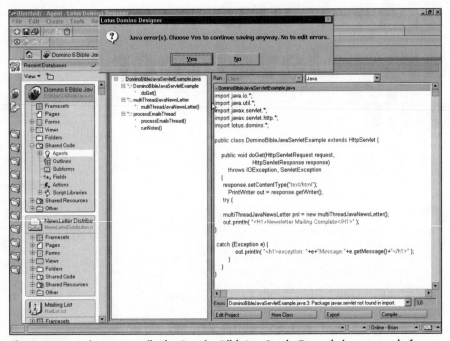

Figure 36-1: Trying to compile the DominoBibleJavaServletExample.java example from Chapter 35 in the Domino Designer Java agent UI

Options for Developing Java Applications and Servlets

Literally hundreds of third-party tools are available for Java developers, ranging from free to outrageously expensive. But a few key factors always play into the tools game, such as large numbers of developers with skills on a platform, and the ability of the company to stay alive and weather today's competitive application developer tools market with deep pockets and good tools, research, and strategies. For this reason, this chapter focuses on the community editions of WebSphere Studio Workbench, and SunONE Studio, the free versions of two widely used, readily available tools. BEA, Borland, Rational, TogetherSoft, and several others have good tools as well, if you are looking for options beyond the tools covered here. Notably, BEA has an integrated-platform approach similar to Domino, combining a J2EE server, administration tools, and an integrated development environment. BEA has a free trial version of its integrated platform available for download at www.bea.com.

Both the IBM and Sun offerings are open-source and focus on J2EE application, servlet, and applet development. Unfortunately for developers, both follow different paths when it comes to development features and user interfaces. IBM offers Java development software based on the open-source Eclipse development tools framework project; whereas Sun's tools are based on the NetBeans open-source tools framework. The Eclipse tools will be more familiar to developers who have been working in Windows. Eclipse follows Windows conventions in their user interface, and for basic tasks like naming menu options. SunONE's interface and task naming more closely follows Unix and Linux standards, so developers that are used to X-windows environments will probably be right at home, even in the Windows version.

Both tools have basic facilities for basic functions such as debugging, compiling, and executing Java applications, applets, and servlets. Both also have rudimentary versions of advanced features, such as functionality for building a basic Java User Interface into an application or applet. More advanced features are available when the full version of each tool is purchased.

Developing Domino Servlets with WebSphere Studio Workbench 2.0.1

IBM has added several plug-ins to the base Eclipse Workbench platform and rebranded it as WebSphere Studio Workbench 2.0.1. The plug-in architecture of Eclipse-based products makes the platform easy to upgrade with customized tools and interfaces. WebSphere Studio Application Developer, for example, is based on the WebSphere Studio Workbench product and ships with major additions and a more advanced UI for enterprise development — along with a hefty price tag. You can download the free version of WebSphere Studio Workbench from `www-3.ibm.com/software/ad/workbench`. Version 2.0.1 supports JDK 1.3 and 1.4, and therefore is acceptable for use with Domino.

Navigating WebSphere Studio Workbench

The Workbench is based on the concept of perspectives, which contain navigators, outlines, and editors — much like Domino Designer contains a Work pane on the left, a Reference pane, and Programmer's pane. On the far left is a shortcut bar that lists and navigates perspectives, much like the bookmark bar on Domino Designer. The name of the active perspective is displayed in the Perspective window title bar. When WebSphere Studio Workbench is opened for the first time, a Welcome screen appears in the default Editor pane, and the Perspective, Navigator, and Outline panes are blank, as in Figure 36-2.

Creating a new project

Before coding can begin, you must first create an ndbible project that will be used to contain the servlet code from Chapter 35. Creating a project in WebSphere Studio Workbench creates a new directory in which to store the code, along with any associated system files. The first dialog box asks for a project type, which in these examples should always be Java Project. The second dialog box asks for a project name, which becomes a subdirectory of the default directory specified in the same box. For example, if the project is named `ndbible`, the default directory of `C:\eclipse\workspace` is chosen for the project, the default directory for the project will be `C:\eclipse\workspace\ndbible`. The third dialog box is where you set the Java settings for the project. Figure 36-3 shows the Java Settings dialog box. You can specify the subdirectory for Java source code in the Java Settings dialog box, as well as libraries that need to be in the build path of the new project, additional files to be imported into the project directory, and output folders for compiled code.

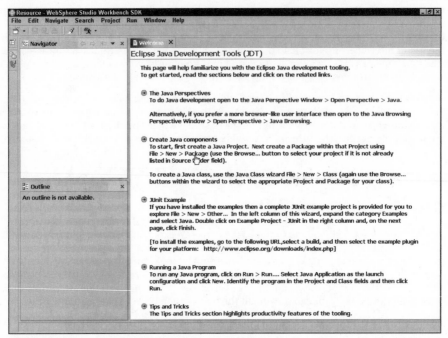

Figure 36-2: The post-installation Welcome screen for the WebSphere Studio Workbench

Figure 36-3: The Java Settings dialog box for
WebSphere Studio Workbench 2.0.1

Importing the servlet source code

The next step is to add an example source code file into the new ndbible project. Figure 36-4 shows the Import File dialog box, with the `DominoBibleJavaServletExample.java` source code file selected.

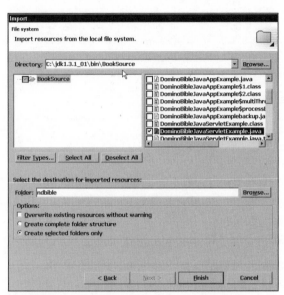

Figure 36-4: The Import File dialog box with the DominoBibleJavaServletExample.java source code file selected

Choosing Finish from this dialog box copies the source code into the WebSphere Studio Workbench project folder, compiles the code, lists all files associated with the project in the Navigator pane, sets up a class hierarchy display in the Outline pane, and displays formatted source code in the Editor pane, as shown in Figure 36-5.

Editing the classpath variable

Figure 36-5 includes several errors highlighted in the Editor pane when the `DominoBible-JavaServletExample.java` source code is imported for the first time. This is because the .jar files required for the source code to function are either not included as part of the import or not listed in the classpath for the project environment. Unfortunately, WebSphere Studio Workbench 2.0.1 does not automatically add the system classpath to a new project, although this would be a great feature. A system's classpath is a way for a Java program to find the classes that it needs to function. Java classes are usually imported in .jar (Java Archive) or .zip files, which contain a number of Java .class files compressed and stored in one archive file. Java programs look for .jar or .zip files by reading files in the order listed in a system's classpath then looking in the files to see whether they contain the classes that the Java program needs to run.

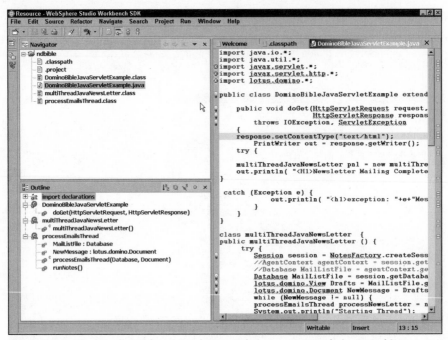

Figure 36-5: The DominoBibleJavaServletExample.java source code imported into WebSphere Studio Workbench

Developers either need to import required .jar and .class files as part of the project, specify a project classpath when a project is created, or edit the .classpath object after a project is created. In this case, you'll edit the project .classpath by selecting the .classpath file object from the View pane on the left and cutting and pasting the system classpath from your system environment variables into the .classpath object's SRC parameter, as shown in Figure 36-6.

The DominoBibleJavaServletExample.java source code needs the NCSO.jar file, which is where the lotus.domino.* classes are imported from at application runtime. Make sure that the NCSO.jar file, which is usually located in the <Notes default directory>\Data\ domino\java subdirectory of a Domino Designer workstation, is in the .classpath for the project.

After you add the classpath setting that includes the reference to the NCSO.jar file, all the default errors go away, because resolution with the imported .jar files that are now visible to the editor has occurred. You can now begin editing and debugging the Java code.

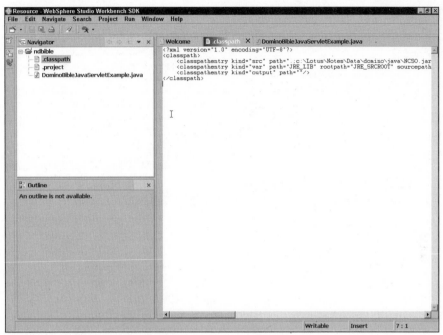

Figure 36-6: Adding the SRC parameter to the .classpath object from the system classpath environmental variables

Editing and debugging Java code

WebSphere studio Workbench has many nice, but basic features as part of the included plug-ins for the Java editor. These include the ability to edit, debug, compile, and run Java applications, applets, and servlets.

Just as in Domino Designer, code is color-coded based on the type of code. By default, core Java is purple, user-defined Java is black, text variables are blue, comments are green, and errors are red. The code is automatically formatted and indented, and there are menu options to force reformatting, to organize imports, and so on. The color scheme as well as font styles and formatting options are configurable by choosing Window ➪ Preferences. One thing that is noticeably absent form the preferences is an option for line wrapping in the Editor pane. Along the left side of the Editor pane is a series of markers for class files, indicated by light bulbs. Clicking one of the light bulbs highlights the class code and opens a dialog box that displays options for accessing and instantiating the class. Figure 36-7 shows these features in a working code Editor pane.

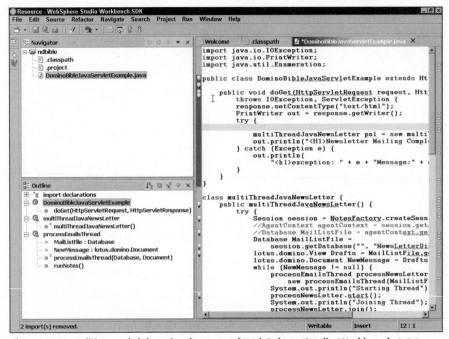

Figure 36-7: Editing and debugging features of WebSphere Studio Workbench 2.0.1

Compiling and running Java code

Code is compiled when it is imported in to the project and can be recompiled when the source code is saved, or when all project code is compiled by choosing Project ➪ Rebuild Project from the main menu. Running the code that is currently being edited is accomplished by choosing Run ➪ Run from the main menu.

Developing Domino Servlets with SunONE Studio 4.0

Sun's open-source, free distribution offering is based on the former Forte Tools for Java. As with the IBM offerings, the plug-in architecture of SunONE-based products makes the platform easy to customize to a developer's liking. The Free SunONE Community edition is the base platform for the much more expensive SunONE Enterprise edition, but like WebSphere Studio Workbench, it still has some very good, if basic, features. All SunONE products are based on the open-source but Sun-controlled NetBeans platform. SunONE Studio can be downloaded from www.sun.com/software.sundev. Like WebSphere Studio 2.0.1, SunONE Studio 4.0 supports JDK 1.3, and therefore, is the best choice for compatibility with Domino applications and servlets. The setup process for SunONE Studio is lengthy and somewhat cryptic the first time it is opened. Figure 36-8 shows the first-time installation screen and the optional Welcome dialog box.

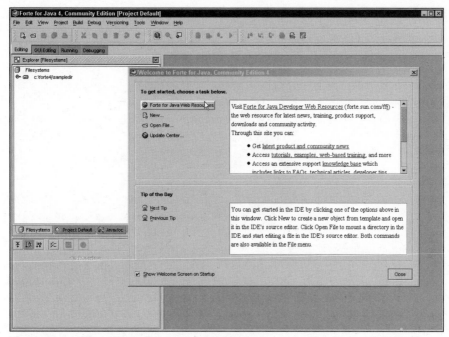

Figure 36-8: The post-installation and setup Welcome screen for the SunONE Studio

Navigating SunONE Studio 4.0

SunONE Studio contains two main panes. The Explorer pane has tabs for code editing, GUI editing, running, and debugging. Below the Explorer pane is a Properties pane, which tracks properties of whatever is being accessed in the Explorer pane. The Editor pane is where code and GUI editing takes place when the Explorer Editing or GUI Editing tab is selected, and where runtime and debugging messages are displayed when the Explorer is in Run or Debug mode. When SunONE Studio is opened for the first time, a Welcome dialog box appears on top of the UI.

Creating a new project

From the Welcome dialog box or the main menu, you can open several types of files and templates, which range from single blank standalone Java files to predefined project templates for JavaBeans, JDBC applications, and Web sites. Templates are an integrated workspace that accommodates certain types of code, such as applets, applications, and servlets. Because you are working with a servlet in this example, you could choose to open a servlet template by selecting the servlet and JSP file template section and selecting a servlet template, but because you opened a project in WebSphere Studio Workbench, you're going to compare opening a project here as well. Figure 36-9 shows the Created Project Template Workspace.

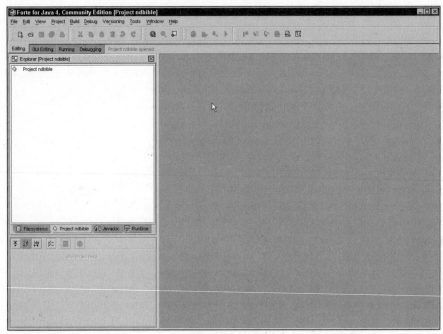

Figure 36-9: The blank template for the ndbible project in SunONE Studio 4.0

Importing the servlet source code

The next step is to add some code to the new ndbible project. Figure 36-10 shows the Import File dialog box, with the `DominoBibleJavaServletExample.java` source code file selected. SunONE has chosen to implement its own file system browser in the Windows version, which takes some getting used to if you're used to the Windows file browser, but is familiar to those who have worked in windowing platforms on Unix or Linux workstations. Choosing Finish from this dialog box copies the source code SunONE Studio Workbench project folder. SunONE Studio does not compile the code automatically, but the code can be compiled by right-clicking the Editor window. Compiling the code in SunONE Studio sets up a Properties box in the lower-left of the screen and also displays any error messages below the Editor pane. The result of compiling the imported `DominoBibleJavaServletExample.java` source code is shown in Figure 36-11.

Figure 36-10: The Open File dialog box with the DominoBibleJavaServletExample. java source code file selected

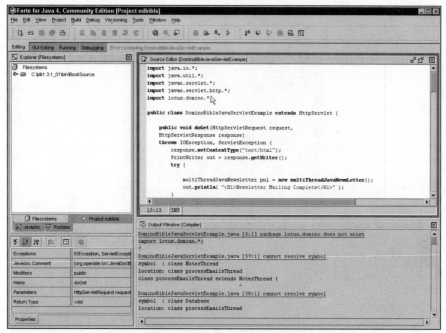

Figure 36-11: The DominoBibleJavaServletExample.java source code imported into SunONE Studio

Mounting the file system with the Notes.jar file

Figure 36-11 includes several errors highlighted below the Editor pane when the `DominoBibleJavaServletExample.java` source code is imported for the first time. As with WebSphere Studio Workbench, this is because the .jar files required for the source code to function were not included as part of the import into the project. Even worse, there is no way to list a classpath for a SunONE Studio project environment. Developers need to import the required .jar and .class files as part of the project, through a process called mounting the file system. To mount a JAR or ZIP archive in the IDE, choose File ⇨ Mount File System from the main menu. In the Choose Template pane of the wizard, choose the Archive/ZIP option, and click Next. Navigate in the file system to the `NCSO.jar` file in your default Lotus directory and click Finish again. Figure 36-12 shows `DominoBibleJavaServletExample.java` after the `Notes.jar` file is mounted and accessible to the `DominoBibleJavaServletExample.java` at runtime.

Editing and debugging Java code

Like WebSphere Studio Workbench, SunONE Studio has many basic features for Java editing, with similar color-coding and formatting options. Like WebSphere Studio Workbench, there is no option for line wrapping in the Editor pane. As for interaction and features inside the Editor's pane, WebSphere Studio Workbench has more sophisticated options and a more intuitive interface for developers used to a Windows environment.

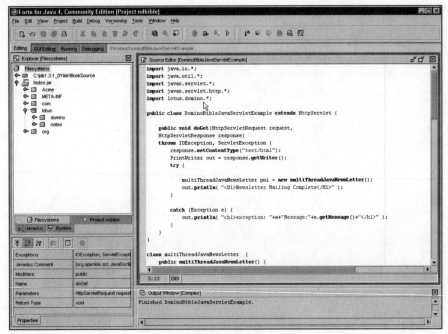

Figure 36-12: The compiled source code in the Editor pane, and Notes.jar in the Filesystems Properties box

Compiling and running Java code

Code is compiled manually by right-clicking the Editor pane. Running the code is accomplished by right-clicking the Editor pane and selecting Execute, which compiles the code and opens a runtime debugging environment. One of the nicer features in SunONE Studio is the integration of the TomCat server in the default installation, which is activated at runtime when a Java program is executed. This helps a great deal when testing and debugging servlets and JSPs.

Summary

In this chapter, you were introduced to third-party developer tools for developing Domino Java applications, including:

✦ Why you need a third-party Java IDE to develop Java applets, applications, and servlets that access Domino objects

✦ Where to find and download free versions of the two most popular Java IDEs

✦ How to configure either IDE to enable access to Domino objects

✦ How to import a Java program

✦ How to edit, debug, and run a Java program

Chapter 37 switches gears and wanders further into unfamiliar territory for Domino developers. Domino 6 has new features that allow servlets to access Domino objects via custom JSP tags. You will review what JSPs are, how the tags work, and see some examples of JSP applications based on the Domino custom tags.

✦　　✦　　✦

Domino Custom JSP Tags

By Brian Benz

In This Chapter

Introducing Java
Server Pages

Introducing JSP tags

Working with Domino
custom JSP tags

Using Domino JSP tags

This chapter illustrates how to access and display Domino views, documents, and forms via servlets by using Domino's custom Java Server Pages (JSP) tags. You learn about servlet development using Domino JSP tags, deployment of JSP and Domino access capability on a remote server, and formatting JSP content. You find out how to add JSP tag capabilities using the example diagnostic servlet from Chapter 35.

Java Server Pages (JSPs) enable integration of specialized tags for content with HTML tags for display. This combination creates dynamic content for the Web. The best comparison in the Domino world is Domino forms and documents versus Domino pages. Domino pages display relatively static information on the Web. Domino documents can contain calculated fields and other objects such as subforms. These objects can be displayed on the Web based on the current Domino session context (user security level, user-defined preferences in a profile document, and so on). Data from Domino documents is applied to the Domino forms, and the result appears as static HTML pages on the Web.

The same comparison can be made of JSP pages and static HTML pages. HTML pages are files that you can edit and save on the server's file system. JSP pages are Dynamic HTML pages that are generated at runtime by a servlet and passed to a Web browser. The servlet that creates the HTML page is generated by an application server that can interpret JSP pages and generate servlet code. JSP tags embedded in a source JSP page tell the application server how to generate the servlet.

JSPs offer developers a way of developing servlets without having to code, debug, and compile Java source code, and then deploy servlet class files. All a developer needs is an HTML editor and reference materials for the JSP tags needed. JSP pages are created using the same markup rules as HTML pages. Instead of saving the HTML page as an `.htm` file, you save it with a `.jsp` extension, and deploy the JSP page to a JSP-compatible Web application server. The Web application server then creates Java servlet source code based on tags in the JSP, then compiles and deploys the servlet. When the JSP is called via a URL on the Web server, the servlet associated with the JSP page generates a static HTML page containing dynamic content and sends the page to the browser.

JSP Tag Libraries and Domino Custom Tags

JSPs are based on Sun's Java Server Pages Specification, which can be reviewed at http://java.sun.com/products/jsp. The JSP version 1.1 specification includes support for custom actions. Custom actions are a way of describing a segment of servlet code and associating it with a reusable JSP tag. Custom actions are based on custom tags that can be embedded in a JSP page. When a servlet is created, the code that is associated with the custom tag is generated as part of the servlet. A collection of custom tags is called a tag library.

The Domino custom tag libraries were written in Java, and are intended to provide Domino Java object functionality to Web developers with little or no Java and limited Domino skills. Web developers can easily add Domino application features to JSP pages by embedding Domino custom JSP as part of the markup on a JSP page.

Domino custom JSP tag libraries are compatible with JSP version 1.1 (the first version of the JSP specification to support custom tags) and Java servlet 2.2 specifications. This, unfortunately, means that they can't run on a Domino server's servlet engine. Domino 6 supports version 2 of the servlet specification and does not contain JSP support. A separate Web server that supports the servlet 2.2 and JSP 1.1 specifications, such as TomCat or IBM WebSphere, has to be used to access Domino 6 server functionality via JSPs.

Understanding JSP Basics

Listing 37-1 shows a basic example of a simple JSP document.

Listing 37-1: **A Simple Java Server Page**

```
<html>
<head>
  <title>A Simple JSP</title>
</head>
<body>
  The Time and Date: <%= new java.util.Date()%>
  <br>
  The Java Version: <%=System.getProperty("java.version")%>
</body>
</html>
```

Listing 37-1 appears to be a regular, if basic, HTML page. The only way to tell that this is a JSP is that it is saved on the file system with a .jsp file extension instead of an .htm or .html extension, and the HTML contains these tags:

```
The Time and Date: <%= new java.util.Date()%>
The Java Version: <%=System.getProperty("java.version")%>
```

When a JSP-compatible application server loads the JSP file, the code contained in the HTML page converts to a servlet. The servlet reproduces the static HTML contained in the page and combines it with the results of the dynamic System.getProperty() call to produce the HTML code shown in Listing 37-2.

Listing 37-2: **HTML Output for a Simple Java Server Page**

```
<html>
<head>
  <title>A Simple JSP</title>
</head>
<body>
  The Time and Date: Wed Oct 16 03:35:53 EDT 2002
  <br>
  The Java Version: 1.3.1_01
</body>
</html>
```

The generated HTML displays two lines in a browser that appear as follows:

```
The Time and Date: Wed Oct 16 03:35:53 EDT 2002
The Java Version: 1.3.1_01
```

The same code on a server running a different version of Java returns different results, depending on the version number returned by the System.getProperty("java.version") call.

Listing 37-1 does not include directions to output the code to the screen or any other destination, because JSP code is automatically assumed to be intended for output to a browser in HTML format. On the JSP-compatible application server, the HTML output tag <%=System.getProperty("java.version")%> is automatically converted to a line in a servlet that directs output to the current device using an out.print() directive:

```
out.print(System.getProperty("java.version"));
```

Listing 37-3 shows a servlet generated from Listing 37-1.

Listing 37-3: **Generated Servlet Code for a Simple Java Server Page**

```
package org.apache.jsp;

import javax.servlet.*;
import javax.servlet.http.*;
import javax.servlet.jsp.*;
import org.apache.jasper.runtime.*;


public class Simple$jsp$jsp extends HttpJspBase {


  static {
  }
  public Simple$jsp$jsp( ) {
  }
```

Continued

Listing 37-3 *(continued)*

```
private static boolean _jspx_inited = false;

public final void _jspx_init() throws org.apache.jasper.runtime.JspException {
}

public void _jspService(HttpServletRequest request, HttpServletResponse
response)
    throws java.io.IOException, ServletException {

    JspFactory _jspxFactory = null;
    PageContext pageContext = null;
    HttpSession session = null;
    ServletContext application = null;
    ServletConfig config = null;
    JspWriter out = null;
    Object page = this;
    String _value = null;
    try {

        if (_jspx_inited == false) {
            synchronized (this) {
                if (_jspx_inited == false) {
                    _jspx_init();
                    _jspx_inited = true;
                }
            }
        }
        _jspxFactory = JspFactory.getDefaultFactory();
        response.setContentType("text/html");
pageContext = _jspxFactory.getPageContext(this, request, response,
        "", true, 8192, true);

        application = pageContext.getServletContext();
        config = pageContext.getServletConfig();
        session = pageContext.getSession();
        out = pageContext.getOut();

        // HTML // begin [file="/Simple.jsp.jsp";from=(0,33);to=(4,19)]
            out.write("\r\n");
            out.write("<html>\r\n");
out.write("<head><title>A Simple JSP</title></head>\r\n");
            out.write("<body>\r\n");
            out.write("The Time and Date: ");
        // end
        // begin [file="/Simple.jsp.jsp";from=(4,22);to=(4,43)]
            out.print( new java.util.Date());
        // end
        // HTML // begin [file="/Simple.jsp.jsp";from=(4,45);to=(6,18)]
            out.write("\r\n");
```

```
        out.write("<br>\r\n");
        out.write("The Java Version: ");
    // end
    // begin [file="/Simple.jsp.jsp";from=(6,21);to=(6,55)]
        out.print(System.getProperty("java.version"));
    // end
    // HTML // begin [file="/Simple.jsp.jsp";from=(6,57);to=(9,0)]
        out.write("\r\n");
        out.write("</body>\r\n");
        out.write("</html>\r\n");
        out.write("");
    // end

    } catch (Throwable t) {
        if (out != null && out.getBufferSize() != 0)
            out.clearBuffer();
        if (pageContext != null) pageContext.handlePageException(t);
    } finally {
        if (_jspxFactory != null) _jspxFactory.releasePageContext(pageContext);
    }
  }
}
```

When the Web application server calls the JSP file via URL, a servlet resembling the one in Listing 37-1 is generated and executed, returning the HTML results in Listing 37-2. This is a great example of the power of JSPs. Instead of having to code, compile, and deploy the previous servlet code to display two lines of basic information in a browser, the developer adds a single tag to a much simpler HTML page in Listing 37-1 and deploys the JSP on a JSP-compatible Web application server. The server takes care of the servlet coding. Each JSP-compatible application server can generate output that may vary from this sample, but follows the same basic pattern. Also, some servlet engines permit JSP-generated servlets to be viewed and saved on the file system, and some servers don't.

One of the free, open-source J2EE editing tools reviewed in Chapter 36, SunONE Developer for Java 4, Community Edition, generated the Servlet code in Listing 37-3. SunONE Developer is bundled with a runtime version of the TomCat J2EE Web application server. The Tomcat server permits the display and editing of servlets generated by JSP files, as well as a preview feature for the servlet output. Because JSPs contain tags that send directives to a J2EE Web application server to generate a servlet, being able to review the generated servlet code is valuable for understanding how a JSP works. The next section takes a look at the different types of JSP scripting elements, and how each type of scripting element affects the generation of a servlet.

Introducing JSP Tags

After you understand how Java Server Pages generate servlet code based on JSP tags, the next step is to understand the different types of tags and how they affect JSP output. Table 37-1 shows the three types of standard JSP scripting elements that JSP developers need to know.

Table 37-1: JSP Scripting Elements

Scripting Element	Description
Expressions	The examples in Listings 37-1, 37-2, and 37-3 all contain expression tags. Expressions are formatted and included as part of the generated servlet's response.
Declarations	Declarations are inserted into the servlet outside of method calls.
Scriptlets	Scriptlets are pieces of Java code inserted in the generated servlet. Scriptlets are inserted into a special method created for JSP servlets called _jspService.

In addition to three types of scripting elements, Table 37-2 shows the two different ways to format each scripting type — standard and XML formats.

Table 37-2: JSP Scripting Element Tags — Standard and XML Formats

Standard Tag Format	XML Format

Expressions:
`<%=expression%>`
	`<jsp:expression>`
	expression
	`</jsp:expression>`

Declarations:
`<%!declaration%>`
	`<jsp:declaration>`
	declaration
	`</jsp:declaration>`

Scriptlets:
`<%scriptlet%>`
	`<jsp:scriptlet>`
	scriptlet code
	`</jsp:scriptlet>`

Both formats are legal for JSP 1.1 pages when inserted in HTML. The XML format is usually a little easier to follow, especially for long expressions, declarations, and scriptlets.

Now that you have an idea of the scripting elements that you can send to a JSP-generated servlet, a line-by-line review of the generated servlet code in Listing 37-3 will show you how a servlet generated from a JSP differs from a regular servlet.

The imports are noticeably different in a JSP servlet as compared to a regular servlet, because of the import of the org.apache.jsp classes as well as the jasper runtime classes. The org.apache.jsp class extends HttpJspBase, which is an extension of javax.servlet. http.HttpServlet. The Apache group, the same people who created the Apache HTTP server on which the IBM HTTP server is based, and the Tomcat J2EE server, write org. apache.jsp and the org.apache.jasper classes, which are an implementation of the JSP 1.1 specification:

```
package org.apache.jsp;
```

```
import javax.servlet.*;
import javax.servlet.http.*;
import javax.servlet.jsp.*;
import org.apache.jasper.runtime.*;
```

The following code is where any declarations sent by declaration scripting elements are located. In this example, there was no need for declarations, so this section is `blank.public class Simple$jsp$jsp extends HttpJspBase {`:

```
static {
}
public Simple$jsp$jsp( ) {
}

private static boolean _jspx_inited = false;

public final void _jspx_init() throws org.apache.jasper.runtime.JspException {

}
```

The next code segment is where any scriptlets would be located. Scriptlets are placed here via scriptlets scripting element. In this example, there was no need for scriptlets, so there are none listed.

The next code segment includes basic variable setup in the `_jspService` method. It's no surprise that most of the classes and methods in a JSP servlet are JSP-specific extensions of `javax.servlet` classes and methods. `jspFactory` helps set up page context and is part of the JSP specification. `pageContext` is an extension of `javax.servlet.ServletRequest`. `servletContext` is an extension of `javax.servlet.ServletContext`. `JspWriter` is the class for the browser output.

```
public void _jspService(HttpServletRequest request, HttpServletResponse
response)
    throws java.io.IOException, ServletException {
    JspFactory _jspxFactory = null;
    PageContext pageContext = null;
    HttpSession session = null;
    ServletContext application = null;
    ServletConfig config = null;
    JspWriter out = null;
    Object page = this;
    String _value = null;
```

The next code segment contains a conditional statement to open a new thread if no thread is open yet. Servlets must have at least one explicitly opened thread to function.

```
    try {

      if (_jspx_inited == false) {
        synchronized (this) {
          if (_jspx_inited == false) {
            _jspx_init();
            _jspx_inited = true;
          }
        }
      }
```

The next code segment sets the output type for the `JspWriter` and gets the current JSP page. After the request and response definitions, the first `true` parameter defines a session, 8192 is a buffer size for reading the JSP page, and the second `true parameter` automatically unloads the page when finished.

```
_jspxFactory = JspFactory.getDefaultFactory();
response.setContentType("text/html");
pageContext = _jspxFactory.getPageContext(this, request, response,
    "", true, 8192, true);
```

The next code pulls a number of items from the `pageContext` class, much like `AgentContext` provides many session objects in a `NotesSession` class of a Domino agent. After defining the servlet context and the configuration parameters for the servlet, you have a session object for the page and the output method. After these objects are in place, the servlet can write output to the browser screen.

```
application = pageContext.getServletContext();
config = pageContext.getServletConfig();
session = pageContext.getSession();
out = pageContext.getOut();
```

The TomCat server generates the comments in the code while generating the servlet. The comments refer to the JSP tags' original lines in the JSP page, and make the connection between the generated servlet and the original JSP page much easier to follow. The first number is the line number and the second number is the characters from the left, starting at 0. The Java code generated for each line or line segment is just below the commented JSP page reference.

```
// HTML // begin [file="/Simple.jsp.jsp";from=(0,33);to=(4,19)]
    out.write("\r\n");
    out.write("<html>\r\n");
out.write("<head><title>A Simple JSP</title></head>\r\n");
    out.write("<body>\r\n");
    out.write("The Time and Date: ");
// end
// begin [file="/Simple.jsp.jsp";from=(4,22);to=(4,43)]
    out.print( new java.util.Date());
// end
// HTML // begin [file="/Simple.jsp.jsp";from=(4,45);to=(6,18)]
    out.write("\r\n");
    out.write("<br>\r\n");
    out.write("The Java Version: ");
// end
// begin [file="/Simple.jsp.jsp";from=(6,21);to=(6,55)]
    out.print(System.getProperty("java.version"));
// end
// HTML // begin [file="/Simple.jsp.jsp";from=(6,57);to=(9,0)]
    out.write("\r\n");
    out.write("</body>\r\n");
    out.write("</html>\r\n");
    out.write("");
// end
```

The rest of the code is standard error catching and a command to release the `pageContext`, which flushes the JSP page from memory, based on the previously defined `getPageContext` method.

```
    } catch (Throwable t) {
      if (out != null && out.getBufferSize() != 0)
        out.clearBuffer();
      if (pageContext != null) pageContext.handlePageException(t);
    } finally {
      if (_jspxFactory != null) _jspxFactory.releasePageContext(pageContext);
    }
  }
}
```

The next section provides a more complicated example using the Domino custom JSP tags.

Domino Custom JSP Tags

The Domino custom JSP tags are stored in XML format in a Tag Library Descriptor (TLD) file. TLDs are useful for storing and sharing JSP tags in a portable format, and are part of the JSP 1.1 specification.

Just as with regular JSP tags, the Domino custom tags enable Web developers to generate servlet code using Domino objects without having to code, compile, and deploy servlets, and with little knowledge of the Java classes being accessed. In this way, the design of Web pages can be somewhat separated from the content, because JSP pages are a lot easier to edit than servlets that produce the same content.

Two Domino JSP Tag Libraries exist: `domtags.tld` contains tags for back-end Domino database and server objects, and `domutil.tld` provides basic J2EE classes and methods needed for most J2EE Web applications.

Using Domino JSP Tags

The SunONE Studio is one of the few J2EE IDEs that has a JSP preview feature. This means that you don't have to spend time coding, compiling, and deploying before you can see results. For this reason, I use the SunONE Studio to illustrate the examples in this section.

 Cross-Reference Refer to Chapter 36 for instructions on installation and setup of the SunONE studio.

Before using the custom library, you have to add `domtags.jar`, `domtags.tld`, and `domutil.tld` to the SunONE developer environment.

To add `domtags.jar`, mount the filesystem with the `domtags.jar` from the `<domino install directory>\data\domino\java` directory using the Mount Filesystem menu option under the File menu.

To add `domtags.tld` and `domutil.tld`, right-click the WEB-INF folder of a SunONE project and choose Add JSP Tag Library from the pop-up menu. The Find in Filesystem submenu option is the best way to reference the file on the file system. Retrieve both files from the `<domino install directory>\data\domino\java` directory.

In the `web.xml` file located in WEB-INF subdirectory directory of your project folder, add the following code:

```
<taglib>
  <taglib-uri>domtags.tld</taglib-uri>
  <taglib-location>/WEB-INF/domtags.tld</taglib-location>
</taglib>
<taglib>
  <taglib-uri>domutil.tld</taglib-uri>
  <taglib-location>/WEB-INF/domutil.tld</taglib-location>
</taglib>
```

The preceding code registers the location of the TLD files with the J2EE Web application, even though you refer to them explicitly in the JSP code in Listing 37-4. It's good practice to install and reference the tag libraries on any JSP-compatible Web application server you are using custom tag libraries with. This saves any issues with code that improperly references tag libraries by name.

Listing 37-4: **All ndbible.com Mailing List Subscribers Using Domino Custom JSP Tags**

```
<%@page contentType="text/html"%>
<html>
<head>
<title>Not So Simple JSP Page - Domino Custom Tags Example</title>
<%@ taglib uri="/WEB-INF/lib/domtags.tld" prefix="domino" %>
<%@ taglib uri="/WEB-INF/lib/domutil.tld" prefix="domutil" %>
</head>
<body>
<h1>Mailing List Contacts</h1>
<domino:session>
<domino:db dbname="ndbible\MailList.nsf">
 <domino:view viewname="Contacts" toponly="true" debug="true" >

  <table border=1>
  <tr><td>Name</td><td>Contact Info</td></tr>
  <domino:viewloop>
      <tr>
        <td><domino:viewitem col="1" format="HTML"/></td>
        <td><domino:viewitem col="2" format="HTML"/></td>
      </tr>
  </domino:viewloop>
  </table>

</domino:view>
</domino:db>
</domino:session>
</body>
</html>
```

Listing 37-4 is a JSP that uses the Domino custom tags in the `domtags.tld` file. The code opens the Mailing List database example database used in Chapters 34 and 35, selects the Contacts view, and displays each contact's name and e-mail address in a row in a table.

The header of this HTML page has three new lines. The first line is a directive to the JSP 1.1 server to send output from the JSP-generated servlet to text and/or HTML, depending on the HTML tags in the page. The tags that start with `taglib uri=` are instructions to the servlet to look in the `="/WEB-INF/lib/domtags.tld` for custom tag definitions of any tag that begins with `domino`. The same goes for `domutil`. The domutil reference refers to J2EE design elements that would be used in a more complex Web UI. Because this is a simple example with very little Web interactivity, the domutil tag library reference is included here for future compatibility. None of the domutil tags are actually used in this basic example.

```
<%@page contentType="text/html"%>
<html>
<head>
<title>Not So Simple JSP Page - Domino Custom Tags Example</title>
<%@ taglib uri="/WEB-INF/lib/domtags.tld" prefix="domino" %>
<%@ taglib uri="/WEB-INF/lib/domutil.tld" prefix="domutil" %>
</head>
```

The next code segment opens a new Domino session, opens the `ndbible\MailList.nsf` database on the local machine, and selects the Contacts view.

```
<body>
<h1>Mailing List Contacts</h1>
<domino:session>
<domino:db dbname="ndbible\MailList.nsf">
 <domino:view viewname="Contacts" toponly="true" debug="true" >
```

The rest of the code loops through the Contacts view using the `viewloop` tag and displays each entry in the view in its own HTML table row, which is generated by hard-coded HTML table tags placed around the Domino custom tags:

```
<table border=1>
<tr><td>Name</td><td>Contact Info</td></tr>
<domino:viewloop>
    <tr>
      <td><domino:viewitem col="1" format="HTML"/></td>
      <td><domino:viewitem col="2" format="HTML"/></td>
    </tr>
</domino:viewloop>
</table>

</domino:view>
</domino:db>
</domino:session>
</body>
</html>
```

Summary

This chapter introduced you to Java Server Pages, including:

✦ How JSPs work

✦ How scripting elements affect JSP servlet output

✦ An example of a simple JSP page and its servlet output

✦ How to read a servlet generated by JSP tags

✦ The Domino custom JSP tags

✦ Using Domino JSP tags

✦ Generating dynamic content in J2EE Web applications

In the next chapter, you're introduced to the WebSphere application server. You learn how to set up WebSphere to work with Domino, including implementing single-sign on capabilities for a DNS domain. You also find out how to deploy servlets and JSPs on WebSphere.

✦   ✦   ✦

Domino and WebSphere

By Brian Benz

WebSphere application server is a Java 2 Enterprise Edition (J2EE) servlet manager that provides scalability, security, and enterprise data access for servlet-based J2EE Web applications. The standard edition of WebSphere server has been bundled with Domino since early versions of R5, and Domino capabilities for accessing servlet functionality via Common Object Request Broker Architecture (CORBA) are incorporated into Domino server. This chapter discusses the issues involved in deploying a servlet on WebSphere that accesses Domino data, and illustrates the issues and procedures for deploying and configuring J2EE Web applications and JSPs using Domino custom JSP tags on a WebSphere server.

Limitations on Using WebSphere with Domino

IBM is bundling WebSphere with Domino 6, just as it did with Domino 5, with some important limitations. The most important limitation is that the WebSphere server must be installed on the same physical server as Domino. The second important factor is that the WebSphere server may act against Domino data only, not relational data such as DB2 or MS SQL server. Also, using the WebSphere Java Connector Architecture (JCA) connectors and Enterprise JavaBeans (EJBs) are prohibited under the license agreement.

With all these restrictions, what can you do with WebSphere that is bundled with Domino? WebSphere supports performance and security management features that Domino does not have, such as connection pooling for performance and servlet access restriction for security.

Hosting Web Services for Domino servers is an example of a good application for an integrated Domino and WebSphere solution, despite the license restrictions. Domino has no support for RPC router functionality that Web Services need. But as with servlets, Web Services hosted on WebSphere are legal only if the data accessed is Domino data, according to the license agreement for WebSphere bundled with Domino.

Cross-Reference   Part XI covers Web Services on Domino in more detail, including an example of a Web Service solution that accesses Domino data from a Java application in Chapter 57.

Another important feature that the Domino and WebSphere bundle provides is Java Server Pages (JSP) processing. As mentioned in Chapter 37, although Domino 6 supports J2EE standards, it does not support the servlet 2.2 specifications, which support the JSP specification 1.1, which supports Domino custom JSP tags. For JSP tags to be used in an application, a separate Web application server must be installed to support JSP pages by converting JSP files into servlets that can generate dynamic HTML when called by a URL.

A few other possibilities exist for legally running WebSphere servlets, Web Services, and JSPs that access data from non-Domino sources. First, you can purchase a full license for WebSphere Advanced Edition from IBM. An option for small development shops is to join the IBM PartnerWorld for Developers program and purchase the Value Pack, which provides developer-only versions of WebSphere, DB2, and many other tools to qualified developers at steep discounts. Another possibility is to download trial versions of WebSphere and DB2 from the IBM WebSphere Developer Domain Web site at `software.ibm.com/wsdd/`. The free trial versions include fully functional, but limited-time versions of the WebSphere application server and DB2 for development use only, without the Domino data-only restrictions of WebSphere bundled with Domino. Finally, you can use the open source and freely downloadable TomCat J2EE Web application server with Domino. TomCat does not support the same Domino integration, performance, and advanced security features that WebSphere does, but it also does not have the same license restrictions as WebSphere bundled with Domino. A group of developers are working on a project to more tightly integrate TomCat with the Domino Java API. You can find more information on this at `www.openntf.org`.

Preparing to Install WebSphere on a Domino Server

Describing installation on specific versions in a book is always tricky. The software versions and installation steps often change before the book is printed, and every six to nine months after that. This is most likely the case for Domino 6.0, DB2 7.2, and the WebSphere Application Server, Advanced Edition 4.03 installation on a Windows 2000 system described in this chapter. Installation instruction updates will be posted on the ndbible Web site when the new versions of WebSphere and Domino become available.

Installation prerequisites — single-server installation

As per the WebSphere license agreement for Domino, the following sections describe the process for installing WebSphere on the same machine as Domino, using DB2 as the WebSphere administration database server.

Here are the prerequisites:

✦ **A pre-installed Domino 6 server and Domino administrator client:** The client can be on the same machine or an administrator's workstation. Consult your Domino server documentation for installation instructions. Installing Domino with the Typical Installation option is all that is required now; you will reconfigure Domino to work with WebSphere after you install DB2 and WebSphere on the server. The Domino server should be installed but not running while WebSphere and DB2, or another relational database for administration settings, are installed.

✦ **1.5-2.5GB of server disk space:** The server must have at least 1.5GB of free space (after Domino is installed). If DB2 and WebSphere files are downloaded from the Web and not installed from CD, 2.5GB of space is preferable for storing and unzipping downloaded files prior to installation.

✦ **A user ID with specific system properties for DB2 (or another relational database) and WebSphere:** The ID must have no spaces to be accepted by DB2 (and most other relational database) naming conventions. Local security settings for this ID must support the following: act as part of the operating system, create a token object, increase quotas, and replace a process-level token.

✦ **A relational database server for storing and managing administration settings:** DB2, Oracle, Informix, Merant, and Sybase are all compatible relational database servers for managing and storing WebSphere administration settings. Check with the documentation of the current release of WebSphere to ensure that the database server version is compatible with WebSphere. DB2 version 7.02 is used in this example.

✦ **WebSphere application server software**: WebSphere Application Server Advanced Edition version 4.03 is used in this example.

Creating or editing a password for use with DB2 (or another relational database) and WebSphere

WebSphere needs a user ID and password preconfigured with the following rights on the server: act as part of the operating system, create a token object, increase quotas, and replace a process-level token. Figure 38-1 shows how these rights look in Windows 2000, which are part of the Local Security Settings under Administrative Tools. For other servers, consult your operating system documentation and/or the WebSphere installation instructions for that specific platform.

Installing DB2 as the WebSphere administration database server

Before installing IBM WebSphere Advanced Edition, DB2 must be installed as the administration server. A DB2 database is created when WebSphere is installed that manages configuration settings for the WebSphere server.

✦ **ID and password issues:** Switch to the OS login ID created or edited in preparation for DB2 before starting the DB2 installation process. Follow the standard installation instructions with the Typical Installation option selected, and remember to enter the ID that was just added/created with sufficient rights on your server to install DB2. If you have any errors while installing the configuration database or the sample database, chances are the ID is incorrect or the rights are not sufficient. Verify the user ID and password and restart the installation process.

✦ **Make sure that DB2 is running JDBC 2.0 or higher:** Before installing WebSphere, ensure that the version of DB2 that you installed is running a WebSphere-compatible DB2 JDBC driver. WebSphere 4.03 needs JDBC 2.0 or higher.

For version 7.x, the DB2 JDBC driver version can be switched by running the `use-jdbc2.bat` file located in the `<DB2 Install Directory>\java12` subdirectory. Running this batch file will ensure that the JDBC Driver is version 2.

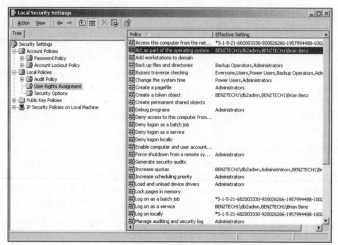

Figure 38-1: User rights assignments for a newly created DB2 and WebSphere ID in Windows 2000

✦ **Verify that DB2 is running:** Open the DB2 control center and navigate to your DB2 control database by choosing Systems ⇨ (Installed Server Name) ⇨ DB2 ⇨ (DB2 Control Server Name–Default is DWCTRLDB) ⇨ Tables. You should be able to view the tables and other objects in the database if the DB2 server is running correctly and the current user has adequate rights to access the DB2 control databases.

Installing WebSphere on a Domino Server

Before installing, shut down Domino and any other Web servers on this machine. DB2 or the compatible relational database you chose for managing and storing WebSphere administration settings must be installed and running at this point.

Installing the WebSphere software

After starting the installation program, follow these steps to install the WebSphere software:

1. Choose Custom Installation. In the first screen that appears, leave all install options chosen, including the IBM HTTP server.

2. In the Choose Web Server Plugin(s) screen, choose the Domino V5.05 or Higher option and uncheck the default IBM HTTP server option, as shown in Figure 38-2. For Domino 6, you copy the file from the Domino server after WebSphere installation. For now, just add the R5 plug-in as part of the installation.

3. In the next screen, choose the ID and password created for use with WebSphere and the relational database, as shown in Figure 38-3.

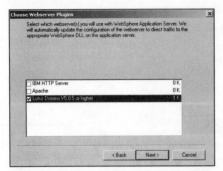

Figure 38-2: The Domino V5.05 or Higher option chosen in the Choose Web Server Plugin(s) screen

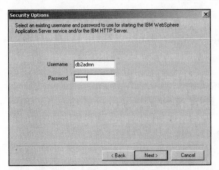

Figure 38-3: The Security Options screen — choose the ID and password created for use with WebSphere and the relational database.

4. For Windows 2000 and XP, you may receive an error message that indicates that the user ID entered has insufficient rights to verify user name and password on the current machine. If you receive this warning, exit the installation and verify the security settings as described in the "Creating or Editing a Password for Use with DB2 (or another Relational Database) and WebSphere" section earlier in this chapter.

5. The next screen prompts you for a database format and type for installation of WebSphere. The database software should be preinstalled before you get to this step. Use the ID and password created for use with WebSphere and the relational database matching the user ID and password used in the Security Options screen, as shown in Figure 38-4.

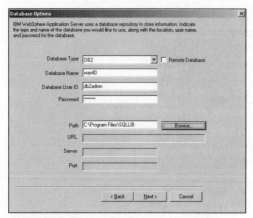

Figure 38-4: The Database Options screen —
choose the database type, the file name, the ID
and password created for use with WebSphere
and the relational database, and the location
of the database working directory.

6. The next screen is the verification screen, which should match what is entered so far. After completing this step, the software is installed.

Verifying the installation of WebSphere

After rebooting the server to finish the WebSphere server installation, you should verify that the server is running by starting all the basic WebSphere tasks on the server. Figure 38-5 shows what the server console looks like after WebSphere installation. Consult your WebSphere documentation for instructions on starting WebSphere for your OS. In Windows 2000, follow these steps:

1. Choose Applications ➪ WebSphere.

2. Start the administrative server by selecting the administrative server icon from the hierarchical tree. Choose the start icon from the menu options at the top of the console.

3. Navigate through the Notes to the server name that was installed and choose Application Servers ➪ Default Server.

4. Right-click the default server icon and select Start from the pop-up menu.

After a few moments, you should get a message similar to the one in Figure 38-5. You now have confirmation that all the server tasks are functioning correctly. You are ready to start and configure Domino for use with WebSphere.

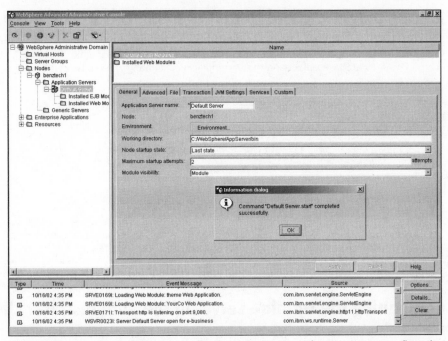

Figure 38-5: The Confirmation screen for the default server. The Server.Start confirmation message verifies that the administration server, administrator console, and the default application server are all functioning correctly.

Installing the WebSphere sample applications

The next step is to install the sample applications. This is an important step, because not only does it verify that the server is running properly, but it also generates a default plugin-cfg.xml file for use on the server, which otherwise has to be generated manually or via a batch file. The generation of plugin-cfg.xml by the sample database creation process also provides good working examples of configuration settings, which you can later edit and readapt for your own application installation purposes. Follow the instructions in the WebSphere documentation for steps on setting up the sample applications.

Configuring the Domino Server for WebSphere

IBM has gone to great lengths to make sure that WebSphere is integrated with Domino at many levels. Installation of the integration features, however, is probably the trickiest part of the installation process.

Each of the steps outlined in this section has to be followed exactly, and in sequence. If a step is missed, it is recommended that you start over rather than try to complete the single step out of sequence.

Editing plugin-cfg.xml to manage NSF URLs

If the IBM HTTP server, WebSphere, and Domino are all running on the same machine, the IBM HTTP server and WebSphere process HTML and servlet URL requests. To enable URLs to access Domino database objects on the Domino server, a change has to be made to `plugin-cfg.xml`.

Open the plug-in configuration file, located at `<WebSphere Install Directory>\config\ plugin-cfg.xml` under the XML element that reads `<UriGroup Name="default_host_ URIs">`, and add the following lines to redirect any URL containing `.nsf`:

```
<UriGroup Name="default_host_URIs">
<Uri Name="/*.nsf*"/>
</UriGroup>
```

Copying domino5_http.dll to WebSphere

The Domino 6 plug-in for WebSphere ships by default with Domino and is located in the `<Domino Install Directory>\domino\plugins` directory. Copy the `domino5_http.dll` file to the default working directory for WebSphere — in this case, `c:\WebSphere\AppServer\ bin\domino5_http.dll`. Add the name and path of the file and save the server document.

Configuring the Domino server in the administrator client

Start the Domino server. After a few moments, you should see a message similar to the following that indicates that the Domino server has started:

```
>Domino Server Started
```

You can now start the Domino administrator to edit server settings. The following list discusses the settings you need to change:

✦ **Edit the DSAPI filter filenames:** Domino server configuration is best performed through the Domino administrator client on a Win32 platform, which should be preinstalled on the Domino server or on an administrator's workstation. To start the Domino administrator, choose Lotus ➪ Domino Administrator from the Windows Applications menu. If the server to administer doesn't open by default, select the name of the server you want to administer by selecting Open Server from the Domino administrator File menu. After opening the server, select the Configuration tab and open the current server document under the Servers option, as shown in Figure 38-6.

Figure 38-6 also shows the DSAPI filter filename, which is located under the Internet Protocols➪HTTP tab of the server document. This is the name of the Domino 6 WebSphere plug-in that was copied in the "Copying domino5_http.dll to WebSphere" section earlier. It should be located in the default working directory for WebSphere — in this case, `c:\WebSphere\AppServer\bin\domino5_http.dll`. Add the name and path of the file and save the server document.

✦ **Edit the Java servlet support setting:** In the same server document, make sure that the Java servlet support setting under the Internet Protocols ➪ Domino Web Engine tab is set to Third Party Servlet Support, and save the server document.

✦ **Verify the WebSphere plug-in installation for Domino:** Ensure that the Domino server HTTP task restarts by typing **TELL HTTP QUIT** and then **LOAD HTTP** in the Domino server console, either directly on the server or via the administrator client console interface. You should receive a message that says `Servlet Engine Initialization Was Successful` if the WebSphere plug-in was installed correctly.

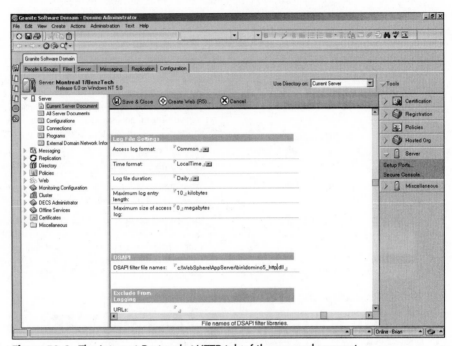

Figure 38-6: The Internet Protocols⇨HTTP tab of the server document

Note `TELL HTTP RESTART` is convenient, but can be flaky in various versions of Domino, depending on what else may be installed. Using `TELL HTTP QUIT` and `LOAD HTTP` is always safer.

Setting Up WebSphere and Domino Single Sign-On Capabilities

One of the key features of WebSphere for Domino developers is the ability to pass tokens back and forth between multiple WebSphere and Domino servers that are located in the same DNS domain. This enables the smooth transition of functionality and navigation between Domino objects and WebSphere objects without requiring a user to log in to each server separately. A user's browser has to be configured to accept cookies for single sign-on (SSO) to function, URLs have to contain the same base DNS domain to be compatible, and multiserver session authentication has to be enabled on the Domino servers in the DNS.

Creating SSO capabilities in a single DNS domain requires four basic steps, which are described in Table 38-1. If the Domino server hosts multiple DNS domains, you can configure each domain with SSO capabilities individually, rather than global setup at the server level. Refer to the latest administration help documentation for more details.

Table 38-1: SSO Setup Steps

Step	Details
Enable session authentication on each Domino server in the same DNS domain	You must first enable session authentication for Web clients in the server document. Each user that used session-based authentication must have a Person document in the Domino Directory.
Create a domain-wide configuration document	You must create a Web SSO configuration document in the Domino Directory.
Enable the Multi-server option	You must enable this option for session-based authentication in the server document.
Enable `HTTPEnableConnectorHeaders` in NOTES.INI	Setting this variable to `1` enables the Domino HTTP service to pass special header information about the front-end server's configuration and user authentication status to Domino applications. This helps to facilitate SSO.

J2EE resource packaging: EARs and WARs

Two types of J2EE application resource packages exist: EARs and WARs. Each one is similar to a ZIP file, with many J2EE application and configuration files compressed into a single, portable container. A WAR (Web Application Resource) can contain HTML, JSPs, and Java code, including `.class` and `.jar` files, as well as access control and back-end resource mappings for deployment on a J2EE Web server. An Enterprise Application Resource (EAR) contains one or more WAR files, as well as the roles for each WAR file.

Accessing Notes objects in J2EE applications

System requirements for accessing Domino objects via J2EE servers are similar to the requirements for Java applications outlined in Chapter 34. The J2EE server's `CLASSPATH` system variable should contain accurate references to `Notes.jar` and `NCSO.Jar`, and the JDK `\bin` directory should be in the server's `PATH` environment. The `JAVA_HOME` environment variable has to be set to the main directory of the server's JDK.

For Windows NT and 2000, environmental variables are set by opening the Control Panel, selecting the System icon, selecting the Advanced tab, and selecting the Environment Variables button.

Listing 38-1 shows a sample setup for a J2EE server, where the Domino 6 server is installed in `c:\Lotus\Domino`, and Java JDK 1.3 is installed in `c:\JDK1.3.1_01`.

Listing 38-1: **Environment Variable Settings for a Typical J2EE Server**

```
SET CLASSPATH =
.;c:\Lotus\Domino\Data\domino\java\NCSO.jar;c:\lotus\Domino\N
otes.jar;
Set PATH=
C:\WINNT;C:\WINNT\COMMAND;C:\jdk1.3.1_01\bin;c:\lotus\domino
set JAVA_HOME=c:\jsdk1.3.1_01
```

Deploying a Web application to WebSphere

You can manually deploy servlets to WebSphere servers via the file system, or more easily, via the Install Enterprise Application wizard. In the wizard, a developer enters the .war, .ear, or .jar file that contains the application, a name for the application, and the context root for the main servlet in the container. The imported .war file, for example, is made up of DiagnosticServlet developed in Chapter 35, and some configuration information. As shown in Figure 38-7, the servlet name is DiagnosticServlet and the context root is diagnostic. The URL for calling this servlet, therefore, is http://(Site URL)/diagnostic/ DiagnosticServlet. You can also assign roles and security settings for the application, and mapping to JNDI and EJBs, in the Install Enterprise Application wizard.

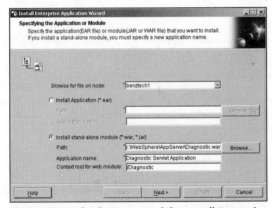

Figure 38-7: The first screen of the Install Enterprise Application wizard, showing the Diagnostic J2EE Web application

Running a Web application on WebSphere

You can configure servlets in J2EE Web applications to run on Web Application server startup, on first access via a URL, or manually from the WebSphere administration console. You can deploy configuration settings for running as part of a .war or .ear file, or you can configure and edit them via the administration console.

Deploying and Running JSPs

Because JSPs generate servlets on a JSP compatible J2EE application server, deploying JSPs to WebSphere is similar to deploying servlets. The JSP must be contained in a .war file, which can be part of an .ear file. The same requirements must be met for the CLASSPATH, PATH, and JAVA_HOME settings if the JSP is accessing Domino objects.

In addition, you need to make sure that the domtags.jar, the domtags.tld, and the domutil.tld files are present on the WebSphere server. You also need to ensure that the domtags.jar file is either in the classpath of the server or included as part of the WAR file for the Web application that makes the JSP calls to Domino objects.

Make sure that the Domino custom Tag Library JSP reference tags listed in Listing 38-2 are in the web.xml file for your application:

Listing 38-2: Domino Custom Tag Library JSP Reference Tags for WebSphere Applications

```
<taglib>
  <taglib-uri>domtags.tld</taglib-uri>
  <taglib-location>/WEB-INF/domtags.tld</taglib-location>
</taglib>
<taglib>
  <taglib-uri>domutil.tld</taglib-uri>
  <taglib-location>/WEB-INF/domutil.tld</taglib-location>
</taglib>
```

You can configure JSPs in J2EE Web applications to generate a servlet, and to be ready to run on Web application server startup, on first access via a URL, or manually from the WebSphere administration console. Likewise, you can deploy configuration settings for running JSPs as part of a .war or .ear file, or you can configure and edit them via the administration console.

Summary

This chapter reviewed tips and tricks for installing and running WebSphere:

✦ Configuring WebSphere

✦ Connecting to Domino objects with WebSphere

✦ Connecting Domino and WebSphere applications with SSO

✦ Running J2EE applications in WebSphere

✦ Serving JSPs in WebSphere and Domino

Part VIII switches gears to cover JavaScript, including client-side data validation, DHTML, and some other cool things that you can do with JavaScript in Domino applications.

✦   ✦   ✦

JavaScript Techniques

JavaScript Basics

By Brian Benz

J avaScript is a platform-independent, event-driven, interpreted programming language that has been part of Domino since R5, and could be used with Domino 4.6 versions of Domino via Pass-Thru HTML. JavaScript should not be confused with Java, which is very different in terms of functionality and language. JavaScript and Java can communicate with each other because the original intention was that a combination of Java applets and JavaScript would represent a complete client-side Web application development platform, but for several technical and non-technical reasons, this never came to fruition.

Today, JavaScript is a common extension to HTML that can enhance the user experience by handling client-side events and application control in browser clients. JavaScript is useful for adding interactivity to Domino Web applications and Notes client applications. The Notes 6 client JavaScript feature set has added more complete access to JavaScript classes and methods than prior implementations, and eliminated many of the bugs that hampered Notes client JavaScript development in R5.

This chapter introduces JavaScript and describes basic techniques for JavaScript document object access and detecting JavaScript client settings. The next chapter covers more about the Notes DOM and JavaScript events in Domino.

Introducing JavaScript

Netscape introduced JavaScript in 1995 as a core component of the Netscape Navigator 2.0 browser. Originally, it was conceived as a client-side complement to Java that could be used as part of a browser environment to link applets together with HTML page objects and events. But after JavaScript was released to the Web-development community, it was seldom used for this purpose, even though those capabilities exist in JavaScript to this day. Instead, it was mainly used as a simple script-driven way to code interactivity into previously static Web pages and forms. Two main factors contributed to JavaScript's success.

The first factor was simplicity. Because it was an interpreted language loosely based on Visual Basic and other scripting languages, Web developers with little or no coding expertise could quickly grasp the language fundamentals and start creating fairly sophisticated interactive functionality, which was easy to test and deploy as part of any Web page.

The second factor was the Web. Because JavaScript is an interpreted language, it is impossible to hide JavaScript code in a compiled version. All JavaScript code that is deployed on the Web is available for anyone to see by viewing the source code of an HTML page. Because of this, it is easy for a novice Web developer to see JavaScript functionality that they need, look at someone else's uncompiled code and re-adapt that code for use in their own site. Aside from this, or as some may argue, because of this, an abundance of script-sharing sites have popped up on the Web, where downloadable JavaScript code and tutorials are available for free. These sites greatly assist in getting JavaScript expertise and functionality rapidly distributed across the Web.

Microsoft introduced its flavor of JavaScript in 1996 as part of Internet Explorer 3, and called it JScript. It is somewhat compatible with the Netscape version, but has differences that are significant enough to require Web developers to test the browser type and version at runtime and create separate JavaScript functions for each flavor of JavaScript that they could potentially encounter. The next few chapters cover the more critical differences and how Domino developers can handle them. These differences exist to this day, with each vendor offering its own JavaScript Document Object Model (DOM) and associated objects.

JavaScript Structure and Syntax

It's important for Domino developers to think about JavaScript from an HTML page point of view, because that's the base from which the JavaScript language was invented. Domino has made some great advances in adapting the JavaScript structure and opening up Domino objects and events to JavaScript objects, but JavaScript remains primarily a development language for Web pages. JavaScript can be effectively used for a few things in the Notes client, such as field validation in forms and image rollovers, but there are usually better ways to implement JavaScript functionality for the Notes client using LotusScript, @functions, and even Java in some cases. The main reason for using JavaScript in Notes and Web applications is ease of coding and maintenance. If the JavaScript code functions as needed in the Web and Notes application, there's no need to rewrite the logic in another language just for the Notes application. If a Notes client code already exists and works in LotusScript, @Formulas, or Java, it's probably not necessary to rewrite the code in JavaScript for the Notes client. In any case, multiplatform code has to be tested in Web and Notes client environments to determine the needs of the application.

Keeping this in mind, examine the JavaScript structure from an HTML page point of view. JavaScript functions are usually included at the top of an HTML page, and JavaScript function calls are included as part of HTML tag names. JavaScript represents a Web page with a document object. The way that a JavaScript document is structured and described to JavaScript is called a Document Object Model (DOM).

Objects and methods for HTML forms within a DOM are referenced through an array located under the `document.forms` object. Because they have the same name, it's easy for Domino developers to confuse Domino forms with HTML forms, but there are critical differences. An HTML page can contain one or more HTML forms, while a Domino document contains references to one form via the `Form` reserved keyword. If an HTML page has been created by a Domino server, the current Domino form properties as represented in JavaScript are available via the first HTML form object, which is accessed via `document.forms[0]`.

The examples illustrated in the JavaScript chapters of this book are contained in the Domino 6 Bible JavaScript Examples database (d6bibleJavaScript.nsf), which is available for download from www.wiley.com/compbooks/benz.

Listing 39-1 shows a document that is generated from the JavaScript document tree example form in the Domino 6 Bible JavaScript Examples database. Listing 39-1 shows how the output looks when the form is opened in a Notes client.

Listing 39-1: Output From the JavaScript Document Tree Example Form in the Domino 6 Bible JavaScript Examples Database

```
document:
alinkColor = #000000
anchors = [object AnchorArray]
applets = [object AppletArray]
bgColor = #ffffff
cookie =
domain =
embeds = [object EmbedArray]
fgColor = #000000
forms = [object FormArray]
images = [object ImageArray]
lastModified =
linkColor = #000000
links = [object LinkArray]
plugins = undefined
referrer = undefined
title =
URL = Notes:///85256C58007B4792/JavaScript Document Tree
Example?OpenForm
vlinkColor = #000000
location = Notes:///85256C58007B4792/JavaScript Document Tree
Example?OpenForm
_DominoForm = [object Form]

forms:
length = 1
_DominoForm = [object Form]

First form:
action =
elements = [object Form]
encoding =
method = POST
name = _DominoForm
target =
length = 1
DocDisplay = <input type="text" name="DocDisplay">

First form Elements:
```

Continued

Listing 39-1 *(continued)*

```
form = undefined
name = _DominoForm
type = undefined
value = undefined
checked = undefined
options = undefined
selectedIndex = undefined
defaultChecked = undefined
defaultValue = undefined
length = 1
```

This output illustrates what a Domino document looks like to JavaScript, and how the document fits into the Document Object Model (DOM) for JavaScript. The output that the same code generates for a Web page using Internet Explorer is far too lengthy to display here, but the Domino output is a subset. To illustrate the way JavaScript accesses objects in forms and documents, take a look at the JavaScript that generated this example output in Listing 39-2.

Listing 39-2: JavaScript Code for the JavaScript Document Tree Example Form in the Domino 6 Bible JavaScript Examples Database

```
function notesDocumentInfotoLayer(){
var docInfo=""
for(var d in document)
docInfo+=d+" = "+document[d]+"\n"
var formInfo=""
for(var f in document.forms)
formInfo+=f+" = "+document.forms[f]+"\n"

var firstFormInfo=""
for(var f1 in document.forms[0])
firstFormInfo+=f1+" = "+document.forms[0][f1]+"\n"
var firstFormElements=""
for(var e in document.forms[0].elements[0])
firstFormElements+=e+" = "+document.forms[0].elements[e]+"\n"
document.forms[0].DocDisplay.value = "document:
 \n"+docInfo+"\nforms: \n"+formInfo+"\nFirst form:
 \n"+firstFormInfo+"\nFirst form Elements:
 \n"+firstFormElements}
```

The JavaScript notesDocumentInfotoLayer() function is called by the document's onLoad event, which is called each time the document is opened on the Web or, as in this case, in the Notes client. Let's go through the code line by line so you can associate the code in this listing with the output for a Notes document. Listing 39-3 shows the document object listing output along with the code that generates the display of the output.

Listing 39-3: JavaScript Code and Output for the Document Object

Code:
```
var docInfo=""
for(var d in document)
docInfo+=d+" = "+document[d]+"\n"
```

Output:
```
alinkColor = #000000
anchors = [object AnchorArray]
applets = [object AppletArray]
bgColor = #ffffff
cookie =
domain =
embeds = [object EmbedArray]
fgColor = #000000
forms = [object FormArray]
images = [object ImageArray]
lastModified =
linkColor = #000000
links = [object LinkArray]
plugins = undefined
referrer = undefined
title =
URL = Notes:///85256C58007B4792/JavaScript Document Tree
 Example?OpenForm
vlinkColor = #000000
location = Notes:///85256C58007B4792/JavaScript Document Tree
 Example?OpenForm
_DominoForm = [object Form]
```

As you can see from this listing, the JavaScript code example cycles through all the objects under the JavaScript document object and lists them in the output. When the output listing value looks like [object x], you know that the values for that object are contained in an array, which can contain many more arrays, nested in a tree structure. Look at the forms array, which appears in the document object as [object FormArray] (see Listing 39-4).

Listing 39-4: JavaScript Code and Output for the document.forms Object

Code:
```
var formInfo=""
for(var f in document.forms)
formInfo+=f+" = "+document.forms[f]+"\n"
```

output:
```
length = 1
_DominoForm = [object Form]
```

In this listing, the JavaScript code is cycling through the document.forms object, which is an array that contains one element. In most cases, an HTML page or a document in a Notes client that was created by a Domino form contains only one HTML form in the JavaScript DOM, which is a basic reference to the form with which the Domino document was created. The first element in the array is accessed by referencing document.forms[0], as shown in Listing 39-5.

Listing 39-5: JavaScript Code and Output for the document.forms[0] Object

```
code:
var firstFormInfo=""
for(var f1 in document.forms[0])
firstFormInfo+=f1+" = "+document.forms[0][f1]+"\n"

output:
action =
elements = [object Form]
encoding =
method = POST
name = _DominoForm
target =
length = 1
DocDisplay = <input type="text" name="DocDisplay">
```

Here you can see the objects in the actual JavaScript DOM form elements created when a Domino form generates an HTML page or a Notes document. Most interactive Domino objects that a developer wants to access, such as fields, views, and document references, are located in document.forms [0].

Browser detection

As mentioned in the introduction to this chapter, the major browser developers, including Internet Explorer and Netscape Navigator, each has its own Document Object Model, which differs enough to require that JavaScript developers test for browser type and adapt their code for each DOM. Compounding this further for Domino developers is the Notes DOM, which is used to access Domino objects when JavaScript is running on the Notes client. In general, Domino developers need to check for at least these three basic DOMS: Notes, IE, and Netscape.

An HTML page can query the state of JavaScript before a function is called using the navigator class in JavaScript. Also, the lack of support for JavaScript can be detected and managed by the <NOSCRIPT> HTML tag. Additionally, Domino developers can use the @BrowserInfo function in a Domino form to detect the client type, JavaScript support, and many other features.

Using the JavaScript navigator class

The output in Listing 39-6 is generated by opening the Navigator example form in the Domino 6 Bible JavaScript Examples database and previewing the design in Internet Explorer. The output shows the objects that the navigator class contains in the Internet Explorer DOM.

Note Depending on your browser version and settings, this example may display different settings when run on your machine.

Listing 39-6: Navigator Class Output from the MS Internet Explorer DOM

```
appCodeName = Mozilla
appName = Microsoft Internet Explorer
appMinorVersion = ;Q321232;Q323759;
cpuClass = x86
platform = Win32
plugins =
systemLanguage = en-us
userLanguage = en-us
appVersion = 4.0 (compatible; MSIE 6.0; Windows NT 5.0)
userAgent = Mozilla/4.0 (compatible; MSIE 6.0; Windows NT
5.0)
onLine = true
cookieEnabled = true
mimeTypes =
```

The `Navigator.appName` object returns Microsoft Internet Explorer in this case. If the same form is previewed in Notes, it looks like the output in Listing 39-7.

Listing 39-7: Navigator Class Output from the Lotus Notes DOM

```
appCodeName = Domino
appName = Lotus Notes
appVersion = 4.0 (compatible; Lotus-Notes/6.0; Windows-NT)
mimeTypes = [object MimeTypeArray]
plugins = [object PluginArray]
userAgent = Mozilla/4.0 (compatible; Lotus-Notes/6.0;
Windows-NT)
```

When previewed in Notes, the same form produces a subset of the IE output, based on the Notes DOM. The `Navigator.appName` object returns Lotus Notes in this case. The JavaScript functions that generate this output are shown in Listing 39-8.

Listing 39-8: The webNavinfotoLayer() and the notesNavinfo() Functions

```
function webNavinfotoLayer(){
var navInfo=""
for(var n in navigator)
navInfo+=n+" = "+navigator[n]+"<BR>"
document.all.Layer.innerHTML = "<font size=\"2\"
```

Continued

Listing 39-8 *(continued)*

```
face=\"Arial\"><b>Navigator Example on the
Web:</b><br>"+navInfo+"</font>"
}

function notesNavinfo(){
 var navInfo=""
for(var n in navigator)
navInfo+=n+" = "+navigator[n]+"\n"
document.forms[0].NavigatorDisplay.value = navInfo
}
```

The use of two functions is an aesthetic choice. Both functions cycle through the `navigator` object, just as in the `document` object in previous examples, and write the contents of the `navigator` class to an object on the Domino form.

The first function, `webNavinfotoLayer()`, writes output to a DHTML layer that is embedded on the Navigator example Domino form. Because this function is writing to the `innerHTML` object of the layer, HTML settings are used to govern the display of the output, including bold with the `<b>` tags and line feeds with the `<br>` tag.

 Cross-Reference For more information about DHTML layers, refer to Chapter 41.

In the `notesNavinfo()` function, you simply write to a Domino field on the form instead of the layer. One of the limitations of the Notes DOM is that the document object does not contain an object for layers, so there is no access to the current layer on the form. On the Notes client, however, the NavigatorDisplay text field expands vertically to display the contents of the navigator adequately, unlike a basic field on the Web, which maintains its original size and is limited to one vertical row. The `\n` at the end of the output adds a line feed to the output via JavaScript, which displays each `navigator` object on a new line, just as the HTML `<br>` tag does in the `webNavinfotoLayer()` function. The NavigatorDisplay field is hidden when the form appears on the Web, via the field properties.

Notes clients and Web browsers enable users to disable JavaScript processing through user preference settings. This is the second thing a developer should check for before running JavaScript code. If an older browser that does not support JavaScript is detected, or if a user turned off JavaScript in the browser or Notes client, the `NOSCRIPT` HTML tag displays its contents, which can contain any HTML-compliant object, including text, images, and links.

The code in Listing 39-9 shows the code in the HTML head content object of the Navigator example form. The code that is stored in the HTML head content object has to comply with @function syntax rules, so it is stored as a text variable with a backslash before each original quote to indicate a Pass-Thru HTML value. Then the page appears on the Web, and the code is evaluated and put into the `<HEAD>` tag of a Web page. Storing the HTML head content in @function format adds the possibility of including @functions to the code to produce dynamically calculated HTML heading content.

Listing 39-9: **The NOSCRIPT HTML Tag Element for the Navigator Example Form**

```
"<NOSCRIPT>JavaScript cannot run on your Client. Click <a
 href=\"JavaScriptInstructionsForm?OpenForm\">here</a> for
instructions on enabling JavaScript.
</NOSCRIPT>";
```

Using @BrowserInfo to check for the client type and JavaScript support

Domino developers have one more way to check for browser type and JavaScript support along with many other settings on a Web page. The @BrowserInfo function was added in Domino 5 and detects the properties of a client by reading and evaluating the HTTP user-agent header sent by the client to the Domino server. Take a look at the results of @Browser-Info via the BrowserInfo examples form in the Domino 6 Bible JavaScript Examples database. When this form is opened in Internet Explorer, it looks like the image in Figure 39-1.

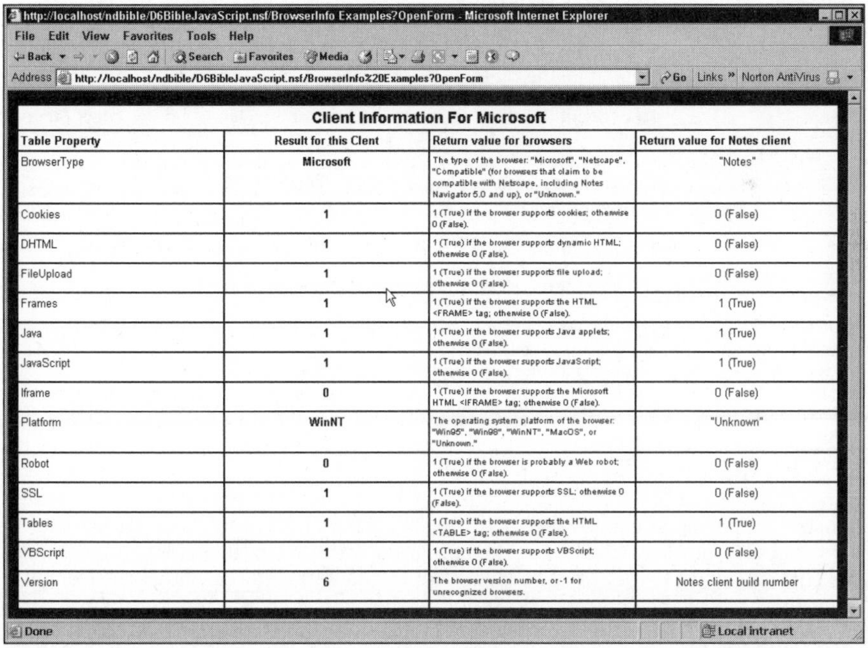

Figure 39-1: The BrowserInfo examples form from the Domino 6 Bible JavaScript Examples database when opened in Internet Explorer

This form displays different results based on the parameters that the @BrowserInfo function can accept from a client. Because of this, it's a great diagnostic tool for checking a user's client settings for remote technical support. A developer can place a database containing this form on a server that is accessible to both Notes and Web browser clients. If users are having issues with client code, the developer can redirect them to the test page and ask them to read the output that is displayed on the screen to see if the client is configured to support the application. Table 39-1 displays a full listing of the settings and the default output for most popular clients.

Table 39-1: @BrowserInfo Output

Table Property	Return Value
BrowserType	The type of the client: Microsoft, Netscape, Compatible (for clients that claim to be compatible with Netscape, including Notes Navigator 5.0 and up), Notes or Unknown.
Cookies	1 (true) if the client supports cookies; otherwise 0 (false).
DHTML	1 (true) if the client supports dynamic HTML; otherwise 0 (false).
FileUpload	1 (true) if the client supports file upload; otherwise 0 (false).
Frames	1 (true) if the client supports the HTML <FRAME> tag; otherwise 0 (false).
Java	1 (true) if the client supports Java applets; otherwise 0 (false).
JavaScript	1 (true) if the client supports JavaScript; otherwise 0 (false).
Iframe	1 (true) if the client supports the Microsoft HTML <IFRAME> tag; otherwise 0 (false).
Platform	The operating system platform of the client: Win95, Win98, WinNT, MacOS, or Unknown.
Robot	1 (true) if the client is probably a Web robot; otherwise 0 (false).
SSL	1 (true) if the client supports SSL; otherwise 0 (false).
Tables	1 (true) if the client supports the HTML <TABLE> tag; otherwise 0 (false).
VBScript	1 (true) if the client supports VBScript; otherwise 0 (false).
Version	The client version number, Notes client build number or -1 for unrecognized clients.

So instead of having to use JavaScript or the NOSCRIPT element to check for browser type or client support, the client can be checked programmatically on the loading of a Domino form. This enables the developer to code JavaScript in different versions within the Domino Designer UI, and use the correct JavaScript for the correct client at runtime. For example, three subforms or JavaScript libraries could be created, one for Internet Explorer, one for Netscape, and one for Notes clients. BrowserInfo could be used when a Domino form is loaded to compute the subform or JavaScript library to use with a specific client. This way the code for each class of client can be separated and debugged without affecting the other code in the same object. The next section of this chapter focuses on how you debug with the Domino Designer UI.

The Domino Designer JavaScript UI

The Domino Designer has several ways to help developers code and debug JavaScript in their Notes and Web applications. Figure 39-2 shows the JSHeader object for the Navigator example form in the Domino 6 Bible JavaScript Examples database.

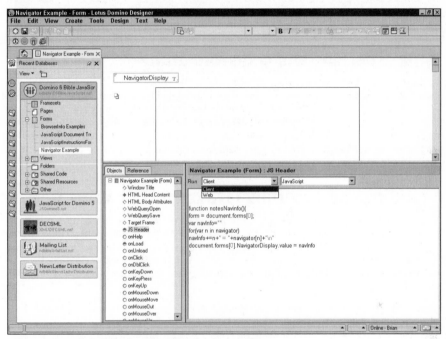

Figure 39-2: The JSHeader object in Domino Designer

Figure 39-2 shows two options above the JSHeader Programmer's pane. Domino 6 now contains two JSHeader objects in each form, page, and subform, one to store code for Web browsers, and one to store code for Notes clients. Domino 5 has one JSHeader object per form, page, or subform, and versions prior to Domino 5 have no JSHeader object. To use the same JSHeader object content for Web and Notes clients, select Common JavaScript from the drop-down list to the right of the Web or client drop-down list.

To the left of the Programmer's pane are two tabs. The Objects tab lists objects associated with whatever is in the Programmer's pane, and the Reference tab provides references to language syntax, classes, and methods for JavaScript. When you select the Reference tab, a drop-down list appears above the list of objects. There are two options: Notes DOM and Web DOM. As described earlier in this chapter, Notes has its own DOM, so it's important to select one DOM or the other for a function. The selection of a DOM affects not only the Reference pane, it also affects how the code is checked before it is saved, and governs the content of the auto-complete pop-ups in the Programmer's pane.

As with the JSHeader object in forms, pages, and subforms, there are a few other objects that support JavaScript in the Notes client. These objects are discussed in detail in the next chapter. When looking at the JavaScript objects under the Objects tab, the background color of the Object placeholder is white for empty objects, blue for JavaScript code for Web clients, and yellow for JavaScript code for Notes clients. If the object contains code for Web and Notes clients, the object placeholders display blue on the top half of the circle and yellow on the bottom half. Figure 39-2 also shows the JSHeader and the onLoad events populated with both Notes and Web client code, and all other JavaScript objects empty for the Navigator example form.

Syntax checking and code formatting

Domino automatically provides JavaScript syntax checking, color-coding of code elements, such as keywords and variables, and code formatting, such as auto-indenting. JavaScript keywords are in blue; user-defined code and variables are in black; strings are pink, and comments are green. JavaScript code is checked for syntax when a page is saved or an attempt is made to move to another object. Any lines or functions containing syntax errors are highlighted in red. Editing the Programmer's pane properties can control colors, fonts, and other display properties, as well as auto-indent and auto-complete.

Importing and exporting JavaScript code using Designer 6

Domino Designer 6 has a new feature for importing and exporting JavaScript code form the file system. To import a JavaScript file into a JSHeader object, right-click in the Programmer's pane and choose Import; or choose File ➪ Import from the main Domino Designer menu. Choose the JavaScript file to import. To export a file to the file system, right-click in the Programmer's pane and choose Export; or choose File ➪ Export from the main Domino Designer menu.

Storing and Referencing JavaScript in a Domino JavaScript Library

JavaScript code can be stored in a JavaScript library for reuse among objects, instead of in a single JSHeader object for a form, page, or subform.

Script libraries are located under the Shared Code section of the Design Bookmark bar on the left side of the screen. Select New JavaScript Library to create a new library object. A JavaScript library supports all the syntax and UI features of a JSHeader object.

To reference a JavaScript Library from a JSHeader object, right-click in the Programmer's pane and choose Insert Resource; or choose Create ➪ Resource ➪ Insert Resource from the main Domino Designer menu. Choose the JavaScript library to include. The functions and methods in that JavaScript library can then be used in your form, page, or subform as if they were part of the JSHeader object. An example of this is in the JSHeader of Navigator Example Using a JavaScript Library form in the Domino 6 Bible JavaScript Examples database. It uses a reference to two libraries, one for Notes client code and one for the Web. With this structure, a change to the JavaScript library code affects the functionality of any form, page, or subform that is linked to the library.

One other handy use for JavaScript libraries is to keep backup versions of JavaScript code while new code is being developed. The old code libraries can be cut, pasted, and numbered. The backup library can be referenced if a code rollback is required in the future.

Summary

This chapter provided an introduction to JavaScript and described JavaScript's structure and syntax, including:

✦ The document, document.forms, and navigator classes

✦ The Domino Designer JavaScript UI

✦ Options for importing and exporting JavaScript files

✦ Techniques for storing and referencing JavaScript in a Domino JavaScript library

The next chapter introduces Domino JavaScript events and describes how and when to use them. Using these events and objects, the chapter illustrates how well JavaScript can handle field validation and browser data manipulation by adding JavaScript field validation to the Web version of an e-mail-enabled mailing list management signup form.

✦ ✦ ✦

Using JavaScript Events

By Brian Benz

I n this chapter, you build on the basic JavaScript examples in the preceding chapter to develop advanced browser client functionality. Illustrations and examples in this chapter exploit JavaScript events, JavaScript actions, and JavaScript libraries to extend the look and feel of the Web-based Mailing List Registration form, which is part of the newsletter management application.

All examples contained in the JavaScript Part of this book, including the databases used in this chapter, can be downloaded from the `www.wiley.com/compbooks/benz` Web site. Please see the Web site for installation Instructions.

Introducing Domino JavaScript Events

It's important to remember that when working with JavaScript object models, the JavaScript code is under the control of the client. And after a Web page or Notes document is loaded in the client, the client interprets and executes the script according to that client's Document Object Model (DOM). Table 40-1 provides an overview of JavaScript events and their corresponding Domino object support.

Table 40-1: Domino Objects and Related JavaScript Events

JavaScript Event/Object	Associated Domino Objects
`JSHeader` object: Where you place any JavaScript functions you want to share with a form, page, or subform.	Forms, pages, and subforms
JavaScript Library: JavaScript Libraries are in the Shared Code section in Domino Designer's Design Bookmarks in Domino 6 and above; references to JavaScript Libraries can be contained in any form, page, or subform.	Forms, pages, and subforms

Continued

Table 40-1 *(continued)*

JavaScript Event/Object	*Associated Domino Objects*
onClick: User clicks an object.	Form (browser only) Page (browser only) Editable fields (browser only) Button Action Hotspot
onDblClick: User double-clicks an object.	Form (browser only) Page (browser only) Field (browser only) Button (browser only) Action (browser only) Hotspot (browser only)
OnFocus: Activated when the field is given focus on the form by the user moving to the field using the tab, mouse click, or arrow keys.	Editable fields Button (browser only) Action (browser only) Hotspot (browser only)
onBlur: Activated when the current field loses focus because the user clicks another field, moves out of the current field using the tab or arrow keys.	Editable fields Button (browser only) Action (browser only) Hotspot (browser only)
OnChange: User adds, deletes, or edits text into a field or selects another option in a keyword field.	Editable fields
OnHelp: Activated if a user presses the F1 key (or the Help key on a Mac) while a button, action, or HotSpot is in focus in the browser.	Button (browser only) Action (browser only) Hotspot (browser only) Form, subform, and -page
OnSelect: User selects a portion of a field.	Editable fields (browser only)
OnKeyDown: Activated when user presses a key.	Form (browser only) Page (browser only) Editable field (browser only) Button (browser only) Action (browser only) Hotspot (browser only)
onKeyPress: Activated when user presses and holds down a key.	Form (browser only) Page (browser only) Editable field (browser only) Button (browser only) Action (browser only) Hotspot (browser only)
onKeyUp: Activated when user releases a key.	Form (browser only) Page (browser only) Editable field (browser only) Button (browser only) Action (browser only) Hotspot (browser only)

JavaScript Event/Object	Associated Domino Objects
`onLoad`: Activated when a page, document, or form is loaded.	Form Subform Page
`onMouseDown`: Activated when user clicks a mouse button.	Form (browser only) Page (browser only) Editable field (browser only) Button (browser only) Action (browser only) Hotspot (browser only)
`onMouseMove`: Activated when user moves the mouse.	Form (browser only) Page (browser only) Editable field (browser only) Button (browser only) Action (browser only) Hotspot (browser only)
`OnMoveOut`: Activated when user moves the mouse pointer out of an area; for use mainly with pictures.	Form (browser only) Page (browser only) Editable field (browser only) Button (browser only) Action (browser only) Hotspot (browser only)
`OnMouseOver`: Activated when user hovers the mouse pointer over an object.	Form (browser only) Page (browser only) Editable field (browser only) Button (browser only) Action (browser only) Hotspot (browser only)
`OnMouseUp`: Activated when user releases a mouse button.	Form (browser only) Page (browser only) Editable field (browser only) Button (browser only) Action (browser only) Hotspot (browser only)
`onReset`: Activated when a user resets a form, usually by pressing a reset button on the form, which restores the form to its original state, before any data was entered.	Form (browser only)
`onSubmit`: Activated when a user submits a form, usually by pressing a Submit button on the form.	Form Page
`onUnload`: Activated when a user leaves or closes a form or page.	Form Subform Page

In this chapter, the examples use many of the field and form events in combination with the JavaScript DOM. The next chapter on DHTML covers some of the mouse- and pointer-related events in more detail.

Form, page, or subform events act as default actions for the entire object. When a user clicks a specific field, for example, if there is JavaScript associated with the onClick event in that field, the field-specific JavaScript is executed; otherwise, the default (form, page, or subform) JavaScript event is activated.

Experienced JavaScript developers may have noticed a few events missing in this example. The onAbort, onDragDrop, onError, onMove, and onResize form events are not supported by the Domino Designer JavaScript UI, but can be added to a form, page, or subform for the Web by adding the events and associated code to the top of a page using Pass-Thru HTML text, or by formatting the code as Function language and storing it in the HTML head object. Either way, the code becomes part of the Web page and can be accessed, as long as the browser client DOM supports the event. Later in this chapter, you can see an example of how to include JavaScript as Pass-Thru HTML at the top of a Web page and integrate that JavaScript with a Domino field, so that the values of the field become part of the JavaScript DOM.

So far, you have learned about the Document Object Model and the events of JavaScript. Let's get started using the DOM and events by adding JavaScript data-entry controls to the Mail List Registration form in the Mail List Management database. This is the form that is used when signing up for the newsletter that provides subscribers with news about updates to the ndbible.com Web site.

Adding Web Data Entry Controls in JavaScript

For efficient field and data entry validation on a form, you should control at least two data entry events, one at the field level and one at the form level. Using JavaScript, developers can control both events before the form is submitted to the server for processing. The example in this section illustrates methods for validating required fields, enforcing field length, and ensuring that a date field is valid and within a certain range. This section also covers mandatory and optional data validation.

At the field level, the onBlur or onChange events validate data entry as a user leaves the field. onBlur is always active, and onChange is triggered only when the field value has changed between the time that a user enters a field and the time the user exits that field. onBlur is used as a trigger for most field-level data validation, such as checking for an empty value. Because onChange is activated only if field data has changed, it can be used with onBlur to enforce controls on changed values in a field.

At the form level, the OnSubmit, onUnload, and onReset events are activated when the user is done with a form and moves on. The onSubmit event is the most commonly associated with form-level data validation. onReset and onUnload are commonly used for warning messages, such as a JavaScript routine that checks for updated but unsaved field data and prompts the user with a message that unsaved data will be lost.

Figure 40-1 shows you the data-entry form used to illustrate the data-entry controls.

You can find the examples in this chapter in the Mailing List database (MailList.nsf), and a copy is stored in the Domino 6 Bible JavaScript Examples database (d6bibleJava-Script.nsf). Both are available for download at www.wiley.com/compbooks/benz.

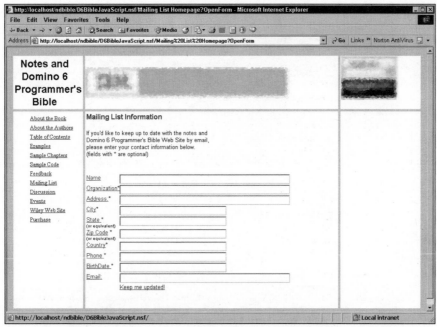

Figure 40-1: The Mailing List home page, which contains the ndbible.com newsletter Mailing List registration form

This form is the place visitors to the ndbible Web site can sign up for newsletters that contain information about updates to the Web site. Registrants have to provide their names and e-mail addresses at a minimum. Other fields are optional. Two fields, however, are optional if blank, but controlled if values are entered. The Phone field requires that a phone number, including area code, be at least ten characters long if a registrant adds a phone number. Birth Date has to be a valid date and earlier than today. (You weren't born yesterday and don't want to send e-mails to anyone who was!)

Field validation occurs at three levels on this form. The onBlur event of the Name field calls a JavaScript function that makes sure that the field is not blank. The onBlur event of the Address field is checked, not only for a nonblank value, but also for a valid e-mail address. The onChange event of the Phone field calls a function to ensure that if a phone number is added or edited, the phone number has at least ten characters. And the Birth Date is checked for validity as well, courtesy of that field's onChange event. Form level controls are enforced when the registrant clicks the Keep Me Updated link at the bottom of the page. When the form gets to the server, the third level of validation occurs via @functions in the input validation event, to make sure that there were no issues associated with client-side JavaScript failure.

Tip Because sometimes client-side JavaScript is not supported on a client because of older software, disabled JavaScript features, or JavaScript errors in a client, it's usually best to have at least two levels of data control: one in the client via JavaScript and one on the Domino server using LotusScript or @functions.

Figure 40-2 shows the same form in Domino Designer.

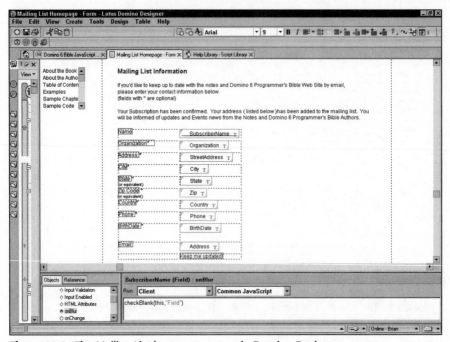

Figure 40-2: The Mailing List home page open in Domino Designer

This section covers many JavaScript-related features. The first thing to point out is the Programmer's pane below the Design window. This shows the onBlur event of the SubscriberName field. The Programmer's pane contains this code:

```
checkBlank(this,"Field")
```

This code calls the checkBlank function, which checks for blank fields. The this parameter passes the current value of the object that is calling the function — in this case the SubscriberName field, which is represented in the DOM by document.forms[0]. SubscriberName. Most developers would probably agree that it's much easier and cleaner to pass this. All properties, objects, and values contained in the DOM of the SubscriberName field are passed using the JavaScript this keyword. The second parameter is not part of the JavaScript DOM, but simply a variable that directs the checkBlank function to handle this function call as field-level validation, not form-level validation.

The checkBlank function code, as well as the rest of the code for data-entry control, is contained in a JavaScript Library in the same database, called the Data Control Library. Listing 40-1 shows the functions in the Data Control Library.

Listing 40-1: Contents of the JavaScript Data Control Library

```
function checkBlank( field, typeOfCheck ) {
if ( field.value == "") {

if (typeOfCheck =="Field") {
alert("This field is required, please enter a value");
field.focus();
return false;
}

if (typeOfCheck =="Form") {
return field.name + " is required, please enter a value\n";
}
}
else {
return "";
}
return true;
}


function checkMinLength( field, typeOfCheck, minLength ) {
if ( field.value.length<minLength ) {

if (typeOfCheck =="Field") {
alert("This field has to be at least " +minLength+"
characters long");
field.focus();
return false;
}

if (typeOfCheck =="Form") {
return field.name+ " has to be at least " +minLength+"
characters long\n"
}
}
else {
return "";
}
return true;
}


function validBirthDate(field, typeOfCheck) {

if (! validDate (field)) {
if (typeOfCheck =="Field") {
```

Continued

Listing 40-1 *(continued)*

```
alert("Please enter a valid date");
field.focus();
return false;
}
if (typeOfCheck =="Form") {
return field.name+ " has to be a valid date\n";
}
}
else {
return "";
}

if (! earlierThanToday (field)) {
if (typeOfCheck =="Field") {
alert("Please enter a date earlier than today");
field.focus();
return false;
}

if (typeOfCheck =="Form") {
return field.name+ " has to be a date earlier than today\n"}
}
else {
return "";
}
}

function validDate(dateField) {
var validDateField = Date.parse(dateField.value);
if ( ! validDateField) {
return false;
}
return true;
}

function earlierThanToday(dateField) {
var validDateField = Date.parse(dateField.value);
var todaysDate = new Date();
if ( validDateField>=todaysDate){
return false;
}
return true;
}

function validEmail (field, typeOfCheck) {
fieldValue = field.value;
var fieldLength = fieldValue.length;
var currentposition = fieldValue.indexOf("@");
var localPart = fieldValue.substring(0,currentposition);
var localPartLength = localPart.length;
var domainPart = fieldValue.substring(currentposition,fieldLength);
```

```
var domainPartLength = domainPart.length;
var periodInDomain = domainPart.indexOf(".");
var isValidEmail = (currentposition > 0 && localPartLength >
0 && domainPartLength > 0 && periodInDomain > 0 );

if ( ! isValidEmail ) {
if (typeOfCheck =="Field") {
alert("Please enter a valid email address");
field.focus();
return false;
}

if (typeOfCheck =="Form") {
return " Please enter a valid email address\n"
}
}
else {
return "";
}

return true;
}

function SubmitMailingList() {
var formProblem=""
formProblem +=checkBlank(SubscriberName,"Form");

if ( Phone.value =="" ) {
var PhoneProblem =""
}
else {
formProblem +=checkMinLength( Phone, "Form", 10 ) ;
}

if (BirthDate.value == "") {
var BirthDateProblem =""
}
else {
formProblem +=validBirthDate(BirthDate, "Form");
}

formProblem +=validEmail (Address, "Form")

if (formProblem == "") {
document.forms[0].submit();
return true;
}
else {
alert("The following errors must be corrected before we can
save this form:\n \n"+formProblem);
return false;
}
}
```

This library contains all the data entry controls that are used for the Mailing List Registration form on the Web, at the field and the form level.

Checking for nonblank fields

The code in listing 40-2 shows the `checkBlank` function, which is called by the `onBlur` event of the SubscriberName field, and checks to make sure that the field is not blank.

This current field is passed to the `checkBlank` function, represented by the field parameter. The second parameter, `typeOfCheck`, tells the function which type of data validation is being requested, field level or form level. The function checks data for both types of validation the same way but reacts differently if it finds a problem. If the `typeOfCheck` is *field*, the function displays an alert box to the user. The function then returns execution focus back to the field that passed the value that caused the error, requesting that the user enter or reenter the data. If the `typeOfCheck` is *form*, the function does not prompt the user right away, but passes a message back to the calling function as a string. What that calling function does with that message is reviewed a little later in this chapter.

Listing 40-2: **Contents of the checkBlank JavaScript Function**

```
function checkBlank( field, typeOfCheck ) {
if ( field.value == "") {

if (typeOfCheck =="Field") {
alert("This field is required, please enter a value");
field.focus();
return false;
}

if (typeOfCheck =="Form") {
return field.name + " is required, please enter a value\n";
}
}
else {
return "";
}
return true;
}
```

Controlling field length

In the mailing list form, the Phone field is an optional field, but there are data restrictions if a value is added to the field. If a phone number is added, you must enforce that the user enters a minimum of ten characters in the field to ensure that it is valid. The optional enforcement functions because the function is called from the `onChange` event to call the `checkMinLength` function illustrated in Listing 40-3, instead of the `onBlur`. With `onChange`, the function is called only if the data has been added or edited while a user is in the Phone field. Here's what the calling code looks like in the `onChange` event of the Phone field:

```
checkMinLength( this, "Field", 10 )
```

Listing 40-3 shows what the code looks like in the JavaScript Data Control Library. Three parameters are passed to `checkMinLength`, compared to the two parameters passed to the `checkBlank` function in Listing 40-2. The first two parameters, `field` and `typeOfCheck`, have the same use in this function, to pass the current field as a parameter and to identify how to react if a data validation error is found. The third parameter in this function specifies the minimum number of characters that the field has to contain to be considered valid data. The `field.value.length` property is used to compare against the `minlength` parameter, and the parameter is sent back out as part of the error message.

Note

Note that the numeric variable passed to the function did not need to be converted to another data type to be included in the string that was sent back in the error message.

Listing 40-3: Contents of the checkMinLength JavaScript Function

```
function checkMinLength( field, typeOfCheck, minLength ) {
if ( field.value.length<minLength ) {

if (typeOfCheck =="Field") {
alert("This field has to be at least " +minLength+"
characters long");
field.focus();
return false;
}

if (typeOfCheck =="Form") {
return field.name+ " has to be at least " +minLength+"
characters long\n"
}
}
else {
return "";
}
return true;
}
```

Controlling date fields

The BirthDate field is validated by using the JavaScript Date object and the `date.parse` method to check for a valid date. The function in Listing 40-4 receives a Date field and a `typeOfCheck` parameter as in the last two examples, but that's where the similarities end. The calling code for this field is in the `onChange` event of the BirthDate field which looks like this:

```
validBirthDate(this, "Field")
```

The function itself checks for a valid date and a date before today, which are broad controls for a BirthDate, but they work well for the purposes of this example. Listing 40-4 shows the `validBirthDate` function.

Listing 40-4: **Contents of the validBirthDate JavaScript Function**

```
function validBirthDate(field, typeOfCheck) {

if (! validDate (field)) {
if (typeOfCheck =="Field") {
alert("Please enter a valid date");
field.focus();
return false;
}
if (typeOfCheck =="Form") {
return field.name+ " has to be a valid date\n";
}
}
else {
return "";
}

if (! earlierThanToday (field)) {
if (typeOfCheck =="Field") {
alert("Please enter a date earlier than today");
field.focus();
return false;
}

if (typeOfCheck =="Form") {
return field.name+ " has to be a date earlier than today\n"}
}
else {
return "";
}
}
```

Combining JavaScript functions

It's important to note here that the validDate and the earlierThanToday function calls are not calling JavaScript classes or methods, but are calling other functions defined in the JavaScript Data Control Library. If the validDate function returns true, the date is valid. If the earlierThanToday function returns true, the date falls within an acceptable range. In this case, registrants of the newsletter must have been born before today.

Aside from providing a practical way to check dates, this structure is also a good illustration of reusing and referring to separate JavaScript functions for specific purposes. Listing 40-5 shows the code for the validDate and the earlierThanToday functions. These functions are simple examples of reusable JavaScript code. In this case, both functions accept a date field as a parameter and perform specific validation tasks, returning either a true or false, depending on validation results.

Listing 40-5: Contents of the validDate and earlierThanToday JavaScript Functions

```
function validDate(dateField) {
var validDateField = Date.parse(dateField.value);
if ( ! validDateField) {
return false;
}
return true;
}

function earlierThanToday(dateField) {
var validDateField = Date.parse(dateField.value);
var todaysDate = new Date();
if ( validDateField>=todaysDate){
return false;
}
return true;
}
```

Controlling e-mail formats

Aside from being a necessary function on most Web-based data entry forms, e-mail validation is also a good example of techniques for parsing strings. In the case of the `validEmail` function (see Listing 40-6), JavaScript is making some basic checks of the e-mail to ensure a skeleton structure. The e-mail address must contain an @ in the address, something before and after the @, and something that follows the @ has to have a period in it. The base structure must look something like this:

```
something@something.something
```

The `validEmail` code in Listing 40-6 checks for each part to make sure that it's there and in the right place. The variables that are set up at the beginning of the `validEmail` function are the key. The `fieldLength` variable measures the length of the value. `CurrentPosition` checks the field by using the `indexOf` method to check for the @. If there is no @, the `indexOf` method returns -1. The `localPart` variable retrieves characters to the left of the @, and the domain variable retrieves characters to the right of the @. Lastly, the `periodInDomain` checks for a period in the domain variable. When all the parts have been collected, the `isValidEmail` variable tries to reassemble a valid e-mail address from the parts that all the other variables have collected. If any parts are missing, the function returns an error message.

Listing 40-6: Contents of the validEmail Function

```
function validEmail (field, typeOfCheck) {
fieldValue = field.value;
var fieldLength = fieldValue.length;
```

Continued

Listing 40-6 *(continued)*

```
var currentposition = fieldValue.indexOf("@");
var localPart = fieldValue.substring(0,currentposition);
var localPartLength = localPart.length;
var domainPart =
fieldValue.substring(currentposition,fieldLength);
var domainPartLength = domainPart.length;
var periodInDomain = domainPart.indexOf(".");
var isValidEmail = (currentposition > 0 && localPartLength >
0 && domainPartLength > 0 && periodInDomain > 0 );

if ( ! isValidEmail ) {
if (typeOfCheck =="Field") {
alert("Please enter a valid email address");
field.focus();
return false;
}

if (typeOfCheck =="Form") {
return " Please enter a valid email address\n"
}
}
else {
return "";
}

return true;
}
```

Controlling the Submit event

The validation examples reviewed so far work only if the user is leaving a field on the form. You also need to code for the possibility that a user does not enter a field that requires validation before moving the mouse to the bottom of the screen and trying to save the form. Form-level validation is facilitated through the `onClick` hotspot event. To make sure that the `SubmitMailingList` function is called when the form is saved, the following code is added to the Keep Me Updated hotspot at the bottom of the data-entry form:

```
return SubmitMailingList() ;
```

This tells the browser to capture and pass event control of the Web page to the `SubmitMailingList` function in the JavaScript Data Control Library. This function checks all validated fields on the form before sending the form to the Domino server for processing.

Listing 40-7 shows the `SubmitMailingList` function. The first thing this function does is set up a variable called `formProblem` that will be reused throughout the function. The next step is to check the SubscriberName field to make sure it is not blank, using the same `checkBlank` function that you used at the field level.

The `checkBlank` function, like all the other functions in this example, returns errors differently if called from a form or a field. For field validation, the user is prompted with an error message and redirected to the field to make a change. But because the function is in the middle of a form validation, the function passes any error messages to the `formProblem` variable instead, which makes all data validation checks for the form and displays all potential error messages at once, instead of one at a time, and one after the other.

Next, the function must check the Phone and the BirthDate fields. Because these are optional fields with data-entry controls if they are not blank, the function checks for a blank field, and then validates the field only if there is something to validate. Finally, the function checks for errors in the required e-mail address. If the function finds any problems, the user is prompted with a list of problems to be corrected via an alert box, and the contents of the `formProblem` variable. If no problem is found, the `formProblem` variable is empty and the form is submitted using the JavaScript `document.forms[0].submit()` command.

Listing 40-7: **Contents of the SubmitMailingList Function**

```
function SubmitMailingList() {
var formProblem=""

formProblem +=checkBlank(SubscriberName,"Form");

if ( Phone.value =="" ) {
var PhoneProblem =""
}
else {
formProblem +=checkMinLength( Phone, "Form", 10 ) ;
}

if (BirthDate.value == "") {
var BirthDateProblem =""
}
else {
formProblem +=validBirthDate(BirthDate, "Form");
}

formProblem +=validEmail (Address, "Form")

if (formProblem == "") {
document.forms[0].submit();
return true;
}
else {
alert("The following errors must be corrected before we can
save this form:\n \n"+formProblem);
return false;
}
}
```

Creating a Web-Based Help System for Domino Applications

Aside from controlling data validation using the document class and alert boxes, JavaScript supports more sophisticated user-interface functionality by using the window class. JavaScript windows can be opened as pop-ups or full screens, closed, reloaded, and have predefined pages loaded into them via JavaScript. Most Web surfers have experienced the JavaScript windows class via pop-up or pop-under advertising generated from a Web page they have visited.

This section covers tips and techniques for using JavaScript and various Domino objects to create an online data-entry form help for Web users of the mailing list registration form. You'll create a system that uses pop-up windows that display information users need to see, when they need to see it. Figure 40-3 shows a pop-up help window on top of the mailing list registration form on the ndbible Web site.

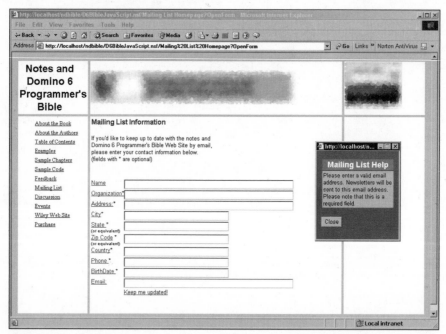

Figure 40-3: The help message for the Email field in the Mailing List Registration form at ndbible.com

The pop-up help window appears when a user clicks one of the field labels to the left of a field. The window appears on top of the current screen and can be closed by clicking the Close button in the pop-up window.

The components of the help system

Several moving parts must work in concert to make the help system function on the Web.

On The Web The Mailing List Help database (`Mailing List Help.nsf`) is available for download from `www.wiley.com/compbooks/benz`.

The Mailing List Help database

The main component of the help system and the component that drives the content is the Mailing List Help database, an adapted Notes help database that contains references to each of the fields on the mailing list registration form. Like the Notes help databases, it opens in its own window when opened from a Notes client. Two small changes were made to the standard help database template. A hidden view called JavaScript Help is used to access the help documentation from the Mailing List Help database, and the body fields in the help forms were changed from rich text to text so they could appear in a view. Figure 40-4 shows the welcome screen for the Mailing List Help database.

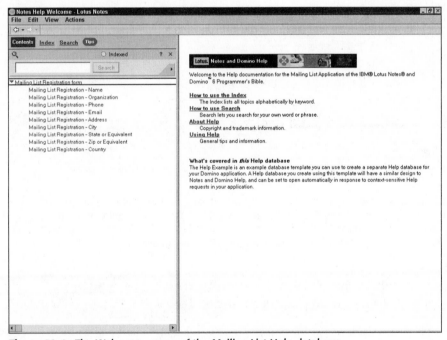

Figure 40-4: The Welcome screen of the Mailing List Help database

Pass-Thru HTML JavaScript functions

At the top of the mailing list registration form is a piece of code that looks like it should probably be part of the JSHeader of that form. Figure 40-5 shows the code. This code is not left over from a previous version of Domino, which is usually when you would use Pass-Thru

HTML to add JavaScript to a page. The contents of the field need to be part of and accessible from the JavaScript DOM, and this is the only way to get this functionality. The Pass-Thru HTML wraps JavaScript code around the results of two @DBColumn queries into the Mailing List Help database.

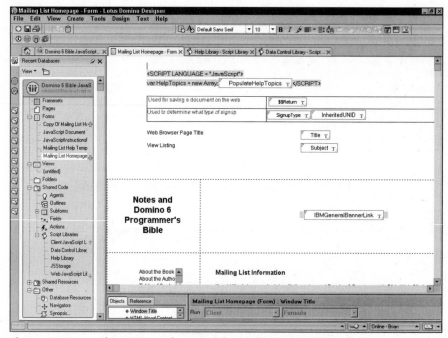

Figure 40-5: Pass-Thru HTML at the top of the Mailing List Registration form

Listing 40-8 shows the contents of the formula that calls two @DBColumn queries. The results of the queries are assembled into an array structure that JavaScript can use to parse and retrieve help values. The first @DBColumn returns field names for the form, and the second @DbColumn returns help text associated with the field names.

Listing 40-8: **Contents of the PopulateHelpTopics Field on the Mailing List Registration Form**

```
HelpTopic :=@Unique(@DbColumn( "" : "NoCache" ; "":"Mailing
List Help"; "(JavaScript Help)" ; 1 ));
HelpMessage :=@Unique(@DbColumn( "" : "NoCache" ; "":"Mailing
List Help"; "(JavaScript Help)" ; 2 ));
@Implode ("HelpTopics[\"" + HelpTopic + "\"] = \"" +
HelpMessage + "\";"; @NewLine)
```

When a document created with this form is opened on the Web, the PopulateHelpTopics field performs the lookups and wraps the JavaScript array formatting around each row of results that is returned. In an HTML page, the results appear similar to Listing 40-9. Each result of the @DBColumn lookup on the help topic becomes an element in the HelpTopics array. Each message in the second @DbColumn is then married to the element as a value.

Listing 40-9: Web Contents of HelpTopics Array Created by the PopulateHelpTopics Field

```
<SCRIPT LANGUAGE = "JavaScript">
var HelpTopics = new Array;
HelpTopics["Address"] = "Please enter a valid email address.
 Newsletters will be sent to this email address. Please
note that this is a required field.";
HelpTopics["City"] = "Please enter a valid city. This is an
optional field";
HelpTopics["Country"] = "Please enter a valid Country. This
is an optional field.";
HelpTopics["Organization"] = "Please enter your Business name
as you would like it to display in the Mailing List. This is
an optional field.";
HelpTopics["Phone"] = "Please enter your phone number,
including country and area code.";
HelpTopics["RegistrationFormHelp"] = "The Mailing List
Registration form is used to record your interest in
receiving Newsletter Updates from the Notes and Domino 6
Programmer's Bible Web Site. The contact information
provided on the form will only be used for internal
identification and communication purposes.";
HelpTopics["State"] = "Please enter a valid State, Province,
County, Arrondissement, Canton, or equivalent. This is an
Optional Field.";
HelpTopics["StreetAddress"] = "Please enter a valid
address.";
HelpTopics["SubscriberName"] = "Please enter your name.
Name is a required field";
HelpTopics["Zip"] = "Please enter a valid Zip Code, Postal
Code, or equivalent. This is an optional field.";
</SCRIPT>
```

Hotspot actions

After you place the help content in the mailing list registration form, the form can access that content from JavaScript. The easiest way to do so is to create a number of links to a JavaScript function that calls a pop-up window and passes a parameter that contains information about which message should be displayed. A hotspot action is added to each field label to the left of a field. The contents of the hotspot action call a JavaScript function that looks like this:

```
helpPopup(HelpTopics["Address"])
```

This code calls the `helpPopup` JavaScript function and passes it a parameter of the field associated with the prompt, Address. This field name matches one of the JavaScript array values in Listing 40-9.

The JavaScript Help Library

The JavaScript function is located in a JavaScript library called Help Library. The code in the library can be added by reference to any form, page, or subform. For more details on JavaScript libraries, refer to Chapter 39. In this example, the form references two JavaScript libraries on the mailing list subform: one for data entry control and one to facilitate the help pop-up functionality.

Tip   You can add references to more than one JavaScript library on any form, page, or subform.

The helpPopup JavaScript function

The JavaScript Help Library contains one function, `helpPopup`, which creates the pop-up help window and displays it on the screen. Listing 40-10 shows the code for the JavaScript `helpPopup` function. The function creates a variable called `winHandle` that is used as the window object for this function. The next thing to do is open the window to a certain height and width. After opening the window, the function writes HTML and the contents of the help pop-up message directly to a document contained inside the window. After writing all the elements to the window, the window is brought into focus, which displays the window on the screen.

Listing 40-10: **Contents of the JavaScript helpPopup Function**

```
function helpPopup(helpTopic) {
winHandle = window.open('','helpWin','height=200,width=192');
winHandle.document.write("<body text=\"#000000\"
bgcolor=\"#5F5F5F\">")winHandle.document.write("<table
border=\"0\"
cellpadding=\"2\" cellspacing=\"2\" border=\"1\">")
winHandle.document.write("<tr valign=\"top\"><td
width=\"192\" bgcolor=\"#808080\">");
winHandle.document.write("<div align=\"center\"><b>");
winHandle.document.write("<font size=\"4\" color=\"#FFFFFF\"
face=\"Arial\">Mailing List
Help</font></b></div></td></tr>");
winHandle.document.write("<tr valign=\"top\"><td
width=\"192\" bgcolor=\"#C0C0C0\"><font size=\"2\"
face=\"Arial\">");
winHandle.document.write(helpTopic);
winHandle.document.write("</font></td></tr></table>");
winHandle.document.write("<form><input type=button
value=Close Window onclick=\"closeWin()\"></form>");
winHandle.document.write("<script>function closeWin() {
window.close(); } </s" + "cript>");
winHandle.focus();
winHandle.document.close();
}
```

JavaScript writing JavaScript

One of the interesting aspects of the JavaScript DOM is that it supports the writing of anything that can be evaluated as text to itself, including JavaScript. The following lines are an example of JavaScript writing itself into the document object of the window.

```
winHandle.document.write("<script>function closeWin() { window.close();
}</s" + "cript>");
```

In this case, the JavaScript function that is written creates the button on the screen that is used by the user to close the pop-up window.

Summary

This chapter extended the introduction of the JavaScript DOM from Chapter 39 to include JavaScript events and their support inside Domino objects. It also covered:

✦ Using DOM and JavaScript events to add JavaScript data controls to Domino forms

✦ Techniques for making JavaScript and Domino objects work together

✦ Building a Web-based pop-up help system based on the Mailing List Help database content.

In the next chapter, you're going to extend your knowledge of JavaScript further to include DHTML and some of its more practical uses in Domino applications.

✦   ✦   ✦

DHTML and Domino

By Brian Benz

T his chapter digs into the details of using DHTML to manage browser UI navigation and image manipulation. DHTML can create a more visually pleasing Web client experience by adding interactive elements to Web applications. In this chapter you update your Web-based newsletter registration application with DHTML UI and navigation features.

DHTML, which stands for Dynamic HyperText Markup Language, is difficult to define because there is no authoritative definition of DHTML. Unlike HTML, XML, and other markup languages, DHTML is not a language, is not completely tag-based, and does not have a centrally standardized W3C specification. This lack of standards exposes DHTML to a multitude of vague and confusing definitions. Is it a language? A set of classes? A grouping of HTML elements? A structure for writing JavaScript? Although these descriptions are close, the truth is that a little of all of them go into DHTML.

In general, any JavaScript function on a Web page that writes to or changes the properties of HTML elements is considered to be DHTML. The display of Web pages is altered by redrawing sections of HTML pages that contain the changed HTML elements. JavaScript or an altered HTML element by itself is not DHTML. Both have to be present and interacting with each other to be considered DHTML. A little DHTML background goes a long way in explaining this uncertain state of affairs.

When Microsoft Internet Explorer 4 and Netscape Navigator 4 were released in 1997, both included support for Cascading Style Sheets (CSS) and DHTML. Both vendors, however, chose to implement DHTML support in different ways inside their DOMs. The Netscape 4 DOM, for example, accesses layers, a critical part of DHTML, via the `document.layers` object; whereas Microsoft accesses the same layer through the `document.all.layer` object.

DHTML had a very slow adoption cycle when it was introduced. Early attempts at DHTML development were difficult for developers. Early DHTML bugs could crash version 4 browsers, and a large installed base of DHTML-incompatible Internet Explorer and Navigator 3 browsers compounded the acceptance of DHTML in Web applications.

Newer browser versions have fixed most of the version 4 DHTML-related JavaScript bugs and added additional Document Object Model (DOM) compatibility. IE and Navigator browsers currently adhere to the W3C's Document Object Model Level 2 core and HTML 4.01 specifications, which can be found at http://www.w3.org/TR/DOM-Level-2-Core and http://www.w3.org/TR/html401, respectively. Unfortunately, differences in each browser's JavaScript references to the DOM still exist. These differences are incompatible enough to require that developers identify the type of client accessing the Web application and provide customized JavaScript functions for each client type to avoid error messages.

To add to Web developer's task lists, the W3C's Document Object Model Level 3 core specification is in its final stages of the W3C recommendation process. Unfortunately, the Level 3 DOM is not compatible with previous DOM versions, so JavaScript and DHTML developers will probably be faced with another client type to be detected when the new DOM is added to future browser versions.

Cross-Reference

Refer to Chapter 39 for more information and examples of detecting the client type in a browser.

Cascading Style Sheets

Cascading Style Sheets (CSS) are great tools for separating HTML content from HTML display. Instead of having to code style settings in HTML for a Web page, you can create a stylesheet that meets your needs and include that stylesheet. Even better, a centrally located stylesheet can be referenced from all the HTML pages for a Web site to ensure the same standardized look and feel for the entire site. This also greatly simplifies the maintenance of display properties for the site. If the stylesheet is centrally located, changing a body style from one font to another, a heading from one color to another, and so on changes the display for that tag across the entire site. In this context, *cascading* means that the styles on a Cascading Style Sheet "cascade" into other Web pages, and controls the fonts, spacing, line height, indents, colors, backgrounds, and other display properties of Web pages. Listing 41-1 shows the code for a simple CSS that controls the font attributes of H1 and H2, body text, and paragraph tags in an HTML page.

Listing 41-1: **A Sample CSS**

```
<STYLE TYPE="text/css">
<!--
  H1 {font-size: 14pt;
      font-family: "Arial";
      font-weight: bold;}

  H2 {font-size: 12pt;
      font-family: "Arial";
      font-weight: bold;
      margin-top: 15pt;}

BODY {font-size: 9pt;
      font-family: "Arial";
      line-height: 10pt;}
```

```
P  {font-size: 9pt;
    font-family: "Arial";
    line-height: 10pt;
    text-indent: 9pt;
    margin-top: 9pt;}
-->
</STYLE>
```

In this example, an HTML page with a reference to this style sheet automatically displays body or paragraph text as Arial 9 font. Anything in a <H1> or <H2> tag picks up the display attributes set in this style sheet as well. All other tags appear with the browser's default display attributes, unless another style sheet is used to control those tag formats as well.

If you want to change the body font to 10 point Times New Roman for pages that use this style sheet, you simply have to change the body style to the following:

```
BODY {font-size: 10pt;
    font-family: "Times New Roman";
    line-height: 10pt;}
```

This display change would cascade through to any Web pages referencing this style sheet.

Of course, Domino developers have had this type of functionality built into the form and document model for a long time. To make the same kind of changes on a Notes application requires a simple change to a form, and all documents that use that form would automatically pick up the new display properties for the form the next time the document was opened on the Web.

There are often situations in Web pages when a style sheet has more specific display control than Domino forms for HTML page display. There are literally hundreds of display attributes for fonts, colors, backgrounds, text, box definitions, group classification, positioning, printing, filtering, and other display properties. More information is available on the W3C CSS Web site at www.w3c.org/Style/CSS. The key to implementing DHTML functionality in a Domino Web site is in using CSSs to define styles and classes, and Javascript to interact with HTML layers and DIV tags.

Layers and DIV Tags

A *layer* is a set of HTML tags defined in a specific block on an HTML page. Layers can be positioned on top of other layers as well as the body of an HTML page. Developers can employ an unlimited number of layers stacked on top of each other and the body of an HTML page, and display different layers by changing the display order via JavaScript. DIV, SPAN, LAYER, and ILAYER tags all represent layers, with slight variations. SPAN tags, for example, function exactly the same as DIV tags, but DIV tags have an HTML line feed (<br>) tag hard-coded at the beginning and end of the block, and SPAN tags don't. This makes SPAN useful for creating a block of text and applying a CSS style to it inline. To apply a CSS class or style, for example, to the middle of a paragraph of text that you don't want interrupted by <br> tags, you can use SPAN instead of DIV.

The DIV tag, which stands for division, is most commonly used to define an area of the HTML document. The code inside the DIV tags is referred to as a layer. The commonly used attributes of a DIV tag are shown in Table 41-1.

Table 41-1: Attributes for the DIV Tag

DIV Tag Attribute	Description
id	Identifies a DIV tag.
Align	Alignment of DIV tag contents. Values: left (default), right, center, and justify.
Style	Formats DIV tag contents based on the CSS style.
class	Formats DIV tag contents based on the CSS class.
lang	Formats DIV tag contents based on any ISO standard two-character language abbreviation.

The id and style attributes are most commonly used to define the display of a layer. The id attribute is used to identify a specific layer. The style attribute controls the position on the screen, the display properties, and the display order of a layer. These attributes are part of the W3C Document Object Model Level 2 style specification, the full text of which can be found at http://www.w3.org/TR/DOM-Level-2-Style.

Following is an example of a DIV element. This was generated from a Domino layer. We discuss setting up layers in the Domino Designer UI a little later in this chapter. For now, a review of a real layer is helpful for illustration. This example shows the two basic attributes, the id, which in this case is called "eventLayer", and several properties of the style attribute:

```
<div id="eventLayer" style="position: absolute; top: 87px;
left: 426px; z-index: 0; width: 273px; height: 254px; font-
family: Arial; font-size: 10pt;"></div>
```

An explanation of the properties and values of the style attribute are listed in Table 41-2.

Table 41-2: Attributes for DIV Tag Styles

Style Attribute	Description
Position	Absolute — Uses the top and left properties to position within the parent object or the HTML body.
	Relative — Uses the top and left properties to position relative to the current position of the parent object or the HTML body.
Left	Position relative to the left of the containing element.
Top	Position relative to the top of the containing element.
Visibility	Visible, hidden, or (inherit from parent object).
z-index	Position of the current object in the display stack, represented by an integer. The lowest number is on the bottom of the stack, the highest on top.

Using CSS classes on layers

Aside from id and style, class attributes can be used across many layers to set and cascade display attributes for a specific layer. The properties and values of layer classes are the same as layer styles, but classes can be applied to more than one style. For the "eventLayer" DIV tag listed earlier, for example, you could define a style called basicText in a CSS defined in the page:

```
basicText {font-family: Arial; font-size: 10pt; }
```

Then you could use a reference to the new basicText class in the DIV tag attributes:

```
<div id="eventLayer" class=" basicText" style="position:
absolute; top: 87px; left: 426px; z-index: 0; width: 273px;
height: 254px"></div>
```

This way, if you ever need to change the font for multiple DIV tags on multiple pages, you simply edit the basicText class in the stylesheet. For example, to change the default font in all layers that use the basicText class to Times New Roman, you simply change the basicText class as follows:

```
basicText {font-family: Times New Roman; font-size: 10pt; }
```

The change is picked up on all DIV tags that have a reference to the basicText class.

CSS in Domino Designer

Domino Designer 6 has new features for storing and referencing Cascading Style Sheets in a Domino database. Prior to Domino 6, developers had three options: to add the stylesheet as part of the HTML head object in a form, store the stylesheet in the HTML directory of a Domino server, or copy the contents of the stylesheet as a page in the database, with an alias name that included the .css extension. If the stylesheet is not included as part of the HTML head object, it could then be included in a form or document by using pass-thru HTML, the HTML @import directive, and a reference URL. For example, to add a stylesheet named defaultStyle located in the HTML directory, the @import directive would appear as follows:

```
@import url(defaultStyle.css)
```

New Feature

Domino Designer 6 has new features for storing and referencing Cascading Style Sheets in a Domino database.

The HTML directive on a page in a Domino database that was formatted with a .css extension would appear as follows:

```
@import url(Databasename.nsf/defaultStyle.css?OpenPage).
```

By contrast, a stored stylesheet in a Domino 6 database is referenced like this:

```
@import url(Databasename.nsf/defaultStyle.css?
OpenCssResource);
```

Storing and editing stylesheets in Domino Designer

Stylesheets are contained in the Design Bookmarks of a Domino database by choosing Shared Resources ➪ Style Sheets. It's important to note that there is no UI for editing stylesheets in Domino, just methods for storing and referencing. The stylesheet listings referenced in the Domino 6 Bible JavaScript Examples database for this chapter are listed in Figure 41-1.

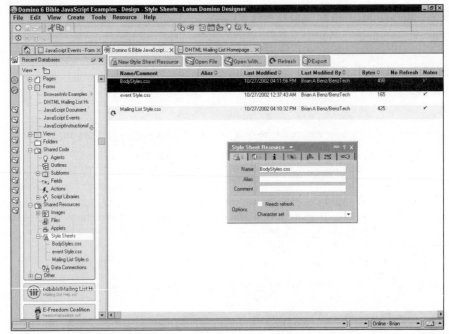

Figure 41-1: The listing of stylesheets used in this chapter, contained in the Domino 6 Bible JavaScript Examples database

As shown in Figure 41-1, there are five buttons across the top of the Domino Designer Style Sheet section. The New Style Sheet Resource button opens a dialog box so you can add a new CSS file into the section. The Open File button opens the stylesheet in whatever UI is configured on the system to edit CSS files. The Open With button lets you choose the tool with which to edit a CSS file. The Refresh button updates the CSS file stored in the database with the file in the original location on the file system. The Export button writes the stylesheet to the file system with a .css extension.

Domino Layers

Domino Designer 6 has new features for creating, editing, and assigning CSS class and style values to layers in the Domino UI, without having to manually edit HTML layer elements. Domino layers can be created and edited in Designer, with full WYSIWYG features. Layers created in Domino can be accessed and manipulated at runtime using JavaScript.

New Feature Domino Designer 6 has new features for creating, editing, and assigning CSS class and style values to layers in the Domino UI.

To create a layer in Domino designer, choose Create ➪ Layer from the main menu. You can size and position the newly created layer in the GUI, or set the position via properties in the Properties box. Style properties of a Domino layer can also be set in the properties box of the layer, and are enclosed in DIV tags as attributes at runtime. Figure 41-2 shows a layer in the Domino Designer UI and its corresponding DIV tag id and style attributes listed in the properties box.

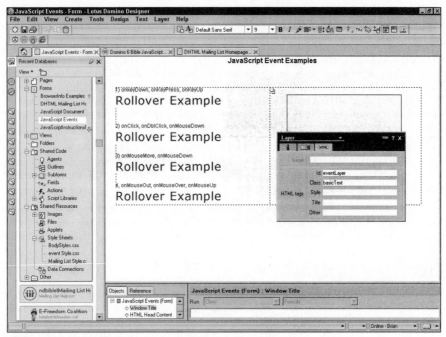

Figure 41-2: The Domino layer eventLayer and associated properties box

In addition to the DIV tag properties, Table 41-3 explains the positioning measurements that are associated with the top and left DIV tag `style` attributes.

Table 41-3: Position Measurements for Domino Layers

Position Measurement	Description
pixels	Pixels from the left/top of the parent object
inches	Inches from the left/top of the parent object
ems	ems are a measurement representing the current font size, horizontally and vertically (for example, if a font is 16 point, one em unit equals 16 point)
percent	Relative position based on the size of the parent object
characters	Relative position based on the parent object's current font size
Auto	Left/top of the parent object; Auto is the same as selecting 0 in any of the previous measurements

Note   If you want to add any predefined CSS styles or classes to the DIV tag, don't forget to reference the stylesheet in the form. To add stylesheets to the body of a page, form, subform, or a specific layer on a page, form, or subform, choose Create ➪ Resource ➪ Insert Resource, or right-click and choose Insert Resource. The Insert Resource dialog box opens, enabling you to select stylesheets as well as other types of resources.

Using DHTML in Domino

There are many uses for DHTML that add additional display and navigation functionality to vanilla Domino applications. Layers can be used to display text messages on a screen dynamically without refreshing the page, and rollovers can add additional features to the overall look and feel of your Web site. DHTML has been a part of some features of Domino since R5. The feature, known as Horizontal Image Resource Sets, was introduced to create image rollover functionality on the Web and in Notes clients. A rollover is an image that appears on a Web page and changes when a mouse pointer is positioned over it.

Beginning with Domino R5, developers simply create two GIF, BMP, or JPG images on top of each other, separated by a one-pixel white space. When Domino Designer saves the image, it is split into two images. At runtime, a JavaScript routine is called to roll one image over the other using the image's mouseOver event.

Of course, as outlined in Chapter 40, many more events can be associated with user interaction in a Web page or a Notes application. The following sections examine other ways to take advantage of some of these events to enhance the user experience in a Domino application.

Creating image rollovers

To see how JavaScript events can work in Domino, take a look at the JavaScript Events form in the Domino 6 Bible JavaScript Examples database. This form highlights all the effects that can be included in Domino applications for the Web and for Notes clients with simple JavaScript calls, including several items on key and mouse events. Figure 41-3 shows the page with several of the events in play.

In this image, you can see the affects of the onDblClick, onMouseMove, and onMouseOut events, as well as a trailing Domino 6 logo that follows the mouse pointer as it moves around the screen. First you review the rollover effects, which contain exactly one line of code each; then we show the code for the trailing Domino 6 logo.

All four of the rollovers are represented on this page by a single graphic in the image resources, called RolloverExample.jpg. But each instance of the JPG image has a different HTML id as specified in the HTML properties tab of the Picture properties box. The HTML id has the same function as an id attribute to a DIV tag. The unique id tag lets JavaScript access each instance of the image as a separate object on the page. The first image has a tag of RolloverExample1, and has JavaScript in the events associated with the key effects: onkeyDown, onKeyPress, and onKeyUp. This is what the code looks like when the Domino form is generated in HTML:

```
<img src="/ndbible/D6BibleJavaScript.nsf/RolloverExample.jpg?OpenImageResource"
width="249" height="34" id="RolloverExample1" name="RolloverExample1"
onkeydown="rolloverExample(RolloverExample1, 'OnKeyDown.jpg');"
onkeypress="rolloverExample(RolloverExample1, 'OnKeyPress.jpg');"
onkeyup="rolloverExample(RolloverExample1, 'OnKeyUp.jpg');" alt="">
```

As you can see here, the image RolloverExample.jpg has an ID of RolloverExample1, which is what JavaScript can use to find this element on a page. But what's really important to this chapter on DHTML is the event code:

```
onkeydown="rolloverExample(RolloverExample1, 'OnKeyDown.jpg');"
onkeypress="rolloverExample(RolloverExample1, 'OnKeyPress.jpg');"
onkeyup="rolloverExample(RolloverExample1, 'OnKeyUp.jpg')"
```

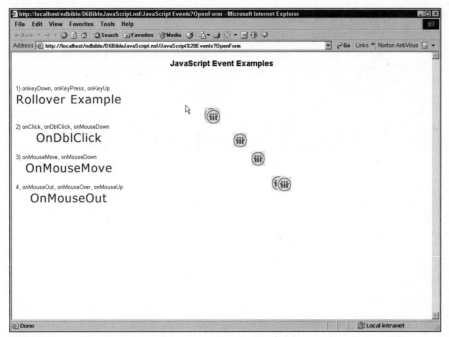

Figure 41-3: A browser view of the JavaScript Events form in the Domino 6 Bible JavaScript Examples database

When a key is pressed, held down, or let go (for `onKeyUp`), a JavaScript function called `rolloverExample` is called and passed to two parameters: the name of the ID and the name of another image. The code for the `rolloverExample` function is in the JSHeader and appears as follows:

```
function rolloverExample(currentImage, newImage){
   if(document.images){
   currentImage.src = newImage;
   }
}
```

It's hard to imagine a simpler function, but it serves a simple purpose. Essentially, after checking to see whether the client machine supports images by checking for the images object array in the document, the function consists of one line that actually does work. It replaces the current image represented by `RolloverExample1` and passed to this function as `currentImage`, with the new image passed to the function and represented here by `newImage`. If all goes well, JavaScript is turned on at the client, and the client DOM supports images and the new image can be found, the new image rolls over the current image.

This technique is repeated in each of the `RolloverExample.jpg` instances, represented by the `onClick`, `onDblClick`, and `onMouseDown` events in `RolloverExample2`, the `onMouseMove` and `onMouseDown` events in `RolloverExample3`, and the `onMouseOut`, `onMouseOver`, `onMouseUp` events in `RolloverExample4`.

Using layers and mouse events together

Now on to a more complicated example: the trailing Domino 6 logo that follows the mouse pointer as it moves around the screen. It's a great example of DHTML graphics manipulation, and of layers and capturing mouse events. Listing 41-2 shows the code that makes this example work. The code is located in the JSHeader of the JavaScript Events form in the Domino 6 Bible JavaScript Examples database.

Listing 41-2: **JavaScript for the Trailing Domino 6 Logo**

```
if (document.all) {
var i =0;
var d = 0;
var D6Images;
var mousePosition;

loadD6Images();
document.onmousemove = catchMouseMove;

function loadD6Images() {
  D6Images = new Array()
  for (i = 0; i < parseInt(6); i++) {
    D6Images[i] = new Image()
    D6Images[i].src = "D6cursor.gif"
  }
  mousePosition = new Array()
  for (i = 0; i < D6Images.length*3; i++) {
    mousePosition[i] = 0
  }
  for (i = 0; i < D6Images.length; i++) {

    document.write('<div id="obj' + i + '" style="position:
absolute; z-Index: 100; height: 0; width: 0"><img src="' +
D6Images[i].src + '"></div>')
  }
  followMouse()
}

function followMouse() {
  for (i = 0; i < D6Images.length; i++) {
    eval("document." + "all.obj" + i + ".style.pixelTop=" +
mousePosition[d])
    eval("document." + "all.obj" + i + ".style.pixelLeft=" +
mousePosition[d+1])
    d = d+2
  }
  for (i = mousePosition.length; i >= 2; i--) {
    mousePosition[i] = mousePosition[i-2]
  }
  d = 0
  var timer = setTimeout("followMouse()",10)
}
```

```
function catchMouseMove() {
    mousePosition[0] = window.event.y+document.body.scrollTop+10
    mousePosition[1] =
window.event.x+document.body.scrollLeft+10
    }

    }
```

Let's review the highlights of this code line by line. Note that the first part of this JavaScript code is at the top of the `JSHeader` object for a document and does not have a function name. This means that the code runs automatically when the page is loaded, without you having to add a function call to the form's `onLoad` event. The first thing the code does is check to see whether the client DOM supports the `.all` object as part of the DOM. This code can be adapted to run on Navigator, but limitations and bugs in Netscape layers cause unreliable results. For now, the code checks for an Internet Explorer DOM and runs only if IE is the client. After some variables are initialized, the `loadD6Images` function is called:

```
if (document.all) {
var i =0;
var d = 0;
var D6Images;
var mousePosition;

loadD6Images();
document.onmousemove = catchMouseMove;
```

`loadD6Images` specifies that any `onMouseMove` events in the current page (represented by `document`) will be passed to the `catchMouseMove` function for processing. The `loadD6 Images` function also creates a new array and instantiates six copies of an image resource. The image resource is located in the Domino 6 Bible JavaScript Examples database and is called `D6Cursor.gif`. It's a screen capture of the Domino 6 icon. Next, the function creates a DIV tag for each of the images in the `D6Images` array. The animation effect is provided by the six DIV tags, which use the calculations in the `followMouse` function to follow the mouse pointer around on the screen. For now, the DIV tags are created in the top-left corner of the screen, one on top of the other:

```
function loadD6Images() {
  D6Images = new Array()
  for (i = 0; i < parseInt(6); i++) {
    D6Images[i] = new Image()
    D6Images[i].src = "D6cursor.gif"
  }
  mousePosition = new Array()
  for (i = 0; i < D6Images.length*3; i++) {
    mousePosition[i] = 0
  }
  for (i = 0; i < D6Images.length; i++) {

    document.write('<div id="obj' + i + '" style="position:
absolute; z-Index: 100; height: 0; width: 0"><img src="' +
D6Images[i].src + '"></div>')
  }
  followMouse()
}
```

Upon completion, the `followMouse` function is called. The `followMouse` function calculates the current position of mouse pointer and moves the six DIV tags a few positions behind when the mouse is moving. It also calls itself recursively to continue following the mouse as long as it is moving.

```
function followMouse() {
  for (i = 0; i < D6Images.length; i++) {
    eval("document." + "all.obj" + i + ".style.pixelTop=" +
mousePosition[d])
    eval("document." + "all.obj" + i + ".style.pixelLeft=" +
mousePosition[d+1])
    d = d+2
  }
  for (i = mousePosition.length; i >= 2; i--) {
    mousePosition[i] = mousePosition[i-2]
  }
  d = 0
  var timer = setTimeout("followMouse()",10)
}
```

The `catchMouseMove` function is activated when the mouse is moved, based on the original `onMouseMove` event call at the top of the `JSHeader` object. It simply tracks the x and y axes of the mouse pointer and passes them to the `mousePosition` array, which `followMouse` uses to place the logos on the screen:

```
function catchMouseMove() {
    mousePosition[0] = window.event.y+document.body.scrollTop+10
    mousePosition[1] = window.event.x+document.body.scrollLeft+10
}
```

Creating DHTML Data Control Functionality for Domino Applications

Now that you've seen a somewhat impractical but fun use for DHTML, here's another example that probably has more use in business applications. We've rewritten the Mailing List Home Page Newsletter Registration form showcased in Chapter 40 to provide help and error messages via layers on the page rather than via JavaScript pop-ups. The new form is called the DHTML Mailing List Home Page. Figure 41-4 shows the form in an IE browser.

In this image the JavaScript help for the e-mail address field is displayed on the right hand column of the screen, as well as an error message prompting the user to enter a valid e-mail address. Just as in the examples in Chapter 40, the user is prompted by an error message if there is something wrong with the format of data in one of the fields, and is not permitted to exit the field until the error is resolved. Unlike the Chapter 40 examples, however, the user is not required to close the pop-up window by clicking the OK button, so the DHTML error messages are a little less intrusive but still enforce the same rules. Also, help text messages automatically appear in the layer on the right when a user enters the field, without the user having to click the link to open a pop-up window.

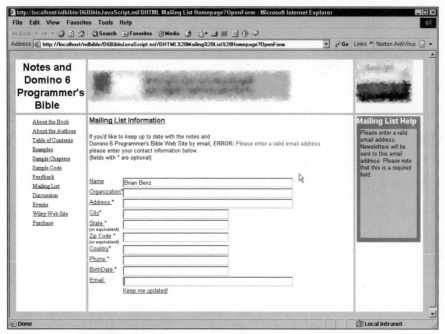

Figure 41-4: The DHTML Mailing List Home Page Newsletter Registration form in the Domino 6 Bible JavaScript Examples database

This functionality is created by adding three Domino layers to the DHTML Mailing List Home Page form and embedding a CSS style sheet, as shown in Figure 41-5.

Adding layers to the Mailing List Home Page form

The first layer to the left, `errorLayer`, has a white background and is empty by default. The second layer is the background layer, `bgLayer`, which has the words Mailing List Help in large letters and a dark gray background. The layer nested in `bgLayer` is called `helpLayer` and is where the help text appears as a user enters each new field. The layer tree in Figure 41-5 shows the independent `errorLayer` and the `helpLayer` nested in the `bgLayer`.

Adding CSS styles and classes to the layers

The Mailing List Style CSS is embedded directly into the DHTML Mailing List Home Page. This code specifies three classes as part of the body of the page. The `helpLayerText` class is for specifying the font for writing help text, which is Black, Arial, and 10 point. The `BGLayerText` class does the same for text displayed in the bgLayer layer, and the same goes for `errorLayerText` for error messages, which are in red.

The next three items in the stylesheet — `helpLayer`, `bgLayer`, and `errorLayer` — are DIV tag styles that are applied to the layers on the page with the same names. The CSS code appears as follows:

```
<STYLE TYPE="text/css">
.helpLayerText { font-family: Arial; font-size: 10pt }
.bgLayerText { font-family: Arial; font-size: 14pt }
.errorLayerText { font-family: Arial; font-size: 10pt }
#helpLayer    { background-color: #5F5F5F; layer-background-color: #5F5F5F }
#bgLayer      { background-color: #808080; layer-background-color: #808080 }
#errorLayer   { background-color: #FFFFFF; layer-background-color: #FFFFFF }
</STYLE>
```

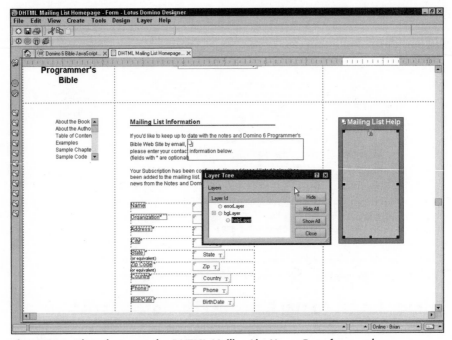

Figure 41-5: Three layers on the DHTML Mailing List Home Page form and an embedded CSS

Using script libraries to add DHTML functionality

The code for the DHTML data validation functionality in this Web page is written in the DHTML Data Control JavaScript Library. This is a good example of the power of script libraries. The function names are the same in both the Data Control Library and the DHTML Data Control Libraries. After developing and testing the new code, the only thing required to add the new DHTML functionality was to swap the reference in the JSHeader from one Script Library to another. Take a look at the contents of the DHTML Data Control Library in Listing 41-3.

Listing 41-3: **The DHTML Data Control Library**

```
function checkBlank( field, typeOfCheck ) {

if ( field.value == "") {
```

```
if (typeOfCheck =="Field") {
errorLayerWrite("This field is required, please enter a
value");
field.focus();
return false;
}

if (typeOfCheck =="Form") {
return field.name + " is required, please enter a
value\n";}
}
else {
return "";
}
return true;
}

function checkMinLength( field, typeOfCheck, minLength ) {
if ( field.value.length<minLength ) {

if (typeOfCheck =="Field") {
errorLayerWrite("This field has to be at least " +minLength+"
characters long");
field.focus();
return false;
}

if (typeOfCheck =="Form") {
return field.name+ " has to be at least " +minLength+"
characters long\n"
}}
else {
return "";
}
return true;
}

function validBirthDate(field, typeOfCheck) {

if (! validDate (field)) {
if (typeOfCheck =="Field") {
errorLayerWrite("Please enter a valid date");
field.focus();
return false;
}
if (typeOfCheck =="Form") {
return field.name+ " has to be a valid date\n";
}
}
else {
return "";
```

Continued

Listing 41-3 *(continued)*

```
}

if (! earlierThanToday (field)) {
if (typeOfCheck =="Field") {
errorLayerWrite("Please enter a date earlier than today");
field.focus();
return false;
}

if (typeOfCheck =="Form") {
return field.name+ " has to be a date earlier than today\n"}
}
else {
return "";
}
}

function validDate(dateField) {
var validDateField = Date.parse(dateField.value);
if ( ! validDateField) {
return false;
}
return true;
}

function earlierThanToday(dateField) {
var validDateField = Date.parse(dateField.value);
var todaysDate = new Date();
if ( validDateField>=todaysDate){
return false;
}
return true;
}

function validEmail (field, typeOfCheck) {
fieldValue = field.value;
var fieldLength = fieldValue.length;
var currentposition = fieldValue.indexOf("@");
var localPart = fieldValue.substring(0,currentposition);
var localPartLength = localPart.length;
var domainPart =
fieldValue.substring(currentposition,fieldLength);
var domainPartLength = domainPart.length;
var periodInDomain = domainPart.indexOf(".");
var isValidEmail = (currentposition > 0 && localPartLength >
0 && domainPartLength > 0 && periodInDomain > 0 );

if ( ! isValidEmail ) {
if (typeOfCheck =="Field") {
errorLayerWrite("Please enter a valid email address");
field.focus();
```

```
return false;
}

if (typeOfCheck =="Form") {
return " Please enter a valid email address\n"
}
}
else {
return "";
}

return true;
}

function SubmitMailingList() {
var formProblem=""
//var SubscriberNameProblem = checkBlank(SubscriberName,"Form");
formProblem +=checkBlank(SubscriberName,"Form");

if ( Phone.value =="" ) {
var PhoneProblem =""
}
else {
formProblem +=checkMinLength( Phone, "Form", 10 ) ;
}

if (BirthDate.value == "") {
var BirthDateProblem =""
}
else {
formProblem +=validBirthDate(BirthDate, "Form");
}

formProblem +=validEmail (Address, "Form")

BirthDateProblem + EmailProblem

if (formProblem == "") {
document.forms[0].submit();
return true;
}
else {
errorLayerWrite("The following errors must be corrected
before we can save this form:\n \n"+formProblem);
return false;
}
}

function errorLayerWrite (errorLayerText) {
ie = (document.all)? true:false

if (ie) {
```

Continued

Listing 41-3 *(continued)*

```
   var HTMLLayer =""
   HTMLLayer += "<font size=\"2\" color=\"#FF0000\"
face=\"Arial\">"
   HTMLLayer += "<b>ERROR: </b>"+errorLayerText
   HTMLLayer += "</font>"
   document.all.errorLayer.innerHTML = HTMLLayer;
   }
   else
   {
   var targetLayer = (layerLevel)?
eval('document.'+layerLevel+'.document.'+Layer+'.document') :
document.layers[errorLayer].document
   targetLayer.className = "errorLayerText";
   targetLayer.open()
   targetLayer.write(errorLayerText)
   targetLayer.close()
   }
 }
```

Although this looks like a great deal of work, it's not as hard as it looks. The code from the DHTML Data Control Library in Listing 41-3 is mostly a copy of the code from the Data Control Library in Listing 40-1 in Chapter 40. After working out what needed to change to add the DHTML functionality, you simply make a new copy of the script library and replace any code that called an alert box:

```
alert("Please enter a valid email address");
```

with code that writes to the errorLayer using the errorLayerWrite function:

```
errorLayerWrite("Please enter a valid email address");
```

 For details on how the data entry controls work, refer to Chapter 40.

The errorLayerWrite function simply writes the same message to the errorLayer instead of sending it to an annoying alert pop-up window. The first thing this function does is check the client type, which determines how the function will access and write to the layer. If the browser is an IE browser, you must write messages to the innerHTML object of the errorLayer layer. If the browser client is anything but IE, you must write the message to the errorLayer object that is nested in the layers array of the document. In the case of non-IE clients, the stylesheets take care of the font type and color.

```
function errorLayerWrite (errorLayerText) {
ie = (document.all)? true:false

if (ie) {
   var HTMLLayer =""
   HTMLLayer += "<font size=\"2\" color=\"#FF0000\"
   face=\"Arial\">"
   HTMLLayer += "<b>ERROR: </b>"+errorLayerText
   HTMLLayer += "</font>"
```

```
document.all.errorLayer.innerHTML = HTMLLayer;
}
else
{
var targetLayer = (layerLevel)?
eval('document.'+layerLevel+'.document.'+Layer+'.document')
: document.layers[errorLayer].document
targetLayer.className = "errorLayerText";
targetLayer.open()
targetLayer.write(errorLayerText)
targetLayer.close()
}
}
```

Creating a DHTML Help System for Domino Applications

As with the data control example, the JavaScript Help Library is copied and edited to support the help display functionality shown on the DHTML Mailing List Home Page form. As a user enters each field, a related help message for that field automatically appears in the right column of the screen, saving the user the trouble of having to click the text to the left to display a pop-up window. (Although they can still do that if they want; the code for the links are still there.) To make the message appear in the layer, we used the onFocus JavaScript event of each field on the form. Here's an example of the code for the SubscriberName field:

```
helpLayerDisplay(HelpTopics[this.name])
```

The helpLayerDisplay function is located in the DHTML Help JavaScript Library. The helpLayerDisplay function passes the array reference to help topics, just as the previous example did in Chapter 40. This time, however, the object being entered has information that matches the help array topics, which are based on the field names on the form. For this reason, a Domino form can pass a reference of the object name, in this case, SubscriberName, to the help function. Listing 41-4 shows the contents of the DHTML Help Library.

 For more details on how the entire help system works, please refer to Chapter 40.
Cross-Reference

Listing 41-4: **The DHTML Help Library**

```
function helpLayerDisplay(helpTopic) {

ie = (document.all)? true:false

if (ie) {
  var HTMLLayer =""
  HTMLLayer += "<font size=\"2\" face=\"Arial\">"
  HTMLLayer += helpTopic
  HTMLLayer += "</font>"
  document.all.helpLayer.innerHTML = HTMLLayer;
  }
```

Continued

Listing 41-4 *(continued)*

```
else
{
var targetLayer = (layerLevel)?
eval('document.'+layerLevel+'.document.'+Layer+'.document') :
document.layers[helpLayer].document
targetLayer.className = "helpLayerText";
targetLayer.open()
targetLayer.write(helpTopic)
targetLayer.close()
}
}
```

As with the DHTML Data Control function that writes to the errorLayer layer, the first thing this function does is check the client type. If the browser is an IE browser, messages are written to the `innerHTML` object of the helpLayer layer, which is nested in the bgLayer background layer. If the browser client is anything other than IE, the message is written to the `helpLayer` object that is nested in the layers array of the document. As with the error messages, the stylesheets take care of the font type and color for non-IE browsers.

Summary

This chapter provided an introduction to DHTML in Domino:

- ✦ An introduction to CSS and layers
- ✦ Using CSS in Domino
- ✦ Domino layers
- ✦ DIV tags
- ✦ Uses for DHTML in Domino
- ✦ Creating DHTML data control functionality for Domino applications
- ✦ Creating a DHTML help system for Domino applications

In Chapter 42, we add even more functionality to Domino applications by showing you how to link JavaScript to Java applets.

✦   ✦   ✦

Combining Domino and Java Applets Using JavaScript

By Brian Benz

♦   ♦   ♦   ♦

In This Chapter

Using Java applets

Using JavaScript
and Java applets

Embedding applets
In HTML pages

Working with
Domino Java applets
in Domino forms

Understanding
Domino applets

Controlling Java applets
in Domino forms

♦   ♦   ♦   ♦

JavaScript and Java applets can be connected to each other in Domino using an interface called LiveConnect, which is supported in the most recent versions of Navigator, MS IE, and the Notes client, and manipulates Java applets using JavaScript through the applet API without the need for Java. However, the Java Applet API must be available or published somewhere in order for this to work.

Domino objects are available to Java applets using the Java `AppletBase` class. Domino has created four applets based on this class that can be embedded into Notes applications; the Outline, View, and Action Bar, and Editor (Rich Text) Applets. Other applets that extend the `AppletBase` class can also be accessed using LiveConnect, if the Applet APIs are published.

This chapter provides some examples of manipulating Java applets from JavaScript using the Domino Designer UI, including isolating Java applet calls, properties, and methods, and using those calls to change properties of an applet embedded in an HTML page. It also covers techniques for embedding the JavaScript to Java calls into existing Domino UI elements.

Java Applets

Java applets were the first technology that Sun developed as part of the Java platform. The idea was to add interactivity to previously static Web pages by passing object behavior along with object data. *Applet* was the term coined to describe this object, which was thought of as a mini-application intended to serve a specific purpose in association with the data on a Web page. This innovation was met with great fanfare in 1995, when it was announced as a core part of the new Netscape Navigator browser. Since then, millions of developers have downloaded Sun's freely distributed Java Developer Kits (JDKs) and are still building applets, applications, and Java servlets.

Unfortunately, the previously bright prospects for complex Java applets, and other types of client-side Java delivered over the Web, have not been realized. Client-side Java has traditionally been plagued with JDK, browser, and client operating system platform compatibility and performance issues. More complicated Java functionality has been pushed back to the server domain, where there are fewer performance and reliability issues due to a more easily controlled environment.

Today, Java applets are frequently used for simple single-purpose functionality on the Web, as they were in 1995. Some of the more complicated functionalities for Web applets can be found in the Domino Outline, View, Action Bar, and Editor applets. We review all the applets in this chapter, and provide some examples of controlling the View applet via JavaScript.

For more information on Java applications and servlets, refer to Part IV.

Java resources — downloads and code

You can find several great resources for downloading and sharing applets on the Web. The applets, as well as other types of Java, are generally available for free; some even include source code for distribution. The following list contains a couple of favorites:

✦ **The Sun Java site:** This site contains an index of applets that you can use in applications. Most are free. There are also several links to other sites with more applets and information (http://java.sun.com/applets/).

✦ **Java Boutique:** This site contains many great examples and lots of code and information, some of it free and some of it for sale. The Java Boutique is the original unofficial Java download source (http://javaboutique.internet.com/).

Understanding JavaScript and Java Applets

JavaScript and Java are often confused due to their similar names. But that's where most of the similarity ends. JavaScript does resemble Java in a few general ways, but it's a lot looser in terms of data typing, and it's an interpreted language, which means that JavaScript code is compiled at runtime by the client. A Java developer using the Java Developer Kit or a built-in compiler in a Java editor compiles Java, and the compiled code is sent to the client machine to be executed by the Java Virtual Machine (JVM) on the client.

Java and JavaScript are both based on object-oriented models, but Java's compiling requirements, specific data typing restrictions, and object hierarchy requirements, as well as the Java syntax, make Java harder to code, but more powerful. Consequently, JavaScript is more widely adopted for simple development requirements, whereas Java is implemented for more complex functionality.

In some instances, however, JavaScript and Java work well together to provide interactive functionality that neither JavaScript nor Java could provide alone. In these cases, JavaScript is used to access and manipulate objects that a Java application provides. For example, Java can provide access to server-side data to provide application state management functionality and keep a session alive. Also, many Java applets are published with parameters that enable developers to access and manipulate the applet with JavaScript.

Embedding Java Applets in HTML Pages

Applets are embedded on an HTML page using a reference to the applet's class file in the `<applet>` HTML tag. Listing 42-1 shows what the `applet` tag and associated parameters look like for a Domino View applet for the Inbox view of a Domino Mail database embedded on an HTML page.

Listing 42-1: **The Applet Tag and Associated Parameters for a Domino View Applet**

```
<applet name="view"
code="lotus.notes.apps.viewapplet.ViewApplet.class"
codebase="/domjava" archive="nvapplet.jar" alt="View"
width="336" height="192" mayscript>
<param name="cabbase" value="nvapplet.cab">
<param name="Database" value="mail/bbenz.nsf">
<param name="ViewName" value="($Inbox)">
<param name="PanelStyle" value="LINE_BORDER">
<param name="ViewUNID"
value="38D46BF5E8F08834852564B500129B2C">
<param name="Expand" value="TRUE">
<param name="bgColor" value="#FFFFFF">
<param name="ShowScrollbars" value="FALSE">
<param name="locale" value="en-us">
<param name="TrashUNID" value="35E60C0DAC14F2A5852566F0006E31B1">
<param name="IconPath" value="/icons">
</applet>
```

Previewing a form that contains an embedded View applet in the MS Internet Explorer browser generates Listing 42-1. This is a fairly typical view of an applet tag, nested elements, and associated parameters. The `applet` tag lists several attributes. Table 42-1 lists the `applet` tag attributes and descriptions:

Table 42-1: Attributes for the Applet Tag

Applet Tag Attribute	Description
name	Identifies an applet by name.
code	The name and location of the `java` class file on the filesystem, or within the archive if an archive is listed.
Codebase (optional)	A path to the directory where the applet class used in the code is located. The full path is codebase + archive.
Archive (optional)	The archive file (usually a `.jar` file) in which the code is located.
Alt (optional)	An alternative name for the applet when embedded on the page.

Continued

Table 42-1 *(continued)*

Applet Tag Attribute	Description
Width	Default (initial) display width for the applet.
Height	Default (initial) display height for the applet.
Mayscript (optional)	Indicates that the applet is deemed by the applet developers to be safe to communicate with JavaScript objects.

Using mayscript

The presence of the mayscript attribute in an applet tag tells JavaScript that the applet is allowed to access JavaScript objects of the Web page. In addition to adding the mayscript tag, the applet developers must code the applet to permit access to JavaScript objects via the JSObject class so that applet objects can write to JavaScript objects on a Web page.

Note   The mayscript tag is necessary if the applet wants to communicate with the JavaScript objects on the page. JavaScript can still access and manipulate parameters of applets that do not have a mayscript tag.

Setting applet parameters

Aside from the applet tag attributes, Listing 42-1 uses several parameters that JavaScript can access. Parameters are the access points for manipulating applets in Domino. Each parameter has two values: the name of the parameter and the value. When an applet is embedded on a Web page, the parameters for that applet are exposed via the document.applets object array. JavaScript can access the parameters in the array by calling on and changing parameter values. More details on applet parameter functionality for each specific Domino applet are listed in the "Using Domino Applets" section of this chapter.

Embedding Java Applets in Domino Forms

Java applets can be embedded on a Domino form, page, or in the rich text field of a document by choosing Java Applet under the Create menu.

Developers can also create an applet resource to be referenced from and shared among several forms, pages, or documents in Domino Designer. You can do so by choosing Applets from the Shared Resources section of Design Bookmarks for a Database, and selecting the applet and associated files to import.

Importing an applet from the file system or using an applet resource

You can import applets from the file system directly into a form, page, or document in Domino. Applets can also be added to the database as an applet resource, and then embedded in the form, page, or document as a reference to the applet resource. When applets are imported directly for the file system, applet files are attached as hidden files to the form, page, or document, and appear on the page as Domino design objects that you can cut, paste, resize, and so on. When applets are added to the database as a shared applet resource, files are stored centrally in the database. Shared applet resources can be reused on more than one form, page, or document, and are linked to the original applet files.

Linking to an applet on a Web server

When a Domino form, page, or document is linked to an applet, nothing is stored in the Domino design object except a URL link to the applet on the Web. This means that there is less for the database to carry around, but that functionality for the Domino application is at the mercy of the current connection to the Web and the state of the server on which the linked applet is stored.

Note   Java applets are supported in most releases of MS Internet Explorer and Netscape Navigator version 4 and up. Domino 5 applets support Java Virtual Machine (JVM) 1.1.8 and up, while Domino 6 applets support JVM version 1.3 and up.

Introducing Domino Applets

The Outline, View, Form, and Editor (Rich Text) applets have been a part of Domino applications since Domino R5, and are intended to provide the same type of functionality in Web browser client applications that Notes client applications support.

Domino Outline, View, and Action Bar applets, as well as rich text objects, have the option of being displayed on the Web as Java or HTML. If Java is chosen as the display type, an associated applet is activated on the Domino server. The Domino applets provide most of the same functionality present in their parent objects in a Notes application. Unlike regular applets, Domino applets support functionality on Domino forms or pages only, not on documents. Editor applets support functionality in Domino forms only, as the parent is a rich text field, which can't be embedded on pages.

Outlines

Outlines are handy for navigation of a Notes application or a Web site. They are particularly useful for creating and reusing a standard set of navigation features by embedding a standardized outline on a page or form.

To enable an outline applet, you can embed an outline in a page or form by choosing Embedded Element ➪ Outline from the Create menu in Domino Designer. Select the outline, choose Element — Outline Properties from the Info tab, and then select Using Java Applet in the Display drop-down menu (the default is Using HTML).

Views

The View applet can be used to represent any Domino view on the Web. The View applet has a great deal of functionality that HTML views on the Web cannot match. The View applet is one of two applets (along with the Editor applet) that include the `mayscript` tag and have parameters that developers can access to manipulate the view represented in the applet.

To enable a View applet, you can embed a view in a page or form by choosing Embedded Element ➪ View from the Create menu in Domino Designer. Select the View, choose Element — View Properties from the Info tab, and make sure that Using Java Applet (the default) is selected in the Web Access drop-down menu.

Action bars

The Action bar is located at the top of a Domino application screen and contains buttons that can call functions or agents. The Action Bar applet replicates the same functionality found in the Action bar of Domino applications. The HTML Action bar contains a smaller subset of features and none of the controls for displaying submenus of the Action bar main menu. The Java Action Bar applet can actually maintain contact between the server and the Web client, so action bar functions that require maintenance of an application state or an unbroken connection to the server can be used with the Java applet. Every Domino form and page has an Action bar as part of the design elements.

To enable an Action Bar applet, in a form or page, choose Design ➪ Action Bar Properties. On the Action Bar Info tab, select Using Java Applet from the Display drop-down menu (the default is Using HTML).

Editors (for rich text fields)

The Editor applet is available when associated with rich text fields on a Domino form only. It contains a subset of Domino functionality, with restrictions on font face, size, color, and so on. Even with these limitations, the feature set of an Editor applet is still far superior to that of an HTML text area, which is the standard HTML representation of a rich text field in Web browsers.

To enable an Editor applet, in a form, choose Field from the Create menu. Open the properties box for the field. Choose rich text as the data type for the field, and choose Using Java Applet from the Display drop-down menu (the default is Using HTML).

Controlling Java Applets in Domino Forms

There are two ways to control Java applets via JavaScript, by accessing documented parameters and methods, and by accessing undocumented parameters and methods. For the purposes of this example, you use the Mailing List View applet example form in the Mailing List database.

The Mailing List database and all other associated databases that contain the examples in this book are available for download from the www.wiley.com/compbooks/benz Web site, under the Downloads link.

The Mailing List View applet example form in the Mailing List database uses several design elements that show the interaction of Domino design elements, Web forms, and Java applets controlled via JavaScript. When the page is first opened, the entire listing of e-mail newsletter recipients appears in the Java applet-enabled embedded view, categorized by e-mail domain. The user selects a unique domain name from the drop-down box on the left, and then clicks the link that says Show Recipients for this Domain Only. The view shortens the list of e-mail recipients to those that match the selected domain only. Similarly, the drop-down box on the right changes the background color of the view. Figure 42-1 shows the Web page in action.

Several interactive Domino, HTML, and Java elements make this page work, and they are described in the following sections.

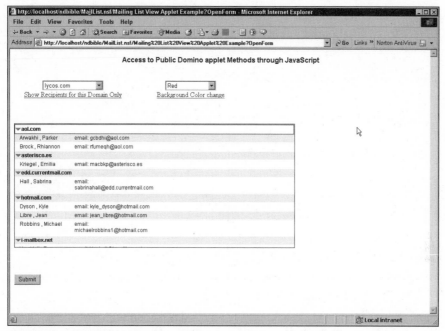

Figure 42-1: The Mailing List View applet example form in the Mailing List database, showing a full listing of mail newsletter recipients and the drop-down combo box that contains a unique listing of domain names

@DbColumn

The unique list of e-mail domain names that appears in the combo box on the left is generated by this @Formula by Domino before the page is sent to the Web:

```
@Unique(@Right(@DbColumn("";"":"";"Contacts";2);"@"))
```

In the center of this code, a @DBColumn function retrieves all the e-mails of the newsletter recipients listed in the Contacts view. The @Right command selects everything to the right of the @ in the e-mail address, which is the domain name if the e-mail address is formatted correctly. The @Unique function makes sure that there are no duplicate e-mail domain names in the list.

List box options

In the first combo box on the screen, you use the @DBColumn function to populate the list of values. For the BackgroundList combo box, the JavaScript function uses the hard-coded values in Listing 42-2.

Listing 42-2: The Hard-Coded Background Color Values for the Backgroundlist Combo Box

```
Red  | FF0000
Red1 | FF421E
Red2 | FF9F9F
Blue | 0000FF
Blue1| 82C0FF
Blue2 | C0E1FF
Back to Original
```

The values to the left of the alias separator (|) are the values that appear on the screen. The values to the right are the color values that will be passed to the applet to change the background color.

Embedded views and Single category views

The By Email Domain view is used for this example. It's categorized in the first field by the same `@Right` function that is used as part of the `@DBColumn` function:

```
@Right(MailAddress;"@")
```

The first field in the By Email Domain view is categorized and sorted for the single category functionality to work in the applet, just as with the same single category function in a Notes client.

Applet parameters – documented and undocumented

Documented parameters for a Java applet are made available at the discretion of the applet author, and are represented by parameters tags nested within the applet tag. In this case, JavaScript is used to access one documented parameter and one undocumented parameter. The documented parameter is `bgColor`, which is listed as part of the HTML tag for this applet, with a default color of white:

```
<param name="bgColor" value="#FFFFFF">
```

The HTML documentation for the undocumented parameters and methods for View applets and Editor applets can be downloaded from the `www.wiley.com/compbooks/benz` Web site.

You may be asking yourself why documentation for undocumented applet calls can be found here. If there is documentation, is the thing not documented? The answer is, actually, no. The reason why these API calls are still officially undocumented is that Lotus may decide to change them on a whim, and if the calls are documented, whim-based editing of the calls will be limited. Basically, Lotus is keeping its options open by not officially publishing methods and making parameters available as part of the applet, but hard-working, brave, and industrious developers can find some information on the calls in the undocumented documentation, just in case they want to play with them.

The undocumented parameter is called `categoryName` and would look like this if it were documented:

```
<param name=" categoryName " value="">
```

If the name of the category is null, all categories are shown. But if you assign a category to this parameter, the View applet displays that single category.

Applet methods – undocumented

This example uses two undocumented methods. The associated parameters, as well as methods and parameters for the Editor applet, are located in the downloads section of the `www.wiley.com/extras` Web site.

Note   These methods are not officially documented by Lotus and could change. You have been warned!

The `setRestrictToCategoryName` method sets the `categoryName` parameter to the text value is passed to it in the browser. The default is `null` and the View applet displays that single category when it is non-null.

The `setBackgroundColor` sets the value of `bgColor`, which is by default, white.

Action hotspots

The action hotspots below the combo boxes tie all the Domino, HTML, and Java elements together. When a user clicks the Show Recipients for this Domain Only link under the left combo box, the following JavaScript code associated with the Action hotspot runs:

```
document.applets(0).setRestrictToCategoryName(RecipientDomainList.options
[RecipientDomainList.selectedIndex].text);
document.applets(0).refresh();
```

This code gets the currently selected value of the RecipientDomainList field by checking the property represented by the `.selectedIndex` object in the `.options` object. After retrieving the currently selected value, the `.text` property is passed to the View applet. The View applet is the only applet on the page, so you know it will always be the first object in the current document's applets object array, which is represented by `document.applets(0)`. The JavaScript function uses the `setRestrictToCategoryName` method to pass the currently selected list item from the RecipientDomainList field to the `categoryName` parameter of the View applet. Because the `categoryName` parameter is now non-null, the view automatically displays the single category matching the `categoryName` parameters when the View applet is refreshed via the `document.applets(0).refresh()` method.

The second action hotspot changes the background color of the View applet. It's a documented parameter this time, but not as cool:

```
document.applets(0).setBackgroundColor(BackgroundList.options[Background
List.selectedIndex].value);
document.applets(0).refresh();
```

As illustrated earlier in this chapter, documented parameters are listed in the HTML tag of the applet when the applet is embedded on a Web page, and can be seen by viewing the source code of the HTML page on which the applet is embedded. Undocumented parameters are not displayed in the parameter list, but may be accessible if the API call for the parameter is known.

This time the code gets the currently selected value of the `BackgroundList` by using the same `.selectedIndex` object in the `.options` object. After retrieving the currently selected value, the `.value` property is passed to the View applet. (The function is dealing with a numeric value this time representing a color, instead of text by which to set a single category.) The View applet is still the only applet on the page, so the function accesses the applet the same way, via `document.applets(0)`. This time the function uses the `setBackgroundColor` method to pass the current color selection from the BackgroundList field to the `bgColor` parameter of the View applet. When the View applet is refreshed via the `document.applets(0).refresh()` method, the new background color takes the place of the previous one. If the last option in the BackgroundList field options is chosen, null is passed to the applet, and the default color for the applet appears on the next `document.applets(0).refresh()` call to the applet.

Summary

This chapter provided an introduction to Java applets and outlined basic concepts of JavaScript versus Java applets:

✦ Working embedded applets in HTML pages

✦ Working with Domino Java applets in Domino forms

✦ Working with Domino applets

✦ Controlling Java applets in Domino forms using JavaScript

✦ Using action hotspots, embedded View applets, and combo box fields to manipulate embedded Java applets

This is the final JavaScript chapter in the book. Other chapters do, however, show tips and techniques to build on these basics. For example, the next chapter covers options for incorporating data entry and UI controls using Domino and JavaScript in a data-integration application.

✦   ✦   ✦

Relational Database Integration

Integrating Enterprise Data with Domino Applications

By Brian Benz

In This Chapter

Learning Domino data integration options

Introducing Domino Enterprise connectivity services and data connection resources

Understanding a Domino 6 DECS/DCR example

Setting up the Domino 6 Bible DECS examples

Domino data integration combines the collaborative, Web-enabled features of Notes and Domino with the vast amount of information that is contained in relational databases, legacy systems, transaction-based enterprise applications, and organizational data warehouses.

This chapter covers tips and techniques for building data integration into Domino applications. After you review the options for data integration, you learn several techniques for including enterprise data in Domino applications by using an application that uses Domino Enterprise Connectivity Services (DECS), ODBC, LotusScript agents, JavaScript, @functions, and Data Connection Resources (DCRs). You can apply the same techniques discussed for DECS and DCRs to all the data integration options in this chapter.

Domino Data Integration Options

Lotus and IBM continuously update data integration options for Domino, as technologies evolve. The real-time Domino data integration options in the following sections represent today's best and most practical integration tools for Domino 5 and 6. This section provides you with a brief overview of DECS, LotusScript Data Objects (LS:DO), Lotus Enterprise Integrator (LEI), Lotus Connector LotusScript Extensions (LC LSX), Lotus Connectors (LC) for Java, Common Object Request Broker Architecture (CORBA), Java Database Connectivity (JDBC), and WebSphere.

Understanding Lotus' connector-based architecture

Connectors are the Lotus standardized data-integration interface for connecting to back-end enterprise data via predefined connection formats. Connectors provide links from Notes and Domino applications to DB2, Oracle, SAP, JD Edwards, PeopleSoft, OLE (for MS SQL Server 7), MQSeries, and ODBC data sources. Connectors are used by Domino Enterprise Connectivity Services (DECS), Lotus Enterprise Integrator (LEI), Lotus Connector LotusScript Extensions (LC LSX), and Lotus Connectors (LC) for Java.

IBM has also developed connector APIs that are customized for IBM hardware and software platforms. MQSeries and CICS have connectors that work with specific tools. MQ Enterprise Integrator (MQEI) supports batch-style replication with MQSeries and CICS. MQSeries can also be accessed from LotusScript if you use the MQSeries LotusScript Extensions (MQ LSX). DB2 has its own LotusScript Extensions that work well with the DB2 connector, and IBM has published a native DB2 JDBC driver as well.

Understanding how connectors work

Connectors make multiple data formats look the same to a Domino application. Notes and Domino applications can call seven classes when using a Lotus connector to access back-end data. Table 43-1 lists the classes that are common across every Lotus connector.

Table 43-1: Lotus Connector Classes

LCSession	Every connection contains a session object. LCSession provides information about available connectors and associated properties and methods. LCSession also handles any errors that occur during a connection.
LCConnection	LCConnection connects and sends queries to the back-end data.
LCFieldlist	LCFieldlist creates a block of field names through an LCConnection to create a result set or to write to a back-end data source.
LCField	LCField stores the data type of a field for all values in an LCFieldList.
LCStream	LCStream is a unicode text and binary data type, including the character set of the data.
LCNumeric	The LCNumeric class contains numbers and is compatible with Domino number field formats.
LCCurrency	The LCCurrency class supports a 19-digit, four-decimal numeric data format, and is the same as the Domino currency data format.
LCDatetime	The LCDatetime class contains date time formats and is compatible with Domino date and time field formats.

You can find more information on implementing data integration solutions using Lotus connectors, as well as an up-to-date listing of available connectors, at the Lotus Enterprise Integration Web site (www.lotus.com/ldd/products.nsf/products/ei).

Lotus Enterprise Integrator

Lotus Enterprise Integrator (LEI) is a tool sold separately by IBM that replicates between Domino and back-end sources in batch. Originally called NotesPump, it contained the real-time capabilities now present in Domino Enterprise Connectivity Services (DECS). When Domino 5 was released, DECS functionality was replicated and is now included as part of the Domino server. DECS also provided the base functionality for Domino 6 Data Connection Resources (DCRs).

LEI still contains real-time tools for data integration, but is mostly purchased and used for batch-style data transfer and replication. Aside from the tools to make data integration possible, LEI also includes a data-integration UI for managing replication. LEI is also useful for replicating data between two Domino databases that are not replicas.

LEI supports LotusScript integration via LEI LotusScript Extensions (LEI LSX), and supports Java functionality via Lotus Connectors for Java.

 Cross-Reference   Refer to Chapter 45 for more detailed information on Lotus Enterprise Integrator.

LotusScript Data Objects

LotusScript Data Objects (LS:DO) uses Open Database Connectivity (ODBC) to connect directly to back-end data from a client or a server. Queries and results pass between the client and the data source via ODBC.

LS:DO features

A set of LotusScript Extension (LSX) files enable functionality for LS:DO. The LSX files are loaded as DLLs in the Notes client and/or Domino server program directory. LS:DO uses Open Database Connectivity (ODBC) to connect back-end data sources to LS:DO classes in a Notes or Domino application. LS:DO contains three LotusScript classes, which differ slightly from their Lotus connector class counterparts. Table 43-2 lists LS:DO classes.

Table 43-2: LS:DO Classes

ODBCConnection	ODBCConnection contains an ODBC session object. It manages the state of the ODBC connection and captures any connection errors.
ODBCQuery	ODBCQuery contains a query associated with an ODBC connection.
ODBCResultSet	ODBCResultSet is the access point for manipulating an ODBC result set.

LS:DO: What developers need to know

LS:DO development requires that a developer have intermediate Domino developmental skills, including advanced LotusScript, some knowledge of LSX installation and integration, ODBC integration, Lotus connector classes, and ODBC classes to adapt application code that uses the LS:DO classes.

For Domino Web applications, LS:DO uses the `WebQueryOpen` and `WebQuerySave` form events to trigger queries and updates to and from back-end data. If you use data query forms, you should also understand the techniques using `$$Return`. For Notes client applications, LS:DO uses the `QueryOpen` and `QuerySave` form events to trigger queries and updates to and from back-end data.

When to use LS:DO

LS:DO has been around for a long time and is included in many legacy Domino applications. ODBC is well known for its performance issues. You should use LS:DO only for Notes applications that require low-volume queries with small numbers of concurrent users. In general, LS:DO applications should never be used for applications that will be supporting over 25MB of data on a server, or more than 100 concurrent users. These numbers may be adjusted depending on the conditions of your network, server, and client machine environments, but serve as a good starting point.

Because LS:DO uses ODBC on a server or a Notes client machine, LS:DO can be useful for building applications that access enterprise data without having to access a Domino server. In this case, you can set up the ODBC driver and connection for the back-end data source on the client machine. Connections can be made directly to the back-end data without a Domino server in the middle.

When not to use LS:DO

Because LS:DO relies on ODBC for connectivity, ODBC drivers for back-end data must exist, and the client and/or server platforms must be able to store and run ODBC drivers, and be ODBC 2.0-compliant. This rules out OS/2, AIX, Solaris, HP-UX, IBM S/390, and OS/400. Also, if LS:DO agents are running on a Domino server, the server must be configured for multi-threaded agents, which may conflict with other Domino software and agents.

Lotus Connector LotusScript Extensions

Lotus Connector LotusScript Extensions (LC LSX) use Lotus connectors to connect to back-end data from a Notes client or a Domino server. Queries and results pass to and from the client to the data source via the Lotus Connector's `LCConnection` class.

LC LSX features

The enabling functionality for LC LSX is a set of LotusScript Extension (LSX) files that are loaded as DLLs in the Notes client and/or Domino server program directory. These files call the Lotus Connector classes in conjunction with a specific Lotus Connector.

LC LSX: What developers need to know

Developers need to have an understanding of Domino development at the intermediate level, including some advanced LotusScript, some knowledge of LSX installation and integration, Lotus Connector integration. Developers must also have a good grasp of the Lotus Connector classes to adapt the methods and properties of the classes for their applications.

Because LC LSX classes were derived from LS:DO classes, LC LSX applications usually use the same `WebQueryOpen` and `WebQuerySave` form events to trigger queries and updates to and from back-end data. If you use data query forms, you should also understand techniques using `$$Return`. For Notes client applications, LC LSX uses the `QueryOpen` and `QuerySave` form events to trigger queries and updates to and from back-end data.

When to use LC LSX

LC LSX uses Lotus Connectors to access back-end data. If you have a choice of using LS:DO via ODBC or LC LSX classes via native connectors, the LC LSX solution always performs better. It doesn't have the performance overhead associated with ODBC. LC LSX is still, however, not a high-volume solution. You shouldn't develop LC LSX solutions for Notes applications that require high-volume queries with large numbers of concurrent users, regardless of the back-end data source performance.

When not to use LC LSX

LC LSX solutions are not recommended for high-volume, transactional solutions with large numbers of users and large sources of data. Also, because LC LSX relies on connectors to access back-end data sources, the connectors must exist for the back-end data source. A C API is available to build connectors for data sources that don't already have one. You can find a list of available connectors, as well as information about the LC LSX API, at the Lotus Enterprise Integration Web site (http://www.lotus.com/ldd/products.nsf/products/ei).

Lotus Connectors for Java (LC for Java)

Lotus Connectors for Java (LC for Java) use Lotus Connectors to connect from Java applets, applications, and servlets to back-end data from a Notes client or a Domino server. Queries and results pass to and from the client to the data source via the Lotus Connector's LCConnection class.

Cross-Reference For more information on Java applications, applets, and servlets, refer to Part VII.

LC for Java features

The enabling functionality for LC for Java is a set of LotusScript Extension (LSX) files that load as DLLs in the Notes client and/or Domino server program directory. These files call the LC for Java Connector classes from Java in conjunction with a specific Lotus Connector.

LC for Java: What developers need to know

Developers must know about Domino development at the intermediate level, including some advanced Java, some knowledge of Java JDK and JRE (Java Runtime Environment) installation, and integration and Lotus Connector integration.

LC for Java applications usually use the WebQueryOpen and WebQuerySave, form events and the contents of a $$Return field, which is triggered when a Web form is saved on a Domino server, to enable queries and updates to and from back-end data.

When to use LC for Java

LC for Java uses Lotus Connectors to access back-end data. If developers are experienced with Java applets, applications, and servlets but not with LotusScript, use the LC for Java classes. If the solution requires a Java applet or Java application with data connectivity features in association with Domino interactivity, LC for Java is a good choice for the back-end data integration portion of the project. Keep in mind that the Java solution needs to be installed on a machine that has a Notes client and/or has access to a Domino server for the LC for Java classes to function. As with LS:DO and LC LSX, LC for Java is not a high-volume solution. You shouldn't develop LC for Java solutions for Notes applications that require high-volume queries with large numbers of concurrent users, regardless of the back-end data source performance.

When not to use LC LSX

LC for Java solutions are not recommended for high-volume, transactional solutions with large numbers of users and large sources of data. Also, connectors must exist for the back-end data source.

Common Object Request Broker Architecture (CORBA)

CORBA is a specification that is not tied to a specific language. But because of their complicated nature, CORBA solutions are usually developed in lower-level programming languages. Java is the most common solution, and C or C++ is a close second in number of implementations and available class libraries. CORBA class libraries conform to CORBA specs such as LiveConnect. CORBA class libraries also support CORBA data modeling and interface standards to make them compatible with most CORBA applications.

CORBA features

Because of CORBA's ability to manage sessions and state, CORBA applications are generally associated with managing session and transaction functionality in an otherwise stateless browser application. An applet is placed on a Web page, which the browser client Java Virtual Machine (JVM) instantiates when the page loads. Typically, this applet sets up a session on a back-end server and manages the session and any related connections.

You can also use CORBA to connect two servers, as long as they both have compatible Object Request Brokers (ORBs). WebSphere and Domino commonly share data via CORBA if both are loaded on the same machine.

CORBA: What developers need to know

A Domino and CORBA solutions developer should have advanced Java development skills, good working knowledge of CORBA classes, properties, methods, Notes client and Domino server ORB (Object Request Broker) structure, the ORB structure for the back-end data source, and that source's associated classes and objects.

When to use CORBA

Because CORBA uses Java applets on the browser client, it enables direct connections to back-end sources without the need to instantiate a Domino form or session event to query form and submit objects to servers. If you need access to Domino objects, the `AppletBase` class can access Notes client and Domino server objects, instantiate sessions, and maintain session info on the Domino server.

Applets that extend the `AppletBase` class or facilitate a back-end data access connection are often used in Domino Web applications as part of a display applet or a pinpoint applet. A pinpoint applet is a tiny applet (not visible to the user) that is included on a Web page. Other types of applets are visible to the user and provide some sort of interactive function. When you embed the applet on the page, it becomes part of the JavaScript Document Object Model (DOM) for that page and can be accessed like any other object via parameters and methods. But when you access the CORBA object, the properties and methods in the applet perform CORBA transactions with Domino and/or a back-end data source and respond with data from those sources. Other objects in the DOM have access to only the current Web page.

When not to use CORBA

CORBA-bound data has to travel through several layers before arriving at its destination. A typical CORBA data request is sent via a Java applet from a browser to a local Object Request Broker (ORB), and then to a remote ORB. A query is then made to the back-end data, which is packaged and sent back to the local ORB, to the applet, and finally to the user's screen through JavaScript. This model, while flexible and useful for Web applications, has negative performance characteristics.

You should not use CORBA for applications that require high-volume, high-speed transactions. And because of the complex nature of developing a CORBA application, development staff capability is an important consideration. Your staff must be experienced with Java and CORBA (and maybe C or C++). Another important factor to remember is that many data sources don't have support for Object Request Brokers (ORBs), so it's critical to make sure that your data sources are CORBA compliant before planning a CORBA solution.

Tip   For more information on supported platforms and tools for CORBA, visit the Object Management Group's Web site at www.omg.org.

Java DataBase Connectivity

Java DataBase Connectivity (JDBC) is a Java-based connection architecture that closely mirrors ODBC, but is implemented in Java. JDBC functionality requires a JDBC driver for the back-end data source, or the implementation of a JDBC to ODBC bridge if the data source supports ODBC. JDBC is generally implemented from a server using servlets, but can also be called from a client as long as the client supports the classes and methods required for the JDBC driver and Java. Unlike ODBC, which is well known for its poor performance, if the JDBC driver is running as part of a Java servlet on a third-party servlet manager, such as WebSphere, JDBC can be used for high-performance, high-volume transactional systems. JDBC is often used as part of a multitier system comprised of browser applications using HTML or JSPs, a servlet manager in the middle, and a back-end data source accessed via JDBC in the servlet.

JDBC: What developers need to know

JDBC and Domino solution developers need intermediate Domino development skills, advanced Java skills to code the JDBC calls and manipulate result sets, and a good understanding of Domino Web application and JDBC/ODBC interactivity, They require knowledge of ODBC driver architecture and DSN naming conventions if no native JDBC driver is available and a JDBC to ODCB bridge architecture is being used, and a good understanding of Domino Web events, which are used to trigger servlets that make JDBC queries.

When to use JDBC

Because of the complex nature of developing a multitier JDBC application solution, you should use JDBC in more complex, high-volume, transactional systems, usually involving servlet development on the middle tier and calls from the Domino Web application to the servlet.

Another consideration for JDBC applications is the ability to use a JDBC driver for the back-end data source. Most large relational database vendors have JDBC drivers available, including MS SQL server, Oracle, and DB2. Domino has its own JDBC driver. Several third-party JDBC driver developers build drivers for other applications.

When not to use JDBC

If a Web application solution doesn't need transactional or high-volume capabilities as part of the application requirements, it's best to go with one of the more simple solutions, such as a LotusScript or Java connector-enable solution, or DECS/DCR.

If a JDBC driver is not available for the back-end data source in the planned application, you can use the JDBC to ODBC architecture for sources that support ODBC. But performance of a JDBC to ODBC architecture is much lower than the performance of a JDBC driver solution. Lotus Connector-based solutions often perform better than JDBC to ODBC architecture solutions. They're also much easier to implement, assuming that there's a Lotus Connector for the back-end data source. As mentioned earlier in the chapter, a C API is available to build connectors for data sources that don't already have connectors.

WebSphere (and other J2EE servers)

Although WebSphere isn't really a data integration tool, it's an important part of an industry-strength multitier Domino Web application that supports back-end data integration. WebSphere is a servlet-management environment that supports high-volume, secure servlet transaction processing. Servlets can contain JDBC, CORBA, or other types of data connectivity, as well as classes and methods for querying data and manipulating data result sets.

Java Server Pages (JSPs) and data integration

Java Server Pages (JSPs) are a way of integrating server-side functionality with HTML tags to create dynamic content for the Web, while separating content from display in a J2EE world. You can compare JSPs to Domino forms and documents versus Domino pages. Domino pages display relatively static information on the Web when compared to Domino documents, which can contain calculated fields and subforms that appear on the Web based on the current Domino session context (user security level, user-defined preferences in a profile document, and so on), even though both appear as HTML pages on the Web. At runtime, the Domino server applies a Domino form to a Domino document and generates a static HTML page that you can view in a browser.

You can make the same comparison of static HTML versus a JSP. HTML is a static file that you can edit and save on the server's file system, whereas JSPs are calculated HTML pages that are generated at runtime by a servlet, which is in turn generated by a JSP page. JSPs are a way of generating servlets on the fly. JSP tags are formatted much like HTML tags. But JSP tags are references to servlet functionality that generate an HTML page on a server at runtime and send the HTML page to a browser.

You can use JSPs to build servlet applications that integrate Domino data and objects via the new Domino 6 custom JSP tags. Domino custom tags provide Web developers with the ability to generate servlet code using Domino objects without having to code, compile, and deploy servlets, and with very little knowledge of the Java classes being accessed. In this way, you can separate the design of Web pages from the content, as JSP pages are a lot easier to develop than servlets that produce the same content.

Cross-Reference   For more information on WebSphere and WebSphere solutions, including JSP solutions, refer to Chapter 37.

WebSphere features

WebSphere provides a management environment to run servlets, JSPs, and Enterprise Java Beans (EJBs). It also supports high-volume transaction processing via connection pooling, transaction processing, load balancing, connection failover, and persistence features. WebSphere also includes administration and management tools.

WebSphere developer profile

A WebSphere and Domino solution developer should have advanced Domino Web site and servlet development skills. HTML page and JSP development skills are also a must, if you're going to use the Domino custom JSP tags. Advanced Java development skills are required to efficiently implement servlet solutions on WebSphere. Experience with WebSphere administration features is desirable as well.

When to use WebSphere

IBM is bundling WebSphere with Domino 6, as they did with Domino 5, with some important limitations. The most important one is that the WebSphere server must be installed on the same physical server as Domino. The second important factor is that the WebSphere server may act only against Domino data, not relational data, such as DB2 or MS SQL server. Using the WebSphere Java Connector Architecture (JCA) connectors and EJBs are also prohibited.

Domino Enterprise Connectivity Services and Data Connection Resources

You now have a basic understanding of the various data integration options for Domino applications. This section covers the features and setup of a Domino Enterprise Connectivity Services (DECS) application. As mentioned earlier, you can apply the same techniques for DECS and Data Connection Resources (DCRs) to all the data integration options discussed in this chapter.

DECS features

DECS enable code-free external data integration from sources via Lotus Connectors. DECS has been available as an add-in for Domino since version 4.63 and was included with Domino R5. In Domino 6, DECS functionality was incorporated into DCRs. The server-based DECS administration database (DECSADM.NSF) is where developers define and manage connections to external data sources and specify events to watch for in databases. For DECS and DCRs to function, the DECS tasks must run on the same server as the DECS administration database, and the same server as the Domino application database. The back-end data can be on any server, as long as it is accessible to the server running the DECS task.

DECS enables you to set up and map data sources directly from external data sources to your Web applications by mapping a single key field in the external data source to a field in the Domino form. DECS connection documents define connections to external data sources, and DECS activity documents define applications databases to watch and specific activities to watch for. You can define connection documents and activity documents using a series of fields and picklists on a page in the DECS administration database. Less experienced DECS developers can also set documents up using wizards.

DCR features

A DCR is new to Domino 6 and based on DECS functionality, but does not use the DECS administration database (DECSADM.NSF). Instead, the connections and activities are defined in the Domino application database, and a DCR-enabled database needs to be put on a Domino server running the DECS tasks to function. As with DECS, the back-end data can be on any server, as long as it is accessible to the server running the DECS task. A Domino form can contain a single DCR via form properties, or multiple DCRs can be used via field properties.

DECS and DCRs: What developers need to know

Because of the ease of setting up connections and activities, DECS and DCR development requires the least amount of Domino development skills of any of the data integration options. Developers need intermediate Domino development skills and enough knowledge of ODBC or Lotus Connector integration to specify data sources and activities via wizards and/or DECS and DCR forms.

Developing applications using DECS involves the use of the `WebQueryOpen` and `WebQuerySave` form events to trigger queries and updates to and from back-end data. If you use data query forms, you should also understand the techniques using $$Return. Notes client DECS applications use the `QueryOpen` and `QuerySave` form events to trigger queries and updates to and from back-end data. DECS activity documents for Notes applications can be triggered when a document is created, opened, closed, or deleted.

Cross-Reference   For more on using DECS and DCRs in applications, refer to Chapter 44.

When to use DECS and DCRs

DECS and DCRs are great tools to set up a low-volume data integration solution that doesn't require a lot of records returned from the back-end data source, and doesn't support a large number of concurrent users. DECS and DCRs are perfect, for example, for small help desk operations that have 5 to 10 concurrent users querying a 10,000 row relational inventory database.

DECS and DCRs are also useful for prototyping the UI for a data integration solution and before spending time implementing the data integration portion in a more robust format.

When not to Use DECS and DCRs

The power and ease of use of DECS and DCRs are balanced out by poor performance. Any application that needs to return more than 500 rows of data in a single query, requires more than 50 concurrent users, and queries more than 100,000 rows of back-end data, probably finds the performance of DECS and DCRs unsuitable. DECS is best for querying data from back-end sources, but has limited features for writing data to back-end sources, especially if the data needs to be written to more than one table. This limits DECS to nontransactional applications with relatively low numbers of transactions.

A Domino 6 DECS/DCRs Example – Quotes

This example uses an MS Access Quote of the Day database. The Access database is used with the permission of the original owners, Newbs Consulting and Sapphire Oak Technologies. You can download the original Quote of the Day Domino database from `www.sapphireoak.com` or `www.newbsconsulting.com`.

The Access Quote of the Day database contains over 1,000 quotes that you can add to e-mails, Web pages, and other types of applications. This example uses an Access table because only the file and the Access ODBC driver are required on the Domino server to run the back-end data examples (plus the Domino server and the DECS task running, of course!). MS Access doesn't need to be on the server unless developers want to view or change the database structure.

The database is named `Quotes.mdb` and contains a single table, called QuoteTable. The data structure of the Quote table is outlined in Table 43-3.

Table 43-3: Quote of the Data Access Database Structure

Date	The date the quote was added to the database.
Source	The source of the quote, or the name of the person who added the quote.
Quote	The quotation.
QuoteKey	Primary key. A unique identifier of the quote for relational purposes.

The Domino 6 Bible DECS Examples database

The Domino 6 Bible DECS Examples (D6BibleDECS.nsf) database contains the sample Quote application and all the DECS and DCR application-side information. Figure 43-1 shows the Query screen of the DECS Quote Example database.

 You can find the examples in this chapter in the Mailing List database (MailList.nsf), and a copy is stored in the Domino 6 Bible JavaScript Examples database (d6bibleJava Script.nsf). Both are available for download at www.wiley.com/compbooks/benz.

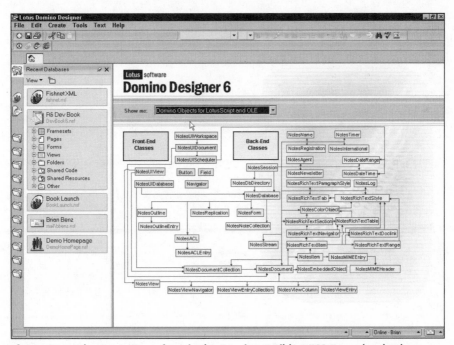

Figure 43-1: The QuoteQuery form in the Domino 6 Bible DECS Examples database

You can find the form in Figure 43-1 in the Domino 6 Bible DECS Examples database. The form has two fields and buttons for queries. The first field and button search for a Quote Source, and the second button searches for text in a quotation. When the query is processed, DECS returns matching values and displays them on the screen. Figure 43-2 shows the results of a query on Bill Gates as the Quote Source.

The applications provide a good example of capturing Domino and Web form events, as well as integrating back-end data with Domino applications. Each quote is stored in the database for logging purposes. Storing the query has maintenance disadvantages but audit trail advantages. The advantage is the ability to log queries. Because the query traced time and dates, you're able to track total queries and query patterns, which helps demonstrating return on investment for the system and assists in determining peak query periods. You can also track successful query statistics and compare them against unsuccessful query statistics, and use the information gathered to enhance data entry controls and improve query results. The potential disadvantage to logging every query is an extra load on application performance and disk space. To counter this, set up a simple agent that moves all result records to an archive database daily.

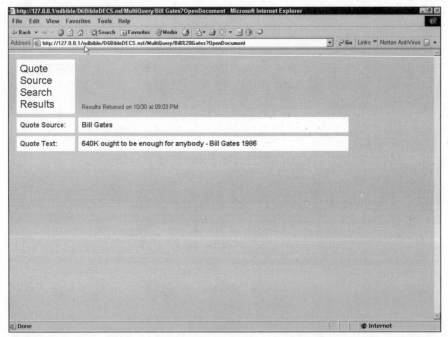

Figure 43-2: The results returned from the QuoteQuery form showing Bill Gates as the Query Source

Setting up the Domino 6 Bible DECS examples

The setup of this example requires administration rights to a Domino server, with enough access to be able to set up an ODBC driver, create new files on the file system, and create new Domino databases and administer the DECS administration database (DECSADM.nsf). Don't forget that the DECS task must be running on the server, the DECS activities must be started, and the ODBC connection and Domino application database have to be present on the same server as the DECS administration database for the queries to work.

Copying the Domino 6 Bible DECS Examples database and the MS Access Quotes database

Copy the Domino 6 Bible DECS Examples database (D6BibleDECS.nsf) and the MS Access Quotes database (Quotes.mdb) from the downloads section of ndbible.com and place them in the <Lotus Domino Install Directory>\data\ndbible\ subdirectory of your Domino server.

Setting up the ODBC driver

Create a custom MS Access ODBC connection to the Quotes.mdb MS Access database called Quotes. Consult the operating system help files for the location of the ODBC driver settings and procedures for setting up a new ODBC driver. No user ID and password are required for the configuration, and the end result should closely resemble the custom driver shown in Figure 43-3.

Figure 43-3: Setting up a custom MS Access ODBC connection to the Quotes.mdb MS Access database called Quotes

Setting up the DECS connection to the ODBC data source

Open the DECS administrator database (DECSADM.nsf) on your Domino server. If no database exists on your server, create a new one using the DECS administration template (DECSADM.ntf). The database must be named DECSADM.nsf for DECS to use it.

To set up the connection for the Quotes.mdb MS Access database, create a new connection and follow the instructions in the Connection Wizard, or add the field values manually by canceling out of the wizard. The connection document should match Figure 43-4 when done.

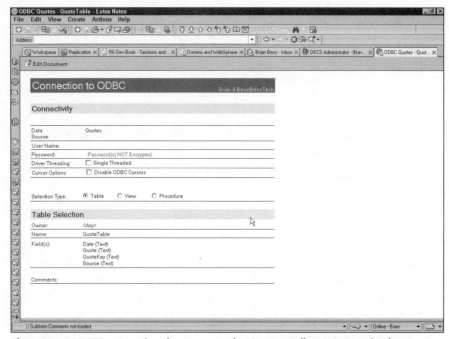

Figure 43-4: DECS connection document to the Quotes.mdb MS Access database

Setting up the DECS activities for the Domino 6 Bible DECS Examples database

After the connection is set up, you're ready to create the first of two activity documents using the new Quotes connection document. Create a new activity and follow the instructions in the Activity Wizard, or add the field values manually by canceling out of the wizard.

Name the first activity Quote Source Query and set the QuoteSourceResults form of ndbible\d6BibleDECS.nsf as the form. Map the QuoteSource Domino field to the Source MS Access field as the key. Then add the QuoteText Domino field mapped to the Quote MS Access field to the field(s). Leave all the rest of the options at their defaults. The result should match the activity in Figure 43-5.

Name the second activity Quote Text Query and set the QuoteTextResults form of ndbible\d6BibleDECS.nsf as the form. Reverse the key and field(s) settings from the first activity. In other words, map the QuoteText Domino field to the Quote MS Access field as the key. Then add the QuoteSource Domino field mapped to the Source MS Access field to the field(s).

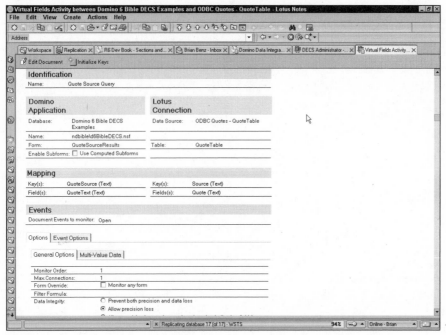

Figure 43-5: DECS activity document for the Quote Source Query activity

Summary

This chapter reviewed Domino data integration options at a high level, with a more detailed introduction to DECS and DCRs, including:

✦ A review of Domino data-integration options

✦ An example application that uses DECS and DCRs

✦ Retrieving data from a back-end Access database

✦ Setting up the Domino 6 Bible DECS Examples database and related files

The next chapter reviews best practices and techniques for creating Domino applications that integrate with enterprise data by showing you how a DECS application works and explaining how to adapt the same techniques for use with other data-integration options.

✦   ✦   ✦

Developing Domino Applications for Data Integration

By Brian Benz

This chapter extends the data integration concepts that you learned in Chapter 43 by illustrating several practical examples of a working data integration solution. The example application uses Domino Enterprise Connectivity Services (DECS) to connect to an access database that contains over 1000 popular quotations. The quotes table in the database contains four columns: A unique key for each quotation, a quotation source, the quotation, and the date that the quotation was added to the database.

The application provides good examples of application, form, and other design element techniques for developing Domino solutions that integrate with enterprise data. The application in this chapter uses Domino Enterprise Connectivity Services (DECS) and Data Connection Resources (DCRs), but you can easily adapt it to use any Domino data integration option using the same techniques.

Cross-Reference For more information on setting up the example database and an introduction to data integration, refer to Chapter 43.

Triggering Simple Queries

For a single-key query that performs a search on the access database for a quotation source, you simply create a Domino form with a single field, which is used to enter the query. Several other fields display the results of the query. The query value field appears when the document is in Edit mode, and the returned data fields appear when the document is in Read mode. The same form can look like the query form when it's in Edit mode and the results form when it's in Display mode.

DECS queries are triggered on a query value when a Domino document with a form name that is specified in a DECS activity document is opened. To trigger a lookup on a Web-based form, three things must happen:

1. The user enters a query value into a Domino document and clicks the Submit button.

2. The document is saved and then reopened via commands placed in an embedded $$Return field.

3. When the document is reopened, a form open activity in the DECS administration database triggers a DECS query. The query passes results to the Domino document.

To the user, this process looks like a simple query and response. But it's important that developers understand the inner workings of the document save-and-reopen model to trigger a query. This is the basic query and response event for all Domino Web applications when using any Domino data integration tool.

Unfortunately for developers, users quickly outgrow simple one-value lookup screens, and generally want more options when querying data. When multiple queries are combined on a single Domino form, developers start to encounter complex issues. For example, data-entry errors that return large partial-key query results can bring a server to a standstill, or users that need to filter queries by more than one key value at a time from a single screen, such as a quotation source combined with a single word contained in a quotation.

The data entry problems are easy to avoid by adding JavaScript to the data entry form to restrict user data entry. For example, a JavaScript function could be written to prevent users from entering less than three letters on a quotation source or quotation, which avoids queries that return large amounts of data based on matching a single letter or number. A prompt can appear warning users that partial quotation sources or short quotations return unpredictable results.

Triggering Multiple Queries by Using Multiple Keys on a Single Query Form

One of the best techniques for managing multiple queries on a single Domino Web form is to fool Domino into thinking a document with a different form name has been opened depending on which query was chosen by the user. DECS activities watch for documents with a specific form name to open. When a document with that form name opens, DECS submits a query to a back-end database to return values based on a query value field on the form. The simple option is to create three query forms, which can be selected depending on the query value. But this means that users have to switch forms constantly to perform queries on different query values, which is confusing and unnecessary when a little deception provides the same functionality on one form. Figure 44-1 shows the data entry form with buttons and fields for searching quotation sources and quotations.

First, one Submit button is added for each data entry field. A user can then select which key value to query on by clicking the appropriate query button. This is the sequence of events that the application follows when users submit a query using the form in Figure 44-1:

Figure 44-1: The Quotation database query form, with options to search on quotation source and quotation

1. A user enters data in one of the two key value fields and clicks the corresponding query button.

2. JavaScript validates the query data and records the key value in a lookup field.

3. The `WebQuerySave` event saves the document with a different form name, depending on which query button was clicked.

4. The $$Return field in the document contains a command that finds the document in the Query view and reopens it. That command is called as soon as the document is saved.

5. Reopening the document triggers a DECS activity based on the document form name. If the query triggered by the activity is successful, and a single query record is returned, the data will appear to the user. If the query triggered by the activity is successful, and multiple query records are returned, multiple rows of result data appear to the user. If the query was unsuccessful, an error message appears to the user with tips on how to improve the query.

Now that you know how the query form works, the next few sections address the features step by step.

Setting the HTML attributes for each button

Each button in the data entry form has an associated `onClick` JavaScript event. To fully understand what the button does, you must look at the generated HTML code attributes:

```
<INPUT TYPE="button" Name=QuoteSourceSubmit VALUE="Search for
Source" onClick="SubmitQS()">
```

Each button's attributes are slightly different. The quotation search button, for example, appears as follows:

```
<INPUT TYPE="button" Name=QuoteTextSubmit VALUE="Search for
Quotation" onClick="SubmitQT()">
```

Clicking the button in the browser activates the JavaScript function associated with the `onClick` event. The QuoteSourceSubmit button, for example, calls the `SubmitQS` JavaScript function.

JavaScript functions in the JSHeader

The JavaScript function called by the onClick event contains data validation for the associated data entry field, and modifies two other fields on the form, called ButtonPressed and ButtonPressedValue. When data passes validation and the two buttons are set without problems, the form is also submitted to the Domino server via JavaScript. Listing 44-1 shows the contents of the JSHeader object for the QuoteQuery form.

Listing 44-1: The Contents of the JSHeader Object for the QuoteQuery Form

```
function SubmitQS() {
form = document.forms[0];
if (form.QuoteSource.value == "")
  {alert("quotation source is required");
  form.QuoteSource.focus();
     return""}
else
form.ButtonPressed.value= "QS";
form.ButtonPressedValue.value= form.QuoteSource.value;
form.submit();
}

function SubmitQT() {
form = document.forms[0];
if (form.QuoteText.value == "")
  {alert("quotation is required");
  form.QuoteText.focus();
     return""}
else
form.ButtonPressed.value= 'QT';
form.ButtonPressedValue.value= form.QuoteText.value;
form.submit()
}
```

Each function is associated with a different button on the form. The SubmitQS function is called when you click the quotation source query button. This code performs a simple check to see whether the QuoteSource field is empty, represented by a blank value, and displays an alert box to the user and returns execution focus back to the QuoteSource field, requesting that the user enter or reenter the data.

If the field is not blank and the data passes validation, two fields are assigned to Javascript variables. The two variables become part of the Domino document when the document is saved, as if they were part of the original form design. ButtonPressed is used by the WebQuery Save event to determine which button was clicked, and the ButtonPressedValue variable becomes a key part of looking up data when the query is triggered:

```
function SubmitQS() {
form = document.forms[0];
if (form.QuoteSource.value == "")
  {alert("Quotation source is required");
  form.QuoteSource.focus();
    return""}
else
form.ButtonPressed.value= 'QS';
form.ButtonPressedValue.value= form.QuoteSource.value;
form.submit()
}
```

Cross-Reference For more information on JavaScript and data validation, refer to Chapter 40.

Adding a WebQuerySave event to change the form name

JavaScript assigns the `ButtonPressed` value based on which button was clicked, and this value is used by the `WebQuerySave` event. The `SubmitQS` JavaScript function saves the value of the button and passes the value to the `WebQuerySave` event to change the form name for the document. The Domino server does not accept changes in the form name made by JavaScript. When the document is saved on the server, Domino simply overwrites JavaScript-assigned form names with the original form name. The `WebQuerySave` event can, however, change form names. The server processes the form name change just before the document is saved. Listing 44-2 shows the contents of the `WebQuerySave` event for the QuoteQuery form. The `WebQuerySave` event contains a simple @If that chooses a new form name based on the value of `ButtonPressed`. If the value was `"QS"`, the form name is set to `QuoteSourceResults`; otherwise, it's set to `QuoteTextResults`.

Listing 44-2: The Contents of the WebQuerySave Event for the
                QuoteQuery Form

```
@If(ButtonPressed="QS";
@SetField("Form";"QuoteSourceResults");
ButtonPressed="QT";@SetField("Form"; "QuoteTextResults");
@Success)
```

Editing the $$Return field associated with the form

On Domino Web documents, the $$Return field embedded on a document is activated automatically when the document is submitted to the Domino server. Domino Web applications can use $$Return to display a submittal confirmation message, or to create any @function formula that evaluates to valid HTML. In the QuoteQuery form, the $$Return reopens the document that has just been saved to the server. When a QuoteQuery document is saved,

$$Return contains a URL that retrieves the first value in the Query view matching the value of the ButtonPressedValue field just submitted. This calls the document to open itself via the URL in the $$Return field. When the document is opened a DECS activity is called that performs a query on a back-end database. The query returns a value associated with the query field. Here's the $$Return in the QuoteQuery form:

```
"[/ndbible/D6BibleDECS.nsf/MultiQuery/" + ButtonPressedValue
+ "?OpenDocument]"
```

Because the first column in the Query view contains the ButtonPressedValue field sorted by the most time and date, the application needs only one view for all $$Return queries. Multiple query values are displayed and retrieved from the same column in the view. Here's what the calculated URL looks like when it's opened in a browser:

```
http://www.ndbible.com/ndbible/D6BibleDECS.nsf/MultiQuery/Roc
ky+Oliver?OpenDocument
```

The ButtonPressedValue of "Rocky Oliver" is placed in the first column of the MultiQuery view, sorted by most recent time and date. This returns the first instance of a document that contains "Rocky Oliver" in the first column.

Switching Forms to Display Single or Multiple Query Results

One of the challenges in building a data integration application is building flexibility into an application to return and display a single-row data result set or a multiple-row data result set. You can't simply change a form name to display single or multiple results, because DECS activities are watching for specific form names to open to trigger queries on that form. And even if you could, you don't know which form to choose until the data result set returns and you know how many rows with which you're dealing. This functionality is available, however, by putting a new spin on an old trick in Domino — using view form selection formulas.

The form selection formula has been a part of view design elements for a long time. It was originally designed to select a form based on client settings, such as @UserName or location settings. View form selection formulas can display more or less information in a document to users by changing the form to use with the document without changing the form name.

The following view form selection formula contains a basic @If statement that checks to see how many elements are contained in the QuoteText field. When multiple row data result sets are returned in Domino, they are contained in multivalue fields, with each field containing one value for each row in the data result sets. Checking for @Elements, which returns the number of values in a multivalue field, or a value of one for a single element, tells you how many records you're dealing with for the result set:

```
@If(@Elements(QuoteText)>1;"MultiResults";form)
```

If the result set contains more than one row of data, the form is swapped when the document opens without changing the value of the form name in the document, via the view's form formula function. The application can still call the query based on the original form name via the DECS activity, but the view of the data is different based on the number of rows returned in a result set.

Figure 44-2 shows a single-row result set from a query against the Quotation database for a quotation source of Bill Gates, who has only one quotation in the database.

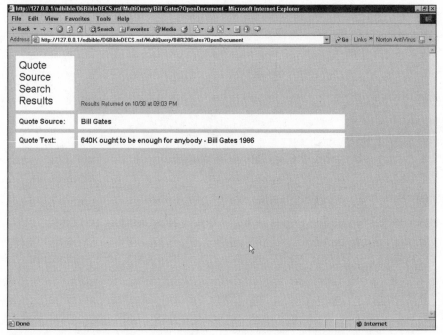

Figure 44-2: A single-row result set from a query against the Quotation database

Figure 44-3 lists results for a source query on Rocky Oliver, which is listed as the source for 102 quotes.

Note   DECS does not return multirow result sets by default. The DECS configuration document for the query has to be configured to accommodate multiple record results by enabling the mutivalue data property under Events ⇨ Options ⇨ Multi-Value Data in a DECS activity form.

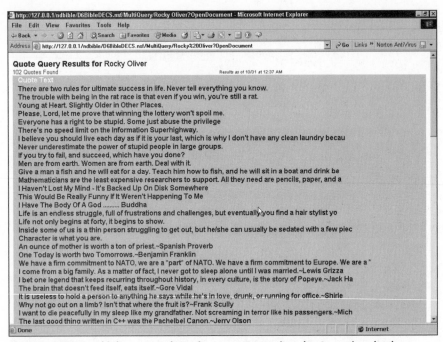

Figure 44-3: A multiple-row result set from a query against the Quotation database

The single-row result uses the original form name, which is QuoteSourceResults. The QuoteSource results form, shown in Figure 44-4, contains four basic fields: a date and time that the document was created, the source of the quotation from the original form, and the text of the single result returned from the query.

The Multiple Results form is slightly more complex. The main difference is that the QuoteText field is set to show multiple values in field properties, and displays each new value on a new line. Instead of using the QuoteSource field as with the QuoteSource form, the query entry shows the ButtonPressedValue field, just in case QuoteText returns multiple values, which would make it hard to display. Users would want to see the source once, and a listing of all the multiple quotations — not a listing of each instance of the same quote source repeated for as many rows as are in the result set. The display of the results returned is facilitated through the `RecordsReturned` field, which contains the following formula:

```
@Text(@Elements(QuoteText))+" "
```

This formula counts the number of elements in the QuoteText field and displays it on the screen as the number of records returned. The Multiple Results form is shown in Figure 44-5.

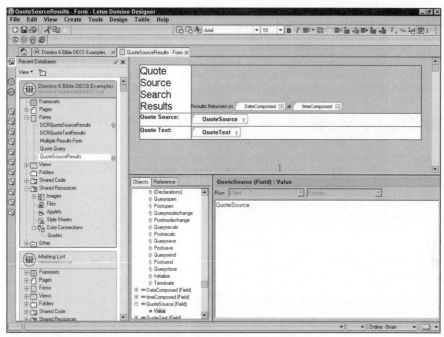

Figure 44-4: The QuoteSource results form in Domino Designer

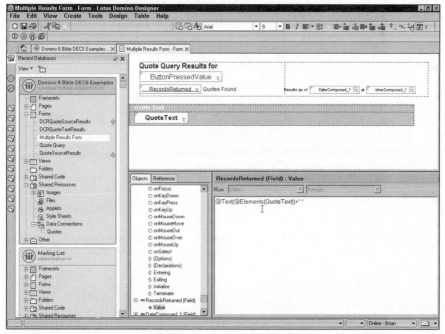

Figure 44-5: The Multiple Results form in Domino Designer

Implementing Data Connection Resources in Domino 6

A Data Connection Resource (DCR) is new to Domino 6 and is based on DECS functionality, but does not use the DECS administration database (`DECSADM.NSF`).

Setting up the DCR

To replicate the functionality of the DECS example with DCRs, an example Data Connection Resource has been set up in the Shared Resources section of the design bookmarks for the Domino 6 Bible DECS Examples database. The DCR is called Quotes to match the ODBC driver source name. It connects to the same Quotes ODBC driver that is used for the DECS examples.

Cross-Reference   For more information on setting up the ODBC drivers and sample database for the DECS and DCR examples, refer to Chapter 43.

Figure 44-6 shows what the Quotes DCR looks like in the Domino 6 Bible DECS Examples database.

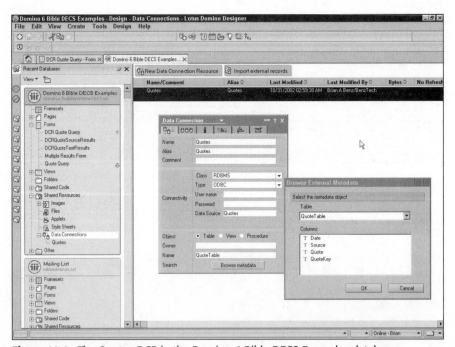

Figure 44-6: The Quotes DCR in the Domino 6 Bible DECS Examples database

By selecting ODBC as the data type and adding the word Quotes in the Data source field, the DCR finds the Quotes custom ODBC driver and populates the Metadata Name field and Alias when you click the Browse Metadata button at the bottom of the dialog box.

Creating new copies of the query and results forms

You can find three new forms in the database: DCRQuoteQuery, a copy of the Original QuoteQuery form, DCRQuoteSourceResults, a copy of the QuoteSourceResults form, and DCRTextSourceResults, a copy of the TextSourceResults form. The original DECS forms are copied and renamed with the DCR prefix, and some minor modifications need to be made to adapt the copied forms for use in a DCR application.

Modifying the query form

Only one small modification is required to make the DECS query form compatible with DCRs. Because you want results to appear in DCR forms and not the old DECS forms, you need to make a change to WebQuerySave so that the new DCR form names are used in place of the old DECS forms:

```
@If(ButtonPressed="QS"; @SetField("Form";"DCRQuoteSourceResults");
ButtonPressed="QT";@SetField("Form"; "DCRQuoteTextResults");
@Success)
```

After making this change, the query form is ready for use with DCRs. When you save the form, the WebQuerySave event changes the form name to the DCRQuoteSourceResults form or the DCRQuoteTextResults form, depending on which button was clicked to submit the query.

Referring to the Quotes DCR in the results forms

The next step is to make the DCRQuoteSourceResults form and the DCRQuoteTextResults form DCR-aware. You do this via the field properties for the QuoteSource and QuoteText fields. As shown in Figure 44-7, you must check the External Data source field property. Additional fields appear at the bottom of the screen. Clicking the Browse button next to the Data source Options line opens the dialog box shown in Figure 44-7. Developers can select the back-end data source field they want to associate with the Domino field. In this case, the source field maps to the QuoteSource field in the Domino 6 Bible DECS Examples database. The QuoteSource field should be marked as a key field, because the value in that field is used to produce query data when a document is opened.

The same steps need to be repeated for the QuoteText field, except that the key field is a data field (the default setting). This is where the results of data based on the QuoteSource key field go.

Both steps must also be repeated for the DCRQuoteTextResults form, reversing the key field and data field settings.

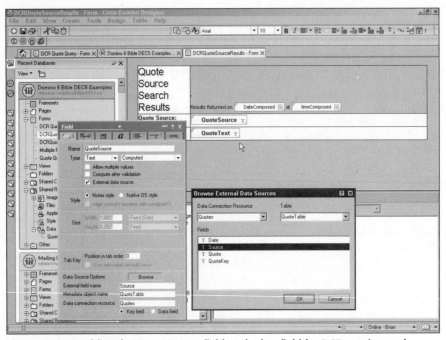

Figure 44-7: Enabling the QuoteSource field as the key field for DCR queries, and mapping it to the back-end data source field

Enabling connections to external databases for DCRs

After setting up the DCR and enabling the forms for connecting to the DCR, you must enable the Allow Connections to External Databases Using DCRs database property for the application to function at runtime. Figure 44-8 shows the settings in the Database properties dialog box:

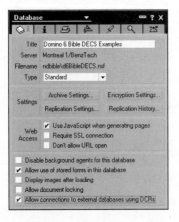

Figure 44-8: Enabling the Allow Connections to External Databases Using DCRs Database property

When the DCR is set up and pointing to the Quotes ODBC driver, the query and result forms are prepared for use with the DCR, and the Allow Connections to External Databases Using DCRs database property is enabled, the application can be run on a server that is running the DECS tasks without having to create connections and activity documents in a DECS administration database.

Summary

In this chapter, you learned more about data integration in Domino Web applications using DECS and DCRs. You saw:

✦ Techniques for triggering simple queries

✦ How to trigger multiple queries by multiple keys on a single query form

✦ Tricks for switching forms to display single or multiple query results

✦ An introduction to Data Connection Resources

✦ Examples of DECS and DCRs in Domino Web applications - the Quotes Sample database for Domino 6

The next chapter provides an introduction to LEI, and concentrates on examples of a significant new feature, virtualization, with a focus on virtual documents.

✦   ✦   ✦

LEI Retrievals and Updates

By Rocky Oliver

◆   ◆   ◆   ◆

In This Chapter

Learning about the
components that
make up LEI

Learning about
connections and
activities

Example: Using baseball
data to illustrate virtual
documents

Introducing integrated
credentials

◆   ◆   ◆   ◆

Since the inception of Notes, one of the most sought-after goals
has been to integrate Notes with other data sources. Notes and
Domino provide world-class collaboration, workflow, security, and
ease of development. Many external data sources, such as relational
databases and ERP systems, contain critical information about your
organization. It makes sense to want the best of both worlds — the
power of Notes combined with the highly scalable relational systems
containing mission-critical data. But the road to data integration has
always been paved with good intentions — and potholes of bad code,
ruts of bad drivers, and foggy functionality.

As Notes has progressed, Lotus has made strides in providing better
data integration. Notes Release 3 introduced @DbLookup and
@DbColumn using ODBC data sources. And even in the Release 3 days,
many vendors jumped on the data integration bandwagon, providing
primitive data integration by adding additional, custom formulas.
Along the way, Lotus bought a product called *NotesPump*, which was
a data integration engine that enabled you to map data fields
between an external source and Notes, and exchange data between
the two. Additionally, NotesPump provided a set of connectors that
allowed a LotusScript developer to work with external data using the
same API, regardless of the back-end data source structure. Lotus
released some other integration tools as well — most notably
LotusScript Data Objects (LS:DO), a set of drivers that wrap ODBC
sources to make it easier to work with them from LotusScript. Around
the release of Notes/Domino 4.5, Lotus made a great move and integrated the real-time capabilities of NotesPump into the Domino
server, and rebranded it as Domino Enterprise Connection Services
(DECS). Developers could now quickly provide real-time access to
external data sources in their Notes applications by simply filling out
a few configuration forms. But there were some drawbacks — most
notably that for every external record you brought into Notes, you
had to have a corresponding key document. This defeated the purpose of using Notes as a pure front-end to external data, because you
still had a ton of documents in your Domino database.

**Cross-
Reference**
Chapter 26 covers using @DbColumn and @DbLookup against
ODBC data. Refer to Chapter 43 for more information on DECS,
LS:DO, and the Lotus connectors LSX.

Lotus took the other part of NotesPump — what was left after adding DECS to Domino — and rebranded it Lotus Enterprise Integrator (LEI). LEI provided scheduled integration between Domino and external sources, and also enabled developers to have additional activities, such as scripted agents that could massage data moved between the two data sources. LEI also included a new set of data drivers known as the Lotus Connectors. DECS included Lotus connectors (which shipped with Domino), but the connectors that shipped with Domino and DECS were not the same as the connectors included with LEI. Although things were getting better, a truly easy way to integrate external data with Domino still didn't exist.

One of the primary goals of the development of Notes/Domino 6 was to make integration with external data as easy as possible. This was accomplished a couple of ways. In previous releases, DECS required the developer to configure the connections through the use of a database called the DECS administrator. This database was usually controlled by the Domino administrator, so the developer had to create the databases that used DECS, and also coordinate with the administrator to configure and enable the connections and activities in the DECS administrator. In Notes/Domino 6, the power is back in the hands of the developer. Domino 6 now includes a new design element known as a *Domino Connection Resource (DCR)*. The DCR represents the connection document found in the DECS Administrator. After you have a DCR, you can indicate in your forms that the data provided for individual fields comes from an external data source, which maps to your DCR. This functionality mimics the activity record found in the DECS Administrator. Now developers can do complete real-time integration as they develop their applications, without the need to involve anyone else or configure some other database. But Lotus didn't stop there.

Cross-Reference   Chapters 43 and 44 cover DCRs in more detail.

One of the most exciting releases recently made by Lotus is the new version of the Lotus Enterprise Integrator, now known as LEI 6. LEI 6 provides many new and exciting features, and improvements in other areas. One great new feature is the concept of *virtualization*, which enables you to have a Domino database act as a pure front-end to relational data, with no documents in the database.

This chapter introduces you to LEI 6, and the powerful integration functionality it provides. You learn some of the basics of LEI, and then go into virtualization features. The chapter concludes with a fairly complex example provided by the LEI development team.

Understanding LEI Basics

LEI 6 is made up of two main components: the LEI server and the LEI Administrator. The LEI server does the work, based on the documents contained in the LEI Administrator. The LEI Administrator is similar to the DECS Administrator — the file name is even the same, `DECSadm.nsf`. The LEI Administrator is where the entire configuration for LEI takes place. The LEI server polls the LEI Administrator for tasks or activities, and then completes them. You can use three other optional databases with LEI 6 — the Script Vault, the LEI Log, and the Integrated Credentials database.

Because LEI and DECS began as the same product, the way that you set them up is virtually identical. Just as in DECS, there is a Connection/Activity relationship. *Connections* define the way LEI (or DECS) connects to data. *Activities* define what is done to the data — move it, replicate it, perform some action against it, and so on. The connections in DECS and LEI are basically the same, except that more connection types are available in LEI. In fact, the Virtual Fields activity in LEI is the same as the Realtime DECS activity. But as with the connections, more activities are available in LEI.

As mentioned earlier, LEI is controlled through the LEI Administrator, which appears in Figure 45-1.

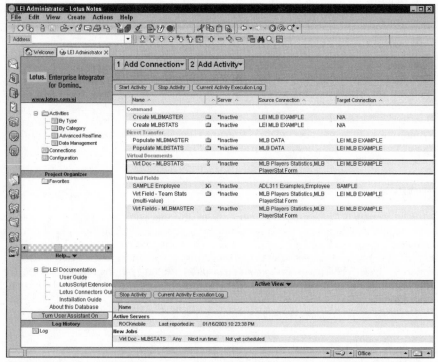

Figure 45-1: The LEI Administrator enables you to manage your entire LEI environment with an integrated and straightforward interface.

The LEI Administrator interface makes it easy to manage your LEI environment. You can create and manage connections and activities, configure your server variables, review the LEI Log, and access the various LEI help databases, all from one place.

Configuring Connections to External Sources

LEI ships with a set of connectors that you can use to build connections to external data sources. You configure the connectors through the LEI Administrator using Connection documents. Connection documents define the parameters needed by LEI to connect to an external data source — things such as a name to reference it by, credentials (user name and password) used to connect to the external data source, the type of external data source (DB2, Oracle, Notes), and so on. Here's a list of external data sources that LEI can connect to out of the box:

✦ DB2

✦ File

✦ Notes

✦ ODBC

✦ OLE DB

✦ Oracle (7 and 8)

✦ Sybase

✦ Text

 Note   You can purchase other connections from Lotus for such external sources as SAP and PeopleSoft.

Configuring a Connection document is similar to the way you configure a DECS Connection document. Later in this chapter you walk through an example that configures and uses a couple of Connection documents.

DCTEST

Before you create a Connection document, make sure that your server can connect to the external data resource using the Lotus connectors. Fortunately, Domino and LEI ship with a handy little command-line tool called DCTEST that tests your connections for you. The DCTEST program tests the capability of the computer to connect to the external data resource. The DCTEST program lives in the program directory of the Domino server. The actual name of the program depends on the operating system of the server, as shown in the following list:

✦ **Win32 platforms:** NDCTEST.EXE

✦ **UNIX platforms:** dctest

✦ **iSeries platform:** call Qnotes/dctest

Remember that this program is also available to Domino for testing connectivity of the DECS and the Lotus connectors.

DCTEST is easy to use. For Win32 systems, open a command prompt window, navigate to the Domino program directory, type NDCTEST, and press Enter. You see the interface shown in Figure 45-2.

You simply choose the type of external resource you are connecting to, and then enter the information needed when prompted. Figure 45-3 shows the results of verifying a connection to a DB2 server.

After you verify the connectivity to the server, you can create your LEI Connection document. Simply fill out the required information for the external resource you need a connection to; then save and close the document. To confirm that you configured your Connection document correctly, LEI includes another tool for testing connectivity through a Connection document — CONTEST.

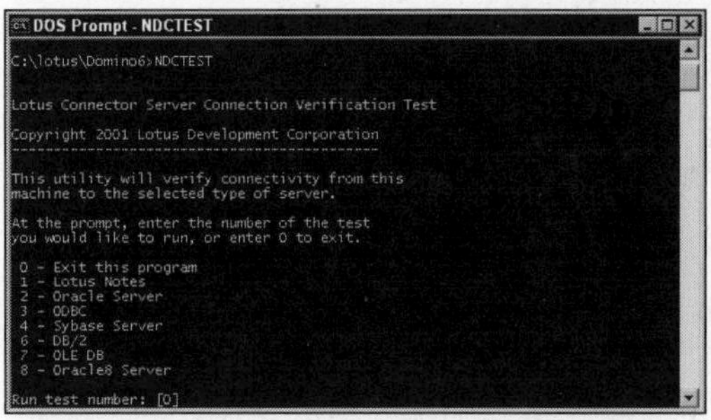

Figure 45-2: The DCTEST program is useful for verifying connectivity to external data resources.

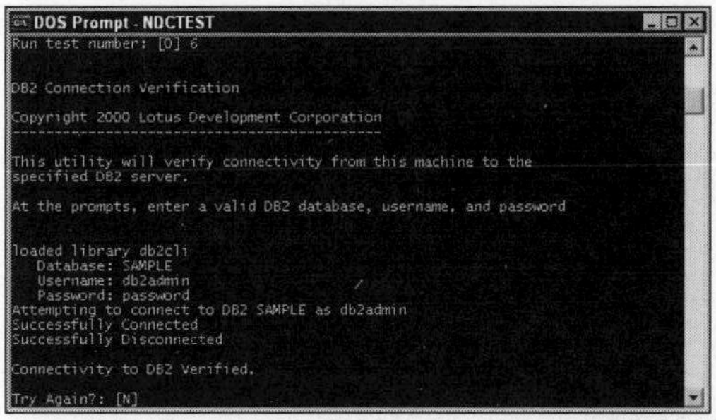

Figure 45-3: The results of the DCTEST program show that the server can connect to the external resource – in this case a DB2 server and database.

CONTEST

The CONTEST program is another command-line program that validates your Connection document. Like DCTEST, CONTEST is called in a slightly different way for each operating system, as shown in the following list:

- ✦ **Win32 platforms:** NCONTEST.EXE

- ✦ **UNIX platforms:** contest

- ✦ **iSeries platform:** call Qnotes/contest

You call CONTEST by navigating to the Domino program directory. Enter the appropriate platform-specific call, followed by the connection name in quotes, at the command prompt. Figure 45-4 shows the results.

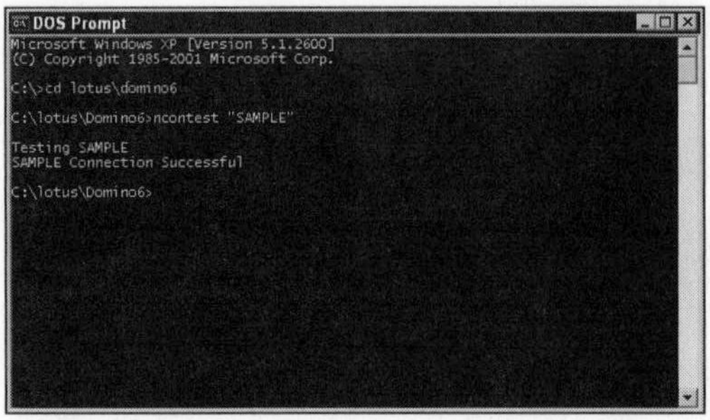

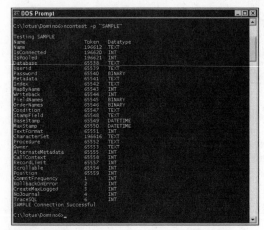

Figure 45-4: CONTEST tests your LEI Connection.

You can obtain a great deal of detailed information from CONTEST by adding a p parameter to the call. This parameter call and the results are shown in Figure 45-5.

Figure 45-5: CONTEST can take an optional p parameter to provide a verbose result, which may help you troubleshoot connectivity issues.

After you create your Connection document and validate that it works, you can create activities that use your newly created Connection.

Configuring LEI Activities

Activities define what is done to or with an external data resource. Two main types of activities exist — declarative and scripted. Declarative activities are form-based, and reside in the LEI Administrator; these include Virtual activities, Command activities, and Direct Transfer activities, among others. Scripted activities are agents written in LotusScript or Java that use the connector LSX to connect and work with external data.

All activity forms have field-level help integrated into the forms as text hotspots. When creating an activity, simply click any label in the form to get help for that particular field.

The following sections briefly review each activity.

Scripted activities

As stated earlier, Scripted activities are agents written in LotusScript or Java that use the connector LSX to connect and work with external data. Agents used for Scripted activities have a corresponding Scripted activity document in the LEI Administrator that manages the execution of the Scripted activity agent. The agent you write to work with the external data, and that is scheduled using the Scripted activity, can be located in any database—you can specify where the agent resides in the Scripted activity document. But most agents used with Scripted activities are stored in the LEI Script Vault, which makes it easier to manage and update the agent.

Declarative activities

Recall that Declarative activities are form-based, and reside in the LEI Administrator. A number of Declarative activities are available. Some of these activities are used once, while others run on a schedule, and still others are started and stay active until they are stopped. The following list introduces you to these activities.

✦ **Admin-Backup and Admin-Purge Log:** Admin-Backup and Admin-Purge Log assist in the maintenance of your LEI environment. Admin-Backup backs up the LEI Administrator, and Admin-Purge Log purges the LEI Log file.

✦ **Archive:** Archive moves documents from one data source to another to archive the documents on a scheduled basis.

✦ **Command:** Command issues commands to an external data resource, such as a DB2 command, or issues an operating system command, such as to delete a file.

✦ **Direct Transfer:** Direct Transfer moves data from one source to another. You normally use this type of activity once to easily set up a new data source. You can use SQL commands or, in the case of Domino databases, @Commands, to help refine the dataset.

✦ **Java:** Java schedules the execution of a Java application. You can specify an alternative JVM to use, and you can set a maximum duration for the activity so that your server isn't unduly taxed.

✦ **Polling:** Polling executes other activities when certain conditions are met. You normally use Polling in conjunction with the Scripted type of activity to check for some certain condition or threshold (for example, when X number of new records are created, and then it calls one or more Scripted activities. These Scripted activities do something like massage, or modify, the data and move it to a Domino database).

✦ **Replication:** Replication is similar to Notes replication, in that it synchronizes data between two data resources. The replication is one-way, however, which means that the target data source is updated to be identical to the source data source.

Virtual activities

When LEI 6 was released, it introduced a new concept called virtualization. *Virtualization* refers to the presentation of data in a Domino database virtually. Specifically, virtualization provides the long-desired feature of being able to have a Domino database act as a pure front-end to relational data, with no documents in the database *at all*. Views, forms, LotusScript, Formulas, and so on all work as if the database has documents, but there isn't a single document in the database. These are known as Virtual Documents. Additionally, you can have real-time Virtual Field activities (the same thing DECS does, except it is called RealTime) that map to documents created by a Virtual Document activity, providing an incredibly powerful and flexible model for front-ending external data. LEI can also present multivalued fields on a document, whereby the multivalue fields are comprised from multiple records in an external data source. Even attachments, OLE objects, and rich text fields can be virtualized!

Three types of Virtual activities exist — Virtual Documents, Virtual Fields (same thing as DECS), and Virtual Agents.

Virtual Document

The Virtual Document activity is the cool activity in LEI 6 that enables you to have a database with no documents in it, but have it act as if it does.

Virtual documents work by tricking the Domino data store into thinking that there are documents in the database. Domino and Notes treats the database as if the virtual documents are real — you can use any of the programming languages, design elements, and so on against these documents. In almost every way these are real documents, at least as far as Notes/Domino is concerned. You can even replicate a database with virtual documents in it. The documents are real in the local replica, and an attempt is made to roll up all changes to the external data source when replication occurs. If there is an issue, such as some of the records have been modified from another source, a replication conflict is created in the local database to reflect that the change to the virtual document cannot be rolled up to the external data source.

Just because the documents are virtual does not mean that the view indexes are virtual. The view indexes are still stored in the Domino database. Any concerns you have about performance in a database with those real documents still exist with virtual documents. Keep this in mind when designing your application.

Most of the mapping of an external data source to Domino is straightforward, similar to a Virtual Fields activity (like DECS). The biggest difference is the way the Virtual Document activity stores the metadata about the virtual document in the external data source — this metadata includes the things you see in the document properties box, any item that begins with a dollar sign ($), the NoteID and UNID, and so on. The external data source must be set up to hold this metadata so that it can trick the Domino database into thinking that there are documents in the database, and this information must be persistent so that the database is the same before and after the Virtual Document activity is stopped and restarted. To do so, you must create four fields in the external data source:

✦ EIMODIFIED: The last time the virtual document was modified. This is a date/time value.

✦ EINOTEID: The NoteID of the virtual document. This is a number value.

✦ EIUNID: The Document Unique ID of the virtual document. This is a text/char value.

✦ EINOTEPROPS: This contains all the other metadata of the document, such as all the items beginning with a dollar sign ($). This is a Binary Large Object (BLOB) data value, of significant size — up to 2GB.

These four fields must exist in the table where the virtualized data resides, or you can create an external table to hold this data. The latter method is the most used — most Database Administrators (DBAs) don't want you to update an existing table with four new fields, especially because one of them is a BLOB of potentially significant size. The Virtual Document activity provides you with a mechanism for creating an external key table automatically. This is a handy feature, which is explained in detail in the LEI help.

The Virtual Document activity also enables you to virtualize attachments in the document. Similar to the way the metadata is supported, you can either create additional fields in the virtual data table, or you can create an external attachment table to house the attachments. Like the external key table, the Virtual Document activity form has a button on it that automatically creates the external attachment table. Because attachments can be any size, they are stored in a BLOB data type field.

Tip

As of this writing, LEI 6 and Virtual Documents had one glaring deficiency. Currently, Virtual Documents don't support Reader and Author Names items. The problem arises from the fact that virtually all Reader and Author Names items are multivalue. But there is good news. First, the LEI 6 development team has acknowledged this deficiency and hopes to have it addressed in a point release — maybe even by the time this book is published. Second, a workaround is available. The functionality that supports the metadata automatically keeps up with all items that begin with a dollar sign. You can prepend your Reader and Author Names items with a dollar sign (`AllowedAuthors` becomes `$AllowedAuthors`), and they are then perfectly preserved in your virtual documents. Before you use this workaround, check whether this deficiency has been addressed in a point release.

Virtualized documents have one drawback — agents that update multiple documents by walking through a view tend to be a bit slower than when the documents were real. The reason is that each changed document requires an update to the external data source. This introduces a bit of latency to the process; however, the advantages for using virtual documents in most applications far outweigh the disadvantages.

You can customize and configure your Virtual Document activity a number of ways. Refer to the LEI 6 help for more information.

Virtual Field activity

No need to say too much about this activity, as it is the same as the DECS Virtual Field/RealTime activity. You can, however, use a Virtual Field activity with a Virtual Document activity, which provides an amazing amount of flexibility and the capability to create innovative combinations of data that best suit your needs.

Cross-Reference For more information on the Virtual Field activity, refer to Chapters 43 and 44.

Virtual Agent activity

Virtual Agent enables you to choose a stored procedure in your external data source, which creates a wrapper agent. This activity then uses the wrapper agent to enable you to schedule that stored procedure for periodic execution. You can then extend the control of your stored procedure to LEI 6.

Example: Using Baseball Data to Illustrate Virtual Documents

Sarah Boucher, one of the amazing people on the Lotus LEI development team, created this example, which shows off some of the neat features of LEI 6.

Note   You must have LEI 6, Domino 6, Notes 6, and DB2 7 or higher. If you don't have these items, you can still download the example from the companion Web site (ndbible.com) and refer to the LEI Administrator to see how it works.

The example uses data about Major League Baseball players. A database, MLB Players Statistics (MLBSTATS.nsf), contains virtual documents showing information about certain players. The virtual documents also show statistics about other players from the same team in the document — and all the data is virtual. Figure 45-6 shows an example virtual document from the database.

Every bit of data in this document — the entire document, including the picture of the player — is not really there. It is virtual.

The chapter doesn't go into all the steps for setting up this example application; instead, only the virtual activities are addressed. If you want to learn more about the setup of this example, download it and follow the instructions.

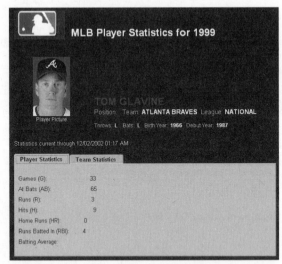

Figure 45-6: All the data in this MLB player document is virtual, including the picture of Tom Glavine.

Virtual Document activity

Virtual Document in this example uses the statistical records stored in DB2 in the LEI MLB EXAMPLE database, the DB2ADMIN.MLBSTATS_ROCK table. The fields in this table are mapped to the fields contained in the MLB PlayerStat form, which is in the MLB Players Statistics database. All of this is shown in Figure 45-7.

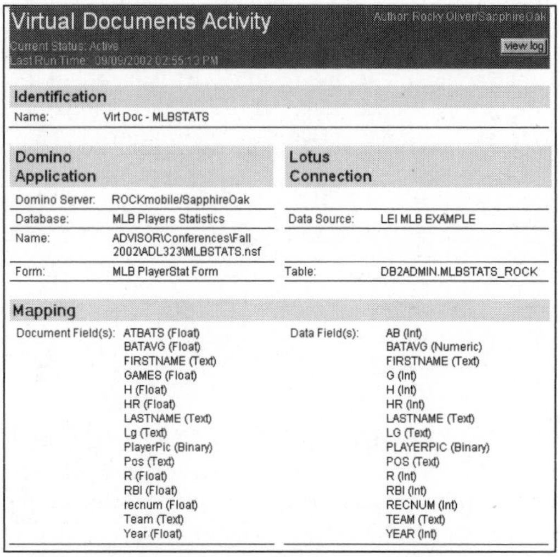

Figure 45-7: The first section of the Virtual Document activity defines the data sources and maps the fields between the two data sources.

The next section of the form is where you specify the key table information, which is where the four fields used for document metadata are stored. Figure 45-8 shows this section of the form.

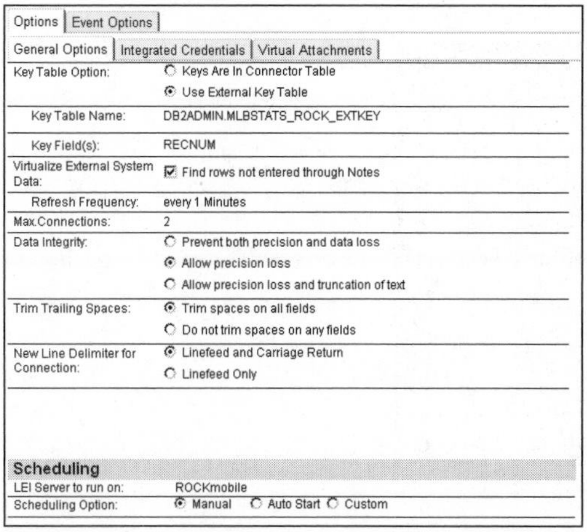

Figure 45-8: The General Options tab is where you define the parameters for the external key table and the various caching and data integrity options.

This section also refines the caching and data integrity settings, such as the cache refresh frequency, the maximum connections, the data precision loss, and more. The section below the tabbed table is where you can set up this activity on a schedule so that it starts and stops automatically.

If you refer back to Figure 45-6, you notice a picture of Tom Glavine. That picture is a graphic in a rich text field. Graphics are a type of attachment, so you need to virtualize them if you want them to be a part of your virtual document. This is done in the Virtual Attachments tab, which is under the Options tab of the Virtual Document activity, which is shown in Figure 45-9.

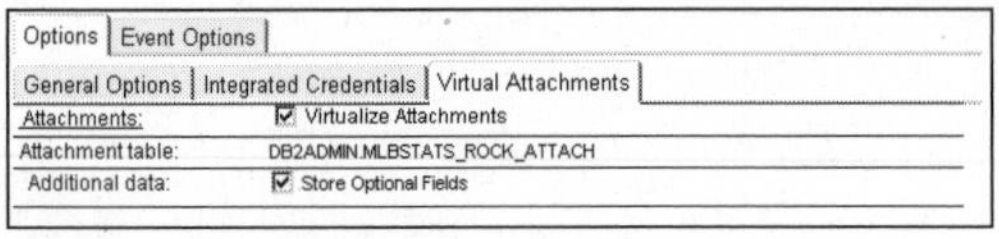

Figure 45-9: You set up Virtual Attachments in the Virtual Document activity document.

You enable Virtual Attachments in this tab. You also define and set up the external table, if desired, to store the attachments — you should use the automated feature for creating this table. The creation of the external table for storing your attachments and related metadata is done through a button that appears on this tab in Edit mode.

Now the Virtual Document activity set up. This activity populates the name, all the statistics on the first tab of the document, and the picture of the player on documents created with the MLB PlayerStat form, as defined in the activity. But the document has another tab, which is shown in Figure 45-10.

It's obvious that this UI could be designed better, but notice that each of the fields on this tab is a multivalue field. These fields are populated from a Virtual Field activity called "Virt Field - Team Stats (multi-value)", which is shown in Figure 45-11.

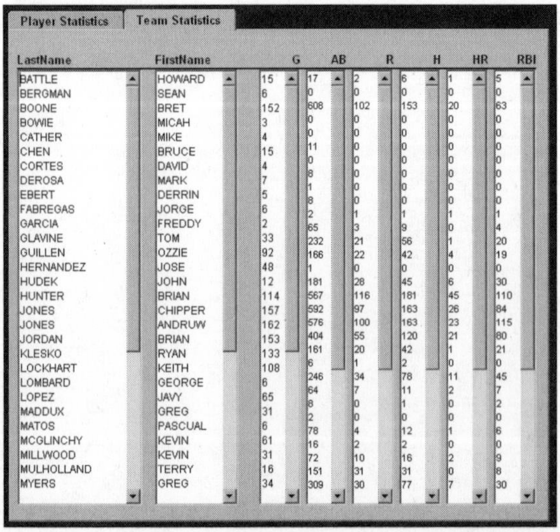

LastName	FirstName	G	AB	R	H	HR	RBI
BATTLE	HOWARD	15	17	2	6	1	5
BERGMAN	SEAN	6	0	0	0	0	0
BOONE	BRET	152	608	102	153	20	63
BOWIE	MICAH	3	0	0	0	0	0
CATHER	MIKE	4	0	0	0	0	0
CHEN	BRUCE	15	11	0	0	0	0
CORTES	DAVID	4	0	0	0	0	0
DEROSA	MARK	7	8	0	0	0	0
EBERT	DERRIN	5	1	0	0	0	0
FABREGAS	JORGE	6	8	0	0	0	0
GARCIA	FREDDY	2	2	1	1	1	1
GLAVINE	TOM	33	65	3	9	0	4
GUILLEN	OZZIE	92	232	21	56	1	20
HERNANDEZ	JOSE	48	166	22	42	4	19
HUDEK	JOHN	12	1	0	0	0	0
HUNTER	BRIAN	114	181	28	45	6	30
JONES	CHIPPER	157	567	116	181	45	110
JONES	ANDRUW	162	592	97	163	26	84
JORDAN	BRIAN	153	576	100	163	23	115
KLESKO	RYAN	133	404	55	120	21	80
LOCKHART	KEITH	108	161	20	42	1	21
LOMBARD	GEORGE	6	6	1	2	0	0
LOPEZ	JAVY	65	246	34	78	11	45
MADDUX	GREG	31	64	7	11	2	7
MATOS	PASCUAL	6	8	0	1	0	2
MCGLINCHY	KEVIN	61	2	0	0	0	0
MILLWOOD	KEVIN	31	78	4	12	1	6
MULHOLLAND	TERRY	16	16	2	2	0	0
MYERS	GREG	34	72	10	16	2	9
			151	31	31	0	8
			309	30	77	7	30

Figure 45-10: The Team Statistics tab in the MLB Player Statistics form shows the statistics for all the other members of that player's team.

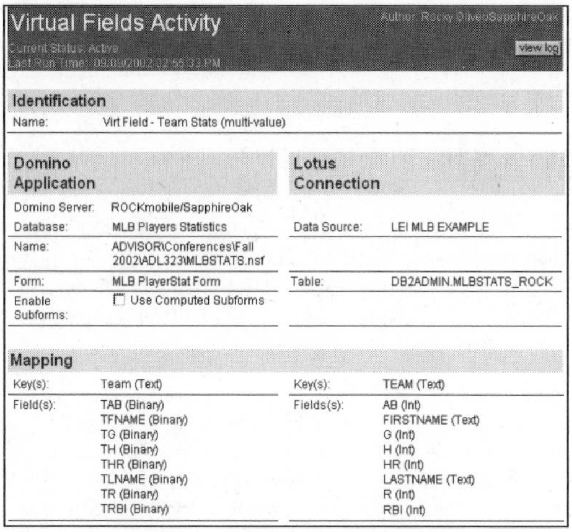

Figure 45-11: The upper part of the Virtual Fields activity is for defining the connection and the field mapping.

The TEAM field is used as the key for this Virtual Field activity. This makes sense because the application is designed to gather player statistics only for the players of the selected team. Then the rest of the fields are mapped. After doing so, you can set up the multivalue field configuration, which is shown in Figure 45-12.

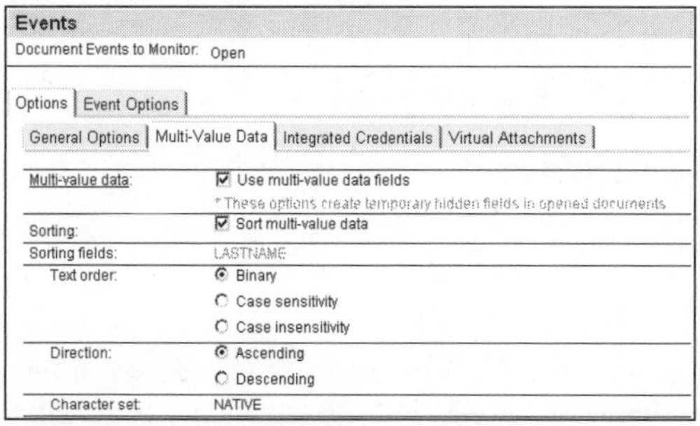

Figure 45-12: The Multi-Value Data tab configures multivalue support for the activity.

The Multi-Value tab shows how you enable multivalue field support, and then you can specify whether you want the data sorted. The nice part of this feature is that this is a *record* sort, not an individual field sort. After the sort is complete, all the data is correct for each alphabetized player.

In the example, only the Open event is being monitored. You can monitor four events — Open, Create, Update, and Delete. Because these fields are for reading access only, the Open event is the only one monitored.

This section provided a quick review of the virtualization example. There is a great deal more to this example, so, if you have all the required software, you should download the example, set it up, and play with it.

Using Integrated Credentials

In DECS and in previous versions of LEI, all connections are done with one user ID and password, which are stored in the Connection document. But in LEI 6, you can specify individual credentials for each person using LEI to access external data. This feature is known as Integrated Credentials.

New Feature   Integrated Credentials is new in LEI 6.

Integrated Credentials enable you to map a name/password value pair to an authenticated user name. When a user logs into the system, and then accesses an LEI-based application that uses Integrated Credentials, the user's authenticated name is used as a key to perform a lookup into the Integrated Credentials database where the name/password value pairs are stored. You must manually create the Integrated Credentials database using the LEI Credentials template from the server where LEI was installed. Figure 45-13 shows the Integrated Credentials form.

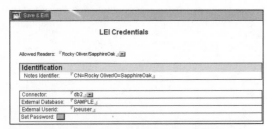

Figure 45-13: The Integrated Credentials form is where you specify an individual user's credentials in order to connect to external data.

The Integrated Credentials are defined by the connector type and database. You provide the user ID and password and save the document. When you want to use Integrated Credentials, you simply specify so in the activity document you're creating, as shown in Figure 45-14.

General Options	Integrated Credentials	Virtual Attachments
Integrated Credentials:	○ Use Connector Credentials	
	⊙ Lookup Credentials	
Missing Credentials:	☑ Use Connector Credentials if none available	
Credentials DB Filepath:	leicred.nsf	
Connection Cache Size:	10	

Figure 45-14: Integrated credentials are enabled in a Virtual activity in the Integrated Credentials tab.

As you can see, you have various options, including:

✦ Defining what happens if an Integrated Credential document can't be found for the authenticated user. The choices are to use the default credentials defined in the Connection document, or deny access to the user altogether.

✦ A path to the Integrated Credentials database to use for this activity. Incidentally, you can have more than one Integrated Credentials database on your LEI server.

When the user accesses the activity, the name/password value pair for the user is returned, and that is used to connect to the external data source, instead of the name/password stored in the Connection document.

Summary

This chapter introduced you to LEI 6. You learned about various features such as:

✦ The various connection and activity types available

✦ The new "virtualization" feature, and the three activities used for virtualization — Virtual Documents, Virtual Fields, and Virtual Attachments

✦ The new Integrated Credentials feature, which allows you to define individual credentials for access to external data sources

Part X introduces you to working with XML in Domino, beginning with Chapter 46, which introduces you to the basics of XML and how it is used within Domino 6.

✦　　✦　　✦

XML

XML and Domino

By Brian Benz

In This Chapter

Introducing XML

Parsing XML

Transforming XML

Using XML data islands

Understanding XML and Domino

Most Domino developers are aware of Domino's power when building flexible applications by separating data from content. XML enhances this capability by adding functionality for sharing applications and data between different systems in a common text-based format. Domino and XML are great compliments to one another, each providing several features that the other lacks.

This chapter provides an introductory overview of Extensible Markup Language (XML), XML structure, parsing and transforming XML, and what XML can be used for in Domino applications. Chapters 47 through 54 drill down into specific topics in more detail, and Chapters 55 through 58 provide details on the most exciting implementation of XML to date, Web services.

Introducing XML

The preceding part of this book provided a lot of information about data integration. It's important to point out that while XML facilitates data integration by providing a transport with which to send and receive data in a common format, XML is not data integration. It's simply the glue that holds data integration solutions together with a multiplatform common denominator that can be shared across platforms and operating systems.

XML does a great job of describing structured and unstructured data as text. It's usually complex and hard for human eyes to follow, but it's important to remember that it's not designed for us to read. XML parsers and other XML-compatible tools are designed to easily interpret XML documents. The Microsoft XML notepad is a good example of a simple tool that parses XML documents to render them manageable by humans. XML documents are converted into a grid format that sheds the original XML tags and replaces them with rows and columns of data. The XML notepad is free and available from `http://msdn.microsoft.com/library/en-us/dnxml/html/xmlpadintro.asp`.

It's important to point out that XML is not HTML, even though it may look like HTML, because its tags and the general format of the data look similar. However, HTML is designed to describe display characteristics of a page to browsers; whereas XML is designed to represent data.

XML structure

Because XML is designed to describe data and documents, the W3C XML recommendation, which can be found at www.w3.org/XML, is strict about a small core of format requirements that make the difference between a text document containing a random set of tags and an identifiable XML document. XML documents that meet W3C XML document formatting specifications are described as being *well-formed* XML documents. Most XML documents start with an optional XML document declaration, which can contain attributes describing the version of XML that the document structure and syntax follow, and the character encoding for the data in the XML document. This is the most common XML document declaration:

```
<?xml version="1.0" encoding="UTF-8"?>
```

Next is an optional reference to a Document Type Declaration (DTD) for data validation. This is the basic structure for a DTD reference that is associated with the rootelement of a document and is located in the same directory as the XML document:

```
<!DOCTYPE rootelement SYSTEM "adtdfilereference.dtd">
```

The root element of the XML document is next, and may contain optional XML namespaces and optional schema references. Other elements, attributes, comments, and text values can be nested under the root element.

Elements

Elements look like this, and always have an opening and closing tag:

```
<element></element>
```

There are a few basic rules for XML document elements. Element names can contain letters, numbers, hyphens, underscores, and periods, and colons when namespaces are used. Element names cannot contain spaces; underscores are usually used to replace spaces. Element names can start with a letter, underscore, or colon, but cannot start with other non-alphabetic characters or a number, or the letters xml.

Aside from the basic rules, it's important to think about using hyphens or periods in element names. They may be considered part of well-formed XML documents, but other systems that use the data in the element name, such as relational database systems, often have trouble working with hyphens or periods in data identifiers, often mistaking them for something other than part of the name.

Attributes

Attributes contain values that are associated with an element, and are always part of an element's opening tag:

```
<element attribute="value"></element>
```

The basic rules and guidelines for elements apply to attributes as well, with a few additions. The attribute name must follow an element name, then an equals sign (=), followed by the attribute value, in single or double quotes. The attribute value can contain quotes, and if it does, one type of quote must be used in the value, and another around the value.

Text

Text is located between the opening and closing tags of an element and usually represents the actual data associated with the elements and attributes that surround the text:

```
<element attribute="value">text</element>
```

Text is not constrained by the same syntax rules as elements and attributes are, so virtually any text can be stored between XML document elements. Note that although the value is limited to text, the format of the text can be specified as another type of data by the elements and attributes in the XML document

Comments

Like JavaScript, comment tags should always follow this format when in XML documents:

```
<!This is an XML document comment---->.
```

Empty Elements

Last but not least, elements with no attributes or text can also be represented in an XML document like this:

```
<element />
```

This format is usually added to XML documents to accommodate a predefined data structure.

DXL, DTDs, Schemas, and Data Validation

Although there are strict rules for the basic structure and syntax of XML documents, several specialized formats of XML documents exist to serve specialized purposes. These formats provide standardized ways of representing certain specific types of data. NewsML, for example, offers a standard format for packaging news and information in XML.

The most important format for Domino developers is DXL, which is the format that Lotus and IBM have created to format Domino data in XML. DXL is described in the Domino DTD and the DXL schema. DTDs and schemas are ways of describing data formats and making sure that data accepted into a system adheres to a certain predefined format. The concept is similar to well-formedness, but relates much more to the content of the XML documents, rather than to the structure and syntax. When an XML document meets the criteria of a Domino DTD or schema, it is said to be valid.

DXL and Domino

DXL is used by the `generateXML()` method of the document class, as well as the `?ReadViewEntries` URL command for Web views and documents. The Java view and editor applets covered in Chapter 42 use DXL to pass data back and forth from Web clients as well. In Domino 6, the Exporter, Transformer, and Viewer DXL utilities in Domino Designer format their output in DXL. Listing 46-1 shows a representation of a Domino memo in DXL format that was created using the DXL Viewer utility , which is located under the Tools menu in Domino Designer.

Listing 46-1: **A Memo Document Represented in DXL**

```
<?xml version='1.0' encoding='utf-8'?>
<!DOCTYPE form SYSTEM
'C:\lotus\notes\xmlschemas/domino_6_0.dtd'>
<form name='DemoMemo' xmlns='http://www.lotus.com/dxl'
version='6.0' replicaid='85256C6100462E1D'
 publicaccess='false' designerversion='6'>
<noteinfo noteid='266'
unid='20A685BB08123ADC85256C630038A5EC' sequence='1'>
<created><datetime>20021031T051844,92-05</datetime></created>
<modified><datetime>20021031T051953,85-
05</datetime></modified>
<revised><datetime>20021031T051953,80-05</datetime></revised>
<lastaccessed><datetime>20021031T051953,85-
05</datetime></lastaccessed>
<addedtofile><datetime>20021031T051953,85-
05</datetime></addedtofile></noteinfo>
<updatedby><name>CN=Brian A
Benz/O=BenzTech</name></updatedby>
<wassignedby><name>CN=Brian A
Benz/O=BenzTech</name></wassignedby>
<body><richtext>
<pardef id='1'/>
<par def='1'>SampleMemo for DXL Demo</par>
<par/>
<par>
<field type='names' kind='editable' name='SendTo'/></par>
<par/>
<par>
<field type='text' kind='editable' name='Subject'/></par>
<par/>
<par>
<field type='text' kind='editable'
name='Body'/></par></richtext></body>
<item name='$$ScriptName'
summary='false'sign='true'><textlist><text>DemoMemo</text></t
extlist></item></form>
```

To understand the structure and syntax reviewed so far, let's break this example down and discuss its components piece by piece, starting with the first two tags.

The first tag in an XML document is usually an optional XML declaration. XML declarations are not actually part of the specifications for a well-formed XML document, but are almost always included as the first element in XML documents. XML declarations provide information about the XML document version and the data encoding for data in the document.

The second tag is optional and contains a reference to one or more Document Type Declaration (DTD) documents for data validation. This style of tag is called a document type definition. In this case, the DXL was generated by the DXL Viewer utility on a developer workstation. The DTD used to validate this data is located in a file called domino_6_0.dtd, and is located in the <notes install drive>\xmlschemas subdirectory of every Notes 6 client installation:

```
<?xml version='1.0' encoding='utf-8'?>
<!DOCTYPE form SYSTEM
'C:\lotus\notes\xmlschemas/domino_6_0.dtd'>
```

The name of the root element of the XML document is form. The XML root element tag separates the XML heading information and the data of the XML document. The form root element has several attributes, such as the form name (DemoMemo) and the version of designer that generated this DXL (6).

The xmlns attribute represents an XML namespace, which is a method for separating and identifying XML elements that may have the same element name on the same page. Namespaces can also be used as specifications to describe specific types of data and other attributes that are contained inside elements that use that namespace. Often the URL in the namespace also resolves to a Web site that provides documentation about the namespace. Unfortunately, the Lotus DXL namespace URL, http://www.lotus.com/dxl, does not.

```
<form name='DemoMemo' xmlns='http://www.lotus.com/dxl'
version='6.0' replicaid='85256C6100462E1D'
publicaccess='false' designerversion='6'>
```

The next tag after the root element, noteinfo, records the noteid of the form and the unid. Several other design elements are also nested inside the noteinfo tag. These elements track more information about the form, such as the dates the form was created, modified, last accessed, and added to the DXL file. All these tags have data format element tags in them that describe the Julian calendar date values as DXL datetime data types.

```
<noteinfo noteid='266'
unid='20A685BB08123ADC85256C630038A5EC' sequence='1'>
<created><datetime>20021031T051844,92-05</datetime></created>
<modified><datetime>20021031T051953,85-
05</datetime></modified>
<revised><datetime>20021031T051953,80-05</datetime></revised>
<lastaccessed><datetime>20021031T051953,85-
05</datetime></lastaccessed>
<addedtofile><datetime>20021031T051953,85-
05</datetime></addedtofile></noteinfo>
```

Now you have more information about who updated the form:

```
<updatedby><name>CN=Brian A
Benz/O=BenzTech</name></updatedby>
<wassignedby><name>CN=Brian A
Benz/O=BenzTech</name></wassignedby>
```

After taking care of the DXL that represents Domino document system data, the rest of the data is comprised of elements and attributes representing nonsystem values that developers and applications have added to the document. In this case, the form that generated this DXL consists of three fields: SendTo, Subject, and Body. The DXL-required body element is assigned as part of DXL. The body element of the DXL document represents rich text, in which other fields and paragraph formatting can be embedded. Nested inside the body are the developer-defined fields, and nested inside the field tags are data type tags for each field. The XML document ends with the closing of the form root tag.

```
<body><richtext>
<pardef id='1'/>
<par def='1'>SampleMemo for DXL Demo</par>
<par/>
<par>
<field type='names' kind='editable' name='SendTo'/></par>
<par/>
<par>
<field type='text' kind='editable' name='Subject'/></par>
<par/>
<par>
<field type='text' kind='editable'
name='Body'/></par></richtext></body>
<item name='$$ScriptName' summary='false'
sign='true'><textlist><text>DemoMemo</text></textlist></item>
</form>
```

Now that you have an understanding of the basic format of XML, let's have a look at what you can do with it in Domino.

Parsing XML

Parsing is the breaking down of an XML document into pieces that are digestible by an application.

There are two mainstream parser families: Document Object Model (DOM) parsers and Simple API for XML (SAX) parsers.

The DOM is an in-memory tree that is used to trace the path of pieces of data, called nodes, and their relationship to other pieces of data in the same XML document. DOM nodes stay in memory and can be assessed and manipulated; whereas the code that created the DOM representation is active.

SAX Parsers pass through an XML document once and break the document down into a series of document events. For example, the beginning of an element and the end of an element are two separate SAX events, and data can be collected from these events as the SAX parser moves through the document.

Cross-Reference The Document Object Model (DOM) parser and the Simple API for XML (SAX) parser are discussed in more detail in Chapter 51.

Transforming XML

XSL Transformations (XSLT) use a transformation engine to parse and then convert data from one format to another using directives contained in an XSL stylesheet. XSLT stylesheets are well-formed XML documents that contain information about source XML documents and elements and specify how to transform those source elements into new types of XML documents and elements. XSLT can transform XML documents to other formats of XML, HTML, and text.

Cross-Reference

Chapter 53 discusses transformations in more detail.

Using XML Data Islands

XML data islands are a combination of the Microsoft XML parser (MSXML), XSLT, DOM parsing, and JavaScript. XML data islands create client-side *islands* of data on a Web page that can be manipulated and managed as separate entities from the Web page on which the island resides.

Cross-Reference

We discuss XML data islands in more detail in Chapter 54.

Domino and XML

In addition to DXL and the DXL Transformer, Viewer, and Exporter utilities; Domino has many tools for generating, working with, and managing XML in Domino applications. The ReadViewEntries URL command displays the data contained in a Domino document or view when added to a URL on the Web. The generateXML method of the Java document class performs the same function in Java applets, applications, servlets, and agents. Transformations and parsing of DXL and other XML formats is supported in Java by the XML4J.jar file, which is in the Notes directory of a developer's workstation.

New Feature

Many new LotusScript classes in Domino 6 support DXL creation, XML parsing, and XSLT transformation.

Several other features support XML in Domino. XML tag elements can simply be added to Domino forms to make Domino documents generate XML documents when opened in a Notes client or on the Web. Developers can also create XML from document data using QueryOpen or WebQueryOpen events and @function agents, LotusScript agents, Java agents, applications, servlets, or C and C++ applications.

Cross-Reference

We cover most of the techniques described in this chapter in more detail in Chapters 47 through 54.

Summary

This chapter provided a quick overview of XML, which we cover in much more detail throughout Part X. You were introduced to XML and shown a simple example of the DXL document format.

✦ XML document structure

✦ XML Syntax

✦ Well-formed XML

✦ Introduction to DXL

✦ Valid XML documents and XML data validation

✦ Parsing and transforming XML

The next few chapters dive much deeper into the methods for generating XML data from Domino data, starting with creating XML data from Domino form events, and then moving on to techniques using LotusScript, Java, and other core Domino languages and functions.

✦   ✦   ✦

XML, DXL, and Domino Data

By Brian Benz

◆   ◆   ◆   ◆

In This Chapter

Using the Notes and
Domino 6 Programmer's
Bible XML Example
database — XMLQuotes

Understanding DXL

Working with
ReadViewEntries
in Domino Web
applications

Using DTDs and
schemas

Using the Exporter,
Transformer, and
Viewer DXL utilities

Generating XML from
Domino forms and fields

Applying a DTD to
custom XML data

◆   ◆   ◆   ◆

This chapter builds on the XML concepts introduced in Chapter 46 by reviewing examples in Domino, starting with the examples in the Notes and Domino 6 Programmer's Bible XML Example database.

The chapter also covers DXL for views and documents. DXL is the XML format that Lotus and IBM have created to represent Domino Data. You're then introduced to the Domino DTD and the DXL schema, which enforce DXL data structure and syntax rules on XML data. Techniques for including the ReadViewEntries command in Domino Web applications will be shown as an introduction to DXL.

After you understand the DXL, DTD, and schema concepts, you learn how to develop custom XML output from Domino forms, and apply a custom DTD to the custom XML output.

Using the Notes and Domino 6 Programmer's Bible XML Example Database — XMLQuotes

The sample XML and Web Services examples in this book use an adaptation of a Domino Quote of the Day database. The database is used with permission of the original owners, Newbs Consulting and Sapphire Oak Technologies. You can download the original Quote of the Day Domino database from the Downloads section of either www.sapphireoak.com or www.newbsconsulting.com.

You can download all the examples contained in Part X of this book, including the XMLQuote.nsf database, from the www.wiley.com/compbooks/benz Web site. See the ndbible Web site for installation Instructions.

The Quote of the Day database contains over 1,000 quotes that you can add to e-mails, Web pages, and applications. The database is named XMLQuotes.nsf and contains several views, forms, and agents that you use throughout Part X of this book. All of the Quotation documents in the database are based on the Quotes form. The data structure of the Quotes form is outlined in Table 47-1:

Table 47-1: Format for the Quote Form in XMLQuote.nsf

QDate	The date the quotation was added to the database
QSource	The source of the quote, or the name of the person who added the quote
Quote	The quotation text
QuoteKey	A unique identifier of the quotation for relational purposes

The Quote of the day database also contains all the XML examples that you are working with in the XML part of this book, including views, agents, forms, and other design objects that are used to generate DXL, the XML format that is used to describe Domino objects.

Understanding DXL

Chapter 46 introduced DXL, the Domino-specific version of XML. DXL describes Domino objects in XML. The Domino DTD, covered later in this chapter, describes elements that make up DXL. DXL can contain XML elements to describe databases, forms, documents, pages, ACLs, and just about every other design element that a Domino database can contain. A full listing of the hundreds of design elements represented in DXL tag elements is available in the Domino Designer help database, under DXL in the index.

Understanding Domino views in DXL

The DXL form and view examples in the XMLQuotes database are a good place to learn how DXL looks in views, forms, and documents. Listing 47-1 shows the output of a single row of data in a Domino view as represented by DXL.

Note

Views and other Domino design objects are rendered as XML documents in DXL. This terminology can be confusing, because most Domino developers are not used to referring to Domino design objects as documents. In the XML world, all data is in documents. For example, a DXL representation of a Domino view is called a DXL View document, and it's (unfortunately) technically correct to refer to a DXL representation of a Domino document as a DXL document.

The DXL View document starts with an optional XML document declaration. The next line gets right into the DXL, with the `viewentries` root element. The `viewentries` element represents all the rows in a view, plus any categories, total rows, and other optional attributes. The `viewentry` element maps to the `ViewEntry` class in LotusScript and Java. The `toplevelentries` attribute value tells you that there are 245 entries in the first column of this view. This number represents the total number of categories in the view, not the number of rows, as the first column of the row is categorized.

The nested `viewentry` element represents a single row in the view, with the position attribute value of `9.1` telling you that this category is the first row of the ninth category in the view. The `unid` and `noteid` attributes represent the unique identifiers for this document — `unid` is the same in any database, and `noteid` is unique for this database. The `siblings` attribute tells you that there is only one `viewentry` at this nesting level in the DXL document.

At the next nested level are two `entrydata` elements, which represent the data in the columns of a view row. Column 1 (Column 0 is represented by the view category, which is in turn represented by `viewentries`) tells you that the original field name for the value is Quote, and that the data type is text via the nested text element. Column 1 then provides the actual quotation in the column nested in the data type elements. Column 2 is identical, except the data source is the QSource field and the value nested in the text data type elements is the source of the quotation. The XML document finishes by closing the nested `viewentry` and `viewentries` elements.

Listing 47-1: **DXL Output for a Single View Row**

```
<?xml version="1.0" encoding="UTF-8"?>
<viewentries toplevelentries="245">
<viewentry position="9.1"
unid="AA79E91C2DB18A6C85256B8800586D25" noteid="173E"
siblings="1">
<entrydata columnnumber="1" name="Quote">
<text>The most incomprehensible thing about the world is that
it is at all comprehensible. - Albert
Einstein</text></entrydata>
<entrydata columnnumber="2" name="QSource">
<text>Albert Einstein</text></entrydata>
</viewentry>
</viewentries>
```

Understanding Domino documents in DXL

Like forms, views, databases and other Domino design objects, documents have their own structure when represented in DXL, with attributes and elements nested under the `<document>` element. Listing 47-2 shows a simple Domino document represented in a DXL document.

The DXL document begins with a `document` root element, just after the XML declaration in the first line. This document was created from a Domino Mail Memo form, so the form name is Memo, as shown in the form attribute value. The next element, `noteinfo`, is where Domino housekeeping information for a DXL document is stored. As with individual view rows in the DXL view document example, the `unid` and `noteid` attributes in `noteinfo` represent the unique identifiers for this document — `unid` is the same in any database and `noteid` is unique for this database. Next, you have the created date and time represented in a `datetime` data type, to end the nested `noteinfo`.

Any values added to a Domino document by a user are represented by item elements, which map directly to the Domino item class in LotusScript and Java. In this case, you have three items: the subject line of the memo in a `text` data type, the date that the memo was sent in a `datetime` data type, and the Body field, in a `richtext` data type. The `richtext` data type, in this case representing a rich text field, contains several elements that identify paragraphs, fonts, and other layout attributes. The document finishes with a close of the final item tag and the document tag.

Listing 47-2: **DXL Output for a Domino Document**

```
<document form="Memo">
<noteinfo unid="9C93469B4BFC2081852567EA0559842"
noteid="942">
<created><datetime>20010808T091500,00-04</datetime></created>
</noteinfo>
<item name="Subject"><text>Sample DXL document</text></item>
<item name="Sent">
<datetime dst="true">20030808T091500,00-04</datetime></item>
<item name="From"><text>Brian Benz</text></item>
<item name="Body"><richtext>
<par def="1">
<run><font style="italic"/>Italic Example</run>This is a
simple rich text example of regular text
</par></richtext></item>
</document>
```

Working with ReadViewEntries in Domino Web Applications

The easiest way to generate DXL from a Domino view is by using the `ReadViewEntries` Domino URL command. `ReadViewEntries` first arrived in Domino version 5, along with the arrival of DXL, and provides a simple way for developers to generate a view or part of a view in DXL. To open the `getQuotesXML` view in a browser, the URL is as follows:

```
http://localhost/ndbible/xmlquotes.nsf/GetXMLQuotes?OpenView
```

To generate a DXL version of the same view, the URL is as follows:

```
http://localhost/ndbible/xmlquotes.nsf/GetXMLQuotes?ReadViewEntries
```

While the `ReadViewEntries` URL may be familiar to developers who work with Domino 5, the parameters associated with the command are not. The parameters for `ReadViewEntries` are some of the most useful features of the URL command, offering detailed control over the generated DXL output of a view. Table 47-2 lists the parameters for the `ReadViewEntries` URL command and their effects on a DXL view.

Table 47-2: **The Parameters for the ReadViewEntries URL Command**

`CollapseView or Collapse=`*n*	The DXL view elements are collapsed, which means that the DXL view elements for the individual rows in the view are not listed in the output DXL. `Collapse=n` means the collapse starts at the nth row of the view. You can use the `@DocNumber` function to determine the current row of a view and pass the value to URL commands.

ExpandView or Expand=*n*	The DXL view elements are expanded, which means that the DXL view elements for the individual rows in the view are listed in the output DXL. Expand=n means the expand starts at the nth row of the view. You can use the @DocNumber function to determine the current row of a view and pass the value to URL commands.
RestrictToCategory=*category*	Displays a single category in a view. You must categorize and sort the first column of the view. See the explanation of the code in Listing 47-4 for an example of using RestrictToCategory.
Count=*n*	Count is used with Start, Collapse, or Expand. It produces n rows of DXL output for the view. See the explanation of the code in Listing 47-3 for an example of using Count.
Start=*n*	Start is usually used with count. It starts at row n to produce DXL output for the view. You can use the @DocNumber function to determine the current row of a view and pass the value to URL commands. See the explanation of the code in Listing 47-3 for an example of using Start.

PreFormat	Converts all data types to text on the server, instead of the DXL-specific data types. A date, for example, without &PreFormat appears as follows:
	
	`<datetime>20030930</datetime>`
	
	The same date using &PreFormat appears as follows:
	`<text>09/30/2003</text>`

StartKey/UntilKey = text or time	If a text string or time is specified as the StartKey for the view, DXL output is generated for the view starting at the first match of the value, and continues until the first match of the UntilKey value. If there is no exact key match, the view output starts at the row after the place that the StartKey should have been, and stops at the next row after the place that the UntilKey should have been. You can use StartKey alone. UntilKey is optional, but must be used with StartKey.
KeyType = string or time	The default data type for StartKey and UntilKey is text. KeyType = time must be used to change the data type if the key values for StartKey and UntilKey are time values.
ResortAscending = column number	Resorts the DXL output to display lowest to highest values on the column specified. Column numbers start with 0.
ResortDescending = column number	Resorts the DXL output to display highest to lowest values on the column specified. Column numbers start with 0.

Figure 47-1 shows an example that uses the `GetXMLQuotes` view in the XMLQuotes database. The example illustrates the control and options that the `ReadViewEntries` URL command offers when combined with the `Start`, `Count`, and `RestrictToCategory` parameters.

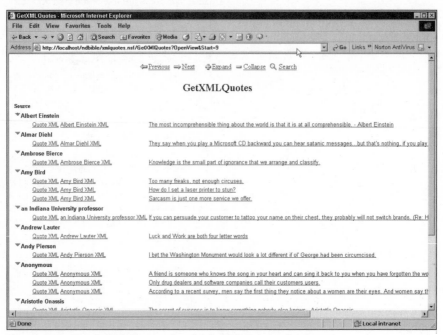

Figure 47-1: The GetXMLQuotes view in the XMLQuotes database

The first two links of all the detail rows shown in the view in Figure 47-1 create DXL output to the browser. The first link, `Quote XML`, produces a DXL document for the Domino document represented in that row of the view. The `Quote <Quote Source Name>` link produces a DXL document that contains all the quotes for the quotation source that matches the value in the current document in the view. Both links use Pass-Thru HTML in a view column to generate the link. The third link, which is the actual quotation itself, uses the standard auto-generated link to the document that represents the row in the view, and opens the document in read mode.

The first link, `Quote XML`, uses the `Start` and `Count` `ReadViewEntries` parameters. This link calculates a URL based on the current document using a subset of the `@DBName` function, which returns the directory location and the Domino database filename on the Domino server. The `ReadViewEntries` URL command is passed as part of the URL, and the formula also passes the row number in the view to the formula using the `@DocNumber` function. Here's the link as it is created in the View column in Domino Designer:

```
"[<A HREF=/"+@Subset(@DbName;-
1)+"/GetXMLQuotesNoViewInfo?ReadViewEntries&Start=" +
@DocNumber + "&Count=1>Quote XML</A>]"
```

And here's what the code looks like in the source code of a Web browser:

```
<A HREF="
/ndbible/xmlquotes.nsf/GetXMLQuotesNoViewInfo?ReadViewEntrie
s&Start=12.1&Count=1">Quote XML</A>
```

This URL uses the Start parameter to begin at the first row of the twelfth category. Amy Bird quotes are located in the twelfth category of the view, and the start document is the first document that appears under that category. Because the row number is dynamically calculated using the @DocNumber function, the correct row and category is always listed in the URL. Count =1 ensures that the URL link generates DXL for the current record only. If Count isn't included, the DXL generates records starting at the twelfth category and displays rows for the rest of the view.

Listing 47-3 shows the DXL output when you click the Quote XML link in the view on the first Amy Bird quotation.

Listing 47-3: DXL Output for a Single Quotation in the GetQuotesXML View

```
<?xml version="1.0" encoding="UTF-8"?>
<viewentries toplevelentries="245">
<viewentry position="12.1"
unid="3A4D4341507CDCAF8525677E00708C3F" noteid="C06"
siblings="3">
<entrydata columnnumber="1" name="Quote">
<text>Too many freaks, not enough
circuses.</text></entrydata>
<entrydata columnnumber="2" name="QSource">
<text>Amy Bird</text></entrydata>
</viewentry>
</viewentries>
```

The link in the second column of the view uses the same technique as the first link to generate the URL dynamically. But this time the link uses the RestrictToCategory parameter to generate DXL for all the quotes that match the value in the Quote Source field of the current document. Here's what the link looks like in Domino Designer:

```
"[<A HREF=/"+@Subset(@DbName;-
1)+"/GetXMLQuotesNoViewInfo?ReadViewEntries&RestrictToCategor
y=" + QSource + "> "+@ReplaceSubstring(QSource; " "; "+") +"
XML</A>]"
```

Here's what the link looks like when it's generated in a browser:

```
<A HREF="
/ndbible/xmlquotes.nsf/GetXMLQuotesNoViewInfo?ReadViewEntrie
s&RestrictToCategory=Amy+Bird"> Amy Bird XML</A>
```

The code that generates the URL dynamically calculates the value of the QSource field, representing the quotation source, and adds that value to the &RestrictToCategory value. The first column of the view is sorted and categorized on quotation source, which means that quotes matching the source of the current document in the view are selected for DXL output. Listing 47-4 shows the DXL output when you click the `Amy Bird XML` link in the view on any of the Amy Bird quotes shown in Figure 47-1.

Listing 47-4: DXL Output for a Single Quotation in the GetQuotesXML View

```
<?xml version="1.0" encoding="UTF-8"?>
<viewentries toplevelentries="3">
<viewentry position="1"
unid="3A4D4341507CDCAF8525677E00708C3F" noteid="C06"
siblings="3">
<entrydata columnnumber="0" name="Quote">
<text>Too many freaks, not enough
circuses.</text></entrydata>
<entrydata columnnumber="1" name="QSource">
<text>Amy Bird</text></entrydata>
</viewentry>
<viewentry position="2" unid="CD83BCD1B05F58BD8525677E00709634"
noteid="145A"
siblings="3">
<entrydata columnnumber="0" name="Quote">
<text>How do I set a laser printer to
stun?</text></entrydata>
<entrydata columnnumber="1" name="QSource">
<text>Amy Bird</text></entrydata>
</viewentry>
<viewentry position="3"
unid="F976C645E79762FC8525677E00706A06" noteid="164E"
siblings="3">
<entrydata columnnumber="0" name="Quote">
<text>Sarcasm is just one more service we
offer.</text></entrydata>
<entrydata columnnumber="1" name="QSource">
<text>Amy Bird</text></entrydata>
</viewentry>
</viewentries>
```

Note that different views are used to calculate URLs and to display the URL links. This is because the `GetXMLQuotes` view contains the columns and URLs for displaying `Quote XML` and `Quote <Quote Source Name>`, and these values would be included in the DXL output if the same view were used. In most cases, users don't want to see these calculated fields in their DXL output. The `GetXMLQuotesNoViewInfo` view is identical to the `GetXMLQuotes` view, except that it does not contain the two columns that create the `Quote XML` and `Quote <Quote Source Name>` URLs, which makes for cleaner output of the DXL.

Another thing to note in Listings 47-3 and 47-4 is how the numbering of the elements differs between the `Start` and `Count` output and the `RestrictToCategory` output. In Listing 47-3, the `viewentry` position is 12.1 for a single row of view output starting at the first row of the twelfth category. In Listing 47-4, which uses `RestrictToCategory` to generate a new view containing a single category of data, the position starts at 1 and runs to 3. Also, `columnnumber` starts at 0 for the `RestrictToCategory` example in Listing 47-4 compared to 1 for the start and count example in Listing 47-3, because there is no category listed in the single category view output.

Understanding Data Type Definitions (DTDs) and Schemas

The DXL discussed in Chapters 46 and 47 is based on the Domino DTD and the DXL schema. DTDs and schemas are documents that describe the contents of XML documents and are used for XML document validation. *DTDs* are text documents that describe data formats in other XML documents. *Schemas* are the next generation of data-validation formats, and like DTDs, they describe data formats in other XML documents. But unlike DTDs, schemas are formatted using XML elements, attributes, and text values.

Using the Domino DTD

Most DXL tools and classes in Domino validate DXL data against the Domino DTD. The DTD contains references to DXL elements, called entities, and lays out the entities for DXL elements and attributes in a hierarchy. This structure must be matched by a DXL document to be valid DXL. The following is an example of the DXL entity representation of a Domino document `unid`:

```
<!ENTITY % unid "CDATA">
```

This entity describes a Notes item called `unid` in a DXL document, and that the data type for a unid is `CDATA` (character data).

Other entities in the DTD refer to the `unid` entity to enforce DXL validation rules. Listing 47-5, for example, shows the `noteid` element described in the DTD.

Listing 47-5: The noteid DXL Element Described in the Domino DTD

```
<!ATTLIST noteinfo
    noteid        %noteid;      #IMPLIED
    unid          %unid;        #IMPLIED
    sequence      %integer;     #IMPLIED
    >
```

This entity says that a `noteinfo` element must have a `noteid`, a `unid`, and a sequence number to be considered valid DXL. Other DXL elements refer to `unid` in a similar way.

For more information on the full listing of DXL elements, DTD entities, and using the Domino DTD for data validation, refer to the Domino Designer help index under DTD. In addition, the Domino DTD is included on every installation of Notes and Domino, and is located in the Notes install directory with the filename `domino_6_0.dtd`.

Using the DXL schema

The Domino DXL schema is a work-in-progress, but it provides much more control over the format of data contained in a DXL document (partly because the validation data is described in XML, not in DTD syntax). The following code shows what the unid element looks like to the DXL schema:

```
<xsd:simpleType name="unid">
  <xsd:annotation>
   <xsd:documentation>Identifier for a
document</xsd:documentation>
   <xsd:documentation>unids are 32 hex
characters</xsd:documentation>
  </xsd:annotation>
  <xsd:restriction base="xsd:binary">
   <xsd:length value="16" fixed="true" />
   <xsd:encoding value="hex" />
  </xsd:restriction>
</xsd:simpleType>
```

This segment of the DXL schema tells you that unid exists and that it must be binary data consisting of 32 hex characters. This is more information than you can get from the DTD, and it's more useful for ensuring data accuracy. unid must be there, and it has to look like a Domino unid. Listing 47-6 shows the noteinfo reference to unid and other attributes. The DXL schema describes a noteinfo element of a DXL document in much more detail, including more information on the format of unid and other data that may or may not be present in the DXL document. The DXL schema can tell you, for example, that unid and noteid are optional, that the created date element (xsd:element name="created") has to be present (minOccurs="0"), that it's a Datetime data type (type="DatetimeType"), and that there can't be more than one created date (maxOccurs="1").

Listing 47-6: The noteid DXL Element Described in the DXL Schema

```
<xsd:element name="noteinfo">
  <xsd:annotation>
   <xsd:documentation>
       "noteinfo" contains identity information about notes,
and is used
       in many elements that represent different kinds of
notes.
   </xsd:documentation>
  </xsd:annotation>
  <xsd:complexType>
   <xsd:sequence>
    <xsd:element name="created" type="DatetimeType"
               minOccurs="0" maxOccurs="1" />
    <xsd:element name="modified" type="DatetimeType"
               minOccurs="0" maxOccurs="1" />
```

```
        <xsd:element name="revised" type="DatetimeType"
                     minOccurs="0" maxOccurs="1" />
        <xsd:element name="lastaccessed" type="DatetimeType"
                     minOccurs="0" maxOccurs="1" />
        <xsd:element name="addedtofile" type="DatetimeType"
                     minOccurs="0" maxOccurs="1" />
    </xsd:sequence>
    <xsd:attribute name="noteid" type="noteid" use="optional"
/>
    <xsd:attribute name="unid" type="unid" use="optional" />
    <xsd:attribute name="sequence" type="integer"
use="optional" />
  </xsd:complexType>
 </xsd:element>
```

For more information, the DXL schema is included on every installation of Notes and Domino. You can find it in the Notes install directory with the filename `DXL.XSD`.

Using the Exporter, Transformer, and Viewer DXL Utilities

Domino Designer 6 gives developers three new and easy menu options for working with Domino design objects in DXL:

✦ The DXL Exporter generates DXL for the currently selected Domino design element and saves it to a file on the file system with an `.xml` file extension. The exporter can be useful for exporting DXL forms, views, and other design objects to be shared with other systems, or to manipulate Domino objects using XML tools.

✦ The DXL Viewer generates the same DXL to a temporary XML file and opens a Web browser to display the file in the default browser. This can be useful for viewing the DXL that a design element generates when developing XML applications. For example, it's handy for prototyping client-side XML applications that need to serve XML to a browser and transform the DXL to HTML for browser display using an XSLT transformation engine in the client. The source DXL of design elements can be easily displayed using the viewer while developing the stylesheet.

✦ The DXL Transformer opens a DXL transformer window. You can select one or more source design elements for DXL generation and a stylesheet from a list of defaults or by browsing the file system. You can display transformation output to the screen or written to the file system by selecting the output method from a drop-down dialog box. This tool can be useful for testing while developing stylesheets for DXL transformations.

All of the options are available by selecting a Domino design object and then choosing Tools ⇨ DXL Utilities from the Domino Designer main menu.

Generating Custom XML from Domino Documents and Fields

DXL is a great format for describing Domino design objects, but is not always the format of choice for output of XML from a Domino application. Fortunately, options exist for generating other forms of XML data from Domino documents.

The simplest method for generating other types of XML from Domino documents is creating hard-coded XML in Domino forms. The form for this example is in the `Quotes.nsf` database and is called XMLQuote. This form is called when the `GetXMLQuotesWithDocument` view is opened in a browser and the `Quote XML` link is chosen from a view row. Figure 47-2 Shows the `GetXMLQuotesWithDocument` view in a browser.

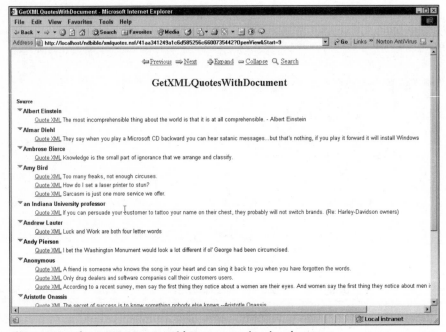

Figure 47-2: The GetXMLQuotesWithDocument view in a browser

Instead of calling a `ReadViewEntries` URL command via Pass-Thru HTML in the browser, the `Quote XML` link in this view opens the document. But because you're using a form formula in the `GetXMLQuotesWithDocument` view that specifies the XMLQuote form, the default quote form is overridden when the document appears. The data appears as an XML document instead of the regular HTML output. Listing 47-7 shows what the custom output looks like in the form.

For the purposes of this example, the XML output is validated by a custom DTD called `XMLQuote.DTD` (covered in the next section of the chapter). After the DTD definition, the code moves right into the custom XML. The root element for the document is `Quote`, and the `QuoteSOurce`, `QuoteText`, and `QuoteKey` elements are nested in the `Quote`.

Listing 47-7: Custom XML Output Form of a Domino Form

```
<?xml version="1.0" encoding="UTF-8" ?>
<!DOCTYPE Quote SYSTEM
"C:\Lotus\Notes\Data\ndbible\DTD\XMLQuote.dtd">
<Quote>
<QuoteSource>Albert Einstein</QuoteSource>
<QuoteText>The most incomprehensible thing about the world is
that it is at all comprehensible. - Albert
Einstein</QuoteText>
<QuoteKey>HNEY-58LLVP</QuoteKey>
</Quote>
```

Figure 47-3 shows the XMLQuote form that generates this output.

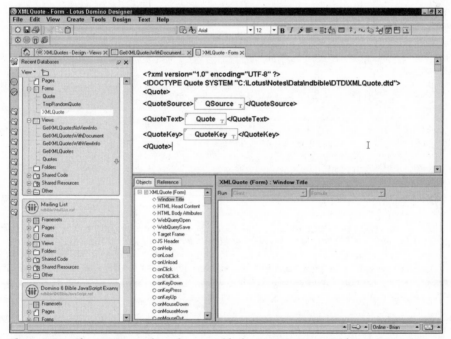

Figure 47-3: The XMLQuote form for use with the GetXMLQuotesWithDocument view in a browser

The XMLQuote form is a basic Domino form with a couple of simple changes that turn it into an XML generator for Domino field data. First, the form property Treat document contents as HTML is enabled, which passes all output of this form directly to the browser without adding any Domino formatting elements.

A hard-coded line above the first field contains the XML declaration, which will be passed to the browser:

```
<?xml version="1.0" encoding="UTF-8" ?>
```

The hard-coded root element is added on the next line and hard-coded XML elements are wrapped around every field on the form. When the fields appear in the browser, the field values become the text values of the elements in the XML document. After all the elements and text values are defined in the form, the close tag for the root element is the last line on the form.

Applying a DTD to Custom XML Data

In most cases where custom XML is generated and shared across organizations, a DTD is used to ensure that the XML being shared is valid data. The DTD is shared with all interested parties and referenced via DTD definitions in the XML documents. This ensures that the XML document matches a specific format and there are no surprises for the applications that are sharing the XML.

The second line of the custom XML output refers to a DTD called XMLQuote in this line:

```
<!DOCTYPE Quote SYSTEM"C:\Lotus\Notes\Data\ndbible\DTD\XMLQuote.dtd">
```

Listing 47-8 shows the contents of XMLQuote.DTD that is referenced in the XML document.

Listing 47-8: **Contents of the XMLQuote DTD**

```
<?xml version="1.0" encoding="UTF-8"?>
<!ELEMENT Quote (QuoteSource, QuoteText, QuoteKey)>
<!ELEMENT QuoteKey (#PCDATA)>
<!ELEMENT QuoteSource (#PCDATA)>
<!ELEMENT QuoteText (#PCDATA)>
```

When compared to the Domino DTD, the XMLQuote DTD enforces simple structure rules for simple output. The XMLQUote DTD specifies that the root element of the XML document must be called Quote, and can contain a QuoteKey, a QuoteSource, and a QuoteText nested element. The elements are required, and they must be nested under the root Quote tag in the order specified by the comma-delimited list: QuoteSource, QuoteText, QuoteKey.

Summary

In this chapter, you built on the XML concepts introduced in Chapter 46 by reviewing examples in Domino, starting with the examples in the Notes and Domino 6 Programmer's Bible XML Example database. The chapter included:

✦ Details of DXL for views and documents

✦ A review of the ReadViewEntries command and its little-known, but powerful, parameters

✦ Working examples for using `ReadViewEntries` and its parameters in Domino Web applications

✦ Uses for DTDs and schemas

✦ An introduction to the Exporter, Transformer, and Viewer DXL utilities in Domino Designer

✦ An easy option for getting custom XML out of Domino documents

✦ How to generate XML from Domino documents and fields

✦ How to apply a custom DTD to XML output

The next chapter delves more deeply into coding applications that generate DXL and custom XML, including several new Domino 6 classes that make a DXL coder's life much easier in LotusScript.

✦   ✦   ✦

LotusScript and XML

By Brian Benz

In This Chapter

Extending the XMLQuotes examples

Generating custom XML using LotusScript

Creating XML files using LotusScript

Generating DXL using LotusScript

This chapter focuses on techniques for creating and using LotusScript to generate flexible XML based on form and document data. Techniques include creating custom XML output, as well as working with the new `NotesDXLExporter` and `NotesStream` classes to generate DXL from Domino data.

Extending the XMLQuotes Examples

In the previous chapter you saw some basic examples for generating DXL and custom XML from Domino forms and views using built-in commands with relatively little coding required. But the options you have seen, while powerful and easy, do not provide the control over the application and the XML data that some Web applications require.

The `ReadViewEntries` techniques in the last chapter, for example, are a good use of existing functionality, but only for DXL output of Domino data that can be contained in a view. Other DXL output, such as rich text, can't be generated using `ReadViewEntries`. And custom XML generation from Domino documents using a custom form is easy, but developers are limited to XML output from single documents using this technique.

LotusScript provides the next level of functionality for generating DXL, especially with the new features available in Domino 6. The combination of LotusScript agents, Script Libraries, and Domino form events, along with the new DXL classes, provide flexible and powerful options for generating XML and DXL in Domino Web applications.

You can download all the examples in Part X of this book, including the `XMLQuote.nsf` database, from the `www.wiley.com/compbooks/benz` Web site. Refer to the Web site for installation instructions. The database design and content is reused with permission from the original owners, Newbs Consulting and Sapphire Oak Technologies. You can download the original Quote of the Day Domino database that `XMLQuotes.nsf` is based on from the Downloads section of `www.sapphireoak.com` or `www.newbsconsulting.com`.

Generating Custom XML Using LotusScript

Chapter 47 reviewed methods for generating custom XML from Domino form data by hard-coding XML elements around field values. LotusScript provides functionality that adds more options to form-based custom XML generation, with the use of LotusScript agents and events on Domino Web forms.

To begin generating custom XML using LotusScript, you're going to start with a simple XML form and agent example. The Domino form you're using for this example is in the XMLQuotes.nsf database and is called LSXMLQuote. This form is called when you open the GetXML-QuotesWithLSAgent view in a browser and the Quote XML link is chosen from a view row. The view is identical in appearance and functionality to the GetXMLQuotesWithDocument view shown in Chapter 47. Behind the scenes, however, things are different. Figure 48-1 shows the GetXMLQuotesWithLSAgent view in a browser.

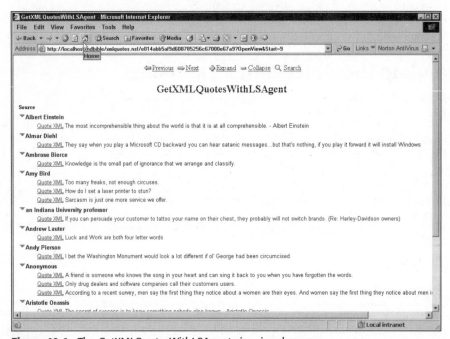

Figure 48-1: The GetXMLQuotesWithLSAgent view in a browser

The Quote XML link in this view opens the document associated with the view row. But because a form formula in the GetXMLQuotesWithLSAgent view specifies the LSXMLQuote form, the default quote form is overridden when the document appears. The data appears as an XML document instead of the regular HTML output. The LSXMLQuote form is a combination of the default quote form and the XMLQuote form that you learned about in Chapter 47, with a few slight variations. Figure 48-2 shows the LSXMLQuote form in Domino Designer.

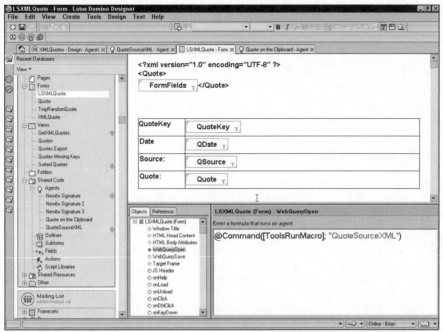

Figure 48-2: The LSXMLQuote form in Domino Designer, showing the form field as well as the WebQueryOpen call to the QuoteSourceXML agent

Like the XMLQuote form, the form property content type is set to HTML. This passes all output of documents created with this form directly to the browser without adding any Domino formatting elements. Also, all the fields listed at the bottom of the form in the table are marked in text properties to be hidden from Web browsers. This needs to be done to avoid HTML output from the fields being included as part of the XML document when it is generated. HTML is not part of well-formed XML documents and would generate XML errors in the browser. But all the fields on the document are visible to the WebQueryOpen agent, which is required. A hard-coded line above the FormFields field containing the XML declaration is passed to the browser:

```
<?xml version="1.0" encoding="UTF-8" ?>
```

You must add the root element on the next line to comply with W3C specifications of well-formed XML. After the root element is the FormFields field, which is always a blank field. In the custom XML example in Chapter 47, XML tags were wrapped around the fields on the form, creating nested XML elements. But in this case, the XML comes from an agent, not hard-coded values on the form. When the document opens on the Web, the WebQueryOpen event calls the QuoteSourceXML agent. The QuoteSourceXML agent is a LotusScript agent that loops through all the Notes items in the Domino document and creates XML elements and text values for each item. Listing 48-1 shows the content of the QuoteSourceXML agent.

Listing 48-1: **The QuoteSourceXML Agent**

```
Sub Initialize
 Dim session As NotesSession
 Set session = New NotesSession
 Dim doc As NotesDocument
 Set doc = session.DocumentContext
 VFF=""
 Forall i In doc.Items
  If ( Instr( i.name, "$" ) = 0 ) Then
   VFF = VFF + "<" + i.name+">"+ i.text + "</" +
i.name+">"+Chr(13)
  End If
 End Forall
 doc.FormFields=VFF
End Sub
```

This agent starts off with basic LotusScript setup code to instantiate the session and get the current document using `Session.DocumentContext`. The `Forall` loop then iterates through all the items in the current Domino document and checks to see whether they have a $ in the item name. If they do, the item is ignored. Most item names that contain a $ are Domino system fields and not part of what you want to include in the XML document. If the item has been added to the form, the agent uses the item name for the tag name and the item text value as the element value. The field named QSource with a value of Albert Einstein, for example, generates the following output in the XML document:

```
<QSource>Albert Einstein</QSource>
```

After looping through all the items in the document, the agent assigns the concatenated text string of newly created elements to the FormFields field on the document and exits the agent. Listing 48-2 shows the generated output. The chr(13) character added to the end of each element provides rudimentary formatting for the XML document, displaying each element and value pair on a new line.

Listing 48-2: **Custom XML Output from a LotusScript Agent**

```
<?xml version="1.0" encoding="UTF-8" ?>
<Quote>
<Form>Quote</Form>
<QuoteKey>HNEY-58LLVP</QuoteKey>
<QDate>03/26/2002</QDate>
<QSource>Albert Einstein</QSource>
<Quote>The mos
t incomprehensible thing about the world is that it is at all
comprehensible. - Albert Einstein</Quote>
<FormFields></FormFields>
</Quote>
```

Using LotusScript to generate custom XML has several advantages over the form-based example in Chapter 47. If, for example, you need to change the structure of the XML document output, you simply need to add, delete, show, or hide fields in the table at the bottom of the form. Because the LotusScript agent loops through all items in the document, it automatically adapts the output depending on what has been placed on the form. Also, you can create several agents to generate different types of XML output. The WebQueryOpen event and values on a document created with the form could calculate which agent to call when a document is opened on the Web.

Creating XML Files Using LotusScript

Another common requirement in Web applications that use XML is saving a generated XML document in a file for sending, downloading, or sharing. Because of Domino's robust security and e-mail integration capabilities, LotusScript is a natural choice for generating and sharing XML files via e-mail or over the Web.

The example in this section uses another slight variation on previous examples. The Domino form is in the XMLQuotes.nsf database and is called LSXMLQuoteToFile. This form is called when you open the GetXMLQuotesWithLSFileAgent view in a browser and the Quote XML link is chosen from a view row. The view is identical in appearance and functionality to the GetXMLQuotesWithLSAgent view shown in Figure 48-1. In this example, however, the XML document that is created is saved to the file system before appearing on the screen.

The main difference between the LSXMLQuoteToFile form and the LSXMLQuote form is that the agent creates a complete well-formed XML document by itself. The previous example used a combination of hard-coded text on the form and Domino fields in the agent. A complete XML document is created in the agent so that the XML can be saved to the file system without using a form, as well as appearing on the Web. Listing 48-3 shows the content of the QuoteSourceXMLToFile agent.

The agent starts with basic LotusScript setup code that instantiates the session and gets the current document using Session.DocumentContext. After setup, the agent creates a new instance of the NotesStream class and assigns a filename of c:\temp\XMLOutput.xml to the stream. Any output written to the stream is saved in this file.

The stream class is new to Domino 6 and provides an easy way to write binary or character data in Domino. The createStream method creates the stream in the agent, and the Open method opens or creates a file. The Bytes property of the stream is checked to see if the file just opened already contains data. If the file is unable to open, or the file exists and already has data, the error message is sent back to the FormFields field on the form. When the document opens, the error message appears in the browser.

If the agent is creating a new, clean file, the agent adds the XML declaration and the root element to the VFF variable before the Forall loop iterates through all the items in the current Domino document.

Listing 48-3: **The QuoteSourceXMLToFile Agent**

```
Sub Initialize
  Dim session As NotesSession
  Set session = New NotesSession
```

Continued

Listing 48-3 *(continued)*

```
Dim doc As NotesDocument
Set doc = session.DocumentContext
Set stream = session.CreateStream
If Not stream.Open("c:\temp\XMLOutput.xml", "binary") Then
 doc.FormFields= "Unable to create c:\temp\XMLOutput.xml"
 Exit Sub
End If
If stream.Bytes <> 0 Then
 doc.FormFields= "c:\temp\XMLOutput.xml already exists"
 Exit Sub
End If
VFF={<?xml version="1.0" encoding="UTF-8" ?>}
VFF=VFF +{<Quote>}
Forall i In doc.Items
 If ( Instr( i.name, "$" ) = 0 ) Then
  VFF = VFF + "<" + i.name+">"+ i.text + "</" +
i.name+">"+Chr(13)
 End If
End Forall
VFF=VFF +{</Quote>}
doc.FormFields=VFF
 Call stream.WriteText(VFF)
End Sub
```

After the agent loops through all the items in the document, the closing tag for the root element is added and the agent assigns the concatenated text string of newly created elements to the FormFields field on the document. The agent then displays the XML document in the browser. Listing 48-4 shows the contents of the generated output.

Listing 48-4: Custom XML Output in c:\temp\XMLOutput.xml

```
<?xml version="1.0" encoding="UTF-8" ?>
<Quote>
<Form>Quote</Form>
<QuoteKey>HNEY-58LLVP</QuoteKey>
<QDate>03/26/2002</QDate>
<QSource>Albert Einstein</QSource>
<Quote>The most incomprehensible thing about the world is
that it is at all comprehensible. - Albert Einstein</Quote>
<FormFields></FormFields>
</Quote>
```

Generating DXL Using LotusScript

LotusScript, especially in Domino 6, has several useful classes, methods, and properties that make generating DXL practical. Before Domino 6, most useful XML generation functionality was in Java. But with the addition of the `NotesStream` and the `DXLExporter` LotusScript classes, generating DXL is simple. Table 48-1 shows some of the new features and how you can use them.

Table 48-1: Useful LotusScript Classes for Generating DXL

Class	Description
`NotesXMLProcessor`	A base class that contains properties and methods common to all XML classes. Used to process DXLExporter when provided an `inputstream` and an `outputstream`.
`NotesDXLExporter`	Exports Domino data from `NotesDatabase`, `NotesDocument`, `NotesDocumentCollection`, and `NotesNoteCollection` to DXL as one of the following formats: `NotesDOMParser`, `NotesDXLImporter`, `NotesRichTextItem`, `NotesSAXParser`, `NotesStream`, and `NotesXSLTransformer`.
`NotesStream`	Two examples of `NotesStream` output are shown in this chapter. Streams XML or DXL to or from a binary or text object.
`NotesNoteCollection`	`NoteCollections` are specific subsets of Domino database objects, or Notes. These can include documents and design objects. `NoteCollections` can, for example, access all documents by using the `SelectDocuments` method, or all agents using the `SelectAgents` method.
`Pipelining`	Pipelining permits the movement of data from one `NotesXMLProcessor` method to another. The `DXLExporter` class, for example, can send DXL data directly to the file system via the `NotesStream` class, or the data can be pipelined to an XSL processor method before being sent to the file system.

The next example uses another slight variation on previous examples. The Domino form is in the `XMLQuotes.nsf` database and is called LSDXLQuoteToFile. This form is called when you open the GetDXLQuotesWithLSFileAgent view in a browser and the `Quote XML` link is chosen from a view row. The view is identical in appearance and functionality to the previous examples in this chapter. In this example, however, the XML document created saves to the file system in DXL format using the LotusScript `NotesDXLExporter` class, and appears on the screen using the `NotesStream.ReadText()` method.

As with the previous example, the agent creates all XML generated for the form, this time using the `NotesDXLExporter` class. Listing 48-4 shows the content of the `QuoteSource XMLToFile` agent.

This agent begins with the same basic LotusScript setup code as the other examples in this chapter to instantiate the session and get the current document using Session. DocumentContext. But the setup of this agent has two different lines, which are used to set up the NotesDXLExporter object and create a new instance. After setup, you create a new instance of the NotesStream class and assign a filename of c:\temp\DXLOutput.xml to the stream. Any output that the NotesDXLExporter class processes is saved in this file.

The createStream method creates the stream in the agent, and the Open method opens or creates a file. If the file is unable to open, an error message is sent back to the FormFields field on the form, and the agent exits. When the document opens, the error message appears on the browser instead of the DXL document.

In the preceding example, the agent checks to see whether the file already exists and warns the user if it does. This agent, however, is a little meaner in the way it handles any previous output data. The stream.truncate class simply clears the existing stream object of any binary data, regardless of whether data was contained in the file. If the agent returns no data, the empty file is deleted from the system when the stream closes.

Now that the agent has a new, clean file, it can create the DXL using the NotesDXLExporter class. The last few lines of the agent set the input as the current document, set the output as the c:\temp\DXLOutput.xml file, and process NotesDXLExporter. The second-to-last line uses the NotesStream.ReadText class to read the DXL output back from the stream and save it to the FormFields field in the current document, using the ReplaceItemValue method. The stream then closes and the agent exits.

Listing 48-4: **The QuoteSourceDXLToFile Agent**

```
Sub Initialize
Dim session As NotesSession
Set session = New NotesSession
Dim exporter As NotesDXLExporter
Set exporter = session.CreateDXLExporter
Dim doc As NotesDocument
Set doc = session.DocumentContext
Dim stream As NotesStream
Set stream = session.CreateStream
If Not stream.Open("c:\temp\DXLOutput.xml", "binary")
Then
  doc.FormFields= "Unable to create
c:\temp\DXLOutput.xml"
  Exit Sub
End If

Call stream.Truncate

Call exporter.SetInput(doc)
Call exporter.SetOutput(stream)
Call exporter.Process
```

```
Call doc.ReplaceItemValue("FormFields", stream.ReadText())
Call stream.Close
End Sub
```

When the document appears in the browser, the DXL output contained in the file appears via the FormFields field on the document. Listing 48-5 shows the contents of the generated output.

Listing 48-5: Custom XML Output in c:\temp\XMLOutput.xml

```
<?xml version='1.0' encoding='utf-8'?>
<!DOCTYPE document SYSTEM 'xmlschemas/domino_6_0.dtd'>
<document xmlns='http://www.lotus.com/dxl' version='6.0'
replicaid='85256C6400115C34'
 form='Quote'>
<noteinfo noteid='1386'
unid='C0C0F4484E0E948585256A180048197D' sequence='1'>
<created><datetime>20010323T080731,17-05</datetime></created>
<modified><datetime>20021031T220946,25-
05</datetime></modified>
<revised><datetime>20010323T080751,54-05</datetime></revised>
<lastaccessed><datetime>20021031T220940,91-
05</datetime></lastaccessed>
<addedtofile><datetime>20021031T220940,91-
05</datetime></addedtofile></noteinfo>
<updatedby><name>CN=Henry Newberry/O=Newbs</name></updatedby>
<item name='QuoteKey'><textlist><text>HNEY-
4V4HE8</text></textlist></item>
<item
name='QDate'><textlist><text>03/23/2001</text></textlist></it
em>
<item name='QSource'><textlist><text>Abraham
Lincoln</text></textlist></item>
<item name='Quote'><textlist><text>No matter how much cats
fight, there always seems to be plenty of kittens.- Abraham
Lincoln</text></textlist></item>
<item name='FormFields'
summary='false'><textlist><text/></textlist></item>
</document>
```

The output is a standard DXL document, with the DTD reference at the top of the document, several Domino system fields represented as nested elements of the root document tag, and the items at the bottom of the document that represent the data contained in the Domino document.

Summary

This chapter extended the examples from Chapter 47 to show you more LotusScript code and form techniques that are useful when working with XML and DXL. It included:

✦ Examples of generating custom XML using LotusScript

✦ Some advantages of using LotusScript to generate XML

✦ Using LotusScript to create XML and DXL files

✦ New classes and methods in Domino 6 for working with DXL and XML in LotusScript, including the `NotesStream` and the `NotesDXLExporter` classes

The next chapter revisits the data integration application covered in Chapters 43 and 44. You learn how to apply a layer of XML at the Domino level as part of a Web-based data integration solution.

✦   ✦   ✦

Using Domino to Serve Relational XML

By Brian Benz

This chapter expands on the DECS-based relational database Access application example you learned about in the data integration part of this book. As you may recall, the example in Chapter 44 uses Domino Enterprise Connectivity Services (DECS) to connect to an access database that contains over 1000 popular quotations. The quotes table in the database contains four columns: A unique key for each quotation, a quotation source, the quotation, and the date that the quotation was added to the database.

The application provides good examples of application, form, and other design element techniques for developing Domino solutions that integrate with enterprise data. In this chapter you learn how to use the same Domino Web application to serve relational datasets or a representation of that data using XML. You also find out techniques for generating DXL from multi-record database queries.

Working with the Notes and Domino 6 Bible DECS Example Database

You can download the Notes and Domino 6 Bible DECS Examples database (D6BibleDECS.NSF) and the MS Access Quotes database (Quotes.mdb) from www.wiley.com/compbooks/benz. The installation and setup instructions are included with the download. The example database is a good introduction to creating data integration solutions using a Domino server as the middle tier in a multitier Web application. The example application uses Domino Enterprise Connectivity Services (DECS) and Data Connection Resources (DCRs), but can be easily adapted to use any Domino data integration option with the same techniques.

Cross-Reference

For more information on Domino data-integration techniques, plus an introduction to the Notes and Domino 6 Bible DECS Examples database, refer to Chapters 43 and 44.

This chapter shows you how to adapt the existing functionality of the current application by adding XML capabilities from some of the XML examples developed in Chapters 47 and 48.

Domino's abilities as a Web server, combined with advanced security and data integration capabilities, make it an excellent choice for quickly developing flexible and robust mid-range data integration solutions. When combined with Domino capabilities for generating dynamic XML based on Domino data or integrated relational data, the strength of Domino can also be used as a powerful XML application server. This is especially true when the new Domino 6 data integration tools and LotusScript capabilities are included in the mix.

You're going to use the same connection that you used in Chapter 43 to connect to a MS Access database using ODBC. To process the new XML Query functions, you must set up two new activity documents using the Quotes Connection document. To do so, you must create a new activity and follow the instructions in the Activity Wizard. More advanced DECS users can add the form and field values manually by canceling out of the wizard. A new feature in the Domino 6 DECS administration database permits cutting, pasting, and renaming of the existing activities, and then editing the form name you want to find. Because the new XML activities are identical to the original activities, except for the form name to watch, cutting, pasting, and then editing the form name field for the new activity documents is a practical option.

Name the first new or copied activity **XML Quote Source Query** and set the XMLQuote-SourceResults form of `ndbible\d6BibleDECS.nsf` as the form. The mappings stay the same as the original QuoteSource activity, which maps the QuoteSource Domino field to the Source MS Access field as the key, and the QuoteText Domino field to the Quote MS Access field to the field(s). All the rest of the options should stay at the default values. The result should match the activity in Figure 49-1.

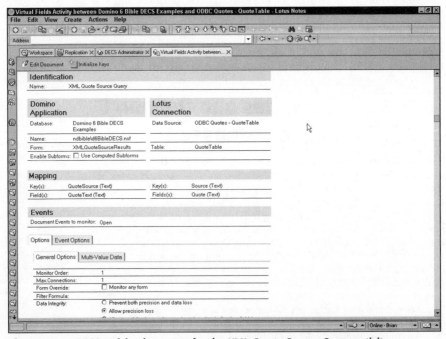

Figure 49-1: DECS activity document for the XML Quote Source Query activity

Name the second activity **XML Quote Text Query** and set the XMLQuoteTextResults form of `ndbible\d6BibleDECS.nsf` as the form. Reverse the key and field(s) settings from the first activity. In other words, map the QuoteText Domino field to the Quote MS Access field as the key. Then add the QuoteSource Domino field mapped to the Source MS Access field to the field(s).

Retrieving XML Documents

For the purposes of this example, a new Query form was added to the Notes and Domino 6 Bible DECS Examples database, called XML Quote Query. Figure 49-2 shows the XML Quote Query form in an IE browser.

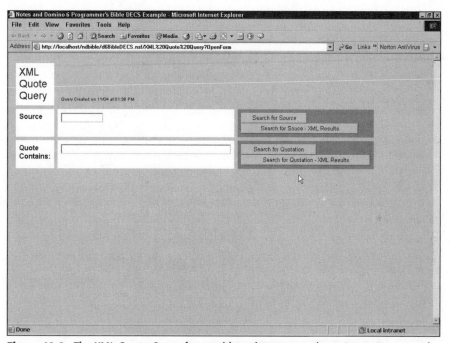

Figure 49-2: The XML Quote Query form, with options to search on Quote Source and Quote Text, and to produce the output as HTML and XML

Note   To open the form in a browser, select the form in Domino Designer, right-click the form, and choose Preview in Web Browser from the pop-up menu. Because the form name has spaces, referring to the form in a browser URL requires that spaces in the form name be replaced with either a plus sign (+) or a space escape character (%20). Domino designer replaces spaces automatically, but if the URL is being manually entered, spaces have to be replaced manually.

The original Quote Query form has two fields, and two buttons that make queries against the Quote Source and the Quote Text, depending on which field is filled in and which button is clicked. The XML Quote Query form adds two new buttons to the form. The buttons generate the Quote Source and the Quote Text results as XML, as well as the original options for generating HTML to the screen.

Cross-Reference   For more details on setting up the example database and how the original Quote Query form works in Domino Web applications, refer to Chapters 43 and 44.

The functionality of the new XML Quote Query form is similar to the original Quote Query form, with some important variations. The following sequence of events happens when using the new form:

1. A user enters data in one of the two key value fields and clicks the corresponding query button, choosing to have the output returned to the screen (as HTML) or to the screen as XML.

2. JavaScript validates the data and records the key value in a lookup field.

3. The WebQuerySave event saves the form with a new name, depending on which button was clicked for which query, and which form of output was selected.

4. The $$Return field on the form finds the form in the Query view and reopens it.

5. Reopening the form triggers a DECS activity based on the new form name.

If the query triggered by the activity was successful, and a single query record is returned, the HTML or XML data appears to the user in the format the user chose when the original form was saved.

If the query triggered by the activity is successful, and multiple query records are returned, multiple rows of HTML or XML result data are displayed to the user in the format the user chose when the original form was saved.

Setting the HTML attributes for each button

As with the original Quote Query form, each button in the XML Quote Query form has an associated onClick JavaScript event. Here's what the generated HTML code attributes look like for the original Search for Source button:

```
<INPUT TYPE="button" Name=QuoteSourceSubmit VALUE="Search for
Source" onClick="SubmitQS()">
```

Here's what the generated HTML code attributes look like for the new Search for Source — XML Results button:

```
<INPUT TYPE="button" Name=XMLQuoteSourceSubmit VALUE="Search
for Souce - XML Results" onClick="SubmitXMLQS()">
```

When a button is clicked in the browser, the JavaScript function associated with the onClick event is activated, which sets values on the form that determine which query to perform, and whether the results should be in HTML or XML. The QuoteSourceSubmit button, for example, calls the SubmitQS JavaScript function, and the XMLQuoteSourceSubmit button calls the SubmitXMLQS JavaScript function.

JavaScript functions in the JSHeader

As in Chapter 44, the JavaScript functions called by the onClick event contain data validation for the associated data entry field and choice of output type. Variables in the function are used to modify two fields on the form, called ButtonPressed and ButtonPressedValue. When data passes validation and the two buttons are set without any problems, the form is submitted to the Domino server via JavaScript. To accommodate the XML source queries, add two new JavaScript functions called by the two new XML Source buttons on the form. Listing 49-1 shows the new XML JavaScript functions in the JSHeader object for the XML Quote Query form.

Listing 49-1: Two New XML JavaScript Functions in the JSHeader Object for the XML Quote Query Form

```
function SubmitXMLQS() {
form = document.forms[0];
if (form.QuoteSource.value == "")
 {alert("Quote Source is required");
 form.QuoteSource.focus();
     return""}
else
form.ButtonPressed.value= "XMLQS";
form.ButtonPressedValue.value= form.QuoteSource.value;
form.submit();
}

function SubmitXMLQT() {
form = document.forms[0];
if (form.QuoteText.value == "")
 {alert("Quote Text is required");
 form.QuoteText.focus();
     return""}
else
form.ButtonPressed.value= 'XMLQT';
form.ButtonPressedValue.value= form.QuoteText.value;
form.submit()
}
```

Each of these functions is associated with one of the XML Source buttons on the XML Quote query form. This code performs a simple check to see whether the QuoteSource field is empty, represented by a blank value. If the value is blank, the function displays an alert box to the user and returns execution focus back to the QuoteSource field, requesting that the user enter data.

If the field is not blank and the data passes validation, two new fields are assigned to the document. The two fields become part of the Domino document when the document is saved, as if they were part of the original form design. ButtonPressed is used by the WebQuery Save event to determine which button was clicked, and the ButtonPressedValue variable becomes a key part of looking up data when the query is triggered.

Here's the code for the SubmitXMLQS function, which is called when the Quote Source Query button is clicked:

```
function SubmitXMLQS() {
form = document.forms[0];
if (form.QuoteSource.value == "")
 {alert("Quote Source is required");
 form.QuoteSource.focus();
    return""}
else
form.ButtonPressed.value= "XMLQS";
form.ButtonPressedValue.value= form.QuoteSource.value;
form.submit();
}
```

Adding a WebQuerySave event to change the form name

JavaScript assigns the ButtonPressed value based on which button was clicked. This value is used by the WebQuerySave event on the Domino form. The function saves the value of the button and passes it to the WebQuerySave event to change the form name, because the Domino server does not accept changes in the form name made by JavaScript. The WebQuerySave event can change form names when JavaScript can't. The changes are processed on the server just before the document is saved. Listing 49-2 shows the contents of the WebQuerySave event for the XML Quote query form.

The WebQuerySave event contains an @If function that chooses a new form name based on the value of ButtonPressed. If the value is "QS", the form name is set to QuoteSource Results. If the value is "XMLQS", the form name is set to XMLQuoteSourceResults. If the value is "QT", the form name is set to QuoteTextResults. If the value is "XMLQT", the form name is set to XMLQuoteTextResults.

Listing 49-2: The Contents of the WebQuerySave Event for the XML Quote Query Form

```
@If(ButtonPressed="QS"; @SetField("Form";
"QuoteSourceResults"); ButtonPressed="XMLQS";
@SetField("Form"; "XMLQuoteSourceResults");
ButtonPressed="QT";@SetField("Form"; "QuoteTextResults");
ButtonPressed="XMLQT";@SetField("Form";
"XMLQuoteTextResults");@Success); @All
```

Editing the $$Return field associated with the form

As with the original Quote Source field, the $$Return field reopens the form that was saved to the server and triggers a DECS activity. When the XML Quote query form is saved, $$Return contains a URL that retrieves the first value in the Query view matching the value of the ButtonPressedValue field that was just submitted, calling the saved form to open itself via a

URL in the $$Return field. A DECS activity then performs a lookup on the back-end database and returns a value or values associated with the key field. The same $$Return field in the XML Quote Query form was in the original Quote Query form:

```
"[/ndbible/D6BibleDECS.nsf/MultiQuery/" + ButtonPressedValue
+ "?OpenDocument]"
```

Because the first column in the Query view is sorted by the most recent time and date and contains the ButtonPressedValue field, you only need one view for all $$Return queries. Multiple query values are displayed and retrieved from the same column in the view. The calculated URL looks the same when opened in a browser:

```
http://www.www.wiley.com/extras/ndbible/D6BibleDECS.nsf/Multi
Query/Albert+Einstein?OpenDocument
```

The URL does not contain a form name, just a document value and the OpenDocument URL command. The ButtonPressedValue of Albert Einstein is passed to the MultiQuery view of the URL, which is sorted by most recent time and date. It returns the first instance of a document that contains the key value of Albert Einstein, which is the value of the ButtonPressedValue field on the form, in the first column of the view.

Adding the XML forms to the database

Adding two new XML forms is the final step in our new XML generation application. The DECS activities are mapped to specific forms in the Domino database. Even though the data is the same in the documents, regardless of the HTML or XML output method chosen, the forms display the HTML output and XML output in different ways. To accommodate this, you add two new forms, called XMLQuoteSourceResults and XMLQuoteTextResults, to the Notes and Domino 6 Bible DECS Examples database. Figure 49-3 shows the layout of the XMLQuoteSourceResults form.

The XMLQuoteSourceResults and XMLQuoteTextResults forms are identical, but you need two forms for output because DECS triggers a separate activity, depending on the form name. The XMLQuoteSourceResults form triggers a query using the Quote Source as the key value, and the XMLQuoteTextResults form triggers a query using the Quote Text as the key value.

The XMLQuoteSourceResults form and the XMLQuoteTextResults form are based on the XMLQuote form introduced in Chapter 47. Both are basic Domino forms with a couple of simple changes that create XML output when the form appears in a browser. First, the form property content type is set to HTML. This passes all output of this form directly to the browser without adding any Domino formatting elements. The next step is to add a hard-coded line above the first field with the XML declaration:

```
<?xml version="1.0" encoding="UTF-8" ?>
```

The root element is then added on the next line, and the nested XML elements are wrapped around every field on the form. When you open the document and trigger the DECS activity, the field values are populated as a result of the query on the MS Access database. When the results appear in the browser, the field values become the element values on the XML document.

Listing 49-3 shows the XML query results for the query on Albert Einstein when the results are sent to the browser via the XMLQuoteSourceResults form.

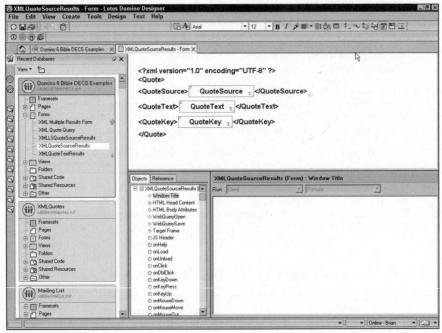

Figure 49-3: The XMLQuoteSourceResults form in the Notes and Domino 6 Bible DECS Examples database

---

Listing 49-3: **XML Query Results Based on the XMLQuoteSourceResults Form**

```xml
<?xml version="1.0" encoding="UTF-8" ?>
<Quote>
<QuoteSource>Albert Einstein</QuoteSource>
<QuoteText> Imagination is more important than
knowledge.</QuoteText>
<QuoteKey></QuoteKey>
</Quote>
```

Cross-Reference For more information on creating forms that generate XML in Domino, refer to Chapters 47 and 48.

Generating Multivalue XML Results from Relational Database Queries

Just as the original QuoteSourceResults and QuoteTextResults forms can generate and display multiple rows of result data, the XMLQuoteSourceResults and XMLQuoteTextResults forms and their associated queries are capable of generating multiple rows of XML result data by exploiting the form selection formula. The form selection formula property of a Domino view changes the form to use with the document without changing the form name just before the document is opened. The original form selection formula for the MultiQuery view appeared as follows:

```
@If(@Elements(QuoteText)>1;"MultiResults";form)
```

You have to add another option to check if the form name contains XML:

```
@If(@Elements(QuoteText)>1;@If(@Contains(form;"XML");"XMLMult
iResults";"MultiResults");form)
```

This function extends the original @If statement that checks to see how many elements are contained in the QuoteText field. When multiple-row data result sets are returned in Domino, they are contained in multivalue fields, each field containing one value for each row in the data result sets. Checking for @Elements that return the number of values in a multivalue field, or a value of one for a single element. This tells you how many records you're dealing with for the result set. If the form name contains the string XML, the code chooses the XMLMultiResults form; otherwise, the original form name is chosen.

If the result set contains more than one row of data, the form is swapped when the document opens without changing the value of the form name in the document, via the view's form formula function. The query is called based on the original form name via the DECS activity, but the view of the data is based on the number of rows returned in a result set, and whether the form name starts with XML.

Adding a new XML form that displays multiple results is the final step in generating XML output for relational database queries that return multirecord results. The form formula redirects XML output with multiple results to the XMLMultiResults form. This form is a basic Pass-Thru HTML form like the other XML results forms. But instead of calculating each field individually and adding them to the XML document, multivalue results are calculated and concatenated in a single field on the document and nested into the hard-coded XML declaration and root element. Figure 49-4 shows the layout of the XMLMultiResults form.

As shown in Figure 49-4, the XMLMultiResults form contains a few lines of hard-coded XML for the XML declaration and the Quote Root element. The QuoteList field is where all the actual work is done to generate the XML for the document. When text values are added to field values in a single-value Domino field, the results that appear are the text and the field value concatenated together. But when a text value is concatenated with multiple value fields on a Domino form, the results displayed are the text concatenated to every value in the multivalue field. If multivalue field A has three elements that look like this:

```
One:two:three
```

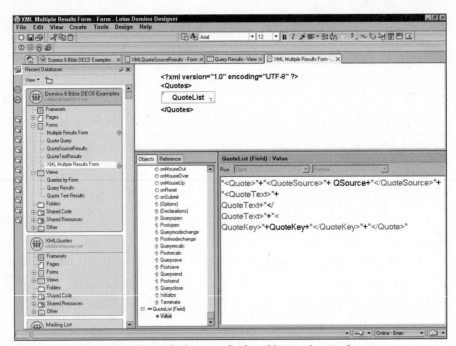

Figure 49-4: The XMLMultiResults form as displayed in Domino Designer

The concatenated results displayed in a Domino form of the formula `value: +A` will look like this:

```
Value: One value: two value: three
```

The QuoteList field in the XMLMultiResults form takes advantage of this feature to wrap nested XML elements around each value that is contained in multivalue relational data results that are on the form. The calculated value of the QuoteList field appears as follows:

```
"<Quote>"+"<QuoteSource>"+ QSource+"</QuoteSource>"+
"<QuoteText>"+QuoteText+"</QuoteText>"+"<QuoteKey>"+QuoteKey+
"</QuoteKey>"+"</Quote>"
```

The preceding code wraps the QuoteSource XML elements around the QSource value, the QuoteText XML elements around the QuoteText value, and the QuoteKey XML elements around the QuoteKey value, for each instance of a new Domino element in a multivalue field.

Listing 49-4 shows the results generated by the XMLMultiResults field for a source query on Amy Bird, which is listed as the source for three quotes.

Listing 49-4: **XML Query Results Based on the XMLMultiResults Form**

```
<?xml version="1.0" encoding="UTF-8" ?>
<Quotes>
<Quote><QuoteSource>Amy Bird</QuoteSource><QuoteText>Too many
freaks, not enough
circuses.</QuoteText><QuoteKey></QuoteKey></Quote>
<Quote><QuoteSource>Amy Bird</QuoteSource><QuoteText>How do I
set a laser printer to
stun?</QuoteText><QuoteKey></QuoteKey></Quote>
<Quote><QuoteSource>Amy Bird</QuoteSource><QuoteText>Sarcasm
is just one more service we
offer.</QuoteText><QuoteKey></QuoteKey></Quote>
</Quotes>
```

Summary

This chapter reviewed techniques for triggering single and multiple queries to generate XML data from a single query form. It also provided

✦ Examples of application, form, and other design element techniques for XML data integration solutions in Domino

✦ The method for generating XML from enterprise data

✦ Techniques for generating DXL from multi-record database queries

✦ A method for generating XML output for single and multiple result sets of relational data

✦ The method for switching forms to display single or multiple XML query results

The next chapter describes how developers can take advantage of the Lotus XML Toolkit and the new Domino 6 Java classes to build stand-alone Java applications that access Domino data and generate DXL output.

✦   ✦   ✦

Developing Java Applications with XML and Domino

By Brian Benz

This chapter expands on the Chapter 34 Java application examples to illustrate how Java applications can access Domino objects and generate DXL and custom XML formats. The example highlighted in this chapter is a fully functional Java application that uses Java Swing classes and AWT events to generate a UI, Domino objects to access Domino data, and Domino and Lotus XML toolkit classes and methods to generate DXL and other types of XML.

Introducing the Java Sample Application — DominoBibleQuoteDXLApplication

The Domino Bible Quote DXL application (`DominoBibleQuoteDXL-Application.java`) is a Java application that interacts with Domino object classes and methods for accessing domino data.

Cross-Reference For an introduction to Java applications, refer to Chapter 34.

Figure 50-1 shows the Java application screen. Amy Bird is the quote source in the top left of the screen. Quotes for Amy Bird are listed in the top right of the screen. The first quote selected in the top right of the screen is the output. The DXL From Document.generateXML() option is the chosen output format, and the resulting DXL output appears in the lower pane of the screen.

Figure 50-1: The DominoBibleQuoteDXLApplication.java Java application screen

How the application works

When a user opens the application window, a class is called that retrieves a list of unique quote sources from the XMLQuotes database, draws the various swing panels on the page, and attaches AWT events to the panels. Users can scroll the list of quote sources in the Source List panel and select a single quote source by clicking it. Clicking a quote source name triggers another query to XMLQuotes.nsf to retrieve all the quotes attributed to the selected quote source, and displays the quotes in the Quote List panel. When a user clicks one of the quotes in the Quote List panel, another Java class is called to generate output for the selected quote and display it in the output panel in the lower half of the form. In the middle of the screen is a combo box that you can use to select output format options. Table 50-1 lists the four options and what they produce.

Table 50-1: Java application output format options

Output format option	Result
Just the Quote	Generates plain quote text in the output window.
XML (Form=Root, Fieldname=Element)	A basic format of a Domino document. The document form name becomes the root element, and document items are nested element values. Item names become XML element names.

Output format option	Result
DXL from Document.GenerateXML	Document DXL from the `GenerateXML` method of the Domino document class.
To File via DXLExporter	Document DXL To File via the Lotus XML toolkit `DXLExporter` class.

Aside from being a cool application, the Domino Bible Quote DXL application is a good example of creating an alternative user interface to Domino using a Java application and UI classes. The Domino Bible Quote DXL application contains examples for accessing Domino views, view entries, view navigators, and Domino documents from a Java application, as well as native methods for generating DXL and XML from Domino data.

This chapter extends the examples in the Domino Quote of the Day database used in previous XML chapters. Download and setup instructions for XMLQuotes.nsf and the DominoBibleQuoteDXLApplication.java application are listed on the ndbible.com Web site. The original Quote of the Day database is used with the permission of the original owners, Newbs Consulting and Sapphire Oak Technologies. You can download the original Quote of the Day Domino database from www.sapphireoak.com or www.newbs consulting.com.

System Prerequisites for Java Applications That Access Domino

Developers need to know which JDK to work with when developing Java applications that access Domino objects. Make sure that the installed JDK on the server matches Domino's Java support requirements. Notes and Domino 5 support Lotus JDK 1.1.8, and Domino 6 supports JDK 1.3. Make sure that the appropriate version is installed on your development machine as well.

CLASSPATH, PATH, and JAVA_HOME variables are usually set when you install a JDK and Domino, but it's best to set these values first if developers are experiencing any Java compile or run errors. At a minimum, your CLASSPATH system variable should contain accurate references to Notes.jar and NCSO.jar for developing Java applications. Your JDK \bin directory should be in the PATH environment variable for Java applications to compile and run correctly, and you must set the JAVA_HOME environment variable to the main directory of your JDK.

For Windows 98 and earlier versions, you can set environmental variables via the autoexec.bat file. For Windows 2000 and later, environmental variables are set by opening the Control Panel, selecting the System icon, clicking the Advanced tab, and clicking the Environment Variables button.

Listing 50-1 shows a sample setup of a typical Java application developer's machine, where the Notes 6 Designer client is installed in c:\Lotus\Notes, and the Java JDK 1.3 is installed in c:\JSDK1.3.1_01. The same settings can be used for a Domino server.

Listing 50-1: Environment Variable Settings for a Typical Domino Developer Client

```
SET CLASSPATH =
.;c:\Lotus\Notes\Data\domino\java\NCSO.jar;c:\lotus\notes\Not
es.jar;
PATH=C:\WINNT;C:\WINNT\COMMAND;C:\jsdk1.3.1_01\bin;c:\lotus\n
otes;c:\lotus\domino
set JAVA_HOME=c:\jsdk1.3.1_01
```

Next, the Lotus XML toolkit needs to be set up. The Lotus XML toolkit is a set of DLLs, a JAR file, and a grouping of examples and utilities for building DXL import and export capabilities into Java and C++ applications on Win32 platforms only, and an old, outdated version of the Domino DTD. The toolkit is available as a separate download from the Lotus Developer Domain Downloads page at http://www.lotus.com/ldd/down.nsf, under the Toolkits and Drivers section. The installation instructions are clear and helpful, and you should read the readme.txt file loaded in the base directory. The main points to remember are to add the DXLTools10.dll to your Win32 directory, and include the DXLTools.jar in your Java class-path before trying to call the DXL utilities.

Reviewing the Java Application User Interface

If the previous setup instructions have been followed, the developer's workstation and the server are now set up to run the servlet code. The next part of this chapter goes under the hood of the Java application by breaking down the Java application source code into topical sections.

The source code for this application is more than 300 lines, and would occupy more than 15 pages of this chapter if listed. Instead, the source code is broken down into segments that relate to a specific topic, rather than showing the source code in its entirety on the pages. You can download the full source code for the DominoBibleQuoteDXLApplication.java application from the www.wiley.com/compbooks/benz Web site.

Defining the public variables and the application window

Listing 50-2 starts with the introductory application setup. Aside from importing the common java.util, java.io, and lotus.domino classes, this Domino application imports the javax.swing classes to handle UI features, and selected java.awt classes to manage action events. Also added are the lotus.dxl classes that are part of the Lotus XML toolkit, and are contained in the DXLTools.jar file.

The rest of this code sets up a JFrame window, which becomes your application's window, and creates an instance of an ActionListener to watch for the window to be closed. When the window closes, the application exits.

Listing 50-2: Defining the Public Variables and the Application Window

```
import javax.swing.*;
import javax.swing.event.*;
import lotus.domino.*;
import java.util.*;
import java.awt.*;
import java.awt.event.*;
import java.io.*;
import lotus.dxl.*;

public class DominoBibleQuoteDXLApplication extends JPanel {
    JTextArea output;
    JList SourceList;
    JList QuoteList;
    ListSelectionModel SourcelistSelectionModel;
    ListSelectionModel QuotelistSelectionModel;
    public String[] listData;
    JComboBox comboBox;

    public static void main(String[] args) {
        JFrame frame = new JFrame("Quote DXL Generator");
        frame.addWindowListener(new WindowAdapter() {
            public void windowClosing(WindowEvent e) {
                System.exit(0);
            }
        });
      frame.setContentPane(new DominoBibleQuoteDXLApplication());
        frame.pack();
        frame.setVisible(true);
    }
```

Now that you have your main application window, you can start building the application UI on top of it.

Setting objects in the window and implementing ActionListeners

Listing 50-3 shows the code that defines the main UI on top of the application window. The first task is to retrieve a unique list of quote sources from XMLQuotes.nsf by calling the GetSourceList() class (covered later in this chapter).

After doing so, the SourceList object is created, and a SourceListSelectionHandler object is attached to the list. When users click a quote source, the SourceListSelectionHandler class is called to handle the action. Next a JscrollPane called SourcePane is created for the list object, which is placed in the top-left area of the application window.

The instantiation steps are repeated for the `QuoteList` object, which displays quotes for a selected source in the top-right corner of the application window. A `QuoteListSelection Handler` object is attached to the quote list.

The hard-coded output options are defined. and the first object is set as the default option. A drop-down combo box containing the application output options is then created and the values are assigned to the combo box. The combo box is located in the center of the application window, just below the Source List and Quote List panes.

The last step is for a `JtextArea` object to be defined and placed in the bottom half of the application window. This is where the XML and DXL output is sent when a user selects a quote from the Quote List pane.

The balance of the code in Listing 50-3 involves swing and AWT class housekeeping to create the details of the layout that the user interface needs.

Listing 50-3: Setting Objects in the Window and Implementing ActionListeners

```
public DominoBibleQuoteDXLApplication() {
    super(new BorderLayout());

    listData = GetSourceList();
    String[] WelcomeMessage={"Click on a Source in the Left Pane to
Retrieve Quotes"};

    SourceList = new JList(listData);

    SourcelistSelectionModel = SourceList.getSelectionModel();
    SourcelistSelectionModel.addListSelectionListener(
    new SourceListSelectionHandler());
    JScrollPane SourcePane = new JScrollPane(SourceList);

    QuoteList = new JList(WelcomeMessage);
    QuotelistSelectionModel = QuoteList.getSelectionModel();
    QuotelistSelectionModel.addListSelectionListener(
    new QuoteListSelectionHandler());
    JScrollPane QuotePane = new JScrollPane(QuoteList);

    JPanel OutputSelectionPane = new JPanel();
        String[] OutputFormats = { "Just the Quote", "XML
        (Form=Root,
        Fieldname=Element)",
    "DXL from Document.GenerateXML" ,"To File via DXLExporter"};

    comboBox = new JComboBox(OutputFormats);
    comboBox.setSelectedIndex(0);
    OutputSelectionPane.add(new JLabel("Select an output Format:"));
    OutputSelectionPane.add(comboBox);
```

```
output = new JTextArea(1, 10);
output.setEditable(false);
output.setLineWrap(true);
JScrollPane outputPane = new JScrollPane(output,
ScrollPaneConstants.VERTICAL_SCROLLBAR_ALWAYS,
ScrollPaneConstants.HORIZONTAL_SCROLLBAR_AS_NEEDED);

JSplitPane splitPane = new JSplitPane(JSplitPane.VERTICAL_SPLIT);
add(splitPane, BorderLayout.CENTER);

JPanel TopPanel = new JPanel();
TopPanel.setLayout(new BoxLayout(TopPanel, BoxLayout.X_AXIS));
JPanel SourceContainer = new JPanel(new GridLayout(1,1));
SourceContainer.setBorder(BorderFactory.createTitledBorder(
"Source List"));
SourceContainer.add(SourcePane);
SourcePane.setPreferredSize(new Dimension(300, 100));
JPanel QuoteContainer = new JPanel(new GridLayout(1,1));
QuoteContainer.setBorder(BorderFactory.createTitledBorder(
"Quote List"));
QuoteContainer.add(QuotePane);
QuotePane.setPreferredSize(new Dimension(300, 500));
TopPanel.setBorder(BorderFactory.createEmptyBorder(5,5,0,5));
TopPanel.add(SourceContainer);
TopPanel.add(QuoteContainer);

TopPanel.setMinimumSize(new Dimension(400, 50));
TopPanel.setPreferredSize(new Dimension(400, 300));
splitPane.add(TopPanel);

JPanel BottomPanel = new JPanel(new BorderLayout());
BottomPanel.add(OutputSelectionPane, BorderLayout.NORTH);
BottomPanel.add(outputPane, BorderLayout.CENTER);
BottomPanel.setMinimumSize(new Dimension(400, 50));
BottomPanel.setPreferredSize(new Dimension(800, 400));
splitPane.add(BottomPanel);
}
```

Defining the actions for the source list

Listings 50-4 and 50-5 show the AWT class `ActionListeners`, which facilitate the UI functionality in the application. The ActionListener detects that the user has selected a quote source. The `GetSingleSourceList` class is called by the ActionListener, which returns a single-category view of the quotes for that source. The quotes are written to the QuoteList object and are displayed in the Quote List pane on the top-right of the application window.

Listing 50-4 shows the code that is called when a user clicks a quote source.

Listing 50-4: Defining the Actions for the Source List

```
class SourceListSelectionHandler implements ListSelectionListener {
    public void valueChanged(ListSelectionEvent se) {
        ListSelectionModel slsm = (ListSelectionModel)se.getSource();
        String [] s =
GetSingleSourceList(SourceList.getSelectedValue().toString());
        QuoteList.setListData(s);


    }
}
```

Defining the actions for the quote list

The code in Listing 50-5 is called when a user clicks a quote in the Quote List pane. When the ActionListener detects that the user has selected a quote, the QuoteListSelectionHandler checks the combo box to see which output format is selected by the user.

If the Just the Quote selection is chosen, the contents of the quote are sent to the output object. If the XML (Form=Root, Fieldname=Element) option is chosen, the GetSingleQuote class is called to generate custom XML for the output. If the DXL from Document.GenerateXML is chosen, the GetSingleQuoteGenerateXML class is called to generate a DXL document from the quote document and send it to the output object. If the To File via DXLExporter option is chosen, the output is sent to an XML file, and a message appears in the output window indicating where you can find the file containing the DXL document on the file system.

Listing 50-5: Defining the Actions for the Quote List

```
class QuoteListSelectionHandler implements ListSelectionListener {
    public void valueChanged(ListSelectionEvent qe) {
        ListSelectionModel qlsm = (ListSelectionModel)qe.getSource();
        String OutputFormatChoice = (String)comboBox.getSelectedItem();

        if (OutputFormatChoice.equals("Just the Quote")) {
            output.setText(QuoteList.getSelectedValue().toString());
        }
        else if (OutputFormatChoice.equals("XML (Form=Root,
        Fieldname=Element)")) {

        output.setText(GetSingleQuote(QuoteList.getSelectedValue().toS
        tring()));
        }
        else if (OutputFormatChoice.equals("DXL from
        Document.GenerateXML")) {

        output.setText(GetSingleQuoteGenerateXML(QuoteList.getSelected
        Value().toString()));
```

```
        }
        else if (OutputFormatChoice.equals("To File via DXLExporter"))
        {

        output.setText(GetSingleQuoteDXLExporter(QuoteList.getSelected
        Value().toString()));
        }
        else {
            output.setText(QuoteList.getSelectedValue().toString());
        }



        }
```

Retrieving a list of sources from XMLQuotes.nsf

The code in Listing 50-6 returns a unique listing of quote sources from the XMLQuotes.nsf database by getting all the values in the UniqueQuoteSources view in an array, and then removing duplicates and trimming the array to match the unique list of sources.

The code starts by creating a ViewNavigator for all entries in the view, and then getting the count of the ViewNavigator entries to define the original array dimension. Next, all the contents of the first column are retrieved into the array, making sure that the current quote source does not match the previous quote source (to generate a unique list). The finalElement variable tracks the number of unique elements by incrementing each time a unique quote source is added. When you're done populating the array, the sourceList array is initialized to the smaller array size. An array copy populates the new, smaller array, and then returns the unique quote source array to the Source List object. The contents of the Source List object are then created by the array.

Listing 50-6: **Retrieving a List of Sources from XMLQuotes.nsf**

```
public String [] GetSourceList() {
    String sourceList [] = null;
    String lastSource = null;
    String thisSource = null;
    try{
        NotesThread.sinitThread();
        Session session = NotesFactory.createSession();
        Database db = session.getDatabase(null,
        "ndbible\\XMLQuotes.nsf");
        View view = db.getView("UniqueQuoteSources");
        ViewNavigator nav = view.createViewNav();
        String [] sourceArray = new String [nav.getCount()];
        ViewEntry entry = nav.getFirst();
        int finalElement = 0;
```

Continued

Listing 50-6 *(continued)*

```
        while (entry != null) {

            Vector v = entry.getColumnValues();
            thisSource=v.elementAt(0).toString();
            if ( ! thisSource.equals(lastSource)) {
                sourceArray[ finalElement ] = thisSource;
                finalElement += 1;
            }
            lastSource = v.elementAt(0).toString();
            entry = nav.getNext();

        }
        sourceList = new String[ finalElement ];
        System.arraycopy( sourceArray, 0, sourceList, 0,
        sourceList.length );
        db.recycle();
        view.recycle();
        nav.recycle();
    }
    catch(NotesException e) {
        e.printStackTrace();
    }
    finally {
        NotesThread.stermThread();
    }

    return sourceList ;

}
```

Retrieving a list of quotes based on the source selected

Listing 50-7 shows another technique for returning a single category from a view. When a user clicks a quote source, the `ActionListener` for the `sourceList` object passes the quote source string value to the `GetSingleSourceList` class, shown in Listing 50-7. This class uses the passed value to retrieve all the quotes for that quote source using the `createViewNavFromCategory` method of the `View` class. This method creates a view navigator for the first instance of a view category that matches the string passed to the view, which in this case is the GetXMLQuotes view.

The count of the navigator is used to dimension an array. The single-dimension array based on the third column in the view is passed to the `singleSourceList` object. The contents of the `singleSourceList` object are then created by the array.

Listing 50-7: **Retrieving a List of Quotes Based on the Source Selected**

```
public String [] GetSingleSourceList(String CategoryName) {
    String singleSourceList [] = null;

try{.......................................................................
..........
        NotesThread.sinitThread();
        Session session = NotesFactory.createSession();
        Database db = session.getDatabase(null,
        "ndbible\\XMLQuotes.nsf");
        View view = db.getView("GetXMLQuotes");
        ViewNavigator nav =
        view.createViewNavFromCategory(CategoryName);
        singleSourceList = new String [nav.getCount()];
        ViewEntry entry = nav.getFirst();
        int quoteElement = 0;
        while (entry != null) {

            Vector v = entry.getColumnValues();

        singleSourceList[ quoteElement ] = v.elementAt(3).toString();
            quoteElement += 1;
            entry = nav.getNext();

        }

        db.recycle();
        view.recycle();
        nav.recycle();
    }
    catch(NotesException e) {
        e.printStackTrace();
    }
    finally {
        NotesThread.stermThread();
    }

    return singleSourceList ;

}
```

When users click a quote in the QuoteList pane, it triggers a call to QuoteListSelection-Handler. This call triggers one of four actions, depending on the output format chosen in the combo box. The first action is to send the plain text directly to the output object. The next action, involving custom XML, is shown in Listing 50-8.

Generating custom XML output

Listing 50-8 is called when you click on a quote in the QuoteList object and you choose the XML (Form=Root, Fieldname=Element) option from the Output Format combo box. The quote text passes to the GetSingleQuote class, which looks up the quote in the GetXMLQuoteTextOnly view. Because you need the Domino document object to generate custom XML based on document items, you retrieve the document from the view using the getDocumentByKey method of the View class.

The code retrieves the Form name and the items from the document and hard-codes the XML declaration to the top of the string that will return the XML document. The next step is to pass the form name as the root element, and then cycle through the items on the Document and generate XML element names and values based on document field names and values.

For XML element names, the XMLSafeName variable is used, which trims off any leading dollar signs ($) from a field name. Several Domino document items start with a $, which some XML processors have trouble with in element names, even though it is not an illegal character for XML.

Listing 50-8: **Generating Custom XML Output**

```
public String GetSingleQuote(String PassedQuote) {
    String XMLDoc=null;

    try{
        NotesThread.sinitThread();
        Session session = NotesFactory.createSession();
        Database db = session.getDatabase(null,
        "ndbible\\XMLQuotes.nsf");
        View view = db.getView("GetXMLQuoteTextOnly");
        Document doc = view.getDocumentByKey(PassedQuote);
        Item Form = doc.getFirstItem("Form");
        String FormName = Form.getValueString();
        Vector items = doc.getItems();
        XMLDoc="<?xml version=\"1.0\" encoding=\"UTF-8\" ?>";
        XMLDoc+= "<"+FormName+">";
        String XMLItemName = null;
        String XMLSafeName = null;
        for (int j=0; j<items.size(); j++) {
            Item item = (Item)items.elementAt(j);
            XMLItemName = item.getName();
            if (XMLItemName.substring(0, 1).equals("$")) {
                XMLSafeName = XMLItemName.substring(1,XMLItemName.length());
            }
            else {
                XMLSafeName = XMLItemName;
            }
            XMLDoc+= "<"+XMLSafeName+">" +item.getValueString() +
"</"+XMLSafeName+">";
        }
        XMLDoc+= "</"+FormName+">";
        db.recycle();
        view.recycle();
```

```
            doc.recycle();
        }
        catch(NotesException e) {
            e.printStackTrace();
        }
        finally {
            NotesThread.stermThread();
        }

        return XMLDoc ;

    }
```

Listing 50-9 shows a sample of the custom XML output for a quote in the application.

Listing 50-9: Custom XML Output Generated by the GetSingleQuote Class

```
<?xml version="1.0" encoding="UTF-8"?>
<Quote>
  <Form>Quote</Form>
  <QDate>05/27/99</QDate>
  <QSource>Amy Bird</QSource>
  <Quote>Too many freaks, not enough circuses.</Quote>
  <QuoteKey>HNEY-4TTLDZ</QuoteKey>
  <UpdatedBy>CN=Henry Newberry/O=Synergistics</UpdatedBy>
  <Revisions/>
</Quote>
```

Generating DXL Output Using Document.generateXML

The basic structure in Listing 50-9 may meet the needs of basic XML applications, but does not describe the data well enough for most applications. A simple way to generate more complicated XML is to use the `generateXML` class of a Domino document to generate DXL.

The code in Listing 50-10 is called when a user selects a quote in the `QuoteList` object and chooses the DXL from Document.GenerateXML option from the Output Format combo box. The quote text passes to the `GetSingleQuoteGenerateXML` class, which looks up the quote in the GetXMLQuoteTextOnly view. Because you need the document object to generate DXL using the `generateXML` method of the Domino document class, you retrieve the document from the view using the `getDocumentByKey` method of the `View` class.

The code creates a new instance of the `StringWriter` class and assigns the output of the `Document.generateXML` class to the `StringWriter` class. The string value that is generated is passed to the `XMLDoc` string, which is returned to the output object in the bottom half of the application window.

Listing 50-10: Generating DXL Output Using Document.generateXML

```java
public String GetSingleQuoteGenerateXML(String PassedQuote) {
    String XMLDoc=null;

    try{
        NotesThread.sinitThread();
        Session session = NotesFactory.createSession();
        Database db = session.getDatabase(null,
        "ndbible\\XMLQuotes.nsf");
        View view = db.getView("GetXMLQuoteTextOnly");
        Document doc = view.getDocumentByKey(PassedQuote);
        StringWriter out = new StringWriter();
        doc.generateXML(out);
        XMLDoc=out.toString();
        db.recycle();
        view.recycle();
        doc.recycle();
    }
    catch(NotesException ne) {
        ne.printStackTrace();
    }
    catch(Exception ioe) {
        ioe.printStackTrace();
    }
    finally {
        NotesThread.stermThread();
    }

    return XMLDoc ;

}
```

Listing 50-11 shows the DXL output of the GetSingleQuoteGenerateXML class for the same Amy Bird quote that appears in Listing 50-9 as custom XML.

Listing 50-11: Custom XML Output Generated by the GetSingleQuote Class

```xml
<document form="Quote">
  <noteinfo noteid="c06" unid="3A4D4341507CDCAF8525677E00708C3F" sequence="2">
    <created>
      <datetime dst="true">19990527T162919,35-04</datetime>
    </created>
    <modified>
      <datetime>20021031T220941,45-05</datetime>
    </modified>
    <revised>
      <datetime>20010210T102813,08-05</datetime>
```

```
    </revised>
    <lastaccessed>
      <datetime>20021031T220939,90-05</datetime>
    </lastaccessed>
    <addedtofile>
      <datetime>20021031T220939,90-05</datetime>
    </addedtofile>
  </noteinfo>
  <updatedby>
    <name>CN=Henry Newberry/O=Synergistics</name>
    <name>CN=Henry Newberry/O=Newbs</name>
  </updatedby>
  <revisions>
    <datetime dst="true">19990527T162920,95-04</datetime>
  </revisions>
  <item name="QDate">
    <text>05/27/99</text>
  </item>
  <item name="QSource">
    <text>Amy Bird</text>
  </item>
  <item name="Quote">
    <text>Too many freaks, not enough circuses.</text>
  </item>
  <item name="QuoteKey">
    <text>HNEY-4TTLDZ</text>
  </item>
</document>
```

Working with the Lotus XML Toolkit

At times XML files need to be shared on the file system as well as displayed on the screen for users. Because the Lotus XML Toolkit classes use the Stream classes for importing and exporting XML, they make ideal candidates for file system functions. This chapter focuses on the DXLExporter class, which exports one or more documents to DXL.

Because the toolkit has been around since the early days of Domino R5, some of the options in the release may seem a little old. But the toolkit is still the only way to generate DXL output in Java to the file system in bulk without having to write your own DXL generation classes. For other applications in Java agents, it may be recommended to try the new Domino 6 NotesDXLExporter before working on a Java solution.

Generating DXL output using the Lotus XML toolkit DXLExporter class

The code in Listing 50-12 is called when you select a quote in the Quote List object and you choose the To File via DXLExporter option from the Output Format combo box. The quote text passes to the GetSingleQuoteDXLExporter class, which looks up the quote in the GetXMLQuoteTextOnly view.

DXLExporter has three parameters — an output destination, a DXLDatabase class, and an optional Notes UNID. If the UNID is omitted, DXLExporter exports every document in the DXL database to the output destination specified. The document object is needed to retrieve the Notes UNID because the view.getDocumentByKey method is not supported in the DXLDatabase class. In this case, you need to open a regular Domino database class, retrieve the UNID using the view.getDocumentByKey method, and then pass the UNID to the DXLDatabase class for exportation.

The code in Listing 50-12 creates a DXLSession and a new instance of the FileOutputStream class, and then assigns the output of the DXLExporter to the FileOutputStream class. Next, the exportDXL method of the exporter class is called, which extracts the document in DXL format and saves it in an XML file on the file system. The last step passes a confirmation message back to users, telling them where to find the generated file, which has been passed to the output object of the applications window.

Listing 50-12: **Generating DXL Output Using the Lotus XML Toolkit DXLExporter Class**

```
public String GetSingleQuoteDXLExporter(String PassedQuote) {
    String XMLDoc=null;

    try{
        NotesThread.sinitThread();
        Session session = NotesFactory.createSession();
        Database db = session.getDatabase(null,
        "ndbible\\XMLQuotes.nsf");
        View view = db.getView("GetXMLQuoteTextOnly");
        Document doc = view.getDocumentByKey(PassedQuote);
        String valStr = new String(doc.getNoteID());
        int noteId = Integer.parseInt(valStr, 16);
        FileOutputStream out = new
        FileOutputStream("C:/TEMP/GetSingleQuoteDXLExporter.xml");
        DXLSession dxlsession = new DXLSession();
        dxlsession.init();
        DXLExporter exporter = new DXLExporter(dxlsession);
        DXLExportOptions options = new DXLExportOptions();
        options.setExportedSchemaName("");
        exporter.setExportOptions(options);
        DXLDatabase DXLdb = new DXLDatabase("ndbible\\XMLQuotes.nsf");
        exporter.exportDXL(DXLdb, out, noteId);

        XMLDoc=("File Saved to C:/TEMP/GetSingleQuoteDXLExporter.xml");

        db.recycle();
        view.recycle();
        doc.recycle();
    }
    catch(NotesException ne) {
        ne.printStackTrace();
    }
    catch(Exception ioe) {
        ioe.printStackTrace();
```

```
    }
    finally {
        NotesThread.stermThread();
    }

    return XMLDoc ;

  }


}
```

Summary

This chapter outlined techniques for generating XML and DXL from Domino using Java applications. It included the following:

- ✦ A sample Java application that generated XML and DXL from Domino data
- ✦ Using best practices for generating XML and DXL from Domino objects
- ✦ Setting up Domino servers and Domino designer workstations to develop Java applications
- ✦ Understanding system prerequisites for Java applications that access Domino
- ✦ Creating a Java application UI
- ✦ Generating DXL with Document.generateXML
- ✦ Generating DXL with the XML toolkit

In Chapter 51, you learn about these techniques in more detail and apply some of them to agents and servlets. The next chapter discusses the other end of XML and DXL transactions — getting XML and DXL data into Domino.

✦   ✦   ✦

Generating XML with Domino Java Agents and Servlets

By Brian Benz

✦ ✦ ✦ ✦

In This Chapter

Using XML Java agents

Writing DXL to the file
system with Java agents

Writing DXL to a
browser window
with Java agents

Using XML servlets

Example: A three-tier
system combining Java
applications, servlets
and Domino

Understanding the
prerequisites for
developing Domino
XML servlets

Running the DXL
application servlets from
a Web browser

Running the DXL
application servlets from
a Java application

Under the hood of the
DXL application servlets

Under the hood of the
DXL Java Application,
Servlet Edition

✦ ✦ ✦ ✦

This chapter focuses on the tools and techniques required to generate DXL from document data using Java agents and servlets. You start with techniques for generating DXL to browser windows and file systems using Java agents. You then move on to techniques for creating servlets that return data to a browser window and finish up with servlets that interact with the DXL Quote Generator Java application showcased in Chapter 50.

As in past XML chapters, views in XMLQuotes.nsf are used to call the Java agents for the examples used in this chapter.

Download and setup instructions for XMLQuotes.nsf are listed on the ndbible and www.wiley.com/compbooks/benz Web site. The original Quote of the Day database is used with permission of the original owners, Newbs Consulting and Sapphire Oak Technologies. You can download the original Quote of the Day Domino database from www.sapphireoak.com or www.newbsconsulting.com.

Using XML Java Agents

Java agents are often overlooked as a solution when you use Java to generate XML from Domino data. But you should consider Java agents as part of any Notes or Web Java solution that generates XML or DXL for the following reasons:

✦ Java agents can be scheduled to run on a Domino server at a specified time or associated with a specific event.

✦ Java agents can be linked to document events, such as the opening or closing of a document.

✦ Java agents can be called by a URL from the Web to dynamically access Domino objects for display in Web pages.

This chapter discusses the capabilities of three Java agents to generate DXL. The first agent generated a DXL document from a Domino document and saves the new DXL document to a file. The second agent retrieves a single document via a passed document UNID parameter. The third agent retrieves a group of documents via a passed category name parameter and formats the output for the Web.

Cross-Reference For an introduction to Java agents, refer to Chapter 32.

Writing DXL to the file system with Java agents

The fist example is a Java agent that generates DXL from a Domino document and saves the generated DXL document to the file system. Figure 51-1 shows the GetDXLQuotesWithJava-FileAgent view in the XMLQuotes.nsf database.

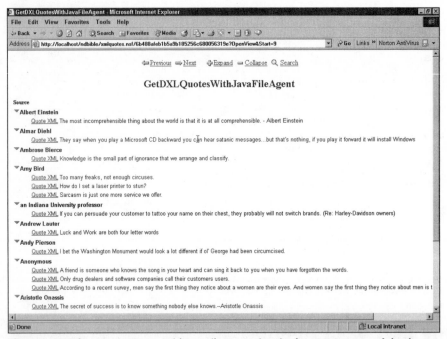

Figure 51-1: The GetDXLQuotesWithJavaFileAgent view in the XMLQuotes.nsf database

The Quote XML links in the view create output to an XML file by creating a DXL document from a Domino document using the Document.generateXML method. The links call the JavaDXLQuoteToFile document, which has a Java agent associated with the WebQueryOpen event called QuoteSourceJavaDXLToFile. When the user clicks a link from a Web browser, the JavaDXLQuoteToFile form opens, which triggers the QuoteSourceJavaDXLToFile Java agent. Listing 51-1 shows the code for the QuoteSourceJavaDXLToFile agent.

The code uses the regular progression of Domino Session, AgentContext, Database, and Document objects to get the current document in the view. From there, a new instance of FileWriter is created, and the Domino Document.generateXML method is called to create a DXL representation of the current document. The document's FormFields field is then updated with a message to the users telling them where they can find the newly created file on the file system. When the document is displayed on the Web, the contents of the FormFields field are displayed.

Listing 51-1: The QuoteSourceJavaDXLToFile Agent Code

```
import lotus.domino.*;
import java.io.*;

public class JavaAgent extends AgentBase {

    public void NotesMain() {

        try {
 Session session = getSession();
        AgentContext agentContext = session.getAgentContext();
        Database db = agentContext.getCurrentDatabase();
        Document doc = agentContext.getDocumentContext();
        FileWriter fw = new FileWriter("c:\\temp\\DXLJavaOutput.xml");
        doc.generateXML(fw);
        doc.replaceItemValue("FormFields", "File saved to
c:\\temp\\DXLJavaOutput.xml");
        fw.close();
        } catch(Exception e) {
           e.printStackTrace();
        }
    }
}
```

Writing DXL to a browser window with Java agents

The next example uses the GetXMLQuotesWithJavaAgentToScreen view of the XMLQuotes.nsf database. Like previous XML examples, the first two links of each row in the view create DXL output that is displayed in a browser. Figure 51-2 shows the view.

The first link, Quote XML, produces a DXL document for the Domino document represented in that row of the view. The Quote <Quote Source Name> link produces a concatenated set of DXL documents in a single XML document. The concatenated DXL document contains all the quotes for the quote source in the current Domino document. Both links use Pass-Thru HTML in a view column to generate the link. But unlike previous examples, the Java agent examples shown here do not call the represented document directly, but make a call to a Java agent via a URL. The URL passes a parameter that includes a reference to the current document.

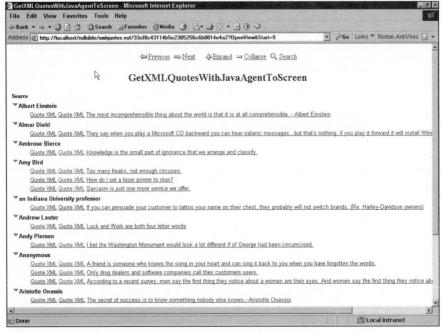

Figure 51-2: The GetXMLQuotesWithJavaAgentToScreen view

Generating DXL for a single document

The first link, Quote XML, looks like this when displayed in Domino Designer:

```
"[<A HREF=/"+@Subset(@DbName;-1)+"/QuoteJavaDXLToScreen?OpenAgent&" +
@Text(@DocumentUniqueID) + ">Quote XML</A>]"
```

This link calculates a URL and a parameter based on the current Domino document using a subset of the @DBName function. The URL returns the directory location and the Domino database filename on the Domino server. The QuoteJavaDXLToScreen?OpenAgent URL command is passed as part of the URL, and the formula also passes a text version of the Domino document UNID via the @DocumentUniqueID function. The & is used by the agent to parse the parameter from the rest of the URL in the Java agent. Here's what the code looks like in the source code of the HTML page that is generated by the view:

```
<A HREF=/ndbible\xmlquotes.nsf/QuoteJavaDXLToScreen?OpenAgent&AA79E91C2DB18A6C
85156B8800586D25>Quote XML</A>
```

This URL passes the UNID (AA79E91C2DB18A6C85156B8800586D25) as a parameter to the QuoteJavaDXLToScreen Java agent. The UNID is passed to the agent and used to locate the Domino document in the database. Listing 51-2 shows the code in the QuoteJavaDXL ToScreen Java agent.

Listing 51-2: QuoteJavaDXLToScreen Java Agent Source Code

```
import lotus.domino.*;
import java.io.*;

public class JavaAgent extends AgentBase {

   public void NotesMain() {

      try {
Session session = getSession();
AgentContext agentContext = session.getAgentContext();
Database db = agentContext.getCurrentDatabase();
Document doc = agentContext.getDocumentContext();
String QueryString = doc.getItemValueString("QUERY_STRING");
String DocumentUnid =
QueryString.substring(QueryString.indexOf("&")+1,QueryString.length());
Document XMLDoc = db.getDocumentByUNID(DocumentUnid);
PrintWriter pw = getAgentOutput();
pw.println("Content-type: text/xml");
pw.println("<?xml version=\"1.0\" encoding=\"UTF-8\" ?>");
   XMLDoc.generateXML(pw);
     pw.close();

      } catch(Exception e) {
         e.printStackTrace();
      }
   }
}
```

As with the previous examples, the code uses the same progression of Domino `Session`, `AgentContext`, `Database`, and `Document` objects as the previous example, but this time the agent doesn't define a view in the `Database` object. This is because the URL is calling the agent directly, and the Document Unique ID is passed to the agent as a parameter. When a parameter is passed to an agent using the `?OpenAgent` URL command on the Web, anything after the ? in the URL is considered a CGI variable, and is passed to the agent's `QUERY_STRING` variable. The `QUERY_STRING` variable becomes part of the document context in the agent context of the current agent. Because the agent needs only the part of the `QUERY_STRING` that is located to the right of the &, a substring of the current `QUERY_STRING` variable is created that starts at the & and ends at the length of the original string. The variable is the UNID of the original Domino document.

```
Session session = getSession();
 AgentContext agentContext = session.getAgentContext();
 Database db = agentContext.getCurrentDatabase();
 Document doc = agentContext.getDocumentContext();
 String QueryString = doc.getItemValueString("QUERY_STRING");
 String DocumentUnid =
QueryString.substring(QueryString.indexOf("&")+1,QueryString.length());
```

After the agent has the UNID that was passed as a parameter, the original Domino document in the database is retrieved using the database `getDocumentByUNID` method. The next step is to create a new instance of the `PrintWriter` class and use the `getAgentOuput` method to redirect any output from the current agent to the `PrintWriter`, which generates output to the browser window:

```
Document XMLDoc = db.getDocumentByUNID(DocumentUnid);
PrintWriter pw = getAgentOutput();
```

Next, the agent directs the `PrintWriter` to treat all output as XML by sending the `Content type: text/xml` directive as the first output. If this step is omitted, the `PrintWriter` assumes that the output is HTML and automatically adds the appropriate `HTML`, `HEAD`, and `BODY` tags to the output before and after it is sent to the screen. The next line adds an optional XML declaration to the top of the new XML document. The XML declaration is not necessary for the XML output to be a well-formed XML document, but it is common to include the declaration at the top of XML documents.

```
pw.println("Content-type: text/xml");
pw.println("<?xml version=\"1.0\" encoding=\"UTF-8\" ?>");
```

The next line generates a well-formed DXL document based on the Domino document retrieved by the `getDocumentByUNID` call and sends the DXL to the `PrintWriter`. Closing the `PrintWriter` sends the completed XML document to the screen.

```
XMLDoc.generateXML(pw);
pw.close();
```

Generating DXL for multiple documents

The next link in the view uses the same technique as the first link to dynamically generate a URL that calls a Java agent and passes a parameter. But this time the agent uses a different approach to return several DXL documents as one XML document. Here's what the link looks like in Domino Designer:

```
"[<A HREF=/"+@Subset(@DbName;-1)+"/SourceJavaDXLToScreen?OpenAgent&" +
@ReplaceSubstring( QSource ; " " ; "+" ) + ">Quote XML</A>]"
```

This link also calculates a URL based on the current document using a subset of the `@DBName` function. The link returns the directory location and the Domino database file name on the Domino server. The `SourceJavaDXLToScreen?OpenAgent` URL command is passed as part of the URL. The URL also passes the QSource field from the current document. As with the preceding example, the & is used by the agent to parse the parameter from the calling string in the Java agent. Here's what the code looks like in the source of an HTML page:

```
<A HREF=/ndbible\xmlquotes.nsf/SourceJavaDXLToScreen?OpenAgent
&Albert+Einstein>Quote XML</A>
```

Tip

Note that there is a + between `Albert` and `Einstein` instead of a space. When a URL is parsed, the `QUERY_STRING` variable stops at the first space in the URL. In this case, the parameter returned is `Albert`, and this parameter reference returns an empty XML document because the full `QUERY_STRING` is not passed. To get around this, the `@ReplaceSubstring` function is used to replace any spaces with plus signs when Domino calculates the URL. You then replace the + with spaces in the agent after the full `QUERY_STRING` is safely passed to the agent.

Listing 51-3 shows the code in the `SourceJavaDXLToScreen` Java agent.

Listing 51-3: **SourceJavaDXLToScreen Java Agent Source Code**

```
import lotus.domino.*;
import java.io.*;

public class JavaAgent extends AgentBase {

    public void NotesMain() {

        try {
      Session session = getSession();
        AgentContext agentContext = session.getAgentContext();
        Database db = agentContext.getCurrentDatabase();
        Document doc = agentContext.getDocumentContext();
        String QueryString = doc.getItemValueString("QUERY_STRING");
      String CategoryName =
QueryString.substring(QueryString.indexOf("&")+1,QueryString.length());
      CategoryName=CategoryName.replace('+',' ');
      PrintWriter pw = getAgentOutput();
        View view = db.getView("GetXMLQuotes");
        ViewNavigator nav = view.createViewNavFromCategory(CategoryName);
        ViewEntry entry = nav.getFirstDocument();
        Document XMLDoc;
        pw.println("Content-type: text/xml");
        pw.println("<?xml version=\"1.0\" encoding=\"UTF-8\" ?>");
        pw.println("<Documents>");
        while (entry != null) {
    XMLDoc = entry.getDocument();
      XMLDoc.generateXML(pw);
    entry = nav.getNextDocument();
            }
    pw.println("</Documents>");
    pw.close();

        } catch(Exception e) {
          e.printStackTrace();
        }
    }
}
```

This agent is similar to the previous agent example, with a few notable differences. The first difference is that the `CategoryName`, which is the `QUERY_STRING` that is passed from the parameter to the agent, uses the `String.replace` method to replace any plus signs in the string with spaces. This restores the parameter to its original condition so that it matches a category in the view.

```
Session session = getSession();
   AgentContext agentContext = session.getAgentContext();
   Database db = agentContext.getCurrentDatabase();
   Document doc = agentContext.getDocumentContext();
   String QueryString = doc.getItemValueString("QUERY_STRING");
   String CategoryName =
   QueryString.substring(QueryString.indexOf("&")+1,QueryString.length());
   CategoryName=CategoryName.replace('+',' ');
```

The next difference is that the agent creates a view navigator that returns all the matching quotes for a category in the GetXMLQuotes view, instead of a single document. After that, a PrintWriter is instantiated and output is defined as XML using the Content-type directive. Next, the optional XML declaration is added to the top of the page.

```
PrintWriter pw = getAgentOutput();
View view = db.getView("GetXMLQuotes");
ViewNavigator nav = view.createViewNavFromCategory(CategoryName);
ViewEntry entry = nav.getFirstDocument();
Document XMLDoc;
pw.println("Content-type: text/xml");
pw.println("<?xml version=\"1.0\" encoding=\"UTF-8\" ?>");
```

The next difference is the placement of the XML declaration for the XML document output. There is a very good reason why generateXML does not include the XML declaration at the top of the page, and that reason is in the next step of this example. The agent creates a root element called Documents for the XML document, and then cycles through the documents in the view navigator. The generateXML method is used to generate DXL for each Domino document. If the XML declaration is included in the generateXML method, as it was in the previous example, the result would be multiple XML declarations in the output document. Well-formed XML documents can have only one XML declaration, at the top of the document, above the root element.

```
XMLDoc = entry.getDocument();
XMLDoc.generateXML(pw);
entry = nav.getNextDocument();
        }
```

When the agent reaches the end of the view navigator, the root Documents tag is closed and the output is sent to the screen by closing the PrintWriter.

```
pw.println("</Documents>");
pw.close();
```

Listing 51-4 shows single-document output from the SourceJavaDXLToScreen Java agent, including the hard-coded Documents tag wrapped around a single DXL document.

> ## Listing 51-4: **Single-Document Output from the SourceJavaDXLToScreen Java Agent**

```
<?xml version="1.0" encoding="UTF-8"?>
<Documents>
  <document form="Quote">
```

```
        <noteinfo noteid="173e" unid="AA79E91C2DB18A6C85156B8800586D25"
        sequence="1">
          <created>
            <datetime>20020326T110551,09-05</datetime>
          </created>
          <modified>
            <datetime>20021031T220948,63-05</datetime>
          </modified>
          <revised>
            <datetime>20020326T110608,68-05</datetime>
          </revised>
          <lastaccessed>
            <datetime>20021031T220941,78-05</datetime>
          </lastaccessed>
          <addedtofile>
            <datetime>20021031T220941,78-05</datetime>
          </addedtofile>
        </noteinfo>
        <updatedby>
          <name>CN=Henry Newberry/O=Newbs</name>
        </updatedby>
        <item name="QuoteKey">
          <text>HNEY-58LLVP</text>
        </item>
        <item name="QDate">
          <text>03/26/2002</text>
        </item>
        <item name="QSource">
          <text>Albert Einstein</text>
        </item>
        <item name="Quote">
          <text>The most incomprehensible thing about the world is that it is
          at all comprehensible. - Albert Einstein</text>
        </item>
      </document>
</Documents>
```

Using XML Servlets

Servlets are made up of Java code that extends the `HttpServlet` Java class, which is the core of the Sun Java Servlet Development Kit (JSDK). Servlet class files are loaded on to a servlet application server and are called via Web browser requests. Every servlet has a call method, which receives servlet requests, and a response, which returns servlet responses. Because of this structure and functionality, servlets are great tools for quickly and flexibly generating XML.

Cross-Reference For an introduction to servlets, refer to Chapter 35. For more details on the functionality of the original Domino application that doesn't use servlets, refer to Chapter 50.

Example: A Three-Tier System Combining Java Applications, Servlets, and Domino

This section breaks up the Java application created in Chapter 50 into a three-tier application. The first tier is the Java application or a Web browser, which provides the user interface to the data. The new second tier contains the Java servlets, which handle data requests from the Java application or browser and retrieve data from the third tier, which contains the Domino server and its associated databases.

Separating the user interface from the data access processes

The Java application, called `DominoBibleQuoteDXLApplicationSE.java`, is based on the swing UI classes and the AWT event classes. This application functions exactly the same as the application in Chapter 50, but instead of running all the Java code on the client and accessing Domino databases over the network, the application makes calls to servlets on a Domino server. The servlets handle data access to Domino objects. In this multitier structure, the client machine doesn't require a Domino client, a `Notes.jar` file, or a `NSCO.jar` file to access Domino objects; all access is via the server. This also means that the application handles the client-side functionality only, and does not have to handle any Notes threading or security issues related to accessing Domino data. The division of processing also makes each side of the application perform better than the original combined application solution from Chapter 50.

Running the servlet examples from the Web

You can also run the servlets in this chapter from the Web using URLs. The functionality is similar, but a more basic user interface. Each servlet contains a setting that is controlled by a parameter. The parameter setting enables response data to be redirected to either a browser window or a Java application object.

Understanding the Prerequisites for Developing Domino XML Servlets

Because you're using client Java, servlets, and a Domino server for this example, there are several steps involved in setting up the application. The following sections review some of the prerequisites for making this application run.

Setting up servlet support in Domino

By default, servlet support is not enabled on a Domino server. Domino can manage its own servlet environment as part of the Domino HTTP task, or can delegate servlet management to a third-party servlet manager, such as the IBM WebSphere server. WebSphere provides a much more robust servlet environment, with more security options, better performance, and more options for running and administrating servlets. The details of working with WebSphere are covered in Chapter 38, but the Domino servlet manager is more than adequate to provide an introduction to servlets for this chapter.

Tip   Ensure that the Domino server has the HTTP task running before enabling Java servlet support. If it's not running on the server, load it by typing **LOAD HTTP** into the Domino administrator console.

To enable servlet support, a person with administration rights on the Domino server has to edit the server document in the Domino Directory. In the server document, click the Internet Protocols tab, click the Domino Web Engine tab, and then scroll to the Java Servlets section. Change the value in the Java Servlet Support field from None to Domino Servlet Manager.

Leave the default values for the servlet URL Path (as `/servlet`) and classpath (as `domino/servlet`). The servlet URL field indicates the trigger that causes Domino to look for a servlet as opposed to a Domino object, such as a database. The classpath field is the location relative to the Domino data directory where the servlet class files are located. If left unchanged, the servlet directory is `<Domino default directory>:\lotus\domino\data\domino\servlet`.

Java servlet support: JDK and JSDK issues

You must know which JDK to use when developing, compiling, and running Java application and servlet code. Domino R5 supports the Sun JDK 1.1.8, and Domino Server 6 supports JDK 1.3 and JSDK 2. Domino Server 6 ships with the `JSDK.jar` in the default Domino program directory. You can download the `JSDK.jar` for a previous version of Domino from Sun's Web site at `www.java.sun.com`.

Editing the Domino server CLASSPATH, PATH, and JAVA_HOME variables

You need to add a Java servlet SDK reference if it's not already in the Domino server's and client machine `CLASSPATH`, which is usually in `<notes program file>jsdk.jar`. Make sure the `jsdk.jar` file is there by searching the Domino Directory on your server for `jsdk.jar` before adding the value to your `CLASSPATH` environment variable. Aside from the JSDK reference, the `CLASSPATH` system variable should contain path references that correctly resolve to the `Notes.jar` and `NCSO.Jar` for supporting Domino servlets. The JDK `\bin` directory should be in the `PATH` environment variable for Java servlets to compile and run correctly, and the `JAVA_HOME` environment variable should be set to the main directory of the server's JDK.

For Windows NT and earlier server versions, you can set environmental variables via the `autoexec.bat` file. For Windows 2000 servers and later, you can set environmental variables by opening the Control Panel, selecting the System icon, clicking the Advanced tab, and clicking the Environment Variables button.

Listing 51-5 shows the minimum required settings to support the compiling and running of servlets in a Domino 6 server environment, where the Domino server is installed in `c:\Lotus\Domino`, and the Java JDK 1.3 is installed in `c:\JSDK1.3.1_01`.

> ### Listing 51-5: **Minimum Environment Variable Settings for Domino Servlet Support**

```
SET CLASSPATH = .;c:\Lotus\Domino\Data\domino\java\NCSO.jar;c:\lotus\
Domino\Notes.jar; c:\lotus\ Domino\JSDK.jar;
PATH=C:\WINNT;C:\WINNT\COMMAND;C:\jsdk1.3.1_01\bin;c:\lotus\Domino;
set JAVA_HOME=c:\jsdk1.3.1_01
```

Setting up JavaUserClasses in notes.ini

Servlets are supported as part of the HTTP task on a Domino server and run under the JVM that is installed as part of the Java JDK. Domino also has its own JVM to run its own classes, such as the lotus.domino classes. To ensure that your servlets are loaded as part of the Domino JVM, add the same JDK and JSDK references to the server's JavaUserClasses variable in the server's notes.ini file. Listing 51-6 shows a standard Domino server JavaUserClasses variable setting for Domino JVM servlet support.

Listing 51-6: JavaUserClasses Value in a Domino Server's Notes.ini

```
JavaUserClasses = .;c:\Lotus\Domino\Data\domino\java\NCSO.jar;c:\lotus\
Domino\Notes.jar; c:\lotus\ Domino\JSDK.jar;
```

Installing the DXL application servlets

You can download all the servlets in this example, as well as the Java application and the Domino database, from the www.wiley.com/compbooks/benz Web site.

The examples in this chapter use four servlets:

✦ DominoBibleQuoteDXLServletGetSourceList gets the first list of unique quote sources for use in the Java application or on the Web.

✦ DominoBibleQuoteDXLServletGetSingleSourceList gets a list of quotes for a single quote source for use in the Java application or on the Web.

✦ DominoBibleQuoteDXLServletGetSingleQuote returns a quote in custom XML format to the Java application or to the Web.

✦ DominoBibleQuoteDXLServletGetSingleQuoteGenerateXML returns a quote in DXL format to the Java application or to the Web.

To test the Domino server servlet configuration, download the .class files for these four servlets from the Web site and copy them to the Domino servlet directory, which is usually <Domino data directory>\domino\servlet.

Note   After loading and copying the new servlets, you must stop and restart the Domino HTTP service. You can easily do so by typing **TELL HTTP RESTART** in the server administrator console.

After loading/reloading the HTTP task, two messages should be displayed in the Domino server administration console.

```
Java Servlet Manager Initialized
```

This message confirms that the servlet manager is running. Check the servlet settings in the server document if this doesn't appear.

```
HTTP Web Server restarted
```

After the HTTP message displays, it's safe to test the servlets.

Installing the XMLQuotes.nsf database

The servlet interface to the XMLQuotes.nsf database can be accessed from any browser via URLs. The Java application, however, needs to have the XMLQuotes.nsf database located in a specific place on the client machine, or the application needs to be edited and recompiled with references that point to the new location of XMLQuotes.nsf.

If changing the application code is not an option, make sure that the database is installed on the same server as the servlets. The database needs to be located in a subdirectory under the data directory called ndbible. If your Domino server, for example, is installed in c:\lotus\domino, you should install the XMLQuotes.nsf database in c:\lotus\domino\data\ndbible\XMLQuotes.nsf.

Installing the DominoBibleQuoteDXLApplicationSE Java application

You must install the DominoBibleQuoteDXLApplicationSE.java application in a directory of a workstation that is accessible to the Java JDK. The Domino server that hosts the servlets and the XMLQuotes.nsf database has to be accessible to the application over a network. Refer to the "Understanding the Prerequisites for Developing Domino XML Servlets" section earlier in this chapter for more details on workstation requirements.

Running the DXL Application Servlets from a Web Browser

You can run the servlet examples in this chapter from the Web as well as from the Java application. After you restart the HTTP task, start any browser and open the following URL:

```
http://<server IP
address>/servlet/DominoBibleQuoteDXLServletGetSourceList?DeliveryMethod=Web&Data
baseName=ndbible\\XMLQuotes.nsf
```

Caution   The Domino servlet manager is case sensitive. URLs must match the filename case exactly. Check the case of your URL first when having trouble with servlets in the Domino environment.

It may take 10 to 15 seconds for the servlet to load the first time due to servlet initialization. If everything is configured properly, you should get results like those in Figure 51-3.

The DominoBibleQuoteDXLServletGetSourceList servlet displays a unique list of quote source links. Clicking one of the links calls the DominoBibleQuoteDXLServletGetSingleSourceList servlet, which generates a list of quotes for a specific quote source by passing a value in the link to the servlet.

A sample Quote source link for Amy Bird looks like this in a browser:

```
<A HREF=/servlet/DominoBibleQuoteDXLServletGetSingleSourceList?
DeliveryMethod=Web&DatabaseName=ndbible\\XMLQuotes.nsf&Catego
ryName=Amy+Bird>Amy Bird</A>
```

Figure 51-4 shows the result of the link for Amy Bird.

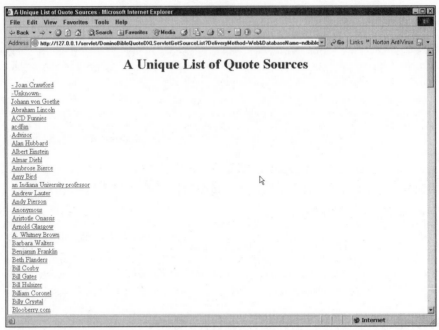

Figure 51-3: The output of the DominoBibleQuoteDXLServletGetSourceList servlet

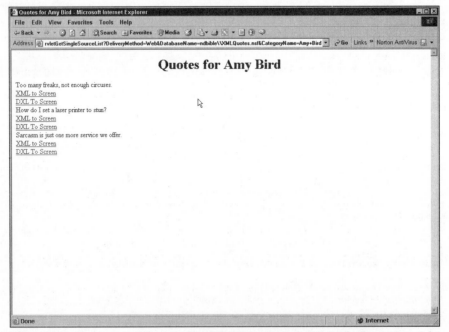

Figure 51-4: The output of the DominoBibleQuoteDXLServletGetSingleSourceList servlet, displaying a list of quotes for a single quote source

Under each quote are two links, XML to Screen and DXL to Screen. The XML to Screen link calls the `DominoBibleQuoteDXLServletGetSingleQuote` servlet to return the associated quote in custom XML format. The following is what the link looks like for the first quote in Figure 51-4:

```
<A HREF=/servlet/DominoBibleQuoteDXLServletGetSingleQuote?
DeliveryMethod=Web&DatabaseName=ndbible\\XMLQuotes.nsf&PassedQuote=Too+many
+freaks,+not+enough+circuses.>XML to Screen</A>
```

The DXL to Screen link calls the `DominoBibleQuoteDXLServletGetSingleQuoteGenerateXML` servlet to return the associated quote in DXL format to the Java application or to the Web. The link appears as follows:

```
<A HREF=/servlet/DominoBibleQuoteDXLServletGetSingleQuoteGenerateXML?
DeliveryMethod=Web&DatabaseName=ndbible\\XMLQuotes.nsf&PassedQuote=Too+many
+freaks,+not+enough+circuses.>DXL To Screen</A>
```

Removing spaces from parameters

The links use plus signs (+) where spaces usually are for the same reasons covered earlier in this chapter. When a value is passed as a parameter via HTTP, parsing of the parameter stops at the first space it encounters. A constant stream of parameter data is expected, so a space indicates the end of a value. The parameter `Amy+Bird`, for example, is received by a servlet or agent as `Amy+ Bird`. The plus sign is replaced with spaces using a simple one-line `string.replace` method in the servlet. But `Amy Bird` is parsed as `Amy` and will not match the correct value when sent as a parameter to another servlet or agent.

Running the DXL Application Servlets from a Java Application

One of the features of the DXL application servlets is that you can run them from the Web or they can be called by a Java application. The Java application example in this chapter is based on the Java Application example in Chapter 50, but is adapted for a multitier system by the addition of the capability to call servlets from the application, instead of containing all the application code and functionality in one Java class file.

After you download the application, you can run it by typing `java DominoBibleQuote DXLApplicationSE` from a command prompt or from the Windows Run menu option. The application appears on the screen in its own Java window. The application's UI is identical to the Java application UI in Chapter 50.

But what's happening behind the scenes is of more interest to developers. The rest of this chapter reviews the servlets, what they do and how they interact with browsers, the Java application, and the Domino server.

Under the Hood of the DXL Application Servlets

The four servlets that (together with the client-side Java UI application) make up the Quote DXL Generator, Servlet Edition application are adaptations of the classes that were showcased in the Java application in Chapter 50.

The DominoBibleQuoteDXLServletGetSourceList servlet

The code in Listing 51-7 is a servlet that returns a unique listing of quote sources from the XMLQuotes.nsf database by first getting all the values in the UniqueQuoteSources view in an array, and then removing duplicates and trimming the array to match the unique list of sources.

> **Listing 51-7: The DominoBibleQuoteDXLServletGetSourceList Servlet Code**

```
import lotus.domino.*;
import java.util.*;
import java.io.*;
import javax.servlet.*;
import javax.servlet.http.*;

public class DominoBibleQuoteDXLServletGetSourceList extends HttpServlet {


    public void doGet(HttpServletRequest request,
    HttpServletResponse response)
    throws IOException, ServletException {

        String DeliveryMethod=request.getParameter("DeliveryMethod");
        String DatabaseName=request.getParameter("DatabaseName");
        String [] SourceList = GetSourceList(DatabaseName);

        if (DeliveryMethod.equals("Web")) {
            response.setContentType("text/html");
            PrintWriter out = response.getWriter();
            String title = "A Unique List of Quote Sources";
    out.println("<HTML><HEAD><TITLE>"+ title+"</TITLE></HEAD>");
            out.println("<BODY><H1 ALIGN=CENTER>" + title + "</H1>");
            for (int i= 0 ; i < SourceList.length; i++) {
                String sl=SourceList[i].replace(' ','+');
                out.print("<A HREF=/servlet/
                DominoBibleQuoteDXLServletGetSingleSourceList");
                out.print("?DeliveryMethod="+DeliveryMethod+"
                &DatabaseName="+DatabaseName);
                out.print("&CategoryName="+sl+">"+
                SourceList[i]+"</A><br>");
            }
            out.println("</BODY></HTML>");
            out.close();
        }
        else {

            response.setContentType("application/x-java-serialized-
            object");
```

```java
        ObjectOutputStream out = new
        ObjectOutputStream(response.getOutputStream());
        out.writeObject(SourceList);
        out.flush();
    }
}

public String [] GetSourceList(String DatabaseName) {
    String sourceList [] = null;
    String lastSource = null;
    String thisSource = null;
    try{
        NotesThread.sinitThread();
        Session session = NotesFactory.createSession();
        Database db = session.getDatabase(session.getServerName(),
        DatabaseName);
        View view = db.getView("UniqueQuoteSources");
        ViewNavigator nav = view.createViewNav();
        String [] sourceArray = new String [nav.getCount()];
        ViewEntry entry = nav.getFirst();
        int finalElement = 0;
        while (entry != null) {

            Vector v = entry.getColumnValues();
            thisSource=v.elementAt(0).toString();
            if ( ! thisSource.equals(lastSource)) {
                sourceArray[ finalElement ] = thisSource;
                finalElement += 1;
            }
            lastSource = v.elementAt(0).toString();
            entry = nav.getNext();

        }
        sourceList = new String[ finalElement ];
        System.arraycopy( sourceArray, 0, sourceList, 0,
        sourceList.length );
        db.recycle();
        view.recycle();
        nav.recycle();
    }
    catch(NotesException e) {
        e.printStackTrace();
    }
    finally {
        NotesThread.stermThread();
    }

    return sourceList ;

}
}
```

This servlet begins with the standard servlet code constructs introduced in Chapter 35, starting with a `doGet` that creates the request and response object that are used to retrieve parameters and return data.

The next two lines get parameters that were passed as part of the URL from the request object. `DeliveryMethod` is used by `doGet` to determine the format for returning response data, and the `DatabaseName` parameter passes the name of the database that contains the quotations.

The last step is to call the `GetSourceList` class, which returns an array of unique sources for quotations from the database. If the `DeliveryMethod` is Web, the servlet returns data in an HTML format that can be read by a Web browser.

```
String DeliveryMethod=request.getParameter("DeliveryMethod");
String DatabaseName=request.getParameter("DatabaseName");
String [] SourceList = GetSourceList(DatabaseName);
```

For Web browser output, the servlet sets the `response.setContentType` to `"text/html"`, and then creates an instance of the `PrintWriter` class. After that, basic HTML tags add a browser window title to the HTML head object and an HTML title for the Web page.

After the basic page layout is set up, the servlet cycles through the array that was created by the `GetSourceList` class and generates a URL for each of the unique quotation sources in the array. The URL is displayed as a link on the HTML page. Each link calls the DominoBibleQuoteDXLServletGetSingleSourceList servlet and passes `DeliveryMethod` and `DatabaseName` as parameters. One new parameter is added, called `CategoryName`. `CategoryName` is based on the name of the quotation source, and retrieves a list of quotes for that source from the `XMLQuotes.nsf` database.

```
if (DeliveryMethod.equals("Web")) {
        response.setContentType("text/html");
        PrintWriter out = response.getWriter();
        String title = "A Unique List of Quote Sources";
        out.println("<HTML><HEAD><TITLE>"+ title +"</TITLE></HEAD>");
        out.println("<BODY><H1 ALIGN=CENTER>" + title + "</H1>");
        for (int i= 0 ; i < SourceList.length; i++) {
            String sl=SourceList[i].replace(' ','+');
            out.print("<A HREF=/servlet/
            DominoBibleQuoteDXLServletGetSingleSourceList");
            out.print("?DeliveryMethod="+DeliveryMethod+
            "&DatabaseName="+DatabaseName);
            out.print("&CategoryName="+sl+">"
            +SourceList[i]+"</A><br>");
        }
        out.println("</BODY></HTML>");
        out.close();
    }
```

For application output, you pass a parameter that can be any value except Web. Instead of preparing the response object to return HTML, a serialized object is returned to the calling application that matches the original data format specified in the application.

This time, the `response.setContentType` is set to `"application/x-java-serialized-object"`, which is a MIME type that can support any serializable Java class. The servlets are working with arrays and strings, so `application/x-java-serialized-object` is a good response format.

Next, the servlet creates a new instance of the `ObjectOutputStream` class, which is an extension of the Java `Stream` class, instead of a `PrintWriter` or other type of writer instance. The Java application that calls the servlet uses an `ObjectInputStream`, which is covered later in the chapter. The `SourceList` is written to the `ObjectOutputStream`, which is an array that was created by the `GetSourceList` class.

```
response.setContentType("application/x-java-serialized-object");
        ObjectOutputStream out = new
        ObjectOutputStream(response.getOutputStream());
        out.writeObject(SourceList);
        out.flush();
```

The `GetSourceList` class is based on the same `GetSourceList` class from the application example in Chapter 50. The class creates a ViewNavigator for all entries in the view, and then gets the count of the ViewNavigator entries to define the original array dimension. Next, the entries in the first column of the ViewNavigator are loaded into the array, checking to make sure that the current quote source doesn't match the previous quote source. This generates a unique list of quotation sources. The number of unique quote sources is counted by incrementing the `finalElement` variable each time a unique quote source is added to the array. When the array has been populated, the `sourceList` array is copied to populate the new, smaller array. The unique quote source array is returned to the `doGet` class to be returned to either a Web browser or a Java application as a servlet response.

```
public String [] GetSourceList(String DatabaseName) {
        String sourceList [] = null;
        String lastSource = null;
        String thisSource = null;
        try{
            NotesThread.sinitThread();
            Session session = NotesFactory.createSession();
            Database db = session.getDatabase(session.getServerName(),
            DatabaseName);
            View view = db.getView("UniqueQuoteSources");
            ViewNavigator nav = view.createViewNav();
            String [] sourceArray = new String [nav.getCount()];
            ViewEntry entry = nav.getFirst();
            int finalElement = 0;
            while (entry != null) {

                Vector v = entry.getColumnValues();
                thisSource=v.elementAt(0).toString();
                if ( ! thisSource.equals(lastSource)) {
                    sourceArray[ finalElement ] = thisSource;
                    finalElement += 1;
                }
```

```
        lastSource = v.elementAt(0).toString();
        entry = nav.getNext();


    }
    sourceList = new String[ finalElement ];
    System.arraycopy( sourceArray, 0, sourceList, 0,
    sourceList.length );
    db.recycle();
    view.recycle();
    nav.recycle();
}
```

DominoBibleQuoteDXLServletGetSingleSourceList servlet

The `DominoBibleQuoteDXLServletGetSingleSourceList` servlet in Listing 51-8 is called when a user clicks a source list link from a Web browser, or clicks a quote source in the Java application. The URL that is sent to the servlet passes `DeliveryMethod`, `DatabaseName`, and `CategoryName` as parameters, and returns an array of quotes for a single quote source back to the Web browser or Java application, depending on the value of the `DeliveryMethod` parameter.

Listing 51-8: DominoBibleQuoteDXLServletGetSingleSourceList Servlet Code

```java
import lotus.domino.*;
import java.util.*;
import java.io.*;
import javax.servlet.*;
import javax.servlet.http.*;

public class DominoBibleQuoteDXLServletGetSingleSourceList extends
HttpServlet {


    public void doGet(HttpServletRequest request,
    HttpServletResponse response)
    throws IOException, ServletException {

        String DeliveryMethod=request.getParameter("DeliveryMethod");
        String DatabaseName=request.getParameter("DatabaseName");
        String CategoryName=request.getParameter("CategoryName");

        String [] SingleSourceList = GetSingleSourceList(CategoryName,
        DatabaseName);

        if (DeliveryMethod.equals("Web")) {
            response.setContentType("text/html");
            PrintWriter out = response.getWriter();
            String title = "Quotes for "+CategoryName.replace('+',' ');
```

```
        out.println("<HTML><HEAD><TITLE>"+ title +"</TITLE></HEAD>");
        out.println("<BODY><H1 ALIGN=CENTER>" + title + "</H1>");
        for (int i= 0 ; i < SingleSourceList.length; i++) {
            String sl=SingleSourceList[i].replace(' ','+');
            out.print(SingleSourceList[i]+"<br>");

            out.print("<A
            HREF=/servlet/DominoBibleQuoteDXLServletGetSingleQuote");
            out.print("?DeliveryMethod="+DeliveryMethod+"
            &DatabaseName="+DatabaseName);
            out.print("&PassedQuote="+sl+">XML to Screen</A><br>");

            out.print("<A HREF=/servlet/
            DominoBibleQuoteDXLServletGetSingleQuoteGenerateXML");
            out.print("?DeliveryMethod="+DeliveryMethod+
            "&DatabaseName="+DatabaseName);
            out.print("&PassedQuote="+sl+">DXL To Screen</A><br>");
        }

        out.println("</BODY></HTML>");
        out.close();
    }
    else {

        response.setContentType("application/x-java-serialized-
        object");
        ObjectOutputStream out = new
        ObjectOutputStream(response.getOutputStream());
        out.writeObject(SingleSourceList);
        out.flush();
    }
}

public String [] GetSingleSourceList(String CategoryName, String
    DatabaseName) {
    String singleSourceList [] = null;

    try{
        NotesThread.sinitThread();
        Session session = NotesFactory.createSession();
        Database db = session.getDatabase(session.getServerName(),
        DatabaseName);
        View view = db.getView("GetXMLQuotes");
        ViewNavigator nav =
        view.createViewNavFromCategory(CategoryName);
        singleSourceList = new String [nav.getCount()];
        ViewEntry entry = nav.getFirst();
        int quoteElement = 0;
        while (entry != null) {
```

Continued

Listing 51-8 *(continued)*

```
                    Vector v = entry.getColumnValues();

                    singleSourceList[ quoteElement ] =
                    v.elementAt(3).toString();
                    quoteElement += 1;
                    entry = nav.getNext();


            }

            db.recycle();
            view.recycle();
            nav.recycle();
        }
        catch(NotesException e) {
            e.printStackTrace();
        }
        finally {
            NotesThread.stermThread();
        }

        return singleSourceList ;


    }


}
```

When the `DominoBibleQuoteDXLServletGetSingleSourceList` **servlet returns data to a Web browser, two links are sent to the screen. If the user clicks the first link,** `DominoBibleQuoteDXLServletGetSingleQuote` **is called. If the second link is chosen, the** `DominoBibleQuoteDXLServletGetSingleQuoteGenerateXML` **servlet is called. Both servlets pass same parameters —** `DeliveryMethod`, `DatabaseName`, **and the new** `PassedQuote` **parameter, which represents the actual quote from the Web page or the Java application.**

```
        out.print("<A
        HREF=/servlet/DominoBibleQuoteDXLServletGetSingleQuote");
                out.print("?DeliveryMethod="+DeliveryMethod+
                "&DatabaseName="+DatabaseName);
                out.print("&PassedQuote="+sl+">XML to Screen</A><br>");

                out.print("<A HREF=/servlet/
                DominoBibleQuoteDXLServletGetSingleQuoteGenerateXML");
                out.print("?DeliveryMethod="+DeliveryMethod+
                "&DatabaseName="+DatabaseName);
                out.print("&PassedQuote="+sl+">DXL To Screen</A><br>");
        }
```

If the servlet is being called from a Java application, the array representing the quote for a single quote source is passed to the `ObjectOutputStream`.

```
response.setContentType("application/x-java-serialized-
        object");
        ObjectOutputStream out = new
        ObjectOutputStream(response.getOutputStream());
        out.writeObject(SingleSourceList);
        out.flush();
```

As with the previous example, the `GetSingleSourceList` class is based on the same `GetSourceList Class` from the application example in Chapter 50, with a few small changes. The `GetingleSourceList` class uses the `CategoryName` to retrieve all the quotes for that quote source using the `createViewNavFromCategory` method of the `View` class. This method creates a view navigator for the first instance of a view category that matches the `CategoryName` string passed to the view, which in this case is the GetXMLQuotes view.

```
NotesThread.sinitThread();
        Session session = NotesFactory.createSession();
        Database db = session.getDatabase(session.getServerName(),
        DatabaseName);
        View view = db.getView("GetXMLQuotes");
        ViewNavigator nav =
        view.createViewNavFromCategory(CategoryName);
        singleSourceList = new String [nav.getCount()];
        ViewEntry entry = nav.getFirst();
        int quoteElement = 0;
        while (entry != null) {

            Vector v = entry.getColumnValues();

            singleSourceList[ quoteElement ] =
            v.elementAt(3).toString();
            quoteElement += 1;
            entry = nav.getNext();
```

After the array is created, it is passed back to the `doGet` class to be formatted for the Web via the `PrintWriter` class, or sent back to the Java application as an array via the `ObjectOutputStream` class.

The DominoBibleQuoteDXLServletGetSingleQuote Servlet

The code in Listing 51-9 is called when a user clicks on the XML to Screen link from a Web browser, or selects the XML (Form=Root, Fieldname=Element) option as the quote output format in the Java application.

> Listing 51-9: **The DominoBibleQuoteDXLServletGetSingleQuote Servlet Code**

```
import lotus.domino.*;
import java.util.*;
import java.io.*;
import javax.servlet.*;
```

Continued

Listing 51-9 *(continued)*

```java
import javax.servlet.http.*;

public class DominoBibleQuoteDXLServletGetSingleQuote extends HttpServlet {

    public void doGet(HttpServletRequest request,
    HttpServletResponse response)
    throws IOException, ServletException {

        String DeliveryMethod=request.getParameter("DeliveryMethod");
        String DatabaseName=request.getParameter("DatabaseName");
        String PassedQuote=request.getParameter("PassedQuote");

        String DXLQuote = GetSingleQuote(PassedQuote, DatabaseName);

        if (DeliveryMethod.equals("Web")) {
            response.setContentType("text/xml");
            PrintWriter out = response.getWriter();
            out.println(DXLQuote);
            out.close();
        }
        else {

            response.setContentType
            ("application/x-java-serialized-object");
            ObjectOutputStream out = new
            ObjectOutputStream(response.getOutputStream());
            out.writeObject(DXLQuote);
            out.flush();
        }
    }

    public String GetSingleQuote(String PassedQuote, String
    DatabaseName) {
    String XMLDoc=null;

    try{
        NotesThread.sinitThread();
        Session session = NotesFactory.createSession();
        Database db = session.getDatabase(session.getServerName(),
        DatabaseName);
        View view = db.getView("GetXMLQuoteTextOnly");
        Document doc = view.getDocumentByKey(PassedQuote);
        Item Form = doc.getFirstItem("Form");
        String FormName = Form.getValueString();
        Vector items = doc.getItems();
        XMLDoc="<?xml version=\"1.0\" encoding=\"UTF-8\" ?>";
        XMLDoc+= "<"+FormName+">";
```

```
            String XMLItemName = null;
            String XMLSafeName = null;
            for (int j=0; j<items.size(); j++) {
                Item item = (Item)items.elementAt(j);
                XMLItemName = item.getName();
                if (XMLItemName.substring(0, 1).equals("$")) {
                    XMLSafeName =
                    XMLItemName.substring(1,XMLItemName.length());
                }
                else {
                    XMLSafeName = XMLItemName;
                }
                XMLDoc+= "<"+XMLSafeName+">" +item.getValueString() +
                "</"+XMLSafeName+">";
            }
            XMLDoc+= "</"+FormName+">";
            db.recycle();
            view.recycle();
            doc.recycle();
        }
        catch(NotesException e) {
            e.printStackTrace();
        }
        finally {
            NotesThread.stermThread();
        }

        return XMLDoc ;

    }

}
```

The servlet is not writing the output as HTML this time, as XML is being generated for the document. In this case, the Web output option is much simpler than the previous two examples. The content type is set to "text/xml" instead of the previous type, "text/html". After doing so, the string that was generated by the GetSingleQuote class in this servlet is returned to the Web as a string.

```
if (DeliveryMethod.equals("Web")) {
        response.setContentType("text/xml");
        PrintWriter out = response.getWriter();
        out.println(DXLQuote);
        out.close();
    }
```

If the servlet is being called from a Java application, the string representing the single quote in XML format is passed from the GetSingleQuote class to the ObjectOutputStream via the servlet's doGet.

```
response.setContentType
("application/x-java-serialized-object");
ObjectOutputStream out = new
ObjectOutputStream(response.getOutputStream());
out.writeObject(DXLQuote);
out.flush();
```

The `GetSingleQuote` class looks up the quote in the GetXMLQuoteTextOnly view. Because you need the document object to generate custom XML based on document items, you retrieve the document from the view using the `getDocumentByKey` method of the `View` class.

```
NotesThread.sinitThread();
Session session = NotesFactory.createSession();
Database db = session.getDatabase(session.getServerName(),
DatabaseName);
View view = db.getView("GetXMLQuoteTextOnly");
Document doc = view.getDocumentByKey(PassedQuote);
```

Next, the servlet retrieves the form name and the items from the document, and hard-codes the XML declaration to the top of the string that returns the XML document. The form name is passed as the root element. Next, the document items are used to generate XML element names and text values based on the original Domino document field names values.

```
Item Form = doc.getFirstItem("Form");
        String FormName = Form.getValueString();
        Vector items = doc.getItems();
        XMLDoc="<?xml version=\"1.0\" encoding=\"UTF-8\" ?>";
        XMLDoc+= "<"+FormName+">";
        String XMLItemName = null;
        String XMLSafeName = null;
        for (int j=0; j<items.size(); j++) {
            Item item = (Item)items.elementAt(j);
            XMLItemName = item.getName();
```

For XML element names, the `XMLSafeName` variable is used, which trims off any leading $ on a Domino item name. Several Domino document items start with a $, which is not an illegal character for XML. Some XSL processors, however, have trouble with the $ in element names, most notably MS Internet Explorer's parser, which is used for XML display in a Web browser.

```
if (XMLItemName.substring(0, 1).equals("$")) {
        XMLSafeName
        XMLItemName.substring(1,XMLItemName.length());
```

After the servlet creates the XML output string, it is passed back to the `doGet` class to be formatted for the Web via the `PrintWriter` class, or sent back to the Java application as an array via the `ObjectOutputStream` class.

The DominoBibleQuoteDXLServletGetSingle QuoteGenerateXML

The code in Listing 51-10 is called when a user clicks the DXL to Screen link from a Web browser, or selects the DXL from the Document.GenerateXML option as the quote output format in the Java application.

Listing 51-10: The DominoBibleQuoteDXLServletGetSingle QuoteGenerateXML Code

```java
import lotus.domino.*;
import java.util.*;
import java.io.*;
import javax.servlet.*;
import javax.servlet.http.*;

public class DominoBibleQuoteDXLServletGetSingleQuoteGenerateXML extends
HttpServlet {


    public void doGet(HttpServletRequest request,
    HttpServletResponse response)
    throws IOException, ServletException {

        String DeliveryMethod=request.getParameter("DeliveryMethod");
        String DatabaseName=request.getParameter("DatabaseName");
        String PassedQuote=request.getParameter("PassedQuote");

        String DXLQuote = GetSingleQuoteGenerateXML(PassedQuote,
        DatabaseName);

        if (DeliveryMethod.equals("Web")) {
            response.setContentType("text/xml");
            PrintWriter out = response.getWriter();
            out.println("<?xml version=\"1.0\" encoding=\"UTF-8\" ?>");
            out.println(DXLQuote);
            out.close();
        }
        else {

            response.setContentType("application/x-java-serialized-
            object");
            ObjectOutputStream out = new
            ObjectOutputStream(response.getOutputStream());
            out.writeObject(DXLQuote);
            out.flush();
        }
    }

    public String GetSingleQuoteGenerateXML(String PassedQuote, String
    DatabaseName) {
     String XMLDoc=null;

     try{
         NotesThread.sinitThread();
         Session session = NotesFactory.createSession();
```

Continued

Listing 51-10 *(continued)*

```
        Database db = session.getDatabase(session.getServerName(),
        DatabaseName);
        View view = db.getView("GetXMLQuoteTextOnly");
        Document doc = view.getDocumentByKey(PassedQuote);
        StringWriter out = new StringWriter();
        doc.generateXML(out);
        XMLDoc=out.toString();
        db.recycle();
        view.recycle();
        doc.recycle();
    }
    catch(NotesException ne) {
        ne.printStackTrace();
    }
    catch(Exception ioe) {
        ioe.printStackTrace();
    }
    finally {
        NotesThread.stermThread();
    }

    return XMLDoc ;

}


}
```

As in the previous example, the servlet output is an XML string, so the content type is set to "text/xml". After doing so, the string that was generated by the GetSingleQuote GenerateXML class in this servlet is returned for display in a Web browser. If the servlet is being called from a Java application, the string representing the single quote in XML format is passed from the GetSingleQuoteGenerateXML class to the ObjectOutputStream via the servlet's doGet.

```
    if (DeliveryMethod.equals("Web")) {
        response.setContentType("text/xml");
        PrintWriter out = response.getWriter();
        out.println("<?xml version=\"1.0\" encoding=\"UTF-8\" ?>");
        out.println(DXLQuote);
        out.close();
    }
    else {

        response.setContentType("application/x-java-serialized-
        object");
        ObjectOutputStream out = new
        ObjectOutputStream(response.getOutputStream());
```

```
out.writeObject(DXLQuote);
out.flush();
}
```

The `GetSingleQuoteGenerateXML` class looks up the quote in the GetXMLQuoteTextOnly view using the `getDocumentByKey` method of the `View` class.

```
Session session = NotesFactory.createSession();
Database db = session.getDatabase(session.getServerName(),
DatabaseName);
View view = db.getView("GetXMLQuoteTextOnly");
Document doc = view.getDocumentByKey(PassedQuote);
StringWriter out = new StringWriter();
doc.generateXML(out);
XMLDoc=out.toString();
```

After the XML output string is created, it is passed back to the `doGet` class to be formatted for the Web via the `PrintWriter` class, or is sent back to the Java application as an array via the `ObjectOutputStream` class.

Under the Hood of the DXL Java Application, Servlet Edition

The Java application in this example is based on the Java application in Chapter 50. Only a few changes are needed to adapt the original DominoBibleQuoteDXLApplication Java application for use in a multitier servlet application. Listing 51-11 shows the changed code in the DominoBibleQuoteDXLApplicationSE Java application.

Two things are changed in the Java application code. First, the imports of the `lotus.domino` and `lotus.dxl` classes are removed. Because processing and access of Domino objects are moved to the middle tier in the servlets, Domino classes don't have to be accessible to the Java application. You can load the application on any workstation that supports Java JDK 1.3.1 or higher, and you don't need a Domino client, the `Notes.jar`, or the `NCSO.jar` loaded on the workstation for the Java application to function.

The second change is the addition of a variable at the top of the application that specifies the server and directory location of the servlets. The `ServletURLBase` string contains a variable that resolves to the location of the servlets. The current value, `http://127.0.0.1/servlet/`, specifies the local machine. This indicates that the servlets are on the same machine as the Java application. If the servlets are running on a server, you need to change the `ServletURLBase` to match the URL of the server and the directory in which the servlets are located.

> **Listing 51-11: Changed Code in the DominoBibleQuoteDXLApplicationSE Java Application**

```
import javax.swing.*;
import javax.swing.event.*;
import java.util.*;
import java.awt.*;
```

Continued

Listing 51-11 *(continued)*

```
import java.awt.event.*;
import java.io.*;
import java.net.*;

public class DominoBibleQuoteDXLApplicationSE extends JPanel {
    JTextArea output;
    JList SourceList;
    JList QuoteList;
    ListSelectionModel SourcelistSelectionModel;
    ListSelectionModel QuotelistSelectionModel;
    public String[] listData;
    JComboBox comboBox;
    String ServletURLBase = "http://127.0.0.1/servlet/";
```

In addition to the two changes to the application code, a few changes are made to the classes that call Domino objects. Instead of containing code that generates lists of quote sources, quotes for a unique source, and XML or DXL output in the application code, the classes now call servlets that pass the correct data back to the application in the required format. Listing 51-12 shows the classes that changed in the DominoBibleQuoteDXLApplicationSE Java application.

Each class in the Java application now builds a URL that calls the appropriate servlet and creates an ObjectInputStream to receive data from the ObjectOutputStream generated by the servlet.

A new instance of the ObjectInputStream is created. A URL is assembled into a string using the ServletURLBase variable assigned at the beginning of the application, the servlet name, and any appropriate parameters that need to be passed to the servlet. A URL object is created from the string, and a URLConnection is created using the newly created URL and the openConnection() method. The openConnection() method calls the servlet, which returns an ObjectOuputStream. The ObjectInputStream then collects the response for the servlet and passes the response back to the application.

The servlet assigns the response from the servlet collected using the ObjectInputStream to an object in the Java application via the ObjectInputStream.readObject method. This example has two formats for responses from the servlets: arrays and strings. An array that contains a unique list of quote sources is received using this code:

```
sourceList = (String []) inputFromServlet.readObject();
```

And a Java string that contains custom XML for a single quote is received using this code:

```
XMLDoc = (String) inputFromServlet.readObject();
```

In either case, the object is passed back to the application and is used as an element of the application UI.

> **Listing 51-12: Changed Classes in the DominoBibleQuoteDXL-**
> **ApplicationSE Java Application**

```
public String [] GetSourceList() {
       String sourceList [] = null;

       try{
           ObjectInputStream inputFromServlet = null;
           String ServletCall = ServletURLBase +
           "DominoBibleQuoteDXLServletGetSourceList";
           ServletCall +="?DeliveryMethod=App";
           ServletCall += "&DatabaseName=ndbible\\XMLQuotes.nsf";
           URL ServletURL = new URL( ServletCall );
           URLConnection ServletConnection = ServletURL.openConnection();
           inputFromServlet = new
           ObjectInputStream(ServletConnection.getInputStream());
           sourceList = (String []) inputFromServlet.readObject();
       }

       catch(Exception e) {
           e.printStackTrace();
       }
       return sourceList ;

   }


   public String [] GetSingleSourceList(String CategoryName) {
       String singleSourceList [] = null;

       try{
           ObjectInputStream inputFromServlet = null;
           String ServletCall = ServletURLBase +
           "DominoBibleQuoteDXLServletGetSingleSourceList";
           ServletCall +="?DeliveryMethod=App";
           ServletCall += "&DatabaseName=ndbible\\XMLQuotes.nsf";
           ServletCall += "&CategoryName="+CategoryName.replace(' ','+');
           URL ServletURL = new URL( ServletCall );
           URLConnection ServletConnection = ServletURL.openConnection();
           inputFromServlet = new
           ObjectInputStream(ServletConnection.getInputStream());
           singleSourceList = (String []) inputFromServlet.readObject();
       }

       catch(Exception e) {
           e.printStackTrace();
       }
```

Continued

Listing 51-12 *(continued)*

```
        return singleSourceList ;

}

public String GetSingleQuote(String PassedQuote) {
    String XMLDoc=null;

    try{
        ObjectInputStream inputFromServlet = null;
        String ServletCall = ServletURLBase +
        "DominoBibleQuoteDXLServletGetSingleQuote";
        ServletCall +="?DeliveryMethod=App";
        ServletCall += "&DatabaseName=ndbible\\XMLQuotes.nsf";
        ServletCall += "&PassedQuote="+PassedQuote.replace(' ','+');
        URL ServletURL = new URL( ServletCall );
        URLConnection ServletConnection = ServletURL.openConnection();
        inputFromServlet = new
        ObjectInputStream(ServletConnection.getInputStream());
        XMLDoc = (String) inputFromServlet.readObject();
    }

    catch(Exception e) {
        e.printStackTrace();
    }


    return XMLDoc ;

}

public String GetSingleQuoteGenerateXML(String PassedQuote) {
    String XMLDoc=null;

    try{
        ObjectInputStream inputFromServlet = null;
        String ServletCall = ServletURLBase +
        "DominoBibleQuoteDXLServletGetSingleQuoteGenerateXML";
        ServletCall +="?DeliveryMethod=App";
        ServletCall += "&DatabaseName=ndbible\\XMLQuotes.nsf";
        ServletCall += "&PassedQuote="+PassedQuote.replace(' ','+');
        URL ServletURL = new URL( ServletCall );
        URLConnection ServletConnection = ServletURL.openConnection();
        inputFromServlet = new
        ObjectInputStream(ServletConnection.getInputStream());
        XMLDoc = (String) inputFromServlet.readObject();
    }

    catch(Exception e) {
```

```
                e.printStackTrace();
        }

    return XMLDoc ;

}
```

Summary

This chapter introduced concepts for developing Java agents that process XML:

✦ Writing DXL to a Web browser

✦ Writing DXL to a Java Application

✦ Building a multitier Java XML application

✦ Methods for building servlets that access Domino objects and generate XML

✦ Techniques for accessing servlets from Java applications and Web browsers

The next chapter covers tips and techniques for getting XML and DXL into Domino applications, as well as using Java and LotusScript to parse data into Domino objects.

✦　　✦　　✦

Getting XML into Domino

By Brian Benz

This chapter focuses on XML document parsing and manipulation using LotusScript and Java. You start with an introduction to XML document parsing, including DOM and SAX. You then review LotusScript and Java agent examples, which include parsing an XML document using DOM and parsing a DXL document using SAX.

There are four ways to get XML and DXL document data into Domino databases:

✦ The easiest way to import DXL documents is to use the new Domino 6 `DXLImporter` LotusScript class. The Domino Designer help has ample documentation on this single-purpose class, which is based on the Lotus XML toolkit `DXLImport` class.

✦ If the DXL or XML document is already in a Domino database as an attachment or contained directly in a rich-text field, you can use the Java `ParseXML` class to parse the attachment into a DOM document. The Domino Designer help also has ample documentation on `ParseXML`. You can easily adapt the Java agent examples in this chapter to use `ParseXML()` to create a DOM document from a rich text field or attachment, using the `ParseXML` examples in the help, instead of creating the DOM document using the parser from a file.

✦ You can use the new LotusScript `NotesSession` methods `CreateDOMParser` and `CreateSAXParser` to parse XML and DXL via SAX and DOM. The chapter provides tips and techniques for working with DOM and SAX in LotusScript, and working with parsed data.

✦ Java agents can implement the `org.w3c.dom` and `org.xml.sax` classes to parse XML and DXL via SAX and DOM. The chapter provides tips and techniques for working with DOM and SAX in Java, and working with parsed data by adapting the LotusScript parsing agent examples into Java agents.

Parsing XML Documents

Parsers are used to integrate data in XML documents with other formats of data. *XML Document Parsing* is the process of identifying and converting XML tags contained in an XML document into nested nodes or document events, depending on the type of XML parser being used. Document Object Model (DOM) parsing breaks a document into nested elements, referred to as *nodes* in a DOM document representation. The Simple API for XML (SAX) parser breaks XML documents down into events in a SAX document representation. After XML documents are parsed, you can use these nodes or events to convert the original XML document tags into other types of data, based on the data represented by the elements and attributes in the nodes or events.

Understanding XML Parsers

Parsers generally fall into the following two categories:

✦ Nonvalidating parsers ensure that a well-formed XML document adheres to the basic XML structure and syntax rules.

✦ Validating parsers have the option to verify that an XML document is valid according to the rules of a DTD or schema, as well as check for well-formed document structure and syntax.

There are several XML parsers on the market, but only three stand out from the pack in terms of standards support and general marketplace acceptance. In addition, one pluggable interface is also available from Sun.

Apache's Xerces

The Xerces parser is a validating parser available in Java and C++. It fully supports the W3C XML DOM (Level 1 and 2) standards, as well as SAX version 2. Support for XML document validation against W3C schemas is also provided. The C++ version of the Xerces parser also includes a Perl wrapper, plus a COM wrapper that works with the MSXML parser, if you're into that sort of thing.

You can download Xerces at `http://xml.apache.org`.

IBM's XML4J

The IBM XML for Java (XML4J) libraries, with some more recent help from the Apache Xerces project and Sun (via project Crimson), is the mother of all Java-based XML parsers, starting with version 1.0 in 1998. IBM and the Apache group work closely on XML document-parsing technologies. Consequently, the IBM XML4J libraries are based on Xerces. The latest version of the XML4J libraries support the W3C XML schema recommendation, SAX 1 and 2, DOM 1 and 2, and some basic features of the as-yet-unreleased DOM 3 standard, currently in the recommendation process. XML4J also adds support for Sun's JAXP (more on that in the next section), plus multilingual error messages.

XML4J is the default parser library shipped with Domino 5 and 6. You can download recent updates to XML4J from `www.alphaworks.ibm.com/tech/xml4j`.

Microsoft's XML parser (MSXML)

Microsoft's XML parser is part of Internet Explorer 5.0 or later. MSXML supports most XML standards and the XML DOM and SAX parsers, as well as schemas. MSXML works with JavaScript, Visual Basic, and C++, but not Java.

The MSXML parser ships as part of Internet Explorer, but MSXML functionality is separate from IE functionality by design. You can download recent MSXML updates from www.microsoft.com/msxml.

Sun's JAXP

Several types of XML parsers are available from a single vendor, plus several versions of each type of parser. The Java API for XML Processing (JAXP) is designed to smooth over the various versions of the SAX and DOM parsers and their associated incompatibilities through a single pluggable interface. A document could be parsed using DOM1, then DOM2, and then updated to DOM3 when the new DOM 3 recommendation arrives through the W3C recommendation process. The code that performs the parse is separated from the parser by the JAXP classes, so the parsing code does not have to change when a new parser is implemented. This provides the best of both worlds; applications have access to better parser performance and functionality, but application code needs less maintenance as parsers evolve.

You can download JAXP from http://java.sun.com/xml/jaxp/.

Using the Document Object Model (DOM)

DOM parsing is the more common, easier method of parsing XML documents. The DOM specification is the only XML document object model officially recommended by the WWW consortium (www.w3c.org). Most Java DOM parsers available on the market adhere to the latest W3C standards by creating a new instance of the org.w3c.dom.Document class. You can use the XML DOM to create XML documents, navigate DOM structures, and add, modify, or delete DOM nodes. DOM can be slower than SAX because it creates a representation of the entire document as nodes, regardless of how large the document is. But DOM can be handy for retrieving all the data from a document, or retrieving a piece of data several times, because the DOM is resident in memory as long as the code that created the DOM representation is running.

What is DOM?

The Document Object Model (DOM) is a tree representation of XML data, with a root element and nested elements, attributes, text values, and processing instructions in an XML document. In Java, the structure is represented by instances of the org.w3c.dom.Node nested inside a single org.w3c.dom.Document class. Each node in the DOM tree represents a matching element, attribute, text value, or processing instruction. Nodes are nested at multiple levels matching the nested levels of the items in the original XML document. The root element always equals the root node in a DOM document, and nested XML elements are located as branches from the DOM root. You can find more information about DOM at www.w3.org/DOM/.

About DOM 1 and DOM 2

The DOM Level 1 and Level 2 specifications are both W3C recommendations. Both specifications are final, and developers who build applications based on either specification can be assured that the standards are complete and will not be updated. But DOM Level 1 is not compatible with DOM Level 2, and there are no guarantees that DOM Level 1 or 2 are compatible with DOM Level 3, which is currently winding its way through the recommendation process at the W3C. DOM 1 supports navigation and editing of DOM nodes in HTML and XML documents. DOM 2 extends Level 1 with namespace support, and a few new features that are similar to SAX functionality, such as filtered views, ranges, and events.

Using Simple API for XML (SAX)

SAX parsing is faster than DOM parsing, but slightly more complicated to code. You might compare SAX parsing to getting information from this chapter of the book by going to the page where the chapter starts, reading the chapter, and stopping when the chapter ends. DOM would extract the same information from this book by reading the entire book, and then looking through the book one more time to find the beginning of the chapter, and reading the chapter. In other words, SAX provides just the chunk of information that you need from an XML document, whereas DOM retrieves the whole document and then extracts the chunk.

What is SAX?

Like DOM, SAX is used to describe, parse, and manipulate XML documents. Unlike DOM, SAX breaks a document into a series of events, such as `StartDocument`, `StartElement`, `EndElement`, `ProcessingInstruction`, `SAXWarning`, `SAXError`, and `EndDocument`. In Java, a SAX 1 driver implements the SAX parser interface and a SAX 2 driver implements the XMLReader interface.

SAX is not developed or recommended by the W3C, although subsequent DOM implementations invariably borrow features from more advanced SAX feature sets. SAX is usually ahead of DOM implementations, because the W3C recommendation process does not hinder SAX development. No official specification of SAX exists, just the implementation of the `XMLReader` class, which is only written in Java at this time. Other implementations of SAX exist on other platforms, but these are a result of bindings to code in the SAX archive file, `sax.jar`, or a complete rewrite of code that simply mimics the functionality of SAX classes.

You can download the latest updates to SAX via the `sax.jar` file at www.saxproject.org/. The site also contains information about parser implementations and bindings, and the FAQ at that site is a fun read. Really.

SAX 1 and SAX 2

Unlike DOM 1 and 2, SAX 2 is backward compatible with SAX 1, although most current parsers implement the SAX 2 interfaces. SAX 1 supported navigation around a document and manipulation of content via SAX events. SAX 2 supports Namespaces, filter chains, plus querying and setting features and properties via SAX events. The LotusScript classes in Domino 6 and the `org.xml.sax` classes that are contained in the `XML4j.jar` file, which ships with Domino 6, are currently based on SAX 1.

Using LotusScript and Java Agents to Parse XML and DXL Documents: Examples

The new LotusScript classes in Domino 6 make it easier to parse DXL and XML documents using LotusScript. Previously, Domino developers had to develop their own parsing routines in LotusScript or use the Java interfaces in a Java agent. As the examples in this chapter illustrate, Domino 6 LotusScript parsing classes and methods are based on DOM 1 and SAX 1 and are best suited for basic parsing of XML. Java supports more advanced features and manipulation of data via the full feature set of DOM and SAX parser classes.

The examples in this chapter parse two source XML and DXL documents that were generated by LotusScript agents in Chapter 48. The first example, XMLOutput.xml, is a basic XML document, with the original Domino form name as the root element, the original Domino field names as the nested element names, and the original field values as the text values. Listing 52-1 shows the sample XMLOutput.xml document.

Listing 52-1: **Format of the XMLOutput.xml Document**

```
<?xml version="1.0" encoding="UTF-8"?>
<Quote>
  <Form>Quote</Form>
  <QuoteKey>HNEY-4V4HE8</QuoteKey>
  <QDate>03/23/2001</QDate>
  <QSource>Abraham Lincoln</QSource>
  <Quote>No matter how much cats fight, there always seems to be plenty
  of kittens.- Abraham Lincoln</Quote>
  <UpdatedB>CN=Henry Newberry/O=Newbs</UpdatedB>
</Quote>
```

The second example, DXLOutput.xml, is a DXL representation of the same original Domino document. Listing 52-2 shows the sample XMLOutput.xml document.

Listing 52-2: **Format of the DXLOutput.xml Document**

```
?xml version="1.0" encoding="utf-8"?>
<!DOCTYPE document SYSTEM 'xmlschemas/domino_6_0.dtd'>
<document xmlns="http://www.lotus.com/dxl" version="6.0"
replicaid="85256C6400115C34" form="Quote">
  <noteinfo noteid="1386" unid="C0C0F4484E0E948585256A180048197D"
  sequence="1">
    <created>
      <datetime>20010323T080731,17-05</datetime>
    </created>
    <modified>
      <datetime>20021031T220946,25-05</datetime>
```

Continued

Listing 52-2 *(continued)*

```
    </modified>
    <revised>
      <datetime>20010323T080751,54-05</datetime>
    </revised>
    <lastaccessed>
      <datetime>20021031T220940,91-05</datetime>
    </lastaccessed>
    <addedtofile>
      <datetime>20021031T220940,91-05</datetime>
    </addedtofile>
  </noteinfo>
  <updatedby>
    <name>CN=Henry Newberry/O=Newbs</name>
  </updatedby>
  <item name="QuoteKey">
    <textlist>
      <text>HNEY-4V4HE8</text>
    </textlist>
  </item>
  <item name="QDate">
    <textlist>
      <text>03/23/2001</text>
    </textlist>
  </item>
  <item name="QSource">
    <textlist>
      <text>Abraham Lincoln</text>
    </textlist>
  </item>
  <item name="Quote">
    <textlist>
      <text>No matter how much cats fight, there always
      seems to be plenty of kittens.- Abraham
      Lincoln</text>
    </textlist>
  </item>
  <item name="FormFields" summary="false">
    <textlist>
      <text/>
    </textlist>
  </item>
</document>
```

All of the parsing examples in this chapter create new Domino documents based on the QuoteFromXML form in the XMLQuotes.nsf database. The Quotes From XML view shows all the documents created using the QuoteFromXML form.

You can download all the examples contained in Part X of this book, including the XMLQuotes.nsf database, the DXLOutput.xml document, and the wmljout.xml document from the www.wiley.com/compbooks/benz Web site. The database design and content are reused with permission of the original owners, Newbs Consulting and Sapphire Oak Technologies. You can download the original Quote of the Day Domino database that XMLQuotes.nsf is based on from www.sapphireoak.com or www.newbs consulting.com.

Figure 52-1 shows the layout of the QuoteFromXML form in the XMLQuotes.nsf Database.

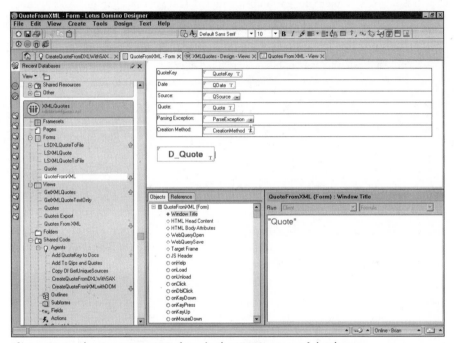

Figure 52-1: The QuoteFromXML form in the XMLQuotes.nsf database

The QuoteFromXML form is based on the Quote form in the same database. The form contains the original four fields, as follows:

- ✦ QuoteKey, a unique key for the quote

- ✦ Qdate, the date the quote was added

- ✦ Qsource, the source the quote is attributed to

- ✦ Quote, the actual quote text

The next two fields are added by the parsing agent:

- ✦ The ParseException field lists any parser errors, fatal errors, and warnings that were encountered during parsing of the XML or DXL document as a text list.

- ✦ The CreationMethod field describes the parsing method (SAX or DOM) and the type of agent (LotusScript or Java).

Parsing XML documents with DOM in a LotusScript agent

The code in Listing 52-3 shows a LotusScript agent that uses the new Domino 6 `DomParser` method of `NotesSession` to parse the XML document shown in Listing 52-1 into DOM document nodes. The agent copies the nodes into a new QuoteFromXML form in the `XMLQuotes.nsf` database.

Note the choice for source documents when parsing DOM and SAX. DOM performs best with smaller XML documents that contain simple data structures. DOM needs to break down every element, text value, attribute, and processing instruction in the document to build a DOM node tree before document nodes can be extracted. Later in this chapter, SAX's event-driven interface example uses the larger and more verbose DXL example document, because SAX is faster at parsing parts of larger XML documents.

Listing 52-3 shows the complete `CreateQuoteFromXMLWithDOMLS` LotusScript agent. The code is broken down into segments and explained after this listing.

> ### Listing 52-3: **Code for the CreateQuoteFromXMLWithDOMLS LotusScript Agent**

```
Sub Initialize
    Dim CurrentItemName As String
    Dim CurrentItemValue As String
    Dim doc As NotesDocument
    Dim session As New NotesSession
    Dim domParser As NotesDOMParser
    Dim db As NotesDatabase
    Set db = session.CurrentDatabase
    Set doc = New NotesDocument(db)

    Dim xml_in As NotesStream
    Dim docNode As NotesDOMDocumentNode
    filename$ = "c:\temp\XMLOutput.xml"
    Set xml_in=session.CreateStream
    If Not xml_in.Open(filename$) Then
        Messagebox "Cannot open " & filename$,, "XML file error"
        Exit Sub
    End If
    If xml_in.Bytes = 0 Then
        Messagebox filename$ & " is empty",, "XML file error"
        Exit Sub
    End If

    Set domParser=session.CreateDOMParser(xml_in)
    domParser.Process

    Set docNode = domParser.Document

    Set QuoteElementName = docNode.DocumentElement.FirstChild

    While numChildNodes < docNode.DocumentElement.NumberOfChildNodes
        If DOMNODETYPE_ELEMENT_NODE Then
            CurrentItemName = QuoteElementName.Tagname
```

```
    End If

    Set QuoteElementValue = QuoteElementName.FirstChild
    If DOMNODETYPE_TEXT_NODE Then
       CurrentItemValue = QuoteElementValue.NodeValue
    End If

    Messagebox " Writing Creating Item Name: "+CurrentItemName+" Value: "
    + CurrentItemValue, MB_ICONINFORMATION
    Call doc.ReplaceItemValue( CurrentItemName, CurrentItemValue )

    Set QuoteElementName = QuoteElementName.NextSibling
    numChildNodes = numChildNodes+1
  Wend

  doc.Form="QuoteFromXML"
  Call doc.ReplaceItemValue( "CreationMethod", "From an XML File via DOM
  in a LotusScript Agent" )
  Call doc.Save(True, False)

End Sub
```

The next part of this chapter reviews the agent code in segments to see how DOM handles an XML document and how the LotusScript agent uses the parsed DOM document to create a new Domino document.

The first part of this agent defines several strings and gets the current database from the NotesSession. The code also defines domParser and creates a new NotesStream object that is used to stream the contents of the simple XML file in Listing 52-1 into the DOM parser for processing.

 New Feature

The LotusScript NotesStream and NotesDOMParser classes are new in Domino 6. Notes Stream represents files as streams of binary or character data. The CreateStream method in the NotesSession class creates new NotesStream objects. NotesStream is also used to pass objects into and out of XML document parsing and transformation processors.

NotesDOMParser parses XML documents into DOM tree nodes. The CreateDOMParser method of NotesSession creates a NotesDOMParser object.

```
Dim CurrentItemName As String
  Dim CurrentItemValue As String
  Dim doc As NotesDocument
  Dim session As New NotesSession
  Dim domParser As NotesDOMParser
  Dim db As NotesDatabase
  Set db = session.CurrentDatabase
  Set doc = New NotesDocument(db)
  Dim xml_in As NotesStream
```

Next the agent creates a new NotesDOMDocumentNode. DOM documents are representations of XML documents, with each element, attribute, text value, or processing instruction in the source XML document represented by a node in the DOM. The job of a developer is to write parsing code that manages the relationships between DOM nodes to create coherent data out of the node structure.

Next, the agent checks to see whether the XML source file can be opened on the file system. If the file can be opened, the XML document in the file is parsed using the NotesDOMParser.

```
Dim docNode As NotesDOMDocumentNode
filename$ = "c:\temp\XMLOutput.xml"
Set xml_in=session.CreateStream
If Not xml_in.Open(filename$) Then
    Messagebox "Cannot open " & filename$,, "XML file error"
    Exit Sub
End If
If xml_in.Bytes = 0 Then
    Messagebox filename$ & " is empty",, "XML file error"
    Exit Sub
End If

Set domParser=session.CreateDOMParser(xml_in)
domParser.Process
```

The DOM parser produces a DOM document node tree based on the XML document, which is used to extract elements and text values. The extracted elements and values create fields in a new Domino document. The QuoteElementName variable is set to the value of the first child node of the first element in the DOM document using docNode.DocumentElement. FirstChild. A count of the nodes in the document is defined using the docNode. DocumentElement.NumberOfChildNodes method to return the number of nodes in the next level of the DOM. Next, the name of the first nested element in the original XML document is retrieved, ignoring the original root element. The DOMNODETYPE_ELEMENT_NODE and DOMNODETYPE_TEXT_NODE references are two of several predefined Domino node types that are used to define node types in DOM trees. ELEMENT_NODE defines elements, and _NODE defines text values.

After the agent has located the element node, the next child element is the text value associated with the element, as in this XML document example:

```
<QuoteKey>  (QuoteElementName)
          HNEY-4V4HE8 (QuoteElementName.FirstChild)
</QuoteKey>
```

The QuoteElementValue variable is assigned the value of the first child node of QuoteElementName. QuoteElementName becomes the field name in the new Domino document, and QuoteElementValue becomes the field value:

```
Set docNode = domParser.Document

Set QuoteElementName = docNode.DocumentElement.FirstChild

While numChildNodes < docNode.DocumentElement.NumberOfChildNodes
    If DOMNODETYPE_ELEMENT_NODE Then
        CurrentItemName = QuoteElementName.Tagname
    End If

    Set QuoteElementValue = QuoteElementName.FirstChild
    If DOMNODETYPE_TEXT_NODE Then
        CurrentItemValue = QuoteElementValue.NodeValue
    End If
```

When the agent has field name and value, a field on the new Domino document is created, as shown in the following code.

The LotusScript `replaceItemValue` method creates a new field for each name and value pair found in the original XML document. After the new fields are created, a text string text describing the parsing process is written to the CreationMethod field and the new Domino document is saved.

```
        Messagebox " Writing Creating Item Name: "+CurrentItemName+" Value: "
        + CurrentItemValue, MB_ICONINFORMATION
        Call doc.ReplaceItemValue( CurrentItemName, CurrentItemValue )

        Set QuoteElementName = QuoteElementName.NextSibling
        numChildNodes = numChildNodes+1
    Wend
doc.Form="QuoteFromXML"
    Call doc.ReplaceItemValue( "CreationMethod", "From an XML File via DOM
    in a LotusScript Agent" )
    Call doc.Save(True, False)

End Sub
```

Parsing DXL documents with SAX in a LotusScript agent

SAX parsing via events is usually difficult to grasp for developers who are used to working with objects. The DOM method of looking for an element or attribute by simply starting at the top of a document and sifting through things you don't want until you find the things you do want is usually more familiar. The SAX approach for reading data from an XML document is to attach processes to events and collect pieces of an XML document as the events are processed. Developers need to have a fairly good knowledge of SAX events and the basic structure of DXL to make SAX parsing happen, and the process is a little more complicated than DOM parsing. The payoff to mastery of the SAX and event-driven interfaces is speed — SAX parsing is invariably faster than DOM parsing.

SAX is great for retrieving small parts of large documents, because SAX events enable developers to drill down into just the parts of the documents that they need for their processing. In this case, the DXL document represented in the `DXLOutput.xml` document in listing 52-2 is a great example of appropriate use for a SAX parser. Although the DXL representation of the document is large and verbose, you only need the elements that represent the Notes items in the DXL document to create a new Domino document. SAX can extract the item elements without having to create a representation of the entire document. A DOM solution would first have to parse the entire document and assemble it into a node tree before extracting the item elements. Listing 52-4 shows the `CreateQuoteFromDXLWithSAXLS` LotusScript agent, which parses the `DXLOutput.xml` document using the new LotusScript SAX classes.

> **Listing 52-4: Code for the CreateQuoteFromDXLWithSAXLS**
> **LotusScript Agent**

```
Declarations:
Dim CurrentElement As String
Dim CurrentItemName As String
Dim doc As NotesDocument
```

Continued

Listing 52-4 *(continued)*

```
Sub Initialize

    Dim session As New NotesSession
    Dim saxParser As NotesSAXParser
    Dim db As NotesDatabase
    Set db = session.CurrentDatabase
    Set doc = New NotesDocument(db)
    doc.Form="QuoteFromXML"

    Dim xml_in As NotesStream
    filename$ = "c:\temp\DXLOutput.xml"
    Set xml_in=session.CreateStream
    If Not xml_in.Open(filename$) Then
        Messagebox "Cannot open " & filename$,, "XML file error"
        Exit Sub
    End If
    If xml_in.Bytes = 0 Then
        Messagebox filename$ & " is empty",, "XML file error"
        Exit Sub
    End If

    Set saxParser=session.CreateSAXParser(xml_in)
    CurrentElement=""
    On Event SAX_StartElement From saxParser Call ReadFieldElements
    On Event SAX_Characters From saxParser Call ReadFieldCharacters
    On Event SAX_Warning From saxParser Call SAXException
    On Event SAX_Error From saxParser Call SAXException
    On Event SAX_FatalError From saxParser Call SAXException

    saxParser.Process

    Call doc.ReplaceItemValue( "CreationMethod", "From a DXL File via SAX
    Events in a LotusScript Agent" )
    Call doc.Save(True, False)

End Sub

Sub ReadFieldElements (Source As Notessaxparser,Byval elementname As
String, Attributes As NotesSaxAttributeList)
    If elementname="item" Then
        If Attributes.Length > 0 Then
            CurrentElement=elementname
            CurrentItemName = Attributes.GetValue("name")
        End If
    End If

End Sub
```

```
Sub ReadFieldCharacters (Source As Notessaxparser, Byval Characters As
String, Count As Long)
   If (CurrentElement ="item") Then
      Messagebox " Creating Item Name: "+CurrentItemName+" Item Value:
 "+Characters, MB_ICONINFORMATION
      Call doc.ReplaceItemValue( CurrentItemName, Characters )
   End If
End Sub

Sub SAXException (Source As Notessaxparser, Exception As NotesSaxException)
   Dim item As NotesItem
   Set item = doc.GetFirstItem( "ParseException" )
   If ( item Is Nothing ) Then
      Call doc.ReplaceItemValue( "ParseException" , Exception.Message    )
   Else
      Call item.AppendToTextList( Exception.Message )
   End If
   Messagebox "Exception - "+Exception.Message, MB_ICONINFORMATION
End Sub
```

You can tell from the first few lines of this agent that you're working with SAX 1, because of the implementation of the SAXParser class instead of the XMLReader class, contained in NotesSAXParser.

The next few lines set up a new Notes document in preparation for the DXL document that the agent is about to parse. Next, the agent checks to see whether the XML source file can be opened on the file system, and if the file is empty. If the file can be opened and contains an XML document, the XML document is assigned to the xml_in NotesStream.

```
Dim session As New NotesSession
Dim saxParser As NotesSAXParser
Dim db As NotesDatabase
Set db = session.CurrentDatabase
Set doc = New NotesDocument(db)
doc.Form="QuoteFromXML"

Dim xml_in As NotesStream
   filename$ = "c:\temp\DXLOutput.xml"
   Set xml_in=session.CreateStream
   If Not xml_in.Open(filename$) Then
      Messagebox "Cannot open " & filename$,, "XML file error"
      Exit Sub
   End If
   If xml_in.Bytes = 0 Then
      Messagebox filename$ & " is empty",, "XML file error"
      Exit Sub
   End If
```

The next code segment creates a new instance of the SAX parser and identifies the SAX events to capture for the parsing of a DXL document into a Domino document.

New Feature

The LotusScript NotesSAXParser class is new in Domino 6. NotesSAXParser parses XML documents using SAX events. The CreateSAXParser method of NotesSession creates a NotesSAXParser object.

Unlike the previous DOM example, SAX passes through a document only once and enables the developers to grab what they need as they go past XML document elements, attributes, and other XML document objects. The CurrentElement variable is an important part of the gathering process, as you'll see later in this code.

Next, the agent sets up five SAX events to watch for while the SAX parser processes the document. The StartElement event calls the ReadFieldElements subroutine. The Characters event calls the ReadFieldCharacters subroutine. The Characters event is called when the parser encounters any characters, which represent text values. All data represented by XML is text, so characters in the XML document that aren't in elements or attributes or some other type of XML construct are, by process of elimination, text values. The final three events catch any exceptions that may occur during parsing:

```
Set saxParser=session.CreateSAXParser(xml_in)
   CurrentElement=""
   On Event SAX_StartElement From saxParser Call ReadFieldElements
   On Event SAX_Characters From saxParser Call ReadFieldCharacters
   On Event SAX_Warning From saxParser Call SAXException
   On Event SAX_Error From saxParser Call SAXException
   On Event SAX_FatalError From saxParser Call SAXException

   saxParser.Process
```

The ReadFieldElements subroutine determines whether an element represents a DXL item, and if so, records the elementname, which is "item", and the value of the ItemName attribute.

```
Sub ReadFieldElements (Source As Notessaxparser,Byval elementname As
String, Attributes As NotesSaxAttributeList)
   If elementname="item" Then
      If Attributes.Length > 0 Then
         CurrentElement=elementname
         CurrentItemName = Attributes.GetValue("name")
      End If
   End If

End Sub
```

The ReadFieldCharacters subroutine uses the passed variable from the element event to determine whether the characters that triggered the Characters event are based on an item. As the SAX parser passes through the DXL document, the parser encounters the first DXL representation of an item:

```
<item name='QuoteKey'><textlist><text>HNEY-4V4HE8</text></textlist></item>
```

The agent encounters an element, which triggers the ReadFieldElements subroutine, which populates the CurrentElement and CurrentItemName variables. The parser then traverses through the nested <textlist> and <text> elements, doing nothing, until it encounters the characters after the <text> element. Now the ReadFieldCharacters subroutine is called, and because the CurrentElement has a value of item, a new field is added to the document called QuoteKey (the value of the `CurrentItemName` variable) with a value of the characters that triggered the character event. This process is repeated for the other DXL items represented in the DXL document.

```
Sub ReadFieldCharacters (Source As Notessaxparser, Byval Characters As
String, Count As Long)
   If (CurrentElement ="item") Then
      Messagebox " Creating Item Name: "+CurrentItemName+" Item Value:
"+Characters, MB_ICONINFORMATION
      Call doc.ReplaceItemValue( CurrentItemName, Characters )
   End If
End Sub
```

If there are any errors, the `SaxException` routine is called and the ParserException field on the Domino document is either created or appended to the text of the warning, error, or fatal error message.

```
Sub SAXException (Source As Notessaxparser, Exception As NotesSaxException)
   Dim item As NotesItem
   Set item = doc.GetFirstItem( "ParseException" )
   If ( item Is Nothing ) Then
      Call doc.ReplaceItemValue( "ParseException" , Exception.Message    )
   Else
      Call item.AppendToTextList( Exception.Message )
   End If
   Messagebox "Exception - "+Exception.Message, MB_ICONINFORMATION
End Sub
```

After the DXL document is parsed, the SAX parser process returns control to the `Initialize` subroutine, the hard-coded `CreationMethod` value is passed to the new Domino document, and the document is saved to the `XMLQuotes.nsf` database.

```
Call doc.ReplaceItemValue( "CreationMethod", "From a DXL File via SAX
Events in a LotusScript Agent" )
   Call doc.Save(True, False)
```

Parsing XML documents with DOM in a Java agent

The `CreateQuoteFromXMLWithDOMJava` agent is a close adaptation of the code in the `CreateQuoteFromXMLWithDOMLS` LotusScript agent shown in Listing 52-3, and performs the same function of parsing a simple XML document and creating a Domino document from the parsed data. This time, however, Java classes are used to illustrate techniques for parsing a DOM document using a Java agent.

> **Listing 52-5: Code for the CreateQuoteFromXMLWithDOMJava Agent**

```
import lotus.domino.*;
import java.io.*;
import com.ibm.xml.parsers.*;
import org.w3c.dom.*;
```

Continued

Listing 52-5 *(continued)*

```java
public class JavaAgent extends AgentBase {

    public String CurrentItemValue = "";
    public String CurrentItemName = "";
    public lotus.domino.Document doc;

  public void NotesMain() {

 try {

            Session session = getSession();
            AgentContext agentContext = session.getAgentContext();
            Database db = agentContext.getCurrentDatabase();
            doc = db.createDocument();
            DOMParser parser = new DOMParser();

            parser.parse("file:///c:/temp/DXLOutput.xml");

            org.w3c.dom.Document docNode = parser.getDocument();

            Node QuoteElementName = null;
            Node QuoteElementValue = null;

        NodeList list = docNode.getChildNodes();
          for (int i=0; i<list.getLength(); i++) {

          QuoteElementName = list.item(i);
            CurrentItemName = QuoteElementName.getNodeName();
        System.out.println(" Writing Name: "+CurrentItemName);

        QuoteElementValue = QuoteElementName.getFirstChild();
        CurrentItemValue = QuoteElementValue.getNodeValue();
        System.out.println(" Writing Value " + CurrentItemValue);

        System.out.println(" Creating Item Name: "+CurrentItemName+" Value: "
+ CurrentItemValue);
        doc.replaceItemValue( CurrentItemName, CurrentItemValue );

        QuoteElementName = QuoteElementName.getNextSibling();

        } //end for

            doc.replaceItemValue("Form", "QuoteFromXML");
            doc.replaceItemValue("CreationMethod", "From an XML File via
DOM in a Java Agent");
            doc.save();

        } //end try
```

```
catch(Exception e) {
        e.printStackTrace();
    }
  }
}
```

The first part of this agent imports the parser classes for the agent, defines several public strings, and then defines the `NotesMain` for the agent. `NotesMain` is the main method of the `AgentBase` class and contains all executable Domino agent code.

```
import lotus.domino.*;
import java.io.*;
import com.ibm.xml.parsers.*;
import org.w3c.dom.*;

public class JavaAgent extends AgentBase {

    public String CurrentItemValue = "";
    public String CurrentItemName = "";
    public lotus.domino.Document doc;

  public void NotesMain() {

 try {
```

The next code segment retrieves a `Session` and the associated `agentContext`, and then gets the `currentDatabase` and creates a new document in that database. Next, the `DOMParser` is defined and the file on the file system is parsed into a DOM node tree. It's best to use the full qualifying class name for the Domino Document class, because both `lotus.domino` and `org.w3c.dom` contain Document objects. The last line of this code segment creates a `NodeList` and counts the number of nested nodes in the DOM node tree. It is also used to refer to each node in the DOM tree.

```
            Session session = getSession();
            AgentContext agentContext = session.getAgentContext();
            Database db = agentContext.getCurrentDatabase();
            doc = db.createDocument();
            DOMParser parser = new DOMParser();

            parser.parse("file:///c:/temp/DXLOutput.xml");

            org.w3c.dom.Document docNode = parser.getDocument();

            Node QuoteElementName = null;
            Node QuoteElementValue = null;

        NodeList list = docNode.getChildNodes();
```

The preceding code collects the name of the element using `QuoteElementName.getNode Name()` and the value of the child node of the element using `QuoteElementName.getFirst Child().getNodeValue()`, represented by the `CurrentItemValue` variable. As with the LotusScript example, the next child node after an element is always the text value associated with the element, which looks like this in the original XML document:

```
<QuoteKey>  (QuoteElementName.getNodeName())
            HNEY-4V4HE8 (QuoteElementName.getFirstChild().getNodeValue())
</QuoteKey>
```

Now that the agent has both the field name and value, a field on the new Domino document can be populated. The siblings of the current node in the `NodeList` can then be processed until the agent runs out of nodes to process.

```
        for (int i=0; i<list.getLength(); i++) {

            QuoteElementName = list.item(i);
            CurrentItemName = QuoteElementName.getNodeName();
        System.out.println(" Writing Name: "+CurrentItemName);

        QuoteElementValue = QuoteElementName.getFirstChild();
        CurrentItemValue = QuoteElementValue.getNodeValue();
        System.out.println(" Writing Value " + CurrentItemValue);

        System.out.println(" Creating Item Name: "+CurrentItemName+" Value: "
+ CurrentItemValue);
        doc.replaceItemValue( CurrentItemName, CurrentItemValue );

        QuoteElementName = QuoteElementName.getNextSibling();

        } //end for
```

Next, the agent writes a text string containing the type of document creation to the CreationMethod field and saves the new Domino document.

```
            doc.replaceItemValue("Form", "QuoteFromXML");
            doc.replaceItemValue("CreationMethod", "From an XML File via
DOM in a Java Agent");
            doc.save();

        } //end try

catch(Exception e) {
        e.printStackTrace();
    }
  }
}
```

Parsing DXL documents with SAX in a Java agent

The next example is a Java conversion of the CreateQuoteFromDXLWithSAXLS LotusScript agent that parses DXL with SAX in Listing 52-4. Like the LotusScript example, the Java agent uses the Java SAX 1 classes to access the same DXL document on the local hard drive, but this time from a Java agent. Listing 52-6 shows the CreateQuoteFromDXLWithSAXJava Java agent.

Listing 52-6: Code for the CreateQuoteFromDXLWithSAXJava Java Agent

```java
import lotus.domino.*;
import java.io.*;
import org.xml.sax.*;
import org.xml.sax.helpers.ParserFactory;

public class JavaAgent extends AgentBase {

    public String CurrentElement = "";
    public String CurrentItemName = "";
    public lotus.domino.Document doc;

    public void NotesMain()  {

        try {
            Session session = getSession();
            AgentContext agentContext = session.getAgentContext();
            Database db = agentContext.getCurrentDatabase();
            doc = db.createDocument();
            doc.replaceItemValue("Form", "QuoteFromXML");

            org.xml.sax.Parser parser =
            ParserFactory.makeParser("com.ibm.xml.parsers.SAXParser");

            HandlerBase handlerbase = new HandlerBase()  {

                public void startElement(String elementname, AttributeList
                Attributes) {
                    if (elementname.equals("item")) {
                        if (Attributes.getLength() > 0) {
                            CurrentElement=elementname;
                            CurrentItemName = Attributes.getValue("name");
                        }
                    }
                }


                public void characters(char [] ch, int nStart, int nLength)
    {

                    try{
                        if (CurrentElement.equals("item")) {
                            String CurrentCharacters =   new
                            String(ch,nStart,nLength);
                            System.out.println("Creating Item Name:
                            "+CurrentItemName+" Value: "+ CurrentCharacters
                            );
```

Continued

Listing 52-6 *(continued)*

```
                        doc.replaceItemValue(CurrentItemName,
                        CurrentCharacters);
                }
            }
            catch (Exception e) {
                e.printStackTrace();
            }
        }

        public void error(SAXParseException saxparseexception)
        throws SAXException {
            try{
    System.out.println("Creating Exception: "+saxparseexception );
                doc.replaceItemValue("ParseException",
                saxparseexception);
                throw saxparseexception;
            }
            catch (Exception e) {
                e.printStackTrace();
            }
        }



        };

        parser.setDocumentHandler((DocumentHandler)handlerbase);
        parser.setErrorHandler((ErrorHandler)handlerbase);

        parser.parse("file:///c:/temp/DXLOutput.xml");

        doc.replaceItemValue("CreationMethod", "From a DXL File
        Events in a Java Agent");
        doc.save();

    } //end try

    catch (Exception e) {
        e.printStackTrace();
    }


}


}
```

Domino 6 agents use an implementation of SAX 1 parser in LotusScript and Java. You can tell from the first few lines of this agent that the agent is using SAX 1 because of the implementation of the SAXParser class, instead of the SAX 2 XMLReader interface.

The agent defines two public strings, one to track the current element, and one to track the current item name, which is extracted from a DXL element representing a Notes item. A `lotus.domino.Document` object is created and declared public, because `replaceItemValue` is used to add fields to the document different classes called by SAX events. It is recommended to specify the full class name for the Domino Document class because both the `org.xml.sax` and `lotus.domino` classes define a Document object.

```
import lotus.domino.*;
import java.io.*;
import org.xml.sax.*;
import org.xml.sax.helpers.ParserFactory;
public class JavaAgent extends AgentBase {

    public String CurrentElement = "";
    public String CurrentItemName = "";
    public lotus.domino.Document doc;

    public void NotesMain()  {
```

The agent creates a new session, gets the current database, and creates a new Domino Document object as part of that database, using the previously defined public document. A form name is specified for the document, and a new instance of the parser using the IBM XML4J `SAXParser` class is created. The XML4J `SAXParser` class provides access to the SAX parser via an implementation-independent interface. A new instance of the `HandlerBase` class is set up, which is part of the `org.xml.sax` interface, and is used to capture SAX events.

```
          Session session = getSession();
          AgentContext agentContext = session.getAgentContext();
          Database db = agentContext.getCurrentDatabase();
          doc = db.createDocument();
          doc.replaceItemValue("Form", "QuoteFromXML");

          org.xml.sax.Parser parser =
          ParserFactory.makeParser("com.ibm.xml.parsers.SAXParser");

          HandlerBase handlerbase = new HandlerBase()  {
```

The `startElement` class is called whenever the SAX parser encounters the start of an element in the DXL document. If the `elementname` is `"item"`, the value of the element is saved in the `CurrentElement` variable, and the `ItemName` attribute is saved in the `CurrentItemName` variable.

```
          public void startElement(String elementname, AttributeList
          Attributes) {
              if (elementname.equals("item")) {
                  if (Attributes.getLength() > 0) {
                      CurrentElement=elementname;
                      CurrentItemName = Attributes.getValue("name");
                  }
              }
          }
```

The characters class is called whenever the SAX parser encounters text values in the DXL document. The class uses the public variables that were assigned by the startElement class to determine whether the characters that triggered the Characters event are based on a DXL item. As with the LotusScript SAX example, when the SAX parser passes through the DXL document, the parser encounters the first DXL representation of an item, as shown in the following line of code:

```
<item name='QuoteKey'><textlist><text>HNEY-4V4HE8</text></textlist></item>
```

This triggers the startElement class, which populates the CurrentElement and CurrentItemName variables. The parser then traverses through the nested <textlist> and <text> elements, doing nothing, until it encounters the characters after the <text> element. The characters class is called, and because the CurrentElement is equal to item, a new field is added to the document called QuoteKey (the value of the CurrentItemName variable) with a value of the characters encountered. This process is repeated for the other DXL items represented in the DXL document. The try and catch in this class are required when using the replaceItemValue method of document, which may throw a NotesException.

```
public void characters(char [] ch, int nStart, int nLength)  {

                    try{
                        if (CurrentElement.equals("item")) {
                            String CurrentCharacters =    new
                            String(ch,nStart,nLength);
                            System.out.println("Creating Item Name:
                            "+CurrentItemName+" Value: "+ CurrentCharacters
                            );
                            doc.replaceItemValue(CurrentItemName,
                            CurrentCharacters);
                        }
                    }
                    catch (Exception e) {
                        e.printStackTrace();
                    }
                }
```

If there are any SAX errors in the Java agent, the error class is called and the ParserException field on the Domino document is either created or appended to the text of the warning, error, or fatal error message. As with the characters class, the try and catch in this class are required when using the replaceItemValue method of the document, which may throw a NotesException.

```
            public void error(SAXParseException saxparseexception)
throws SAXException {
                try{
          System.out.println("Creating Exception: "+saxparseexception );
                    doc.replaceItemValue("ParseException",
saxparseexception);
                    throw saxparseexception;
                }
                catch (Exception e) {
                    e.printStackTrace();
                }
            }
```

The DocumentHandler watches for the startElement, characters, and error SAX events. The DocumentHandler is attached to the parser, and the DXL document is set to be passed from the file system. After the DXL document is parsed, the agent writes a message into the CreationMethod field on the new Domino document explaining how this document was created. The document is then saved to the XMLQuotes.nsf database.

```
parser.setDocumentHandler((DocumentHandler)handlerbase);
        parser.setErrorHandler((ErrorHandler)handlerbase);

        parser.parse("file:///c:/temp/DXLOutput.xml");

        doc.replaceItemValue("CreationMethod", "From a DXL File via SAX
Events in a Java Agent");
        doc.save();
```

Summary

This chapter introduced the methods and tools for parsing XML documents. The following subjects were covered:

✦ Popular XML parsers

✦ The Document Object Model (DOM)

✦ The Simple API for XML (SAX)

✦ LotusScript and Java agents for parsing XML documents using DOM

✦ LotusScript and Java agents for parsing DXL documents using SAX

✦ Writing parsed XML document data to Domino documents

The next chapter discusses XSL transformations and shows several examples that change the structure of data from one XML document format to another, and also transformations from XML to HTML.

✦   ✦   ✦

Transforming XML with XSLT

By Brian Benz

In the last chapter, you discovered how to parse and assimilate XML and DXL data into Domino documents. This chapter covers tips and techniques for transforming XML documents into other XML formats and HTML using Extensible Stylesheet Language Transformation (XSLT).

Examples include writing LotusScript and Java agents that perform XSL transformations, tips for writing XSL stylesheets for Domino-generated data, how to integrate XSL transformations for added display flexibility, and using the DXL Transformer for transforming Domino design elements.

XSL stands for eXtensible Stylesheet language. The W3C XSL Transformation Recommendation document describes the process of applying an XSL stylesheet to an XML document using a transformation engine, and also specifies the XSL language covered in this chapter. XSLT is based on DSSSL (Document Style Semantics and Specification Language), which was originally developed to define SGML document output formatting. XSLT 1.0 became a W3C Recommendation in 1999, and the full specification is available for review at http://www.w3.org/TR/xslt.

The XSLT Recommendation should not be confused with the named Extensible Stylesheet Language (XSL) Version 1.0 Recommendation, which achieved W3C Recommendation status on 15 October 2001. This recommendation has more to do with XSL: Formatting Objects (XSL:FO) than XSL transformations (XSLT). The Extensible Stylesheet Language (XSL) version 1.0 Recommendation can be viewed at http://www.w3.org/TR/xsl/.

Another W3C Recommendation that affects XSLT is the XML Path Language (XPath). XPath is a tree-based representation model of an XML document that is used in XSLT to describe elements, attributes, text data and relative positions in an XML document. The full recommendation document can be seen at http://www.w3.org/TR/xpath.

Version 2.0 of XSLT and XPATH are currently in the W3C Recommendation process, and are expected to become final W3C Recommendations sometime in late 2003. The current documents and their status can be reviewed at http://www.w3.org/TR/xslt20req and http://www.w3.org/TR/xpath20req.

Transformation engines support a variety of programming languages, usually based on the language that they are developed in. At the time of this writing there is no comprehensive list of XSLT engines available, but the Open Directory Project provides a good overview at `http://dmoz.org/Computers/Data_Formats/Markup_Languages/XML/Style_Sheets/XSL/Implementations/`. Despite a multitude of XSLT engines supporting a multitude of languages, mainstream XSLT engines are split into two platform camps: Java and Microsoft.

One of the first Java transformation engines was the LotusXSL engine, which IBM donated to the Apache Software Group, where it became the Xalan Transformation engine. Since then, Apache has developed Xalan version 2, which implements a pluggable interface into Xalan 1 and 2, as well as integrated SAX and DOM parsers. Both Java versions of Xalan implement the W3C Recommendations of XSLT and XPath. More information on Xalan can be found at `http://xml.apache.org/xalan-j/index.html`.

Microsoft support for XML 1.0 and a reduced implementation of the W3C XSLT recommendation began with the MS Internet Explorer 5, which also supported the Document Object Model (DOM), XML namespaces and beta support for XML Schemas. XML and XSL functionality was extended in later browser versions and separated from the browser into the MSXML parser, more recently renamed the Microsoft XML Core Services. MSXML is for use in client applications, via Web browsers, Microsoft server products, and is a core component of the .NET platform.

How an XSL Transformation Works

Developers create code that identifies the XML source, the XSL stylesheet, and the output method and destination, and then call the XSLT engine to perform a transformation. The XSLT engine reads the source XML document and performs a transformation of the XML document based on instructions in the XSL stylesheet.

In the Domino world, the LotusScript and Java implementations of XSL processor code use the same method of passing an XML document, XSL stylesheet and output destination to an XSL processor, as you will see in our examples later in this chapter.

XSLT stylesheets are well-formed XML documents that conform to W3C syntax standards. XSLT namespaces are defined in the heading of an XSL document, along with any other namespaces that are used in the document. Output format is specified in the XSL document as well, and can be HTML, text, or XML.

XSL and XPath

XSLT is based on pattern matching. The `match` attribute of a `template` element can be used to match a pattern in an XML document, to detect the root element in an XML document (/), or the DXL document element (`dxl:document`), as shown in these two examples:

```
<xsl:template match="/">
<xsl:template match="dxl:document">
```

The `match` attribute is one of several XSLT pattern-matching attributes that are used to find nodes in an XML source document. Pattern matching is facilitated through XPath expressions, which refer to the parsed nodes of an XML document. XPath follows a syntax that closely mirrors file system paths, but in the context of an XML document. XPath tree representations break XML documents down into a series of connected root, element, text, attribute, namespace, processing instruction, and comment nodes.

Imagine that the XSLT processor parses a document and places each of the elements in the document into a directory on a file system, and defining attributes, namespaces, and text data in each directory with special identifiers. The new file system starts with the root directory (/), and each descendant element can be found in a subdirectory under the root. XPath doesn't work *exactly* like this, but on the surface it appears to, and the directory metaphor is a good point of reference for starting to understand how XPath really does work. Table 53-1 shows the basic location operators for XPath expressions:

Table 53-1: XPath Location Operators

Operator	Description
.	The current node
..	The parent node
/	The root element
//	All descendants
@	Attribute Identifier
*	All child nodes

The Location operators are actually abbreviations of commonly used XPath node axes. Node axes are expressions that relate to the current node and radiate out from that node in different directions, to locate parents, ancestors, children, descendants, and siblings, in relation to the current node. Table 53-2 lists and describes the XPath node axes:

Table 53-2: XPath Node Axes

Axis	Description
self	The current node.
ancestor	Ancestors, excluding the current node.
ancestor-or-self	The current node and all ancestors.
attribute	The attributes of the current node.
child	Children of the current node.
descendant	Descendants, excluding the current node.
descendant-or-self	The current node and all descendants.
following	The next node in the document order, including all descendants of the next node, and excluding the current node descendants and ancestors.
following-sibling	The next sibling node in the document order, including all descendants of the sibling node, and excluding the current node descendants and ancestors.
namespace	All namespace nodes of the current node.

Continued

Table 53-2 *(continued)*

Axis	Description
parent	The parent of the current node.
preceding	The previous node in the document order, including all descendants of the previous node, and excluding the current node descendants and ancestors.
preceding-sibling	The previous sibling node in the document order, including all descendants of the sibling node, and excluding the current node descendants and ancestors.

XPath axes, attributes, and namespaces

XPath axis nodes treat attributes and namespaces differently than they treat elements, text values, processing instructions and comments, depending on the axis and the current node. This is because attributes and namespaces in the document are not part of the hierarchy of elements, text values, processing instructions, and comments, but are located separately in the node tree.

✦ Attributes are only available from element nodes or the root node, not from other attribute and namespace nodes.

✦ The child, descendant, following, following-sibling, preceding, and preceding-sibling axes do not contain attributes or namespaces, and are empty if the current node is an attribute or a namespace node.

✦ Attributes of the current node can be accessed using the attribute axis or the attribute identifier (@), as long as the current node is an element node.

The example XSL stylesheet segment below creates a new element based on the name of an attribute in the XML document tree. For the purposes of this example, the current node is an attribute. XPath has limitations on what can be accessed if the current node is an attribute or Namespace. To get around this limitation, the XSLT name() function is used to pass the name of the current attribute node to the new element declaration. The XPath location operator representing the self node (.) is used to pass the value of the attribute into the value of the new element using the value-of select element, and then the new element is finished with a hard-coded closing tag:

```
<xsl:element name="{name()}">
    <xsl:value-of select="."/>
</xsl:element>
```

The name() function is one of many functions that can be used in Stylesheets. Unlike other types of XML, XPath supports five types of data representation, even though the data itself remains text.

✦ **Boolean objects:** True or false values

✦ **Numbers:** Any numeric value

✦ **Strings:** Any string

✦ **Node-sets:** A set of nodes selected by an XPath expression or series of expressions

✦ **External objects:** A set of nodes returned by an XSLT extension function other than an XPath or XSLT expression. Support for external objects depends on the XSLT processor support for extensions.

There are also several functions related to each data type that can be used in XSL Stylesheets. Table 53-3 describes the functions supported for each data type:

Table 53-3: Functions by data type

Function	Description
Boolean Functions	
boolean()	Convert an expression to the Boolean data type value and returns true or false.
true()	Binary true.
false()	Binary false.
not()	Reverse binary true or false. (not(true expression)=false, not(false expression)=true).
Number Functions	
number()	Convert an expression to a numeric data type value.
round()	Round a value up or down to the nearest integer. round(98.49) = 98, round(98.5) = 99.
floor()	Round a value down to the nearest integer. floor(98.9) = 98.
ceiling()	Round a value up to the nearest integer. ceiling(98.4) = 99.
sum()	Sum the numeric values in a node-set.
count()	Count the nodes in a node-set.
String Functions	
string()	Convert an expression to a string data type value.
format-number()	Convert a numeric expression to a string data type value, using the decimal-format element values as a guide if the decimal-format element is present in a Stylesheet.
concat()	Convert two or more expressions to a concatenated string data type value.
string-length()	Count the characters in a string data type value.
contains()	Check for a substring in a string. Returns Boolean true or false.
starts-with()	Check for a substring at the beginning of a string. Returns Boolean true or false.
translate()	Replace an existing substring with a specified substring in a specified string data type value.
substring()	Retrieve a substring in a specified string data type value starting at a numeric character position and optionally ending at a specified numeric length after the starting point.
substring-after()	Retrieve a substring of all characters in a specified string data type that occur after a numeric character position.

Continued

Table 53-3 *(continued)*

Function	Description
substring-before()	Retrieve a substring of all characters in a specified string data type that occur before a numeric character position.
normalize-space()	Replaces any tab, newline, and carriage return characters in a string data type value with spaces, then removes any leading or trailing spaces from the new string.
Node Set Functions	
current()	The current node in a single-node node-set.
position()	The position of the current node in a node-set.
key()	A node-set defined by the key element.
name()	The name of the selected node.
local-name()	The name of a node without a prefix, if a prefix exists.
namespace-uri()	The full URI of a node prefix, if a prefix exists.
unparsed-entity-uri()	The URI of an unparsed entity via a reference to the source document DTD, based on the entity name.
id()	A node-set with nodes that match the id value.
generate-id()	A unique string for a selected node in a node-set. The syntax follows well-formed XML rules.
lang()	A boolean true or false depending on if the xml:lang attribute for the selected node matches the language identifier provided in an argument.
last()	The position of the last node in a node-set.
document()	Builds a node tree from an external XML document when provided with a valid document URI.
external object functions	(Note: these functions may also apply to other data types)
system-property()	Returns information about the processing environment. Useful when building multi-version and multi-platform Stylesheets, in conjunction with the fallback element.
element-available()	A boolean true or false based on if a processing instruction or extension element is supported by the XSLT processor.
function-available()	A boolean true or false based on if a function is supported by the XSLT processor.

Now that you have the basic concepts of XSL, its building blocks, and syntax, you're ready to move on to some examples of XSL in Domino.

You can download all the examples from this chapter from the `www.wiley.com/ compbooks/benz` Web site. Installation instructions are included with the download. Note that the stylesheets and source XML documents have to be in the directories specified in the installation instructions for the examples to function properly.

Learning DXL Transformation Techniques

As mentioned earlier, XML has three basic output styles—other forms of XML, text, and HTML. This section shows you techniques for transforming XML, and specifically DXL, into other forms of XML and HTML.

All the examples use the same source XML file, which is a DXL document based on a quotation by Abraham Lincoln from the XMLQuotes.nsf database. The agents in Chapters 47 and 48 generated the sample DXL document. Listing 53-1 shows the DXL document, named `DXLOutput.xml`, which is referred to in the next few examples:

Listing 53-1: **The Contents of DXLOutput.xml**

```
<?xml version="1.0" encoding="utf-8"?>
<document xmlns="http://www.lotus.com/dxl" version="6.0"
replicaid="85256C6400115C34" form="Quote">
   <noteinfo noteid="1386"
   unid="C0C0F4484E0E948585256A180048197D" sequence="1">
      <created>
         <datetime>20010323T080731,17-05</datetime>
      </created>
      <modified>
         <datetime>20021031T220946,25-05</datetime>
      </modified>
      <revised>
         <datetime>20010323T080751,54-05</datetime>
      </revised>
      <lastaccessed>
         <datetime>20021031T220940,91-05</datetime>
      </lastaccessed>
      <addedtofile>
         <datetime>20021031T220940,91-05</datetime>
      </addedtofile>
   </noteinfo>
   <updatedby>
      <name>CN=Henry Newberry/O=Newbs</name>
   </updatedby>
   <item name="QuoteKey">
      <textlist>
         <text>HNEY-4V4HE8</text>
      </textlist>
```

Continued

Listing 53-1 *(continued)*

```
        </item>
        <item name="QDate">
            <textlist>
                <text>03/23/2001</text>
            </textlist>
        </item>
        <item name="QSource">
            <textlist>
                <text>Abraham Lincoln</text>
            </textlist>
        </item>
        <item name="Quote">
            <textlist>
                <text>No matter how much cats fight, there always
                seems to be plenty of kittens.- Abraham
                Lincoln</text>
            </textlist>
        </item>
        <item name="FormFields" summary="false">
            <textlist>
                <text/>
            </textlist>
        </item>
</document>
```

XML to XML

Transforming XML to other forms of XML is probably the second-most common type of transformation, after XML to HTML transformations. In this situation, you must know and identify the elements needed in the source and target of the transformation. This example uses the source DXL document to produce a smaller XML file. The DXL form name becomes the root element name for the new XML document. The DXL item elements are transformed into elements in the new XML document. The names for the transformed elements form the name attribute of each DXL item element. Listing 53-2 shows the code for the DXLtoXML.xsl stylesheet.

Listing 53-2: The Code for the DXLtoXML.xsl Stylesheet

```
<?xml version="1.0" encoding="UTF-8"?>
<xsl:stylesheet
xmlns:xsl="http://www.w3.org/1999/XSL/Transform"
version="1.0" xmlns:dxl="http://www.lotus.com/dxl">
<xsl:output doctype-system="XMLQuote.dtd"/>
```

```
<xsl:output method="xml"/>

<xsl:template match="/">
<xsl:apply-templates/>
</xsl:template>

<xsl:template match="dxl:document">
<xsl:element name="{@form}">
<xsl:apply-templates select="dxl:item">
</xsl:apply-templates>

</xsl:element>
</xsl:template>


<xsl:template match="dxl:item">
<xsl:element name="{@name}">
<xsl:value-of select="."/>
</xsl:element>
</xsl:template>

</xsl:stylesheet>
```

The stylesheet declares the XSL stylesheet as an XML document, because XSL is well-formed XML. After that, two namespaces are declared, one for the XSL elements in the stylesheet, and one for the DXL items in the source document.

```
<?xml version="1.0" encoding="UTF-8"?>
<xsl:stylesheet
xmlns:xsl="http://www.w3.org/1999/XSL/Transform"
version="1.0" xmlns:dxl="http://www.lotus.com/dxl">
```

The output is defined as XML, and XPath pattern matching is started at the root element. The XSL processor is then instructed to apply the template to all elements in the source document.

```
<xsl:output doctype-system="XMLQuote.dtd"/>
<xsl:output method="xml"/>
<xsl:template match="/">
<xsl:apply-templates/>
</xsl:template>
```

The next match deals with dxl:document, which is the equivalent of a Notes document in DXL. A new element is created using the XSL element command, and the name of the element is passed from the current value of the form attribute for the document element ({@form}), which is Quote. This provides the root element for the new XML document, based on the old DXL form name. The XSL processor is then instructed to select any items found on the source document and applies a template to them.

```
<xsl:template match="dxl:document">
<xsl:element name="{@form}">
<xsl:apply-templates select="dxl:item">
```

```
</xsl:apply-templates>

</xsl:element>
</xsl:template>
```

The item template creates an element for each item element in the original DXL document, and uses the value of the name attribute (`{@name}`) as the new element name. The text value associated with each item is passed to the new element using the `value-of select` command.

```
<xsl:template match="dxl:item">
<xsl:element name="{@name}">
<xsl:value-of select="."/>
</xsl:element>
</xsl:template>
```

Listing 53-3 shows the final transformation output, with a new XML document with elements based on attributes of the original DXL document.

Listing 53-3: **Transformation Output from DXLtoXML.xsl Stylesheet**

```
<?xml version="1.0" encoding="UTF-8"?>
<!DOCTYPE Quote SYSTEM "XMLQuote.dtd">
<Quote>
  <QuoteKey>HNEY-4V4HE8</QuoteKey>
  <QDate>03/23/2001</QDate>
  <QSource>Abraham Lincoln</QSource>
  <Quote>No matter how much cats fight, there always seems to
  be plenty of kittens.- Abraham Lincoln</Quote>
  <FormFields></FormFields>
</Quote>
```

XML to HTML

The next example is based on the `DXLtoHTML.xsl` stylesheet shown in Listing 53-4. In this example, the same DXL source document is transformed into an HTML document. In addition to knowing and identifying the elements needed in the source and target of the transformation, you also need the intended layout of the resulting HTML page. Listing 53-4 shows the code for the `DXLtoHTML.xsl` stylesheet.

Listing 53-4: **The Code for the DXLtoHTML.xsl Stylesheet**

```
<xsl:stylesheet
xmlns:xsl="http://www.w3.org/1999/XSL/Transform"
version="1.0" xmlns:dxl="http://www.lotus.com/dxl">
<xsl:output method="html"/>
```

```
<xsl:template match="/">
  <xsl:apply-templates/>
</xsl:template>

<xsl:template match="dxl:document">
  <html>
  <head><title>Output based on a DXL Form: <xsl:value-of
  select="@form"/></title></head>
  <body TEXT="000000" BGCOLOR="#000000">
  <font SIZE="3" COLOR="FFFFFF" FACE="Arial">
  <h2>Output based on a DXL Form: <xsl:value-of
  select="@form"/></h2>
  <table BGCOLOR="FFEFCE" cellpadding="3" cellspacing="5"
  WIDTH="100%" align="center">
  <font SIZE="2" COLOR="0000FF" FACE="Arial">

<xsl:apply-templates select="dxl:item">
  </xsl:apply-templates>
  </font>
  </table>
  </font>
  </body>
  </html>
</xsl:template>

<xsl:template match="dxl:item">
  <tr><td>
  <xsl:value-of select="@name"/>
  </td><td>
  <xsl:value-of select="."/>
  </td></tr>
</xsl:template>

</xsl:stylesheet>
```

As in the preceding example, the stylesheet starts by declaring the document as an XML document and defines the same two namespaces, one for the XSL elements in the stylesheet, and one for the DXL items in the source document. This time the output is specified as HTML, and XPath pattern matching starts at the same root element.

```
<xsl:stylesheet
xmlns:xsl="http://www.w3.org/1999/XSL/Transform"
version="1.0" xmlns:dxl="http://www.lotus.com/dxl">
<xsl:output method="html"/>

<xsl:template match="/">
  <xsl:apply-templates/>
</xsl:template>
```

This time the `dxl:document` match template creates an HTML head element. The window and Web page title are based on the original DXL form element's name attribute value. Next, a body element is created for the output page and cosmetic enhancements for fonts and colors are added to the body using HTML tags. Next, the columns and rows are filled with item element data in the next template.

```
<xsl:template match="dxl:document">
  <html>
  <head><title>Output based on a DXL Form: <xsl:value-of
  select="@form"/></title></head>
  <body TEXT="000000" BGCOLOR="#000000">
  <font SIZE="3" COLOR="FFFFFF" FACE="Arial">
  <h2>Output based on a DXL Form: <xsl:value-of
  select="@form"/></h2>
  <table BGCOLOR="FFEFCE" cellpadding="3" cellspacing="5"
  WIDTH="100%" align="center">
  <font SIZE="2" COLOR="0000FF" FACE="Arial">

  <xsl:apply-templates select="dxl:item">
  </xsl:apply-templates>
  </font>
  </table>
  </font>
  </body>
  </html>
</xsl:template>
```

The item template cycles through all the items in the DXL document and extracts the value of the name attribute and the text value. Table rows and columns are wrapped around each item name attribute and text value. The table is completed when the last item element is encountered in the source DXL document. After that, the table and the HTML tags are closed for the Web page.

```
<xsl:template match="dxl:item">
  <tr><td>
  <xsl:value-of select="@name"/>
  </td><td>
  <xsl:value-of select="."/>
  </td></tr>
</xsl:template>
```

Figure 53-1 shows the final transformation output, with an HTML document displaying items from the original DXL document.

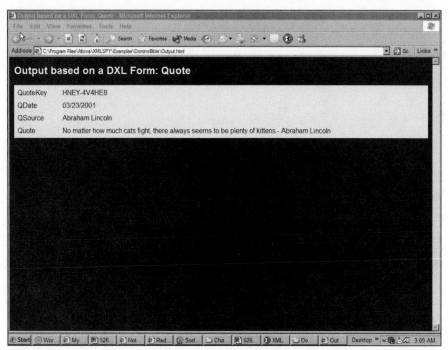

Figure 53-1: The final transformation output for the DXLtoHTML.xsl stylesheet, with an HTML document displaying items from the original DXL document

Using the DXL Transformer Utility

One of the easiest ways to perform DXL transformations in Domino Designer 6 is to use the DXL Transformer utility. Unfortunately, despite its simple functionality, the DXL Transformer is only available in Domino Designer for transforming DXL generated by design elements.

There is currently only one DXL stylesheet that ships with Domino. It's up to developers to create more for their own needs. The stylesheet, called REPORT-AllLSinForm.xsl, is a useful beginner's example of extracting data from DXL documents. It generates a display of all the LotusScript for a chosen Domino form. The stylesheet is located in the XSL directory under the data directory, on a Domino Designer client machine. If developers create their own stylesheets for Domino design objects, a copy should be located in the data/xsl/ directory so that the transformer utility can have access to the stylesheet.

To transform the XML for one or more design elements using the DXL Transformer utility, choose Tools⇨DXL Utilities⇨Transformer from the main menu, select an XSL file, and then select the method of output (Display or File). Figure 53-2 shows the DXL Transformer in action.

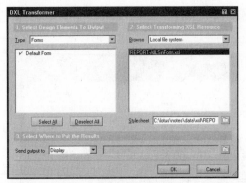

Figure 53-2: With the DXL Transformer, developers can select one or more design element sources, stylesheets, and output methods.

Using the LotusScript NotesXSLTransformer Class

NotesXMLTransformer is a new LotusScript class that transforms XML documents when provided with a source XML document, a stylesheet, and a destination. Listing 53-5 shows the code for the NotesXSLTransformerExample agent.

Four important things are happening in the following code. First three NotesStream objects are declared in the declarations of the agent, which are used to work with the DXL source file, the XSL stylesheet, and the destination XML output. After the objects are opened, the transformer reads from the DXLSource stream and writes to the XMLOut stream, using the stylesheet as a guide for the transformation. After the transformation is complete, a message box appears to the users telling them where they can find the output file.

Listing 53-5: Code for the NotesXSLTransformerExample Agent

```
Declarations:
Dim DXLSource As NotesStream
Dim StyleSheet As NotesStream
Dim XMLOut As NotesStream
Sub Initialize

    Dim session As New NotesSession

    Set DXLSource=session.CreateStream
    If Not     DXLSource.Open("c:\lotus\notes\data\ndbible\
xsl\DXLOutput.xml") Then
        Messagebox "Cannot open DXL Source File",,
        "c:\lotus\notes\data\ndbible\xsl\DXLOutput.xml"
        Exit Sub
    End If
    If DXLSource.Bytes = 0 Then
```

```
    Messagebox
    "c:\lotus\notes\data\ndbible\xsl\DXLOutput.xml does not
    exist or is empty",, "XML file error"
    Exit Sub
 End If

 Set StyleSheet=session.CreateStream
 If Not
StyleSheet.Open("c:\lotus\notes\data\ndbible\
xsl\DXLtoXML.xsl") Then
    Messagebox "Cannot open StyleSheet",,
    "c:\lotus\notes\data\ndbible\xsl\DXLtoXML.xsl"
    Exit Sub
 End If

 Set XMLOut=session.CreateStream
 If Not XMLOut.Open("c:\lotus\notes\data\ndbible\
xsl\DXLtoXMLResultLS.xml") Then
    Messagebox "Cannot Open Destination",,
    "c:\lotus\notes\data\ndbible\xsl\DXLtoXMLResultLS.xml"
    Exit Sub
 End If

 Dim transformer As NotesXSLTransformer
 Set transformer=session.CreateXSLTransformer(DXLSource,
 StyleSheet, XMLOut)
 transformer.Process
 Messagebox "Transform Complete",, "Results are in
 c:\lotus\notes\data\ndbible\xsl\DXLtoXMLResultLS.xml"

End Sub
```

Transforming DXL with Java

Like the preceding LotusScript agent example, the TransformXMLExample Java agent transforms DXL and XML documents when provided with a source XML document, a stylesheet,
and a destination. Listing 53-6 shows the code for the TransformXMLExample agent.

Listing 53-6: **Code for the TransformXMLExample Agent**

```
import org.apache.xalan.xslt.*;
import org.apache.xalan.*;
import lotus.domino.*;
import java.io.*;
```

Continued

Listing 53-6 *(continued)*

```java
public class TransformXMLExample extends AgentBase {

    public void NotesMain() {

        try {
            String DXLSource = "c:/lotus/notes/data/ndbible/
            xsl/DXLOutput.xml";
            String StyleSheet = "c:/lotus/notes/data/ndbible/
            xsl/DXLtoXML.xsl";

            XSLTInputSource DXLSourceIS = new
            XSLTInputSource(DXLSource);
            XSLTInputSource StyleSheetIS = new
            XSLTInputSource(StyleSheet);

            FileWriter fw = new
            FileWriter("c:\\lotus\\notes\\data\\ndbible\\xsl
            \\DXLtoXMLResultJava.xml");
            org.apache.xalan.xslt.XSLTResultTarget XMLOut =
            new org.apache.xalan.xslt.XSLTResultTarget(fw);

            XSLTProcessor XSLTransformer =
            XSLTProcessorFactory.getProcessor();

            XSLTransformer.process(DXLSourceIS, StyleSheetIS,
            XMLOut);

            System.out.println("Transform complete - results
            are in c:\\lotus\\notes\\data\\ndbible\\
            xsl\\DXLtoXMLResultJava.xml");
        }
        catch (Exception e) {
            e.printStackTrace();
        }
    }
}
```

The agent imports the `org.apache.xalan.xslt` classes to get the transformation job done. The `lotus.domino` package also contains XSLT classes, but these classes are deprecated in more recent versions of Xalan, so this agent references the Xalan base classes instead.

```java
import org.apache.xalan.xslt.*;
import org.apache.xalan.*;
import lotus.domino.*;
import java.io.*;

public class TransformXMLExample extends AgentBase {
```

```
public void NotesMain() {

    try {
```

As in the LotusScript example, the DXL source file, the XSL stylesheet, and the destination XML output are opened. The DXL input source and the stylesheet are specified as XSLTInputSources.

```
String DXLSource = "c:/lotus/notes/data/ndbible/
xsl/DXLOutput.xml";
String StyleSheet = "c:/lotus/notes/data/ndbible/
xsl/DXLtoXML.xsl";

XSLTInputSource DXLSourceIS = new
XSLTInputSource(DXLSource);
XSLTInputSource StyleSheetIS = new

XSLTInputSource(StyleSheet);
```

Next the `org.apache.xalan.xslt.XSLTResultTarget` is defined as the output destination. The full class path is listed in the package, because both `org.apache.xalan.xslt` and `lotus.domino` contain `XSLTResultTarget` classes.

```
FileWriter fw = new
FileWriter("c:\\lotus\\notes\\data\\ndbible\\xsl
\\DXLtoXMLResultJava.xml");
org.apache.xalan.xslt.XSLTResultTarget XMLOut =

new org.apache.xalan.xslt.XSLTResultTarget(fw);
```

After the XML document, the stylesheet and the output destination are defined, the agent creates an `XSLTProcessor` and instructs the processor to read from the `DXLSource` stream and write to the `XMLOut` stream using the stylesheet as a guide for the transformation.

```
XSLTProcessor XSLTransformer =
XSLTProcessorFactory.getProcessor();

XSLTransformer.process(DXLSourceIS, StyleSheetIS,

XMLOut);
```

After the transformation is complete, a message is sent to the Java console telling the users where they can find the output file.

```
System.out.println("Transform complete - results

are in c:\\lotus\\notes\\data\\ndbible\\

xsl\\DXLtoXMLResultJava.xml");
```

The Java TransformXML method

Another handy way to facilitate DXL and XML transformations in Java is the Domino `TransformXML` method. TransformXML can use a Notes item retrieved from an embedded object, item, or MIMEEntity as the DXL input source for the transformation, instead of a file. The Notes item does not have to be converted to a stream, unlike other types of XML source documents. The code for retrieving the input source from a rich text item instead of a file appears as follows:

```
Item DXLSource = StyleDoc.getFirstItem("Body");
if (DXLSource == null) System.out.println(
"DXL Source is null!");
XSLTResultTarget XMLOut = new XSLTResultTarget();

XMLOut.setFileName("c:\\lotus\\notes\\data\\ndbible\\xsl\\DXL
toXMLResultJava.xml");
                xml.transformXML(StyleSheetIS, XMLOut);
```

Summary

This chapter provided an introduction to XSL, including:

✦ XSL Stylesheets

✦ XSLT functions

✦ XPath

✦ Transforming DXL to XML

✦ Transforming DXL to HTML

✦ Using the DXL Transformer utility

✦ Using the LotusScript NotesXSLTransformer class

✦ Using Xalan in a Java agent

✦ Transforming DXL with Java using the TransformXML method

The next chapter puts all the lessons you've learned about XML, XML parsing, and transformations to use on the client side with JavaScript. The chapter shows you how to create interactive XML data islands on Web pages.

✦   ✦   ✦

XML Data Islands

By Brian Benz

This chapter combines many of the previous XML, XSL, JavaScript, and DHTML examples to show you how to use the Microsoft MSXML parser and Domino design elements to create JavaScript-based XML parsing and XSL transformation.

You use MSXML parsing and transformation features to create a Web page that gathers DXL from a view via the `?ReadViewEntries` command, transforms the data, parses the data into a table, and then adds buttons to the top of the page to facilitate client-side sorting of the data.

Introducing XML Data Islands

A *data island* describes tagged data embedded on an HTML page. The data can be physically embedded into the HTML, added to the page using a reference to an XML page with a `src=` attribute (just like an image), or loaded onto the page using JavaScript XMLDOM and XML-HTTP ActiveX objects. This chapter includes examples of using the most common method, loading an XMLDOM ActiveX object via JavaScript.

User interface-related XML tasks, such as XML filtering and sorting, are more efficient when processed on the client, where the user interface resides. This takes pressure off organizational networks and servers as well, in the same way that client-side JavaScript data validation for forms provides better performance for users, networks and servers. The downside is that developers usually have to rely on running JavaScript in an unknown and uncontrollable client environment.

As mentioned in previous JavaScript chapters, you must be aware that despite Mozilla and Navigator 6.0 advances in client-side DHTML and XML handling, the JavaScript and client-side XML and XSL examples in this chapter work most reliably on Microsoft Internet Explorer browser clients.

The Microsoft XML Core Services

Microsoft XML Core Services (formerly known as the Microsoft XML Parser, which is a little closer to the MSXML acronym) is shipped at no charge with Internet Explorer 5 and up. However, for the example in this chapter, developers will need the MSXML 4.*x* parser from Microsoft, which began shipping with IE 6. The separate MSXML Dynamic Link Library (DLL) can be downloaded for free and added to browsers without requiring a full browser upgrade. For developers who are unsure which version they have on their machines, Microsoft provides a free utility for verifying MSXML installation and checking the version of the install. The tool can be downloaded from `http://support.microsoft.com/default.aspx?scid=KB;en-us;q278674`, and the latest MSXML version can be downloaded from `http://msdn.microsoft.com/library/default.asp?url=/nhp/default.asp?contentid=28000438`.

The DXLDataIslandExample Page

All of the examples contained in this chapter, including the `XMLQuotes.nsf` database, XSL stylesheets, and source XML documents, can be downloaded from the `www.wiley.com/compbooks/benz` Web site, in the Downloads section. See the ndbible Web site for installation instructions. The database design and contents is reused with permission of the original owners, Newbs Consulting and Sapphire Oak Technologies. The original Quote of the Day Domino database that `XMLQuotes.nsf` is based on can be downloaded from the downloads section of either `www.sapphireoak.com` or `www.newbsconsulting.com`. This chapter uses the MSXML 4 parser to load a DXL representation of a view into an HTML page, and then transform the DXL into something more digestible for client-side parsing and transforming. The examples include a generic stylesheet that transforms DXL entry data elements and attributes into simple nested XML elements. Next, techniques are shown for parsing XML data into a table that can be sorted by a second XSL stylesheet. Figure 54-1 shows the final result in the DXLDataIslandExample page of the `XMLQuotes.nsf` database.

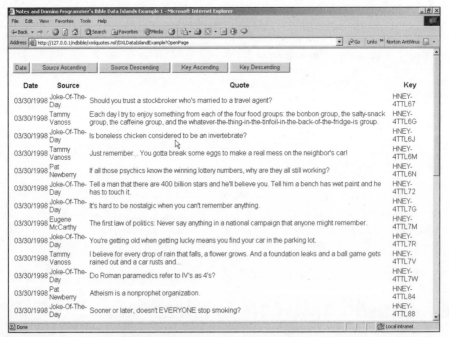

Figure 54-1: The DXLDataIslandExample page of the XMLQuotes.nsf database, with buttons for client-side data island sorting

Creating a data island using JavaScript and MSXML

The HTML page shown in Figure 54-1 calls the getTransformedXML() JavaScript function via the page's onLoad event. The getTransformedXML() function and two deceptively small XSL stylesheets contain most of the functionality for this example. The getTransformedXML() function in shown in its entirety, and then broken down in segments so that each step can be reviewed in more detail. Listing 54-1 shows the code for the getTransformedXML() function.

Listing 54-1: **The Code for the getTransformedXML() Function**

```
var dxlDoc;
var xslSheet;
var transformedXML;
var sortSheet;
var strResult;

function getTransformedXML()
    {

    dxlDoc = new ActiveXObject
    ("Msxml2.FreeThreadedDOMDocument.4.0");
    dxlDoc.async = false;
    loadSuccess = dxlDoc.load
    ("Quotes+Export?ReadViewEntries&PreFormat");

    xslSheet = new ActiveXObject
    ("Msxml2.FreeThreadedDOMDocument.4.0");
    xslSheet.async = false;
    loadSuccess = xslSheet.load("DXLViewtoXML.xsl");

    sortSheet = new ActiveXObject
    ("Msxml2.FreeThreadedDOMDocument.4.0");
    sortSheet.async = false;
    loadSuccess = sortSheet.load("SortXML.xsl");
    sortSheet.setProperty("SelectionNamespaces",
    "xmlns:xsl='http://www.w3.org/1999/XSL/Transform'");
    transformedXML= new
    ActiveXObject("Msxml2.FreeThreadedDOMDocument.4.0");
    dxlDoc.transformNodeToObject(xslSheet, transformedXML);

    NodeList = transformedXML.documentElement.childNodes;

    var vHTML = "<table border=0><tr><thead><th>Date</th>
    <th>Source</th><th>Quote</th><th>Key</th></thead>";

    for (var i=0; i<NodeList.length; i++) {

        ChildList = NodeList.item(i).childNodes
            for (var j=0; j<ChildList.length; j++) {
                Child = ChildList.item(j);
```

Continued

Listing 54-1 *(continued)*

```
                vHTML += "<td>" + Child.text + "</td>";
            }
        vHTML += "</tr>";
    }
    transformedXMLOutput.innerHTML = vHTML;
}
```

As mentioned earlier, the XML Island code makes heavy use of the Microsoft XML Core Services XMLDOM ActiveX object. The rest of the code looks deceptively short and simple, but there are many moving parts lurking under the surface. The next two sections go through each segment of code and get into the details of what's happening on the page.

Retrieving view data using the ?ReadViewEntries URL command

The first thing the Domino page does when it is opened is load the DXL for the Quotes Export view from the XMLQuotes.nsf database into an XML data island on the HTML page by creating a new ActiveX object.

```
dxlDoc = new ActiveXObject
("Msxml2.FreeThreadedDOMDocument.4.0");
dxlDoc.async = false;
loadSuccess = dxlDoc.load
("Quotes+Export?ReadViewEntries&PreFormat");
```

The DXL contents of the view are loaded into the dxlDoc object on the page. The async property is set to false, which means that JavaScript execution is paused until the data is loaded. This does not represent a noticeable delay and saves developers from having to write code to check and see whether a data island has completed population before something is done with the data. In this case, you're transforming the data after the dxlDoc object loads, so it's best to wait for the object to complete loading instead of taking the chance on generating transform errors on an incomplete DXL view.

You also use the &PreFormat URL command parameter on the view data, which returns all data as text in the dxlDoc object. This is ideal for converting to a simpler XML data format later.

Loading the DXL to XML and the sorting stylesheets

The next step is to load each of two XSL stylesheets: The first sheet, represented by the xslSheet object, transforms data from DXL view data to a much more simple XML format. The second stylesheet, represented by the sortSheet object, facilitates client-side sorting of data island data. The sorting mechanism is reviewed later; the next section takes a look at how the DXL to XML transformation takes place.

```
xslSheet = new ActiveXObject
("Msxml2.FreeThreadedDOMDocument.4.0");
xslSheet.async = false;
loadSuccess = xslSheet.load("DXLViewtoXML.xsl");

sortSheet = new ActiveXObject
("Msxml2.FreeThreadedDOMDocument.4.0");
sortSheet.async = false;
loadSuccess = sortSheet.load("SortXML.xsl");
```

Transforming a DXL View to an XML Data Island

After the page loads the XML data island source and the XSL stylesheets, the next step is to transform the DXL in the `dxlDoc` object into XML using the `xslSheet` stylesheet. To facilitate this, the JavaScript function creates a new object called `transformedXML`, and you use the `transformNodeToObject` method of the `XMLDomNode` class to apply the `xslSheet` object and create the new XML document.

```
transformedXML= new
ActiveXObject("Msxml2.FreeThreadedDOMDocument.4.0");
dxlDoc.transformNodeToObject(xslSheet, transformedXML);
```

The document is rebuilt and child nodes are replaced. The XML transformation can also be sent to a stream, but you're using it on the page, so replacing the `transformedXML` object is best.

The DXLViewtoXML stylesheet facilitates the transformation. The contents are shown in Listing 54-2.

The elements in the DXLViewtoXML stylesheet start at the root `viewentries` element and add a new root element for the XML document, called "`Quotes.`" Next the stylesheet traverses the DXL view document until it gets to the `viewentry` element. The `viewentry` element is replaced by the `QuoteEntry` element in the new XML document. All the `entrydata` elements under the `viewentry`, which represent the columns in a view, are replaced with simple elements that use the `entrydata` name attribute as the element name and pass the `entrydata` value as the value of the new element.

Cross-Reference   For more information on XSL transformations, refer to Chapter 53.

Listing 54-2: The DXLViewtoXML Stylesheet

```
<?xml version="1.0" encoding="UTF-8"?>
<xsl:stylesheet xmlns:xsl="http://www.w3.org/1999/XSL/Transform"
version="1.0">
  <xsl:output method="xml"/>
  <xsl:template match="/viewentries">
    <xsl:element name="Quotes">
      <xsl:apply-templates/>
    </xsl:element>
  </xsl:template>
  <xsl:template match="viewentry">
    <xsl:element name="QuoteEntry">
      <xsl:apply-templates select="entrydata">
</xsl:apply-templates>
    </xsl:element>
  </xsl:template>
  <xsl:template match="entrydata">
    <xsl:element name="{@name}">
      <xsl:value-of select="."/>
    </xsl:element>
  </xsl:template>
</xsl:stylesheet>
```

Here's the first view row in the original Quotes Export view DXL:

```
<?xml version="1.0" encoding="UTF-8"?>
<viewentries toplevelentries="1057">
  <viewentry position="1"
  unid="06D70500B19F244C852565D7004FD4C7" noteid="94A"
  siblings="1057">
          <entrydata columnnumber="0" name="Date">
              <text>03/30/1998</text>
          </entrydata>
          <entrydata columnnumber="1" name="QSource">
              <text>Joke-Of-The-Day</text>
          </entrydata>
          <entrydata columnnumber="2" name="Quote">
              <text>Should you trust a stockbroker
              who&apos;s married to a travel agent?</text>
          </entrydata>
          <entrydata columnnumber="3" name="QuoteKey">
              <text>HNEY-4TTL67</text>
          </entrydata>
  </viewentry>............
```

And here's what the same data looks like after being transformed to a simpler XML format:

```
<?xml version="1.0" encoding="UTF-8"?>
<Quotes>
  <QuoteEntry>
          <Date> 03/30/1998</Date>
          <QSource> Joke-Of-The-Day</QSource>
          <Quote> Should you trust a stockbroker who's married
          to a travel agent?</Quote>
          <QuoteKey> HNEY-4TTL67</QuoteKey>
  </QuoteEntry>...........
```

Parsing Data Island Data into a Table

After the data is modified into a much more readable format, it can be parsed into a table and displayed onscreen. The following code parses the transformed data into nodes, which are then nested in table rows and columns.

```
NodeList = transformedXML.documentElement.childNodes;

    var vHTML = "<table border=0><tr><thead><th>Date</th>
    <th>Source</th><th>Quote</th><th>Key</th></thead>";

    for (var i=0; i<NodeList.length; i++) {

        ChildList = NodeList.item(i).childNodes
          for (var j=0; j<ChildList.length; j++) {
              Child = ChildList.item(j);
              vHTML += "<td>" + Child.text + "</td>";
          }
        vHTML += "</tr>";
```

```
        }
        transformedXMLOutput.innerHTML = vHTML;
    }
```

After the data is parsed into HTML table format, it is passed to the `transformedXMLOutput` DIV tag on the screen for display.

Cross-Reference   For more information on DIV tags and their uses, refer to Chapter 41.

Linking XSL with Domino page design elements

At this point the data is transformed and parsed into the XML data island, yet the output looks — well, it looks just like output from a very basic Domino HTML view. But there's a reason for all of this trouble of creating, transforming, and parsing the XML data island — to facilitate client-side sorting of the data island output. Before getting to that, you need to add some elements to the Domino page to make sorting work. In this case, you need five buttons and another JavaScript function in the JSHeader.

Figure 54-2 shows the DXLDataIslandExample page in Domino Designer, with the button for sorting added at the top.

Of course, it would be great if just adding the buttons made the XML data sortable, but you still have some work to do before the example is fully functional.

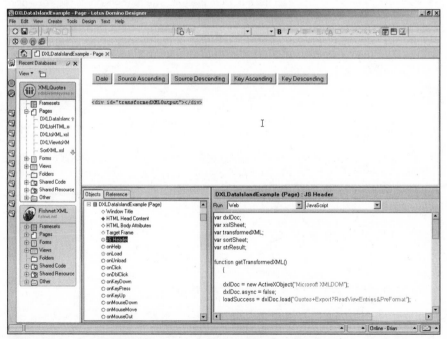

Figure 54-2: The DXLDataIslandExample page in Domino Designer

Sorting Data Islands Using JavaScript and XSL

The five buttons along the top of the DXLDataIslandExample page call the JavaScript sort function and pass parameters with instructions on how to sort the data island data. Here are the Date, Source Ascending, and Source Descending buttons in JavaScript code:

```
sort('Date', 'ascending')
sort('QSource', 'ascending')
sort('QSource', 'descending')
```

Listing 54-3 shows the sort function, which is added to the JSHeader of the DXLDataIslandExample page.

At the time that this chapter is being written, there is a quirk in the MSXML parser that requires a property be set for the xsl: namespace before sorting can be done. This should be fixed in a future MSXML parser version 4.x and up. If you are getting an error that says "Reference to undeclared namespace prefix: 'xsl'", you need to add the following line to your JavaScript code. Place it just after the declaration of the stylesheet that sorts the XML island data:

```
sortSheet.setProperty("SelectionNamespaces",
"xmlns:xsl='http://www.w3.org/1999/XSL/Transform'");
```

This code adds the xsl: namespace prefix to the MXSML rendering of the stylesheet.

The sort function passes the parameters from the JavaScript button code, which becomes the strSortBy and strOrder variables in the function. The function calls the sortSheet stylesheet and the selectSingleNode method of the XMLDOMNode class, which returns the first node that matches the value passed by the Sort button. Next, the code assigns the nodeValue for the XML element and the sort method (ascending or descending), and transforms the data using the transformNode method of the XMLDOMNode class.

Listing 54-3: **The JavaScript sort Function**

```
function sort(strSortBy, strOrder) {

    var objSelect = sortSheet.selectSingleNode
    ("//xsl:sort/@select");
    var objOrder = sortSheet.selectSingleNode
    ("//xsl:sort/@order");

    objSelect.nodeValue = strSortBy;
    objOrder.nodeValue = strOrder;

    strResult = transformedXML.transformNode(sortSheet);

    transformedXMLOutput.innerHTML = strResult;
}
```

Cross-Reference For more information on JavaScript functions and events, refer to Chapter 40.

The transformation is based on the SortXML stylesheet, which is shown in Listing 54-4.

Listing 54-4: The SortXML Stylesheet

```
<?xml version="1.0" encoding="UTF-8"?>
<xsl:stylesheet xmlns:xsl=http://www.w3.org/1999/XSL/Transform
version="1.0">
  <xsl:template match="/">
    <html>
      <head>
        <title>Notes and Domino Programmer's Bible Data
        Islands Example 1</title>
      </head>
      <body>
        <table border="0" cellpadding="10">
          <tr>
            <th align="left">Date</th>
            <th align="left">Quote Source</th>
            <th align="left">Quote</th>
            <th align="left">Quote Key</th>
          </tr>
          <xsl:apply-templates select="/Quotes/QuoteEntry">
            <xsl:sort select="Date" order="ascending"/>
          </xsl:apply-templates>
        </table>
        <p/>
      </body>
    </html>
  </xsl:template>
  <xsl:template match="QuoteEntry">
    <tr>
      <td>
        <xsl:value-of select="Date"/>
      </td>
      <td>
        <xsl:value-of select="QSource"/>
      </td>
      <td>
        <xsl:value-of select="Quote"/>
      </td>
      <td>
        <xsl:value-of select="QuoteKey"/>
      </td>
    </tr>
  </xsl:template>
</xsl:stylesheet>
```

The SortXML stylesheet is a rough sketch of the DXLDataIslandExample page, laid out in an XSL stylesheet. The top half of the code sets up the HTML page title, the fonts and layouts via an embedded stylesheet, and a default display if none is specified for page loading.

When the JavaScript `sort` function calls this stylesheet, it sets the `nodeValue` for the XML element, which can be Date, Source, Quote, or QuoteKey, and the `sort` method, which is ascending or descending. After these default nodes are set, the transformation result pivots around the default notes and produces a sorted XML document, which is rewritten to the `transformedXMLOutput` DIV tag.

Summary

This is the last Chapter in the XML Part of this book, and the examples bring together many of the lessons learned so far together into a single solution:

✦ Techniques for combining XML, XSL, JavaScript, and DHTML

✦ Working with the MSXML parser

✦ Creating an XML data island from Domino design elements

✦ Working with XML data islands

✦ Using JavaScript XML parsing and XSL transformation

In the next chapter and the next part of the book, you'll get into one of the hottest technologies and the most interesting applications of XML around today — Web Services. In Part XI, you learn how to leverage Domino as a Web Service provider and how to use the Notes client as a practical and useful Web Services client.

✦　　✦　　✦

Web Services

Web Services Introduction

By Brian Benz

Web Services are service-oriented, component-based, self-describing applications that are based on an architecture of emerging standards. This chapter introduces Web Services and how they relate to Domino applications, starting with the basic concepts of Web Services architecture; Simple Object Access Protocol (SOAP), Web Services Description Language (WSDL), and Universal Description, Discovery and Integration (UDDI).

Web Services are a method of integrating data and applications via W3C-compliant XML formats across computing platforms and operating systems. Web Service-enabled applications make calls and send responses to each other using a standardized XML document format called Simple Object Access Protocol (SOAP). Web Services are described to Web Service clients and other server applications by using another standard XML format called Web Services Description Language (WSDL), which is associated with all W3C-compliant Web Services. A description and location of your Web service can be published to a Universal Description, Discovery and Integration (UDDI) registry.

A good place to see where Web Services are and where they're going is the Xmethods Web site, at `www.xmethods.com`. Xmethods is a Yahoo!-like hierarchical directory of Web Services available on the Web, along with some great beginner tutorials and examples.

The logical place to navigate Web Services is a UDDI registry's Web site, but the current UDDI sites can be somewhat inscrutable for the Web Services newbie. The listing of Web Service examples at Xmethods range from simple temperature or flight status call-and-response applications, to complex, multilayer, looping, and brokered services.

The promise of Web Services is not in simple or even complex call-and-response applications. The practical applications that are emerging tend to feature several Web services that appear as though they function together as a single entity. Each individual Web Service can access many types of data on several disparate software platforms and operating systems. The Web service client, or a client proxy, is used to connect the services together into one specialized user interface.

Most readers, for example, have probably had the experience of booking a flight or renting a car or hotel room on a Web site. The promise of Web Services is to take this common task and extend the experience via a smart client and Web Services to coordinate your flight booking with simultaneous hotel and car bookings, based on pre-defined preferences and expense limits. You could then update a calendar and expense-tracking system with final booking data. On the day of travel, a smart Web Services client could notify the traveler of any flight delays or schedule changes. All the data would be incorporated in several back-end and client systems and coordinated by the smart client. Web Services and related emerging technologies promise this kind of seamless functionality, and they are starting to deliver.

Web Services Standards

The specifications for the main building blocks of Web Services are still in development, even though most of the technologies and specifications are based on W3C (World Wide Web Consortium) standards. Several organizations are working on the development of these specifications, hopefully with backward compatibility for the existing components that make up many of today's core Web Services.

The organization that's grabbing most of the attention these days is the Web Services Interoperability Organization (WS-I). WS-I is an industry organization that represents most of the major Web Service players, including Oracle, IBM, Microsoft, BEA Systems, and most recently, SUN. Their charter is to provide Web Services interoperability (hence the name) across platforms, applications, and programming languages.

Aside from providing a forum to hammer out compatibility and standards, several WS-I deliverables may be of interest to Web Service developers:

✦ Profiles are sets of specifications that work together to support specific solutions, such as design patterns. Profiles outline best practices in Web Services standards rather than application architectures.

✦ Sample implementations are team-assembled test applications based on profiles. They provide valuable documentation on performance and functionality flashpoints.

✦ Implementation guidelines are a result of the sample implementations, which are based on profiles. Implementation guidelines can be based on W3C recommendations or on other Web Service-related topics. They aren't specifications per se, but more like best practices developed by documenting sample implementations.

✦ Sniffer and analyzer tools are for monitoring and logging Web Service interaction. The sniffer runs at runtime and produces a log file that the analyzer reads. The sniffer and analyzer produce results that are based on implementation guidelines.

You can find more information about the WS-I and its deliverables at www.ws-i.org/.

Most of the current efforts and implementations at the WS-I are based on specifications being developed by the World Wide Web Consortium (W3C). The WS-I cooperates with the W3C on developing the SOAP, WSDL, and related specifications. The W3C publishes a Web Services activity statement at www.w3c.org/2002/ws/Activity. The document describes all the Web Service-related initiatives at the W3C, including the XML protocol, Web Services architecture, Web Services description, and Web Services choreography working groups. W3C Working groups are where the W3C recommendations are produced.

Most developers are surprised when they learn that UDDI registry specifications are not controlled by the W3C. They are managed and developed by the UDDI project, which is a part of the Organization for the Advancement of Structured Information Standards (OASIS). OASIS is a non-profit e-business industry consortium that influences Web standards. While UDDI registry development is separated from the W3C and the WS-I, the UDDI registry is based on W3C standards. UDDI registries are actually W3C compliant Web services. More information about OASIS can be found at `www.oasis-open.org`, and the UDDI project home page is located at `www.uddi.org`.

Despite the individual efforts of the W3C, WS-I and UDDI project, the groups work together when possible. The WS-I provides implementation testing and support for applications based on emerging specifications, whereas the W3C and UDDI projects provide specifications, which are often extended and updated by the efforts of the WS-I deliverables.

Web Services Building Blocks

Now that you have an understanding of what Web Services are and where they come from, it's time to review the SOAP, WSDL, and UDDI building blocks that are currently in development. The next three chapters cover these building blocks in more detail, but the following sections review the basic concepts.

SOAP (Simple Object Access Protocol)

SOAP is a messaging format that describes XML data according to W3C standards, and represents call and response data in an envelope and message format. You can view the current W3C specification-in-progress at `www.w3.org/TR/SOAP/`.

Domino developers can compare a basic SOAP structure to a Domino mail memo. SOAP documents are XML documents that contain an envelope. The envelope contains a description of the contents of a message (but not the message). Envelopes also contain serialization (encoding) rules for application-defined data types (represented as text serializations of data according to XML specifications), and optional remote procedure call (RPC) formats for server method calls and responses. SOAP can be sent and received using HyperText Transfer Protocol (HTTP) and Simple Mail Transfer Protocol (SMTP).

WSDL (Web Services Description Language)

WSDL, which is based on the W3C XML standard, describes what Web Services are, what they do, and how they can be accessed. All W3C standard Web Services are described in an associated WSDL document. WSDL can be complicated and verbose, but it enables clients or other Web Services to develop or adapt application interfaces based on WSDL document specifications. Several tools currently exist that enable developers to create a client and/or server interface to a Web Service by parsing a service's WSDL and automatically building code to handle calls and responses to the Web Service. These tools include the IBM Web Services Tool Kit (WSTK) for Java, as well as several tools from Microsoft for Windows and .NET applications.

Most of these tools create and adapt a proxy class from WSDL. The proxy class can act as a client interface from an application to the Web Service. A proxy class manages SOAP calls and responses to and from the client or another Web Service via the generated classes. The Web Services activity group at the W3C is currently developing WSDL. You can see the working draft of the specification at `www.w3.org/TR/2002/WD-wsdl12-20020709/`.

Universal Description, Discovery and Integration

Universal Description, Discovery and Integration (UDDI) is the directory standard for Web Services, developed and maintained by the UDDI project, which is a part of the Organization for the Advancement of Structured Information Standards (OASIS) and not part of the W3C. No auto-indexing or discovery features exist as are common with Web-crawler search engines for HTML pages on the Web. Each Web Service and provider must be manually registered on a UDDI server, either at one of the current UDDI Web sites, or via a UDDI registry Web Service client. Currently, IBM, Microsoft, SAP, and NTT Telecom host versions of the UDDI directory, which are kept in sync via replication. You can find URLs for registry sites, as well as the latest version of the UDDI specification, at http://uddi.org/.

At this stage in Web Service development, public UDDI registries are not as universally popular as private UDDI registries. Private UDDI registries are used by organizations and partners to internally publish Web Services for a select audience. Public registry entries are available to be viewed by anyone with access to the public registry. For security and technical reasons, many organizations are reluctant to post UDDI registry entries for public viewing.

Understanding Web Services Architecture

Due to the developing nature of the Web Services specification and community, vendors such as IBM, and organizations such as the WS-I have developed several Web Services architectures and published specifications. The most advanced and complete architecture for general Web Services based on current W3C recommendations are contained in a publication developed by the W3C Web Services architecture working group. The full publication is available at www.w3.org/2002/ws/arch/.

Basic Web Services architecture

Basic Web Services are applications that employ standard specifications for SOAP, WSDL, and UDDI to exchange messages, describe Web Services, and publish Web Service descriptions. The official term for applications that handle Web Services is *agents*. Agents can be consumers or servers of a Web Service, but consumers must be able to find descriptions of Web Services via WSDL associated with a Web Service provider agent.

Added to the mix is the role of the service discovery agency, which uses UDDI to publish registered Web Services to Web Service consumers, much like a real estate agency puts buyers and sellers together for homes (but without the commission — yet). The concept is that a consumer finds a Web Service they need at a service discovery agency, follows the registration information to the service location, and then accesses the service according to instructions in the published WSDL document. Figure 55-1 shows the layout of a basic Web Service architecture, including an optional service discovery agency.

Extended Web Service architectures

Extended Web Service architectures involve support for more complicated message exchange patterns (MEPs) that create full multilayered transactions from simple call and response mechanisms. These transactions can include security and authentication, event chaining to other Web Services, and confirmation and rollback functionality.

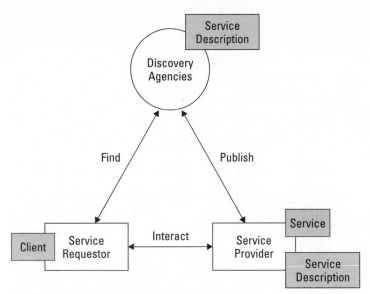

Figure 55-1: The basic Web Service architecture
* Copyright (c) 2002 World Wide Web Consortium

Extended Web Service architectures also take advantage of more recent developments in W3C and UDDI specifications. SOAP attachments can represent several transactions accumulated or concatenated during a complicated multilayer transaction. Message authentication can optionally be employed via user ID and password, application authentication tokens, or authenticated X.509 certificates.

Other initiatives include development of encryption for SOAP messages, digital signatures, fixed message routing, and session handling between messages and services.

Figure 55-2 shows the layout of an extended Web Service architecture, illustrating how the different components work together. Most of the operational load falls on the SOAP messages, with additional support for authentication and security in the WSDL documents, and no significant changes in the optional UDDI directory role.

Web Service workflow is also being developed. The Business Process Execution Language for Web Services (BPEL4WS) is developing into a practical method for handling synchronized Web Service execution. BPEL4WS is being developed as a joint effort between IBM, Microsoft, and BEA Systems. You can find more information on the specifications at `www-106.ibm.com/developerworks/library/ws-bpel/`.

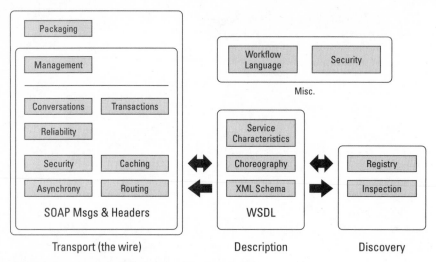

Figure 55-2: Extended Web Service architectures
* Copyright (c) 2002 World Wide Web Consortium

Web Service Architecture Models

Beyond the specifications, you can break down basic and extended Web Service architectures into three real-world models: call and response, brokered calls, and chained.

The call and response model

The basic format for a Web Service is a default call and response mechanism from one calling agent to a serving agent. In this scenario, the calling agent is either a Web Service client or a Web Service provider.

The calling agent has already discovered the serving agent, usually without the aid of UDDI. The calling agent simply interacts with the serving agent via SOAP calls and responses. The call is made to the serving agent via a dynamic generation of a SOAP envelope. The SOAP call is formatted by the WSDL document of the serving agent. The interface that generates the SOAP call is created by a developer who has read the WSDL and created a compatible SOAP interface, or by a WSDL interface generation tool. Figure 55-3 illustrates a basic call and response Web Service model, with WSDL being interpreted and SOAP calls and responses generated based on the WSDL.

The call and response model is the most common method of Web Service interaction today. Most Web Service clients are Web browsers or specialized smart clients such as Java or Windows applications. These clients access a predetermined Web Service at a predetermined location. If interactions with multiple Web Services are required for a transaction, the client usually controls the Web Service call and response flow by waiting for one Web Service to return data before the next Web Service is called.

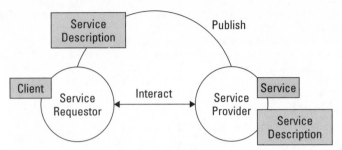

Figure 55-3: The call and response model
* Copyright (c) 2002 World Wide Web Consortium

The brokered calls model

The brokered calls model is similar to the call and response model, but with the addition of a Web Service between the calling and providing agents. The function of the middle-tier Web service is not the same as the service discovery agency role described in the basic Web Service architecture. Instead of acting as an agent that puts calling agents together with appropriate providing agents, the middle-tier Web Service acts like an application proxy for the calling agent. It processes one or more call and response mechanisms on behalf of the original calling agent to one or more serving agents. The middle-tier Web Service then returns concatenated responses to the calling agent. As with the previous scenario, the calling agent is either a Web Services client or another Web Services provider. You can also use the middle-tier Web Service to centrally enforce security and authentication standards between Web Services.

A multitier Web Services architecture simplifies client application maintenance by simplifying the application requirements for the calling agent, and by providing a layer for the Web Service to adapt to changes in the environment (such as a server move or WSDL change for a serving agent). Figure 55-4 illustrates a brokered calls model, with WSDL being interpreted and SOAP calls and responses generated based on the WSDL, through an intermediate Web Service.

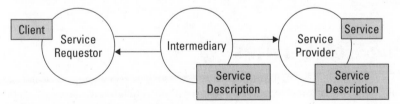

Figure 55-4: The brokered calls model
* Copyright (c) 2002 World Wide Web Consortium

The chained model

The chained model implements several new features of SOAP and a few features of more recent WSDL specifications. SOAP attachments can represent several transactions accumulated or concatenated during a complicated multilayer chained transaction. Messages can be authenticated and SOAP envelopes can be signed. Chained transactions support commit and rollback functionality and workflow specifications, such as the Business Process Execution Language for Web Service (BPEL4WS).

Web Service interaction is still facilitated through calls and responses in the chained model, but the calling and responding agents can also call and respond to other agents to get their jobs done, rolling the series of calls and responses into a single network transaction that eventually finds it way back to the calling agent. The chain can start at the client or server level via the brokered calls model. Figure 55-5 illustrates a chained model, with WSDL being interpreted and SOAP calls and responses generated based on the WSDL along every link of the chain.

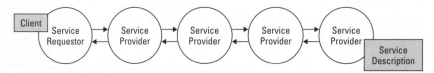

Figure 55-5: The chained model
* Copyright (c) 2002 World Wide Web Consortium

Serving Web Services

You can serve Web Services from any platform that can support data binding to the HTTP or SMTP protocols. A related WSDL document has to be published to describe the functionality and the location of the Web Service. You can also optionally register the Web Service to a UDDI server or other registry, such as Xmethods.com for Web Service clients to access.

In most cases Web Services are implemented in Java or one of the MS Visual Studio.NET languages. Application development tools and languages that support Web Services enable the service to take advantage of platform-specific tools, utilities and class libraries that make Web Service development more of a practical endeavor.

Most Java implementations of Web Services, for example, use one of the UI tools for development, such as WebSphere Studio Application Developer, SunONE Developer for Java, or the IBM Web Services Tool Kit to speed up Web Service development time. In almost all cases, Java implementations of Web Services use the Apache SOAP class libraries as their SOAP implementation.

Consuming Web Services

Calling a Web service from a Web Service client is referred to as consuming a Web Service. You can call Web Services from any platform that supports data binding to the HTTP or SMTP protocols and can read and interpret a Web Service provider's WSDL document.

Web Services shine when a smart client with a rich application UI and easy integration with tools such as calendars, to-do lists, and e-mail are available. In this case, browsers are marginal Web Service clients. The best Web Service clients tend to be Windows applications, because of the Web Service integration features in Windows and Office XP, and the ease of development for Web Service client applications via Visual Studio.NET tools.

The Notes client also makes a good Web Services client, because of the integrated UI and development features. Chapter 57 covers tips and techniques for making a Notes 6 client a great Web Services client.

Summary

This chapter provided an introduction to Web Services and covered the following topics:

✦ The developing Web Service standards and specifications

✦ An introduction to Web Service building blocks — SOAP, WSDL, and UDDI

✦ Web Service architecture

✦ Web Service models — call and response, brokered calls, and chaining

✦ Serving and consuming Web Services

The next chapter goes deeper into the basic building blocks of Web Services by illustrating examples of SOAP, WSDL, and UDDI.

✦   ✦   ✦

SOAP, WSDL, and UDDI

By Brian Benz

Chapter 55 introduced you to the concepts behind Web Services, the architecture of Web Service prototypes, and common Web Service models. This chapter continues the introduction by digging deeper into the main building blocks of Web Services — SOAP, WSDL, and UDDI — and illustrating how each component works together in a Web Services environment.

Simple Object Access Protocol (SOAP)

SOAP is an evolutionary result of the development of distributed computing over the Web. In recent years, the need has increased for a way to invoke application calls and responses in a format that travels easily through corporate firewalls and the Internet. This format also needs to be able to describe complicated call and response data in an accurate and detailed way. As most developers know, applications and data usually start out simple and quickly get complicated as layers of complexity build. The following code, for example, is a simple servlet URL call to the `XMLQuotes.nsf` database used in Chapter 51:

```
<Web Server
URL>/servlet/DominoBibleQuoteDXLServletGetSingleSourceList?
        DeliveryMethod=W
eb&DatabaseName=ndbible\\XMLQuotes.nsf&CategoryName=Amy+Bird
```

This call passes three parameters with the servlet URL, which are then passed to the servlet and used to return all the quotations in the `XMLQuotes.nsf` database for Amy Bird. The URL is already too long to fit along the top of a Web browser screen, and this is a simple example. It's not uncommon to have 20 or even 100 parameters passed to a servlet in an unreadable URL string. When (not if) the need arises to start describing the data format of parameters for distributed applications, the list can easily grow by three or four times. It starts to become obvious that a new way is needed to pass values from one distributed application to another that includes a detailed description of the data being sent. XML is a natural format for sending this data, because of its transportability and rich formatting capabilities for representing complex data formats in a hierarchy. Add messaging capabilities, encoding for data representation, and RPC descriptors, and you have SOAP.

SOAP format

The W3C SOAP specification is based on XML and describes objects that make calls and responses in Web Services and other distributed applications over HTTP.

SOAP can be broken down into several components that are used to deliver calls and responses:

✦ The HTTP header indicates the method being invoked by this call for HTTP requests and responses.

✦ The SOAP endpoint is an HTTP-standard URL, with an optional URI and SOAPAction. A SOAPAction can be used by Web Service agents to filter SOAP request messages without having to parse the SOAP envelope.

✦ The SOAP envelope describes what is in a message and what should be done with the message.

✦ The SOAP encoding rules describe serialization of data based on general or application-specific data types. SOAP data serialization describes a SOAP element's original data type. When the SOAP envelope arrives at its destination, the data is deserialized into its original form. Data types can be simple and complex. Simple types are standard data types that all SOAP-compliant servers understand. Complex data types are described by the creator of the SOAP envelope, and can contain simple types.

✦ One or more SOAP methods (for calls via HTTP POST) can call a Web Service. Each method is identified by a namespace URI (more on namespace URIs a little later in this chapter).

✦ The optional SOAP RPC representation can represent remote procedure calls and responses.

✦ The SOAP body contains the call or response message described by the envelope and encoded according to the encoding rules.

A SOAP request

Now that you have an overview of SOAP components, it's time to examine an actual SOAP call and response to a Web Service. The example in this chapter is the Delayed Quote example on the Xmethods Web site (www.Xmethods.com). The Xmethods Web site is a great starting point for developers who want to get familiar with Web Services. It provides several practical working examples, tutorials, and a place for Web Service developers to post and share their Web Services.

The HTTP header

The HTTP header is used to make requests to a Web service over HTTP. HTTP header values are generated based on values in the WSDL file for the Web Service, which you see later in this chapter. Listing 56-1 shows the HTTP request header.

Listing 56-1: Xmethods Stock Quote SOAP Request HTTP Header

```
HTTP Header:
POST /soap HTTP/1.1
Host: 66.28.98.121:9090
Content-Type: text/xml; charset=utf-8
SOAPAction: "urn:xmethods-delayed-quotes#getQuote"
```

POST and GET

The first line of the HTTP header for the SOAP request contains the following: the HTTP method (POST), the request URI (/soap), and the HTTP protocol version (1.1). HTTP GET is the regular HTTP method when surfing the Web, which sends a URL and optional parameters (such as port number). Calls to Web Services use POST, which tells the HTTP server to expect more than just a URL as part of the request. The HTTP method is blank for HTTP server responses.

URIs, URLs, and URNs

HTTP URIs are a format specification for Uniform Resource Locators (URLs) and Uniform Resource Names (URNs).

✦ A URI is the name that can be assigned to a URN or a URL. The term *URI* is also used to refer to URNs and URLs in most W3C SOAP and Web Service documentation.

✦ For Web surfers, URLs are the most common and familiar form of URI. URLs are used to specify a location-specific resource on the Web, such as www.ibm.com.

✦ URNs describe a relative value that could be at any Web location, such as a /servlet subdirectory. URNs usually mask a complicated namespace or a value for later reference; similar to the way DNS replaces an IP address with a URL.

In Listing 56-1, the request URI is a URN that identifies the soap subdirectory as the target of the request. If no URI is specified in an HTTP POST, the default HTTP directory of the server is used.

SOAPAction

A SOAPAction is used with URLs and URIs to further identify the location of the Web Service on the server. SOAPAction is optional and usually describes a Web Service method or other information about the request that can't be included in the other header objects. Web Services use the SOAPAction to filter requests without having to parse the SOAP envelope to find more information about the request.

In most implementations, the URI and the SOAPAction header have the same value. In Listing 56-1, however, the SOAPAction is "urn:xmethods-delayed-quotes#getQuote", which indicates the method name of getQuote and the URN name of urn:xmethods-delayed-quotes.

The HTTP header assembles the HOST URL and request URI of the HTTP POST to find the Web Service endpoint. A Web Service endpoint is the place where the Web Service calling methods are located. In the example in Listing 56-1, the endpoint is the /soap directory at 66.28.98.121:9090, and the SOAPAction tells you that you need to use the getQuote method of the service in your request.

The SOAP request envelope

After you identify the target of the HTTP POST, you can use the SOAP envelope to make the call to the Web Service method listed in the SOAPAction, and pass the contents of the SOAP envelope to the Web Service for processing. Listing 56-2 shows the SOAP request envelope.

Soap envelope structure

Like the HTTP header in a SOAP request, the SOAP envelope is based on values declared in the WSDL file for the Web Service, which provide instructions about how requests and responses to the Web Service are structured. Because SOAP messages are well-formed XML documents, the SOAP envelope starts with an XML declaration, followed by a single <SOAP-ENV:Envelope> root element. <SOAP-ENV:Envelope> contains several namespace declarations, which are covered in the next section.

In the mandatory <SOAP-ENV:Body> element, you find the getQuote method call as an element name. The nested value in the getQuote element is the parameter that passes to the getQuote method when the SOAPAction in the HTTP header calls it (the value is the stock symbol for IBM). All parameters for a method must be contained in child elements of the procedure call element.

Namespaces, URNs, and SOAP encoding

Unlike most basic forms of XML, namespaces and Schemas are important parts of Web Services. The DXL schema that was introduced in Part X of this book has a namespace of dxl and a URL of www.lotus.com/dxl, which could point to a schema for DXL, but doesn't (nothing is located at www.lotus.com/dxl). All the other URLs specified by SOAP envelope namespaces in Listing 56-2 resolve to real Schema documents or HTML pages describing the structure of the elements and attributes represented by that namespace. Each URL namespace is assigned to a URI for use in the SOAP envelope.

Schemas define SOAP data encoding as well as element and attribute structures. Any nested elements in the getQuote method, for example, use the namespace xsi, which resolves to www.w3.org/2001/XMLSchema-instance, which in turn describes basic data types for elements, such as float and string. Developers can either use standard data-encoding formats or develop their own and an associated Schema to go with them.

Cross-Reference   For more information on Schemas and DXL, refer to Chapter 46.

The URL represented in the following line of code, for example, is assigned a namespace URI of SOAP-ENV that resolves to the SOAP envelope Schema URL:

```
xmlns:SOAP-ENV="http://schemas.xmlsoap.org/soap/envelope/"
```

When you define the body of the envelope, you can use

```
<SOAP-ENV:Body>
```

which is easier to follow than

```
< http://schemas.xmlsoap.org/soap/envelope/:Body>
```

Both are legal references, but the URI version makes the SOAP envelope much easier to follow, allows the reuse of the smaller URI, and keeps the size of SOAP envelopes smaller. Also, if the URL reference changes, it's much easier to change one URI reference at the start of the envelope instead of hard-coded references in the envelope elements.

Listing 56-2: **Xmethods Stock Quote SOAP Request**

```
<?xml version="1.0" encoding="UTF-8" standalone="no"?>
<SOAP-ENV:Envelope xmlns:SOAP-
ENV=http://schemas.xmlsoap.org/soap/envelope/
xmlns:tns="http://www.themindelectric.com/wsdl/net.xmethods.s
ervices.stockquote.StockQuote/"
xmlns:electric="http://www.themindelectric.com/"
xmlns:soap="http://schemas.xmlsoap.org/wsdl/soap/"
xmlns:xsd="http://www.w3.org/2001/XMLSchema"
xmlns:soapenc="http://schemas.xmlsoap.org/soap/encoding/"
xmlns:wsdl="http://schemas.xmlsoap.org/wsdl/"
xmlns:xsi="http://www.w3.org/2001/XMLSchema-instance">
  <SOAP-ENV:Body>
    <mns:getQuote xmlns:mns="urn:xmethods-delayed-
    quotes" SOAP ENV encodingStyle=
    "http://schemas.xmlsoap.org/soap/encoding/">
    <symbol xsi:type="xsd:string">IBM</symbol>
    </mns:getQuote>
  </SOAP-ENV:Body>
</SOAP-ENV:Envelope>
```

A SOAP response

After you make the SOAP request, the Web Service returns a response. The body of the response is formatted according to the same SOAP envelope structure and encoding rules. But in this case it contains fewer namespaces and a slight variation on the method name (see Listing 56-3).

In the response envelope, the single Body element contains the original method name with the word Response added to the end of it, which makes for easy calculation of the response element name for parsing and transformation of the response data. The response to the request is located in the same nested element of the method as the request was located, using the same encoding namespace — xsi.

Web Services process the request on whatever back-end system is handling Web service requests. The main feature of Web Services is that requests and responses are formatted in XML, and passed to the Web Service. The Web Service back-end code can be running on any platform (Windows Server, UNIX, Linux, and Mainframe platforms) and can be written in any programming language (C, Java, LotusScript, PERL, Basic, and so on). It's up to the back-end system to parse the SOAP envelope and generate the SOAP response.

Listing 56-3: **Xmethods Stock Quote SOAP Response**

```
<?xml version="1.0" encoding="UTF-8"?>
<soap:Envelope
xmlns:soap=http://schemas.xmlsoap.org/soap/envelope/
xmlns:xsi="http://www.w3.org/2001/XMLSchema-instance"
```

Continued

Listing 56-3 *(continued)*

```
xmlns:xsd="http://www.w3.org/2001/XMLSchema"
xmlns:soapenc="http://schemas.xmlsoap.org/soap/encoding/"
soap:encodingStyle="http://schemas.xmlsoap.org/soap/encoding/
">
  <soap:Body>
    <n:getQuoteResponse xmlns:n="urn:xmethods-delayed-
    quotes">
      <Result xsi:type="xsd:float">84.9</Result>
    </n:getQuoteResponse>
  </soap:Body>
</soap:Envelope>
```

Web Service Description Language

Web Service Description Language (WSDL) defines what SOAP calls and responses should look like, and helps Web Service calling agents define appropriate interfaces for the Web Service at hand.

WSDL format

Most Many developers are overwhelmed when they see a WSDL document for the first time. WSDL is based on XML, but with the addition of namespaces, parts, ports, and so on, the format can be intimidating. It's important to remember that WSDL isn't meant for humans to read — its purpose is to inform Web Service clients and other Web Services how to access the functionality of a Web Service. The verbosity of WSDL is actually a very good feature of Web Services. The detail enables Web Services to avoid any misinterpretations when conversing with each other.

The good news is that most development tools in the Java and Windows application world have some sort of WSDL generation tools to free developers from the drudgery of WSDL coding. Also, more advanced tools are becoming available that enable clients and other Web Services to create and adapt interfaces to other Web Services. The theory is that the calling agent should be able to adapt to any updated functionality described in the WSDL from the serving agent.

The WSDL file for the Xmethods Stock Quote Web Service is shown in Listing 56-4. The list below briefly describes each element of the WSDL file. A full description of each element and examples are covered after Listing 56-4.

WSDL is formatted as several elements that are combined to describe a Web Service:

✦ **definitions** define a Web Service. As with SOAP, this is followed by namespace declarations as parameters of the definitions element.

✦ **documentation** can be contained under the definitions element, in a documentation tag.

✦ **types** describe the structure of the data to be contained in call and response SOAP messages.

✦ **messages** group types together to describe an input, output, or fault message.

✦ **parts** describe the data format of the request and response calls of a message.

✦ **operations** group input, output, and fault messages into a unit.

✦ **portTypes** can group together one or more operations. All operations must be contained in at least one portType.

✦ **bindings** tie portTypes to a specific protocol.

✦ **ports** tie bindings together with specific Web Service endpoints.

✦ **services** tie one or more ports together.

Listing 56-4: **Xmethods Stock Quote WSDL**

```
<wsdl:definitions
xmlns:tns="http://www.themindelectric.com/wsdl/net.xmethods.
services.stockquote.StockQuote/"
xmlns:electric=http://www.themindelectric.com/
xmlns:soap="http://schemas.xmlsoap.org/wsdl/soap/"
xmlns:xsd="http://www.w3.org/2001/XMLSchema"
xmlns:soapenc="http://schemas.xmlsoap.org/soap/encoding/"
xmlns:wsdl="http://schemas.xmlsoap.org/wsdl/"
xmlns="http://schemas.xmlsoap.org/wsdl/"
targetNamespace="http://www.themindelectric.com/wsdl/
net.xmethods.services.stockquote.StockQuote/"
name="net.xmethods.services.stockquote.StockQuote">
  <message name="getQuoteResponse1">
    <part name="Result" type="xsd:float"/>
  </message>
  <message name="getQuoteRequest1">
    <part name="symbol" type="xsd:string"/>
  </message>
  <portType name="net.xmethods.services.
   stockquote.StockQuotePortType">
    <operation name="getQuote" parameterOrder="symbol">
      <input message="tns:getQuoteRequest1"/>
      <output message="tns:getQuoteResponse1"/>
    </operation>
  </portType>
  <binding name="net.xmethods.services.
   stockquote.StockQuoteBinding"
   type="tns:net.xmethods.services.
   stockquote.StockQuotePortType">
   <soap:binding style="rpc"
    transport="http://schemas.xmlsoap.org/soap/http"/>
   <operation name="getQuote">
     <soap:operation soapAction="urn:xmethods-delayed-
      quotes#getQuote"/>
     <input>
       <soap:body use="encoded"
       encodingStyle="http://schemas.xmlsoap.org
```

Continued

Listing 56-4 *(continued)*

```
      /soap/encoding/" namespace="urn:xmethods-delayed-
      quotes"/>
    </input>
    <output>
      <soap:body use="encoded"
      encodingStyle="http://schemas.xmlsoap.org
      /soap/encoding/" namespace="urn:xmethods-delayed-
      quotes"/>
    </output>
  </operation>
</binding>
<service name="net.xmethods.services.
 stockquote.StockQuoteService">
<documentation>net.xmethods.services.
  stockquote.StockQuote web service</documentation>
  <port name="net.xmethods.services.
   stockquote.StockQuotePort"
   binding="tns:net.xmethods.services.
   stockquote.StockQuoteBinding">
    <soap:address
     location="http://66.28.98.121:9090/soap"/>
  </port>
</service>
</wsdl:definitions>
```

Using WSDL

This example shows several WSDL elements combined hierarchically in a single WSDL document. The following sections break down the document and review the role of each element.

Definitions

The definitions root element defines several namespaces for structure and data encoding, just as the soap:Envelope root element did in the SOAP examples. The targetNamespace attribute names the class on the Xmethods server that is used for the Web Service (net.xmethods.services.stockquote.StockQuote).

```
<wsdl:definitions
xmlns:tns="http://www.themindelectric.com/wsdl/net.xmethods.
services.stockquote.StockQuote/"
xmlns:electric=http://www.themindelectric.com/
xmlns:soap=http://schemas.xmlsoap.org/wsdl/soap/
xmlns:xsd=http://www.w3.org/2001/XMLSchema
xmlns:soapenc=http://schemas.xmlsoap.org/soap/encoding/
xmlns:wsdl=http://schemas.xmlsoap.org/wsdl/
xmlns="http://schemas.xmlsoap.org/wsdl/"
targetNamespace="http://www.themindelectric.com/wsdl/
net.xmethods.services.stockquote.StockQuote/"
name="net.xmethods.services.stockquote.StockQuote">
```

parts, types, and messages

The parts become part of the request and response calls in the SOAP messages that access this Web Service. The `Result` parameter is a `float`, and the symbol parameter is a `string`. The parts and types are grouped into input and output messages:

```
<message name="getQuoteResponse1">
  <part name="Result" type="xsd:float"/>
</message>
<message name="getQuoteRequest1">
  <part name="symbol" type="xsd:string"/>
</message>
```

operations and portTypes

The input and output messages are grouped into an operation, and then into a portType. The portType is named `net.xmethods.services.stockquote.StockQuotePortType`.

```
<portType name="net.xmethods.services.
  stockquote.StockQuotePortType">
    <operation name="getQuote" parameterOrder="symbol">
      <input message="tns:getQuoteRequest1"/>
      <output message="tns:getQuoteResponse1"/>
    </operation>
</portType>
```

bindings

Next, the `net.xmethods.services.stockquote.StockQuotePortType` portType is bound to remote procedure call (RPC) over HTTP. This means that the SOAP envelope must conform to SOAP RPC formats, and the envelope can only be received via the HTTP protocol, not via SMTP.

The namespace and SOAPAction are defined next. The `SOAPAction` attribute of the `soap:operation` element describes the same method as the operation element. Web Service servers can use the SOAPAction to route and/or filter requests without having to parse the SOAP envelope to read the operation element. The SOAPAction (`urn:xmethods-delayed-quotes#getQuote`) can be passed in the HTTP POST header of any SOAP request that calls the Web Service via HTTP. The RPC binding, including the SOAPAction, is named `net.xmethods.services.stockquote.StockQuoteBinding`.

```
<binding name="net.xmethods.services.
  stockquote.StockQuoteBinding"
  type="tns:net.xmethods.services.
  stockquote.StockQuotePortType">
   <soap:binding style="rpc"
    transport="http://schemas.xmlsoap.org/soap/http"/>
   <operation name="getQuote">
     <soap:operation soapAction="urn:xmethods-delayed-
      quotes#getQuote"/>
     <input>
       <soap:body use="encoded"
       encodingStyle="http://schemas.xmlsoap.org
       /soap/encoding/" namespace="urn:xmethods-delayed-
       quotes"/>
     </input>
     <output>
```

```
      <soap:body use="encoded"
      encodingStyle="http://schemas.xmlsoap.org
      /soap/encoding/" namespace="urn:xmethods-delayed-
      quotes"/>
    </output>
  </operation>
</binding>
```

services and ports

Next, the `net.xmethods.services.stockquote.StockQuoteBinding` is bound with the reference to the SOAPAction of the Web Service endpoint. The port is named `net.xmethods.services.stockquote.StockQuotePort,` and is bound to the `net.xmethods.services.stockquote.StockQuoteService` Web Service.

```
  <service name="net.xmethods.services.
   stockquote.StockQuoteService">
  <documentation>net.xmethods.services.
    stockquote.StockQuote web service</documentation>
   <port name="net.xmethods.services.
    stockquote.StockQuotePort"
    binding="tns:net.xmethods.services.
    stockquote.StockQuoteBinding">
     <soap:address
      location="http://66.28.98.121:9090/soap"/>
   </port>
  </service>
</wsdl:definitions>
```

When a client or another Web Service reads the WSDL, the HTTP header creates references to the endpoint and the SOAPAction from the binding, and generates a SOAP envelope with input and output messages and appropriate nested parameters from the portType.

Universal Description, Discovery, and Integration

Universal Description, Discovery, and Integration (UDDI) is the final piece of the Web Service puzzle. It links consumers of Web Services with providers. UDDI is a specification created by the UDDI project, which is a part of the Organization for the Advancement of Structured Information Standards (OASIS), and is not part of the W3C. Currently, IBM, Microsoft, SAP, and NTT Telecom host public versions of the UDDI directory, which are kept in sync via a form of replication. You can find URLs for registry sites as well as the latest version of the UDDI specification at `http://uddi.org/`.

UDDI structure

UDDI is a platform-independent framework for sharing information about Web Services and the organizations that provide them. Industry-standard Web Service formats can be shared among organizations on public UDDI servers. Although the UDDI project is not part of a regular standards body, such as the W3C or the IETF (Internet Engineering Task Force), the structure of UDDI is based on Web Service standards, which means that UDDI registries are theoretically accessible through the same means as all other Web Services.

Finding Web Services with UDDI

Each of the four public UDDI registries (IBM, Microsoft, SAP, and NTT) has its own interface and UI to access their registry via the Web. The Web sites for each interface can be found at `http://www.uddi.org`. Regardless of the interface provided, the UI is notoriously hard to navigate for Web developers that are used to more user-friendly HTML search sites. But like WSDL, the main users of the UDDI registries are intended to be Web Services rather than developers. As a testament and/or a response to this, Microsoft, IBM, and a few smaller players have released UDDI SDKs, which make developing Web Service front-ends to UDDI registries more accessible to anything on the other end of the SDK (human or machine). You can download Microsoft SDKs at `http://uddi.microsoft.com/`, and you can download the IBM UDDI for Java (UDDI4J) as part of the IBM Web Services Tool Kit from `http://alphaworks.ibm.com/tech/webservicestoolkit`.

You can also use these tools, as well as a few others, to set up private UDDI servers for use within an organization or via VPN. Private UDDI servers are useful for groups that want the full benefits of a complete set of Web Services technologies, but don't want to share their Web Services with the world on one of the public sites. Private organizational UDDI servers are the most common use of UDDI today. Organizations are reluctant to share Web Service information on a public server, for security reasons. Private UDDI servers provide an easy way for an organization to share information about internal Web Services while controlling who has access to the Web Service.

Registering Web Services

UDDI servers do not support auto-indexing or discovery features that are common with HTML Web crawler search engines. You must manually register each Web Service provider and service on a UDDI server, either at the one of the public UDDI Web sites, or via a UDDI registry Web Service client. Anyone can register their company and one or more Web Services on a public UDDI server. Records are given a unique key, called a Universally Unique Identifier (UUID) or Globally Unique Identifier (GUID). The structure of the unique ID is based on the ISO/IEC 11578:1996 structure and generation algorithm standard. More information on the unique ID is available at `www.iso.ch`.

Each record is unique, and provider and Service information replicates with other public UDDI site(s), or private sites if you have a UDDI VPN. Each Web Service reference contains a discovery URL that points to the WSDL for the Web Service, with an optional copy stored on the UDDI server.

TModels

As part of the registration process, registrants can reuse or develop their own tModels for use as classification for their Web Service. tModels describe a Web Service format. tModels can be shared among interested parties on public UDDI servers to standardize a Web Service interface. Several airlines, for example, may someday decide to create a common flight status tModel, with the same parameters and methods regardless of the airline. tModels store the name of the model, the publisher, the categories that describe the service type, pointers to related technical specifications, interface definitions, message formats, message protocols, security protocols, and other definitions that aid in lowest-common-denominator compatibility.

Industry-standard taxonomies defined as tModels are available for review on public UDDI sites. Examples include business classification code models for SIC (Standard Industrial Classification), NAICS (North American Industry Classification System), UNSPSC (Universal Standard Products and Services), ISO 3166 Geographic taxonomy, and GeoWeb Geographic classification.

You can find more information on UDDI and links to public servers and tModels at `http://uddi.org/`.

Summary

This chapter reviewed the building blocks of Web Services:

✦ Simple Object Access Protocol (SOAP)

✦ Web Service Description Language (WSDL)

✦ Universal Description, Discovery, and Integration (UDDI)

In the next chapter, you begin working with SOAP and WSDL by creating Web Services that can be served from any Domino server.

✦　　✦　　✦

Serving Web Services from Domino

By Brian Benz

In This Chapter

Walking through an example: A three-tier Web Services system combining Java applications, Web Services, and Domino

Learning the prerequisites for developing Domino Web Services

Deploying the Web Service class, WSDL, and WSDD files

Running the DXL application Web Services from a Java application

Dissecting the DXL application Web Services

Dissecting the DXL Java application — Web Services Edition

This chapter focuses on creating Java classes that accept SOAP requests and return SOAP data in a Domino server environment. The chapter also covers tools for generating WSDL for Domino Web Services and deploying Web Service agents.

You can download all the examples in Part XI of this book, including the XMLQuote.nsf database and the Quote DXL Generator — Web Services Edition, plus associated WSDL and WSDD files, from the ndbible Web site. See the Web site for installation instructions. The database design and content are reused with permission of the original owners, Newbs Consulting and Sapphire Oak Technologies. You can download the original Quotation of the Day Domino database that XMLQuotes.nsf is based on from www.sapphireoak.com or www.newbsconsulting.com.

Domino developers can use LotusScript and Java agents to provide Web Services, even though Domino servers have no native facility for handling SOAP calls and responses. Consequently, Domino-only solutions tend to be awkward and kludged, especially in LotusScript:

+ **LotusScript agents:** Web Services send an XML document as part of the Request_content CGI variable. Using this variable, a LotusScript agent can parse the contents of the SOAP envelope, and the values in the body can be used as passed parameters. The Domino 6 help includes an example of a LotusScript agent that serves a simple Web Service using LotusScript to manually parse a SOAP request and rebuild the SOAP response.

+ **Java agents:** You can pass the same Request_content CGI variable to a Java agent, making calls to methods in a class file that is part of the Java agent. You can manually parse and rebuild the SOAP envelope, or you can use Java XSL transformation classes to parse and/or rebuild the data. The Domino 6 help includes an example of a Java agent that serves a simple Web Service using custom Java classes to manually parse a SOAP request and rebuild a SOAP response.

✦ **Serving Web Services via a J2EE Web server and SOAP/RPC router:** The third option is the one covered in this chapter, and the only option that can accommodate more than a few users simultaneously and handle the most recent SOAP standards. These standards include the SOAPAction directive in the HTTP `POST` header and use of an RPC router to manage SOAP requests.

The examples in this chapter focus on the most practical solution for hosting Web Services in industrial-strength server environments. For Domino solutions, this involves serving the Web Service through a third-party application server such as WebSphere or TomCat. Domino objects can be called from the Web Service via imported Domino classes from that server.

In this chapter the three-tier Java and servlet application created in Chapter 51 is converted into a Web Services application. The first tier is the Java application, which provides the user interface to the data. The next tier includes the Java-based Web Services, which handle requests for data from the Java application and retrieve data from the third-tier, which is the Domino server and its associated databases. Figure 57-1 shows the UI for the Quote DXL Generator — Web Services Edition.

Figure 57-1: The UI for Quote DXL Generator — Web Services Edition

The Java application, called `DominoBibleQuoteDXLApplicationWSE.java`, is based on the Swing UI classes and the AWT event classes. The application functions exactly the same as the application examples in Chapters 50 and 51, but instead of running all the Java code on the client and accessing Domino databases over the network or via servlets, the application makes calls to Web Services on a Domino server, which handles data access to Domino objects. As with the servlet edition of the application, the client machine does not need a Domino client, `Notes.jar` or `NSCO.jar` files to access Domino objects; all Domino access is via the server. This also means that the application handles all the client-side functionality only. This division of processing makes each side of the application perform better than a combined solution, and the addition of Web Services adds another layer of flexibility in the application.

Prerequisites for Developing Domino Web Services

Because you're using Web Services and a Domino server for this example, some work is required to set up the application before you can start using it. You must first review some of the prerequisites for making this application run.

Downloading and installing AXIS

You must first install the latest implementation of the Apache SOAP toolkit, which is now called AXIS. AXIS stands for Apache eXtensible Interaction System, but is still based on the W3C SOAP recommendation. You can download the entire library from `http://xml.apache.org` as a ZIP or TAR file and install it on your file system.

If you're running a J2EE application server, move the AXIS subdirectory to the WEB-INF or WebApps directory, depending on the server; then restart the server. If you're not running an application server, the latest version of AXIS comes with a client-side server tool that you can use for testing on a Domino server or a Domino Designer workstation (discussed later in this chapter).

Java Web Services support: JDK and JSDK issues

You must know which JDK to use when developing, compiling, and running Java application and Web Service code. Domino R5 supports the Sun JDK (Java Development Kit) 1.1.8, and Domino Server 6 supports JDK 1.3. Domino Server 6 ships with the `JSDK.jar` in the default Domino program directory. R5 developers have to download and install JDK 1.3 or higher to work with the examples in this chapter. To download the JDK1.3 and the `JSDK.jar` file for previous versions of Domino, go to the download section of Sun's Web site at `http://www.java.sun.com`.

Edit the Java CLASSPATH

After downloading and installing AXIS, you must make some edits to the Java `CLASSPATH` for the AXIS router to function correctly. The `CLASSPATH` system variable should also contain accurate references to `Notes.jar` and `NCSO.jar` for supporting Domino servlets. You should set the `JAVA_HOME` environment variable to the main directory of the server's JDK. For Windows NT and earlier server versions, you can set environmental variables via the `autoexec.bat` file. For Windows 2000 servers and later, you set environmental variables by opening the Control Panel, selecting the System icon, clicking the Advanced tab, and clicking the Environment Variables button.

Listing 57-1 shows the minimum required `CLASSPATH` reference settings to properly route and run Web Services in a Domino 6 Designer environment, where the Domino Designer is installed in `C:\Lotus\Notes`, and the Java JDK 1.3 is installed in `C:\JSDK1.3.1_01`. On a Domino server, the directory references would be changed, usually to `C:\Lotus\Domino`.

Listing 57-1: Minimum Environment Variable Settings for Domino Web Service Support

```
CLASSPATH:
.;C:\xml-axis-10\lib\axis.jar;C:\xml-axis-10\lib\axis-
ant.jar;C:\xml-axis-10\lib\commons-discovery.jar;C:\xml-axis-
10\lib\commons-logging.jar;C:\xml-axis-10\lib\jaxrpc.jar;C:\xml-axis-
10\lib\log4j-1.2.4.jar;C:\xml-axis-10\lib\saaj.jar;C:\xml-axis-
10\lib\wsdl4j.jar;c:\lotus\notes\Notes.jar;c:\Lotus\Notes\Data\domino\java\
NCSO.jar;c:\lotus\notes\jsdk.jar;

PATH:
C:\WINNT;C:\WINNT\COMMAND;C:\jsdk1.3.1_01\bin;c:\lotus\Domino;
set JAVA_HOME=c:\jsdk1.3.1_01
```

Deploying the Web Service Class, WSDL, and WSDD Files

The Web Service examples in this chapter use the following four classes:

- ✦ `DominoBibleQuoteDXLWebServiceGetSourceList` gets the first list of unique quotation sources for use in a Java application.

- ✦ `DominoBibleQuoteDXLWebServiceGetSingleSourceList` gets a list of quotations for a single quotation source for use in a Java application.

- ✦ `DominoBibleQuoteDXLWebServiceGetSingleQuote` returns a quotation in custom XML format to a Java application.

- ✦ `DominoBibleQuoteDXLWebServiceGetSingleQuoteGenerateXML` returns a quotation in DXL format to a Java application.

You also use four associated WSDL files and four Web Service Deployment Descriptor (WSDD) files with the same names as the Java class files. WSDD files are used to manage back-end programs that are called from an application server. In this case, they map Web Service operations to Java classes. WSDD files are covered in more detail later in this chapter.

 You can download all the Web Services in this example, as well as the Java application, deployment descriptors, WSDL files, Web Service classes, source files, and the `XMLQuotes.nsf` Domino database, from the ndbible Web site.

Running the Web Services from a J2EE application server

After downloading all related Web Service files from the `www.wiley.com/compbooks/benz` Web site, copy the class and WSDD files to the AXIS\class directory on the J2EE server or the designer workstation. In a J2EE server environment, the WSDD files can be located elsewhere if your organization does not load them in the class directory.

After copying the files, if the Web Services are being deployed on a J2EE application server, consult that server's documentation on deploying the Web Services and maintaining the WSDD files with application-specific variables.

Running the Web Services without a J2EE server

The latest version of AXIS contains an implementation of a simple Web Services router and server environment, which you can run from a command line without installing a J2EE server. Future versions are supposed to be multithreaded and faster, but for now the simple AXIS server is useful as a single-user testing environment.

If you do not have access to or do not want to install a J2EE application server on your Domino Server machine, the simple Web Services router and server environment can run on a Domino server. The Web Service servlets can run on the Domino server as well. To set up the SOAP router/server on a Domino server, follow the steps in the next few sections.

Running the AXIS Simple SOAP Server

If the Java CLASSPATH is set up as directed earlier, type the following in a command prompt:

```
java org.apache.axis.transport.http.SimpleAxisServer -p 8080
```

You should see the following message:

```
- SimpleAxisServer starting up on port 8080.
```

This indicates that the server has started. You receive no confirmation message and the startup confirmation message is the last message that runs in the prompt window. You must keep the prompt window open for the Simple AXIS Server to run.

Deploying the Web Services to the AXIS Simple SOAP Server

After loading the AXIS Simple SOAP Server, you must deploy the Java class files to the server. Deployment is facilitated by calling the java org.apache.axis.client.AdminClient and referencing the WSDD files. The WSDD files contain instructions to locate and run the class files for the Web Services. The Java class files must be in the same AXIS/class directory as the WSDD files. From a separate command prompt, go to the AXIS/Class directory and type the following four commands:

```
java org.apache.axis.client.AdminClient
deployDominoBibleQuoteDXLWebServiceGetSourceList.wsdd
java org.apache.axis.client.AdminClient
deployDominoBibleQuoteDXLWebServiceGetSingleSourceList.wsdd
java org.apache.axis.client.AdminClient
deployDominoBibleQuoteDXLWebServiceGetSingleQuoteGenerateXML.wsdd
java org.apache.axis.client.AdminClient
deployDominoBibleQuoteDXLWebServiceGetSingleQuote.wsdd
```

The contents of the WSDD files are explained later in this chapter. For now, you just need to know that these commands load the class files into the AXIS simple SOAP server and establish rules for running and accessing the Web Services and associated Java class files.

Testing the server status and deployment

To test the server implementation and ensure that the Web Services deployed as necessary, open a browser window and type the following URL, substituting the IP address if necessary:

```
http://127.0.0.1:8080/axis
```

You should see a basic HTML Web page that looks like this:

```
Content-Type: text/html; charset=utf-8 Content-Length: 977
And now... Some Services
AdminService (wsdl)
AdminService
DominoBibleQuoteDXLWebServiceGetSingleSourceList (wsdl)
GetSingleSourceList
DominoBibleQuoteDXLWebServiceGetSingleQuote (wsdl)
GetSingleQuote
DominoBibleQuoteDXLWebServiceGetSingleQuoteGenerateXML (wsdl)
GetSingleQuoteGenerateXML
DominoBibleQuoteDXLWebServiceGetSourceList (wsdl)
GetSourceList
Version (wsdl)
getVersion
```

The page confirms that the Web Services have deployed. Two system Web Services are at the top and bottom of the page, and the rest are the Web Services classes that are deployed by your prompt commands, followed by the single registered method name for each class.

If you receive an error on this screen, or not all the classes and methods are installed, the first place to check is the AXIS references in the CLASSPATH, followed by the location of the class and WSDD files.

Installing the XMLQuotes.nsf database

To avoid changing and recompiling the Java application client code, make sure that the database is installed on the same server as the Web Services, in a subdirectory under the data directory called ndbible. If your Domino data directory is, for example, in C:\lotus\ Domino\data\, you should install the XMLQuotes.nsf database in C:\lotus\Domino\ Data\ndbible\XMLQuotes.nsf. Check the instructions that are downloaded with the XMLQuotes.nsf in case there are any updated installation instructions.

Installing the DominoBibleQuoteDXLApplicationWSE Java application

You can download the DominoBibleQuoteDXLApplicationWSE Java application, as well as all the Web Services and the XMLQuotes.nsf Domino database, from the ndbible Web site.

You must install the DominoBibleQuoteDXLApplicationWSE Java application Java class files in a directory of a workstation that is accessible to the Java JDK on the same machine, as well as accessible to the Domino server over a network.

Installing the WSDL files

You must copy the WSDL files associated with the Web Service to a Web server for clients who want to access the Web Services in a remote environment. In a Domino server environment, the WSDL files for the Web Services should be located in the server's HTML directory. On a J2EE application server, refer to the application server's documentation for correct placement of the WSDL. Manually test the WSDL file URL in a browser before publishing a discovery URL for the WSDL file in a UDDI registry entry or creating other references to the service.

Running the DXL Application Web Services from a Java Application

After downloading the application and completing the installation, run the application by typing **java DominoBibleQuoteDXLApplicationWSE** from a command prompt or the Windows Run menu option. The application appears on the screen in its own Java window. The application is identical in function to the Java application in Chapters 50 and 51.

As with the servlet example in Chapter 51, it's what's happening behind the scenes that is of more interest to developers. The rest of the chapter describes how the application works and how the Web Services interact with the Java application and the Domino server.

Dissecting the DXL Application Web Services

The Quote DXL Generator — Web Service Edition application is an adaptation of the example Java code that was created for the regular Java application in Chapter 50, and the servlet-based application in Chapter 51. The following sections go under the hood of each Web Service to show how it works.

The DominoBibleQuoteDXLWebServiceGetSourceList Web Service

Unlike previous Java application examples, each servlet that represents a Web Service in the Quote DXL Generator — Web Service Edition application has two files associated with it — a Web Services Description Language (WSDL) file and a Web Service Deployment Descriptor (WSDD) file. Each WSDL and WSDD file is almost the same as its counterpart, except for the names of the classes, the names of the methods, and the data types returned. The DominoBibleQuoteDXLWebServiceGetSourceList class, WSDL, and WSDD files serve as examples of how all four Web Services are set up.

The code in Listing 57-2 is the Java class file for the DominoBibleQuoteDXLWebService GetSourceList Web Service. The Web Service returns a unique listing of quotation sources from the XMLQuotes.nsf database by first retrieving all the values in the UniqueQuoteSources view in an array and then removing duplicates and trimming the array to match the unique list of sources.

Listing 57-2: The DominoBibleQuoteDXLWebServiceGetSourceList Web Service Code

```java
import lotus.domino.*;
import java.net.URL;
import java.io.*;
import com.ibm.xml.parsers.*;
import org.w3c.dom.*;
import java.util.*;

public class DominoBibleQuoteDXLWebServiceGetSourceList {


    public String [] GetSourceList(String DatabaseName) {
        String sourceList [] = null;
        String lastSource = null;
        String thisSource = null;
        try{
            NotesThread.sinitThread();
            Session session = NotesFactory.createSession();
            Database db = session.getDatabase(session.getServerName(),
DatabaseName);
            View view = db.getView("UniqueQuoteSources");
            ViewNavigator nav = view.createViewNav();
            String [] sourceArray = new String [nav.getCount()];
            ViewEntry entry = nav.getFirst();
            int finalElement = 0;
            while (entry != null) {

                Vector v = entry.getColumnValues();
                thisSource=v.elementAt(0).toString();
                if ( ! thisSource.equals(lastSource)) {
                    sourceArray[ finalElement ] = thisSource;
                    finalElement += 1;
                }
                lastSource = v.elementAt(0).toString();
                entry = nav.getNext();

            }
            sourceList = new String[ finalElement ];
            System.arraycopy( sourceArray, 0, sourceList, 0,
            sourceList.length );
            db.recycle();
            view.recycle();
            nav.recycle();
        }
        catch(NotesException e) {
            e.printStackTrace();
        }
        finally {
            NotesThread.stermThread();
```

```
        }

        return sourceList ;


    }
}
```

The Quote DXL Generator – Web Service Edition application WSDL and WSDD files

Listing 57-3 shows the WSDD file associated with the DominoBibleQuoteDXLWebService GetSourceList Web Service.

The code declares the name of the Web Service, two XML namespaces, and the service data-binding format as Java remote procedure call (RPC). Next, the service's class name is defined as DominoBibleQuoteDXLWebServiceGetSourceList. The code then permits access to all methods contained in the class.

The deployment descriptor describes a Web Service from a server point of view. It adds another level of flexibility and security by linking a back-end program to a named Web Service. If a change is made to the location or the platform, or even the language of the back-end program, the WSDD can be updated with this information. The published WSDL and the named Web Service do not need to change.

Listing 57-3: **DominoBibleQuoteDXLWebServiceGetSourceList WSDD Code**

```
<deployment name="DominoBibleQuoteDXLWebServiceGetSourceList"
xmlns="http://xml.apache.org/axis/wsdd/"
    xmlns:java="http://xml.apache.org/axis/wsdd/providers/java">
  <service name="DominoBibleQuoteDXLWebServiceGetSourceList"
provider="java:RPC">
    <parameter name="className"
value="DominoBibleQuoteDXLWebServiceGetSourceList" />
    <parameter name="allowedMethods" value="*" />

<typeMapping
        xmlns:ns="http://www.ndbible.com/wsdl/default/"
        qname="ns:ArrayOf_xsd_string"
        type="java:java.lang.String[]"
        serializer="org.apache.axis.encoding.ser.ArraySerializerFactory"
        deserializer="org.apache.axis.encoding.ser.
ArrayDeserializerFactory"
        encodingStyle="http://schemas.xmlsoap.org/soap/encoding/"
      />
</service>

</deployment>
```

As mentioned in Chapter 56, reading a WSDL file can be a daunting task, but if everything goes well, humans should rarely have to read a Web Service. WSDL files are a way of defining a Web Service interface programmatically to another Web Service or a smart client. Listing 57-4 shows the WSDL interface for the `DominoBibleQuoteDXLWebServiceGetSourceList` Web Service.

In this WSDL example, two messages are defined: a string going in called `DatabaseName`, and an array of strings coming out, called `GetSourceListReturn`. Both messages are rolled into an operation called `GetSourceList`, which is rolled into a `portType` called `DominoBible QuoteDXLWebServiceGetSourceList`. Next, you bind the `portType` to RPC and standard SOAP encoding, and then create a port with an address of `http://127.0.0.1:8080/axis/servlet/AxisServlet` where the Web Service can be found.

Listing 57-4: DominoBibleQuoteDXLWebServiceGetSourceList WSDL Code

```
<?xml version="1.0" encoding="UTF-8"?>
<wsdl:definitions targetNamespace=http://www.ndbible.com/wsdl/default/
xmlns=http://schemas.xmlsoap.org/wsdl/
xmlns:apachesoap=http://xml.apache.org/xml-soap
xmlns:impl=http://www.ndbible.com/wsdl/default/
xmlns:intf=http://www.ndbible.com/wsdl/default/
xmlns:soapenc=http://schemas.xmlsoap.org/soap/encoding/
xmlns:wsdl=http://schemas.xmlsoap.org/wsdl/
xmlns:wsdlsoap=http://schemas.xmlsoap.org/wsdl/soap/
xmlns:xsd="http://www.w3.org/2001/XMLSchema">
 <wsdl:types>
  <schema targetNamespace=http://www.ndbible.com/wsdl/default/
  xmlns="http://www.w3.org/2001/XMLSchema">
   <import namespace="http://schemas.xmlsoap.org/soap/encoding/"/>
   <complexType name="ArrayOf_xsd_string">
    <complexContent>
     <restriction base="soapenc:Array">
      <attribute ref="soapenc:arrayType" wsdl:arrayType="xsd:string[]"/>
     </restriction>
    </complexContent>
   </complexType>
   <element name="ArrayOf_xsd_string" nillable="true"
   type="impl:ArrayOf_xsd_string"/>
  </schema>
 </wsdl:types>
  <wsdl:message name="GetSourceListRequest">
     <wsdl:part name="DatabaseName" type="xsd:string"/>
  </wsdl:message>
  <wsdl:message name="GetSourceListResponse">
     <wsdl:part name="GetSourceListReturn"
      type="intf:ArrayOf_xsd_string"/>
  </wsdl:message>
```

```
<wsdl:portType name="DominoBibleQuoteDXLWebServiceGetSourceList">
    <wsdl:operation name="GetSourceList" parameterOrder="DatabaseName">
        <wsdl:input message="intf:GetSourceListRequest"
        name="GetSourceListRequest"/>
        <wsdl:output message="intf:GetSourceListResponse"
        name="GetSourceListResponse"/>
    </wsdl:operation>
</wsdl:portType>
<wsdl:binding
name="DominoBibleQuoteDXLWebServiceGetSourceListSoapBinding"
type="intf:DominoBibleQuoteDXLWebServiceGetSourceList">
    <wsdlsoap:binding style="rpc"
    transport="http://schemas.xmlsoap.org/soap/http"/>
    <wsdl:operation name="GetSourceList">
        <wsdlsoap:operation soapAction=""/>
        <wsdl:input name="GetSourceListRequest">
            <wsdlsoap:body
            encodingStyle=http://schemas.xmlsoap.org/soap/encoding/
            namespace=http://www.ndbible.com/wsdl/default/
            use="encoded"/>
        </wsdl:input>
        <wsdl:output name="GetSourceListResponse">
            <wsdlsoap:body
            encodingStyle=http://schemas.xmlsoap.org/soap/encoding/
            namespace=http://www.ndbible.com/wsdl/default/
            use="encoded"/>
        </wsdl:output>
    </wsdl:operation>
</wsdl:binding>
<wsdl:service name="DominoBibleQuoteDXLWebServiceGetSourceListService">
    <wsdl:port
    binding="intf:DominoBibleQuoteDXLWebServiceGetSourceListSoapBinding"
    name="DominoBibleQuoteDXLWebServiceGetSourceList">
        <wsdlsoap:address location="
        http://127.0.0.1:8080/axis/servlet/AxisServlet"/>
    </wsdl:port>
</wsdl:service>
</wsdl:definitions>
```

Putting the WSDD, Java class, WSDL, and SOAP together

So far this may look like much more work to set up than the previous examples in Chapters 50 and 51, but keep in mind that the WSDD, Java class, WSDL, and SOAP files play an important role in dividing the processing of the application, and adding flexibility along the way. You can use the deployment descriptor, for example, to redirect calls to another Java class file or another platform entirely, or to adapt to new security or other scenarios without having to change the name of the Web Service.

The Web Service WSDL is not important for the day-to-day functionality of the Web Service, but it is important for Web Service clients who want to access the Web Service. The WSDL file specifies the format for a SOAP call and response related to the Web Service. The WSDL file paves the way for a dynamic client that can read the WSDL file for a Web Service, and adapts the calling agent interface to the serving agent. The WSDL can also be used with a tool, such as the IBM Web Services Toolkit, to generate Java proxy class code for the Web Service that can be incorporated into an application. Listing 57-5 shows the SOAP request envelope contents for the `DominoBibleQuoteDXLWebServiceGetSourceList` Web Service.

The method name in this example SOAP request envelope maps directly to the incoming message in the WSDL file. The `DatabaseName` parameter nested in the `GetSourceList` method call maps to the message name in the WSDL file.

Listing 57-5: The DominoBibleQuoteDXLWeb ServiceGetSourceList SOAP request envelope

```
<SOAP-ENV:Envelope xmlns:SOAP-ENV="http://schemas.xmlsoap.org/soap/envelope/"
xmlns:SOAP-ENC="http://schemas.xmlsoap.org/soap/encoding/"
xmlns:xsi="http://www.w3.org/2001/XMLSchema-instance"
xmlns:xsd="http://www.w3.org/2001/XMLSchema"
SOAPENV:encodingStyle="http://schemas.xmlsoap.org/soap/encoding/">   <SOAP-
ENV:Body>
     <m:GetSourceList xmlns:m="http://www.ndbible.com/wsdl/default/">
        <DatabaseName xsi:type="xsd:string">
        ndbible\\XMLQuotes.nsf</DatabaseName>
     </m:GetSourceList>
   </SOAP-ENV:Body>
</SOAP-ENV:Envelope>
```

The DominoBibleQuoteDXLWebServiceGetSingle SourceList Web Service

The `DominoBibleQuoteDXLServletGetSingleSourceList` Web Service is called when a user clicks a quotation source in the Java application. The `DatabaseName` and `CategoryName` parameters are passed in the SOAP envelope, and the Web Service returns an array of quotations for a single quotation source back to the Java application. Listing 57-6 shows the `DominoBibleQuoteDXLWebServiceGetSingleSourceList` code.

Listing 57-6: The DominoBibleQuoteDXLWeb ServiceGetSingleSourceList Web Service Code

```
 import lotus.domino.*;
import java.util.*;
import java.io.*;

public class DominoBibleQuoteDXLWebServiceGetSingleSourceList {
```

```
public String [] GetSingleSourceList(String CategoryName, String
DatabaseName) {
    String singleSourceList [] = null;

    try{
        NotesThread.sinitThread();
        Session session = NotesFactory.createSession();
        Database db = session.getDatabase(session.getServerName(),
        DatabaseName);
        View view = db.getView("GetXMLQuotes");
        ViewNavigator nav =
        view.createViewNavFromCategory(CategoryName);
        singleSourceList = new String [nav.getCount()];
        ViewEntry entry = nav.getFirst();
        int quoteElement = 0;
        while (entry != null) {

            Vector v = entry.getColumnValues();

            singleSourceList[ quoteElement ] =
            v.elementAt(3).toString();
            quoteElement += 1;
            entry = nav.getNext();

        }

        db.recycle();
        view.recycle();
        nav.recycle();
    }
    catch(NotesException e) {
        e.printStackTrace();
    }
    finally {
        NotesThread.stermThread();
    }

    return singleSourceList ;

}

}
```

The DominoBibleQuoteDXLWeb ServiceGetSingleQuote Web Service

The code in Listing 57-7 is called when a quotation is selected by choosing the XML (Form=Root, Fieldname=Element) option as the quotation output format in the Java application.

The string representing the single quotation in XML format is passed from the GetSingleQuote class back to the Web Service as a string.

The GetSingleQuote class looks up the quotation in the GetXMLQuoteTextOnly view. Because you need the document object to generate custom XML based on document items, the class retrieves the document from the view using the getDocumentByKey method of the view class.

Next, the form name and the items are retrieved from the Domino document, and the XML declaration is hard-coded at the beginning of the string that returns the XML document. The form name is passed as the root element; then all the items in the Domino document are used to generate XML element names. The XML document element names and text values are based on Domino document field names and field values.

For XML element names, the XMLSafeName variable is used, which trims off any leading $ from a field name. Several Domino document items start with a $, which is not an illegal character for XML, but some XSL processors have trouble with the $ in element names (most notably MS Internet Explorer's stylesheet for XML display in a Web browser).

After you create the XML output string, it is passed back to the Java application using a SOAP response envelope.

Listing 57-7: The DominoBibleQuoteDXLWeb ServiceGetSingleQuote Web Service Code

```
import lotus.domino.*;
import java.util.*;
import java.io.*;

public class DominoBibleQuoteDXLWebServiceGetSingleQuote {


        public String GetSingleQuote(String PassedQuote, String
        DatabaseName) {
         String XMLDoc=null;

         try{
             NotesThread.sinitThread();
             Session session = NotesFactory.createSession();
             Database db = session.getDatabase(session.getServerName(),
             DatabaseName);
             View view = db.getView("GetXMLQuoteTextOnly");
             Document doc = view.getDocumentByKey(PassedQuote);
             Item Form = doc.getFirstItem("Form");
             String FormName = Form.getValueString();
             Vector items = doc.getItems();
             XMLDoc="<?xml version=\"1.0\" encoding=\"UTF-8\" ?>";
             XMLDoc+= "<"+FormName+">";
             String XMLItemName = null;
             String XMLSafeName = null;
             for (int j=0; j<items.size(); j++) {
                 Item item = (Item)items.elementAt(j);
                 XMLItemName = item.getName();
                 if (XMLItemName.substring(0, 1).equals("$")) {
```

```
            XMLSafeName =
            XMLItemName.substring(1,XMLItemName.length());
        }
        else {
            XMLSafeName = XMLItemName;
        }
        XMLDoc+= "<"+XMLSafeName+">" +item.getValueString() +
        "</"+XMLSafeName+">";
    }
    XMLDoc+= "</"+FormName+">";
    db.recycle();
    view.recycle();
    doc.recycle();
}
catch(NotesException e) {
    e.printStackTrace();
}
finally {
    NotesThread.stermThread();
}

return XMLDoc ;

}


}
```

The DominoBibleQuoteDXLWeb ServiceGetSingle QuoteGenerateXML Web Service

The code in Listing 57-8 is called when a quotation is selected by choosing the DXL from Document.GenerateXML option as the quotation output format in the Java application.

The `GetSingleQuoteGenerateXML` class looks up the quotation in the GetXMLQuoteTextOnly view. You retrieve the document from the GetXMLQuoteTextOnly view using the `getDocumentByKey` method of the view class.

As with the previous example, after the XML output string has been created, it is passed back to the Java application via the SOAP response envelope.

Listing 57-8: The DominoBibleQuoteDXLWeb ServiceGetSingleQuoteGenerateXML Code

```
import lotus.domino.*;
import java.util.*;
import java.io.*;
```

Continued

Listing 57-8 *(continued)*

```
public class DominoBibleQuoteDXLWebServiceGetSingleQuoteGenerateXML {

        public String GetSingleQuoteGenerateXML(String PassedQuote, String
        DatabaseName) {
         String XMLDoc=null;

        try{
            NotesThread.sinitThread();
            Session session = NotesFactory.createSession();
            Database db = session.getDatabase(session.getServerName(),
            DatabaseName);
            View view = db.getView("GetXMLQuoteTextOnly");
            Document doc = view.getDocumentByKey(PassedQuote);
            StringWriter out = new StringWriter();
            doc.generateXML(out);
            XMLDoc=out.toString();
            db.recycle();
            view.recycle();
            doc.recycle();
        }
        catch(NotesException ne) {
            ne.printStackTrace();
        }
        finally {
            NotesThread.stermThread();
        }

        return XMLDoc ;

    }
}
```

Dissecting the DXL Java Application — Web Service Edition

The Java application in this example is based on the sample Java applications in Chapters 50 and 51. Listing 57-9 shows the code adapted for Web Services in the DominoBibleQuoteDXLApplicationWSE Java application.

Two things changed in the Java application code. First, imports of the lotus.domino and lotus.dxl classes have been removed. Several references to AXIS packages that are used to generate calls to the Web Services have been added. That means that the application can be loaded on any workstation that supports Java JDK 1.3.1 or higher with the AXIS JAR files loaded. The workstation does not have to have a Domino client and the Notes.jar, or the

NCSO.jar loaded on the workstation for the Java application to function. Another change is the addition of a variable at the top of the application that specifies the database name for XMLQuotes.nsf, which is used by all Web Services.

Listing 57-9: Changed Code in the DominoBibleQuoteDXLApplication-WSE Java Application

```
import javax.swing.*;
import javax.swing.event.*;
import java.util.*;
import java.awt.*;
import java.awt.event.*;
import java.io.*;
import java.net.*;
import org.apache.axis.*;
import org.apache.axis.client.*;
import java.rmi.*;
import com.ibm.xml.parsers.*;
import org.apache.axis.encoding.*;
import org.apache.axis.utils.*;

public class DominoBibleQuoteDXLApplicationWSE extends JPanel {
    JTextArea output;
    JList SourceList;
    JList QuoteList;
    ListSelectionModel SourcelistSelectionModel;
    ListSelectionModel QuotelistSelectionModel;
    public String[] listData;
    JComboBox comboBox;
    String DatabaseName = "ndbible\\XMLQuotes.nsf";
```

In addition to the two changes to the application code, a few changes were also made to the classes that connect to Domino data. Instead of containing code that generates lists of quotation sources, quotations for a unique source, and XML or DXL output in the application code, the classes now call Web Services that pass the correct data back to the application in the required format. Listing 57-10 shows the classes that changed in the DominoBibleQuote DXLApplicationWSE Java application.

Each class in the Java application builds a SOAP request envelope and endpoint URL to call the appropriate Web Service and receives a SOAP response envelope from the Web Service.

A new instance of a SOAP call is created and assigned a Web Service target endpoint of http://127.0.0.1:8080/axis/servlet/AxisServlet. This endpoint accesses the AXIS Simple Server, which reads the SOAP envelope and the HTTP POST header, parses out the data, and routes the parameters in the SOAP envelope to the appropriate Web Service class. Routing of the Web Service data is based on information in the Web Service Deployment Descriptor (WSDD) file associated with each Web Service. Two parameters are passed to the Web Service — CategoryName and DatabaseName.

Next, a new instance of a string array is created by encoding the response as `ArrayOf_xsd_string`, a standard SOAP data type. Encoding data types is an integral part of Web Services. Data encoding allows typed data to flow between platforms and operating systems by being serialized and deserialized when sending and delivering the SOAP envelope.

Next, the class calls the Web Service, sends the parameters in the SOAP envelope, and then waits for a SOAP response envelope. The response parameter is assigned to the `single SourceList` string array variable, which is passed back to the application for display in the UI.

Listing 57-10: Changed Classes in the DominoBibleQuoteDXL-ApplicationWSE Java Application

```
public String[] GetSourceList() {
    String sourceList [] = null;
    try {
        Service  service = new Service();
        Call call = (Call) service.createCall();
        call.setTargetEndpointAddress( new
        java.net.URL("http://127.0.0.1:8080/axis/servlet
        /AxisServlet") );
        call.setOperationName( new
        javax.xml.namespace.QName("DominoBibleQuote
        DXLWebServiceGetSourceList", "GetSourceList") );
        call.addParameter( "DatabaseName", XMLType.XSD_STRING,
        javax.xml.rpc.ParameterMode.IN );
        call.setReturnType(new
        javax.xml.namespace.QName("http://www.ndbible.com
        /wsdl/default/", "ArrayOf_xsd_string"));
        sourceList = (String [] ) call.invoke( new Object[]
        {DatabaseName});

    }
    catch(Exception e) {
        e.printStackTrace();
    }
    return sourceList ;
}


public String [] GetSingleSourceList(String CategoryName) {
    String singleSourceList [] = null;

    try{
        Service  service = new Service();
        Call call = (Call) service.createCall();
        call.setTargetEndpointAddress( new
```

```
                java.net.URL("http://127.0.0.1:8080/axis/servlet
                /AxisServlet") );
                call.setOperationName( new javax.xml.namespace.QName
                ("DominoBibleQuoteDXLWebServiceGetSingleSourceList",
                "GetSingleSourceList") );
                call.addParameter( "CategoryName", XMLType.XSD_STRING,
                javax.xml.rpc.ParameterMode.IN );
                call.addParameter( "DatabaseName", XMLType.XSD_STRING,
                javax.xml.rpc.ParameterMode.IN );
                call.setReturnType(new
                javax.xml.namespace.QName
                ("http://www.ndbible.com/wsdl/default/",
                "ArrayOf_xsd_string"));
                singleSourceList = (String [] ) call.invoke( new Object[]
                {CategoryName, DatabaseName});
            }

        catch(Exception e) {
            e.printStackTrace();
        }

        return singleSourceList ;

    }

    public String GetSingleQuote(String PassedQuote) {
        String XMLDoc=null;

        try{
            Service  service = new Service();
            Call call = (Call) service.createCall();
            call.setTargetEndpointAddress( new
            java.net.URL("http://127.0.0.1:8080/axis/servlet
            /AxisServlet") );
            call.setOperationName( new
            javax.xml.namespace.QName(
            "DominoBibleQuoteDXLWebServiceGetSingleQuoteGenerateXML",
            "GetSingleQuote") );
            call.addParameter( "PassedQuote", XMLType.XSD_STRING,
            javax.xml.rpc.ParameterMode.IN );
            call.addParameter( "DatabaseName", XMLType.XSD_STRING,
            javax.xml.rpc.ParameterMode.IN );
            call.setReturnType(new
            javax.xml.namespace.QName(
            "http://www.ndbible.com/wsdl/default/", "string"));
            XMLDoc = (String ) call.invoke( new Object[] {PassedQuote,
            DatabaseName});
```

Continued

Listing 57-10 *(continued)*

```
        }

        catch(Exception e) {
            e.printStackTrace();
        }


        return XMLDoc ;

    }

    public String GetSingleQuoteGenerateXML(String PassedQuote) {
        String XMLDoc=null;

        try{
            Service  service = new Service();
            Call call = (Call) service.createCall();
            call.setTargetEndpointAddress( new
            java.net.URL("http://127.0.0.1:8080/axis/servlet/AxisServlet")
            );
            call.setOperationName( new
            javax.xml.namespace.QName(
            "DominoBibleQuoteDXLWebServiceGetSingleQuote",
            "GetSingleQuoteGenerateXML") );
            call.addParameter( "PassedQuote", XMLType.XSD_STRING,
            javax.xml.rpc.ParameterMode.IN );
            call.addParameter( "DatabaseName", XMLType.XSD_STRING,
            javax.xml.rpc.ParameterMode.IN );
            call.setReturnType(new javax.xml.namespace.QName(
            "http://www.ndbible.com/wsdl/default/", "string"));
            XMLDoc = (String ) call.invoke( new Object[] {PassedQuote,
            DatabaseName});
        }

        catch(Exception e) {
            e.printStackTrace();
        }

        return XMLDoc ;

    }
```

Summary

This chapter rolled several examples from earlier in the book into a multitier Java application that calls Web Services:

✦ Combining Java applications, Web Services, and Domino

✦ Prerequisites for developing Domino Web Services

✦ Setting up and AXIS simple SOAP server on a Domino server

✦ Deploying Web Services, WSDL, and WSDD files

✦ Calling Web Services from a Java application

Chapter 58 takes a look at the other side of Web Services, namely using Notes clients as smart clients for Web Services. Notes clients have the potential to be great Web Services clients. Readers are introduced to SOAPConnect, which enables Web Service access via SOAP from LotusScript and an example of a Notes client accessing Web Services from a Java agent using AXIS.

✦   ✦   ✦

Consuming Web Services in Notes Client Applications

By Brian Benz

This chapter illustrates the great potential of the Notes client to become a full-featured Web Services client. You're introduced to SOAPConnect, which enables Web Service access via SOAP from LotusScript. You also work through examples of a Notes client accessing Web Services from a Java agent using AXIS.

For those readers who skipped Chapter 57, AXIS stands for Apache eXtensible Interaction System, and is based on the W3C SOAP recommendation. More details on AXIS and how to set it up on your workstation come later in this chapter.

Chapter 55 described a Smart Web Service client that could coordinate the booking of a flight, hotel and car, then update a calendar and expense tracking system with final booking data, and notify the traveler of any flight delays or schedule changes. The integration needed for such an application is beyond the scope of today's application platforms. This type of application would need a flexible yet powerful data storage model, security, support for calendars and email, and integrated Web access. The platform would also need a standardized UI, and probably some kind of integrated developer tool to make application development practical.

The Notes client has provided almost all of these features for several years, except the Web integration with external applications. Web Services provide the final piece of the puzzle by providing a way to integrate external data in a standardized way. With the addition of Web Service functionality to the Notes client (and a little development work), Notes clients can become integrated, smart Web Service application clients with native functionality that other application platforms can only dream of.

However, developers are currently waiting for Web Service providers to catch up with meaningful applications to integrate with. There are many providers deploying Web Services every day, and the WS-I is working hard to make sure that the standards that are emerging embrace the spirit of Web Services interoperability.

Options for Consuming Web Services from Notes Clients

In this chapter, you're going to work with two simple Web Service agents, one that accesses the current temperature for a given ZIP code, and one that returns a stock quote when provided with a stock symbol. The examples are written in Java agents using AXIS, and then ported to LotusScript agents using SOAPConnect.

As of Domino 6, you have two options for connecting to Web Services. The first option is to connect to a Web Service from a LotusScript agent using the SOAPConnect download from the Lotus developer domain. The second option is to write a Java agent that is called by Notes to access the Web Service and return values.

The LotusScript option is the easiest to implement, because of the great examples that come with the SOAPConnect download. The Java agent solutions are a little more complex, because examples of Java accessing Web Services are almost never in the context of access from Domino agents (until now), and the code can be much more complex. A good working knowledge of Java, SOAP, WSDL, and the Notes Java classes is required. The payoffs for the Java solutions are speed and flexibility, complex and user-definable data types, and more advanced SOAP handling classes that are embedded in AXIS.

You can cut and paste the examples in this chapter into any Notes database that contains a Calendar view and the standard Appointment form, including a user's mail database. The scheduled agents are designed to reach out to the Web and retrieve a temperature for a provided ZIP code, and a stock quote for a provided stock symbol. The agents retrieve data from Web Services and create a Notes calendar Appointment form in reminder format. If the agent is running in a user's Mail database, this provides a daily update of a stock price and a temperature at the top of the calendar listings for a given day.

Both Web Services are hosted as examples by Xmethods (www.Xmethods.com). Detailed documentation of the WSDL, SOAP, and sample client code is available there for review.

Learning About SOAPConnect

You can download SOAPConnect from the Lotus developer domain at the IBM Web Site (www.lotus.com/ldd). After following the installation instructions, you can reference the SOAP samples database for examples. The SOAPConnect help also has fairly good documentation on the classes that you can use to access Web Services. LotusScript agents become SOAPConnect agents with the addition of the %INCLUDE "SOAPConnect" directive in the Options container of the agent.

You can open and review the SOAPConnect LSS API file with Notepad, because it's a text file that contains a set of LotusScript classes that describe data and method interfaces to Web Services. The code in the classes also enforces data formats for Web Service call and response parameters, at runtime and at compile time.

Working with an Example: Accessing the Stock Quote Web Service from Notes via SOAPConnect

The first example, shown in Listing 58-1, uses LotusScript and SOAPConnect to retrieve temperature data from the Xmethods.com Temperature Web Service. You can review the WSDL file for the service at www.xmethods.net/sd/2001/TemperatureService.wsdl.

Cross-Reference For more information about WSDL files, refer to Chapter 56.

Listing 58-1: **The SOAPConnect Temperature Web Service**

```
%INCLUDE "SoapConnect"
Sub Initialize
    Dim ret As Single
    Dim endPoint As String
    Dim Method As String
    Dim zipcode(0) As Variant
    Dim zipName As String
    Dim retStr As String
    Dim session As New NotesSession
    Dim db As NotesDatabase
    Dim doc As NotesDocument
    Dim dt As NotesDateTime
    Dim webServiceTarget As String
    Dim targetNamespace As String
    Set db = session.CurrentDatabase
    Set doc = New NotesDocument ( db )
    zipcode(0) ="90210"
    zipName="Beverly Hills"
    Set dt = New NotesDateTime( "Today" )

    webServiceTarget =
    "http://services.xmethods.net:80/soap/servlet/rpcrouter"
    Method = "getTemp"
    targetNamespace="urn:xmethods-Temperature"
    Dim webService As New SOAPClient(webServiceTarget )
    ret = webService.invoke(targetNamespace, Method, zipcode)
    retStr=Cstr(ret)

    doc.Form = "Appointment"
    doc.AppointmentType= "4"
    doc.MeetingType= "1"
    doc.ScheduleSwitcher= "1"
    doc.StartDate= dt.DateOnly
    doc.CalendarDateTime= dt
    doc.StartDateTime= dt
    doc.StartTime= dt.TimeOnly
```

Continued

Listing 58-1 *(continued)*

```
doc.StartTimeZone= dt.TimeZone
doc.EndDate= dt.DateOnly
doc.EndDateTime= dt
doc.EndTime= dt.TimeOnly
doc.EndTimeZone= dt.TimeZone

doc.Subject= "Today the temperature is "+retStr+" in "+zipName
doc.Body = "Today the temperature is "+retStr +" in "+zipName
Call doc.Save( True, True )
```

```
End Sub
```

Let's review the code for the SOAPConnect agent line by line. The first part of this code sets up the variables needed to make the Web Service call and also to create the Appointment form once the response is returned. The ret variable is single, which maps to a float data type when SOAPConnect passes the value to the Web Service. The method maps to the operation name of the Web Service, and the zipcode variant (all outgoing Web Service parameters must be variants) becomes the string value passed to the Web Service. Next, the agent performs a basic instantiation of session, database, and a new document. Values are assigned to the zipcode and zipName variables, which are used in the return message for the agent. The dt variable sets up the Appointment form after a response is received.

```
%INCLUDE "SoapConnect"
Sub Initialize
    Dim ret As Single
    Dim Method As String
    Dim zipcode(0) As Variant
    Dim zipName As String
    Dim retStr As String
    Dim session As New NotesSession
    Dim db As NotesDatabase
    Dim doc As NotesDocument
    Dim dt As NotesDateTime
    Dim webServiceTarget As String
    Dim targetNamespace As String
    Set db = session.CurrentDatabase
    Set doc = New NotesDocument ( db )
    zipcode(0) ="90210"
    zipName="Beverly Hills"
    Set dt = New NotesDateTime( "Today" )
```

Next, the agent assigns the target URL value for the Web Service. The rpcrouter on the Xmethods.com Web site handles parsing and routing of the Web Service SOAP envelopes.

Cross-Reference   Refer to Chapter 57 for more information on how a server handles Web Services.

The namespace URI is provided for the operation associated with the Web Service's operation—in this case, `urn:xmethods-Temperature`.

After the agent has collected all the necessary parts, it makes the Web Service request by creating a new SOAPConnect `SOAPClient` object, and invoking the object using the target namespace, method, and the `zipcode` value. The response of the Web Service is stored in the `ret` variable, which is then converted to a string for concatenation in Notes fields on the Appointment form.

```
webServiceTarget = "http://services.xmethods.net:80/soap/servlet/rpcrouter"
Method = "getTemp"
targetNamespace="urn:xmethods-Temperature"
Dim webService As New SOAPClient(webServiceTarget )
ret = webService.invoke(targetNamespace, Method, zipcode)
retStr=Cstr(ret)
```

The response creates a new Appointment form, adding variations of the value of the previously updated `NotesDateTime` object, and then adding text based on the Web Services response to the subject and the body of the Appointment form:

```
   doc.Form = "Appointment"
doc.AppointmentType= "4"
doc.MeetingType= "1"
doc.ScheduleSwitcher= "1"
doc.StartDate= dt.DateOnly
doc.CalendarDateTime= dt
doc.StartDateTime= dt
doc.StartTime= dt.TimeOnly
doc.StartTimeZone= dt.TimeZone
doc.EndDate= dt.DateOnly
doc.EndDateTime= dt
doc.EndTime= dt.TimeOnly
doc.EndTimeZone= dt.TimeZone

doc.Subject= "Today the temperature is "+retStr+" in "+zipName
doc.Body = "Today the temperature is "+retStr +" in "+zipName
Call doc.Save( True, True )
```

The next Web Service (see Listing 58-2) is similar, but gets a stock quote when a symbol is provided via a different Web Service at Xmethods. You can review the WSDL file at `http://services.xmethods.net/soap/urn:xmethods-delayed-quotes.wsdl`.

Listing 58-2: **The SOAPConnect Stock Quote Web Service**

```
%INCLUDE "SoapConnect"
Sub Initialize
   Dim ret As Single
   Dim Method As String
   Dim symbol(0) As Variant
   Dim retStr As String
```

Continued

Listing 58-2 *(continued)*

```
Dim session As New NotesSession
Dim db As NotesDatabase
Dim doc As NotesDocument
Dim dt As NotesDateTime
Dim webServiceTarget As String
Dim targetNamespace As String
Set db = session.CurrentDatabase
Set doc = New NotesDocument ( db )
symbol(0) ="IBM"

Set dt = New NotesDateTime( "Today" )

webServiceTarget = "http://66.28.98.121:9090/soap"
Method = "getQuote"
targetNamespace="urn:xmltoday-delayed-quotes"
Dim webService As New SOAPClient(webServiceTarget )
ret = webService.invoke(targetNamespace, Method, symbol)
retStr=Cstr(ret)

doc.Form = "Appointment"
doc.AppointmentType= "4"
doc.MeetingType= "1"
doc.ScheduleSwitcher= "1"
doc.StartDate= dt.DateOnly
doc.CalendarDateTime= dt
doc.StartDateTime= dt
doc.StartTime= dt.TimeOnly
doc.StartTimeZone= dt.TimeZone
doc.EndDate= dt.DateOnly
doc.EndDateTime= dt
doc.EndTime= dt.TimeOnly
doc.EndTimeZone= dt.TimeZone

doc.Subject = symbol(0)+ " is at "+retStr
doc.Body = symbol(0)+ " is at "+retStr
Call doc.Save( True, True )
```

```
End Sub
```

The functionality is almost the same as the preceding example, except for the following differences:

```
symbol(0) ="IBM"

Set dt = New NotesDateTime( "Today" )

webServiceTarget = "http://66.28.98.121:9090/soap"
```

```
Method = "getQuote"
targetNamespace="urn:xmltoday-delayed-quotes"
Dim webService As New SOAPClient(webServiceTarget )
ret = webService.invoke(targetNamespace, Method, symbol)
retStr=Cstr(ret)
```

In the preceding code, a symbol variant is used to access the stock quote service, and the target URL, method, and target namespace URI are different. The only other difference in the code is the line that creates a new subject and body for the new appointment document:

```
doc.Subject = symbol(0)+ " is at "+retStr
doc.Body = symbol(0)+ " is at "+retStr
```

Both values are based on a string converted from the `float` data type returned by the Web Service, which was converted to a single LotusScript data type.

The next examples show how AXIS can be used in a Java agent to build calls and responses to the same Web Services.

An Example: Accessing the Stock Quote Web Service from Notes via Java Agents using AXIS

As with the previous examples, both Java agents that use AXIS call the same Xmethods Web Services. This is a good example of the power of Web Services to bridge platforms — the Web Services handle the Java calls and the LotusScript calls exactly the same, because each platform creates a compatible SOAP envelope for calls and responses. Instead of trying to map compatible methods and data types for serialization and deserialization, SOAP acts as the lowest common denominator to handle the integration. You don't need to know what the back-end platform is, nor does the Web Service need to know what your client platform is.

Listing 58-3: The AXIS Temperature Web Service

```
import org.apache.axis.AxisFault;
import org.apache.axis.client.*;
import org.apache.axis.encoding.*;
import org.apache.axis.utils.*;
import javax.xml.namespace.*;
import javax.xml.rpc.*;
import lotus.domino.*;
import java.net.*;

public class AxisDailyTemperatureAgent extends AgentBase {

public void NotesMain() {

String zipcode="90210";
String zipname="Beverly Hills";
```

Continued

Listing 58-3 *(continued)*

```
try {
 Session session = getSession();
 AgentContext agentContext = session.getAgentContext();
 Database db = agentContext.getCurrentDatabase();
 Document doc = db.createDocument();
 DateTime dt = session.createDateTime("Today");

 org.apache.axis.client.Service  service = new
 org.apache.axis.client.Service();
 org.apache.axis.client.Call call = (org.apache.axis.client.Call)
 service.createCall();
 call.setTargetEndpointAddress( new
 java.net.URL("http://services.xmethods.net:80/soap/servlet/rpcrouter"));
 call.setOperationName( new QName("urn:xmethods-Temperature", "getTemp") );
 call.addParameter( "zipcode", XMLType.XSD_STRING, ParameterMode.IN );
 call.setReturnType( XMLType.XSD_FLOAT );

 Object ret = call.invoke( new Object[] {zipcode} );
 System.out.println("Today the temperature is "+String.valueOf(ret)+" in
 "+zipname);

        doc.appendItemValue("Form", "Appointment");
        doc.appendItemValue("AppointmentType", "4");
        doc.appendItemValue("MeetingType", "1");
        doc.appendItemValue("ScheduleSwitcher", "1");
        doc.appendItemValue("StartDate", dt.getDateOnly());
        doc.appendItemValue("CalendarDateTime", dt);
        doc.appendItemValue("StartDateTime", dt);
        doc.appendItemValue("StartTime", dt.getTimeOnly());
        doc.appendItemValue("StartTimeZone", dt.getTimeZone());
        doc.appendItemValue("EndDate", dt.getDateOnly());
        doc.appendItemValue("EndDateTime", dt);
        doc.appendItemValue("EndTime", dt.getTimeOnly());
        doc.appendItemValue("EndTimeZone", dt.getTimeZone());

        doc.appendItemValue("Subject", "Today the temperature is
        "+String.valueOf(ret)+" in "+zipname);
        RichTextItem rti = doc.createRichTextItem("Body");
        rti.appendText("Today the temperature is "+String.valueOf(ret));
        rti.appendText(" in "+zipname);
        doc.save();

        db.recycle();
        doc.recycle();
        dt.recycle();
        rti.recycle();
```

```
      } catch (Exception e) {
        e.printStackTrace();
      }


}


}
```

The first part of the code sets up the import from AXIS, `Javax`, and Domino packages. The `java.net` class is used to create the URL object used for the Web Service's target URL. Next, the agent defines and assigns the `zipcode` string variable needed to make the Web Service call. Next is the basic Notes agent instantiation of a session, a database, and a new document. As in the SOAPConnect example, the `dt` variable is used to create the Appointment form after a response is received form the Web Service.

```
import org.apache.axis.AxisFault;
import org.apache.axis.client.*;
import org.apache.axis.encoding.*;
import org.apache.axis.utils.*;
import javax.xml.namespace.*;
import javax.xml.rpc.*;
import lotus.domino.*;
import java.net.*;

public class AxisDailyTemperatureAgent extends AgentBase {

public void NotesMain() {

String zipcode="90210";
String zipname="Beverly Hills";

try {
 Session session = getSession();
 AgentContext agentContext = session.getAgentContext();
 Database db = agentContext.getCurrentDatabase();
 Document doc = db.createDocument();
 DateTime dt = session.createDateTime("Today");
```

Next, a new AXIS service and AXIS call are created for invoking the temperature Web Service. The agent uses fully distinguished class names for `org.apache.axis.client.Service` and `org.apache.axis.client.Call`, because the `javax.xml.rpc` packages have classes with the same names, so you need to specify that you're making a client call via AXIS.

Next, the agent assigns the target endpoint URL and defines the URI for the SOAPAction operation name. The `getTemp` method is defined as the method that the Web Service should run. Next, the agent adds the `zipcode` string containing the value passed to the `getTemp` method, and defines the type of data to be returned (float).

Now the agent has all the necessary values assigned and is ready to send a request envelope to the Web Service. The request is made by invoking the call using the target namespace, method, and the `zipcode` value. The response of the Web Service is stored in the `ret` object, which is then converted to a string using the `valueOf` method of `java.lang.String`. The new string is used for concatenation in Notes fields on the Appointment form.

```
org.apache.axis.client.Service  service = new
 org.apache.axis.client.Service();
 org.apache.axis.client.Call call = (org.apache.axis.client.Call)
 service.createCall();
 call.setTargetEndpointAddress( new
 java.net.URL("http://services.xmethods.net:80/soap/servlet/rpcrouter"));
 call.setOperationName( new QName("urn:xmethods-Temperature", "getTemp") );
 call.addParameter( "zipcode", XMLType.XSD_STRING, ParameterMode.IN );
 call.setReturnType( XMLType.XSD_FLOAT );

 Object ret = call.invoke( new Object[] {zipcode} );
 System.out.println("Today the temperature is "+String.valueOf(ret)+" in
 "+zipname);
```

The Web Service response is used by the agent to create a new Appointment form, adding variations of the `DateTime` object, and then adding text to the subject and the body of the Appointment form:

```
        doc.appendItemValue("Form", "Appointment");
        doc.appendItemValue("AppointmentType", "4");
        doc.appendItemValue("MeetingType", "1");
        doc.appendItemValue("ScheduleSwitcher", "1");
        doc.appendItemValue("StartDate", dt.getDateOnly());
        doc.appendItemValue("CalendarDateTime", dt);
        doc.appendItemValue("StartDateTime", dt);
        doc.appendItemValue("StartTime", dt.getTimeOnly());
        doc.appendItemValue("StartTimeZone", dt.getTimeZone());
        doc.appendItemValue("EndDate", dt.getDateOnly());
        doc.appendItemValue("EndDateTime", dt);
        doc.appendItemValue("EndTime", dt.getTimeOnly());
        doc.appendItemValue("EndTimeZone", dt.getTimeZone());

        doc.appendItemValue("Subject", "Today the temperature is
        "+String.valueOf(ret)+" in "+zipname);
        RichTextItem rti = doc.createRichTextItem("Body");
        rti.appendText("Today the temperature is "+String.valueOf(ret));
        rti.appendText(" in "+zipname);
        doc.save();

        db.recycle();
        doc.recycle();
        dt.recycle();
        rti.recycle();

    } catch (Exception e) {
      e.printStackTrace();
    }
```

As with the SOAPConnect examples, the Stock Quote Web Service in Listing 58-4 contains only slight variations from the Temperature Web Service example.

Listing 58-4: **The AXIS Temperature Web Service**

```
import org.apache.axis.AxisFault;
import org.apache.axis.client.*;
import org.apache.axis.encoding.*;
import org.apache.axis.utils.*;
import javax.xml.namespace.*;
import javax.xml.rpc.*;
import lotus.domino.*;
import java.net.*;

public class AxisDailyStockQuoteAgent extends AgentBase {

public void NotesMain() {

String symbol="IBM";

 try {
Session session = getSession();
AgentContext agentContext = session.getAgentContext();
Database db = agentContext.getCurrentDatabase();
Document doc = db.createDocument();
DateTime dt = session.createDateTime("Today");

org.apache.axis.client.Service  service = new
org.apache.axis.client.Service();
org.apache.axis.client.Call call = (org.apache.axis.client.Call)
service.createCall();
call.setTargetEndpointAddress( new
java.net.URL("http://66.28.98.121:9090/soap"));
call.setOperationName( new QName("urn:xmltoday-delayed-quotes", "getQuote")
);
call.addParameter( "symbol", XMLType.XSD_STRING, ParameterMode.IN );
call.setReturnType( XMLType.XSD_FLOAT );

Object ret = call.invoke( new Object[] {symbol} );
System.out.println(symbol + " is at "+String.valueOf(ret));

        doc.appendItemValue("Form", "Appointment");
        doc.appendItemValue("AppointmentType", "4");
        doc.appendItemValue("MeetingType", "1");
        doc.appendItemValue("ScheduleSwitcher", "1");
        doc.appendItemValue("StartDate", dt.getDateOnly());
    doc.appendItemValue("CalendarDateTime", dt);
        doc.appendItemValue("StartDateTime", dt);
```

Continued

Listing 58-4 *(continued)*

```
        doc.appendItemValue("StartTime", dt.getTimeOnly());
        doc.appendItemValue("StartTimeZone", dt.getTimeZone());
        doc.appendItemValue("EndDate", dt.getDateOnly());
        doc.appendItemValue("EndDateTime", dt);
        doc.appendItemValue("EndTime", dt.getTimeOnly());
        doc.appendItemValue("EndTimeZone", dt.getTimeZone());

        doc.appendItemValue("Subject", symbol + " is at
"+String.valueOf(ret));
        RichTextItem rti = doc.createRichTextItem("Body");
        rti.appendText(symbol + " is at "+String.valueOf(ret));
        doc.save();

        db.recycle();
        doc.recycle();
        dt.recycle();
        rti.recycle();

    } catch (Exception e) {
      e.printStackTrace();
    }


}


}
```

The only difference between the Java AXIS Stock Quote and Temperature agents is a change in the target namespace URI, the target Web Service URL, and the method being called. The new variable, which is still a string data type, is symbol, and the response is a float data type.

```
call.setTargetEndpointAddress( new
java.net.URL("http://66.28.98.121:9090/soap"));
call.setOperationName( new QName("urn:xmltoday-delayed-quotes", "getQuote")
 );
call.addParameter( "symbol", XMLType.XSD_STRING, ParameterMode.IN );
call.setReturnType( XMLType.XSD_FLOAT );
```

The only other difference is the message that is added to the body and subject items of the new appointment document:

```
doc.appendItemValue("Subject", symbol + " is at "+String.valueOf(ret));
RichTextItem rti = doc.createRichTextItem("Body");
rti.appendText(symbol + " is at "+String.valueOf(ret));
```

The subject item is updated by the agent based on the Web Service response, and a new rich text item containing the same Web Service response data is appended to the body.

Summary

This chapter illustrated the power of Web Services for platform-free data integration, as well as the potential for the Notes client to be a powerful Web Services client. The main points included:

✦ The advantages of the Notes client as a Web Services client

✦ Tips for accessing Web Services from Notes agents

✦ Accessing the Xmethods.com Temperature and Stock Quote Web Services

✦ Accessing Web Services using LotusScript and SOAPConnect

✦ Accessing Web Services using Java and AXIS

✦　　✦　　✦

Index

Continued

Continued

Continued

Continued

Continued

Continued

F

Continued

Continued

Continued

Continued

Continued

Continued

Continued

Continued

Continued

Continued